THE BOOK OF 1000 PLAYS

Compiled and Edited by
STEVE FLETCHER AND NORMAN JOPLING

With Contributions from:
David Hallam
David Griffiths
Cathy McMahon
Scott Ewings
Lucy Jopling
Barbara Matthews

Facts On File
New York • Oxford

The Book of 1000 Plays

Library of Congress Cataloguing in Publication Data
Fletcher, Stephen.
   The Book of 1000 Plays: a comprehensive guide to the most frequently
performed plays/[compiled and edited by] Stephen Fletcher, Norman
Jopling.
      p.   cm.
   Includes index
   ISBN 0-8160-2122-8
      1. Drama--Stories, plots, etc. 2. Drama--Bibliography. 3. Drama--
Dictionaries and encyclopedias. 4. English drama--Stories, plots, etc. 5.
American drama--Stories, plots, etc. 6. English drama--Translations from
foreign languages--Stories, plots, etc. 7. Drama--Translations into English-
-Stories, plots, etc.
I. Jopling, Norman. II. Title. III. Title: Book of one thousand plays.
PN6112.5.F54 1989809.2--dc19   88-38121
ISBN 0-8160-2122-8

This book was designed and produced by
Amanuensis Books Ltd
12 Station Road
Didcot
Oxfordshire
OX11 7LL
UK

Cover design: Peter Laws
Editors: Kim Richardson; Ann Marangos;
Lynne Gregory; and Loraine Fergusson

Thanks for typing and suggestions to
Janet Chandler-Smith
Special thanks to all the staff at
The British Theatre Association Library, London,
and in particular Enid Foster

CONTENTS

Preface

Every year hundreds of plays come and go in the English speaking theatre. Some are new, some are revivals, some are adaptations. Thus it has been for a very long time. No amount of electronic wizardry can diminish the magic and creativity of the live theatre: each performance is a unique event, inviting performer and spectator to partake of the essence of the other in a subtle interaction of artistic effort and audience appreciation, or not.

Theatre will never die because it is a fundamental activity of mankind, and it enables mankind to examine every aspect of the human condition from seemingly countless perspectives, at the same time artfully creating a drama that aims to make some sense of existence. These dramas, encapsulating and exemplifying, entertaining and electrifying, run a breathtaking gamut across all shades of the spectrum of human activity. From profound tragedy to coarse comedy, musical to mystery, they figure all human types in infinite interplay.

The play's the thing, and plays have been preserved for thousands of years, constantly dusted-off and renewed, so that a huge body of work is now available to the theatre and the theatregoer. It is not possible to say which are the best plays, but it is possible to say which plays are the most popular. These most popular plays constitute, with certain exceptions, the superstructure of the modern theatre; they are its reference points and its dogma.

Quite a few are fairly obscure but successful and popular in their limited way. For a few of those few their greatest popularity is yet to come, as is occasionally the way in the unpredictable world of theatre. There are surprise hits and - rather more often - mystifying flops. Dead certs are as hard to come by in the theatre as they are on the race course. Part of the medium's fascination concerns what does and doesn't make money - by tempting Angels (backers), cajoling government subsidies, commercial sponsorship or foundation grants, and - the real trick - actually selling tickets, giving value and making palms pound.

Everyone interested in the theatre knows (more or less) which plays are the most popular, but until now there has been no definitive guide. This book attempts to remedy this, bringing together through statistical analysis details of these most popular plays; title, author, date and place of first production, objective synopsis of the plot, and dramatis personae. This book is intended for both the specialist user - amateur dramatic societies, schools, colleges etc - and for any reader interested in enjoying the plots of famous plays.

The choice of plays is based upon: (a) the longest-running plays over the past eighty years in London's West End and on Broadway (b) the most popular plays in regional British theatres and off-Broadway (c) the most popular plays with British and American dramatic societies (d) the most frequently performed and studied plays in school and college syllabuses. No definite statistics for (c) and (d) exist, so the information has been gathered through various sources including theatrical associations, play libraries and educational departments of colleges, universities and schools.

The book is the result of an idea by Steve Fletcher, whose wife, theatrical agent Wendy, frequently asked him details of play plots and characters. Often unable to answer, Steve discovered no playguide existed. Determined to remedy this, he enlisted collaborator Norman Jopling and several contributors and thus the work was born. All involved in its compilation and production hope its readers gain from it at least a little more understanding of, and delight at, the richness of the English-speaking theatre.

Introduction

An invitation to contribute some synopses to a book about the plots of 1,000 plays seemed just the ticket. I had the opportunity to describe, with love and care, some of my happiest experiences of theatre, cinema and television. Even better, I could read some plays I had long been curious about but had never seen. Of course, I had to take my share of difficult or tedious scripts but there were interesting surprises: occasionally, after long study, more merit could be discerned in a story than was realised during one viewing in a theatre. Rather more often, I fear, what had seemed fairly dazzling, as produced, turned out to be a triumph of cunning stagecraft over banal writing. Fortunately, I was well equipped to cope with this because, in the early years of ITV, I used to write the Playbill feature in TV Times which involved reading all the network's playscripts about a month before the plays were screened - live in those days. If lucky, I might see a little bit of script-in-hand early rehearsal. Nowadays, thanks to the invention of videorecording, plays are taped many months ahead of transmission and the press previewers can watch the completed production.

Most plays can be read, by the imaginative, with almost as much pleasure as seeing them in the theatre, though the pleasure is as different as that of reading a book from watching a film. The reader does not enjoy seeing the parts fleshed out by actors; he sees the characters in his mind's eye. But there is a sort of linking device: plays are usually published with at least the original cast listed. If the performers are known to you, and are congenial, you can use them in your imaginary 'production'. Indeed, there are actors and actresses so well known in certain characterisations that it would take a great effort to expunge them from memory - Olivier as *The Entertainer*, Pleasence in *The Caretaker*, Brando and Leigh in *A Streetcar Named Desire*, Edith Evans in *The Importance of Being Earnest* are just a few of my unforgettables.

One joy of some theatrical experiences that can't really be imagined is the sumptuously beautiful and ingenious set, though for production purposes some playbooks provide helpful drawings and photographs of the stage layouts.

Also, an aspect of theatrical experience that cannot be conveyed in words is the show's pacing. An obvious example of this is Arnold Wesker's little drama *The Kitchen*. Much of it reads dully but in performance, starting slowly and building in speed, noise and tension as the whole kitchen operates at full blast for the packed, unseen restaurant, it is weirdly exciting. Very difficult to stage well, though.

This is not a judgemental book. We have tried to avoid critical assessment though, inevitably, a few hints of enthusiasm or irritation will have crept into a synopsis or two.

But please be advised that the length or brevity of a plot summary is not related to the show's merit. That is because some stories can be quite marvellous and at the same time capable of a quick summing-up. Others, especially farces and historical pageants, are far too elaborate to be adequately described in a book of this size. There is a further problem we've had to wrestle with. The dénouement. In revealing so much plot we may have gone further than a reader who would like to see the play might wish. The remedy is to place a piece of paper over the entry and move it down so that you can read some but not all of the plot. With plays where the raison d'être is almost entirely whodunnit we have stopped short of the final revelation. I for one have suffered too often from library books in which somewhere past half way a malicious joker has pencilled in something like 'It was the butler'.

David Griffiths

Abelard and Heloise
Ronald Millar
Tragedy 2 Acts
Exeter 1970

Millar bases this tragedy on the famous twelfth-century love affair between Peter Abelard, a brilliant scholastic philosopher and Master of the Schools of Notre Dame and Heloise, niece to Canon Fulbert of those same schools.

The play opens in 1131 at the Abbey of the Paraclete, Troyes, France, where Abelard, the Abbot, welcomes Heloise, Abbess of Argenteuil, and the young nuns under her care. Abelard is a resigned, devout and ageing fifty-two; Heloise a haunting and beautiful thirty-two, and still passionately in love with him.

Through a series of flashbacks to a time seventeen years earlier we see the growth of a wildly unconventional love affair between the two after Abelard is asked by Canon Fulbert to move into his home and act as a tutor to the young Heloise. They are discovered by Fulbert, who gradually develops such a hatred of Abelard (especially after Heloise gives birth to their bastard child) that he sends a gang of thugs to castrate the young man.

Abelard initially reacts to his mutilation with a sense of agonised loss but gradually grows into a life of supreme and serene commitment to the church. Heloise enters the same Benedictine order, becomes with the passage of years its Abbess, but goes on loving Abelard and regards her religious life as hypocrisy.

In a long and impassioned final scene, where the action has returned to the meeting of the lovers at the Abbey of the Paraclete, Abelard prevails on Heloise to abandon their love for the love of God.

Peter Abelard
Heloise
Alain
Gerard
Phillip
Robert de Montboissier, Peter's
* student*
Guibert, Peter's betrayer
Gilles de Vannes, Peter's patron
Jehan
Fulbert, Heloise's father
Belle Alys, a prostitute
Abbess of Argenteuil, Heloise's
* confidante*
Sister Laura
Sister Constance, Heloise's friend
Sister Gochic
Mariella
Gisella
Alberic of Rheims, Master of the
* School at Rheims*
Bernard of Clairvaux
Denise, Peter's sister
Hugh, Denise's husband

Abie's Irish Rose
Anne Nichols
Comedy 3 Acts
New York 1922

Solomon Levy is looking forward to his son Abie finding a nice Jewish wife and joining the family business, but the boy has secretly married Rose Mary Murphy, an Irish Catholic. He introduces her to his father as his fiancée Rose Murpheski, daughter of a clothing manufacturer, and Solomon is impressed and arranges the 'vedding'. He decorates the reception with oranges to make 'Rosie' (from California) feel at home, so when her father, Patrick, and a priest arrive they are horrified to think she is about to marry a Protestant.

The secret comes out and both fathers demand that the marriage be anulled, but the couple are determined and marry again in a Catholic ceremony and are both disowned.

A year later finds the couple poor but happy as they prepare for Christmas. Their fathers arrive secretly and leave presents for their grandchild but when they meet a row follows about the infant's gender. It transpires that Rose has had twins who are named respectfully after their grandparents. This, of course, reconciles the feuding families as the Christmas bells ring out.

Mr Isaac Cohen
Mrs Cohen
Dr Jacob Samuels
Solomon Levy
Abraham 'Abie' Levy
Rose Mary Murphy
Patrick Murphy
Father Whalen
A flower girl

Abigail's Party
Devised by Mike Leigh
Drama 2 Acts
Hampstead 1977

Beverly is domineering and pushy with ghastly taste, vainly unaware of her uncultured values. Laurence is her serious, hard-working estate agent husband. Tony, a computer operator, and his nurse wife Angela, have been invited round for a would-be convivial evening. Laurence has to go out for a while to see a client, much to Beverly's annoyance, though at least he can bring back some goods from the off-licence. The conversation and attitudes expressed are often gruesomely funny as the flirtatious Beverly tries to be a charming hostess. Quiet and more upper-class divorcee Susan is most uneasy but has been invited round because her daughter Abigail is having a noisy teenage party nearby about which Susan worries while Beverly tries ineptly to be soothing and helpful. There is a dark undertone and Beverly and Laurence's bickering gets increasingly strident until Laurence has a heart attack. Far from silencing Beverly, she just prattles tipsily and insensitively on. An ambulance is sent for while Angela does her best, but Laurence's troubles are over and Beverly's evening has been quite ruined.

Beverly
Laurence
Angela
Tony
Susan

Abraham Lincoln
John Drinkwater
Drama 6 Scenes
London 1918

In 1860, with Northern and Southern Democrats divided over slavery, and civil war looming, a delegation comes to Lincoln's house in Springfield, Illinois, to ask if he will become the Republican candidate for the Presidency. He is not keen to go to Washington and is horrified by the thought of killing, but he accepts because he loathes slavery and feels the South must be defeated, the breakaway Confederacy stopped and the nation reunited.

President Lincoln's task is dreadful but he carries it out resolutely and as humanely as possible. General Lee surrenders to General Grant. A few days later, at the theatre, the President makes an inspiring speech about the end of the war, and the nation, under God, now being able to look forward to a new birth of freedom with government of, by and for the people.

John Wilkes Booth creeps into the theatre box and shoots Lincoln dead.

Two chroniclers
Mr Stone, a farmer
Mr Cuffney, a storekeeper
Susan, a maid
Mrs Lincoln
Abraham Lincoln
William Tucker, a merchant
Henry Hind, an attorney
Elias Price, a lay preacher
James Macintosh, editor of a Republican journal
William H. Seward, Secretary of State
Johnson White, Caleb Jennings, Representatives of the Confederate States
John Hay, a secretary
Hawkins, a clerk
Salmon P. Chase, Secretary of the Treasury
Montgomery Blair, Postmaster General
Cabinet members: *Simon Cameron, Caleb Smith, Burnet Hook, Gideon Welles*
Mrs Goliath Blow
Mrs Otherly
William Custis, a negro
Edwin M. Stanto, Secretary of War
Gen. Grant
Capt. Malins
Dennis, an orderly

William Scott, a soldier
Gen. Meade
Capt. Sone
Robert E. Lee
John Wilkes Booth

Absent Friends
Alan Ayckbourn
Drama 2 Acts
Scarborough 1974

Diana has invited Colin to a tea-party so his friends can show support after the drowning of his fiancée, whom they never met.

When Colin arrives he proves to be the only happy one among them. Uptight Diana correctly suspects Evelyn of a fling with her successful and philandering husband Paul. Marge is pestered by phone calls from her overweight hypochondriac husband Gordon, laid up in bed at home but still heaping disasters - and medicines - upon himself. Evelyn's jittery husband John keeps trying to hustle a cat food deal with Paul, while being tremendously understanding of his wife and Paul's affair, which is now common knowledge.

Colin's relaxed attitude plays havoc with the status quo and Diana has to be led upstairs after having hysterics. When at last Colin leaves, everything begins to return to its normal state of comfortable equilibrium.

Paul
Diana
John
Evelyn
Colin
Marge

Absurd Person Singular
Alan Ayckbourn
Black Comedy 3 Acts
Scarborough 1972

The author calls this piece his first 'offstage action play'. Three different couples, in three consecutive years, give Christmas drinks parties for their neighbours. The action is set in the kitchen of each couple's home, not with the main body of guests.

In the first act, Sidney, a hectoring bully and his wife Jane, play host to their neighbours, Ronald, Marion, Geoffrey, Eva and others who remain offstage. From a welter of comic misunderstanding that verges on slapstick; flyspray mistaken for room deodorant, drink spilled, people accidentally locked out, there gradually emerges a portrait of six people who thoroughly fail to understand one another.

The second party is given by Geoffrey and Eva and brings to the surface the hysterical tension latent in the earlier one. Geoffrey announces to Eva that he will leave her on Boxing Day, to which she replies with a series of futile suicide attempts, variously ignored and not noticed by her guests. Geoffrey escapes to find a doctor for Eva and the party ends with the guests, led by Eva in a drunken stupor, singing, *On the First Day of Christmas.*

The action becomes nearly grotesque in the last act which takes place in Ronald and Marion's kitchen. After dropping by to visit a drunk and bedridden Marion, Eva sits down to a drink with Ronald.

They are joined by Geoffrey and then by Sidney and Jane. The last pair, who were unwelcome, drunkenly let themselves into the kitchen and eventually organize a game of forfeits (which the others do not wish to play), along with wild dancing to an interminable Scottish reel.

Sidney
Jane
Ronald
Geoffrey
Marion
Eva

Accidental Death of an Anarchist
Dario Fo
Satirical Farce 2 Acts
Varese 1970

On 12 December 1960, bombs exploded simultaneously in banks in Rome and Milan. A member of an ineffectual anarchist club, Guiseppe Pinelli, was arrested by police for the crimes. During interrogation, police later claimed, he jumped to his death from a fourth floor window at their headquarters.

Fo builds his farce out of the testimony the police gave concerning the anarchist's death; especially out of its internal contradictions. The play is dominated by a fool who plays first a lunatic, then an investigating magistrate, a Captain of Police from the Scientific Division, a bishop and, in one of the play's alternate endings, a magistrate again.

In all these roles, the Fool exposes the inconsistencies and grotesqueries in the police's version of events. Various officers make claims that would require that the anarchist had three feet, could jump while dead and be able to fly out of the window in a quasi-religious rapture and so on.

In one ending, the Fool, having exposed the police to an investigative reporter, is himself thrown to his death only to be resurrected again as yet another investigating magistrate.

In another he escapes arrest for impersonation by threatening to send a recording of police testimony to the press.

The Fool
The Sergeant
Inspector Bertozzo
Captain Pisani
Chief Bellati
The Reporter

Accrington Pals, The
Peter Whelan
Drama 2 Acts
London 1981

Greengrocery stallholder May, in her late twenties, is an independent and strong-willed young woman whose sensitive and artistic lodger Tom, nineteen, has volunteered for the 'Accrington Pals' - Accrington in Lancashire being the smallest town in Britain to raise a whole battalion for Kitchener's New Army in 1915. Clerk Ralph has also volunteered and his millworker girlfriend Eva comes to live with May in Tom's old room; May is slightly shocked at Eva's admission that she has slept with Ralph. Neighbour Annie, who bullies her teenage son Reggie mercilessly, sees religious fanatic husband Arthur volunteer, and Sarah, another millworker, also sees her husband leave. May and Tom love each other but cannot bring themselves to get too close. She tries to persuade C.S.M. Rivers not to take Tom, but in vain.

The men leave for training and the women wait and work, frustrated and fraught. As the war progresses though, there is more work and money around and the women gain a kind of independence. May plans to buy a local corner-shop, and the women study the letters and tokens sent by their menfolk. Their attitude is realistic and intelligent but then they learn that the men have been sent off to France and the Somme, where the men finally go over the top. Subsequent newspaper reports are mere propaganda but the appearance of Arthur's wounded homing pigeon from France is an awful omen. The women learn from the trickle of survivors that terrible things have happened. The fact is that all the Pals are dead. May hallucinates an encounter with C.S.M. Rivers and Tom, and the women mourn and get on with their lives.

May
Tom
Ralph
Eva
Sarah
Bertha
Annie
Arthur
Reggie
C.S.M. Rivers

Acharnians, The
Aristophanes
Comedy 1 Act
Athens 425BC

For six years Athens has been suffering in the Peloponnesian war. The Acharnians, who live at the border of Athenian territory, have suffered the worst of the horrors.

A demi-god appears to Dikaiopolis, an Athenian farmer, sent by the gods to negotiate a peace between

Athens and the Spartan enemy. Unfortunately, the demi-god has not enough money to make the trip to Sparta. In return for the travelling money he needs, the demi-god agrees to fix a treaty between Sparta and Dikaiopolis himself. The beleaguered Acharnians are furious at the farmer's opportunism, and interrupt his joyous celebrations to condemn him to death. Before his execution he is allowed to make a speech pleading for mercy, which the Acharnians grant, despite the vigorous protests of their general, Lamachus.

After a series of vignettes which comically illustrate the folly of war and the virtue of peace, Lamachus marches defiantly off to war. He returns, badly wounded, to find Dikaiopolis in a drunken revel with Bacchus, the god of music and wine.

Dikaiopolis, Athenian farmer
Deputies
Crier
Amphitheos, a demi-god
Ambassadors
Theoros
Soldiers
Dikaiopolis's wife
Dikaiopolis's daughter
Kephisophon, Euripedes' servant
Euripedes
Lamachus, Acharnian general
Chorus
Farmers
Servants
Messengers

Action Replay
Fay Weldon
Drama 2 Acts
Birmingham 1979
Three girl students, all very different, share a flat. It is 1952. Helen is beautiful and difficult, Shirley is pretty and ordinary, Judy is plain and sexy. Young Jewish architect Saul is in love with Helen, pursues her, and weds her against the wishes of his orthodox family. His younger brother Stephen, a drop-out painter, weds Shirley, and eventually Judy has a baby by married man Jonathan, who then divorces his wife and marries her. But everyone has affairs with everyone else, all their marriages break up, Stephen is killed in Israel and Jonathan commits suicide. The play ends twenty-five years later as it begins, with Saul begging hard-hearted Helen to let him in for coffee, while the other two girls sit in the flat. She relents and lets him in.

An extra dimension enhancing the realism of the relationships is obtained by presenting different 'takes' for each scene, the various 'takes' being alternative possibilities of action and dialogue within that particular situation - some subtle, some more radical.

Helen
Judy
Shirley
Saul
Stephen
Jonathan

Adam the Creator
Josef and Karel Capek
Drama 6 Scenes
Prague 1927
Adam has destroyed the world with his cannon of negation and is left in an empty landscape with nothing but a mound of clay. The voice of God orders him to create from the clay to see how difficult being a creator can be.

Henceforth Adam makes nothing but ill-prepared mistakes; a perfect man and woman who disdains him as an imperfect being; a doting wife who demands too much attention; and an Alter-Ego who opposes his every idea, to the point of dividing the world (and the clay) in two. Alter-Ego creates the crowd and before long, war is raging between the two sides. After a reconciliation, they decide to create together but the result is a new race who deny their creators. God finally asks Adam what he will do with his new world. Adam says he will leave well alone, and God agrees.

The voice of God
Adam
Alter-Ego
Superman Miles
Eve
Lilith
Alter-Ego's wife
Persons created by Adam: *Orator, Poet, Scholar, Romanticist, Hedonist and Philosopher*
Persons created by Alter-Ego*: First Alter-Ego, Second Alter-Ego, Third Alter-Ego, Fourth Alter-Ego, Fifth Alter-Ego and Sixth Alter-Ego*
Oddly-Come-Short
Drunkard
High Priest
Novice
Watchman
Policeman

Adding Machine, The
Elmer Rice
Play 7 Scenes
New York 1923
This expressionist piece is a grim satire about an anti-hero, Mr Zero, in a world of automation.

Zero, a middle-aged accounts clerk, is nagged at home by his wife and argues at work with Daisy, after whom he lusts. His twenty-five years of faithful service as a bookkeeper are rewarded by the Boss telling him that he is to be replaced by an adding machine.

Dinner at Zero's house, with his boring friends Mr

and Mrs One, Two, Three and so on, is followed by a nationalistic outburst in which they all curse foreigners and ethnic minorities. Zero calmly announces that he has murdered the Boss.

His defence at his trial is another nationalistic tirade; he is found guilty, executed and goes up to heaven. Daisy too arrives, after committing suicide and pronounces her love for Zero, but he is totally preoccupied operating a huge adding machine. A heavenly official explains that after 'cosmic laundering' Zero is to be returned to earth as a mindless, lustful super adding machine operator.

Mr Zero
Mrs Zero
Daisy Diana Dorothea Devore
The Boss
Mr and Mrs One
Mr and Mrs Two
Mr and Mrs Three
Mr and Mrs Four
Mr and Mrs Five
Mr and Mrs Six
Policeman
Judy O'Grady
Young man
Shrdlu
A head
Lieut Charles
Joe

Admirable Crichton, The
J. M. Barrie
Comedy 4 Acts
London 1902

In the early years of the twentieth century the progressive Lord Loam has instituted a monthly tea hour, which all the family and servants attend, to point up the artificiality of class distinctions. His views are not shared by his loyal and efficient butler, Crichton, who wants to preserve his position in the servant hierarchy.

On a world cruise the household is shipwrecked on a remote desert island, and Crichton, being the most resourceful, soon becomes 'Guv', loved and honoured by all, especially Loam's haughty daughters who vie for his favours. All the castaways become marvellously happy in their primitive idyll, and Crichton decides to take as his mate the beautiful Lady Mary.

When a ship eventually appears the ever-dutiful Crichton makes the decision to be rescued, despite the pleas of Lady Mary.

Back home at the manor house, the status quo is resumed and as everyone is embarrassed at Crichton's presence, he decides to leave his Lordship's service. Lady Mary will of course marry an aristocrat, but she finally admits to Crichton that he is the best man among all of them.

Earl of Loam

Hon. Ernest Wooley
Revd John Treherne
Lord Brocklehurst
A naval officer
Crichton
Tompsett
Lady Mary Lasenby
Lady Catherine Lasenby
Countess Brocklehurst
Fisher
Eliza (Tweeny)

Affairs of State
Louis Verneuil
Comedy 3 Acts
New York 1950

When Constance Russell tells her US elder statesman husband Philip that she seeks a separation, he guesses correctly that she is in love with his friend, Senator George Henderson, a younger man, so Philip cunningly and temporarily thwarts George's immediate ambitions, telling him he will only scale the political heights with a good wife by his side. He then plants the idea that George should consider a marriage of convenience, and George and Constance fall into his trap when they pick as a candidate Philip's studious schoolteacher niece Irene, spending her holidays arranging George's vast library. George strikes up a deal with her, to be terminated when he is free to wed the woman he loves. Irene agrees, but as their 'marriage' proceeds, she plays the part so well and blossoms so much that she becomes invaluable to George who begins to fall in love with her.

This is all part of Philip's devious plan, and when he sees George's involvement with Irene is sufficiently well-established, he tells Constance he will grant her separation and that he himself intends to take a world cruise. Constance, who has already revealed the truth to Irene, accepts the inevitable and gracefully concedes George to her. She then asks Philip if she can accompany him on the world cruise - and he produces two tickets.

Philip Russell
Lawrence
Constance Russell
George Henderson
Irene Elliott
Byron Winkler

After the Fall
Arthur Miller
Drama 2 Acts
New York 1964

In this thinly disguised autobiography, Miller reviews his life and attitudes towards love, guilt and responsibility.

The central character Quentin, a forty-year-old lawyer, addresses the audience as to a psychiatrist, and attempts to make some sense of his life which is presented as a series of scrambled scenes. These include his failures with various women, his mother who deceives him, his two wives, and his German girlfriend, who suffers from guilt about concentration camps, which figure throughout. The men in his life include his father, brother and friends who have been investigated by a congressional committee, one of whom has killed himself.

Quentin's second marriage to Maggie (an obvious reference to Marilyn Monroe) is examined further. She craves love and understanding but he urges her to live her own life and when he will not take responsibility for her, she commits suicide.

He seeks to find some meaning for his ruined life, 'after the fall', and leaves with his German bride.

Quentin
Felice
Dan
Mother
Elsie
Louise
Carrie
Chairman
Holga
Father
Maggie
Lou
Mickey
Lucas
Harley Barnes
Nurses
Porters
Passers-by
Boys

After the Rain
John Bowen
Drama 3 Acts
Hampstead 1966

Two hundred years after the Great Rain - a second deluge which drowned the world as we know it - a new society has evolved, founded by nine survivors from a raft and based on a very imperfect tradition of life in Britain during the 1960s. At a university lecture hall, a group of prisoners under hypnosis are acting out life aboard the raft, based upon the diaries of Alan Armitage, and a religious work, the *Book of Arthur*. The crime of each actor has a parallel in the conduct of the person he is representing, but the actual 'crimes' themselves tend to be all types of antisocial behaviour - from psychosomatic asthma and public sarcasm to murder.

In the drama, leader Arthur Henderson takes Armitage and Sonya aboard the already crowded boat, but Alan is not convinced of Henderson's omniscience; nevertheless he and the others do obey Arthur's commands and they do survive. Ex-accountant

Henderson is calculating and ruthless, and with an awareness of the mythic implications of their survival he eventually proclaims himself a god and is worshipped by the others, some more and some less enthusiastically. Then he changes his mind and decides he is mortal but must be the god's high priest, and decides a sacrifice is needed - Sonya's unborn child. He is then challenged by Tony, Sonya's friend, an impotent body-builder. Tony kills Arthur - not only in the staged drama but in real life - at Arthur's own command. The implications - that Arthur chose his own death - overwhelm the lecturer presiding over the play and he forbids any further discussion.

The lecturer
Two assistants
Capt. Hunter
Arthur Henderson
Gertrude Forbes-Cooper
Tony Batch
Wesley Otterdale
Muriel Otterdale
Harold Banner
Alan Armitage
Sonya Banks

Agamemnon (Oresteia, Part 1)
Aeschylus
Tragedy 1 Act
Athens c. 458BC

A watchman waits on the roof of King Agamemnon's palace in Argos for the beacon announcing the fall of Troy. In quick succession the beacon flares, a herald announces Agamemnon's return, and the king himself arrives with Cassandra, his captive. The Chorus of Argive citizens celebrate the victory, but there is an undercurrent of anticipated doom in what they say. All remember that Agamemnon has sacrificed Iphegenia, his daughter by Queen Clytemnestra, to ensure his triumph over Troy. All fear Clytemnestra's revenge. Feigning a mood of devoted welcome, Clytemnestra leads her husband into the palace. But Cassandra, who has forseen his death and her own, bewails her fate in a frenzy. She follows Agamemnon into the palace only to hear his death agony, and to die herself at Clytemnestra's hand.

Clytemnestra comes boldly before the Chorus of citizens with her victims' corpses, and glories in her vengeance. Her lover Aegisthus joins her, but their joy is undercut by the fearful reproaches of the rest of Argos.

Watchman
Clytemnestra, Queen of Argos
Agamemnon, King of Argos
Cassandra, Agamemnon's captive
Aegisthus, Clytemnestra's lover
Chorus
Herald

Agnes of God
John Pielmeier
Drama 2 Acts
Louisville 1979
Dr Martha Livingstone has, with the help and hindrance of Mother Miriam Ruth, to sort out - for legal reasons - the hideous problem of how one of Mother Miriam's convent nuns, the apparently innocent twenty-one-year old Agnes (who has never read a book, seen a film or watched television), came to give birth to a baby that was strangled with its umbilical cord and dumped in a wastebasket.

The Doctor, an obsessive smoker, stops when she become obsessed with this case, and Mother Miriam used to smoke heavily herself. The connections pile up. The Doctor was a cradle Catholic who now is hostile to the faith and its superstitions. Her sister died in a convent.

Mother Miriam was married for twenty-three years, has two daughters and grandchildren. Her tremendously promiscuous sister was Agnes's mother and she used to sexually interfere with Agnes. Under hypnosis it emerges that Agnes is not so innocent or ignorant as she seems and that Mother has been more involved than she has let on. Agnes can bleed stigmatically from her hands.

The Mother Superior tries, with increasing hostility, to save Agnes from too much interrogation and from a possible manslaughter charge, but a court case results in Agnes being sent to a hospital where she stops singing and eating, and dies. The Doctor resumes menstruating for the first time in several years, and goes to confession. No rapist or seducer or seducee, of or by Agnes, is identified. A little miracle may or may not have occurred.
Dr Martha Livingstone
Mother Miriam Ruth
Agnes

Ah! Wilderness
Eugene O'Neill
Comedy 4 Acts
New York 1933
The play follows the Miller family and especially the relationship between Nat Miller, his wife Essie and their seventeen-year-old son Richard during a two day crisis that sees Richard pass from adolescence to manhood.

The Miller family have gathered to celebrate American Independence Day, but their preparations are interrupted by David McComber, who comes to complain about Richard's attachment to his daughter, Muriel.

Richard, a devotee of Swinburne, Wilde and Omar Khayyam, has outraged McComber by sending Muriel florid passages from their works. McComber leaves Nat a letter from Muriel breaking off relations with Richard.

Devastated, Richard allows himself to be tempted into a night of drinking with a tart in a local bar. He returns late to find his family anxiously waiting for him but since Richard is too drunk to be coherent, he is packed off to bed by his Uncle Sid, himself a noted carouser.

The next day Muriel sends a second letter explaining that she was forced to write the first, but in fact still loves Richard. They are re-united, to the relief of Richard's family.
Nat Miller, newspaper owner
Essie Miller, Nat's wife
Arthur, Richard, Mildred, Tommy, Nat's children
Sid Davis, Essie's brother
Lily Miller, Nat's sister
David McComber
Muriel McComber, Richard's girl
Wint Selsby
Belle
Norah
Bartender

Alcestis
Euripides
Drama 1 Act
Athens 438BC
Helped by his friend Apollo, King Admetus of Pherae has persuaded the Fates to postpone his death on condition that he finds someone to die in his place. Of all the King's relatives, only his wife Alcestis is ready to be sacrificed.

Alcestis looks forward to her death with dignity and solicitude for the future of her children. Her attitude is in sharp contrast to Admetus's maudlin but self-seeking glorification of his wife's loyalty. Pheres, Admetus's aged father, arrives and faces the king's hypocritical anger for being afraid of death. The old man points out that his son is the worse coward for letting his own wife die in his place.

In shamed fury, Admetus drives his father away, but goes on to reflect that death would have been preferable to a life of cowardice. The giant Heracles (Hercules) arrives and is made elaborately welcome by Admetus. Although he knows the welcome is sycophantic, Heracles feels pity for Alcestis, and wrestles with death so her life may be spared.
Apollo
Death
Female servant
Alcestis, Admetus's wife
Admetus, King of Pherae
Son of Admetus
Daughter of Admetus
Heracles
Pheres, Admetus's father
Male servant
Chorus

Alchemist, The
Ben Jonson
Comedy 5 Acts
London 1610

In and around the absent old Lovewit's London house, Subtle, usually dressed as a doctor, Face, his accomplice (Lovewit's butler), and their bawdy colleague Dol Common squabble and scheme to fleece people. Dapper, a lawyer's clerk wants to win at gambling and is offered a magic ritual. Drugger, a tobacconist is given astrological advice about his shop.

Sir Epicure Mammon, accompanied by sceptical Surly, receives a *tour de force* torrent of alchemical 'information'. Two men of the cloth from Amsterdam also seek the Philosopher's Stone and want to cast gold coins. Angry young man Kastril wants to be able to live profitably by his wits and study under Subtle; his widowed sister Dame Pliant has her fortune told by palmistry.

Lovewit returns unexpectedly to be told by excited neighbours that there have been extraordinary goings on at his home. Bewildered, he seeks an explanation from Face and is reassured until Mammon, Surly, Kastril and the clerics return with police officers. But 'alchemist' Subtle and Dol have gone, Face survives as the butler thanks to his master's gullibility, and Dame Pliant's fortune comes strangely true; she is betrothed to a very happy old Lovewit.

Subtle, an alchemist
Face, housekeeper
Dol Common
Dapper, Clerk
Drugger, a tobacco man
Lovewit, master of the house
Sir Epicure Mammon
Pertinax Surly, a gamester
Tribulation, a pastor of Amsterdam
Ananias, a deacon
Kastril
Dame Pliant, Kastril's sister
Parson
Neighbours
Officers
Mutes

Alfie
Bill Naughton
Drama 3 Acts
London 1963

Alfie is a bright Cockney womanizer whose success with the 'birds' has inspired him to devise a homespun philosophy/training manual about women - what they want and how to manipulate them. He proceeds to demonstrate his charms on various women including Siddie, an attractive married woman out of his class and also out for 'a bit of the other' on the side; then there is Gilda, his domesticated stand-by girl; Annie, whom he picks up in a motorway café; and Ruby, a rich older woman.

Everything is kept skin-deep with Alfie; he shies from real emotional involvement and the less glamorous aspects of female physical problems rub his essentially prissy nature up the wrong way. Gilda becomes pregnant and when Alfie refuses to commit himself she marries her stand-by, Humphrey. Alfie is upset, especially as he is becoming attached to his child, and finally Gilda tells him to leave. His vanity then leads to a rudeness which Annie finds unforgivable and she leaves him. When Alfie then decides to settle down and marry Ruby, he discovers she is deceiving him. A spot of TB leads to a brief fling with Lily, the pleasant wife of a fellow-patient. But this goes horribly wrong and there is a painful abortion scene which even touches Alfie. Just as he appears resigned to suffer for his sins, along comes Siddie again and off they go ...

Alfie
Siddie
Gilda
Humphrey
Woman doctor
Harry Clamacraft
Joe
Lily Clamacraft
Carla
Perc
Lacey
Flo
Annie
Lofty
Ruby
Sharpey
Vy
Mr Smith

Alibi for a Judge
Henry Cecil
Felicity Douglas
Basil Dawson
Comedy Mystery 3 Acts
London 1965

Bank clerk William Burford is accused of a bank robbery - some of the stolen notes are found on him. He maintains that he was given them in payment for placing bets on behalf of Thompson, a man with a mysterious past who cannot be found but who is alleged to have anonymously framed Burford.

Partly because of the Judge's prejudicial and compulsive interference during the trial and summing up, Burford is convicted. The Judge later feels uneasy about this and so he agrees to visit race courses with Burford's pretty wife, Lesley, who says Thompson makes a living from a tax-dodging scheme involving Tote tickets. But though there seem to be near misses, Thompson remains elusive. Lesley, and the Judge's, hopes for a retrial are not helped by her rather frequent lying, sometimes for practical reasons, sometimes foolishly and mischievously.

As the plot twists and turns the possibilities are that Thompson is the villain, or died in the war, or never existed, and Lesley is trying to extract money from the Judge by false pretences and perhaps by sexually compromising and then blackmailing him. He resolves to mend his case-meddling ways...

Lesley Burford
Mr Hunt
Thomas Empton QC
William Burford
Mr Justice Carstairs
Mr Bell
Superintendent Neale
Usher
Police Constable Griffin
Clerk of the Court
Foreman of the Jury
Mr Honeyman
Ernest Mott
George
Mr Campbell
Mrs Campbell
Joe
Rob
Inspector Martin
Warder
Court Policeman
Lady Second to Empton QC
Two jurymen

All for Love or The World Well Lost
John Dryden
Tragedy 5 Acts
London 1677

Set in Alexandria, this is the story of Antony and Cleopatra. Antony, having been defeated at Actium, is urged to fight on by Ventidius who chides him for losing an empire for the love of a woman, Cleopatra. Antony agrees to continue the war. Cleopatra comes to his camp and professes true love, her proof being a letter from Octavius offering her Egypt if she will betray Antony, which she has rejected.

After a minor victory Ventidius and Dollabella advise Antony to make peace and return to his family. His wife Octavia, the emperor's sister, meets Cleopatra and accuses her of trying to destroy Antony, but she defends her love for him.

Ventidius plots to ruin the romance by making Antony jealous of Dollabella, which succeeds, and Antony banishes him. The Egyptian army goes over to Caesar, and Cleopatra is urged to leave Antony and make her own peace with Octavius. With Caesar at the gates, a servant deceives Antony that Cleopatra has killed herself, and he and Ventidius take their own

lives. Before Antony has died Cleopatra enters and the lovers are united fully when she too commits suicide, by snake bites.

Mark Antony
Ventidius, his General
Dollabella, his friend
Cleopatra, Queen of Egypt
Alexas, Queen's eunuch
Octavia, Antony's wife
Serapion, a priest
Myris, a priest
Charmion, a maid
Iras, a maid

All my Sons
Arthur Miller
Drama 3 Acts
New York 1947

High summer in the back yard of the Keller home on the outskirts of an American town a couple of years after World War Two. Joe Keller, sixty, is enjoying a relaxed conversation with his doctor, Jim Bayliss, and they are joined by another neighbour, Frank Lubey, then by Jim's wife Sue, and by Frank's young wife Lydia. A little boy, Bert, comes in and the conversation starts to get a little strange with Bert wanting to talk about guns and jails.

Soon there is an undercurrent of tension. Mother - Joe's wife and Chris's mother - is worried because Anne has come to visit them from New York and she used to be Mother's other son Larry's girl. Anne is also the daughter of Joe's disgraced partner, Deever, who is serving a jail sentence for knowingly fitting P40 fighter planes with faulty cylinders, thus causing the deaths of twenty-one pilots. But Deever had done the fitting on Keller's telephoned instructions while Keller had stayed away pretending to be ill in bed so that nothing could be pinned on him. Though arrested and briefly imprisoned Keller had got out on appeal leaving Deever to take the blame.

Mother does not want Anne to marry Chris because she insists on believing, on flimsy astrological grounds and against all probability, that Larry is still alive - he was presumed killed in action flying a plane, though not a P40.

George, Deever's son, has been at last to see the bitter old man in jail and knows the truth. Now he has come to take his sister away from any further involvement with the monstrous Kellers but Anne still wants to marry Chris who is horrified at confirmation of his half-suspicions about his father's greedy deed. Forced to reveal the truth about Larry, Anne shows Mother a letter from him saying he's going to kill himself because of his father's crime. After seeing the letter Joe Keller goes off and blows his brains out.

Joe Keller
Kate Keller (Mother)

Chris Keller
Anne Deever
George Deever
Dr Jim Bayliss
Sue Bayliss
Frank Lubey
Lydia Lubey
Bert

All's Well That Ends Well
William Shakespeare
Comedy 5 Acts
London 1604
Young Bertram becomes the Count of Roussillon on the death of his father and, because he is under twenty-one, is made the ward of the King of France who is old and ill. Helena, daughter of a late great physician, has been cared for by Bertram's mother and is secretly in love with Bertram though she thinks, with reason, that her status is too low to be acceptable to him. She follows Bertram to Paris bearing a prescription left by her father that might cure the King. It does, and so he offers her any bachelor of the court she chooses. Bertram objects but the King insists on the marriage. Bertram promptly abandons her and goes off with the worthless braggart and liar Parolles to the wars of Tuscany.

Helena returns to Roussillon where she receives a letter from Bertram saying he'll only be her husband if she can get hold of a ring he always wears, and have a child by him. Helena disguises herself as a pilgrim and goes to Florence where she lodges with a widow whose virginal daughter, Diana, Parolles has attempted to procure for Bertram.

Helena gets Diana to pretend to succumb to Bertram's desires and to obtain the ring for her. Helena then takes Diana's place in bed and in the dark gives Bertram a keepsake ring that was given to her by the King of France. Helena is thought to be dead, and the King, seeing his ring, believes Bertram has killed her and has him arrested. Diana too gets in trouble with the King for apparently lying but then Helena turns up pregnant and all is straightened out.

King of France
Duke of Florence
Bertram, Count of Roussillon
Lafeu, an old Lord
Two Brothers Dumaine, French Lords
Parolles, a follower of Bertram
A French gentleman
Renaldo, steward to the Countess of Roussillon
Lavache, a clown
A page
Countess of Roussillon
Helena
Widow Capilet of Florence
Diana, the widow's daughter
Violenta and Mariana, neighbours of the widow
Lords
Attendants
Soldiers

Along Came Ruth
Holman Day
Comedy 3 Acts
New York 1914
Israel Hubbard runs a furniture store at the turn of the century, and business has become slack. Indeed, the whole town is in a slump. Into the store comes Ruth Ambrose, looking for accommodation and work. Such is her charm and enthusiasm that within minutes she gets both, vowing to transform the business for Israel. This she does, charming the whole town in the process. Soon the store is flourishing and Ruth's encouragement of an advertising campaign has made the place a boom town. Israel's son Allen has fallen in love with Ruth, and by the play's end, his proposal is accepted and a rosy future is predicted for all.

Israel Putnam Hubbard
Mrs I. P. Hubbard
Allen Hubbard
Priscilla Hubbard
Ruth Ambrose
Col Miles Standish Bradford

Alphabetical Order
Michael Frayn
Drama 2 Acts
London 1975
An enchanting chaos reigns in the library of a provincial newspaper, with files, sundry bundles, envelopes and accumulated newspaper debris piled and 'filed' under the easy-going disorganized system run by librarian Lucy. Her pleas for an assistant have been answered by the arrival of Leslie, shy but efficient, who is soon treated to the intimacies and foibles of the editorial staff; rumpled and rambling college man John, who writes the leaders and has an on-off relationship with Lucy; well-disposed Geoffrey; waggish Wally; awkwardly obvious Nora, who is after large slow Arnold. As the relationships are explored, the conviviality of the situation becomes apparent.

A few weeks later things have changed. Leslie has tidied up and set everything in meticulous order; she is also engaged to be married to the not entirely willing John. Everyone is now down in the dumps. The magic has vanished. News that the paper is to fold leads them enthusiatically to demolish Leslie's new system, scattering files and papers, but their destruction is premature. Leslie is determined the staff will take over the running of the paper and leads the editorial staff for talks with the other workers. John manages to make a date with Lucy, who just sits alone and smiles.

Leslie   *Lucy*
Geoffrey   *Nora*
Arnold   *Wally*
John

Amadeus
Peter Shaffer
Tragedy 2 Acts
London 1979

Peter Shaffer sets out in Amadeus his imaginative reconstruction of the last ten years of the life of Wolfgang Amadeus Mozart (1766-91). The composer's slow decline into poverty and premature death is portrayed as the result of the subversion of his career at the Austrian court by a rival composer, Antonio Salieri, who eventually himself becomes senior composer.

The story is laid out by Salieri in a series of almost episodic flashbacks which show his own suave progress at court, and modest musical achievement, in contrast to Mozart's vulgar, graceless court appearances and consummate, effortless virtuosity. Salieri becomes obsessed with undermining Mozart at court, tries to seduce his wife and even disguises himself as the ghost of Mozart's dead father in a ploy to drive the starving younger composer mad.

Returning from the series of flashbacks to the last hour of his own life, Salieri writes a confession to having murdered Mozart as a last desperate attempt to participate, however vicariously, in the glory, which Salieri is sure will forever surround Mozart's name.

The Venticelli brothers, gentlemen of the court
Valet to Salieri
Antonio Salieri, court composer
Johann Kilian Von Strack
Count Orsini-Rosenberg, advisors to Joseph II
Baron Von Sweiten
Constanze Weber, Mozart's wife
W. A. Mozart
Major-Domo
Joseph II
Servants and citizens of Vienna

Amazing Dr Clitterhouse, The
Barrie Lyndon
Drama 3 Acts
London 1936

When likeable, forty-ish, Dr Clitterhouse returns to his surgery late one night, faithful Nurse Ann accidentally discovers he is responsible for a string of local burglaries. He explains he is writing a book on the physical reactions to the stress of criminal activity and needs first-hand information. Later, the doctor wheedles information on 'fencing' stolen goods from his unsuspecting friend Chief Inspector Charles of the Yard, then goes to see top fence Benny Kellerman at his private drinking club in Holborn. Benny is nasty and suspicious but agrees to do business with 'Clit', who strikes up a friendship with Benny's cronies 'Pal' Green, 'Oakie', 'Tug' Wilson, 'Badger' Lee and Daisy. This gives Clit a circle of accomplices and the opportunity to pull more jobs, including a daring furs robbery in which he is able to gain valuable data for his book; Pal tends to lose his voice under pressure, and Badger faints.

Although Clit remains anonymous, he rewards his associates well and gives his own proceeds to charity. But Benny is jealous of Daisy's affection for Clit, and after slyly discovering who he is, attempts to blackmail him. However, Clit knocks Benny out with heroin in a glass of scotch, and later drowns him in a river outside his country bungalow. This also gives Clit a chance to assess his stress reactions during murder, which will complete his book. Unfortunately for him, the post mortem on Benny reveals he died before drowning, and Clit discovers he has made other mistakes. The net tightens around him and he tells barrister Sir William Grant the story of a 'friend' who is in identical trouble. Sir William replies he would stake his reputation the man would get off - because he was obviously mad. Inspector Charles arrives and Clit acts a little crazy, says goodbye to Ann for a while and engages the services of Sir William.

Nurse Ann
Dr Clitterhouse MD MRCP
Chief Inspector Charles
Benny Kellerman
'Pal' Green
Daisy
Sergeant Bates
'Oakie'
'Tug' Wilson
'Badger' Lee
Sir William Grant QC
A constable

Amber for Anna
Arthur Watkyn
Mystery 3 Acts
London 1964

A group of friends in a country village near Brighton return from the theatre to the Marsh's home and discuss the murder mystery they have just seen. Penny Brett says all such plays are ridiculous, but the others - Carol and Andrew Marsh, Helen and Paul Ritchie, and German émigré Herman Voss, disagree. They point to a decorative knife on the mantelpiece as a typical domestic weapon. Later that evening, the Marsh's German au pair Anna is found dead upstairs stabbed by the same knife. One of the guests must be guilty. Inspector Elliott arrives to investigate, and discovers a trail of red herrings leading from Freda Schultz, the Ritchie's au pair girl, who is not all she seems. The au pairs are brought over to England through a company run by Andrew Marsh, whose wife Carol is having an affair with Paul Ritchie. There is also a rumour that Voss is a disguised Nazi and had been recognized by Anna. The identity and motive of the murderer are not revealed until the end since the Inspector cannot find the evidence to pin the crime(s) on him/her. Until, that is, Penny's husband Clive, who was drunk on the fateful evening, contributes the vital clue.

Carol Marsh
Penny Brett
Helen Ritchie
Paul Ritchie
Andrew Marsh
Herman Voss
Anna Klein
Police Constable Wright
Police Inspector Elliott
Clive Brett
Freda Schultz

Amédée
Eugène Ionesco
Comedy 3 Acts
Paris 1954

In a nondescript quarter of Paris, sometime in the mid-fifties, Amédée Buccinioni, a failed playwright, and his wife Madeleine, who runs a surreal telephone switchboard from their flat, sit arguing about a guest who has been occupying their bedroom for many years. As they argue, the guest, who turns out to be a corpse, gradually expands to fill first the bedroom and then the sitting room.

As Amédée and Madeleine range from mild bickering to mutual recrimination and back again, it becomes plain that the corpse must be removed or it will finally crowd them out. They finally manage to push its immense length out the window to the ground below, where Amédée tries to haul it away to the river.

On the advice of an American soldier who has been ejected drunk from a local bar, Amédée wraps the corpse around himself so it will be easier to move. Instead, the corpse unfurls like a giant kite and drags Amédée into the heavens. Despite his wife's pleas and the exhortations of neighbours and the police, Amédée flies off and vanishes.

Amédée Buccinioni, a failed playwright
Madeleine, Amédée's wife
Amédée II, Amédée's double
Madeleine II, Madeleine's double
A postman
Two American soldiers
Mado
Bar owner
Two policeman
A man
A woman

Amen Corner
James Baldwin
Tragedy 3 Acts
Vienna 1965

The redoubtable Margaret Alexander is pastor of a fundamentalist black church in Harlem in the mid-sixties. She is supported in her ministry by her spinster sister Odessa, and by her eighteen-year-old son David.

Members of her congregation and several elders of the church have become unhappy with Maggie's high-handed ways. Their discontent surfaces when Maggie forbids one of them to take up a job driving a van for a liquor company, such work being 'ungodly'. Maggie is further undermined when her estranged husband, Luke, a jazz 'great' now dying of tuberculosis, returns to Harlem from the South and has to be given room in her home. David, having discovered that Maggie first came to New York after abandoning Luke and abducting his son, leaves the church to take up jazz.

The resentment of the elders, Maggie's self-righteous harshness to Luke, David's growing bohemianism and the suggestion that Maggie has not properly accounted for church funds, all lead to her removal as pastor. Stripped of their home and the church, Maggie and Odessa face the future alone.

Margaret Alexander (Maggie), Pastor
Odessa
Church elders:
Ida Jackson
Sister Moore
Sister and Brother Boxer
David
Luke
Members of the congregation

American Buffalo
David Mamet
Drama 2 Acts
Chicago 1975

In a run-down second-hand shop, somewhere in the urban Midwest of the USA, three characters from the margin of American society try to plan and carry out a robbery.

Don Dubrow, owner of the shop, has sold a rare Buffalo-head nickel to a sophisticated collector for ninety dollars. Fearing after the sale that he has made a bad bargain, he resolves to steal it back from the collector: so he plans a robbery with his assistant Bob, a young junkie. Bob's place is then usurped by Walter Cole, nicknamed Teach, who convinces Don that Bob is wrong for the job.

Teach talks to Don of efficiency, honest practice and loyalty, while in fact setting out to poison him against both Bob and the other prospective partner in the crime, Fletch. The impending robbery and Teach's treachery make Bob the scapegoat for both older men when their nerve cracks and their plans begin to go awry. Teach beats Bob so violently that the robbery must be abandoned to take the younger man to hospital.

Don Dubrow, owner, Don's Resale Shop
Walter Cole (Teach)
Bob, Don's assistant

American Dream, The
Edward Albee
Drama 1 Act
New York, 1961

Droll satire set in a living room where Mommy and Daddy, who seem to represent the worst kind of American inanity, live with Grandma, who by virtue of her age and constant parading of the infirmities of the old, seems a little more real. Grandma brings in lots of parcels and waits in fear for the van man to come and take her away, a threat wielded by Mommy and Daddy.

Local woman's club chairman Mrs Barker arrives and Grandma reminds her how, twenty years before, Mrs Barker once brought childless Mommy and Daddy a bundle of joy from the Bye Bye Adoption agency. Unfortunately the bundle turned out unsatisfactory, was mutilated and then died. Mrs Barker leaves to think things over and along comes a gorgeous young man looking for work. He is the American Dream, but he explains to Grandma that although he looks great, he is incomplete; he was separated at birth from his identical twin brother and ever since has been emotionless.

Mrs Barker returns and Grandma suggests she pretends that the Bye Bye agency has now sent along the young man to be Mommy and Daddy's new bundle. Everyone seems happy at the arrangement, although Mommy finds there is something familiar about the young man she can't quite place.

Mommy
Daddy
Mrs Barker
Grandma
The young man

Amorous Prawn, The
Anthony Kimmins
Comedy 3 Acts
London 1959

When Maj.- Gen. Sir Hamish Fitzadam has to go to the USA for several months, his wife Lady Fitzadam and the staff at his official army residence at Glenmally House, Argyll, turn the place into a luxury hotel to help pay for the General's retirement. Two Americans, svelte Larry Hoffmann and crude Sam Goulensky turn up and compete for the biggest salmon, helpfully supplied by the local poacher, and the staff - sexy Suzie, cheeky Cpl Sydney Green, chef Willie et al, make the guests very much at home. Everything goes well until the General gets back early. He's just had an insulting letter from army bureaucrats and to everyone's relief goes along with the hotel scheme. Then the Prawn - Lord Vernon - arrives and also falls in love with the place. Unfortunately he is also Secretary of State for War, and discovers the ruse. However, it is not his wife he has brought along for the night, but a local barmaid, so he wants to keep things quiet too. The General gets what he wants from the army - a peaceful retirement.

Cpl Sydney Green
Pte Biddy O'Hara WRAC
Pte Suzie Tidmarsh WRAC
Lady Fitzadam
Maj. Gen. Sir Hamish Fitzadam KBE CB DSO
Pte Albert Huggins
Pte Willie Maltravers
Sam Goulansky
Larry Hoffman
The Prawn
Uncle Joe

Amphitryon
Jean Giradoux
Comedy 3 Acts
Paris 1929

Giradoux originally called this play *Amphitryon 38*, in reference to the number of dramatic treatments of this story produced by his predecessors, most notably Plautus (d. 184BC).

Jupiter (Zeus) has decided to seduce Alcmena, loyal wife of Amphitryon, Prince of Thebes, so that she may give birth to the demi-god Hercules. Aided by Mercury, his scheming son, Jupiter sets out to subvert Alcmena's loyalty, but instead becomes so taken with her that he impersonates Amphitryon rather than force Alcmena to accept unwelcome advances.

Unaware that she has already given herself to the god, and having been told by a joyous Theban population that Jupiter is on his way to claim her, Alcmena tries to avoid his attentions by substituting Leda, Queen of Sparta, for herself. In so doing, however, she mistakenly offers Leda the genuine Amphitryon. She escapes Jupiter's anger only because he has already seduced her, disguised as Amphitryon, and been spellbound by her charm and loyalty.

Alcmena, Amphitryon's wife
Amphitryon, Prince of Thebes
Mercury
Sosios, a slave
Trumpeter
Warrior
Eclissa, Alcmena's nurse
Leda, Queen of Sparta
Echo, heavenly voices

Amphitryon
Plautus
Comedy 1 Act
Athens 195BC

Jupiter has fallen in love with Alcmena, the wife of Amphitryon, commander of the army of Thebes. While Amphitryon is away at war, Jupiter assumes his identity and enters Thebes accompanied by Mercury in the guise of Amphitryon's trusted slave, Sosia.

As Mercury has explained in a prologue, Jupiter is

distinguishable from Amphitryon only by a gold tassel on the god's hat, and Mercury from Sosia only by a tiny helmet plume. When Amphitryon and Sosia return unexpectedly to Thebes, a farce of mistaken identities ensues, and arouses Amphitryon's suspicion concerning Alcmena's fidelity. Jupiter is thus forced to appear to Amphitryon without disguise and to explain that he has seduced and impregnated Alcmena while posing as her husband.

Amphitryon, Theban General
Alcmena, Amphitryon's wife
Sosia, Amphitryon's slave
Jupiter
Mercury
Blepharo
Bromia
Other slaves

Anastasia File, The
Royce Ryton
Drama 2 Acts
London 1978

An Inspector comes to interview Mrs Manaham who tells him she will see him because his father was kind to her, but then asks him to leave her alone. He says she holds the key to a mystery; she says there is no mystery.

In a flashback to a psychiatric hospital in Berlin in 1922 a doctor and nurse are discussing a girl patient with the Inspector's father. The girl, who does not speak, is obviously someone quite special. Her deportment, her pedicure, all indicate great wealth. When she begins to speak, she does so in perfect German - although she is not German - and perfect English. She also understands Russian but will not speak it. She is very knowledgeable in political affairs. At last another patient at the hospital recognizes her. She is Anastasia, daughter of the murdered Tzar of Russia, the only survivor from the revolutionary massacre of the Russian royal family at Ekaterinburg. She has suffered terribly and as the news of her survival breaks, her tortures continue. Her family refuse to recognize her after she reveals the Tzar had deposited millions of roubles in gold in the Bank of England and if she is proven to be the Tzar's daughter, she will inherit the fortune. The bank also does not want to pay out. The Inspector likes her, gives her a home, and takes her to the USA to try to prove her identity. Unsuccessful, she returns to Europe and is forgotten, only finding some peace in her marriage.

Years later when the son of the Inspector once again goes over the central question of what happened between the time of the massacre and the time she was found, Mrs Manahan says something new and enigmatic which only deepens the mystery.

Inspector
Mrs Manahan
Actor and actress, playing many roles

Anatol
Arthur Schnitzler
Drama 7 Acts
Vienna 1890

Seven linked one-act plays about the sex life of the active Anatol.

The Crucial Question. Max tells his friend Anatol how much he envies Anatol's apparently hypnotic power over women but Anatol is very worried about Cora's possible infidelity. He hypnotizes her and sends Max out of the room before he asks the crucial question. Then he funks it.

Christmas Shopping. Anatol meets Gabrielle, with whom he has not had an affair, and carries her parcels for a while, as she asks about his latest mistress. Gabrielle sends the unknown girl some flowers with a message to the effect that she too might have loved Anatol as much - if she had had the courage.

Episode. Anatol visits Max, bringing a parcel containing souvenirs of past affairs. It emerges that they have shared a woman, Bianca, and now she is back in Vienna and coming to visit Max. She barely remembers Anatol who slinks off into the night.

Souvenirs. Anatol is engaged to Emilie who catches him searching the drawers of her desk. He finds two stones - a ruby which Emilie has kept as a memento of her loss of virginity at sixteen to a young man she cannot remember. The other stone, she reveals with greedy pride, is a black diamond. Anatol throws it in the fire and calls her a whore.

Farewell Supper. Max and Anatol are dining at the expensive Hotel Sacher and waiting for Annie of whom Anatol is tired. She is about to be replaced but, before Anatol can break this to her, Annie reveals that she is going to marry a young man in her ballet company. Anatol, who had told Max he had wanted the parting to go smoothly, is furious.

Agony. Anatol is tormented by 'love' for Elsa who declares she loves only him but often fails to turn up, or only stays a few minutes, and in any case refuses to leave her husband.

The Morning of Anatol's Wedding. Max visits Anatol a couple of hours before the scheduled wedding. Max is extremely disconcerted to find that Anatol has spent the night with Ilona whom he had picked up at the Masquerade. At first, Ilona cannot believe Anatol is really off to be married. She has no intention of giving him up.

Anatol
Max
Cora
Gabrielle
Bianca
Emilie
Annie
Elsa
Franz, manservant
Ilona

Anatomist, The
James Bridie
Drama 3 Acts
Edinburgh 1930

This historical piece is a character study of Dr Robert Knox, the Scottish anatomist. Knox needs cadavers for his dissections, but is not concerned from whence they come and becomes involved with the notorious Burke and Hare resurrectionists.

Knox's assistant argues with his fiancée about the body snatchers' activities and seeks comfort in the arms of a local tart, who is subsequently murdered by Burke and Hare and presented as a corpse for Knox. The assistant recognizes the body and is horrified at Knox's refusal to concern himself with where it came from.

Burke is arrested and hanged and Knox is implicated. Threatened by a mob, he goes to the home of his assistant's fiancée, ready to shoot her, but he is rescued by his students to whom he delivers an impassioned anatomy lecture on the subject of the heart.

Mary Belle Dishart
Amelia Dishart
Walter Anderson
Jessie Ann
Dr Knox
Raby
Landlord
Mary Paterson
Janet
Davie Paterson
Burke
Hare

And a Nightingale Sang
C. P. Taylor
Drama 2 Acts
Newcastle-upon-Tyne 1977

The fortunes of the working-class Stott family from Newcastle-upon-Tyne during World War Two are chronicled from the day war breaks out, revealing their personal preoccupations and modest adventures set against a vivid backdrop of air raids and deprivation. Daughter Helen, in her early thirties, is narrator; she's matter-of-fact and sensible and not as pretty as younger sister Joyce, engaged to soldier Eric. But Joyce isn't sure she really wants to marry Eric. She does, though, with considerable trepidation and later they part. Dad (George) is always playing popular songs of the day on the piano, and also mocking Mam Peggy's fervent Catholicism. Old Andie, the grandad, stoical and fatalistic, moves shiftlessly from one place to another, never completely welcome, until a local wife scares him off with a proposal and he creeps back to the fold.

When Eric brings round mate Norman, he and Helen fall in love and set up house together, much to Ma's dismay; Norman is a married man, but Helen has a wonderful time and just can't help herself. George becomes a fully-fledged Marx-spouting communist and gets strafed by the Luftwaffe while firewatching; everyone thinks he's dead and then he wanders in dazed with a bandage on his head. Circumstances eventually draw reluctant Norman back to his family, which takes the edge off VE Day for Helen. Eric returns to Joyce and is surprised to see how Helen has blossomed. They celebrate victory with a happy dance...

Helen Stott
Joyce Stott
George
Peggy (Mam)
Andie
Eric
Norman

And So To Bed
J. B. Fagan
Comedy 3 Acts
London 1926

This historical romp finds diarist and 'father of the Admiralty' Samuel Pepys rescuing lovely singer Mrs Knight from a violent pick-purse, then slyly arranging a musical tryst with her that evening. His dinner guests include young francophile dandy Pelham Humphries and brazen Mrs Pierce and Mrs Knepp, but Pepys declares he has urgent business at the Navy office. His attractive wife sees him dress up, and knowing his ways with women, doesn't believe his story. When she finds the note with Mrs Knight's address she pursues Sam.

Meanwhile her amorous husband is using all his flowery lines on Mrs Knight when her former lover King Charles II arrives. Sam is forced to hide in a chest where he hears little good of himself. Then it's Charles's turn to hide as Mrs Pepys arrives, ranting and raving after Samuel, but she's brought to heel upon discovering not Sam, but his Majesty behind a curtain. Charles, the archetypal ladies' man, flirts with Mrs Pepys before sending her home, then demands that sulking Mrs Knight open the chest. Charles and an uncomfortable Sam lecture each other, but upon leaving Sam forgets his flageolet (a musical instrument) which Charles then sends to Mrs Pepys; now both know what the other has been up to.

Back home Sam and wife confront one another with various accusations, protestations and extractions of mutual promises of fidelity. It is now past midnight, their adventures are over... and so to bed.

Charles II
Samuel Pepys
Creed
Pelling, the Potticary
Pelham Humphries
Prodgers, Groom of the Chamber
W. Caesar, a lutanist
Boy to Pepys
Boy to Creed
Pelling's 'prentice
A pick-purse

First watchman
Second watchman
Mrs Pepys
Mrs Knight
Mrs Pierce
Mrs Knepp
Doll, a blackamoor
Lettice
Sue
Julia

Androcles and the Lion
George Bernard Shaw
Comedy Prologue 2 Acts
London 1913

The original, probably apocryphal, story of Androcles had him meet, in the ring of the Colosseum, a lion he had treated for a poisoned paw when the animal was in the wild. Shaw shows how Androcles' timid kindliness had won the lion's trust, moves forward in time to show the old Androcles entering Rome in a group of condemned fellow-Christians, and draws a portrait of the different kind of faith shown by each of the Christians in the face of death.

Lavinia, a patrician convert, is at first haughtily steadfast, but later recants the 'god of the future'; Ferrovius, a born warrior, abandons his faith and defends his friends from death; and Spintho dies accidentally trying to escape his meeting with the lions. As a counterpoint to the Christians' deep moral dilemma, Shaw portrays Caesar as an opportunist, utterly debauched and cynical, who persecutes the new religion purely as a matter of political expediency.

Emperor Caesar
Captain, admirer of Lavinia
Androcles
Lion
Lentullus, Metullus, Roman dandies
Ferrovius, a warrior convert
Spintho, a once debauched convert
Centurion
Editor
Call Boy
Secutor
Lavinia, a patrician convert
Retarius
Menagerie keeper
Slave driver
Megaera

Andromache
Jean Racine
Tragedy 5 Acts
Paris 1667

Andromache, widow of the Trojan hero Hector, has been given to Pyrrhus, son of Achilles and King of Epirus, as part of the spoils of the Trojan war. Ignoring the enmity his people feel towards the Trojans, Pyrrhus falls in love with Andromache although he is pledged to marry Hermione, daughter of Helen of Troy and King Menelaus of the Greeks. Andromache, however, loves only Hector's memory and their son Astyanax, captive with her in Epirus.

The kings of the Greek city states send Orestes, son of the great King Agamemnon, to persuade Pyrrhus that Astyanax will present a threat to them all if the boy is allowed to reach manhood. Drawn to Epirus more by his own unrequited love for Hermione than by his duties as envoy, Orestes realizes that the threat he presents to Astyanax will cause Pyrrhus and Andromache to come closer together. He hopes that when they do, Hermione may still become his.

Purely to save Astyanax's life, Andromache marries Pyrrhus and this brings about Hermione's humiliation. She, in turn, goads Orestes into murdering Pyrrhus with the promise that in avenging her, Orestes will win her hand. When Orestes brings news that Pyrrhus is mortally wounded, Hermione reverts to her earlier love, curses Orestes and commits suicide. Driven mad by guilt and Hermione's betrayal, Orestes is taken away from Epirus by his comrades-in-arms.

Andromache, Hector's widow
Pyrrhus, King of Epirus and Achilles' son
Orestes, Agamemnon's son
Hermione, Pyrrhus' betrothed
Pylades, Orestes' confidant
Cleone, Hermione's confidant
Cephisa, Andromache's confidant
Phoenix, Pyrrhus' confidant
Soldiers, servants etc

Andromache
Euripides
Tragedy 1 Act
Athens 431BC

As part of the spoils of victory over Troy, Andromache has been given to Neoptolemus of Thessaly, by whom she has had a son, Molossus. Ten years after her capture, Neoptolemus has gone on to marry Hermione, daughter of King Menelaus.

Hermione remains childless and blames her infertility on Andromache, whom she believes to be a witch. While Neoptolemus is away consulting the Delphic oracle, Hermione, in league with Menelaus, tries to murder both Andromache and Molossus. The intervention of Peleus, Neoptolemus's grandfather, saves both mother and child.

Orestes, to whom Hermione was at one time betrothed, arrives unexpectedly, having murdered Neoptolemus at Delphi, and abducts Hermione. Neoptolemus's death is announced, but the goddess Thetis confers immortality on the aged Peleus, although in so doing she may just be mocking his credulity.

Andromache, Hector's widow, Neoptolemus's
  concubine
Old slave woman

Hermione, *Neoptolemus's wife*
Menelaus, *King of Sparta*
Molossus, *son of Andromache and Neoptolemus*
Peleus, *Neoptolemus's grandfather*
Nurse
Orestes
Messenger
Thetis, *sea nymph*
Chorus

Angel City
Sam Shepard
Drama 2 Acts
San Francisco, 1976

In a surreal movie office in smog-ridden LA, Rabbit is brought in by Lanx to dream up an awesome and totally new major movie disaster idea to save the studio from bankruptcy. All the while, Tympani drums away trying to create a new rhythm, a jazz saxophonist lonesomely wails a 'soundtrack', and glamorous secretary Miss Scoons waits to be discovered for one of her many talents. As everyone poo-poos everyone else's ideas, boss Wheeler gets greener and slimier and more monster-like, and eventually comes up with his own disaster scenario. But by this time he's been out-slimed by Rabbit who takes over the studio.

Lanx
Wheeler
Miss Scoons
Rabbit
Tympani
Sax

Animal Farm
Adapted by Peter Hall from the novel by George Orwell
Lyrics by Adrian Mitchell
Music by Richard Peaslee
Musical Play 2 Acts
London 1984

As an eight-year-old boy reads *Animal Farm* the scene unfolds before him and he acts as narrator.

Farmer Jones is an old drunkard and his Manor Farm has run down so much and the animal inhabitants are so hungry that they decide to take over. Pig Napoleon soon emerges as a natural leader and in no time has organized the other gullible creatures into a strict socialist-style regime, Animal Farm, which is strong enough to repel an attack from Jones and his cronies. Napoleon consolidates his position by rumours, propaganda and coercion and the pigs become a privileged group. Exploitation of the other animals begins, hens have to give up their eggs, cows their milk, and dissent is met with brutal reprisals and even execution.

Trade begins with the outside and humans visit the model establishment; Napoleon decides it might be better if they were to revert to the old name - Animal Farm becomes Manor Farm again.

The boy
Cat
Hens
Pigeons
Cows
Mr Jones
Mrs Jones
Mr Whymper
Old Major
Mr Pilkington
Minimus
Muriel
Napoleon
Squealer
Clover
Moses
Mollie
Benjamin
Napoleon's dog
Snowball
Pigs
Sheep
Stable lad
Farmers

Anna Christie
Eugene O'Neill
Tragic Comedy
New York 1921

After years of neglect and abuse, first as a foster child and then as a prostitute, Anna Christie arrives in the brutal New York docks of the twenties to look for her father, Chris Christopherson, an old seaman. The two are reunited, and despite Anna's resentment and Christopherson's bad conscience, they quickly come to a prickly, but tender regard for one another. Anna's worldly past is clear to others but she is careful to keep her father ignorant of it. To help Anna's recovery from the illness which drove her back to him, Christopherson moves her into the cabin of the coastal barge of which he is now captain. For Anna, life on the coastal waters brings a sense of cleansing and rebirth, and with it a wry tolerance of Christopherson's endless tirades against 'Dat ole davil Sea.' Anchored in the outer harbour of Provincetown, Mass. they save the lives of four sailors adrift from the wreck of their ship. Anna falls in love with one of the survivors, Mat Burke, a huge roistering Irishman. As Mat and she become closer, Christopherson rails ever more violently against the sailors and the sea. He is relieved when Anna refuses Mat's offer of marriage, only to be thrust into despair when she reveals to both men that her refusal arises from the shame of having been a prostitute. In a tempestuous final act, Mat comes to the barge to kill Anna but finally, and with ambivalence, offers to marry her.

Johnny (Johnny-the-Priest), barman
Larry, Johnny's assistant
Chris Christopherson, barge captain

Marthy Owen, Christopherson's mistress
Anna
Johnson, a bargeman
Mat Burke

Anna Lucasta
Philip Yordan
Drama 3 Acts
New York 1944

The working-class Lucasta family get a message from the father's old friend Otis that he is sending up son Rudolph from Alabama with 800 dollars in search of a wife.

Tough son Frank and wife Stella plan to palm Rudolph off with wayward sister Anna, now in Brooklyn. They figure Rudolph is a country fool who will soon part with his money - to them. Nice sister-in-law Katie objects but her husband Stanley is dominated by Frank. The mother, though, is thrilled at the prospect of seeing her beloved Anna again, and Frank forces father, a near psychopath, to fetch Anna from Noah's bar in Brooklyn. Meanwhile, Rudolph arrives and turns out to be no hick, but a prize agricultural student. Nevertheless, he and Anna fall deeply in love, but she does not reveal her sordid past.

Father hates Anna with an unhealthy passion and when Anna's ex-boyfriend, sailor Danny, arrives just after the wedding, the father threatens to tell Rudolph, and then reveals he has already written about Anna to Otis and to Rudolph's prospective employers. Anna flees with Danny.

Three days later Rudolph and Katie go looking for Anna, and just after they leave Noah's bar, Anna returns drunk, together with Danny and his friend Lester. She is frantic and suicidal, and when the sailors have to return to their ship, Noah locks up and tells Anna of her family's bust-up; Pa died of a heart attack and Ma hid the money so Frank got none.

Noah also tells Anna of Rudolph's obvious devotion, to which Anna replies that she left him for his own good. Then Rudolph's voice is heard calling from outside - he has left his bag in the bar. Anna takes it out to him.
Katie
Stella
Theresa
Stanley
Frank
Joe
Eddy
Noah
Blanche
Officer
Anna
Danny
Lester
Rudolph

Anne of the Thousand Days
Maxwell Anderson
Tragedy 3 Acts
New York 1948

Anderson refashions the character of Anne Boleyn, and replaces the shy, ineffectual historical figure (Henry VIII's second wife) with a disillusioned romantic who gives herself to the King to ensure her family's prosperity by providing an heir to the throne.

The play uses flashbacks from Anne's reflections on the eve of her execution to show the course of her life with Henry. The King is attracted by Anne's indifference to him and though he pursues her with unrelenting flattery she agrees to be his lover only if he divorces his wife, Catherine of Aragon. To meet her condition Henry must defy the Pope's sanction on the divorce, and so eventually execute all his subjects who oppose a break with Rome.

When Anne does give herself to the King his interest wanes, and then ceases altogether when she gives birth to a girl (the future Elizabeth I) instead of the son he craves. On refusing to cooperate with Henry's attempt to have the marriage annulled, so that he can marry yet again, Anne finds herself falsely accused and sentenced to death for adultery.
Anne Boleyn
Mary Boleyn, her sister
Thomas Boleyn, her father
Elizabeth Boleyn, her mother
Cardinal Wolsey
Henry VIII
Henry Morris and Mark Smeaton, King's courtiers
Jane Seymour, Henry's mistress
Duke of Norfolk
Earl of Northumberland
Thomas More
Thomas Wyatt
Servant
Attendant
Three musicians
Three singers
Madge Smeaton
Bishop Fisher
John Houghton
Kingston
Clerk

Anne of Green Gables
Alice Chadwicke
Drama 3 Acts
New York 1935

Middle-aged brother and sister Matthew and Marilla Cuthbert live in a beautiful house called Green Gables. After some persuasion the stern and stony Marilla allows Matthew to adopt a boy to help with the farm work. Their friend Nancy Spencer goes to the orphanage to choose a suitable child; however, she is a scatterbrain and sends noisy imaginative Anne Shirley to Green Gables. Matthew is completely taken with Anne, but Marilla is determined to send her back to the orphanage the very next day. Anne, after much crying and begging, is allowed to stay.

She goes to school and makes friends, especially with Diana Barry. She makes enemies with Gilbert Blythe, the richest and best looking boy at school, because he laughed at her freckles. After Anne had been living at Green Gables for two years, disaster strikes as Marilla discovers the bank holding all their money has gone bankrupt. Luckily, Anne had changed their banks because she didn't like the manager. For the first time Marilla shows affection towards Anne for having been such a clever girl. At that moment Marilla's old beau, Ira, walks in and it turns out that he is Anne's uncle. Anne then makes friends with Gilbert Blythe, Ira proposes to Marilla and at last Anne doesn't have to fantasize about her future any more because now she is truly happy.

Anne Shirley
Florence Remsen
Minnie Stearn
Mrs Alexander Spencer
Matthew Cuthbert
Marilla Cuthbert
Mrs Rachel Lynde
Diana Barry
Mrs Allan
Josie Pye
Moody Spurgeon
Gilbert Blythe
Ira Mills

but none of them have the proof needed - except, that is, Miss Hannigan's con-man brother Rooster and girlfriend Lily who arrive in disguise and have all the appropriate documents as well as one half of Annie's locket. Their fraud is thwarted when F.D.R. comes to the rescue with an FBI report that Annie's parents are dead.

Warbucks offers to adopt Annie and she gratefully accepts; her orphan pals are liberated from Miss Hannigan's and can go to school; F.D.R. has his New Deal; and Annie's own special surprise Christmas present is ... Sandy.

Songs include: 'Tomorrow'; 'Something was Missing'; 'You're Never Fully Dressed Without a Smile'

Molly	*Justice Braneis*
Pepper	*Harry*
Duffy	*F.D.R.*
July	*Sophie*
Tessie	*Cecille*
Kate	*Star-to-be*
Annie	*Bonnie Boylan*
Miss Hannigan	*Perkins*
Bundles McCloskey	*Grace Farrell*
Sound Effects Man	*Drake*
Ickles	*Mrs Pugh*
Dog Catcher	*Connie Boylan*
Jimmy Johnson	*Annette*
Honor guard	*Ronnie Boylan*
Bert Healy	*Oliver Warbucks*
Hull	*Rooster Hannigan*
Sandy	*Lily*
Kaltenborn's voice	*Fred McCracken*
Lt. Ward	*Hopkins*
Morganthau	*N.B.C. Page*

Annie

Thomas Meehan
Lyrics by Martin Charnin
Music by Charles Strouse
Musical 2 Acts
New York, 1977

Little orphan Annie (based on the cartoon character) lives in an orphanage run by the cruel Miss Hannigan. After one failed escape attempt she tries again, this time hiding in a laundry hamper; it works. She makes friends with a dog she names Sandy and they stay at a 'Hooverville', a depression-era shantytown. Soon Annie is caught and sent back to the orphanage, but Sandy escapes. However, Annie's luck is in when Grace, secretary to very rich Oliver Warbucks comes and chooses Annie to be a guest at the Warbucks' mansion over Christmas. Oliver meets Annie and thinks she's wonderful; he even takes her to the White House where her ebullient rendition of *Tomorrow* inspires F.D.R. to conceive the New Deal!

Warbucks decides to help Annie find her parents and over the radio he offers 50,000 dollars if they get in touch with him. A thousand fakes present themselves

Annie Get Your Gun

Richard Rodgers and Oscar Hammerstein
Music by Irving Berlin
Book by Dorothy Fields
Musical 2 Acts
New York 1949

Chick hick tomboy Annie Oakley is a crack shot even though she has only a beat-up old rifle. She goes to the visiting Buffalo Bill's Wild West Show and discovers that it offers a five dollar shooting match with Frank Butler, 'the world's foremost sharpshooter', who sure believes in his own publicity. She doesn't realize that she is talking to the swollen-headed champ and he tries to warn her off, but she just knows she's the best. She takes a fancy to him but, although she has an earthy sexiness, he explains that the girl he will marry will have to be the dainty kind. Then she discovers that he is the famed marksman and to everybody's amazement she beats him. Because the show needs a boost Buffalo Bill wants her to join the act but Frank does not care for that idea.

Their rival Pawnee Bill (and his Far East Show) visits them, bringing one of his stars Chief Sitting Bull, who is only temporarily around as he's not interested in show business; he wants to farm his territory but can't because it's too full of oil - and you can't eat oil. They try to persuade him to help with his oil profits, but he refuses although he greatly admires little sure-shot Annie and adopts her into the tribe as his daughter.

Frank gets more displeased as the tour goes on and Annie becomes the main attraction, but in the end Sitting Bull fixes it for Frank to win the contest by bending Annie's gun sights. Annie loses her bet, a big one this time, and despite the previously expressed view that you can't get a man with a gun - she does, and the show is saved.

Songs include: 'I Got the Sun in the Morning'; 'There's No Business Like Show Business'; 'Anything You Can Do'; 'They Say It's Wonderful'

Little Boy	Mrs Little Horse
Charlie Davenport	Mrs Blacktooth
Mac, property man	Mrs Yellowfoot
Foster Wilson	Trainman
Dolly Tate	Waiter
Tommy Keeler	Porter
Frank Butler	Riding Mistress
Annie Oakley	Maj. Gordon Lillie
Little Jake	Chief Sitting Bull
Nellie	Sylvia Potter-Porter
Jessie	Indians
Minnie	Singers
Col William F. Cody	Dancers

Anniversary Waltz
Jerome Chodorov and Joseph Fields
Comedy 3 Acts
New York 1954

Alice and Bud Walters are celebrating their fifteenth anniversary at their Manhattan apartment together with teenage children Okkie and Debbie, and Alice's parents Mr and Mrs Gans. Bud had returned home from work already tipsy with partner Chris and dumb blonde Janice, and during the evening he indiscreetly reveals to his parents-in-law that he and Alice had indulged in pre-marital sex. They storm out, and enraged Bud kicks in the new TV set Alice's folks just gave them.

Next day Chris replaces the set but when Bud turns it on, precocious Debbie appears on a chat show talking about her parents' problems and the pre-maritals. The show is blanked off the air and once more Bud kicks in the set. Chris arrives and is horrified with Bud, and then Mr and Mrs Gans arrive and discover that their present too has been smashed. Everyone rounds on Bud, who leaves home for a week. When he returns, suitably contrite, he makes up with Chris and his parents-in-law but by now Alice is sick of his tantrums. Now it's her turn to want to leave, but she gets a call from her doctor - she's pregnant. She's angry and frustrated, but then yet another TV arrives, this time from Bud, and the loving note with it moves Alice to forgive and forget.

Millie	Sam
Okkie Walters	Mr Gans
Alice Walters	Mrs Gans
Debbie Walters	Handyman
Bud Walters	
Chris Steelman	
Janice Revere	
Harry	

Another Country
Julian Mitchell
Drama 3 Acts
Greenwich 1981

In Gascoigne House at an English public school in the thirties, seventeen-year-old Guy Bennett and Tommy Judd are rebels; Bennett with his series of homosexual crushes is beginning to embarrass the house, and Judd is already a confirmed and vociferous Marxist. Uptight prefect Fowler is continually on their case, but when classmate Devenish declares he is leaving, school politics dictate that the two rebels may have to be persuaded to become prefects. Meanwhile, there is a suicide, after one of two boys, caught *in flagrante* by a master, hangs himself. The school cannot afford any more scandals.

Devenish's uncle, literary intellectual Vaughan Cunningham gives a lecture and has tea in the library with the boys, his nephew, liberal prefect Menzies, Judd (who walks out) and Bennett, who senses in gay Cunningham a useful outside sponsor. The prefect problem is settled when Devenish decides to stay on, and Judd, who had reluctantly decided to accept prefectship is no longer needed and conveniently made to seem as if he had compromised his communist principles.

Bennett, realizing he will always have to hide his true nature, resolves to become a prefect as the first step on the long ladder towards working within the system, while at the same time betraying it.

Guy Bennett
Tommy Judd
Donald Devenish
Jim Menzies, house prefect
Fowler, house prefect
Sanderson, house prefect
Barclay, head of house and member of Twenty Two
Delahay, member of Twenty Two
Wharton, a fag
Vaughan Cunningham

Another Part of the Forest
Lillian Hellman
Drama 3 Acts
New York 1946

Marcus Hubbard, a ruthless and greedy ex-black marketeer, is despised by the inhabitants of Bowden,

Alabama, in 1880. His love of good music and the arts is matched by his contempt for his do-gooder wife and his sons Benjamin and the weak Oscar. He is manipulated, however, by his favourite daughter Regina, who tries to arrange a loan for her lover's family, but she withdraws when she learns that brother Ben is involved and trying to make a profit for himself.

When Oscar, who is infatuated by a local whore, brings her to a family party, she insults the Hubbards and Marcus ends up throwing both of his two sons out of the house. Ben finds evidence of his father's dirty dealing during the Civil War and threatens to expose him. Marcus, now a broken man, has no power to stop his wife leaving to open a school for poor Negroes.

Ben, who has now become the family tyrant, orders Oscar to marry a plantation owner's daughter and Regina to marry a banker.

Regina Hubbard
John Bagtry
Lavinia Hubbard
Coralee
Marcus Hubbard
Benjamin Hubbard
Jacob
Oscar Hubbard
Simon Isham
Birdie Bagtry
Harold Penniman
Gilbert Jugger
Laurette Sincee

Antigone
Jean Anouilh
Tragedy 1 Act
Paris 1942

This play is a close adaptation of Sophocles' original. Eteocles and Polynices, the sons of Oedipus and brothers of Antigone, have killed one another in single combat, each trying to wrest sole control of Thebes from the other. Instead, Creon, Antigone's uncle, has become King of Thebes and decrees that Polynices was a rebel whose corpse must not be buried but left to rot. Antigone defies the decree and is arrested by Creon's guards, despite the fact that Creon's son, Haemon, is her fiancé. To avoid embarrassment, Creon offers to murder the guards who arrested her and to suppress news of the burial if Antigone maintains silence about the incident and obeys him in the future.

Although he goes on to explain that both her brothers were plotting against the state, and that he chose to bury one and revile the other for purely political reasons, Antigone remains determined to bury Polynices. She is condemned to die by starvation in a walled-up cave, where she hangs herself. Haemon and his mother, Queen Eurydice, both commit suicide. Creon is left to rule, alone and friendless.

Chorus

Antigone
Nurse to Antigone
Ismene, Antigone's mother
Haemon, Antigone's betrothed
King Creon, Haemon's father
Three guards
Messenger
Page
Queen Eurydice

Antigone
Sophocles
Tragedy 1 Act
Athens c. 445BC

The war with Argos has ended in death for Oedipus's son, Polynices as well as for Oedipus's second son, Eteocles. Order has been restored to Thebes under the authoritarian hand of Creon, Oedipus's brother-in-law.

To make the point that insurrections against authority are bound to fail, Creon has ordered that Polynices's body shall not be honoured with burial but must rot outside the precincts of Thebes. At the same time he has decreed full honours for Eteocles, who defended the city.

Antigone and Ismene, Oedipus's daughters, arrive in Thebes, Antigone having already resolved to defy the ban on burial. She is adamant that her duty to both Polynices and to the Gods demands disobedience. She asks Ismene to help her. Ismene is fearful and ambivalent, so Antigone resolves to act alone. Caught by the guard that Creon has set over the corpse, Antigone is brought before the King, with whom she argues the claims of her personal obligation against the needs of the state for order. Creon, unmoved, condemns her to death.

Creon's son Haemon, who is betrothed to Antigone, pleads for her pardon, on the grounds that the populace will sympathize with her. The King rails against his son, refuses to drop the matter and orders Antigone to be shut up in a mountain cave. After a further impassioned plea for clemency from Thebe's blind prophet Teiresias, the King relents.

Fired with fear of the dire consequences that Teiresias has predicted for Thebes in the event of Antigone's death, Creon rushes to release Antigone. He arrives too late to prevent her suicide and is futher powerless to prevent Haemon following her lead. Finally Queen Eurydice also commits suicide in her grief for Haemon. Creon, utterly broken, faces desolation.

Antigone, Oedipus's daughter
Ismene, Oedipus's daughter
Creon, King of Thebes
Haemon, Creon's son
Teiresias, a prophet
Eurydice, Queen of Thebes
Chorus
Soldiers
Messenger
Attendants etc.

Antony and Cleopatra
William Shakespeare
Tragedy 5 Acts
London 1607

Antony, brilliant war-hardened soldier and magnanimous general, attempts to protect the interests of the eastern Roman Empire, but instead carouses with Cleopatra, beautiful and fascinating Queen of Egypt. When Antony's relatives in Rome cause trouble for Octavius Caesar and there is the threat of a mighty rebellion by General Pompey, Antony takes unwilling leave of Cleopatra and goes to help Rome with his friend Enobarbus. No one in Rome trusts love-smitten Antony, so a marriage is arranged between Caesar's widowed sister Octavia and Antony. The Empire is then divided up between Caesar (the west), Antony (the east) and Lepidus (the south), and during peace talks everyone gets drunk on board Pompey's galley.

Later, Pompey is defeated, Caesar seizes Lepidus and Antony returns to Cleopatra. An enraged Caesar determines to avenge his sister's honour and against his better judgement, Antony lets himself be persuaded by Cleopatra to fight Caesar at sea. During the battle, Cleopatra's galley flees and to his everlasting shame Antony pursues her instead of fighting. Enobarbus deserts Antony for Caesar, but when Antony sends him his treasure and 'gentle adieus', Enobarbus kills himself in remorse. Antony fights a final land-battle with Caesar but is betrayed by the Egyptians. He rages at Cleopatra, who is so afraid she hides and then sends him the message that she died with his name on her lips. Distraught, Antony wounds himself mortally; meanwhile Cleopatra relents and sends him another message that she is alive. Dying, Antony is brought to her and dies in her arms.

Caesar weeps at the news of the death of the great Antony and promises mercy and good treatment to Cleopatra. She, however, arranges for a deadly asp to be brought to her, concealed in a basket of fruit, and kills herself. Caesar buries her with Antony.

Triumvirs: *Antony, Octavius Caesar and Lepidus*
  Sextus Pompeius
Friends to Antony: *Dometius Enobarbus, Ventidius,*
  Eros, Scarus, Dercetus, Demetrius, Philo and
  Maecenas
Friends to Caesar: *Agrippa, Dolabella, Proculeius,*
  Thadias and Gallas
Friends to Sextus Pompeius: *Menas, Menecrates*
  and Varrius
Taurus, Lieutenant-General to Caesar
Canidius, Lieutenant-General to Antony
Silius, an officer in Ventidius's army
A Schoolmaster, ambassador from Antony to Caesar
Attendants on Cleopatra: *Alexas, Mardian,*
  Seleucus, Diomedes, a soothsayer and a clown
Cleopatra, Queen of Eqypt
Octavia, sister to Caesar, wife to Antony
Charmain and Iras, attendants on Cleopatra
Officers
Soldiers
Messengers
Other attendants

Any Wednesday
Muriel Resnik
Comedy 2 Acts
London 1965

Ellen is John's tax-deductible mistress; everything John touches has to be tax-deductible because he is so successful. His company bought her apartment and he sees her every Wednesday. He is also exhausted every Thursday. She is a bit scatty, nearly thirty and lovely, she writes children's books and longs to see more of John. He is around fifty, suave and svelte, and not above spinning a line. He did not get where he is by kindness.

Enter Cass, whose firm has been bought by John's and is being closed down - for tax purposes. Cass is in New York out to get something on John and he has been steered to the flat - purportedly a company executive suite - by mistake by John's new secretary. Cass assesses the situation and realizes he has something on John, but when John's wife Dorothy comes along, he has to pretend to be Ellen's husband. Dorothy invites them both to dine with her and John, and it all goes horribly wrong. Cass is not hard enough to blackmail John by threatening to tell nice Dorothy, and Dorothy insists on 'doing up' the executive flat, much to Ellen's horror. Dorothy soon realizes what is going on and divorce is in the air. John moves in with Ellen but it does not work. Cass, of course, is in love with Ellen, and when John leaves for good, Cass comes back. He now has Ellen, and his company - John has given him a reprieve.

John
Ellen
Cass
Dorothy

Anything Goes
Howard Lindsay, Russell Crouse, Guy Bolton and P. G. Wodehouse
Music and Lyrics by Cole Porter
Musical Comedy 2 Acts
New York 1934

Nightclub singer Reno Sweeney likes Billy Crocker, but he's still smitten with ex-fiancée Hope. Reno embarks on a liner voyage to England to find Billy also aboard; he's come to say goodbye to Hope, also a passenger, but realizing he still loves her he stows away. Ticketless and passportless, he manages to acquire both when the dodgy Revd Dr Moon's crooked confederate doesn't show up. In fact, the Doc is public enemy number 13, although actually a mild-mannered man with acute criminal ambitions. Billy switches back and forth in and out of disguise, confusing both Hope and Reno, and after Moon is apprehended, the ship's captain holds a revival meeting for passengers who want to confess their sins.

When they reach London, Billy is distraught to find Hope plans to wed Sir Evelyn Oakleigh, but it is a marriage of financial convenience. Luckily, business matters get sorted out, several million dollars are made, and Hope and Billy are reunited. Sir Evelyn takes a fancy to Reno and Moon is dubbed 'harmless' by an FBI report, aggravating him severely.

Songs include: 'Anything Goes'; 'You're the Top'; 'I Get a Kick Out of You'; 'All Through the Night'

Elisha J. Whitney
Steward
Hope Harcourt
Sir Evelyn Oakleigh
Mrs Wadsworth T. Harcourt
Reporter
Photographer
Bishop
Ching
Ling
Reno Sweeney
Purity
Chastity
Charity
Virtue
Billy Crocker
Purser
Bonnie
Moon
Captain
Three girl passengers

Applause

Betty Comden and Adolph Green
Music by Charles Strouse
Lyrics by Lee Adams
Musical Play 2 Acts
New York 1970

Eve Harrington, an 'innocent' theatre fan, manages to charm her way into the dressing room of star Margot Channing on the opening night of her successful new play and spends the rest of the evening with Margot's entourage in Greenwich Village. She soon becomes an indispensable member of Margot's household, a girl Friday who models herself on her idol so successfully that producer Howard Benedict suggests she becomes Margot's understudy. Margot eventually begins to resent the attention that Eve is getting especially when Margot's favourite writer decides to do his next script for Eve, and his wife arranges for Margot to be stranded in the country so that understudy Eve can go on. Eve uses her charms on any man who can advance her career, and is herself used by Howard, but she has no luck with Margot's boyfriend, director Bill Sampson who remains loyal to Margot even when she accepts retirement. Later at an awards ceremony Margot publicly acknowledges Eve's meteoric rise to fame.

Songs include: 'But Alive'; 'Who's that Girl?'; 'The Best Night of My Life'

Tony awards announcer
Tony host
Margot Channing
Eve Harrington
Howard Benedict
Bert
Buzz Richards
Bill Sampson
Duane Fox
Karen Richards
Bartender
Dancer in bar
Peter
Bob
Piano player
Stan Harding
Danny
Bonnie
Carol
Joey
Musicians
TV director
Fan

Apple Cart, The

George Bernard Shaw
Comedy 3 Acts
Warsaw 1929

Writing in 1928 Shaw set this play about authority and party politics in the imaginary future England of 1962.

The Prime Minister, Proteus, and his cabinet of squabbling and generally corrupt colleagues have decided to present King Magnus with an ultimatum; either the monarch will refrain from public speaking, press manipulation, and all mention of his power to veto legislation, or his government will go to the country for a mandate to force him to do so. Although he faces a cabinet supposedly united in the aim of restraining him, Magnus is still able, by flattery and a clearer understanding of the issues, to win the day. When he threatens to upset the apple cart of the play's title by abdicating all of his titles in order to enter parliamentary politics, Proteus and the Cabinet are obliged to withdraw their ultimatum or face the prospect of competing with the King's overwhelming popularity.

Pamphilius
Sempronius, Magnus's secretary
Boanerges, President of the Board of Trade
King Magnus
Proteus
Foreign Secretary
Colonial Secretary
Chancellor of the Exchequer
Home Secretary
Postmistress General

Powermistress General
Orinthia, Magnus's mistress
Queen Jemima, Magnus's wife
American Ambassador

Arcadians, The
Mark Ambient, A. M. Thompson and Robert
Courtneidge
Lyrics by Arthur Wimperis
Music by Lionel Monckton
Fantasy Musical 3 Acts
London 1909

Arcady is a Garden of Eden that Time forgot, nestling somewhere near the North Pole. But the climate is beautiful, as is everything and everyone. Into this idyll crashes balloonist Smith, scaring the innocent and pure inhabitants who have only just heard of the 'monsters' from the outside world from Father Time. Wily restaurateur Smith is no match for the Arcadians' innocence and they push him down the Well of Truth. He emerges transformed, physically, and together with Arcadian girls Sombra and Chrysea and Astrophel, a boy, returns to London with the help of Father Time to convert the Londoners to honest ways.

Smith, now Simplicitus, and the Arcadians swiftly become the new rage and their ability to talk to the animals helps Simplicitus win the Askwood horse race and financially rescue Jack, smitten with Eileen. Jack is fascinated, though, by the female Arcadians too, and there is the usual quota of misunderstandings and interrupted romancings before Jack and Eileen finally marry.

Mrs Smith meanwhile has turned her husband's white elephant of a restaurant into a flourishing concern - by making it all Arcadian, waitresses as nymphs, etc. and she's smitten with her husband Simplicitus whom she doesn't recognize. Eventually all is revealed after Simplicitus tells a lie and resumes his old form. The real Arcadians give up London as a bad job and return to their paradise.

Classic song: 'Merry Merry Pipes of Pan'

Amaryl	
Strephon	*Peter Doody*
Chrysea	*Men about town*
Damoetas	*Waitresses*
Daphne	*Ladies at races*
Sombra	*Chorus of Arcadians*
Time	*Gentlemen*
Astrophel	
Jim Smith	
Lady B	
Percy	
Jack Meadows	
Bobby	
Reggie	
Sir George Paddock	
Eileen Cavanagh	
Mrs Smith	

Arms and the Man
George Bernard Shaw
Comedy 3 Acts
London 1896

Set in Bulgaria, 1885, this mild satire highlights the illusions of war, romance and class.

The fleeing Bluntschli, a Swiss mercenary officer fighting with the Serbs against the Bulgarians, takes refuge in Raina's bedroom. She is the daughter of Major Petkoff of the Bulgarian army. Against her high-minded principles, she is both intrigued and disgusted by Bluntschli's matter-of-factness in military matters, such as filling his cartridge case with chocolates instead of bullets. In complete contrast is her heroic fiancé Sergius, whose hot-headed cavalry charge against machine-guns (supplied with the wrong ammunition) had routed the Serbs. Raina helps Bluntschli escape, but when her father and Sergius return shortly from the war, Bluntschli reappears in order to return her father's coat which Raina had lent him. Louka, an insubordinate servant girl, knows of Raina's association with Bluntschli and uses the information to ensnare Sergius, whose passion for her is far earthier than his 'higher love' for Raina. The couplings are completed when Raina realizes her true love is in fact the chocolate-cream soldier Bluntschli, who conveniently happens to inherit a string of Swiss hotels from his father.

Raina Petkoff
Catherine Petkoff, Raina's mother
Louka, the Petkoff's servant girl
The man (Bluntschli), a Swiss mercenary
A Bulgarian officer
Nicola, the Petkoff's servant
Major Petkoff, Raina's father
Sergius, Raina's fiancé

Arsenic and Old Lace
Joseph Kesselring
Comedy 2 Acts
New York 1941

Abby and Martha Brewster are lovely old sisters, known for their many kindnesses and good works. They live in a big old house in Brooklyn with nephew Teddy, a harmless madman who believes he is Teddy Roosevelt, and his brother Mortimer, a theatre critic. While courting neighbour Elaine, Mortimer discovers a corpse under the window seat and jumps to the conclusion Teddy was responsible, but Abby and Martha tell him the body is just another of their charitable endeavours - putting lonely old men out of their misery (with poisoned elderberry wine). Horrified Mortimer then learns that another eleven are buried in the cellar - where Teddy is digging the Panama Canal.

Enter long-lost brother Jonathan, the real black sheep of the family, together with dubious plastic surgeon Dr Einstein who has disguised Jon to look like Boris Karloff. Jon is a psychotic criminal and mass-murderer who hates Mortimer and he and Einstein have brought along a corpse of their own to dispose of. Mortimer attempts to get Jon to leave but Jon and Einstein plan to set up a 'factory' at the house to disguise wanted criminals, and their hand is strengthened when they too discover the grisly secret of the cellar.

Meanwhile, Teddy's incessant late-night bugle fanfares have so infuriated the neighbours that he has to be certified insane, and when the police arrive they find Jon, who is then arrested. His attempts to tell them of the bodies in the cellar are considered to be ravings of a lunatic. Abby and Martha decide to leave the deadly house and join Teddy in the Happy Dale home, and they reveal to Mortimer that he isn't really part of the family. Mortimer can now marry Elaine without fear of congenital insanity. And as a parting gesture, the sisters offer Witherspoon, stern but lonely head of Happy Dale, a glass of elderberry wine...

Abby Brewster
Revd Dr Harper
Teddy Brewster
Officer Brophy
Officer Klein
Martha Brewster
Elaine Harper
Mortimer Brewster
Mr Gibbs
Jonathan Brewster
Dr Einstein
Officer O'Hara
Lieut Rooney
Mr Witherspoon

As You Like It
William Shakespeare
Comedy 5 Acts
London 1599

A wrestling match between Orlando and court champion Charles ends in Orlando's unexpected victory, displeasing Frederick, who has usurped the throne from his brother the Duke; Orlando is the youngest son of the Duke's faithful companion Sir Rowland de Boys. Less distressed are Frederick's daughter Celia and her beloved cousin Rosalind, daughter of the banished Duke and kept from him by Frederick to be Celia's companion. Rosalind and Orlando fall in love, but paranoid Frederick then banishes Rosalind who, together with Celia, flee to the forest where the Duke and his men hide. Rosalind disguises herself as a boy, Ganymede, and Celia as country girl Aliena, and they take with them the clown Touchstone. Orlando also flees with old servant Adam and is pursued by his antagonistic elder brother Oliver, henchman to Duke Frederick.

Lovesick Orlando and faithful Adam are saved from starvation by the good Duke and his merry men, including the not-so-merry melancholy philosopher Jacques, and to everyone's displeasure, Orlando goes about disfiguring trees with love poems to Rosalind.

She appears to him as Ganymede and begins an intricate teasing game; at the same time parallel romances take place between Touchstone and wench Audrey, and between shepherd Silvius and shepherdess Phebe, which is complicated by Phebe's falling for Ganymede. The charmingly rustic comings-and-goings are resolved when Orlando rescues Oliver from a lioness and the brothers are reconciled and Oliver falls for Aliena (Celia). Ganymede (Rosalind) decides to stop teasing and reveals herself to her father and to Orlando, and persuades Phebe to love Silvius. Touchstone weds Audrey and to cap it all, Rowland de Boys' middle son Jacques appears with news of Duke Frederick; he had come to the forest to slay his brother, but met an old religious man, was converted to the good, and has now bequeathed the crown and estates to the banished Duke. Finally Rosalind, as one of Shakespeare's few women to have a leading part, speaks the epilogue.

Duke, living in exile
Amiens, Jacques, noblemen in attendance on him
Duke Frederick, his brother, the usurper
Le Beau, a courtier
Charles, a wrestler
Oliver, Jacques and Orlando, sons of Sir Rowland de Boys
Adam , Dennis, servants of Oliver
The Clown, alias Touchstone
Sir Oliver Martext, a country vicar
Corin, Silvius, shepherds
William, a country youth, in love with Audrey
Rosalind, daughter of Duke Senior
Celia, daughter of Duke Frederick
Phebe, a shepherdess
Audrey, a country wench
A masquer representing Hymen
Lords, pages, attendants

Ashes
David Rudkin
Drama 3 Acts
London 1974

Colin and Anne are an ordinary, intelligent, youngish couple who are trying to have children. They cannot succeed, no matter what they do or whom they consult, and as their failures become more poignant their desperation increases. All of the possible reasons for non-conception are investigated; his sperm count, too much acid in her vagina, various coital positions, her ovulations, etc. Despite assurances from the seminologist - 'the guru' - to the contrary, Colin cannot help but blame his own homosexual impulses. When Anne finally manages to conceive, miscarriages result and eventually her womb is removed. They are turned down for adoption, their hopes for parenthood lying in ashes. Throughout the play Anne and Colin narrate and explain their indignities with wry humour and little self-pity, finally left with only each other and whatever unknown road is now open for them.

Colin
Anne
Doctor
Surgeon
Guru
Jennifer
Receptionist
Valerie

Aspern Papers, The
Henry James
Comedy 3 Acts
Newcastle 1959

Henry Jarvis, an American man of letters, has come to Venice in 1895 to try to befriend Juliana Bordereau, a transplanted American who was once the lover of America's first great poet, the consuming interest of Jarvis's life, Jeffrey Aspern. Juliana, however, is now a recluse and resists any literary interest in Aspern's work or person.

Jarvis realizes that a direct approach would be useless and instead manages to play upon Juliana's wish to provide capital for her niece, Tina, by offering an exorbitant rent to become their lodger. He ingratiates himself with Tina, in an attempt to reach Juliana through her, and both women hope that Jarvis may become Tina's suitor. When he discovers that Juliana has a chest full of Aspern's intimate correspondence, Jarvis overplays his hand with Tina.

To test his affection, following Juliana's sudden death, Tina pretends to have burnt Aspern's papers. As she had feared, Jarvis loses all interest in her and leaves Venice. Ironically, it is only then that she consigns Aspern's literary remains to the fire.

Assunta, a maid
Mrs Prest
Henry Jarvis, American writer
Miss Tina Bordereau
Miss Juliana Bordereau
Pasquale, Jarvis's servant

Astonished Heart, The
Noël Coward
Play 1 Act
London 1935
See: *Tonight at 8.30*

Auntie Mame
Jerome Lawrence and Robert E. Lee
Comedy 2 Acts
New York 1956

Mame is an exotic flapper, with fascinating friends, whose glitzy heart melts and turns to gold when her dead brother's little boy Patrick is placed in her care. Her eccentric but loving upbringing of the boy is continually thwarted by ultra-conservative banker Babcock who controls Pat's bonds but whose best (or worse) efforts cannot stop him from returning to his aunt's wild lifestyle.

Mame loses her money in the 'crash' but marries rich Southern playboy Beauregard after a wild hunting fling on his old plantation. Widowed on their eighth honeymoon when Beau slips on a glacier, she later writes her memoirs aided by casanova Irish poet O'Bannion. Pat grows up and wants to wed robot beauty Gloria whose rich parents horrify Mame. She thwarts their marriage plans at a dinner party and introduces Pat to the more suitable Pegeen. Finally Mame travels again, this time showing Pat and Pegeen's little boy Michael the wonders of the world.

Norah Muldoon
Patrick Dennis, the boy and the young man
Ifo
Vera Charles
Osbert
Ralph Devine
Bishop Elaftharoosees
Lindsay Woolsey
Auntie Mame
Mr Waldo, a paperhanger
Mr Babcock
Al Linden, a stage manager
Theatre manager
Assistant stage manager
Maid
Butler
Lord Dudley
Customer
Customer's son
Mr Loomis, a floor walker
Beauregard Jackson
Pickett Burnside
Cousins Jeff, Fan and Moultrie
Sally Cato MacDougal
Mother Burnside
Fred, a groom
Huntsman
Dr Shurr, a vet
Agnes Gooch
Brian O'Bannion
Gloria, Doris and Claude Upson
Pegeen Ryan
Michael Dennis
A great many friends of Aunt Mame

Baal
Bertolt Brecht
Drama 22 Scenes
Vienna 1923

Baal is a poetic but boorish Bohemian layabout who sings and womanizes in cheap clubs and bars as he travels around. Sexually ambivalent and physically primitive, he is nevertheless attractive to women and he seduces, uses and discards all that he can get his dirty hands on. As he drinks and brawls his way around, his conquests include a seventeen-year-old girl, a benefactor's wife and a girl he grabs off the street, who loves him and is left pregnant. He repays her adoration with brutality and she commits suicide, much to the horror of Baal's travelling companion, Ekart, for whom he has desires. Baal becomes enraged when he sees Ekart flirting with a waitress and he kills him before escaping to hide in a forest. Alone and dying in a hut, Baal implores some woodcutters to help him, but it is now his turn to be cruelly rejected.

Baal, a poet
Mech, Baal's publisher
Mrs Mech (Emily)
Dr Piller
Johannes Schmidt
Johanna
Ekart, Baal's friend
Louise

Two sisters	*Googoo*
Landlady	*Old beggar*
Sophie Barger	*Maja*
Burn	*Young woman*
Lupu	*Watzman*
Mjurk	*Waitress*
Chanteuse	*Two Rangers*
Pianist	*Teamsters*
Parson	*Farmers*
Bolleboll	*Lumberjacks*

Babes in Arms
Music by Richard Rodgers
Lyrics by Lorenz Hart
Comedy 3 Acts
New York 1937

A group of talented youngsters, the children of touring vaudeville performers, are threatened by the County Sheriff that they will be sent to a work farm until their parents return from the tour. The plucky kids, therefore, organize a show hoping to make enough money to bail themselves out.

Their show proves to be an artistic success, but a financial flop, so it looks like the work farm for the kids after all. Then fate takes a hand. A famous French aviator, making a trans-Atlantic flight, is forced down on the work farm and decides the kids need his help.
Songs include: 'My Funny Valentine'; 'Where or When'; 'I Wish I Were in Love Again'; 'Johnny One Note'; 'Lady is a Tramp'

Maizie La Mar	*Sam Reynolds*
Dan La Mar	*Dolores Reynolds*
Val La Mar	*Lincoln Vanderpool*
Nat Blackstone	*Peter*
Emma Blackstone	*Baby Rose*
Marshall Blackstone	*Ivor De Quincey*
Billie Reynolds	*Rene Flambeau*
Gus Fielding	*Phil McCabe*
Booker Vanderpool	*Dr Snyder*
Pinkie	*Elenore*
Lee Calhoun	*The Gang - twenty kids*

Bacchae, The
Euripides
Tragedy 1 Act
Athens c. 405BC

The god Dionysus arrives in Thebes, where his mother Semele has died, to celebrate his rites. As the god of wine and ecstasy, whose predominantly female worshippers are customarily moved to wild - even orgiastic - expression of their devotion, Dionysus represents a threat to the arrogant and order-loving Theban king, Pentheus.

The women of Thebes ignore Pentheus's displeasure and enter into the celebration of the rites, which rise to a din throughout the city. The King's grandfather, Cadmus, and the prophet Teiresias, plead with the King not to rouse the god to fury by refusing to join in the rites. He not only refuses, but imprisons some of the celebrants, and lays plans to disrupt the god's main celebration on Mount Cithaeron. Pentheus promotes a suspicion that the celebrants are using the rites as an excuse for wantoness.

The King's guard provoke the celebrant women, who put the guard to flight and, in a rage, rip a number of live cattle limb from limb. The King resolves to call in the army to restore order.

This provokes the dark side of the god's ecstasy. Disguised as one of his own priests he bewitches the King. Together they visit the celebrations on Mount Cithaeron, the King disguised as a woman. Dionysus drives the women into a blood frenzy and, led by the King's mother, Agave, they dismember Pentheus, under the delusion that he is a lion.

Dionysus, son of Zeus and Semele
Cadmus, father of Semele, grandfather of Pentheus
Pentheus, King of Thebes
Agave, mother of Pentheus
Teiresias, a prophet
Chorus, soldiers, messengers

Bad Seed
Maxwell Anderson
Tragedy 2 Acts
New York 1954

Richard Bravo, a famous crime reporter, has kept secret from his daughter Christine the fact that she is adopted from a natural mother who was a psychotic mass murderer. Christine, happily married to Col Kenneth Penmark, has in turn a daughter, Rhoda, now eight-years-old. Although Rhoda appears to be immaculately well behaved, Christine notices a glacial detachment and manipulativeness in her daughter.

As the action develops, the audience discovers, with Christine, that Rhoda has murdered a classmate in an argument over a penmanship medal. Eventually Christine discovers her own true origins from Bravo and, further burdened with the knowledge that Rhoda has committed a second murder, tries to kill the child with a dose of sleeping pills. Christine then commits suicide. Rhoda survives and is seen coolly manipulating her grieving father as the play ends.

Rhoda Penmark
Col Kenneth Penmark
Christine Penmark
Monica Breedlove
Emory Wages
Leroy
Miss Fern
Reginald Tasker
Mr and Mrs Daigle
Messenger
Richard Bravo, Christine's adoptive father

Balcony, The
Jean Genet
Play 9 Scenes
London 1956

Set in a brothel in a modern European city, torn by revolution, this piece symbolically attacks society by comparing and confusing it with the sex games played by whores and their clients. Within the bordello various customers become a bishop, a general, a judge and a tramp, while the whores play at being a penitent, a thief, a virgin and finally a queen. The brothel proprietress, Irma, observes the various charades on closed circuit television and is protected by her impotent ex-lover, the Chief of Police.

Meanwhile, revolution is erupting outside; the royal palace and the rulers are destroyed and an envoy persuades the brothel's inhabitants to act out their roles in order to placate the public. These become so successful that the impersonators begin to assume the real roles and even the rebels find the illusions more attractive than the realities.

The scheming Chief of Police regains his virility and plans new charades with Irma, while outside another rebellion is beginning to break out.

Bishop	Second photographer
Judge	Third photographer
Executioner (Arthur)	Irma (The Queen)
General	Woman (Rosine)
Chief of Police	Thief
Beggar	Girl
Roger	Carmen
Court envoy	Chantal
First photographer	

Barber of Seville, The
Pierre Beaumarchais
Comedy 4 Acts
Paris 1761

The young Sevillian, Count Almaviva, has fallen madly in love with the fair Rosine, and daily, disguised as a student, Lindor, he goes to catch a glimpse of her and leave notes for her at the house of her tyrannical guardian and fiancé, Dr Bartholo.

Wily Figaro offers to help the Count, as he has access to the house as the doctor's barber. They devise a plan to get the Count into the house disguised as a drunken soldier. This fails, but on a second attempt they manage to get him into the house by telling Bartholo that he is a student of Rosine's music teacher come to help with the wedding arrangements. Old Bartholo is nevertheless suspicious and Figaro has to devise a number of ploys to let the lovers be alone. They plan to escape the house that night, but the doctor gets wind of this and arranges to be married right away.

While Bartholo goes off to get the police to arrest the 'student' Lindor, Figaro brings a notary to perform the wedding ceremony for the Count and Rosine.

Bartholo returns and his anger at the wedding is soon forgotten when the merciful Count offers to let him keep Rosine's ward money.

Count Almaviva, a Spanish grandee
Figaro
Rosine, a young lady of noble birth
Bartholo, a physician
Bazile, a music master
Wakeful, Bartholo's servant
Youthful, an old servant
A notary
An alcade
Servants

Barefoot in the Park
Neil Simon
Comedy 3 Acts
New York 1964

Corrie and Paul Bratter are moving into a 48th Street New York apartment, a five-flight walk-up that wears out visitors such as the telephone man, the delivery man, and Corrie's mother. But not Victor Velasco, an eccentric (like the other, unseen, neighbours) who lives above them in an attic.

Corrie and Paul are only just recovering from their honeymoon but are quarrelling - he because she is scatty, she because he is such a stuffed shirt that he will not go walking barefoot in the park just because it is freezing. They are witty in their hostility but peculiarly stupid: they do not cover over a hole in the skylight, thus enabling the snow to fall amusingly through.

The impecunious Velasco persuades them to go to an Albanian restaurant on Staten Island. Corrie's widowed mother, in particular, has a bad time but ends up staying the night (innocently but promisingly) at Velasco's. Corrie and Paul turn exceedingly nasty with each other but, really, they are still in love and in the end she decides he is no fuddy duddy; he is dependable and strong and they are going to live happily ever after.

Corrie Bratter
Telephone man
Delivery man
Paul Bratter
Mrs Banks
Victor Velasco

Barretts of Wimpole Street, The
Rudolph Besier
Drama 5 Acts
London 1930

In London, 1845, the invalid Elizabeth Barrett and her brothers and sisters are tyrannized by their pious father Edward Moulton-Barrett, who refuses to let any of them marry. Her sister Henrietta despairs of ever wedding the admirer who has asked for her hand.

The handsome, intense young poet Robert Browning is, however, allowed to visit and he declares his love for

Elizabeth and her work. Encouraged by this ardour she begins to make a remarkable recovery and is advised by her doctors to take a trip to Italy. Father forbids this and orders the whole family to the country.

Browning proposes to Elizabeth, who has reservations about leaving her father but these are dispelled when he brutally assaults her sister who has asked to be allowed to marry. Elizabeth secretly marries Browning and plans to make her departure.

Barrett, who is beginning to realize the effects of his harsh treatment of his children, in a fit of self-doubt tries to explain to Elizabeth his obsessive possessiveness, but it is too late and she leaves. Reverting to his former behaviour, her bitter father orders that her pet dog, Flush, be destroyed.

Dr Chambers
Elizabeth Barrett Moulton-Barrett
Henrietta Moulton-Barrett
Arabel Moulton-Barrett
Octavius Moulton-Barrett
Septimus Moulton-Barrett
Alfred Moulton-Barrett
Charles Moulton-Barrett
Henry Moulton-Barrett
George Moulton-Barrett
Edward Moulton-Barrett
Bella Hedley
Henry Bevan
Robert Browning
Dr Ford Waterlow
Capt. Surtees Cook
Flush

Bartholomew Fair
Ben Jonson
Comedy Spectacle 5 Acts
London 1614
Early in the morning of the Feast of St Bartholomew (24 August), at the house of Proctor John Littlewit and his wife Win, visitors are looking forward to the fair. At the fair, throughout the day a large cast go through their paces, mostly roguish, crazy and bawdy. The action is centred around the grotesque lavatory attendant, Ursula the Pig Woman, whose sideline is procuring. Fools are robbed and conned by knaves and rather deserve their fates. The villains go unpunished. The upright sober moralists get their come-uppances: Judge Overdo who is embarrassed to find his wife disguised as a whore, and Zeal-Of-The-Land Busy is bested in argument by a puppet in a play-within-the-play. The day ends pleasantly with Overdo inviting everybody home for supper.

John Littlewit, a Proctor
Solomon, his man
Mistress Win Littlewit, his wife
Dame Purecraft, her mother and a widow
Zeal-Of-The-Land Busy, her suitor
Ned Winwife, his rival
Tom Quarlous, his companion

Bartholomew Cokes, a squire
Humphrey Wasp, his man
Adam Overdo, a judge
His wife
Grace Wellborn, his ward
Lantern Leatherhead, a hobby-horse-seller
Joan Trash, a gingerbread-woman
Ezekiel Edgeworth, a cutpurse
Nightingale, a ballad-singer
Ursula, a pig-woman
Mooncalf, her tapster
Jordan Knockem, a horse-courser
Val Cutting, a roarer
Captain Whit, a bawd
Punk Alice, mistress 'o the game
Trouble-All, a madman
Toby Haggis
Davy Bristle
Poacher
Watchman
Costermonger
Passengers

Beautiful People, The
William Saroyan
Comedy 2 Acts
New York 1941
Little old lady Harmony Bluesblossom arrives unexpectedly to see her old friend Jonah Webster at his house on Red Rock Hill in San Francisco. Only fifteen-year-old son Owen is there and he introduces her to the Webster world of whimsy; Owen is a poet, scientist and author and tells of his sister, seventeen-year-old 'St Agnes of the Mice' and how much she cares for the little mice and how they in turn worship her and spell her name in flowers. Agnes returns, anxious for a missing mouse, and then when father Jonah comes back (a little tipsy), she tells him she has met a boy and love is not what she expected it to be.

The family live on a regular pension cheque which arrives in error, and when company vice-president William Prim arrives to get the cheque cancelled, he is so taken with this fetching family who immediately befriend him that he not only cancels the cancellation but also raises the money. Owen finds the lost mouse in the steeple of the nearby Catholic Church and anxious Father Hogan follows him home. Jonah assures Hogan that Owen is quite sane and explains about the mouse. Agnes is still looking for her boy and when at last she finds him she is happy again.

Jonah has brought up his children to believe in goodness as the greatest coin of exchange but is nevertheless worried about his eldest son Harold, a musician who is in New York. But when a cornet is heard approaching, everyone becomes silent; Harold appears with homeless friend Steve, and everything is all right.

Owen Webster
Harmony Bluesblossom
Agnes Webster
Jonah Webster
William Prim
Dan Hillboy
Harold Webster
Steve
Father Hogan

Beaux' Stratagem, The
George Farquhar
Comedy 4 Acts
London 1707

In the London of the early eighteenth century young rollicking gentlemen Aimwell and Archer, having spent nearly all their money, decide to try their luck in the country.

They arrive at Litchfield, disguised as Lord and servant, and they learn from garrulous innkeeper Will Boniface of the wealthy widow Lady Bountiful and her beautiful daughter Dorinda. Boniface suspects that the two are thieves and, in league with local highwaymen, he aims to relieve them of the little money they have, which they are using to impress the locals.

Aimwell and 'servant' Archer manage to wheedle their way into the Bountiful household where they make an impression on Dorinda and her frustrated sister-in-law, Mrs Sullen. When Boniface's gang of villians come to rob the house, Aimwell and Archer in the course of various assignations manage to thwart their efforts and become heroes to all.

Aimwell, now about to marry the fair Dorinda, confesses that he is a fraud, but she forgives him knowing in fact, that he will succeed to a title and she gives a fortune to his good friend Archer, who is planning on winning Mrs Sullen.

Thomas Aimwell
Francis Archer
Count Bellair, a French officer
Squire Sullen, a blockhead
Sir Charles Freeman, Mrs Sullen's brother
Foigard, a priest
Gibbet, a highwayman
Houndslow, his companion
Bagshot, his companion
Boniface, landlord of the inn
Scrub, servant of squire Sullen
Lady Bountiful
Mrs Sullen
Dorinda
Gipsy, maid
Cherry, Boniface's daughter
Tapster
Coach-passengers
Countryman and woman
Servants

Becket
Jean Anouilh
Tragedy 4 Acts
New York 1960

The life of Thomas à Becket (1118 -70) was the inspiration for two famous mid-century plays; Anouilh's *Becket* and Eliot's *Murder in the Cathedral*.

Anouilh concentrates on the elusiveness of Becket's character and the ambivalence of his motivation in resisting Henry's designs against the Church. By changing Becket's (historic) nationality from Norman to Saxon, Anouilh is able to portray a character riven by opposing allegiances, and Henry's ruthless appropriation of Becket's mistress introduces a strand of sexual jealousy into the action. At the same time, we witness a close bond of love between the King and Becket, and Becket's greatness as a Lord Chancellor.

The scene moves on to France where Becket is shown in conflict with Henry's knights, who wish to sack the French towns they have won in battle. Becket prefers to bribe the towns into acquiescence, so that he may deliver their unspoilt riches to Henry. While the English are in the field the incumbent Archbishop of Canterbury dies and Henry appoints Becket to the post, although Becket argues that this will destroy their friendship.

With his appointment, Becket begins to defend the Church against Henry's incursions. The two men quarrel and Becket flees to France under the protection of the French king, then on to Rome to seek the Pope's authority for his battle against Henry. Under the terms of a treaty between Henry and the French king, Louis, the Archbishop returns to Canterbury. However, four of Henry's barons, having heard the King's wish to rid himself of Becket, enter Canterbury Cathedral and murder the 'turbulent priest'.

The play closes as it had begun with Henry being scourged by the Canterbury priests as a sign to the rebellious Saxons that he repents Becket's death.

Henry II, King of England
Thomas Becket
Archbishop of Canterbury, Becket's predecessor
Gilbert Folliot, Bishop of London
Gwendolen, Becket's mistress
Queen Mother, Henry's mother
Queen, Henry's wife
Louis, King of France
Barons
Peasants

Bed-sitting Room, The
Spike Milligan and John Antrobus
Comedy 3 Acts
London 1963

Extravagantly lunatic black comedy begins in Capt. Kak's surgery and Government Surplus Store not long after atomic World War Three. Lord Fortnum confesses to Kak his morbid fear of turning into a bed-sitting room, and Acts Two and Three take place inside him after he has done so. Mate (Arthur Scroake) and other surreally silly characters whizz in and out, spouting non sequiturs and nonsensically apeing aspects of their pre-bomb existence.

Clothed in an array of rags and junk, the few survivors resolutely ignore the reality of their predicament. Only Mate has glimpses of the awful ramifications of what has happened, but like everyone else is amazed when Kak's heartbroken wife Penelope asks God to give her back her dead monster babe - and the thing revives. They all crowd around...

Capt. Pontius Kak
Lord Fortnum of
  Alamein
Mate/Arthur Scroake
Shelter Man
Plastic Mac Man
Underwater Vicar
Brigadier/Sergeant
Chest of Drawers/
  Gladys Scroake
Penelope
Diplomat
First announcer
Sea captain
Second announcer

Delivery man/chauffeur
Seaman
Coffin man
Pianist
Third announcer
Phantom
Old soldier
Orderly

Bedfull of Foreigners, A
Dave Freeman
Farce 2 Acts
Croydon 1974
A seedy, incompetent, hotel in France near the German border. It is out of season - late October - and despite the apparent fact that the guests have been taken off to hospital with food poisoning, the place is alleged by head porter Karak and manager Heinz to be short of accommodation. Tourists Brenda and Stanley are offered one large room with a sometimes-used partition down the middle. Brenda finds she has lost her valuable wedding ring, probably in a gas station some while back in their journey. She drives off to try to find her ring. Helga, who speaks English with a slight German accent, turns up because she knows her husband Claude, an English biscuit salesman, is in the village on business. She does not know that this business is actually Simone, a French 'exotic' dancer.

The married couples, plus Simone, find themselves sharing the same sometimes partitioned room and bathroom in various combinations, apart from Brenda who does not return until the end when, just to add a little complication, she discovers that Karak had found her ring in the car park and is, incidentally, her long-lost father. Stanley's feeling that they should have vacationed in Skegness is vindicated.

Karak
Heinz

Stanley Parker
Brenda Parker
Helga Philby
Claude Philby
Simone

Bedroom Farce
Alan Ayckbourn
Comedy 2 Acts
Scarborough 1975
The action takes place entirely in three bedrooms, events switching rapidly from one to the other. They are the bedrooms of late middle-aged Ernest and Delia, younger Malcolm and Kate, and also younger Nick and Jan. Malcolm and Kate are throwing a party, but it's ruined by the arrival of Trevor (son of Ernest and Delia) and wife Susannah, who are not hitting it off - just hitting. Jan, Trevor's ex, arrives without Nick who is bedbound with a bad back, and a quick embrace between Trevor and Jan doesn't help matters. Malcolm wants to throw Trevor out and eventually Trevor ends up staying with Nick and Jan, sleeping on their sofa. Susannah goes to her parents-in-law and ends up turfing out poor Ernest and sleeping with Delia. With the maximum amount of inconvenience caused to their friends and relatives, Trevor and Susannah eventually make up - in Kate and Malcolm's bed.

Ernest
Delia
Nick
Jan
Malcolm
Kate
Trevor
Susannah

Before Dawn (In Praise of Love II)
Terence Rattigan
Drama 1 Act
London 1973
In this fanciful re-working of the narrative climax of Sardon's Tosca, Rattigan gives a more worldly version of the sacrifice of this great beauty to the lust of Baron Scarpia, who heads the royalist Bourbon secret police in Naples.

A taste for intrigue in furthering the Bonapartist cause in Italy has led Tosca's presumed lover, Mario Cavaradossi, to a cell in Scarpia's prison stronghold, the Castel Sant'Angelo, condemned to death. Scarpia offers to spare Mario if Tosca agrees to sleep with him, to which she eventually agrees. The Baron is mortally embarrassed when he proves unable to consummate his lust, and decides to do away with both Mario and Tosca.

It transpires that Mario is not Tosca's lover - he is homosexual - but that she loves his commitment to Bonaparte. Her disillusion is therefore total when Scarpia reveals that Mario was betrayed to the Bourbons by the French themselves. As Mario is put in a carriage for

London, following his fake execution, Scarpia's lust for Tosca is again roused and he falls on her avidly.

Baron Scarpia
The Lackey
Capt. Schiarrone
Tosca
Mario Cavaradossi

Beggar's Opera, The
John Gay
Ballad Opera 3 Acts
London 1728

The author of the piece, the beggar, introduces himself to the audience; his is not a high-falutin' lords-and-ladies play - instead it's a 'fine moral tale' of highwaymen and whores, acted by beggars and harlots. The muses of the gods flow through every man, the beggar says.

Notorious fence and informer Peacham and his wife are horrified to find that their daughter Polly has secretly married Capt. MacHeath, bold king of the highwaymen. Peacham determines to inform on MacHeath and have him hanged, but Polly warns her husband and they have to part. MacHeath, however, denied Polly's bed, goes for comfort to the brothel where he is betrayed by Jenny Diver and sent to Newgate prison. Jailer Lockit's daughter, Lucy, is already pregnant by MacHeath, and with her connivance he escapes, but not before there is the first of several fights between Lucy and Polly over who is his rightful wife. MacHeath rejoins his friends the highwaymen for more escapades and further womanizing, but once again he is caught, delighting the scheming pair Lockit and Peacham. He is taken to the gallows and is about to be hanged, concluding the 'fine morality' of the tale, when the crowd, the women, and MacHeath's cronies demand a reprieve. 'This cannot be' replies the playwright beggar, 'the piece must be realistic...truth must surely out'. But when informed that a happy ending will ensure longer runs (and more money) for his play, the author relents, and at once a messenger comes with a royal pardon for MacHeath, who falls into Polly's arms.

The Beggar, the author of the piece
Mr Peacham, a notorious fence and informer
Mrs Peacham, his common-law wife
Polly Peacham, their daughter
Filch, their servant
Mr Lockit, chief jailer at Newgate prison
Lucy Lockit, his daughter
Capt. MacHeath, a famous highwayman
MacHeath's gang: *Jemmy Twitcher, Crooked-fingered Jack, Wat Dreary, Robin of Bagshot, Nimming Ned, Henry Paddington, Matt of the Mint and Ben Budge*
Ladies of the town: *Mrs Coaxer, Dolly Trull, Mrs Vixen, Betty Doxy, Jenny Diver, Mrs Slammekin, Suky Tawdry and Molly Brazen*
Two constables
Servants at Peacham's warehouse
Mrs Diana Trapes, a brothel keeper
The Judge
Four women with babies
Jack Ketch, the hangman
A messenger

Bell, Book and Candle
John Van Druten
Comedy 3 Acts
New York 1950

Gillian Holroyd, her aunt Miss Holroyd and Tony Henderson all live in the same house in different flats. Tony has had quite enough of finding Miss Holroyd in his flat and fiddling with the phone so he complains to Gillian. He also wonders how she could have got into his flat without a key; little does he know that both Gillian and her aunt are witches. Gillian has taken a liking to Tony and decides to use her feminine charms to ensnare him. However, when she finds out he is engaged to her childhood enemy Merle Kittredge she 'magics' him with the help of her cat Pyewacket to fall in love with her. The spell works, Tony cancels his engagement and for two weeks they are happy together, even though if Gillian were truly to fall in love she would be able to cry and blush but also would lose her magical powers.

Problems arise when Nicky, her warlock brother, begins working on a book all about witches. Gillian 'magics' the book so it won't be published, so Nicky threatens to tell Tony that she is a witch (Tony has read Nicky's book and doesn't believe a word of it). Gillian decides to let the cat out of the bag and tell him herself, revealing that she cast a spell on him. When at last he believes her, he storms out of her house and pays another witch a thousand pounds to have the spell removed.

One evening Tony visits Gillian to pay some back rent (which she refuses) and to use the phone. As he leaves, Gillian blushes and then she starts to cry. Tony realizes she is no longer a witch and he too discovers that he is in love with her, even without being 'magicked'.

Gillian Holroyd
Antony Henderson
Miss Holroyd
Nicholas Holroyd
Sidney Redlitch

Belle of New York, The
Hugh Morton
Music by Gustave Kerker
Musical Comedy 2 Acts
New York 1897

Harry Bronson, a playboy, is about to marry the opera singer Cora Angelique (previously married nine times) when his rich eccentric father Ichabod turns up in town with his entire corps of Young Men's Rescue League and Anti-Cigarette Society to fight vice in New York. The old man is not averse to considerable flirting but when he hears Harry has two other fiancées, Kissy and Fifi, he cuts him off without a cent and gives his money to a Salvation Army lass, Violet Gray. Penniless Harry falls for Violet who has now founded the Purity Brigade and she plans to get Harry his fortune back by shocking old Ichabod by performing as a French floozy.

No one is fooled and despite being sued for breach of promise by Cora, Harry becomes an honest Joe and gets a job as a soda-jerk before he and Violet find happiness together.

Songs include: 'Stop the Wedding'; 'The Anti-Cigarette League'; 'The Purity Brigade'; 'At Ze Naughty Folies Bergère'

Ichabod Bronson, President of the Young Men's
  Rescue League of Cohoes
Harry Bronson, his son
Doc Snifkins, father of Cora Angelique, the Queen of
  Comic Opera
Karl von Pumpernick, a polite lunatic
Blinky Bill M'Guirk, a mixed ale pugilist
Kenneth Mugg, low comedian of The Cora Angelique
  Opera Company
Count Ratsi Rattatoo, Count Patsi Rattatoo, twin
  Portuguese noblemen
Mr Twiddles, Harry Bronson's private secretary
Fricot, a French chef
Mr Snooper, a newspaper reporter
Mr Peeper, a press photographer
William, a butler
Violet Gray, a Salvation Army lassie
Fifi Fricot, a little Parisienne
Cora Angelique, the Queen of Comic Opera
Kissy Fitzgarter, a music-hall dancer
Pansy Pinns, a soubrette
Mamie Clancy, a Pell Street girl
Chorus

Bells Are Ringing
Betty Comden and Adolph Green
Music by Jule Styne
Musical 2 Acts
New York 1956

Ella Peterson works for Susanswerphone, a friendly service that takes messages from a variety of clients, most quite legitimate, but the Vice Squad has suspicions of other activities. However, Ella does have the habit of listening in on calls and trying to put people's lives to right using assumed identities. She becomes romantically involved with struggling playwright Jeff Moss whom she brings together with aspiring songwriter, dentist Dr Kitchell, and arranges delivery of their script to an agent, but then Ella decides that things are getting too complicated and she prepares to go back home.

Ella's boss, Sue, is conned by her boyfriend Sandor into letting him set up a record company in the office which is, in fact, a front for a bookie racket.

Jeff eventually tracks Ella down when he comes to the office looking for one of her assumed personalities, Mom, to whom he turns in time of trouble and the lovers are happily reunited.

Songs include: 'Just in Time'; 'The Party's Over'; 'On My Own'

Sue Summers	Master of ceremonies
Gwynne Smith	Singer at nightclub
Ella Peterson	Waiter
Carl	Maître d' Hotel
Inspector Barnes	Police officer
Frances	Mme Grimaldi
Sandor	Mrs Mallet
Jeff Moss	Dancers
Larry Hastings	Singers
Telephone man	
Ludwig Smiley	
Charles Bessemer	
Dr Kitchell	
Blake Barton	
Clerk	
Olga	
Hoods	
Carol	
Paul Arnold	
Michelle	

Bent
Martin Sherman
Drama 2 Acts
London 1979

Max lives with dancer Rudy in an apartment in Berlin during the early years of the Third Reich. One morning Max is badly hung-over, unable to remember what he did last night at Rudy's club, but is soon reminded by the hulking presence of Wolf, a storm-trooper he brought home. Last night was also the Night of the Long Knives, and with the murder of Ernst Rohm, homosexuals now have no official protector; Wolf is seized and killed by the Gestapo, and shortly afterwards Max and Rudy are taken prisoner. Rudy is badly beaten and left to die on the transport train and Max is befriended by Horst who gives him survival tips.

Max, an aggressive hustler, takes Horst's advice for survival to its extremes and through a dreadful deed manages to get himself a yellow 'Jew' star instead of the pink 'Homosexual' star; in the eyes of the prisoners and guards alike, the homosexuals are the lowest of the low. Inside the concentration camp, Max connives and hustles and gets Horst on his rock-carrying duty - one of the easiest and safest in the camp - but Horst is dubious about Max's seeming betrayal of his sexuality. Horst becomes ill and Max even fellates the hated Nazi Captain in order to get Horst medicine, but to no avail. The Captain sadistically kills Horst. In a final act of defiance, Max stands up for his own nature and takes Horst's shirt with the pink star, puts it on and walks towards the electrified fence.

Max	Corporal
Horst	Lieutenant
Rudy	Guard on train
Wolf	Second Lieutenant
Freddie	Kapo
Greta	Captain
Victor	Officer

Bequest to the Nation, A
Terence Rattigan
Drama 2 Acts
London 1970

George Matcham, his wife Katherine (Horatio Nelson's sister), and their son George Jr are preparing for a visit to Lady Hamilton, Lord Nelson's mistress. To his parents' horror, schoolboy George makes fun of the stories of threesomes with Nelson, Emma Hamilton and her late 'obliging' husband. Lady Nelson turns up, defying etiquette, because she still loves her husband and wants a letter conveyed to him. The adults refuse to see her but she manages to see young George and persuades him to deliver the letter.

Lady Hamilton, whom Nelson has not seen for two years, clearly reveals herself to be crude and alcoholic. She disgusts Nelson's friend Capt. Hardy but has a power of sexual attraction over Nelson that the sickly Lady Nelson cannot compete with. Young George manages to deliver the letter and when Lord Nelson finds out he is outraged. He humiliates the boy, who idolizes him, but later has to apologize and try to explain to George the nature of sexual love.

However, Nelson has another, just as powerful, love - the Navy. He dies at Trafalgar. In mourning, the wife and the mistress meet and Lady Nelson admits that she was waiting for Horatio's old age when she hoped he would return. Now there will be no old age and the two women fumble toward mutual understanding. It appears that Emma Hamilton, against expectation, is the more pitiable.

George Matcham Senr	Lord Minto
Katherine Matcham	Capt. Hardy
Betsy	Revd William Nelson
George Matcham Jr	Sarah Nelson
Emily	Horatio
Frances, Lady Nelson	Capt. Blackwood
Nelson	Midshipman
Lord Barham	Footmen
Emma Hamilton	Sailors
Francesca	Maids

Best Little Whorehouse in Texas, The
Adapted by Larry King from the book
by Peter Masterson
Music and lyrics by Carol Hall
Musical Comedy 2 Acts
New York 1978

After the bandleader has given a potted history of the notorious Chicken Ranch, a friendly service to the males of Texas, two prospective ladies come for an interview with the madame, Miss Mona. She explains the strict, but fair, house rules and the new recruits set to work. One is Shy, by name and nature, and needs some help getting started but there are plenty of female, and male, hands about to show her the ropes.

However, the smooth running of the Ranch is about to be upset in the shape of do-gooder, local TV reporter, greasy Melvin Thorpe. Looking to his own ends, he starts a scurrilous campaign to have the place closed down much to the dismay of the local sheriff, Dodd, and several local politicians. Thorpe organises a raid when the local football team is being 'entertained' and the ensuing scandal makes closure a certainty.

The girls pack up and leave as Thorpe receives an award for his services to morality.

Songs include: 'Girl You're a Woman'; 'Good Old Girl'; 'Texas Has a Whorehouse in It'

Rio Grande Band	Melvin P. Thorpe
Six girls	Soundman
Four cowboys	Stage Manager
Farmer	Melvin Thorpe Singers
Shy kid	Sheriff Ed Earl Dodd
Miss Wulla Jean	Cameraman
Travelling salesman	Scruggs
Slick dude	Mayor Rufus Poindexter
Choir	Edsel Mackey
Amber	Doatsy Mae
Shy	Five townspeople
Jewel	TV announcer
Mona Strangley	Anglettes
Eight girls at Miss Mona's	Aggies
Leroy Sliney	Reporters
The Dogettes	Photographers, others etc

Best Man, The
Gore Vidal
Drama 3 Acts
New York 1960

At a political convention in Philadelphia, intelligent but rather too intellectual Senator Bill Russell is preparing for the vote which will determine whether he or his rival, Cantwell, will be their party's candidate for the presidency. With Russell is his (secretly) estranged wife Alice, and his shrewd agent Dick Jensen, National committee woman Mrs Gamadge, who considers Bill too intellectual but likes Alice, gives Russell homely advice for garnering female votes, but the most important visitor is ex-president Hockstader who tells Bill he is reserving his support for the moment. He also confides in Bill that he is terminally ill, but Bill gathers that although the ex-president likes him, he will be supporting Cantwell whom Hockstader considers the stronger candidate.

Hockstader then goes to Cantwell's suite; Cantwell

is competent but his methods are suspect; he believes the ends justify the means. Hockstader tells him that in politics there are only means. They argue, and Cantwell reveals he has procured a (stolen) psychiatric report on Russell with details of a nervous breakdown, and that he intends shortly to use the information. Hockstader changes his mind about backing Cantwell, but when he returns to Russell's suite, Russell has uncovered evidence of Cantwell's covert homosexuality. Russell, however, despite pressure from his agent, does not want to use it.

The balloting begins and although Cantwell releases the information he has on Russell, his rival refuses to respond. The voting is close, and when Hockstader suddenly dies, Cantwell's cold-bloodedness disgusts Russell. He decides the chief priority is to keep the unscrupulous Cantwell from the White House, so he withdraws from the race, instructing his delegates to support the third contestant Merwin, who, with Russell's votes, will now win.

Cantwell is finished, Russell and Alice are reconciled; Russell tells reporters he is happy the best man won.

Dick Jensen	Arthur Hockstader
First Reporter	Mabel Cantwell
William Russell	Bill Blades
Mike	Joseph Cantwell
Second Reporter	Senator Carlin
Third Reporter	Dr Artinian
Fourth Reporter	Sheldon Marcus
Alice Russell	Reporters
Assistant to Dick Jensen	Delegates
Mrs Gamadge	

Betrayal
Harold Pinter
Drama 9 Scenes
London 1978

In a pub 1977. Jerry and Emma, who have not met for quite a while, are asking each other how they are. Jerry is a literary agent and his (not seen) wife is a doctor. Emma runs an art gallery and her husband Robert is a publisher. They talk about the popular writer Casey whom Jerry represents and Robert publishes. Jerry says he has heard she is seeing quite a bit of Casey. Emma says it is nothing but that anyway her marriage to Robert is finished as she has discovered he has been betraying her with other women for years. Emma has told Robert about the long affair she had with Jerry.

Jerry's house 1977. He and Robert are having a difficult conversation about their long-standing friendship (Jerry had been best man at Robert's wedding). Robert says he thinks Emma is now having an affair with Casey.

Flat 1975. It is the Jerry-Emma love-nest. They are ending the affair.

Robert and Emma's house 1974. Jerry calls. Emma is putting a child to bed. Robert and Jerry discuss temperamental differences between little boys and girls. Jerry and Robert agree to play squash as soon as Jerry gets back from an American business trip.

Hotel room Venice 1973. Emma and Robert are talking about a new writer, Spinks, whom she thinks is good and has been discovered by Jerry but who has been turned down by Robert. Emma has received a letter via the American Express office from Jerry, which by chance, Robert had seen there and recognized the writing on the envelope. Emma confesses that Jerry is her lover. Robert says he has always liked Jerry rather more than he likes Emma.

Flat 1973. Jerry and Emma are in the middle of their affair and talking about Spinks and Jerry's worries about wife Judith finding out about Emma.

Restaurant later in 1973. Jerry and Robert are lunching and talking about Robert's holiday and about publishing.

Flat 1971. Near the start of the affair. Emma tells Jerry she has seen Judith off to luncheon with a woman at Fortnum and Mason's, which Jerry thinks is odd. Jerry says Judith has an admirer; another doctor. Emma says she is pregnant - by her husband.

Robert and Emma's bedroom 1968. There is a party in the rest of the house. Emma is combing her hair. Jerry comes in, tells her she is irresistibly beautiful, kisses her. Robert enters and Emma tells him his best friend is drunk. Jerry says he has been telling Emma what a beauty she is - 'I speak as your oldest friend. Your best man.' Robert: 'You are, actually.' He clasps Jerry's shoulder then leaves Emma and Jerry alone.

Emma
Robert
Jerry
A waiter

Beyond the Horizon
Eugene O'Neill
Tragedy 3 Acts
New York 1920

The two sons of James Mayo, a tough farmer on the north eastern seaboard of the USA, are about to take the fundamental decisions by which they will step from adolescence to maturity. After a sickly, semi-invalid childhood, Robert, the younger, has decided to go to sea with his uncle, while Andrew, his elder brother, plans to marry their childhood friend and neighbour, Ruth Atkins, and to take over running the family farm.

However, in the course of saying farewell to Ruth, Robert confesses his love for her and is astonished to discover that she returns it, although both her family and his expect her to marry Andy. When Robert announces to his family that he will not after all go to sea, but wants instead to marry Ruth and settle on the farm, a heartbroken Andy goes in his place.

Robert settles in to run the farm with his father, but Andy's departure has devastated the older man, who dies. Under Robert's inept guidance the farm gradually goes to ruin, and with it his marriage to Ruth, who realizes, too late, that she has all along loved Andy.

When Andy returns from sea Ruth resolves to reveal her change of heart but before she can do so, Andy lets her know that his new career was for the best - that he never really loved her. Andy leaves again, and Robert and Ruth sink into destitution when first Robert's mother, and then their daughter Mary die.

Andy returns once more to find Robert dying of consumption, and he is left alone with Ruth to survey the wreckage of what might have been.

James Mayo,
Kate Mayo, James's wife
Capt. Dick Scott, Kate's brother
Andrew Mayo
Robert Mayo
Ruth Atkins, Robert's wife
Mrs Atkins, Ruth's widowed mother
Mary, Robert and Ruth's daughter
Ben , a farm worker
Dr Fawcett

Big Knife, The
Clifford Odets
Drama 3 Acts
New York 1949

Top movie star Charlie Castle lives in tasteful luxury in Beverly Hills. Successful and sensitive, Charlie's marriage with Marion is in trouble and columnist Patty Benedict is on the scent. Patty comes to his house and they argue, and when his friend, publicity agent Buddy, butts in, Patty mentions a recent drink-driving rap when Buddy killed a child and threatens to bring it up again publicly if she doesn't get the news on Charlie's marriage. Marion arrives and Patty leaves, and it is apparent that Marion is fed up with Hollywood. She wants Charlie to go back east to the theatre and be true to himself instead of re-signing with studio head Marcus Hoff for another fourteen years. Hoff, powerful and unscrupulous, arrives and Charlie gives in and signs.

More trouble arrives when it is revealed that Buddy in fact took the rap for Charlie, and a girl, Dixie Evans, who was in the car is threatening to spill the beans. She is a starlet who has been shabbily treated by the studio and Charlie sympathizes with her. But later, when Hoff's factotum Coy arrives suggesting the only way out is to murder Dixie, Charlie realizes one wrong is being heaped upon another and says he won't work any more for Hoff. There is a brutal scene when Hoff arrives, and he leaves threatening to break Charlie. Marion and Charlie embrace and Charlie goes upstairs for a bath; Coy returns with the news that Dixie has been killed in an accident. But it is too late; Charlie has committed suicide.

Russell
Buddy Bliss
Charlie Castle
Patty Benedict
Marion Castle
Nat Danziger
Marcus Hoff
Smiley Coy
Connie Bliss
Hank Teagle
Dixie Evans
Dr Frary

Billy Liar
Keith Waterhouse and Willis Hall
Comedy 3 Acts
London 1960

Billy, a lower middle-class lad from the North East has big ideas of fame and fortune but has neither the intellect nor the courage to make anything of himself. His family and employer, an undertaker, have to suffer the consequences of his fantasies and habitual lying, things coming to a head when he becomes engaged to two girls at the same time. Barbara, his 'official' fiancée, whom he tries unsuccessfully to seduce, comes to tea with the family and announces wedding plans, but unfortunately her visit coincides with both the death of Billy's grandmother and a visit from his other 'fiancée' Rita. A fight ensues. Arthur, a friend, tells Billy that Rita's brother is after him, and Billy plans his escape to London to be a TV scriptwriter with Liz - yet another girlfriend. Mum and Dad have strong ideas about all this. Throughout the play, Billy finds refuge from his problems in vivid daydreams in which among others he becomes a doctor, a politician and a general.

Billy Fisher, a slight nineteen-year-old
Florence Boothroyd, Billy's grandmother
Geoffrey Fisher, Billy's father
Alice Fisher, Billy's mother
Arthur Crabtree, Billy's mate
Barbara, Billy's 'fiancée'
Rita
Liz

Birds, The
Aristophanes
Comedy 1 Act
Athens 414BC

Elderly Athenian gentleman Pithetaerus and companion Euelpides are fed up with war, tax and litigation in Athens and leave the city to seek Tereus, former King of Thrace and now a hoopoe. After some difficulties from Tereus's suspicious fellow-birds, they succeed in convincing all birds that it will be in their interests to retrieve their rightful places as gods, overthrow usurper Zeus and his like, and be worshipped once more by mankind, instead of being exploited.

The delighted birds elect Pithetaerus as their now-winged leader and with great organization and ingenuity they succeed in dominating the skies, until mankind, enthralled by the novelty of bird gods, no longer sacrifices burnt offerings to the old gods. Zeus and his fellow-Olympians are enraged, and Prometheus, friend to mankind, tells the birds that when the gods come down to strike a truce, that Pithetaerus should bargain for Zeus's bird-sceptre to be returned, and that Zeus should assign the Sovereign Bride, a maid in charge of all political life, as Pithetaerus's wife.

The gods' ambassadors, Heracles, Poseidon and Triballian arrive; Pithataerus outsmarts them and they concede his demands. A compromise is then reached whereby the birds will assist the gods in ruling mankind and keeping them obedient. A merry wedding ceremony rounds off the successful coup d'état.

Pithetaerus, an elderly   *Iris, the goddess*
  Athenian gentleman   *A herald*
Euelpides, his companion *A father-beater*
Tereus, former King of   *Kinesias, the lyric poet*
  Thrace, a hoopoe   *An informer*
Trochilus, servant to   *Prometheus*
  Tereus   *Poseidon*
A priest   *Heracles*
A poet   *Triballian*
A prophet   *Messengers*
Meton, the astronomer   *Servant*
A commissar   *Chorus of birds*
A law-monger

Birthday Party, The
Harold Pinter
Drama 3 Acts
Cambridge 1958

Meg, a sentimental sixty-year-old, runs a seedy boarding house with her dull husband Petey. Her only boarder is Stanley Webber, an ex-pianist, upon whom she dotes, but he returns her clumsy affection with contempt and anger.

Two strangers arrive, Goldberg and McCann; they have a job to do. Stanley appears to be expecting them with great dread and slips out of the house. Goldberg flatters Meg into telling all about Stanley, and on learning that it is his birthday suggests that they organize a party. Stanley returns and is given a present, a toy drum, by Meg and young neighbour, Lulu, whose advances he finds disturbing. He begins to beat the drum, slowly at first, then in total frenzy.

Stanley is obviously very frightened of the two men and insists that he is not the man they think he is, but they subject him to a cruel interrogation and remove his spectacles. During the party Stanley is ignored as Goldberg flirts with Lulu and Meg drinks with McCann. A game of blind man's buff follows during which Stanley is blindfolded and taunted. He tries to strangle Meg and attacks Lulu before being menaced by Goldberg and McCann. The following morning Goldberg is in need of support when Lulu accuses him of seducing her. McCann frightens her away. Stanley has been

prepared to leave, he is neatly dressed, but appears to be in a daze. Petey is worried about him but eventually does nothing as he is taken away.

Petey tells Meg nothing when she returns and recalls what a wonderful party it was.

Meg, a woman in her sixties
Petey, Meg's husband
Stanley Webber
Lulu, a girl in her twenties
Nat Goldberg
Seamus McCann

Bishop's Bonfire, The
Sean O'Casey
Comedy 3 Acts
Dublin 1955

All the inhabitants of a small Irish town, led by Councillor Reiligan and Canon Burren, join in preparation for the visit of their bishop, a local man who has been many years away from his home. It is intended that the highlight of the visit should be a bonfire on which will be burned anything irreligious, especially secular books owned by any townsperson.

In their anxiety to please the bishop, Reiligan and the Canon have hectored and cajoled the whole town into hasty but maladroit attempts to freshen the town's look. Work centres on Reiligan's property, where it is intended the bishop will stay during his visit. Under pressure of deadlines, the masons doing Reiligan's repairs quarrel over religion and drink; one of Reiligan's daughters, Keelin, pursues her lover in a fever of distraction, while the other, Foorawn, avoids hers to save herself for the Church; and Reiligan himself becomes ever more churlish and domineering. As the festivities begin, Reiligan is rewarded for his efforts with a title from the Papal Court. Reiligan's triumph is ruined when he is shot by Foorawn's suitor, and Keelin is told to give up her lover in favour of a political marriage to one of her father's older cronies.

Dick Curranaun, a mason
Richard Rankin, a mason
Councillor Reiligan
Very Revd Timothy Canon Burren
Manus Moanroe
Daniel Clooncoohy
Keelin, Reiligan's daughter
Codger Sleehaun
Foorawn, Reiligan's daughter
Father Boheroe
Lieut Michael Reiligan
A railway porter

Bitter Sweet
Noël Coward
Operetta 3 Acts
London 1929

In 1929, during a party at the Grosvenor Square home of the ageing Lady Shayne, Dolly Chamberlayne realizes that she is in love with the déclassé orchestra leader, Vincent Howard, and not with her fiancé Lord Henry Kekyll. To Lady Shayne's intense distaste, Dolly dithers at choosing between the two; and the reason for this distaste becomes clear in a series of flashbacks which sketch Lady Shayne's life from 1875 onwards.

Like Dolly, the young Lady Shayne had fallen in love with a musician, her Austrian music teacher Carl Linden, while engaged to a well known diplomat. Far from dithering over her choice, Lady Shayne had eloped with Linden to a bohemian life in Austria. But just as this new life was poised on the brink of success, Linden had been killed in a duel, by a brutal cavalry officer who tried publicly to seduce Lady Shayne.

Far from being defeated by Linden's death, Lady Shayne had dedicated herself to performing and popularizing his songs throughout Europe, where Lord Shayne had seen and fallen in love with her. They had then married in what was for her, a realization of deep friendship, but not love.

In a very short final act, we see Lady Shayne acting as hostess in 1895, to all her old London set, including her former fiancé, at the same Grosvenor Street home in which the play opens.

The Marchioness of Shayne, Sarah Millick
Dolly Chamberlayne
Lord Henry Kekyll, guest of Lady Shayne's first party
Vincent Howard
Carl Linden, Lady Shayne's first husband
Mrs Millick, Lady Shayne's mother
Hugh Devon, Lady Shayne's fiancé
London friends of Lady Shane: *Victoria, Harriet,*
  Gloria, Honor, Jane and Effie
Austrian friends of Lady Shayne: *Lotte, Freda,*
  Hansi, Gussi and Manon (La Crevette)
Capt. August Lutte, Carl Linden's killer
Lieut Tranisch, Capt. Lutte's subordinate
Herr Schlick, Carl Linden's employer

Black Chiffon
Lesley Storm
Drama 3 Acts
London 1949

The Christie family are well-off and live in a house on Chelsea Embankment. Son Roy, handsome and sensitive, is about to marry fiancée Louise; married daughter Thea (who lives just round the corner) is pregnant. Mistress of the house is their mother Alicia, attractive and in her mid-forties, but there is a serious family problem. Alicia's husband Robert is jealous of Roy's place in his mother's affections and has been for some years. Robert has often been away working abroad, sometimes for two years at a time, and their family life has not been normal.

Alicia, happy for Roy's marriage, is at the same time upset at losing him. Her self-control helps hide her deeper feelings, but a few days before the wedding she goes shopping and is hours late getting back. She returns distraught, and has to tell her family she has been charged with shoplifting - a black chiffon nightgown. Robert is horrified and the children devastated in their compassion for her. Due to appear in court on the day before Roy's wedding, she is advised by Bennett Hawkins, a psychiatrist employed by her defence council to plead 'not guilty'. Her only defence, he explains to her privately, is for him to explain how 'locked together emotionally' mother and son are, and submit this explanation for her behaviour on the eve of Roy's wedding.

Alicia becomes frantic at the implications of this idea, but calms down and declines Hawkins' suggestion. She refuses to use this line of defence, so open to suggestions and so potentially destructive to her own and her son's marriage. With Hawkins' grudging admiration she resolves to plead straightforwardly guilty, calmly organizes her household and leaves for court, knowing that she and her family will recover more easily from a prison sentence than from the indignity of such a defence.

Alicia Christie   *Thea Christie*
Robert Christie   *Bennett Hawkins*
Roy Christie
Louise, nannie

Black Coffee
Agatha Christie
Mystery 3 Acts
London 1930

Stingy physicist Sir Claud Amory has just bombarded the atom and discovered a new and terrible explosive. Unfortunately for mankind, the formula has been stolen from his safe. Claud gathers the household together, turns out the lights and gives the thief a chance to return the document. When the lights go back on, Sir Claud is dead - poisoned - and at that moment ace Belgian sleuth Hercule Poirot enters, summoned earlier by Sir Claud.

Suspicion falls on Claud's son Robert and his lovely Italian wife Lucia, but despite her messing around with the deadly poisons, liberally available in this particular household, she is in fact innocent; her suspicious meanderings are due to being blackmailed by horrid Dr Carelli, a fellow-Italian, who has threatened to reveal to Richard that Lucia is the daughter of infamous double-agent Selma Goetz. Naturally, Richard cares nothing about this, and after reuniting the lovebirds, Poirot's razor-sharp brain zones in to tackle the real murderer, who could be: the butler, the secretary, the eccentric aunt, the niece, or even the policeman...

Tredwell, the butler
Lucia Amory
Miss Caroline Amory, Sir Claud's sister
Richard Amory
Barbara Amory, Sir Claud's niece
Edward Raynor, Sir Claud's secretary

Dr Carelli
Sir Claud Amory
Hercule Poirot
Capt. Arthur Hastings OBE
Dr Graham
Inspector Japp
Johnson, a constable

Black Comedy
Peter Shaffer
Comedy 1 Act
London 1965

Young modern sculptor Brindsley Miller and his fiancée Carol Melkett are awaiting the arrival of deaf millionaire art connoisseur George Bamberger. They hope he will buy a piece or two. Also expected is Carol's fierce father Col Melkett. Brindsley is a slob but has spruced up his flat with various bits of antique furniture and expensive porcelain (including a valuable Buddha) temporarily borrowed without permission from absent neighbour Harold Gorringe, an effete and fastidious antiques dealer. Then a main fuse blows and all the lights in the house go out. The play uses the device of having the stage fully lit while the action is supposedly in darkness, and vice-versa.

Prissy neighbour Miss Furnival comes down from upstairs and Carol manages to phone the Electricity Board. Col Melkett then arrives and there follows a series of fumblings and stumblings which increase greatly upon the unexpected return of Harold. This produces desperate attempts by Brindsley to replace Harold's chattels in the darkness. Brindsley's other girlfriend Clea arrives and upon discovering that Brindsley and Carol are engaged, plays various catty pranks on everyone, while Miss Furnival gets progressively drunker.

Electricity Board man Schuppenzigh enters, is mistaken for Bamberger and unashamedly flattered by the others until they discover his true identity, whereupon he is vilified and bundled down through a trap door to the main fuse box. Harold finds out about the antiques and his petulant anger turns to rage when he accidentally smashes the precious Buddha. Together with now-scorned Carol and her enraged father, Harold advances on Brindsley to hit him, but then the real Bamberger arrives. Unfortunately he falls through the trap door, just as the lights go on - and the stage plunges into darkness.

Brindsley Miller
Carol Melkett
Miss Furnival
Col Melkett
Harold Gorringe
Clea
Schuppenzigh
George Bamberger

Blacks, The
Jean Genet
'A Clown Show'
Paris 1959

On the upper part of a split level stage, a group of stereotyped whites (Negroes wearing masks), a queen, a judge, a missionary and a general, watch a group of equally stereotyped blacks performing their grisly dance-like rituals.

A black master of ceremonies, Archibald Absolom Wellington, introduces the cast of a stylized play in which a white woman is raped and ritually murdered, very savagely, by a group of Negroes. The whites demand 'stamp out the blacks'.

News arrives that the blacks all over the world are rising against the whites and the 'white' audience is killed and mutilated.

Archibald then has the dead whites arise to join the blacks and makes a speech on the absurdities of racial intolerance. The actors don their white masks and go off to Hell.

Newport News
Bobo
Virtue
Village
Felicity
Archibald
Diouf
Snow
The Judge
The Queen
The Valet
The Missionary
The Governor General

Bless the Bride
A. P. Herbert
Music and Lyrics by Vivian Ellis
Musical Play 2 Acts
London 1947

At the genteel home of the Willows, the family play croquet and look forward to the wedding, the next day, of Lucy Willow to the Hon. Thomas Trout, but Lucy does not love him and she suspects him of being a liar. Thomas invites some French actor friends to the house, which shocks the conservative Willows, but they are taken in when he passes them off as French diplomats. One of these, Pierre, immediately falls in love with Lucy, who responds; they elope on the wedding day and escape to France, where the Franco-Prussian war is looming.

The Willows follow the lovers and thinly disguised as Frenchmen watch them in a restaurant, but they are suspected by the locals of being Prussian spies and Lucy has to rescue her family just as Pierre goes off to join the army.

Pierre is reported killed and back home in England.

Thomas, who has reformed and become an army officer, offers to marry Lucy again, but before she can accept, her true love returns. The report of his demise had been fabricated by an old flame.

Songs include: 'Ma Belle Marguerite'; 'This is My Lovely Day'; 'Bless the Bride'

Alice Charity Willow
Cousin George
Archdeacon Gurney
Lucy Verity Willow
Hon. Thomas Trout
***Lucy's sisters:** Ann Fidelity, Elizabeth Prudence, Frances Fortitude and Millicent Punctuality*
Pierre Fontaine
Suzanne Valdis
Augustus Willow, father
Mary Willow, mother
Albert Willow, grandfather
Harriet Willow, grandmother
Nanny
Buttons
Two gendarmes
Maître d'Hotel
Waiters
M. Frontenac
Marie Duval
Two customers

Blithe Spirit
Noël Coward
Farce 3 Acts
Manchester 1941

In this farce Coward poses and answers, mischievously, the question, 'What might happen if it were all true?' about psychic phenomena which fascinated the English middle classes during the first quarter of this century.

Charles Condomine, a cynical and mildly pompous writer, stages a séance conducted by a medium who lives in his Kent village, in an effort to learn the 'tricks' which he is certain will prove to be its only real substance. He plans to use this inside knowledge in a novel. Instead the medium, Mme Arcati, falls into a trance, during which the 'shade' of Charles's late wife, Elvira, appears to him. She does not, however, appear to the other participants in the seance; Charles's present wife, Ruth, and their mutual friends, Dr and Mrs. Bradman.

At first Ruth believes Charles is joking about Elvira's visitation; then that he is suffering mental strain. Elvira, however, moves into the Condomine home, and proves her presence to Ruth by pranks like knocking over the furniture. It slowly emerges, through a series of clearly bogus accidents, that Elvira is trying to kill Charles so that she may have him again on the 'other side.' Instead, she mistakenly kills Ruth, and the 'shades' of the two women alternately bicker and nag Charles until he is driven to dematerialize both of them.

Mme Arcati once more comes to Charles's aid by discovering that the Condomines' maid, Edith, has unconsciously raised Elvira's 'shade'. Edith is hypnotized and, under Mme Arcati's guidance unconsciously dematerializes both 'shades'. Free of henpecking for the first time in his life, Charles leaves to travel abroad.

Charles Condomine, a writer
Ruth, Charles's wife
Dr Bradman
Mrs Bradman
Mme Arcati, a medium
Elvira, the shade of Charles's first wife
Edith, the Condomine's maid

Blood Brothers
Willy Russell
Musical 2 Acts
Liverpool 1983

Deserted by her husband, Mrs Johnstone already has five children and is expecting twins. She cleans house for childless Mrs Lyons who offers unofficially to adopt one of the babies. Mrs Johnstone agrees, albeit reluctantly, knowing the child will be well brought up in a prosperous household. But there is a prophesy that twins parted at birth will die when they discover the truth, and both mothers do their best to keep the twins, Mickey Johnstone and Edward Lyons, well separated. The situation becomes harder for both women when Mickey and Edward meet while playing in the street and an immediate bond is forged. They become 'blood brothers', and distraught Mrs Lyons eventually moves to the countryside. Soon after, Mrs Johnstone is rehoused nearby and the boys meet again and fall in love with the same girl, Linda.

But as Edward goes on to higher education, Mickey must take a boring job, and after marrying Linda and losing his job, he turns to crime and gets caught. He is jailed, and when released becomes dependent on tranquillizers. Linda turns to Edward, now a councillor, for help, and he gets Mickey a job and a house. Then Mrs Lyons tells Mickey that Edward is having an affair with Linda and Mickey goes after Edward with a gun. He finds him at a meeting but cannot shoot him - until Mrs Johnstone bursts in and tells them the truth. Mickey kills Edward and is himself killed by the police.

Songs include: 'Marilyn Monroe'; 'Shoes upon the Table'; 'My Child'

Mrs Johnstone
Mickey
Eddie
Sammy
Linda
Mrs Lyons
Mr Lyons
Narrator
Chorus

Blood Wedding
Federico García Lorca
Tragedy 3 Acts
Madrid 1933

On the eve of an arranged wedding in the stark Andalusian countryside, the mother laments to her son, the bridegroom, the murders of her husband and other son. She is filled with foreboding, especially as the bride was formerly betrothed to Leonardo of the family who murdered her men. Leonardo's wife is now pregnant but he is still obsessed with the bride. The bride and bridegroom meet and pledge their love, and the respective parents discuss their hopes. The bride is prepared for the wedding and goes through with the ceremony, but immediately afterwards flees with Leonardo.

The others pursue them, and watched by the moon and death (as a beggar woman), Leonardo and the bride declare their hopeless love. Later we learn the bridegroom and Leonardo have killed each other. The bride offers herself to the mother to be killed. The action is classic, stylized and poetic.

The mother
The bride
The mother-in-law
The wife of Leonardo
The servant
Girls
Leonardo
The bridegroom
The father of the bride
The moon
Death (as a beggar woman)
Woodcutters
Young men

Blossom Time
Dorothy Donnelly
Adapted by Sigmund Romberg
Operetta 3 Acts
New York 1921

Loosely based on the life of composer Franz Schubert, this Viennese tale opens with the young composer in love with Mitzi. But, too shy to declare his love or to sing her the songs she has inspired, he (Cyrano-like) asks his best friend Baron von Schober to perform the chore. Von Schober sings *Song Of Love* (adapted from the First movement of Schubert's *Unfinished Symphony*) and of course Mitzi is smitten with Schober.

After losing both sweetheart and friend, Schubert writes his final work, deliberately leaving it unfinished. The work is premièred but Schubert is heart-sick and in the throes of his final and fatal illness he writes his last great song, *Ave Maria*.

Songs include: 'Three Little Maids'; 'Once to Every Heart'; 'My Springtime Thou Art'

Kuppelweiser
Vogel
Flower girl
Von Schwindt
Bellabruna
Count Sharntoff
Schubert
Mitzi
Fritzi
Kitzi
Erkman
Binder
Domeyer
Kranz
Schober
Rosi
Mrs Kranz
Emmy
Novotney
Mrs Coburg
Danseuse

Blues for Mr Charlie
James Baldwin
Tragedy 3 Acts
New York 1964

A young black man, Richard Henry, returns to his home in the deep South to rebuild his life and recover from drug addiction. A white bigot, Lyle Britten, owner of the local general store, murders Richard because the young man does not 'know his place'.

The story of his murder and its background is told in flashback by various witnesses at Lyle's eventual trial. Parnell James, editor of the local newspaper, is at the same time Lyle's closest friend and the only local white who supports the black man's right to equality before the law. He had also nursed for years a secret love for Juanita, the beautiful black woman with whom Richard was to have eloped on the day of the murder. James is caught between conflicting loyalties, and when his evidence to the court helps to secure Lyle's release, he loses his friends in the black community.

From the black community, at the same time, Richard's father, Revd Meridian Henry, whose restraining calm has always fostered relations with the local whites, gives evidence in his son's favour, and so is branded a communist agitator by the white community.

As the play concludes, the black community prepares to march in protest at the acquittal. The white community prepares to stop them.

Meridian Henry, black minister
Juanita, a beautiful black girl
Mother Henry, Meridian's mother
Lyle Britten, white businessman
Jo Britton, Lyle's wife
Parnell James, newspaper editor
Richard, Meridian's son
Papa D., juke joint owner
Black students: *Tom, Ken, Arthur, Lorenzo and Pete*
White townspeople: *Hazel, Lillian, Susan, Ralph, Ellis, Revd Phelps and George*
The State Counsel for the Bereaved
Congregation
Pallbearers
Blacktown
Whitetown

Bodies
James Saunders
Comedy Drama 2 Acts
London 1977

Two couples are seen at the same time in their respective living rooms. Anne and Mervyn and Helen and David are members of the chattering class - verbose, analytical and neurotic. In addition to their conversations some of their thoughts are spoken directly to the audience.

Some years back Anne had realized that her Mervyn was having an affair with her best friend Helen so she'd done the smart thing and started an affair with Mervyn's friend David. For a while they'd switched partners completely. But that had fizzled out and David and Helen had gone to live and work in the United States.

Now they're back in England and Mervyn has invited his and Anne's former lovers round for an evening of friendly conversation and catching-up on how they all are. Mervyn is now a headmaster and his evening is rather clouded by the knowledge that a clever but unsettling student has apparently tried to commit suicide by crashing his motor bike and Mervyn is waiting to hear from the hospital if the youth has died.

The get-together becomes steadily more intense as David talks about the psychotherapy that has 'cured' him and Helen of their problems and taught them to inhabit their bodies happily without worrying about the significance and the meaning of life. Somewhat bested by David's sober 'logic', the tipsy Mervyn speaks up for the motivating value of neuroses and illogical absurdity... and if all else fails he might buy a motor bike.

Anne
David
Helen
Mervyn

Boeing-Boeing
Marc Camoletti and Beverley Cross
Comedy 2 Acts
London 1962

Parisian man-about-town Bernard is having breakfast with American air-hostess fiancée Janet. As she leaves for work, Bernard's old school friend Robert turns up out of the blue from Aix and Bernard offers him a room in his flat until he finds accommodation of his own. He also explains his 'polygamous' life; in fact he has three 'fiancées' - Janet, German air-hostess Judith, and French air-hostess Jacqueline. Thanks to his meticulously-planned timetable, he is able to balance the comings-and-goings of each girl without their suspecting the existence of each other. All it has hitherto required is a cool nerve and the assistance of grumpy cook-housekeeper Bertha - who has to change menus with each girl.

Robert gets to meet both other girls during a tight but well-planned day, and he falls for Judith. That evening, however, circumstances beyond Bernard's control ensure that for maximum farcical pandemonium all three girls invade the flat at more or less the same time. The strain is almost too much for Bernard, but Robert, the country bumpkin, proves surprisingly cool in shunting the girls in and out of bedrooms and bathrooms while Bernard attempts unsuccessful trysts in the country. The situation is happily resolved when Janet announces she's leaving Bernard - she's been two- or three-timing too, and Judith and Robert decide to get engaged. That just leaves Bernard and Jacqueline, and much-relieved Bertha.

Bernard
Janet
Bertha
Robert
Jacqueline
Judith

Bolt Hole
Langton Smith
Comedy 3 Acts
Altrincham 1974

Elderly spinster sisters Jo and Tessa Hamshaw and their older widow sister May inherit and have to go to live in a big old remote house on Dartmoor during the early thirties. The work involved in renovating the house and garden seems daunting, but the arrival of escaped convicts Pretty Boy Willis and Basher Cox provides the answer. After an initial tussle, Willis agrees to help out, and in three years time everything is transformed. The place is lovely, the old ladies are in the business of helping escaped criminals (but only those who want to turn over a new leaf) and a whole escape system of tunnels has been constructed.

Trouble comes when niece Tammy brings home fiancé Michael, a police inspector. He finds a piece of stolen jewellery and begins to investigate and eventually surly Basher is caught. But Basher doesn't give the game away and his silence enables Willis and fellow-convict Harrison to escape. The old ladies are in the clear and resolve to stop their activities, but at the end of the play, sure enough, they are tempted once again.

Joanna Hamshaw
Tessa Hamshaw
May Jones (née Hamshaw)
Police Constable Harris
Pretty Boy Willis
Basher Cox
Paul Harrison
Tammy Hamshaw
Michael Harvey

Born Yesterday
Garson Kanin
Comedy 3 Acts
New York 1946

Harry Brock, a roughneck racketeering junk metal dealer, is in Washington with his hangers-on to buy the services of Senator Norval Hedges who, with his dowdy wife, comes to Brock's hotel suite to get his orders. Ashamed of his beautiful but simple mistress Billie Dawn, Harry hires Paul Verrall, a reporter for *New Republic* magazine, to give her some instruction in culture and class. Paul succeeds embarrassingly well and Billie starts to get real smart. Teacher and pupil fall in love and decide to blow the whistle on the corrupt machinations of Brock and entourage. Brock attempts to bribe Paul into silence and tries to laugh it off when Paul and Billie spurn his efforts.

Billie Dawn	The Assistant Manager
Harry Brock	Helen, a maid
Paul Verrall	Two bellhops
Ed Devery	A barber
Senator Norval Hedges	A manicurist
Mrs Hedges	A bootblack
Eddie Brock	A waiter

Boy Meets Girl
Bella and Samuel Spewack
Comedy 3 Acts
New York 1935

At the Hollywood office of producer C. Elliot Friday (C.F.), screenwriters Benson (married to a spendthrift woman) and Law (who wants to return to Virginia to do some real writing) are kicking around ideas for screen cowboy Larry Toms' next film; Larry's career is waning, and the idea has got to be good. The jokey pair get inspired by lovely waitress Susie who brings in lunch then collapses, heavily pregnant. They decide a baby will save Larry's bacon; the brainwave is approved by studio head B.K. and sure enough, baby Happy does the trick. Larry is reluctant about playing second fiddle to Happy but at least he's a star again. However, when Larry decides to marry Susie to safeguard his career - now dependent on Happy - a Benson and Law scam to prevent this backfires. Everyone then discovers Happy has a skeleton in the closet, namely he's illegitimate, Susie having married a bigamist. A bout of measles soon enables the studio to replace Happy with a baby of better credentials. But that's OK with Susie, as things get patched up between her and her true love, English actor Rodney - a lord's son, of course, - and they aim to return to the UK and bring up Happy properly. All Benson and Law's attempts to keep him - including fake telegrams from Europe - fail, and the movie craziness continues.

Robert Law	Susie
Larry Toms	A nurse
J .Carlysle Benson	Doctor
Rosetti	Chauffeur
Mr Friday (C.F.)	Young man
Peggy	Studio officer
Miss Crews	Cutter
Rodney Bevan	Another nurse
Green	Maj. Thompson
Slade	

Boyfriend, The
Sandy Wilson
Musical 3 Acts
London 1953

Mme Dubonnet's Finishing School is the setting for this send-up of 1920s romantic values and ethics - love rules and money definitely helps. The premise is that every young lady needs a boyfriend. However, Polly Browne is denied this right because her millionaire father believes that all men are fortune-hunters.

She persuades a messenger-boy to be her partner at the Carnival Ball and he accepts believing her to be an ordinary secretary and hides his true identity; he is the Hon. Tony Brockhurst.

Numerous opportunities arise for young lady débutantes and their beaux to burst into song and dance routines. After several misunderstandings love triumphs and social statuses remain fully intact.

Songs include: 'The Boy friend'; 'Won't you Charleston with Me?'; 'Sur le Plage';'I Could be Happy with You'

Hortense, a French maid
Maisie, Dulcie, Fay and Nancy, débutantes
Polly Browne
Marcel Pierre
Alphonse
Mme Dubonnet
Bobby Van Husen
Percival Browne
Tony
Lord Brockhurst
Lady Brockhurst
Gendarme
Waiter
Pepe and Lolita, speciality dancers
Guests

Boys from Syracuse, The
George Abbot
Lyrics by Lorenz Hart
Music by Richard Rodgers
Musical Comedy 2 Acts
New York 1938

This musical adaptation of Shakespeare's *Comedy of Errors* lifts the setting, plot and main characters, but only two of the original lines ('... the venom clamours of a jealous woman/poisons more deadly than a mad dog's tooth').

In ancient Greece, Antipholus of Syracuse and his servant Dromio arrive at Ephesus where, because of striking mutual resemblances, they are confused with the local and identically-named Antipholus and servant Dromio. In the case of each Antipholus this is not surprising because they are actually twins separated as babies during a storm at sea. The Dromios resemblance is simply coincidence.

Ephesian Antipholus is married to Adriana, whose lovely sister is Luciana; his Dromio is married to Luce. All kinds of bawdy and amusing scrapes based on mistaken identity take place, and when Antipholus of Syracuse fancies Luciana, she rejects him, thinking he is her brother-in-law. Luce chases both Dromios, and after a hilarious climax at a feast, the Ephesian pair are thrown into jail, suspected of being crazy, and the Syracusian pair hide in a priory. Finally, the misunderstandings are sorted out by the twins' father, happy at the return of his missing son, with help from the Duke of Ephesus.

Songs include: 'Sing for Your Supper'; 'Falling in Love with Love'; 'This Can't be Love'.

Sergeant	Corporal
Duke	Luce
Aegeon	Andriana
Antipholus of Ephesus	Luciana
Dromio of Ephesus	Maids
Tailor	Sorcerer
Antipholus of Syracuse	Courtesans
Dromio of Syracuse	Fatima
Merchant of Syracuse	Seeress
Apprentice	Emelia
Angelo	

Boys in the Band, The
Mart Crowley
Comedy Drama 2 Acts
New York 1968

Michael and his homosexual cronies throw a birthday party for Harold, a clever thirty-year-old dark lean Jew with a penchant for pills and pot. Other guests are Donald who, like Michael, is undergoing psychoanalysis and is the nearest to a real friend that Michael has; Emory who is the only one who is a blatantly obvious screaming queen; Hank who has left his wife and children to live with Larry; and Bernard, a tall Negro.

As his present for Harold, Emory has rented a gorgeous blond hustler, Cowboy. While waiting for Harold and his live present to arrive, the boys make with the brittle jokes and bitchiness, tending to refer to everybody as 'she', to use girlish names and refer to such favoured stars as Rita Hayworth, Gloria De Haven and, of course, Judy Garland. It soon becomes clear that they are all more or less seriously disturbed, with Bernard perhaps the most balanced, and Michael quite the nastiest. Like the others he is troubled about growing old and losing his looks and his hair. He has flitted around the world and is now permanently in debt. A heavy drinker, he has been on the wagon for five weeks but the party events soon make him reach for the bottle - and booze makes him more hostile, sarcastic and brutally abusive. He particularly takes against the dumb but harmless Cowboy. Eventually he turns the full force of his malice on Alan with whom Michael roomed at college in the days when Michael concealed his homosexuality. Alan has quarrelled with his wife and turns up unexpectedly, unaware that he is among homosexuals - apart from the obvious Emory whom he assaults for being a freak. Michael tries to organize a 'game' of phoning the people they most love, part of the object of which is to induce Alan to confess that he, too, is one of them. Michael fails miserably and the party disintegrates.

Michael
Donald
Emory
Larry
Hank
Bernard
Cowboy
Harold
Alan

Brand
Henrik Ibsen
Verse Drama 5 Acts
Copenhagen 1885

In mid-nineteenth-century Norway, the iron-willed pastor Brand battles against the enemies of man's salvation - dull heartedness, light heartedness and wild heartedness.

He unsuccessfully urges his mother to renounce her earthly wealth and warns his future wife Agnes of his stern self-sacrificing ways. After three years of happy marriage, his mother dies and his child becomes ill and in need of sunshine and light, but he refuses to move, convinced by a gypsy that he must save his flock from demons and trolls. The child's death is God's will, which Agnes must accept, and Brand insists that she give the child's clothes to a poor gypsy. This she does joyfully but dies herself soon after. Although lonely without Agnes, Brand plans a new church, which is initially opposed by the village authorities. But political expediency lets the church building go ahead, which Brand interprets as compromise; he inspires and leads his congregation up to the mountains. The harsh conditions soon produce disillusionment and the people are tricked into rejecting and eventually stoning Brand. A vision of Agnes appears to Brand asking for compromise which he cannot accept and he dies in an avalanche caused by a gypsy who mistakes him for Christ.

Brand
A guide
Guide's son
Agnes
Ejnar
Gerd
Mayor
Woman from the headland
A villager
Brand's mother
Doctor
Gypsy woman
Sexton
Schoolmaster
Provost

Breaking the Silence
Stephen Poliakoff
Drama 2 Acts
London 1984

Outside Moscow in 1920, the once-rich Pesiakoffs - Nikolai, wife Eugenia, son Sasha and maid Polya - have had their big house requisitioned by the army and must now live in a railway carriage. Eccentric, urbane and arrogant Nikolai has been given the job of Telephone Surveyor of the Northern Railway by his working-class boss Alexei Verkoff. But Nikolai has no intention of doing the job. As soon as the carriage is shunted a thousand miles northward, he immediately continues his research into recording sound on to film. He spends all his time and the government money on his project. Helped in his work by Polya and son Sasha, he still attempts to maintain his pre-revolutionary dignities and delicacies. He completely ignores communications from his superiors and eventually Eugenia surreptitiously has to do his job for him in order to avoid discovery by the authorities.

Four years later everything has changed. Eugenia is no longer pampered and precious, but has mucked in with Polya; they are now more friends than mistress and servant. Sasha has grown up and despises his father whom he considers a parasite, but the death of Lenin puts an end to Nikolai's activities. He is to be investigated and learns that Verkoff in fact has been his protector. When the guards come to arrest them, it is Eugenia who convinces them they will be making a mistake. Polya must stay in Russia, but Nikolai, Eugenia and Sasha can leave, albeit reluctantly. Nikolai must now abandon his grand project.

Polya
Master Alexander (Sasha)
Eugenia Pesiakoff
Nikolai Pesiakoff
Two guards

Breezeblock Park
Willy Russell
Drama 2 Acts
Liverpool 1975

Sisterly rivalry between Betty and Reeny runs rife at their respective homes on a Northern council estate. However, their working-class snobbery, materialism and general tastelessness sicken Betty's daughter Sandra, whose taste for a more cultivated lifestyle has been ignited by southerner Tim, her middle-class student boyfriend.

One Christmas Eve, Betty and husband Syd are visited by her near-alcoholic brother Tommy and lively wife Vera, and later by Reeny with car-proud know-it-all husband Ted and valiumized son John. Sandra and Tim then arrive and she announces she is pregnant and intends to live with Tim - who seems dubious about the scheme. Betty is humiliated in front of her family, but next day at Reeny's she has recovered and is full of grandmotherly plans for little 'Wayne'. They include marrying off Sandra and Tim and converting the upstairs of their house into a flat for the couple and 'Wayne'. The men take Tim to the pub to persuade, or threaten, him into agreeing to the scenario, but when confronted with the plans, Sandra sees her dreams of a more cultured existence slipping away and she tries to leave. The family, including treacherous Tim, block her way, only her mother eventually lets her through. Tim is sent off to find her, and the close-knit family huddle up for yet another TV Christmas.

Betty
Syd
Sandra
Vera
Tommy
Reeny
Ted
John
Tim

Brief Lives
John Aubrey
Drama 2 Acts
Hampstead 1967

Adapted by Patrick Garland from diarist John Aubrey's *Lives*, this dramatized monologue features Aubrey aged seventy, a year before his death in 1697, pottering about his room in Bloomsbury one winter's day, reminiscing, grumbling, gossiping, talking to friends and acquaintances long gone, reciting anecdotes, and generally describing events that happened just before and during his life. His fascinating minutiae of detail is reflected in the cluttered room itself which is jam-packed with knick-knacks from a life lived through a great many changes of government and religion, including the Civil War. Street sounds come and go, and the lighting indicates the progression of the day from morning to night. Aubrey, perky and still mentally agile, reveals his personal segment of the past with a vividness and humanity that brings it once more to life.

John Aubrey

Brigadoon
Alan Jay Lerner and Frederick Loewe
Musical 2 Acts
New York 1947

Tommy and Jeff, two twentieth-century American men, happen upon the carefree eighteenth-century Scottish village of Brigadoon, on the wedding day of Jean and Charlie. Jean's older sister, Fiona, is captivated by Tommy, who is enchanted and bewitched by Brigadoon while Jeff becomes homesick. They discover that, miraculously, Brigadoon will remain untouched because it appears only once a century. If one native leaves the whole place vanishes forever. A stranger, however, can stay if he loves a villager and is willing to forego everything else.

During the wedding festivities, Harry declares his undying love for Jean and threatens to leave Brigadoon but falls to his death after a wild chase when Tommy accidentally trips him. Tommy and Fiona express their love but he cannot trust his feelings and returns to New York. Months later, he rejects his fiancée, flees to Scotland, where his love and belief in Fiona is strong enough to miraculously reawaken Brigadoon long enough for him to join their eighteenth-century world. Songs include: 'Almost Like Being in Love'; 'The Heather on the Hill'; 'Come to Me, Bend to Me'; 'I'll Go Home with Bonnie Jean'

Tommy Albright	*Fiona*
Jeff Douglas	*Jean*
Angus MacMonies	*Charlie Cameron*
Donald Ritchie	*Mr Murdoch*
Sandy	*Two sword dancers*
Maggie Abernethy	*Piper*
MacGregor	*Frank*
Stuart Cameron	*Jane Ashton*
Harry Ritchie	*Singers*
Meg Brockie	*Dancers*
Andrew MacKeith	

Brighton Beach Memoirs
Neil Simon
Drama 2 Acts
New York 1984

Family frustrations and fulfilments are the theme of Simon's autobiographical memoirs set in a crowded wooden frame house in Brighton Beach, a poorish but respectable ethnic neighbourhood in Brooklyn, New York. It is 1937 and budding writer Eugene Jerome is nearly fifteen and discovering his sexuality, enlightened reluctantly by adored big brother Stanley. The Jeromes are a decent Jewish family but life is tough, especially for father Jack who supports not only wife Kate and Eugene, but also widowed sister-in-law Blanche and her two girls, lovely Nora and 'delicate' Laurie. Everyone has problems, everyone has their private moans and grievances and everyone brings them to Jack. He works two jobs and eventually has a mild heart attack. Kate blames this on the pressure put on by Blanche and her family. The sisters fight and things are said, and Blanche says she will have to leave ... but to where?

Stanley almost gets fired from his job for upholding a principle, then in an attempt to make more money for his family he loses a week's wages in a game of poker. Nora gets the chance of a Broadway audition, but Blanche does not want her sacrificing her college education. Jack forgives Stanley and promises to teach him poker; Nora knuckles under, and Kate and Blanche make up. Stanley affirms his great faith in Eugene's talent insisting he must go to college, and Eugene's comments enliven proceedings considerably. Then comes some good news. Their Polish cousins have

managed to escape from the Nazis. All seven will be here in a week. It will be tough, but everyone is happy.

Eugene
Blanche
Kate
Laurie
Nora
Stanley
Jack

Brimstone and Treacle
Dennis Potter
Drama 4 Scenes
Sheffield 1977

Conventional Mr and Mrs Bates have a brain-damaged but very attractive, daughter, Pattie. Martin, a blazered young man who looks as though he stepped out of a 'tennis, anyone?' play, calls at their home, having found Mr Bates' wallet. His attempts to communicate with the gibbering Pattie give the Bates hope of some kind of a miracle, but the specious young man is demonic and, left alone with the poor girl, he rapes her. This leads to her doing a little talking to her father. She remembers something and screams.

Mr Bates
Mrs Bates
Martin Taylor
Pattie

Broadway
Phillip Dunning and George Abbott
Drama 3 Acts
New York 1926

Talented dancer Roy Lane is upset that his dance partner, innocent and beautiful Billie, is showing special interest in rich and handsome Steve Crandell, a good customer at Nick's Paradise Night Club where Roy performs together with Billie and other chorus girls Mazie, Grace, Ruby, Pearl and Ann. Once attractive Lil Rice plays the piano and is being wooed by Porky, one of Steve's cronies, but neither Porky nor club owner Nick are around when secret bootlegger Steve is visited by fellow-mobster 'Scar' Edwards, sore at Steve for muscling in on his territory. Steve shoots Scar in the back and together with accomplice Dolph dumps the body, pretending it's a drunk. Billie sees, but Steve swears her to secrecy.

Detective Dan McCorn arrives to investigate but despite his suspicions he can get nothing on Steve. There is a fight between Steve and Roy over Billie, but despite various ups and downs, Billie predictably ends up in Roy's arms. Unknown to Steve, chorus girl Pearl was Scar's fiancée and finally she confronts Steve and kills him. McCorn turns a blind eye to this and reports the death as suicide. Porky weds Lil and Roy and Billie gets an offer for the 'big time'.

Nick Verdis	*Steve Crandell*
Roy Lane	*Dolph*
Lil Rice	*'Porky' Thompson*
Katie	*'Scar' Edwards*
Joe	*Dan McCorn*
Mazie Smith	*Benny*
Ruby	*Larry*
Pearl	*Mike*
Grace	*Gangsters*
Ann	*Waiters*
'Billie' Moore	

Brother Rat
John Monks Jr and Fred R. Finklehoffe
Comedy 3 Acts
New York 1936

Joyce Winfree and Claire Ramm return to Lexington, Virginia, for a short vacation. Claire's father is the new Commandant of the Virginia Military Institute. Bing Edwards, the Institute's star baseball player, who secretly married the previous year, discovers his wife is pregnant and inadvertently misses roll-call. Col Ramm postpones his punishment for one day so that he may pitch in the big game.

Meanwhile, Billy Randolph, Bing's room-mate, has bet Bing's allowance of fifty dollars on the home team. Realizing that Bing is below par, he pawns Bing's ceremonial sabre, using the money to bet on the opposing team. Col Ramm discovers the illegal pawning of the sabre and places the boys on punishment duty. Bing's chemistry exam is the day after that duty ends, and he must pass in order to graduate. With the aid of Claire, he passes with flying colours. The play thus ends with a double celebration; Bing's graduation and the birth of his baby boy.

Mrs Brooks	*'Newsreel' Scott*
Joyce Winfree	*'Tripod' Andrews*
Claire Ramm	*'Mistol' Bottome*
Harley Harrington	*Slim*
Bing Edwards	*Lieut 'Lace Drawers'*
Billy Randolph	*Rogers*
Kate Rice	*Col Ramm*
Dan Crawford	*Three members of the*
A. Furman Townsend Jr	*guard*

Brothers Karamazov, The
Adapted by Jacques Copeau and Jean Crove, from the novel by Fyodor Dostoevsky
Drama 5 Acts
New York 1927

Set in the nineteenth century, a bitter feud takes place between Dimitri Karamazov and his father Feodor, who has cheated him of his mother's legacy. Dimitri has left his fiancée Katerina, taking 3,000 roubles she entrusted to him, to be with Grouchenka, the object of his desire. However, he is furious that his passion for Grouchenka is shared by his father, who is wooing her with the money left to Dimitri by his mother.

Brother Ivan hates his father also, but has tended to avoid the situation, although he is secretly in love with Katerina. When Feodor is murdered and the legacy stolen, Dimitri is immediately accused and convicted of the crime, though he protests his innocence. On the night of the murder, Ivan had admitted his desire to see his father dead to Smerdiakov, Feodor's lackey, who subsequently carried out the crime, convinced of Ivan's support. The realization of his involvement and guilt sends Ivan to the brink of madness.

Aliocha Karamazov
Dimitri Karamazov
Smerdiakov
Ivan Karamazov
Feodor Karamazov
Father Zossima
Katerina Verhovtseva
Agrafena Alexandrovna Svetlov
A maid
Grigori Vassiliev
Lieut Moussialovitch
Vroubleski
Trifon Borisitch
Andvley
Stevanida
Chief of Police
Monks
Peasants, soldiers

Browning Version, The
Terence Rattigan
Play 1 Act
London 1948

Andrew Crocker-Harris, a once-brilliant academic, is ill and about to leave his post as master of the Lower Fifth, where he is loathed and feared by his pupils. His wife too hates him and is having an affair with a younger master. The headmaster comes to inform 'The Crock' that he has no pension rights and also asks him to step down at a college leaving ceremony in favour of a younger man. His growing awareness of his 'utter failure as a schoolmaster' is heightened when he learns that his nickname is 'The Himmler of the Lower Fifth'.

One pupil, however, does respect him and brings a parting gift, a copy of Robert Browning's version of *Agamemnon*. This moves him greatly, but his wife is very cynical of the boy's motives. Her lover, however, does not share her views and tries to reassure Crocker-Harris, who then reveals that his wife enjoys informing him of her affairs; their life together is a sham.

Later his wife tries to taunt him that her affair will continue, but Crocker has now come to terms with her and with himself. He tells the headmaster he will not defer to the younger colleague at the leaving ceremony.

John Taplow	*Dr Frobisher*
Frank Hunter	*Peter Gilbert*
Millie Crocker-Harris	*Mrs Gilbert*
Andrew Crocker-Harris	

Buried Child
Sam Shepard
Tragedy 3 Acts
San Francisco 1978

Somewhere in the American Midwest, an old alcoholic, Dodge, argues with his wife Halie as she gets ready to go out. He and his eldest son, Tilden, who has deteriorated from football hero to petty criminal, sit husking corn and trading insults. Halie reminisces about her son Ansel, who was killed on military service; and about her disappointment with Tilden and his brother Bradley, an amputee with a wooden leg. Dodge denies Tilden is his son, and says his real son is buried in the back yard. When Halie leaves, Dodge becomes drowsy and asks Tilden to prevent Bradley, if he arrives, from forcing a haircut on him while he sleeps. Dodge falls off to sleep and Tilden instead leaves.

Dodge is woken by Vince, Tilden's son, who has not seen the family in six years, and by Vince's girlfriend Shelley. Vince has stopped off to visit his grandparents before moving West. Dodge claims not to know Vince, making Shelley feel odd, dislocated. Tilden returns and also seems not to recognize his son. Dodge sends Vince for whiskey, and Shelley is left with Tilden who tells her that Dodge murdered the buried child. As they stand in conversation, Bradley arrives, frightens Tilden into leaving and starts to insult Shelley.

In time, Shelley settles warily into the family and waits for Vince, gone missing while on Dodge's errand. She asks Dodge about the buried child, but he evades answering. When Halie arrives with Father Dewis, the questions stop.

Taken aback by Shelley's arrival, Halie is further upset when she argues with Bradley and taunts him by moving his false limb beyond reach. This, with Shelley's hints about the dead child, and Vince's reappearance, drunk, causes Father Dewis to leave. Vince taunts Bradley with his false limb as Dodge dictates a will leaving Vince his estate. The mounting tension drives Shelley away, Halie into hysteria and Dodge to a fatal heart attack. Tilden reappears, carrying a child's rotting corpse and Halie falls into disjointed reverie.

Dodge
Halie, Dodge's wife
Tilden, Dodge's eldest son
Bradley, Dodge's middle son
Vince, Tilden's son
Shelley, Vince's girlfriend
Father Dewis

Burning Glass, The
Charles Morgan
Drama 3 Acts
London 1954

Set in the near distant future, this play warns of the dangers of unbridled scientific progress and its destructive consequences.

High-minded scientist Christopher Terriford has discovered a means of harnessing the rays of the sun to selectively burn any part of the world. He informs the Prime Minister, a former admirer of his mother, of his 'burning glass' but will not reveal details of the operation of the equipment, other than for a military emergency, fearing man's weaknesses. The secret of the machine is known only partially to two other people, one being his wife Mary, who is forced to demonstrate it for an enemy when Christopher is kidnapped. His assistant, who loves Mary, learns the secret during the demonstration, but fearing his own instability commits suicide, leaving Christopher and Mary as the custodians. The Prime Minister sees the suicide as an optimistic gesture for the future of man.

Christopher Terriford
Mary Terriford
Tony Lack
Lady Terriford
Tamas Dokomos Hardlip
Lord Henry Strait, Prime Minister's staff
Montagu Winthrop, Prime Minister
Inspector Wigg, policeman

Bus Stop
William Inge
Romance 3 Acts
New York 1955

Grace owns a restaurant by a bus stop in Kansas. One evening a terrible blizzard storms the town; a bus pulls up outside and in rushes dizzy blonde chanteuse Cherie. She tells Grace and young waitress Elma that a man on the bus has abducted her and intends to marry her with or without her consent. However, the bus has to stop all night and soon Carl, the driver, Will, the sheriff, Dr Lyman, a drunk and cowboys Bo and Virgil are all in the restaurant. Bo is treating Cherie as though he owns her, and eventually Virgil gets the message across that Cherie is not in love with him. Meanwhile Grace and old pal Carl have gone to Grace's apartment, and Elma is listening completely fascinated to everything Dr Lyman has to say.

To cheer themselves up, Elma and Lyman act out a scene from *Romeo and Juliet*, Cherie sings a song while Virgil plays guitar. This really drives Bo crazy; he molests Cherie again and Will has to fight him. Bo is beaten, and after the fight feels utterly defeated and humiliated, but this humbles him enough to apologize to everyone including Cherie. He tells her that she was the first girl he had ever been with and that he truly loves her. Cherie softens and agrees to go to Montana with him. As Bo and Cherie come together we see the aloneness of the others: Dr Lyman, a drunk professor who hangs around schools; Virgil, as he announces to Bo he won't be going to Montana with him and is left alone in the cold; and Grace as she settles down and closes her restaurant all alone.

Elma Duckworth
Grace Hoylard

Will Masters
Cherie
Dr Gerald Lyman
Carl
Virgil Blessing
Bo Decker

Business of Murder, The
Richard Harris
Drama 2 Acts
London 1981

Stone and Detective Superintendent Hallett wait at Stone's flat for his son to arrive. The boy is in trouble with drug dealers and wants protection. But he does not arrive and when Hallett leaves, Stone begins acting suspiciously. That evening Dee Redmond arrives at the flat; she is a crime writer and has come in answer to Stone's letter to encourage his sick wife, also a crime buff. While Stone's wife remains (apparently) asleep in the other room, the conversation between Stone and Dee turns to murder and becomes menacing. Stone leaves to get some urgent pills for his wife but before he returns, Hallett comes back. Hallett and Dee are surprised - they are in fact lovers. Hallett tells Dee that Mrs Stone is dead and when they go into the bedroom there is a dummy in the bed.

Stone returns and the mystery unfolds. Several years ago, Stone's wife and son had been horribly murdered and Hallett had arrested and brutally interrogated Stone, who was later released. Hallett told the story to Dee, who has got her break as a murder writer with a sanitized TV version of the story. Now Stone wants revenge. He has plotted everything to the last imaginable detail and has apparently killed Hallett's wife, with all the clues pointing to Hallett. But Hallett claims he had known of Stone's game all the time and had been hunting the hunter. The final twist comes when the two men fight and Stone forces Hallett to kill him, thus gaining his revenge. Hallett will now have to face a charge of murder.
Hallett
Stone
Dee

Butley
Simon Gray
Drama 2 Acts
London 1971

Butley is a typically unkempt and shambling university lecturer and today is not his day - and he makes the most of it. He shares his college office and also his flat with his pal Joey, former star pupil and homosexual; Butley has recently moved back in with Joey after the break-up of his marriage to Ann. She arrives at the college and tells Butley she intends moving in with and soon marrying teacher Tom, dubbed by Butley 'the most boring man in London'. Though upset, Butley does not want Ann back despite Joey encouraging reconciliation. Butley mischievously tries to make trouble for Tom, but this and his other cruelties to Joey, fellow-lecturer Edna, and his pupils, are suitably rewarded when Joey's new boyfriend Reg appears. He tells Butley that Joey will be moving in with him. Butley's devastating repartee hurled at Reg upon hearing of the end of his most stable relationship results in Reg hitting Butley, followed by Joey moving his things out and into Edna's empty office. Devastated, Butley takes it out on promising pupil Mr Gardner, whom he insults and rejects.
Ben Butley
Joseph Keyston
Miss Heasman
Edna Shaft
Anne Butley
Reg Nuttall
Mr Gardner

Butterflies are Free
Leonard Gershe
Comedy 2 Acts
New York 1969

Don, in his early twenties, is on the phone to his mother from his apartment on Manhattan's lower East side. It is his first apartment and his mother sounds over-protective. When his new neighbour, nineteen-year-old swinger Jill invites herself in for coffee, it takes her a while to realize that Don is blind; he is careful, methodical and well-organized, without a trace of self-pity. His only problem, he says, is other people's attitudes. The couple make love almost immediately, and soon afterwards Don's mother, Mrs Baker, arrives. She does not approve of the flat, the furniture, the neighbourhood and most especially not of Jill, an LA girl from a broken home.

Would-be actress Jill leaves for an off-Broadway audition, planning dinner that night with Don. She is late, though, and finally arrives with Ralph Austin, director of the show in which she now has got a minor part, involving much nudity, crudity, drug addiction and death. She leaves with Ralph, intending to move in with him, and Don is upset, which in turn upsets his mother. Now she has changed her mind about wanting Don to come back home and is not impressed by his new-found self-pity. She thinks it will be better for him to endure things on his own. When she leaves and Jill returns Don accuses her of being emotionally retarded and too scared to make a commitment. Jill leaves again but then returns, ready at last to make that commitment.
Don Baker
Jill Tanner
Mrs Baker
Ralph Austin

Bye Bye Birdie
Michael Stewart
Lyrics by Lee Adams
Music by Charles Strouse
Musical Comedy 2 Acts
New York 1960

Inspired by Elvis's stint in the US Army, this early rock musical opens with idol Conrad Birdie getting his call from Uncle Sam. His hordes of teenage fans are so enraged they threaten to secede from the Union, but even more worried is songwriter Albert Peterson; it looks like his title song for Birdie's next movie will be shelved, and Albert needs the money it will earn to break away from his horrendously possessive mother.

At fiancée Rose's suggestion, Albert comes up with a gimmick; a song titled *One Last Kiss* which Rose arranges for Birdie to sing to (and plant on) a lucky fan - on the Ed Sullivan coast-to-coast TV show. Kiss winner is Kim MacAfee from Sweet Apple, Ohio, and the Birdie circus heads there for the necessary preparations. Birdie gets a big welcome in Sweet Apple and stays with the MacAfees, making Kim's boyfriend Hugo jealous. To compound the problems, Albert's mother arrives, threatening suicide if her son weds Rose. Birdie and Kim, bored with all this, sneak off for fun at the ice rink, thus worrying her folks sick. Rose and Hugo drink to forget, and Rose storms into a Shriners' convention where she does a wild dance.

Albert finally finds her and they are reconciled. He promises to marry her and settle down in Pumpkin Falls, Iowa. Hugo and Kim make up after she gets disillusioned with egoistic Birdie, who then leaves at last for the Army.

Songs include: 'A Lot of Livin' To Do'; 'One Boy'; 'What Did I Ever See In Him?'

Albert Peterson	*Teen Trio*
Rose Alvarez	*Sad Girl*
Helen	*Another Sad Girl*
Nancy	*Mae Peterson*
Alice	*Reporters*
Margie Ann	*Conrad Birdie*
Penelope Ann	*Guitar Man*
Deborah Sue	*Conductor*
Suzie	*Cheerleaders*
Linda	*Mayor*
Carol	*Mayor's wife*
Martha Louise	*Hugo Peabody*
Harold	*Randolph MacAfee*
Karl	*Mrs Merkle*
Harvey	*Old Woman*
Henry	*Neighbours*
Arthur	*Gloria Rasputin*
Freddie	*Ed Sullivan's voice*
Peyton	*TV stage manager*
Ursula Merkle	*Charles F. Maude*
Kim MacAfee	*Bar customers*
Mrs MacAfee	*Dish washer*
Mr MacAfee	*Shriners*

Cabaret
Joe Masterhoff
Lyrics by Fred Ebb
Music by John Kander
Musical 2 Acts
New York 1966

This is a musical version of John Van Druten's play *I Am a Camera*, which is itself an adaptation of earlier Christopher Isherwood stories.

Cliff Bradshaw, a young American writer comes to jazz-age Berlin of 1929. Decadence and political upheaval pervade the atmosphere. He encounters a young German smuggler, Ernst Ludwig, who shows him how to get around in the city, and takes a room in the seedy house of Frau Schneider who has a Jewish suitor. In the sleazy Kit Kat Klub cabaret he meets Sally Bowles, an English chanteuse, with whom he is soon smitten, but problems arise for Cliff when Ernst, revealed as a Nazi money courier, asks him to help with smuggling. Cliff declines, and decides that he should leave Germany and take Sally with him, particularly after Frau Schneider's house is attacked. Sally, however, wants to stay and when Cliff goes to the Kit Kat Klub to see her he gets into a brawl and is beaten up by some of Ernst's Nazi thugs. His parting is hastened when he learns that Sally has had an abortion. He starts writing his reminiscences on the train out of Germany.

Songs include: 'Willkommen'; 'Tomorrow Belongs To Me'; 'The Money Song'; 'Cabaret'.

Master of Ceremonies	*Sally Bowles*
Clifford Bradshaw	*Two ladies*
Ernst Ludwig	*Sailors*
Customs official	*Frau Wendel*
Frau Schneider	*Herr Wendel*
Herr Schultz	*Frau Kruger*
Fraulein Kost	*Herr Erdmann*
Telephone girl	*Kit Kat girls*
Kit Kat Kittens	*Bobby*
Maître D'	*Victor*
Max	*Greta*
Bartender	*Felix*

Cactus Flower
Abe Burrows
Comedy 2 Acts
New York 1975

Beautiful, young and romantic Toni is just saved from suicide by struggling young writer Igor who lives in the next apartment and has smelled gas. The cause of her distress is the older Dr Julian Winston, an affluent dentist and philanderer, who has told her he is married with children so as to protect his bachelorhood. When he hears of Toni's suicide bid, though, Julian hurries round to propose marriage, promising to get a divorce but the sentimental Toni, worrying about the wife and three children to be deserted on her account, insists on meeting the wife even though Julian assures her the wife doesn't care and has a gentleman friend herself.

Julian persuades his somewhat dowdy nurse assistant Stephanie, a woman nearer his age, to play the part of his wife. A cadging patient, Harvey, is offered free dental treatment for himself and his real girl friend, to play Stephanie's younger lover. Senor Arturo Sanchez is also there, looking for a bit of fun with Stephanie.

In a dark nightclub they all collide - Toni with Julian, Stephanie with Harvey, then Harvey with his real girl, which leads to Stephanie with the Senor and Julian's explanation that Stephanie is a nymphomaniac. Toni gets more and more sympathetic to Stephanie, who is becoming steadily more glamorous. Eventually, Stephanie visits Toni and confesses to being only the spinster nurse and so Toni is free to marry Julian. Not knowing about this revelation, Julian - who has become suspicious of Igor's involvement with Toni - turns up and says his wife won't give him a divorce. When Igor comes out of Toni's bathroom wearing only a towel, Julian clears off and leaves the lovers to each other. Back at the dentist's office Julian and Stephanie make their long-delayed confessions of true love.

Toni Simmons	*Senor Arturo Sanchez*
Igor Sullivan	*Customer*
Stephanie Dickinson	*Waiter*
Mrs Dixon Durant	*Botticelli's Springtime*
Dr Julian Winston	*Music lover*
Harvey Greenfield	

Caesar and Cleopatra
George Bernard Shaw
A History in 5 Scenes
New York 1906

As the conquering Caesar sweeps across Egypt in 48BC, the young princess Cleopatra flees to the desert to escape him. She hides near the Sphinx and when Caesar comes to pay homage to the statue, she mistakes him for an ordinary soldier. He takes her back to her palace, encouraging her in the art of ruling, but her fear of him is not allayed until she learns his real identity.

Caesar plans to replace the boy king, Ptolemy, with Cleopatra, but this idea is opposed by a rival Roman faction, one of whom, Pothinus, tries to convince Caesar that Cleopatra will betray him once she is queen. She has Pothinus murdered, much to Caesar's dismay; he sees political intrigue as a normal part of life, and this act precipitates an uprising.

When Cleopatra's servant, Ftatateeta, is murdered, she demands revenge, but Caesar sees it as expedient and calms her by promising her that he will send handsome young Mark Antony to her from Rome.

Julius Caesar	*Pothinus*
Cleopatra	*Theodotus*
Rufio	*Achillas*
Britannus	*Belzanor*
Lucius Septimus	*Bel Affris*
Apollodoms	*Ftatateeta*
Ptolemy XIV	

Cage Aux Folles, La
Harvey Fierstein
Music by Jerry Herman
Musical Comedy 2 Acts
New York 1983

Georges runs the Cages aux Folles drag club in St Tropez, where he presents shows featuring the glamorous chorus of 'Les Cagettes' and the star performer Zaza, who is Albin, his faithful and loving companion of many years. Georges, during a drunken lapse twenty years earlier, has fathered a son, Jean Michel, and the couple have brought him up well, he is a charming and loving son. But now Jean Michel wants to get married to Anne and naturally his fiancée's parents want to meet his family. Unfortunately Anne's father is a leading right-wing politician, with a particular interest in defending morals.

Georges arranges for their normally 'camp' house to be straightened up and Michel requests that his real mother be asked to come to the dinner party meeting, but she refuses and Albin, who has been 'masculinized' to appear as Uncle Al for the occassion, steps in and becomes mother. Things go reasonably well, despite some *faux pas* by butler/maid Jacob, until at the party 'mother' is asked to sing and whips off her wig as a finale. Anne's father is outraged, but has to succumb to blackmail and embarrassment before allowing the young couple to marry.

Songs include: 'We Are What We Are'; 'I Am What I Am'; 'The Best of Times'

Georges
Francis
Jacob
Albin
Jean Michel
Anne
Jacqueline
M. Renaud
Edouard Dindon
Mme Dindon
St Tropez citizens
'Les Cagettes': Chantal, Monique, Dermah, Nicole, Hanna, Mercedes, Bitelle, Lo Singh, Odette, Angelique, Phaedre and Clo-Clo

Caine Mutiny Court Martial, The
Herman Wouk
Drama 2 Acts
New York 1954

At a US Navy court-martial in 1945, Lieut Stephen Maryk is defended reluctantly by young Jewish lawyer Lieut Greenwald. Well-meaning Maryk had forcefully relieved his superior officer, Capt. Queeg, of command of the minesweeper *Caine* during a typhoon in the Philippines. Maryk had considered Queeg was cracking up under pressure, and Greenwald knows that in order to get an aquittal he must convince the court that Queeg was indeed insane during the crisis.

Calamity Jane

The Captain himself is a fastidious and neurotic character, but Greenwald discovers Maryk had been insidiously egged on by Lieut Keefer, a writer working on a war novel. Greenwald cleverly forces Queeg to demonstrate panic under pressure, Maryk wins the case, and Queeg is destroyed. Later, Greenwald gets drunk and attends Keefer's party celebrating the publication of his novel, and after expressing his contempt for Keefer, Greenwald throws a glass of wine in his face and leaves.

Lieut Stephen Maryk
Lieut Barney Greenwald
Lieut-Com. John Challee
Capt. Queeg
Capt. Blakely
Lieut Thomas Keefer
Signalman Third class Junius Urban
Lieut (Jr Grade) Willis Seward Keith
Capt. Ranolph Southard
Dr Forrest Lundeen
Dr Bird
Stenographer
Orderly

Calamity Jane
Charles K. Freeman
Music by Sammy Fain
Lyrics by Paul Webster
Musical 2 Acts
New York

When song-and-dance man Francis Fryer arrives at Deadwood City's Golden Garter saloon instead of female entertainer Frances Fryer, proprietor Miller is stuck with a saloonful of rowdy cowpokes. Hard-bitten gun-totin' tomboy Calamity Jane heads for Chicago to round up pin-up singer/actress Adelaide Adams for the boys' delectation, but by mistake brings back Ade's glamorous starstruck maid Katie Brown. Katie and Calamity soon become friends and after a shaky start Katie is a big hit, especially with Lieut Danny Gilmartin whom Calamity is sweet on. Local hero Wild Bill Hickock also falls for Katie's charms.

Katie shows Calamity how to dress feminine, and the transformation wows the townsfolk at the local hop, because beneath that drag, Calamity is all woman. But when she finds Katie and Danny canoodling, Calamity gets so 'darn ornery' that Katie skedaddles. Wild Bill and Calamity soon realize they love each other and Calamity brings back Katie for the inevitable triple wedding: Katie and Danny, Francis and Miller's niece Susan, and of course Calamity and Wild Bill.

Songs include: 'The Black Hills of Dakota'; 'The Deadwood Stage'; 'My Secret Love'

Calamity Jane	Susan
Wild Bill Hickock	Francis Fryer
Lieut Danny Gilmartin	Adelaide Adams
Katie Brown	Rattlesnake
Henry Miller	'Doc' Pierce

Joe	Trappers
Hank	Indians
Pete	Women of the town
Colonel of Fort Scully	Chorus girls
Cowpunchers	Officers
Bullwhackers	Soldiers and wives
Prospectors	Stage coach passengers

California Suite
Neil Simon
Comedy 2 Acts
New York 1976

A series of four separate playlets, all set in Suite 203-4 of the Beverley Hills Hotel.

Visitor from New York. Brittle Hannah Warren has come to see ex-husband Billy about seventeen-year-old daughter Jenny wanting to move from Mom's to Dad's. Their touching and often painful meeting ends with Hannah relinquishing control of Jenny.

Visitor from Philadelphia. Millie, has flown in to join husband Marvin (separate planes for safety) for a family bar-mitzvah. Trouble is, her brother Harry set Marvin up with a girl who is still out stone cold in Marvin's bed when Millie arrives. Though upset, she graciously forgives him after suitable martyrdom and extracts the promise of a spending spree.

Visitors from London. Actress Diana and her bisexual husband Sydney are the visitors. She has been nominated for an Oscar but loses, and afterwards, disappointed and desperate, they examine their unsatisfactory (to her) relationship which is nevertheless essential to them both.

Visitors from Chicago. Couples Mort and Beth, and Stu and Gert are best friends on holiday together, their forced proximity has made them end up resenting and hating each other, and their anger erupts into ridiculous fights, injuries and a final physical humiliation for Stu as Mort tries to force him to say he will go on holiday with them again next year.

Hannah Warren	Diana Nichols
William Warren	Mort Hollander
Marvin Michaels	Beth Hollander
Bunny	Stu Franklyn
Millie Michaels	Gert Franklyn
Sydney Nichols	

Caligula
Albert Camus
Tragedy 4 Acts
Paris 1945

The young emperor Caligula, whose early career held promise that he would develop into a great ruler, has suddenly become the embodiment of absurdly arbitrary power. Members of his court believe that grief over the recent death of Drusilla, his sister and lover, has catapulted Caligula into madness. The Emperor himself declares that his absolute power can and must, by a kind of bent logic, ignore moral law and challenge any supposed impossibility in the physical world. Accordingly, he sets out utterly to debase the ruling families of Rome, and launches a bizarre expedition, led by his only remaining friend, Helicon, to bring the moon to earth.

Caligula's mistress Caesonia abandons herself to serving his debauchery; nobles dine as his guests while off-stage he rapes their wives; fortunes are sequestrated from the rich men who are then executed. In time the emperor is utterly isolated and open to assassination. Chief amongst the assassins is Cherea, who admits that he acts only out of concern for his personal security. Realizing that the plotting against him is nearly ripe, Caligula strangles the loving Caesonia and then dies under the knives of Cherea's mob.

Caligula, Emperor of Rome
Caesonia, Caligula's mistress
Helicon, Caligula's friend
Scipio and Cherea, Caligula's opponents
The Old Patrician
Mereia
Mucius
The Intendant
Patricians
Knights
Guards
Servants

Call Me Madam
Howard Lindsay and Russel Crouse
Music by Irving Berlin
Musical Play 2 Acts
New York 1950

Sally Adams, a dynamic lady with meagre qualifications, is nevertheless appointed as the new Ambassador to the small European state of Lichtenburg, of which she has never heard. When she arrives in the country with her new assistant, Kenneth Gibson, she soon upsets the US Chargé d'Affaires with her informal brand of diplomacy and her lack of knowledge of protocol, but she does make an impression on local cabinet minister Cosmo Constantine, with whom she falls head over heels in love. Assistant Kenneth also takes a liking to Europeans in the shape of Princess Maria.

Cosmo is an honest and idealistic politician, and despite Sally's offer of a massive US loan he refuses; he wants his country to stand on its own feet. Eventually Sally's antics at court and her active promotion of Cosmo in an election cause her to be recalled to Washington, but not before she has successfully engineered the romance between Kenneth and the Princess and helped sort out Lichtenburg's economic problems. Cosmo becomes Prime Minister of his country and when he comes to the US to present an honour to Sally he also brings his promise of undying love.

Songs include: 'The Best Thing for You'; 'You're Just in Love'; 'It's A Lovely Day Today'

Mrs Sally Adams	*Cosmo Constantine*
The Secretary of State	*Pemberton Maxwell*
Supreme Court Justice	*Clerk*
Congressman Wilkins	*Hugo Tantinnin*
Henry Gibson	*Sebastian Sebastian*
Kenneth Gibson	*Princess Maria*
Senator Gallagher	*Court Chamberlain*
Miss Phillips	*A maid*
Butler	*Grand Duchess Sophie*
Senator Brockbank	*Grand Duke Otto*

Camelot
Lyrics by Alan Jay Lerner
Music by Frederick Loewe
Musical 2 Acts
New York 1960

Up until his wedding to Guenevere, boyish King Arthur (known as Wart) has let magician Merlyn do his thinking for him. Thus, he is a bit rusty at it. Then he meets Guenevere, in fact falls out of a tree on her while she is dithering whether or not to go and face her intended groom King Arthur. They become friends, she then discovers who he is, all is well, and Wart truly becomes King Arthur. Five years later Arthur has an idea: The Round Table. Might for Right, knights for chivalry instead of bullying. Everything is idyllic until self-righteous French knight Lancelot du Lac appears. Eventually Guenevere falls for him and saddened Arthur, who loves them both, cannot do a thing about it, and by now poor Merlyn has been turned into a bat.

The problem is compounded when Arthur's wicked bastard son Mordred appears. This nasty piece of work conspires to get Arthur out of the castle and imprisoned for a night by fairy Morgan le Fey, thus putting temptation in the paths of Lancelot and Guenevere. Mordred catches them together, cries 'Treason' and Lancelot escapes, but Guenevere is sentenced to be burned at the stake, much to Arthur's dismay. Luckily Lancelot rescues her but kills half the Knights of the Round Table in the process. On the final battlefield, the threesome meet: Lancelot and Arthur embrace and Lancelot leaves. Guenevere goes to a nunnery and Arthur meets a young lad, Tom of Warwick, who is urged to spread the word of the glory that was Camelot.

Songs include: 'In Camelot'; 'If Ever I Should Leave You'; 'I Loved You Once in Silence'

Sir Dinadan	*Sir Sagramore*
Sir Lionel	*Clarius*
Merlyn	*Lady Anne*
Arthur	*Lady Sybil*
Guenevere	*Knights*
Nimue	*Morgan le Fey*
Lancelot	*Tom*
Mordred	*Ladies*
A page	
Squire Dap	
Pellinore	

Camille
Pam Gems
Drama 2 Acts
Stratford-upon-Avon 1984

Parisian society whores and decadent aristocrats - at the Opera House, then in Marguerite Gautier's salon - make would-be amusing remarks, humorously insulting each other, and flirt. Armand gets sentimentally serious with Marguerite and they spend the night together. He reveals he has little experience of love but used to love his father's riding master. Marguerite tells of her past: daughter of a Marquis' servant, interfered with by assorted men, deflowered by her uncle, taken into the Marquis' bed at fifteen, made pregnant and dismissed penniless. Her cousin had given her gold coin for sex and she thought this the key to the good life. Nevertheless Armand wants to marry her but she hesitates, unwilling to abandon the independence her profession provides.

In Armand's Paris apartment Prince Bela has tried to commit suicide by slashing his wrists. He loves Armand whose father, the Marquis, arrives to berate his son for the degenerate company he keeps and the money he is wasting. The Marquis tries to forbid Armand to marry Marguerite, not wanting a harlot in the family. Armand insists that they love each other and all will be well, so the Marquis goes to see Marguerite and tells her he will withdraw financial support but is prepared to buy her off and adopt her - and his - son and have him educated. She is persuaded to write to Armand saying she prefers her former existence and it's all over between them.

They meet again at the opera where Marguerite is plying her trade. He hits her. In Marguerite's room she is about to bed a drunken Russian Prince when she has a massive haemorrhage and dies. For the others, life goes on as before and Armand is invited to join the fun.

Auctioneer	Jean
Armand Duval	Jean-Paul
Gaston de Maurieux	Yvette
Prudence de Marsan de	Upholsterer
Talbec	Two gravediggers
Clemence de Villeneuve	Inspector
Sophie de Lyonne	Pierre
Count Druftheim	Armand's father, the
Le Duc	Marquis de Saint-Brieuc
Girl	Two waiters
Prince Bela Mirkassian	Russian Prince (Sergei)
Marguerite Gautier	Man
M. de Sancerre	Priest
Janine/Olympe	

Camino Real
Tennessee Williams
Play 16 Scenes
London 1953

Set somewhere in Latin America, this phantasmagoria features America's mythical World War Two hero Kilroy, an amicable down-and-out boxer.

Camino Real or 'Royal Highway' is a squalid wasteland where nothing honest is tolerated, and is populated by various historical and legendary figures. Among others Casanova, king of cuckolds, is ever hopeful of further conquests, Lord Byron tells the story of Shelley's cremation and Esmeralda (of Hugo's Hunchback of Notre Dame) praises the world's misfits.

Kilroy attempts to escape from all this but after a chase, he is captured, humiliated and narrowly escapes death by snatching his heart back from the hands of medical students. Finally, baptized by the contents of a slopbucket, he is given hope for the future by Don Quixote who leads him through the Triumphal Arch.

Don Quixote	Kilroy
Sancho Panza	Nursie
Gutman	A Ratt
Casanova	Baron de Charlus
Olympe	Esmeralda
Rosita	Lord Mulligan
The Dreamer	Lady Mulligan
La Madrecita	Marguerite Gautier
The gypsy	Byron

Can Can
Abe Burrows
Music and Lyrics by Cole Porter
Musical Comedy 2 Acts
New York 1953

In the Parisian demi-monde at the turn of the century handsome young judge, Aristide Forestier, is sent to look into reports of provocative can-can dancing at the night club run by La Mome Pistache. He soon falls in love with the lady and helps her to get the dance legalized by bringing the gentlemen of the bench to make an on-the-spot investigation at the club, where they are all enchanted and conquered by the 'grisettes'. Forestier marries Pistache.

In a sub-plot one of the dancers, Claudine, is pursued by two rival suitors, a Bulgarian sculptor Boris, and art critic, Hilaire. The critic jealously denounces Boris's work which leads to a farcical duel on the Paris rooftops. Songs include: 'C'est Magnifique'; 'I Love Paris'; 'Allez-vous En'; 'It's All Right With Me'

Bailiff	Waiter
Registrar	La Mome Pistache
Judge Paul Barriere	Cafe waiter
Court President	Second waiter
Judge Aristide Forestier	Café customer
Claudine	Jailer
Gabrielle	Model
Marie	Mimi
Celestine	Second
Hilaire Jussac	
Boris Adzinidzinadze	
Hercule	
Theophile	
Etienne	

Can You Hear Me at the Back?
Brian Clark
Drama 2 Acts
London 1979

Corporate architect Philip Turner lives on a private estate - one of the few - overlooking Feltonly, a large New Town he designed fifteen years ago. Now he hates it, and in his disillusionment he intends to leave everything behind; the town, his doctor wife Sarah, his Marxist student son Colin, and his life of planning. Sarah accuses him of 'planned spontaneity' and indeed Philip can't escape from his own intellectualizing, his too-clever ripostes, and his emotional remoteness.

When headmaster friend Jack's wife Margery declares her desperate love for Philip and willingness to become his mistress, Philip remains passive, unable to make any commitment except flight. Margery is comforted by Colin whose humanity has not yet been overcome by routine - just - and the general distress is shared by Sarah and Jack, both of whom are anxious and frustrated by the ramifications of Philip's 'decision'. Finally he leaves, and the actor playing Philip then relates to the audience a short anecdote which, he states, says as much as all this play put together.

Philip Turner
Sarah Turner
Colin Turner
Jack Hartnoll
Margery Hartnoll

Can't Pay? Won't Pay!
Dario Fo
Comedy 2 Acts
London 1981

Political farce set in a working-class suburb of Milan opens with Antonia and Margherita staggering into Antonia's flat laden with bags of shopping 'liberated' from the supermarket; all the local housewives have had enough of raised prices and have helped themselves. Antonia dares not tell her husband Giovanni, an unliberated factory worker who prides himself on his honesty. When he comments on Margherita's bulging clothes, they spin him a yarn that she is pregnant. The lies snowball and Margherita's dubious pregnancy leads to all sorts of complications including a fascist police inspector tricked by the two woman into believing their outrageous tale of the Feast of St Eulalia - the patron saint of fertility - and the inspector's subsequent religious conversion.

'Struggles', feminism and general left-wing togetherness permeate the non-stop action and humour. Giovanni and his friend Luigi, Margherita's husband, also become involved in 'liberation' - liberating food from the back of a truck. Finally, after the two women are forced to reveal the truth to their husbands, Giovanni sees the (political) light and realizes that the workers are going to have to pull themselves up by their bootstraps. They end by singing a revolutionary song.

Antonia
Margherita
Giovanni
Sergeant
Inspector
Old man
Undertaker
Luigi

Candida
George Bernard Shaw
Comedy 3 Acts
London 1900

Revd James Morrell is a vigorous Church of England clergyman of forty; sensible, benevolent, bold and sure - a Christian Socialist and unconsciously a bit smug. He is hero-worshipped by his brisk secretary Proserpine and his curate Lexy, but his world is shattered when he takes pity on nervy young aristocratic poet Marchbanks, who then announces he's in love with Morrell's charming wife Candida. To Morrell's dismay he finds himself undermined by Marchbank's higher vision and appreciation of Candida.

Meanwhile, Candida's father, the crude and avaricious Burgess, arrives to make up his three-year quarrel with Morrell, and starts fawning over lordly Marchbanks, who in his quivering intense way is now scoring all the points in his arguments with Morrell for the love of Candida. She, however, with her wise and transcendental feminism, is able to ascertain the true strengths and weaknesses of both men, and she maternally chooses the weaker man - her husband. Her decision enables Marchbanks to at last become a man, and he willingly forgoes happiness in order to follow his nobler nature, and leaves without either Morrell or Candida knowing the secrets of his poet's heart.

Revd James Mavor Morrell
Proserpine Garnett
Revd Alexander Mill
Burgess
Candida Morrell
Eugene Marchbanks

Candide
Lillian Hellman
Lyrics by Richard Wilbur
Music by Leonard Bernstein
Comic Operetta 2 Acts
New York 1956

Dr Pangloss the eternal optimist has tutored Candide in the philosophy that all's for the best in this the best of all possible worlds. Poor but worthy (and naive) Candide is engaged to equally pure but rich Cunegonde, daughter of Baron Thunder Ten Trouch of Westphalia, whose effete son Maximilian disapproves of the marriage. On the wedding morning the Hessians invade Westphalia and everyone is scattered.

Pangloss and Candide meet again in Lisbon, where the good doctor even manages to justify the effects of syphilis. Candide then travels to Paris where he arrives just in time to save Cunegonde from a fate as a courtesan, spurred on by her hanger-on, the Old Lady. Candide accidentally kills two men and they all flee with pilgrims to the New World. En route they are enslaved by the unscrupulous ship's captain, and in Buenos Aires they meet Martin, who looks like Pangloss but is his exact opposite - an eternal pessimist. He frees the pilgrims but tells Candide his pessimism got him thrown out of fabulous Eldorado, but recommends it to Candide who, thinking he has killed a revived Maximilian, goes there.

While waiting for Candide, Cunegonde needs protection and becomes the governor's mistress, but he eventually packs her (literally) back to Europe. Candide returns rich from Eldorado and the corrupt governor sells him a rotten boat to go after Cunegonde. It sinks and Martin disappears, but up comes Pangloss and they journey on a raft to Venice.

In Venice, Cunegonde has been further reduced to hustling in a casino, where still-wealthy Candide arrives with Pangloss. Both men are masked, and Candide is mugged by Cunegonde and her accomplice Sofronia. The masks come off and all is forgiven, but by now both Pangloss and Candide are disillusioned. They return to Westphalia where Candide finally rejects the philosophy of eternal optimism, and becomes a realist, rejecting his illusions of Cunegonde's honour and the stupid things he has done to preserve it. Nevertheless he still wants to wed her, but now he determines to love her realistically - simply to do their best.

Dr Pangloss	Beggars
Cunegonde	French lady
Candide	Old lady
Baron	Marquis Milton
Maximilian	Sultan Milton
King of Hesse	Pilgrim Father
Hesse's General	Pilgrim Mother
Man	Captain
Woman	Martin
Dutch lady	Governor of Buenos Aires
Dutch man	Officers
Atheist	Ferone
Arab Conjurer	Madame Sofronia
Infant Casmira	Duchess
Lawyer	Prefect of Police
Very, very old Inquisitor	Prince Ivan (Fat Man)

Canterbury Tales, The
Geoffrey Chaucer
Adapted by Phil Woods and Chris Barnes
Leicester 1975

The tales themselves concern a disparate group of pilgrims travelling one Spring from London to Canterbury to pay homage at the shrine of (recently) martyred St Thomas à Becket. To pass the time on the journey, each must tell two tales going, and two tales coming back. The genial tavern host agrees to ride with them, be their guide, and be the judge of the best tales.

This adaptation is an updated version which sets out to recreate the humour and bawdiness of the original. There is much interaction between the storytellers and

the audience with the M.C. free to exchange jokes as banter as he feels appropriate. The tales covered here are those of the Knight, the Reeve, the Cook, the Wife of Bath, the Franklyn, the Nun's Priest, the Pardoner, the Merchant and the Miller.

Seven men
Five women

Captain Brassbound's Conversion
George Bernard Shaw
Play 3 Acts
London 1899

Lady Cecily Waynflete comes to Morocco in the 1890s with her brother-in-law, Sir Howard Hallam, escorted by a cockney villain Drinkwater and a young brigand, Capt. Brassbound. Hallam is, in fact, Brassbound's uncle, has cheated him out of his father's estate and caused his mother's death. They go on an expedition to a bandit-infested mountain area, and Brassbound, intent on revenge, has his Arab friends capture Hallam. Cecily persuades him of the folly of his ways, and when a rescue party arrives and all are taken into custody, Brassbound is at Hallam's mercy.

Cecily tells all to an inquiry and procures Brassbound's release with his promise that he will destroy some incriminating evidence about Hallam. She is becoming increasingly infatuated by the new honourable Brassbound, even considering marriage, but she is relieved when he eventually decides to return to his former pirate life.

Capt. Brassbound
Sir Howard Hallam
Felix Drinkwater
Redbrook
Johnson
Marzo
The Cadi
Sheik Sidi-el-Assif
Osman
An American Bluejacket
Lady Cecily Waynflete
Krooboys
Arab tribesmen
Officers
Bluejackets

Caretaker, The
Harold Pinter
Drama 3 Acts
London 1960

Into a shabby room, full of miscellaneous objects, comes Davies, a scruffy tramp, and the tenant, Aston, who has offered to put him up for a while till he gets straightened out. Davies, who has the alias Jenkins, needs to buy some shoes so that he can get down to Sidcup in South London to recover his papers and belongings, but he constantly finds excuses for not going. After a night's sleep Aston wakes Davies abruptly and complains that he has been groaning in his sleep. When Aston leaves, Davies starts to sort through the contents of the room but is surprised and set upon by Mick who alternately accuses him of being an intruder and claiming that he is an old acquaintance. Aston returns and explains that Mick, his brother, has to decorate the house and he offers Davies the job of caretaker. Mick later repeats the offer, but says that he must see the references that Davies claims are down in Sidcup. Aston again complains of the noises that Davies makes in his sleep and then goes on to recall his time in a mental institution.

Two weeks later Davies is desperately trying to play one brother off against the other, fearful that he might be thrown out when the work on the house is finished. He still has not been to South London. Confrontations continue, threats and accusations abound as Davies tries to wheedle his way into Aston and Mick's confidence. Both ultimately reject him, but he continues blustering till the end.

Mick, a man in his late twenties
Aston, a man in his early thirties
Davies, an old man

Carmen Jones
Oscar Hammerstein
Musical 2 Acts
New York 1943

Faithful update of Bizet opera in which the cigarette factory in Seville becomes an American parachute factory in a Southern town. Army corporal Joe has his affections stolen from his sweetheart Cindy Lou by temptress Carmen. He goes AWOL and the pair flee to Chicago where flighty Carmen falls for boxer Husky Miller and leaves Joe. He pleads for her to return, but she refuses. He stabs her to death outside the rink on the night of Husky's championship fight.

Songs include: 'Dat's Love'; 'Beat Out Dat Rhythm on a Drum'; 'My Joe'

Cpl Morrell	*Girl*
Foreman	*Husky Miller*
Cindy Lou	*Dancing Girl*
Sgt Brown	*Poncho*
Joe	*Bullet Head*
Carmen	
Sally	
T-Bone	
Tough Kid	
Drummer	
Bartender	
Waiter	
Myrt	
Frankie	
Rum	
Dink	
Boy	

Carousel
Oscar Hammerstein and Richard Rodgers
Musical 2 Acts
New York 1945
See: *Liliom*

Transposed to the USA of 1875 this is an adaptation of Ferenc Molnàr's successful play in which the main character of Liliom becomes the Yankee fairground barker Billy Bigelow and the Hungarian background becomes that of a small New England fishing town.

Songs include: 'If I Loved You'; 'June is Bustin' Out All Over'; 'You'll Never Walk Alone'; 'Carousel Waltz'

Caste
Thomas Robertson
Play 3 Acts
London 1867

Despite the objections of his class-conscious friend Capt. Hawtree, the Hon. George D'Alroy is determined to marry beautiful dancer Esther Eccles, who has the misfortune to possess a drunken father. Her sister Polly, by contrast, has a poor but honest plumber as her suitor.

George and Esther marry and live in luxury for six months until he is posted to India on active service and is reported killed. George's mother, the snooty Marquise de St Maur, demands the custody of her grandson from the now impoverished Esther, but the plucky young mother resists and declares her intention of returning to dancing to support herself and her child.

George reappears from India, having escaped his captors, unaware of his fatherhood, and is justifiably proud of his wife's independent stand and of his new son. Polly and Sam, now married, prove to be good friends and help to reunite George and his family with the Marquise, and even Hawtree is beginning to realize that caste is humbug ... up to a point. He magnanimously offers to send old Eccles off to live in Jersey so that he can drink himself to death.

Hon. George D'Alroy
Capt. Hawtree
Mr Eccles
Polly Eccles
Esther Eccles
Marquise de St Maur
Dixon

Cat and the Canary, The
John Willard
Melodrama 3 Acts
New York 1922

Twenty years after the death of eccentric old Mr West, his six surviving relatives gather one night in his spooky old house on the Hudson to hear the reading of his will by solicitor Crosby. They are: ingratiating Charlie Wilder, hard Harry Blythe, ditherer Paul Jones, nice Cecily Young, not-so-nice Susan Sillsby and heroine Annabelle West. The will reveals that Annabelle gets the legacy unless the 'family failing' - insanity - manifests itself - then the inheritance goes to someone else who is named in a sealed envelope. The seal, however, has been broken ... and the six are going to have to stay the night.

Strange things occur. Old voodoo housekeeper 'Mammy' Pleasant tells of spirits and demons in the house and predicts a death that night. Local asylum guard Hendricks arrives, revealing that a cat-like homicidal maniac has escaped. Crosby disappears, a priceless hidden necklace is recovered then lost, a ghastly hand emerges from the wall; all these events make the others, especially Susan, doubt Anna's sanity, but when Crosby is discovered dead, her mental health is vindicated.

Although Charlie and Harry vie for Anna's affections, it is the unlikely Paul who inspires her with courage and they realize they are in love. He tells Anna he believes the wierd happenings are part of a plot to make her lose her sanity. Finally the homicidal monster itself confronts Anna, but as Hendricks comes to the rescue, Anna whips off its mask to reveal Charlie. He and Hendricks are in league, but she is rescued by the timely reappearance of Harry and Paul. The culprits are led off and Paul produces a minister who will marry him and Anna immediately. She is delighted at his decisiveness.

Roger Crosby
'Mammy' Pleasant
Harry Blythe
Susan Sillsby
Cicely Young
Charles Wilder
Paul Jones
Annabelle (Anna) West
Hendricks
Patterson

Cat on a Hot Tin Roof
Tennessee Williams
Tragedy 3 Acts
New York 1955

The rich, tyrannical owner of a cotton plantation, Big Daddy, returns home from a clinic unaware that he is dying of cancer. Except for his wife, the older members of Big Daddy's family, two sons and two daughters-in-law, all know his true condition. Indeed, it is really because of Big Daddy's illness and the hope of featuring in his will that his eldest son Gooper has taken time off from his law practice to bring his wife and children to visit the plantation.

The excuse for the visit is that Big Daddy's homecoming coincides with his birthday. As Gooper and his wife angle for advantage over Big Daddy's favourite son, the retired football player Brick, they flaunt their brood of six children, and deride Brick's drink problem and barren marriage to Margaret. Brick and Big Daddy retire after the birthday celebrations for an awkward, intimate conversation during which it is revealed that Brick's alcoholism was precipitated by the suicide of his closest friend. Discovering from Big Daddy that family and friends all thought the friendship 'unnatural' Brick angrily reveals Big Daddy's true condition in reprisal. At the same time, it becomes evident that Brick's marriage is barren because he has rejected Margaret, after learning that she had once successfully tried to seduce this same friend.

Big Daddy retires to his room, furious and fearful, where he is followed by a hysterical Big Mama after she, too, learns the truth. The play closes with Margaret trying to seduce Brick in the hope that she will conceive and produce an heir for Brick and Big Daddy's fortune.

Margaret, Brick's wife
Brick, Big Daddy's youngest son
Mae (Sister Woman), Gooper's wife
Dixie, Gooper's daughter
Big Daddy, the paterfamilias
Big Mama
Revd Tooker
Gooper (Brother Man), Big Daddy's eldest son
Dr Baugh
Lacey and Sookey, black servants
Children

Catch 22
Joseph Heller
Comedy 2 Acts
Long Island 1971

A US Air Force base off the coast of Italy, World War Two. Aviator Yossarian - like all the characters - behaves as if he is trying to wisecrack his way into a Marx Brothers' movie. Catch 22 is Yossarian's famous situation in which, trying to get out of flying missions because he is crazy, he is unable to because he must clearly be sane to want to avoid the risks of combat. Though of Italian extraction he says he is the last surviving Assyrian and wants to preserve himself. There is a Major whose surname is Major so he is Maj. Major; a Texan who is good-natured, generous and likeable - so after three days nobody can stand him; Aarfy, who barks like a dog (arf, arf) and who had to kill a maid after he'd raped her because he couldn't let her go around saying bad things about him; and sexy Luciana who won't marry Yossarian because he is crazy, which he must be if he wants to marry her. Doctors squabble over what's wrong with patients according to the afflictions they specialize in. Nurse Duckett shrieks when Yossarian touches her bottom; and when a doctor tells him to take his hands off her she snuggles against Yossarian and is disappointed when he says he won't goose her again.

Every night, according to Yossarian, he dreams of holding a live fish in his hand and Nurse Duckett knows about this because she is in the dream. A psychiatrist shows Yossarian some ink blots to get his reaction; they remind him of sex because everything does. Wintergreen and Milo have various black market lines, competing in Zippo lighters, and Milo is unhappy because he's cornered the market in Egyptian cotton and can't unload it but he has peas on the high seas, cork from New York, shoes from Toulouse, nails from Wales, ham from Siam, etc. Yossarian censors letters and signs them 'Washington Irving'. Nurse Duckett is horrified by Yossarian's anti-God remarks even though she is an atheist but the God she doesn't believe in is a good, merciful and just God. Yossarian has a fight with a whore, is hospitalised but aided by Maj. Major and with the good wishes of the Chaplain runs off.

Yossarian	Cpl Whitcombe
Chaplain	Psychiatrist
Texan	Nately
Clevinger	Nately's father
Doc Daneeka	Nately's mother
Maj. Major	Nately's whore
Sgt Towser	Old woman
Luciana	Old man
Wintergreen	McWatt
Milo	Gus
Nurse Duckett	Wes
English intern	Mrs Daneeka
Doctors (two to four)	Daneeka's mother-in-law
Patient	CID Man
Patient's father	First Investigating Officer
Patient's mother	Second Investigating
Patient's brother	Officer
Col Catchcart	Aarfy
Lieut Col Korn	Two MPs
Capt. Black	Snowden

Caucasian Chalk Circle, The
Bertolt Brecht
Verse and Prose
Play 6 Scenes
Northfield 1948

World War Two has just ended and a group of Caucasian villagers hold a meeting to decide the future of their valley community and agree to run it as a fruit growing collective. After a communal feast, an ancient story is performed to illustrate the wisdom of their decision.

A kitchen maid, Grusche, rescues the child of a cruel landowner during a revolt and brings it up as her own. To legitimize the infant, she marries a wealthy peasant, but still loves her soldier sweetheart, Simon, who is away at war. The child's real mother turns up demanding its return (she needs it for legal reasons) but Grusche takes the case to court. The case is heard by a very eccentric scoundrel judge, Azdak, noted for his bizarre judgements invariably favouring the poor. He applies the 'chalk test' in which the true mother is the one who can pull the child out of a chalk-marked circle, and awards the child to Grusche, who marries Simon. This demonstrates that children are awarded to the motherly so that they might thrive, and therefore the valley goes to the fruit growers so that it may bring forth fruit.

Old man on the right	Old peasant with milk
Peasant woman on the right	Corporal
	Private
Young peasant	Peasant and wife
Very young worker	Lavrenti Vahnadze,
Old man on the left	Grusche's brother
Peasant woman on the left	Aniko, his wife
	Peasant woman,
Agriculturist Kato	Grusche's mother-in-law
Girl tractorist	Jussup, her son
Wounded soldier	Monk
The delegate from the capital	Azdak, judge
	Shuawa, policeman
The singer	Grand Duke
Georgi Abashwili, Governor	Doctor
	Invalid
Natella, his wife	Limping man
Michael, their son	Blackmailer
Shalva, adjutant	Ludovica
Arsen Kazbeki, fat prince	Innkeeper
Messenger from the capital	Stableboy
	Poor old peasant woman
Niko Mikadze, Mika	Irakli, bandit
Loladze, doctors	Three wealthy farmers
Simon Shashava, soldier	Illo Shuboladze, Sandro
Grusche Vashnadze,	Ololadze, lawyers
Kitchen maid	Old married couple

Cause Célèbre
Terence Rattigan
Drama 2 Acts
London 1977

When Alma Rattenbury, attractive but emotionally self-indulgent young wife of past-it Francis 'Ratz' Rattenbury hires strapping young George Wood as odd-job boy, it is bad news all round. In a clever series of flashbacks and composite settings, this dramatization of a real-life 1935 murder trial weaves the story of Alma, seventeen-year-old lover George and murdered husband Ratz in with that of jury forewoman Mrs Davenport, a prude who is losing her beloved son to her ex-husband and who in the course of the trial finds kindred sympathy with love-victim Alma. Both George and Alma are prepared to lie to protect each other, but the clever barristers get Alma rightly acquitted (she did not encourage George to murder), and George himself is found guilty but with a recommendation for mercy. However, George's reprieve from the rope comes too late for tragic Alma - the former songwriter has stabbed herself to death. It is also too late for Mrs Davenport who swayed the jury to acquit Alma and who is now socially outcast.

Alma Rattenbury	George Wood
Francis Rattenbury	Edith Davenport
Christopher	John Davenport
Irene Riggs	Tony Davenport

Stella Morrison	Clerk of the Court
Randolph Browne	Joan Webster
Judge	Sergeant Bagwell
O'Connor	Porter
Croom-Johnson	Warder
Montegu	Coroner

Cavalcade
Noël Coward
Drama 3 Acts
London 1931

Cavalcade follows thirty years, from 1899 to 1930, in the interlocked lives of three families, the Marryots, the Bridges and the Harrises.

The first part of the play traces the effects of the Boer war on the wives and children who are left behind when Robert Marryot, butler Bridges and friend Jim Harris go off to the fight. Robert wins a VC, while Bridges gets a taste for independence and leaves the Marryots' employ on his return to England to manage a pub.

In the following years, Bridges sinks into alcoholism and finally dies in a car accident, but his daughter, Fanny prospers as a dancer, falls in love with Joe Marryot, Robert's youngest son, and is engaged to marry him but he is killed in the Great War. Edward, the elder son, is drowned during his honeymoon cruise. By 1930, the Marryots are aged and white-haired, alone in a home which had once promised such a full future.

Jane Marryot	Annie
Robert Marryot, Jane's husband	Flo Grainger
	George Grainger
Ellen Bridges, the Marryots' servant	Mirabelle
	Lieut Edgar Tyrell
Bridges, the Marryots' butler	Ton Jolly
	Ada (Rose Darling)
Edward and Joe Marryot, the Marryots' sons	Daisy Devon
	Marion Christie
Edith Harris	Neta Lake
Fanny Bridges	Connie Crawshaw
Margaret Harris	Tim Bateman
Mrs Snapper	Douglas Finn
Cook	Lord Martlett

Chairs, The
Eugène Ionesco
Tragifarce 1 Act
Paris 1952

Set in a large empty room on top of a tower surrounded by water, this piece has only three 'live' characters, but many invisible, inaudible ones.

An old man and his wife reminisce as they await visitors to their tower. A boatload of guests arrive and as they come in, chairs are provided for them, but they are invisible. The old man chats to his childhood sweetheart while the old woman disgracefully flaunts herself with an engraver. Other invisible guests come in and out as doors open and shut, including the Emperor, and finally the Orator appears live on stage. The old man tells his invisible guests of how the Orator will communicate his message to save mankind and then full of joy, he and his wife jump off the tower.

The Orator, a deaf mute, scribbles nonsense on a blackboard, bows to the audience and leaves a stage full of empty chairs.

Old man
Old woman
Orator
Many other invisible characters

Chalk Garden, The
Enid Bagnold
Comic Thriller 3 Acts
New York 1955

Eccentric Mrs St Maugham has engaged the enigmatic Miss Madrigal to be governess to her granddaughter at her country manor house in Sussex in the 1950s. The house has a garden with a difficult chalky soil. Equally difficult to manage is the girl, a precocious liar who fabricates salacious stories about her childhood.

The household is mystified by the congenial Miss Madrigal who is later revealed as a murderess who has served fifteen years in prison. She sees a lot of herself in the disruptive girl and finally persuades her to give up fantasizing and return to her mother, whom she despises.

Now alone, Mrs St. Maugham asks the governess to stay on with her, and although still curious about her crime she accepts her offer to help make the chalk garden flourish.

Miss Madrigal
Maitland
Second applicant
Laurel
Thin applicant
Mrs St Maugham
Nurse
Olivia
The Judge

Changeling, The
Thomas Middleton and William Rowley
Tragedy 5 Acts
London 1622

Beautiful and passionate Beatrice lives with her father Vermandero in Alicante. She is betrothed to Alonzo de Piracquo, but shortly before her wedding falls in love with visiting nobleman Alsemero. The family's ugly servant De Flores is absolutely smitten with Beatrice and she treats him like dirt - until, that is, she decides to use him to rid her of Alonzo. She persuades De Flores to murder Alonzo, which he does, then offers him gold in payment, hoping he will leave. But De Flores now has Beatrice in his power. He wants her, not gold, and she submits her virginity to him. With Alonzo disappeared, arrangements are made for Beatrice to wed Alsemero, despite the suspicions of Alonzo's brother Tomazo. Beatrice is now afraid Alsemero will discover she is not a virgin, but she manages to thwart his suspicions by various cunnings, including substituting her virgin waiting-woman Diaphanta for her on her wedding night. Afraid she could now be under Diaphanta's power, she then gets De Flores to kill Diaphanta. Beatrice is now so heavily embroiled with De Flores - and obviously enjoying their sexual relationship - that their indiscretions are overheard, and when Alsemero confronts Beatrice she confesses all. De Flores is then taken, and he manages to mortally wound Beatrice before killing himself. Alsemero, Vermandero and Tomazo are left to mourn.

A sub-plot concerns the machinations of Antonio and Franciscus who pretend to be madmen in order to woo jealous asylum doctor Alibius's lovely wife Isabella. They are both thwarted and aided by the doctor's man Lollio and eventually unmasked and even unjustly accused of Alonzo's murder. The doctor hoped to make plenty of money by having his asylum inmates perform at Beatrice's wedding.

Vermandero	Madmen
Tomazo de Piracquo	Servants
Alonzo de Piracquo	Beatrice
Alsemero	Diaphanta
Jasperino, his friend	Isabella
Alibius	
Lollio	
Pedro, friend to Antonio	
Antonio	
Franciscus	
De Flores	

Changing Room, The
David Storey
Drama 3 Acts
London 1971

This is the straightforward and vivid tale of behind-the-scenes activities at a Rugby League match in the north of England one freezing Saturday afternoon. The players, a bunch of ordinary blokes from varied walks of life, enter in ones, twos and threes, and prepare themselves for the match. They joke, swear and brag with mostly good-humoured male banter while they change, get strapped up and greased, and generally prepare for the match, helped by masseur Luke, paranoid old cleaner Harry, and trainers Sandford and Crosby.

Profuse encouragement also rains down on them from club secretary Mackendrick and Chairman Sir Frederick Thornton ('Nay, no bloody titles here, old lad.') During the match there is one injury; Kendal (who has just bought a new electric drill which he's been showing off) has his nose broken and is temporarily blinded, and on goes eager young reserve Moore. The team return victorious to the changing room where they clean up, goof around, and finally all depart, leaving Harry to sweep up.

Harry, cleaner	Harry Copley, scrum-half
Patsy, wing-threequarter	Bryan Atkinson, forward
Fielding, forward	Billy Spencer, reserve
Mick Morley, forward	John Clegg, hooker
Luke, masseur	Frank Moore, reserve
Fenchurch, wing-threequarter	Danny Crosby, trainer
	Cliff Owens, stand-off-half
Colin Jagger, centre-threequarter	Tallon, referee
	Thornton, chairman
Trevor, full back	Mackendrick, club
Walsh, forward	secretary
Sandford, assistant trainer	
Jack Stringer, centre-threequarter	

Charley's Aunt
Brandon Thomas
Comedy 3 Acts
London 1892

Set in Oxford, c.1882, this classical English farce follows the ludicrous events that arise when two students, Jack and Charles, take the excuse of the imminent visit of Charles' aunt to invite their young ladies, Kitty and Amy, to meet her at their rooms. A telegram arrives postponing the visit of aunt Donna Lucia, but the boys bluff a friend, Lord Fancourt-Babberly, into impersonating her. 'Babbs' soon begins to enjoy the attention 'she' gets from the girls, sharing their little secrets, but problems really begin to arise when the real aunt turns up under an assumed identity and begins to reveal intimate details about 'her' husband. Babbs also has to deal with the attention 'she' is receiving from Amy's money-chasing uncle Stephen Spettigue and the fact the he is attracted to Donna Lucia's companion, Ela Delahay. Events turn out happily in the end with the prospect of several impending marriages.

Jack Chesney, a student of Olde College, Oxford
Charles Wykeham, a student of Olde College, Oxford
Col Sir Francis Chesney, late Indian Service
Stephen Spettigue, a solicitor
Lord Fancourt-Babberly, a student
Brasset, a college servant
Donna Lucia, a Brazilian lady
Kitty Verdun, Spettigue's ward
Amy Spettigue, Spettigue's niece
Ela Delahay, an orphan

Chemin de Fer (La Main Passé)
Georges Feydeau
Farce 4 Acts
Paris 1904

Set in Paris at the turn of the century, this farce compares marriage to the card game of the title.

Françine Chanal is bored with her trusting husband and has taken a lover, Fedot. She also has another admirer, Coustouillu. Chanal stumbles across Françine's plans for a liaison in a hotel room with Fedot, mistakenly assumes her lover to be Coustouillu and sends him off to the meeting place in disgust.

Meanwhile, Françine and Fedot have overslept, realize that they will be discovered by their respective husband and wife, and are in turn discovered by the unwitting Coustouillu. Chanal is now prepared for divorce, one of the terms being that Fedot must in turn divorce his wife and marry Françine. Fedot turns out to be a most oppressive husband and Françine, once again discontented with her lot, takes Coustouillu as her new lover and the 'game' continues.

Chanal
Françine Chanal
Etienne
Hubertin
Coustouillu
Fedot
Germal, a police commissioner
Sophie Fedot
Cecile
Auguste
Belgenie
Platelou, a police commissioner
Capige, a bricklayer
Madeleine

Cheophori, The (Oresteia, Part II)
Aeschylus
Tragedy 1 Act
Athens 458BC

Orestes, exiled son of the murdered King Agamemnon of Argos, returns home secretly with his friend Pylades, to offer a lock of his hair to the spirits at his father's grave. A group of Argive women, led by Agamemnon's daughter, Electra, have been ordered to worship at the tomb by Clytemnestra, murderess and former wife of the King, who fears the gods' revenge.

Electra recognizes her brother's lock, is reunited with him and joins his pact with the god Apollo to have revenge on Clytemnestra. Orestes and Pylades, both in disguise, get close to Clytemnestra's lover, Aegisthus, by pretending to be messengers with news of Orestes' death. Orestes kills Aegisthus and then Clytemnestra, whom he has dragged screaming into the palace. The furies appear, to torment Orestes, and again he flees Argos.

Orestes, son of Agamemnon of Argos
Pylades, Orestes' friend
Chorus
Electra, daughter of Agamemnon
Male servant
Clytemnestra, wife of Agamemnon
Orestes' nurse
Aegisthus, Clytemnestra's paramour
Male servant
Furies

Cherry Orchard, The
Anton Chekhov
Tragicomedy 4 Acts
Moscow 1904

After five years of lavish living in France, Mme Lyubov Ranevsky and her daughter Anya have been obliged to return to their heavily mortgaged Russian estate where, with the rest of their family, they haphazardly set about saving the estate from bankruptcy. They arrive home in May, when their beloved cherry orchard, the pride of the estate, is in full bloom. Unless they can contrive to pay their creditors, the orchard will have to be sold by August. It is suggested by Lopakhin, the rich *arriviste* suitor to Varya, Mme Ranevsky's stepdaughter, that the orchard should be levelled and then developed as a holiday resort. This the family utterly refuse to do and instead leave it to Mme Ranevsky's brother, Gayev Andreyevitch, to raise money by other means. Gayev's efforts come to nothing and the whole estate must eventually be sold at auction. To the surprise of the Ranevskys, Lopakhin himself buys the estate. The Ranevsky's all move out, including Varya, to whom Lopakhin has become indifferent.

In a gloomy final scene, Feers, a freed serf who has spent his whole life in the Ranevsky's service, surveys from his deathbed the beginnings of the demolition with which Lopakhin inaugurates his period of ownership.

Mme Ranevsky (Lyubov Andreyevna), owner of
the cherry orchard
Anya, her daughter
Vanya, her adopted daughter
Gayev (Leonid Andreyevich), her brother
Lopakhin (Yermolay Alexeyevich), a merchant
Trofimov (Pyotr Sergeyevich), a student
Simeonov-Pishchik, a neighbour
Yepikhodov (Semyon Panteleyevitch), the estate clerk
Dounyasha, a maid
Feers, an old servant
Yasha, a young servant
A stranger
Station master
Post Office clerk
Visitors
Servants

Chicago
Maurine Dallas Watkins and Bob Fosse
Music by John Kander
Lyrics by Fred Ebb
Musical
New York 1973

Crime certainly pays for 'heroine' Roxie Hart who drunkenly shoots her lover Fred Casely in Chicago in the late 1920s. Her pleasant husband Amos believes her story about Fred being a burglar and tries to cover for Roxie, but the truth comes out and she is sent to jail

to await trial. Other women on Death Row include singer-dancer celebrity Velma Kelly, Finn Hunyak, Annie and June; they all want lawyer Billy Flynn to defend them because he always gets the women off. He is an unscrupulously mercenary showman and poor Amos mortgages everything to pay Billy - but it still is not enough. So Billy conducts a bizarre 'sale' of Roxie's things which will be all the more valuable if she is condemned to death. Velma is upset and upstaged when Roxie declares she is pregnant and gains national sympathy, then steals all Velma's other tricks for the trial and wins an acquittal. Velma too gets off (but the innocent Hunyak has been hanged) and the two murderesses form a successful double-act and hit the road, cynically singing the praises of American 'justice'. Songs include; 'And All That Jazz'; 'Mister Cellophane'
Velma Kelly
Roxie Hart
Fred Casely
Sergeant Fogarty
Amos Hart
Liz
Annie
June
Hunyak
Mona
Martin Harrison
Matron
Billy Flynn
Mary Sunshine

Chicken Soup with Barley
Arnold Wesker
Drama 3 Acts
Coventry 1958
The first part of *The Wesker Trilogy* (together with *Roots* and *I'm Talking About Jerusalem*) follows the Kahn family from 1936 to 1956. It begins with the resistance of the Kahns and their friends to the famous Fascist East End march; matriarch Sarah Kahn is fiery, energetic and a committed socialist, but her husband, Harry, though likeable, is a cowardly weakling.

Over the years, Sarah sees her friends and family change, their political extremism modified, their fortunes change for better and worse. Only her husband stays the same - lifeless, slovenly, eventually a senile invalid. Even her lively son Ronnie, whose enthusiasm matches his mother's, becomes disillusioned and finally begins to understand and sympathize with his father. His mother, though, rallies against Ronnie's disillusion, telling him he has got to care or he will die.
Sarah Kahn
Harry Kahn, her husband
Monty Blatt
Dave Simmonds
Prince Silver
Hymie Kossof, Sarah's brother
Cissie Kahn, Harry's sister, a Trade Union Organizer

Ada Kahn, daughter of Sarah and Harry
Ronnie, son of Sarah and Harry
Bessie Blatt, wife of Monty

Children of a Lesser God
Mark Medoff
Drama 2 Acts
New Mexico 1979
James, in his mid-thirties, is a speech teacher at a State School for the deaf, and the play takes place in his mind, the characters and events stepping out from his memory. He becomes intrigued with Sarah, deaf from birth and now in her mid-twenties whose obvious high intelligence belies her deliberate inability to lip-read or attempt speech. Her stubbornness is deep-rooted; her father left her mother when Sarah's problems became apparent, and her mother is reluctant to help James help Sarah. They grow closer and become lovers and then marry, but their relationship and Sarah's growing interaction with the outside world are fraught with problems, not least from partial-hearing teenager Lydia who fancies James, and from star pupil Orin Dennis, who believes Sarah is betraying her own kind.

The pride and independence of the deaf characters with their own code and ethos are set against their frustrations at both James and particularly supervising teacher Mr Franklin, and eventually their residual anger and frustration come to a head with a complaint to the Equal Opportunities Commission about hiring practices at the school. Lawyer Edna Klein is consulted, but Orin wants the case put to the Commission by people who are deaf. Sarah becomes involved and after a while the mounting tensions and misunderstandings between her and James lead them to break up. She leaves him to live with her mother and perhaps establish at last a decent relationship with her.
James Leeds
Sarah Norman
Orin Dennis
Mrs Norman
Mr Franklin
Lydia
Edna Klein

Children's Hour, The
Lillian Hellman
Drama 3 Acts
New York 1934
Karen and Martha run a small New England boarding school which admits the neurotic young Mary Tilford as a pupil. The girl causes trouble and runs away from school, justifying her act to her grandmother by lying that the schoolmistresses have a lesbian relationship. Grandmother withdraws Mary from the school and convinces other parents to do the same. Karen's fiancé, a local doctor, soon exposes Mary's lies, but the devious girl blackmails a fellow pupil into corroborating her

story and the school is forced to close.

The doctor tries to get Karen to marry him but she is having doubts about her own sexual preferences, and Martha, having similar feelings, resorts to suicide.

Mrs Tilford discovers the awful truth about her granddaughter's misdemeanours and offers all she has to help undo the wrongs that Karen has suffered but it is now too late.

Peggy Rogers
Catherine
Lois Fisher
Mrs Lily Mortar
Evelyn Munn
Helen Burton
Rosalie Wells
Janet
Leslie
Mary Tilford
Karen Wright
Martha Dobie
Dr Joseph Cardin
Mrs Amelia Tilford
Grocery boy

Chiltern Hundreds, The
William Douglas Home
Comedy 3 Acts
London 1947

At General Election time in 1945, the eccentric 'huntin', shootin', fishin'' Lord Lister and wife are waiting, along with their son Tony's pushy American girlfriend June, at Lister Castle to find out if Tony has been elected a Member of Parliament. He has not.

They have the winner, Labourite Cleghorn, to dinner, during which Prime Minister Attlee rings up to ask the new MP, for tactical reasons, to take a Peerage. It is against Cleghorn's previously expressed principles but he agrees. This creates a by-election, which Tony - with an eye on the main chance - decides to fight as a Socialist. This shocks June who incites butler Beecham to fight the seat as a Conservative. June and Tony fall out and he takes up with the romantic maid Bessie.

Beecham wins. Lord Cleghorn persuades him, however, that he is far too much of a professional to be a successful politician, which is a job for amateurs, so Beecham applies for the Chiltern Hundreds, the only means whereby a sitting member may resign his seat. He also takes Bessie off Tony's hands who then returns to June's embrace. They are all back in their proper stations, and happy.

The Earl of Lister, Lord Lieutenant
The Countess of Lister
June Farrell of the American Embassy
Bessie
Beecham
Lord (Tony) Pym, Lister's son
Lady Caroline Smith, Lister's sister
Mr (Lord) Cleghorn

Chips with Everything
Arnold Wesker
Drama 2 Acts
London 1962

Appalled by the squalor he has witnessed in London's East End, aristocrat Pip Thompson insists on joining the ranks when he is conscripted into the RAF. He and his fellow conscripts are subjected to brutal drilling and humiliations by their NCOs and officers to make them conform, but Pip has radical ideas about the revolutionary working class engendered by his own romantic notions of the French Revolution. He is determined to stay one of the boys who eats 'chips with everything' and fends off officers who try to win him back to the ruling class. This results in his comrades suffering mass reprisals until the officers get through to Pip by suggesting that his real motive is power seeking. Among his own class he is nothing, among the working class he can be king.

A rebellion by the airmen, justified by their ill treatment, is averted by the now commissioned Pip who has become an honest member of the 'hard working' establishment.

Cpl Hill	*Squadron Leader*
239 Cannibal, Archie	*Pilot Officer*
252 Wingate (Chas)	*PT Instructor Flight*
276 Thompson (Pip)	*Sergeant*
247 Seaford (Wilfe)	*Recruit*
284 McClure, Andrew	*Night guard*
272 Richardson (Whitney)	*First corporal*
277 Cohen (Dodger)	*Second corporal*
266 Smith (Dickey)	*First airman*
279 Washington (Smiler)	*Second airman*
Wing Commander	

Chorus Line, A
Michael Bennett
Music by Marvin Hamlisch
Lyrics by Edward Kleban
Musical 2 Acts
New York 1975

Director-choreographer Zach is auditioning dancers for the chorus line of a Broadway show. He needs eight dancers and whittles down the original bunch of eager aspirants to nine woman and eight men. The short-listers present their photos and CVs, but Zach wants to know more. So instead of getting them to do conventional readings, he asks them to talk about themselves. After initial trepidation, they begin to discuss their dreams, backgrounds, ambitions, idiosyncrasies, sexual proclivities, strengths, hopes and vulnerabilities; all are revealed in speech, song and dance. The final choice is complicated by the presence in the troupe of Zach's ex-lover Cassie; he is super-critical of her and his personal guilt and affections strain his judgement.

At last, having heard all their stories, Zach must choose. He tells them he would like to hire them all, but

... he calls forward the losers, apologizes and dismisses them. Among the winners is Cassie.

Roy	Don
Kristine	Bebe
Sheila	Connie
Val	Diana
Mike	Zach
Butch	Mark
Larry	Cassie
Maggie	Al
Richie	Frank
Tricia	Greg
Tom	Bobby
Judy	Paul
Lois	Vikki

Chu Chin Chow
Oscar Asche
Music by Frederick Norton
Musical Play 2 Acts
London 1916

Abu Hassan is a clever robber, who disguises himself to gain entry into the houses of the rich to discover their wealth so that he and his band of thieves can rob them. He comes to Kasim Baba's house in the guise of a rich Chinese trader, Chu Chin Chow, where Zahrat, his spy, is a servant. Kasim's brother, Ali Baba, and his son Nur, have desires on the ladies of Kasim's house and try to buy them out, but they have no money until they stumble onto Abu Hassan's secret cave of treasures, Sesame, and rob it themselves. Kasim is tricked into going to the cave and is killed by Abu Hassan, but Zahrat, who hates Hassan, suggests that he get his fortune back by smuggling his men into Ali Baba's house hidden inside jars of oil. She double-crosses the robber and his men suffer a gruesome demise in the jars as Ali Baba and Nur enjoy themselves with their lovers. Songs include:'I Am Chu Chin Chow of China'; 'Marjanah's Song'; 'Open Sesame!';'I Sit and I Cobble'

Abu Hassan (Chu Chin Chow)	Alcolom
	Mahbubah
Kasim Baba	Bostan
Ali Baba	Zanim
Nur Al-Huda-Ali	Fitnah
Abdullah	Marjanah
Otbah	Zahrat Al-Kulub
Baba Mustafa	Buyers
Mukbill	Slaves
Musab	Dancers
Khuzaymah	Robbers

Cid, The
Pierre Corneille
Drama 5 Acts
Paris 1636

In medieval Seville, Chimene, the beautiful daughter of the Count De Gormas, is especially sought after by Don Roderick and Don Sancho. The Count remarks to her duenna Elvira, whose help has been sought, that both are suitable but he tends to prefer Roderick, the one Chimene favours. King Ferdinand's daughter, the Infanta, is saddened by this because, she confides to her lady in attendance, Leonora, she too loves Roderick but feels he is unsuitable because he is not of royal blood.

Don Diegue, Roderick's father, is appointed to tutor the young Prince of Castile, much to the annoyance of the jealous Count. The two men fall out, Diegue is insulted but is too old to fight a duel. If Roderick does not avenge the insult on behalf of his father, he will lose honour. If he does, he will surely lose Chimene. He decides to fight and the Count thinks that with his arrogance and skill he will surely defeat the young man. But Roderick kills him.

This leaves Chimene no choice but to demand the head of the man she loves. The King hesitates to grant her less than sincere request. The Moors intervene by invading and Roderick replaces the late warrior Count to lead the Spaniards to victory, routing the plunderers and capturing two Moorish kings. He is given the title of Cid - Moorish for Lord - and is a national hero.

Still Chimene is driven to demand his death. She will marry whomever kills her beloved Roderick. Sancho volunteers. The King agrees to allow just one duel, no more, and that will be the end of the matter. The combatants go off to fight alone. Sancho returns with Roderick's sword and a grief-stricken Chimene refuses to honour the deal but then Sancho says he is the defeated one and Roderick had refused to kill him for acting out of love of Chimene. Instead he has sent his sword with which Chimene may kill Roderick if she wishes. With honour more or less satisfied, and Roderick required to go and smite the Moors some more, he ends up serving the king and winning Chimene.

The King, Ferdinand The First of Castile
The Infanta
The Count De Gormas
Don Diegue
Roderick
Chimene
Don Arias
Don Alonso
Don Sancho
Leonora
Elvira
A page
Courtiers
Guards

Cider With Rosie
Laurie Lee and James Roose-Evans
Drama 2 Acts
London 1982

Dramatization of poet Laurie Lee's autobiography opens with the Lee family - indomitable Mother and her six children - moving to a small Gloucestershire village at the end of World War One. Grown-up Laurie's subsequent nostalgic and evocative narration covers his boyhood and adolescence during the inter-war years until his own coming-of-age (with Rosie) and the gradual de-isolation of village life.

Young Laurie (Loll) begins school, fat, lazy and frightened, but soon mucks in and mucks around. Village characters, memorable events, feuding neighbours and the foibles of relatives are all brought to life, but above all Laurie's mother dominates the scene. Her strengths, her sensitivities, her scattiness and her infinite qualities are shiningly demonstrated, from her bringing up of her family without her husband to her final years of unkempt serenity.

Narrator (the grown	*Loll (the young Laurie*
Laurie Lee)	*Lee)*
Mother	*Jack*
Miss B.	*Squire's old gardener*
Doth	*The vicar*
Granny Wallon	*Tony*
Baroness von Hodenburg	*Vincent*
Marge	*The Squire*
Mrs Davies	*Mr Davies*
Mrs Pimbury	*Uncle Sid*
Rosie	
Phyll	
Granny Trill	
Jo	

Circle, The
W. Somerset Maugham
Comedy 3 Acts
London 1921

Urbane Lord Champion-Cheney is curious to see how his wife Kitty, who left him and their son Arnold thirty years before, has fared in that time. At a party given by his daughter-in-law, Elizabeth, he meets Kitty with her long-time lover Lord Porteus; they are an absurd and empty-headed couple. He has noticed that Elizabeth is about to emulate his wife and run off with a young business man, Edward Luton, and he strongly advises her against such folly, but she is determined to discuss the matter with Arnold. Champion-Cheney tells his son that the best course is to give her her freedom and that given the choice she will ultimately see sense. Lord Porteus and Kitty also add their weight to this view, with the benefit of hindsight, and all are confident that Elizabeth will stay. They have not, however, reckoned with irresistible love and as they all smugly laugh about the predicted outcome, the lovers run off.

Arnold Champion-	*Butler*
Cheney, MP	*Lady Catherine*
Footman	*Champion-Cheney*
Mrs Shenstone	*Lord Porteus*
Elizabeth	
Edward Luton	
Clive Champion-Cheney	

City Sugar
Stephen Poliakoff
Drama 2 Acts
London 1975

Thirty-five-year-old disc-jockey Leonard Brazil has a charm and radio manner that makes him something of a star on local commercial radio in Leicester. Underneath he seethes with contempt for the rubbish he presents and the audience that appreciates him. Self-important, opinionated, garrulous, he is demanding of his colleagues, whom he bullies. He particularly takes it out on Rex, his twenty-one-year-old sound engineer who is eager, naive (but learning), ambitious and cocky. Big John, the news reader, also gets kicked around by Leonard. After some fairly good-natured patter on air Leonard becomes increasingly acerbic and nasty, though he never quite goes too far when the microphone is live.

He is running the 'Competition of the Century', as inane as a competion could be, the prize for the winner being a trip to London to meet Ross, one of the Yellow Jacks, America's top pop music group of the moment. Nicola, aided by her fellow supermarket assistant Susan, enters. She is sixteen, calm and serious, a bit enigmatic, while Susan is much more lively. Nicola first wins an LP for almost getting a question right: Leonard generously lets her have it because from the start he is attracted by something in her voice over the phone.

Nicola is one of the two finalists but after a somewhat harrowing live quiz her rival Jane wins and goes off to meet Ross. Left alone in the studio with Nicola, Leonard makes an oblique semi-play for her, but she is unresponsive. Rex, who has been fired by Leonard for his pushiness, unexpectedly gets given airtime and responsibility, for Leonard has been offered a job with the bigger station, Capital, London. He makes a farewell speech to the doubtless desolate Leicester listeners that is boastful, rambling and more than slightly mad.

Leonard Brazil
Rex
Nicola Davies
Susan
Big John
Jane
Mick

Class Enemy
Nigel Williams
Drama 2 Acts
London 1978

Five lads from class 5K in a broken-down South London school are real no-hopers, the uncontrollables, abandoned after vicious baiting of every teacher sent to them. They wait to see if there will be yet another teacher. The 'hard man' is Iron, aggressive and needling, feuding with Sky-Light and bullying everyone - pretty Sweetheart, little Racks and punk Nipper. When their black pal Snatch arrives, Iron forces everyone to get up in front of the class and be teacher.

Sweetheart rambles on about sex, Racks explains his dad's window-gardening, and after Snatch is temporarily removed by a master, Nipper expounds his racialist theories of why blacks are responsible for all the problems. Snatch returns and entertainingly explains his fetish for smashing windows. All the while Iron, ever critical, nihilistic and bursting with violent frustration continues to goad the more reasonable Sky-Light, while Sweetheart sees - or imagines - their dream teacher, the one who will be able to actually teach them, approaching the classroom. Sky-Light uses his turn to give a recipe for bread-and-butter pudding, explaining that he is the household cook because both his parents are blind.

Sky-Light's further message is that Iron is incapable of appreciating the joys of life. The two boys fight and Sky-Light is beaten up, but when a master arrives, Sky-Light doesn't inform on Iron. When the master leaves, after telling the boys they're written off, Iron has his turn. His lesson is self-defence, how to fight, but the others are sickened by his treatment of Sky-Light and fail to respond. Iron goes beserk, relents in his treatment of Sky-Light, and screams his frustrations out in a message of hate at the whole world, savagely punching at the air. Sky-Light finishes with a plea for patience and hope and Sweetheart claims he sees their dream teacher once more, coming towards their classroom.

Sweetheart (Sowerthwaite)
Racks (Rakes)
Nipper (Napier)
Sky-Light (Skellet)
Iron (Herron)
Snatch (Cameron)
Master

Claudia
Rose Franken
Comedy 3 Acts
London 1942

Young married couple Claudia and architect husband David live at their lovely farm, seventy miles from New York together with cook/housekeeper Bertha and handyman husband Fritz. Claudia is beguilingly childlike but over-attached to her mother, Mrs Brown, who reveals to David she may be terminally ill. David's loving but patronizing attitude towards Claudia is shaken when he catches novelist neighbour Jerry making a pass at her, but the incident reveals his wife in a new light and helps consolidate their relationship, which is helped not a little by Claudia's announcement that she is pregnant.

When family friend Julia arrives with diva Mme Daruschka, the wealthy singer makes a tempting offer for the farm and Claudia accepts, hoping to spend her pregnancy in the city with Mom. Then she overhears her mother phoning David to confirm news of her fatal illness, and when Mrs Brown arrives, both strive to accept the inevitable and its consequences. Claudia and David decide not to sell the farm so Mrs Brown can live out her last days with them in their idyllic environment.

Mrs Brown
David Naughton
Claudia Naughton
Bertha
Fritz
Jerry Seymour
Mme Daruschka
Julia Norton

Cloud Nine
Caryl Churchill
Drama 2 Acts
London 1979

Traditional male Clive imposes his (conventional) sexual and political ideals on his household in a British Colony in Africa in Victorian times. It is a facade, however, and the point is emphasized by having: Betty, Clive's wife, played by a man (because she wants to be what men want her to be); Joshua, the black servant, played by a white man (because he wants to be what white men want him to be); young son Edward, played by a girl (because he is effeminate); and baby daughter Victoria, played by a dummy. The arrival of Clive's explorer friend Harry agitates everyone and when outraged Clive discovers Harry is homosexual, he tries to cure him by marrying him off to Edward's lesbian governess Ellen, who fancies Betty. Clive is unaware of most of the myriad deviations, but himself lusts after widow neighbour Mrs Saunders, who comes and goes.

Act Two takes place twenty-five years later, though it is set in 1979. Victoria is grown-up and married to Martin, who understandingly tries to espouse feminism, and they have a son, Tommy. The marriage will not work and Victoria moves in with lesbian friend Lin and 'lesbian homosexual' brother Edward for a menage-à-trois, together with Lin's aggressive daughter Cathy who is played by a man. All the other characters in this act are played 'normally'. Betty decides to leave disillusioned Clive, and she also makes friends with Edward's long-term uninhibited lover Gerry. Everyone ends up a little more reconciled to their true natures.

Act One:
Clive
Betty, his wife
Joshua, his black servant
Edward, his son
Victoria, his daughter
Maud, his mother-in-law
Ellen, Edward's governess
Harry Bagley, an explorer
Mrs Saunders, a widow
Act Two:
Betty
Edward, her son

Victoria, her daughter
Martin, Victoria's husband
Lin
Cathy, Lin's daughter, aged five
Gerry, Edward's lover

Clouds
Michael Frayn
Comedy 2 Acts
London 1976

Owen and Mara meet in Cuba; both have been commissioned to do pieces for rival Sunday colour magazines. He's slightly miffed because he's a regular journalist while she's only a 'lady novelist' and occasionally he gets professionally superior. Their adventures begin as they meet Ed, an enthusiastic and energetic Spanish-speaking American writing a book; and their official 'guide' to Cuba, Angel, a sleepy hypochondriac cigar chain-smoker. Off they go to enjoy the sugar mills, sewage farms and so on, all writing their pieces with their different styles and angles, and being driven by good-humoured Hilberto, a black Cuban chauffeur. It's a kind of a 'road' play, and as the characters get to know each other things get both better and worse between them. All the men are interested in Mara but she, surprisingly, turns out to be interested in Owen ... but inclines towards the others at times. Owen and Mara's ignorance of Cuba is enlightened by Angel's reminiscences, but at the end of the play Owen, Angel and Ed are sulking after a silly fight, while Hilberto and Mara are full of the joys of Cuba.
Owen
Mara
Ed
Angel
Hilberto

Clouds, The
Aristophanes
Comedy 1 Act
Athens c. 423BC

Strepsiades, an Athenian arriviste, who has married above himself, faces financial ruin on account of his dissolute son, Pheidippides, who has run up huge debts. In a desperate bid to save himself, Strepsiades enrols as a student of Socrates, whose philosophy can show that black is white, right is wrong and Strepsiades hopes, ruin is plenty.

Unfortunately, Strepsiades proves to be an inept student and he can make no sense of Socrates' dialectic. Instead he turns his son over to the philosopher for instruction. Pheidippides uses the new learning, not just against the family's creditors, but against Strepsiades himself. For revenge, Strepsiades burns Socrates' school to the ground.
Strepsiades, an Athenian merchant
Pheidippides, his son

Socrates
True Logic
False Logic
Pasias, a money lender
Amynias, a money lender
Chairephon, a student of Socrates
Hermes, a god
Slave, students and witness
Chorus of clouds

Coastal Disturbances
Tina Howe
Drama 2 Acts
New York 1986

Lifeguard Leo Hart, twenty-eight, oversees a stretch of private beach on the North Shore of Massachussetts. It is the last two weeks in August and among those on the beach is Holly Dancer, an arty New York photographer in her twenties, having a breakdown and trying to recover from her relationship with gallery owner André. There's also Faith, five months pregnant, with her adopted daughter Miranda, and Faith's friend Ariel and her son Winston. The kids are noisy, quarrelsome and funny, the women talk and pass the time telling each other about themselves, and their lives unfold in casual detail. Leo is also just off a relationship, and he falls for Holly. After her initial trepidation she allows herself to become involved with him.

Retired eye surgeon Hamilton Adams and M. J., his wife, an amateur painter, also frequent the beach, adding the threads of their lives to those of the others. There are games, laughs, photographs taken, tears and upsets. André arrives and convinces Holly to go back to New York. Leo doesn't like svelte and probably insincere André and tries to persuade Holly to join him when he leaves for the Florida Keys. She decides to return to New York, but at least gives him her address and phone number.
Leo Hart
Holly Dancer
Faith Bigelow
Miranda Bigelow
Ariel Took
Winston Took
M.J. Adams
Dr Hamilton Adams
André Sor

Coat of Varnish, A
Ronald Millar
Drama 2 Acts
London 1982

Elderly Lady Ashbrook together with her doctor and confidante Perryman, grandson Capt. Loseby and girlfriend Susan Thirkill, and distant cousin Humphrey Leigh are anxiously awaiting the phone to ring with the results of her ladyship's medical tests; the doctor is not optimistic and neither is her ladyship. But the news is good and everyone celebrates. Two weeks later Lady Ashbrook is murdered, seemingly by a burglar who stole cash and silver and smashed her head in with a hammer. The police, led by Chief Superintendent Briers, discover Lady Ashbrook had first been strangled. The hammer and the burglary are red herrings and although the police mount a huge search, Briers believes the murder must have been committed by someone known to Lady Ashbrook; either Leigh (Briers' old chum from the Secret Service), Perryman or Loseby.

Painstaking investigations clear Loseby after a series of dubious alibis, and although Leigh is a professionally-trained killer, Briers realizes all motives point to the doctor, who had been handling Lady Ashbrook's money for her in order to dodge the Inland Revenue. He confronts the doctor and paints a realistic scenario of the murder, but the doctor does not crack. His final words to Briers are 'prove it'. Finally Leigh and Briers meet in the house, now closed down. A blood-stained suit has just been found buried by a nearby garden and it will convict the doctor. The suit was planted by Briers, and although both men know Perryman was guilty, they disagree as to whether the end should justify the means.

Chief Superintendent Frank Briers
Lady Ashbrook
Dr Perryman
Loseby
Susan Thirkill
Humphrey Leigh
Sergeant Tanner
Chief Inspector Rees
Inspector Shingler
Professor Morgan
Maria
Police photographer
Stenographer
Policewoman

Cock-a-Doodle Dandy
Sean O'Casey
Comedy 3 Acts
London 1949

Michael Marthraun and Sailor Mahan, the two prominent businessmen in a small Irish town in the 1940s, sit arguing over a contract. They are interrupted when Marthraun's daughter, Loreleen, attracts his scorn for her light-hearted teasing manner. He is convinced that she, along with his young second wife Lorna, and their servant Marion, are all under the influence of demons. At this juncture, a handsome black rooster wanders into his home and panics when the women chase after it. The bird knocks over the family altar and various religious pictures before escaping. Marthraun and Mahan, urged on by an old madman called Shanaar, conclude that the

rooster is a demon and inaugurate a frantic search for the creature in which the bigoted parish priest, the local Civic Guard and a number of local peasants all maladroitly take part.

They stir up a frenzied witch hunt which leads to the death of an innocent man, and the banishment of Loreleen followed by the disgusted departure of Lorna, Marion and Marion's boyfriend, Robin Adair.

The Cock	*A mace bearer*
Michael Marthraun	*The messenger*
Sailor Mahan	*The bellman*
Lorna	*A porter*
Loreleen	
Marion	
Shanaar	
Two roughs	
Father Domineer	
The Serjeant	
Jack	
Julia	
Julia's father	
One-eyed Larry	
A mayor	

Cocktail Party, The
T. S. Eliot
Verse Comedy 3 Acts
Edinburgh 1949

Edward and Lavinia Chamberlayne, both of whom have taken lovers, reach a point of crisis in their marriage and in their individual lives. Edward is obliged to host a cocktail party, apparently arranged by his wife, who seems meanwhile to have left him. A guest at the party, later identified as the psychiatrist Sir Henry Harcourt-Reilly, by probing, teasing and ruthless logic, shows the couple, along with Edward's lover Celia Coplestone, that they have all been living a tired illusion.

Edward and Lavinia are gradually reconciled to the path of mutual tolerance, underpinned by private loneliness, as the best way out of their crushing unhappiness. Celia chooses instead to follow a lonely, almost mystical quest for salvation through service; and eventually dies in the East as a missionary, crucified by the people she tries to serve.

The play concludes with another cocktail party at which Celia's death is discussed as a counterpoint to the fragile accord reached by Edward and Lavinia.

Edward Chamberlayne
Julia Shuttlethwaite, older friend of Edward's
Celia Coplestone, Edward's mistress
Alexander MacColgie Gibbs, Edward's friend
Peter Quilpe
An unidentified guest (later identified as Sir Henry Harcourt-Reilly)
Lavinia Chamberlayne, Edward's wife
A nurse/secretary
Two caterers' men

Collection, The
Harold Pinter
Drama 1 Act
London 1962

Harry, in his forties, shares a house with Bill, in his twenties. At four in the morning Harry answers the phone and a voice says he wants a word with Bill. Harry refuses to wake him and the voice refuses to identify itself but says it will be in touch. James, the voice, in his thirties, lives in a flat with wife Stella, also in her thirties. They work together in the clothing trade. That day James says he is not going to the shop. He is asked if he is going out. Pause. She asks if he will be in tonight. Pause, no answers.

Bill and Harry are having a pause-packed breakfast interspersed with repetitive conversation. The phone rings, Bill answers and James, still anonymous, says he will be round right away. But Bill goes out. Harry answers the door. James denies being the mysterious caller and goes away. Later James catches Bill in, alone, and invites himself in. After many a pause, meaningful and less according to taste, James says he knows that Bill spent the night with Stella in Leeds last Friday, during a business trip...

Harry goes to see Stella who between pauses denies that she knows Bill and can't understand why her husband should make up such a fantastic story. Later Harry assures James that his wife had made up the whole thing and still later James apologizes to Bill for the false accusation and then invites his wife to confirm that she'd only discussed with Bill what they might do. Her expression is friendly and sympathetic as she fails to make any reply.

Harry
James
Stella
Bill

Come As You Are
John Mortimer
Play 4 Acts
London 1970

Each act is a separate play, though all are set in London and are concerned with diverse sexual entanglements.
Mill Hill. Peter Trilby arrives in Denise Blundell's bedroom to consummate their affair, but must first confess his perversion - they must wear Elizabethan costumes, he to play Sir Walter Raleigh, she the Virgin Queen. Their preliminaries are unexpectedly interrupted by her husband Roy, but when they tell him they are rehearsing for an amateur production, he soon shows Peter exactly how Sir Walter should be played and ends up exactly where Peter wanted to be.
Bermondsey. Middle-aged but still attractive publican Bob Purvis is thinking of leaving his pub and family and going up-market with mini-skirted barmaid Rosemary. It is Christmas Eve and close family friend Pip, an upper-class friend of Bob's from army days, is staying.

To save her marriage, Bob's wife Iris tells Pip she knows that he and Bob are lovers and that if they both want to save Bob, Rosemary must be got rid of. When Rosemary, curious about Pip, demands to know what's going on, Bob tells her - and she leaves.
Gloucester Road. Toby Delgardo is a lodger at the Thomson's maisonette and is quite blatant about fancying Bunny, wife of his friend and landlord Mike. The possibility that Bunny might be unfaithful keeps the relationships together. She is not, but the arrival of hippy Clare upsets the delicate balance. When Clare leaves and Mike is sure, once again, that his friend and wife are having a secret affair he is, once again, miserably happy.
Marble Arch. Fading film-star Laura Logan lives in an expensive flat just above her long-time married lover Max - Labour peer and tycoon Lord Hammersmith. She is fed up with their once-a-week liaison, but one morning finds him collapsed in her bathroom, presumably dead. Frantic attempts to remove him via porter McNee result in farce-like activity involving Laura, McNee, reporter Miss Parker and of course the revived Max who was only asleep. Once again Laura finds herself dangling on the string.

Mill Hill:	*Gloucester Road:*
Denise Blundell	*Bunny Thomson*
Peter Trilby	*Mike Thomson*
Roy Blundell	*Toby Delgardo*
Bermondsey:	*Clare Dobson*
Iris Purvis	***Marble Arch:***
Bob Purvis	*Laura Logan*
Pip Lester	*McNee*
Rosemary	*Miss Parker*
	Max

Come Back, Little Sheba
William Inge
Drama 2 Acts
New York 1949

In a rundown section of a Midwestern city, failed MD and reformed alcoholic Doc Delaney has to tolerate the slovenly behaviour of his fat, doting wife Lola as she rambles on and on about their courtship, their lost baby and her long lost puppy, Sheba. He compares her unfavourably with their lodger Marie, an attractive student, and is enraged when Lola encourages her to have her lover, an athlete, stay overnight in her room. He hits the bottle again, after a year's abstinence, smashes up the flat and tries to kill Lola. Friends in AA take him to hospital and Lola is left alone. Returning from 'drying out' Doc is now resigned to his fate and thankful for Lola's cloying, but faithful love; she is beginning to realize that her daydreaming has got to stop and they must get on with living.

Doc
Marie
Lola
Turk

Postman
Mrs Goffman
Milkman
Messenger
Bruce
Ed Anderson
Elmo Huston

Come Blow Your Horn
Neil Simon
Comedy 3 Acts
New York 1961
Playboy Alan Baker lives in an apartment on New York's Upper East Side, neglects his job with Dad's wax fruit company, and has just returned from a long skiing weekend with lovely, dumb Peggy Evans. When kid brother Buddy arrives, fed up with their nagging father and neurotic worrier of a mother, Alan despairs of ever 'educating' his bookish brother. But while Alan tries to keep his favourite girl Connie at arm's length and fend off the unwelcome attentions of his parents, Buddy slowly learns the ropes from the master, his first assignment being to impersonate a Hollywood movie producer to get Peggy off Alan's hands.

Dad is so peeved with Alan's inefficiency and Buddy's bid for freedom that he sacks both sons, thus alienating Mom who moves in with the boys. Soon, Alan has to make the choice between losing Connie or marrying her, and in the midst of a family showdown he announces his engagement. Dad is reluctantly impressed, especially when it also transpires Alan has obtained orders for the wax fruit from important new clients. He is ready to settle down, but by now Buddy has really got into his stride; he has learned how to handle women and is ready to fill his brother's shoes as the family 'swinger'.
Alan Baker
Peggy Evans
Buddy Baker
Mr Baker
Connie Dayton
Mrs Baker
A visitor

Comedians
Trevor Griffiths
Play 3 Acts
Nottingham 1975
It is a wet and dreary evening as the members of a night class for comedians arrive at a secondary school in Manchester to prepare for their acts. They are a mixed bunch of individals, an Irish docker, an insurance agent, a Jew, a milkman, etc. but they all have notions of making it as stand-up comics. All that is, perhaps, except for Price. The teacher, Waters, arrives to give them a final briefing: humour is a serious business that has strong psychological undertones and involves knowing how to gauge the audience responses. He also

tells the aspirants about the man who is to judge their performances, Bert Challoner - up from London.

They make their way to a small club where they are to perform between the bingo sessions. As they go through their routines a familiar pattern of often vicious jokes about sex, ethnic minorities and physical disabilities emerge with varying degrees of success. The act which defies comment is that of Price; he goes through a weird, surreal pantomime with stuffed dummies, blood and social jokes completely over the audience's heads.

They return to the classroom for the post-mortem, Challoner attempting to offer useful advice which the class generally accept. He has no words of wisdom for Price, he found his act 'repulsive' and incomprehensible.

The class leave but Price stays behind with Waters; they discuss further their attitudes towards the function of humour.
Caretaker
Gethin Price
Phil Murray
George McBain
Sammy Samuels
Mick Connor
Eddie Waters
Ged Murray
Mr Patel
Bert Challoner
Club Secretary
Teddy
Pianist

Comedy of Errors, The
William Shakespeare
Farce 5 Acts
London 1594
The setting is Ephesus, a town renowned for swindling and sorcery, where there is great enmity between its people and the citizens of Syracuse.

The story opens with a potential tragedy: old Aegeon, a Syracusan, is sentenced to death unless he can pay the Duke of Ephesus the required ransom. Asked why he had risked putting ashore in Ephesus, Aegeon explains to the Duke that many years ago in a storm at sea he had lost his wife and one of their infant identical twins, plus one of another pair of identical twins whom Aegeon had bought from their poor parents to be brought up as his servants. After eighteen years his son Antipholus and their servant Dromio had left Syracuse to see if they could find their twins.

They too had disappeared and that was how Aegeon had come to be seeking them in Ephesus. The Duke is sympathetic to the old man's plight and gives him twenty-four hours to try to come up with the money. The 'other' Antipholus and Dromio soon put in appearances to everyone's confusion and of course witchcraft is suspected as the wrong identities become hopelessly entangled until the last act when Aegeon is freed and reunited with his long-lost wife and the parents and children get together.

Solinus, Duke of Ephesus
Aegeon, a merchant of Syracuse
Antipholus of Ephesus, Antipholus of Syracuse, twin brothers
Dromio of Ephesus, Dromio of Syracuse, twin brothers and servants
Balthasar, a merchant
Angelo, a goldsmith
Dr Pinch, schoolmaster
Emilia, Abbess at Ephesus, Aegeon's wife
Adriana, wife of Antipholus of Ephesus
Luce, her maid
Luciana, her sister
Two merchants
Courtesan
Jailor
Officers
Headsman
Attendants

Company
George Furth
Music and lyrics by Stephen Sondheim
Musical Comedy 2 Acts
New York 1970

A bunch of New York high-rise apartments filled with couples, either married or about to be. Except for Robert, a thirty-five-year-old bachelor boy whose friends want to get him married off. All he gets, and wants, is a night with air hostess April. The rest of the show is one long hymn to the joys of company, friendship, togetherness and being alive. Along the way are marital spats, copious references to asses (usually being kissed), dope smoking and getting drunk in a niterie. At the end there is a hint of cynicism about the need for other people.

Songs include: 'The Ladies who Lunch'; 'Side by Side by Side'

Robert	*Amy*
Sarah	*Paul*
Harry	*Joanne*
Susan	*Larry*
Peter	*Marta*
Jenny	*Kathy*
David	*April*

Complaisant Lover, The
Graham Greene
Comedy 2 Acts
London 1959

Middle-aged Mary Rhodes is fed up with the boring aspects of marriage and rearing children and is having an affair with bookseller Clive Root. Victor, her jovial husband, is a dentist who is fond of practical jokes and has no suspicion of his wife's liaison. When she goes off for a secret weekend with her lover to Amsterdam, Victor turns up at the same hotel for a dental convention. On discovering his wife's infidelity he is devastated and even briefly contemplates suicide, but when Mary suggests that they can come to an arrangement and 'have our cake and eat it' he is prepared to compromise. His generous attitude is not, however, shared by Clive who refuses to become 'a complaisant lover', although after due consideration he is having doubts.

Victor Rhodes
William Howard
Clive Root
Ann Howard
Margaret Howard
Mary Rhodes
Robin Rhodes
Hotel valet
Dr van Droog

Conduct Unbecoming
Barry England
Drama 3 Acts
Bristol 1969

Into a British Army Officers' Mess in India, in the late 1800s, come two young officers who are joining the Regiment. Drake is keen to be accepted and do well in his chosen career. Millington is not but he is following the family tradition. To Drake's increasing embarrassment, disgust and horror, Millington - almost from the moment of their arrival - behaves badly. He drinks recklessly, speaks out of turn, and on seeing a stained and torn scarlet tunic mounted on a dummy in a showcase demands to know what such a scruffy, smelly, filthy thing is doing in the Mess. This is calculated outrage: he knows it was the tunic of Capt. Scarlett who died heroically in battle.

He also goes against the 'done thing' by flirting with Mrs Hasseltine, an attractive widow who is considered the 'property' of certain senior officers. Though the Mess is on the surface a haven of tradition, gentlemanliness and careful manners, there lurks in it something quite nasty, symbolized by a taste for pig-sticking, enthusiastically practised for in the Mess by using a stuffed boar on wheels which the 'sportsmen' charge and stab in the hindquarters with their swords.

In the morning of a Mess ball, there are screams outside and Mrs Hasseltine scrambles on all fours onto the verandah calling for help. She is dishevelled, her dress torn and she is terrified. She has been attacked and accuses Millington. A subalterns' court martial, which is unofficial but has the merit of keeping the scandal within the confines of the Regiment, is convened and Millington chooses Drake to defend him. Drake takes his duty seriously, insists that Mrs Hasseltine give evidence and it emerges that although Millington, as part of his strategy to get out of the Regiment, has made advances, he was not the attacker. Some other officer, who fancied himself as a reincarnation of Capt. Scarlett, had been lurking in the grounds and had slashed at the lady's bottom with his sword. Once the truth has come out Mrs Hasseltine admits she has nothing but praise for Millington - the only gentleman she has ever met in the Regiment; the rest are stupid, cruel scum who treat pigs and women as objects. The guilty officer is left alone with a gun.

Millington	Boulton
Drake	Winters
The Colonel	Hutton
Roach	Pradah Singh
Wimbourne VC	Head waiter
The doctor	Mrs Hasseltine
The adjutant	Mem Strang
The junior subaltern	Mrs Bandanai
Hart	Ladies at the ball
Truly	Waiters

Confidential Clerk, The
T. S. Eliot
Drama 3 Acts
Edinburgh 1953

The confidential clerk of the title is Colby Simpkins, thought to be the bastard son of City financier, Sir Claude Mulhammer. In an attempt to ease Colby into his family business and then on to his fortune, Mulhammer has provided Colby with a position as his confidential clerk and personal assistant. He hopes that Colby will impress Lady Mulhammer enough that she herself can be brought to suggest that the young man be adopted as their joint heir.

Lady Elizabeth Mulhammer, who is an eccentric spiritualist, decides that Colby is in fact her own long lost son, and so precipitates a series of discoveries of hidden identities. Through these discoveries it is revealed that all the main characters are ignorant of their origins, and so of their true natures.

Sir Claude Mulhammer
Egerson, Mulhammer's retired clerk
Colby Simpkins
Kaghan
Lucasta Angel
Lady Elizabeth Mulhammer
Mrs Guzzard
Colby's adoptive mother

Confusions
Alan Ayckbourn
Five Playlets
London 1976

Mother Figure. Neglected by philandering traveller husband Harry, Lucy has 'reverted' to being a total mother figure. She has three small children, she is always in dressing-gown and slippers, and doesn't answer the phone or doorbell. When neighbour Rosemary comes in through the back door to tell her that Harry has been trying to make contact, Lucy is unable to treat her as an adult. Rosemary's husband

Terry arrives, and Lucy's attitude is infectious; the couple quarrel, behave like, and are treated like, small children by Lucy, who successfully forces them to 'make up'.

Drinking Companion. Husband Harry tries to get young perfume demonstrator Paula up to his room. He succeeds in getting her tipsy, but the arrival of her more experienced friend Bernice puts paid to his pathetic seduction attempts.

Between Mouthfuls. In the same hotel dining-room, the conversations of two couples are overheard by the waiter. Mrs Pearce is convinced her husband Walter, just back from Italy on business, has been having an affair. At another table, out of their sight, sit Walter's job-obsessed employee Martin and wife Polly. She is so infuriated at Martin's lack of interest in her that she confesses her solo holiday was spent with boss Walter. The two women storm out, the two men meet and leave together, laughing and chatting.

Gosforth's Fête. Mrs Pearce is the guest speaker at a charity 'do' organized by whirlwind publican Gosforth. The event is a total shambles, with his helper Millie telling Gosforth she is pregnant by him and the news being inadvertently broadcast around the field on the PA system, much to the humiliation of her cubmaster fiancé Stewart. Rain, the Vicar, naughty cubs and an electrocuted Mrs Pearce put paid to the rest of the event.

A Talk in the Park. Five characters on four park benches shift around and attempt to strike up a conversation with each other, only to be rebuffed. Total alienation is the result. Everybody wants somebody to dump on, nobody wants to be dumped upon.

Mother Figure:	Gosforth's Fête:
Lucy	Mrs Pearce
Rosemary	Milly
Terry	Gosforth
Drinking Companion:	Vicar
Harry	Stewart
Paula	**A Talk in the Park:**
Bernice	Arthur
Waiter	Beryl
Between Mouthfuls:	Charles
Waiter	Doreen
Pearce	Ernest
Mrs Pearce	
Martin	
Polly	

Connection, The
Jack Gelber
Drama 2 Acts
New York 1959

Avant-garde documentary film-maker Jim is set up to shoot *The Connection*, written by Jaybird who has been living for the past few months with a group of junkies who will be the actors, improvising on Jaybird's themes. Two photographers are there also, and a four-piece jazz section hang around, filling in the spaces with be-bop music. They all wait in Leach's room for Cowboy, their supplier, and as the play progresses, exposing their individual characters, the diverse types of relationships between them become apparent, as does the connection - heroin - that they share.

Leach, fussy and discontent, has arranged the 'score'; he is a small-time 'businessman' who claims he cannot get high anymore. Ernie used to play saxophone and still keeps up the musician pretence, but he is a vulnerable know-all with a violent streak. Sam is black, uneducated, and a real nice guy, and Solly is his buddy, well-educated and continually philosophical.

Cowboy finally arrives with Sister Salvation in tow as cover to get past the police. She sits around knowing something is going on, but not quite what. The guys go into the bathroom in turn to fix, and Jaybird and the second photographer are so overwhelmed with curiosity they try some too. Leach, chasing a high, takes an overdose, and the musicians quickly leave, together with Ernie; Cowboy and the others look after Leach who eventually revives from a coma. This has all got too much for Jim who complains about the laid-back action, the lack of story, and says he should have brought along some dames. But Jaybird at least now understands.

Jim Dunn
Jaybird
Leach
Solly
Sam
Ernie
First musician
Fourth musician
First photographer
Second photographer
Second musician
Third musician
Harry
Sister Salvation
Cowboy

Constant Wife, The
W. Somerset Maugham
Comedy 3 Acts
London 1927

Happily married Constance Middleton has no wish to be informed of her husband John's affair with her silly friend Marie-Louise; she has enjoyed her marriage which has matured from passion to genuine affection over the past fifteen years. Her interest in romance is rekindled, however, when she is visited by an old flame Bernard Kersal, who still loves her, and John, in order to pursue his own deceptions and because he cannot conceive of his wife transgressing, encourages them to go out together. Later Constance has to admit that she knows about her husband's transgressions but explains that she cannot complain about his attitude because:

'He bought a toy, and if he no longer wants to play with it, why should he?' She realizes that marriage is based on economic considerations and so she finds herself a well-paid job and in six months has earned enough to announce that she and Bernard are going on holiday for six weeks. John protests but cannot blame her for doing what he has done himself. Constance still loves John. 'I may be unfaithful, but I am constant.'

Mrs Culver
Bentley
Martha Culver
Barbara Fawcett
Constance Middleton
Marie-Louise Durham
John Middleton, FRCS
Bernard Kersal
Mortimer Durham

Conversation Piece
Noël Coward
Comedy 3 Acts
London 1934

The play is set amidst the brittle sophistications of Regency Brighton, 1811.

Paul, Duc de Chaucigny-Varennes, has arrived in Brighton as a landless émigré from the terrors of the French Revolution. With him is Melanie, a beautiful young girl he passes off as his ward and the daughter of a murdered friend, the Marquis de Tramont; although we learn early on that she is a dance hall singer.

Their purpose is to marry Melanie to a rich husband and she quickly attracts the attention of Edward, the young Marquis of Sheere, who asks for her hand. With the help of Lady Julia Charteris, who secretly loves Paul, Edward presses his claims, only to discover that Melanie herself has also all along secretly loved Paul. Lady Julia proposes marriage to Paul and with it the comforts of her fortune. Melanie, desperate to win him for herself, declares her love but only succeeds in plunging him into consternation. In the hope that she can shock him into understanding how close they have become, Melanie feigns a departure for France, leaving no forwarding address. The ploy works and they at last come together.

Paul, Duc de Chaucigny-Varennes
Melanie, his protégée
Rose, Melanie's maid
Edward, Marquis of Sheere, Melanie's suitor
The Duchess of Benedon, Edward's mother
The Duke of Benedon, Edward's father
Lady Julia Charteris, Paul's friend
Ladies
Gentlemen
Courtesans
Maids
Soldiers

Coriolanus
WilliamShakespeare
Tragedy 5 Acts
London 1623

The hungry Roman citizenry are mutinous and suspect that the patricians are making excessive profits, the main object of their hatred being Caius Marcius who has performed valorous deeds but not, they feel, for the State so much as to please his mother Volumnia and for his own pride. Caius Marcius does not help by contemptuously denouncing commoners as unreliable and envious cowards.

News is brought that the neighbouring Volscians, led by Tullus Aufidius, are up in arms. Generals Titus Lartius and Cominius, with Caius Marcius, set off to Corioli, the Volscian capital, to suppress the insurrection. After an initial setback they are cursed back into action by Caius Marcius and, following bloody fighting, the Volscians are defeated. Cominius dubs Caius Marcius with the name Coriolanus to honour his victory. Aufidius vows revenge.

Coriolanus receives a hero's welcome in Rome and is elected as consul, but tribunes of the people, repelled by his scornful manner, soon regret their choice and determine to bring Coriolanus down. They incite the mob to seize him but he escapes and goes to Antium, where Aufidius is living after the Volscian defeat, still planning to bring Coriolanus down. At Aufidius's house, Coriolanus doffs humble disguise and offers either his throat for cutting or his revengeful services to subdue the Romans. The arch enemy is delighted but the latest twist is that the people have begun to regret banishing Coriolanus; Aufidius is jealous of this popularity but believes that some arrogant defect of judgement will destroy Coriolanus's victory.

As they advance on Rome, they are met by mother Volumnia and Coriolanus's wife and young son who plead for reconciliation between the Roman and the Volscian people. Coriolanus at first refuses to spare Rome, but then agrees, and although the Volscian crowd welcomes Coriolanus and the peace treaty, Aufidius accuses him of treason before the Volscian Senate. He is stabbed to death.

Caius Marcius/Coriolanus
Titus Lartius
Cominius
Menenius Agrippa
Sicinius Velutus, Junius Brutus, tribunes of the
  people
Young Marcius
Tullus Aufidius
Volumnia
Virgilia, wife to Coriolanus
Valeria, friend to Virgilia
Nicanor, a Roman
Adrian, a Volscian
Roman herald
Lieutenant to Aufidius

Conspirators with Aufidius
A citizen of Antium
Two Volscian guards
Gentlewoman attending on Virgilia
Roman and Volscian senators
Patricians, ædiles, and lictors
Soldiers
Magistrates
Attendants, citizens and servants

Corn is Green, The
Emlyn Williams
Drama 3 Acts
London 1938

When kindly spinster Miss Moffat comes to reside in the small Welsh village of Glansarno, she is shocked at the illiteracy of the locals and she decides to set up a school and, despite opposition from the greedy local mine owner, she proves to be very successful.

Morgan Evans, a local boy, makes a deep impression on Miss Moffat with his beautifully described pieces about life down the mines, and she is determined that such genius deserves a university education. Unfortunately Morgan is unwise enough to become involved with the provocative daughter of Miss Moffat's cockney servant and as he awaits the results of his Oxford entrance examination, she turns up carrying his baby. Reluctantly, he resolves to do the right thing by her but Miss Moffat cannot allow a talent like his to go to waste, so she adopts the child as her own as the village celebrates the arrival of Morgan's exam results.

Mr John Goronwy Jones *Will Hughes*
Miss Ronberry   *John Owen*
Idwal Morris   *Morgan Evans*
Sarah Pugh   *Old Tom*
A groom   *Boys*
The squire   *Girls*
Bessie Watty   *Parents*
Mrs Watty
Miss Moffat
Robbart Robbatch
Glyn Thomas

Country Girl, The
Clifford Odets
Drama 2 Acts
New York 1950

Georgie, the country girl, is married to a once famous but now alcoholic actor Frank Elgin. She is younger than him, but loves him dearly although through a chronic lack of self-confidence and self-esteem, he does use her as an excuse for his failings.

A young director has enough confidence in Frank to offer him the lead in a new play, but despite his bluff exterior Frank finds the pressure too much to bear and although Georgie encourages him all she can, he finally cracks and goes on a boozing binge during the out-of-town run of the play. Georgie is drawn to the young director but she remains faithful to Frank, and her confidence is rewarded when Frank turns in a brilliant performance at the play's opening in New York.

Bennie Dodd, a director
Larry, stage manager
Phil Cook, a producer
Paul Unger, an author
Nancy Stoddard, an ingénue
Frank Elgin, an actor
Georgie Elgin, his wife
Ralph, a dresser

Country Wife, The
William Wycherley
Comedy 5 Acts
London 1674

In a London that seems to be almost entirely populated by lechers, cuckolds, whores, flirts, spuriously respectable women and clapped-out old men, Horner is the most dedicated and unscrupulous seducer of them all. And he has hit upon a wheeze to gull cuckolds and gain ready access to women and their beds. He persuades his doctor, Quack, to put it about that Horner has become impotent - in effect, a eunuch. Among his cronies - one can't really call them friends - Sir Jasper Fidget is most readily exploited, especially as Sir Jasper is more concerned with business than with keeping his wife occupied so as to keep her from sexual straying. Sparkish is trying to marry the lovely Alithea for her money and she is the sister of Pinchwife who has married the lusty country girl Margery: unlike the others, Margery is not wise to the ways of the wicked townies and she is frankly susceptible to handsome men, especially actors. She is keen to get out and about and is flattered by male attention to the fury of the jealous Pinchwife who, oddly, is the only one who has not heard of Horner's affliction and is therefore making desperate, vain attempts to keep tabs on the crafty predator.

Pinchwife's efforts to keep Margery to himself only result in her wising up to various stratagems, from the use of disguise to letters of assignation. Horner has his way, Margery her extra-marital satisfaction but they come to no harm and the men end up doing the dance of cuckolds.

Mr Horner	*Mrs Squeamish*
Mr Harcourt	*Old Lady Squeamish*
Mr Dorilant	*Quack*
Mr Pinchwife	*Lucy, Alithea's maid*
Mr Sparkish	*Waiters*
Sir Jasper Fidget	*Servants*
Mrs Margery Pinchwife	*Attendants*
Alithea	*Boy*
My Lady Fidget	
Mrs Dainty Fidget	

Creditors
August Strindberg
Tragicomedy 1 Act
Copenhagen 1889

This psychological study of three people is allegedly based on Strindberg's own marriage.

Adolf, an ailing artist, takes the credit for having made his wife Tekla into a successful writer. While she is away on a trip, Adolf falls under the influence of the hypnotic Gustav, a teacher and widower, who makes him reveal intimate details of his marriage. He convinces Adolf that Tekla is responsible for his ill health by draining away his talent and using it for herself, and also that she is unfaithful. To prove the point, he arranges an assignation with her when she returns. Adolf witnesses this meeting which reveals that Gustav is, in fact, her first husband about whom she has written a scandalous book. The shock causes Adolf to have a fatal fit and Tekla shows her true love of him and weeps for forgiveness.

Tekla
Adolf
Gustac
Two ladies
A porter

Crime Passionel
Jean-Paul Sartre
Drama 7 Scenes
Paris 1948
See: *Dirty Hands*

Crimes of the Heart
Beth Henley
Drama 3 Acts
New York 1981

Lenny McGrath, plain and thirty, looks after her grandfather, at present in hospital. Her cousin Chick, something of a social climber, visits the house in a small Mississippi town, and obviously is not happy about an item in the newspaper, nor the impending arrival of Lenny's black sheep sister Meg from Los Angeles. Chick leaves and Meg arrives. She is twenty-seven and pretty, and she and Lenny discuss the problem; their young sister Babe, twenty-four, has shot and seriously wounded her husband, prominent local lawyer Zachary, and all Babe is saying is that she did not like his looks.

Chick returns with Babe, out on bail, and lawyer Barnette Lloyd arrives, a clever young man with an almost fanatical hatred of corrupt Zachary. He has evidence of Zachary brutalizing Babe, but advises Babe to say nothing of her adultery with coloured boy Willie Jay. The sisters talk, reminisce and sympathize; they also argue and pick up on old grudges and generally behave in a sisterly fashion. Meg and Babe want Lenny to come out of her shell and stop being nursemaid to grandfather, but Lenny is shy with men because of a shrunken ovary.

Meg goes out with an old flame, Doc, now married, and does not return till the morning; but it was all innocent stuff, explanations and mutual forgiveness. News has arrived that grandfather has had a stroke and will not recover, so Meg and Babe persuade Lenny to call her only old flame Charlie to tell him that she only stopped seeing him because she could not have children. Charlie says he does not care and he will be right over.

Meanwhile, some incriminating photos of Babe and Willie Jay have been found and Barnette arranges to settle everything out of court. Babe is desperate and half-heartedly attempts suicide, but then realizes that, unlike her mother (who killed herself), she is not alone. It is Lenny's birthday and so the girls sit down to the cake Meg and Babe have bought, and Lenny makes a nice wish.

Lenny
Meg
Chick
Babe
Doc Porter
Barnette Lloyd

Critic, The or A Tragedy Rehearsed
Richard Brinsley Sheridan
Comedy 3 Acts
London 1779

Mrs Dangle reads the paper for hard news and politics, but Mr Dangle is obsessed only by things theatrical. He is a celebrated critic and to his wife's dismay their house is a beacon for fellow-critics, actors and dramatists. Fellow-critic Sneer arrives, living up to his name by slyly demolishing the suspect talent of the next visitor, dramatist Sir Fretful Plagiary. Then Mr Puff arrives, a verbose wordsmith, a journalist and advertising copywriter, master of the verbal 'Puff' and would-be dramatist. He invites Dangle and Sneer to a rehearsal of his play The Spanish Armada and they are treated to a spectacle in which the cast have cut - or mutilated - the play far beyond Puff's expectations.

In The Spanish Armada, Tilburnia, daughter of the Governor of Tilbury Fort, loves prisoner Don Whiskerandos, son of the Spanish admiral leading the oncoming Armada. As the 'tragedy' proceeds, Puff explains the clumsy comings-and-goings to now-dubious Dangle and Sneer whose comments enliven the amateurish production as cliché piles upon cliché. The play ends with Sneer bemused at the closing spectacle of an actor playing 'The Thames' with two more players 'The Banks of the Thames' on either side of him during a final procession. More rehearsals tomorrow, promises patient and enthusiastic Puff.

Dangle
Sneer
Sir Fretful Plagiary
Signor Pasticcio
Ritornello
Interpreter
Under-prompter
Puff
Mrs Dangle
Two Italian girls
Characters of the Tragedy:
Lord Burleigh
Governor of Tilbury Fort
Earl of Leicester
Sir Walter Raleigh
Sir Christopher Hatton
Master of the Horse
Beefeater
Justice
Son
Constables
Thames
Don Ferolo
Whiskerandos
Two Nieces
Justice's lady
Confident
Tilburnia
Guards
Servants
Chorus
Rivers and banks
Attendants

Crown Matrimonial
Royce Ryton
Drama 2 Acts
London 1972

Essentially the abdication drama of Edward VIII told from the viewpoint of his mother Queen Mary, this 'insider' peep at the famous royal crisis highlights the conflicts between personal feelings and duty - not only with Edward (known here familiarly as David) but also his younger brother the Duke of York (Bertie) who soon assumed the succession. Queen Mary has dedicated her life to the Royal Family and the concept of monarchy; she displays so little emotion that when a chink appears in her armour it is especially poignant.

Informed and assisted by her friend, lady-in-waiting Mabell, Countess of Airlie, Queen Mary goes through agony after agony, first as the King's travels with Mrs Wallis Simpson are the subject of worldwide gossip, then as David himself tells her he is prepared to abdicate rather than give up the woman he loves, and finally when she is alone with her son the timid Duke of York and he almost breaks down at the prospect of kingship, for which he feels himself ill-prepared. Nevertheless he has his strong wife Elizabeth to support him and Queen Mary realizes that Bertie will in fact make a better king than his brother. Several years later, after the war, David returns to visit his mother; now, with the monarchy once more firmly entrenched, she is able to send a message of kindness to the now-Duchess of Windsor.

Mabell, Countess of Airlie
Queen Mary
The Hon. Margaret Wyndham
Queen's Page (John)
King Edward VIII (David)
The Princess Royal (Mary)
The Duchess of Gloucester (Alice)

Crucible, The
Arthur Miller
Tragedy 4 Acts
New York 1953

Miller based this play on records of a series of 'witch' trials in Salem, Massachusetts in 1692. The core of the Miller version of these events is a love triangle involving John and Elizabeth Proctor and their former servant Abigail Williams.

Along with a number of Salem girls, Abigail has been seen dancing naked in the forest by the vicious and priggish Revd Parris, the local preacher. His daughter Betty, discovered with other girls, collapses into delirium in fear of her father's wrath. Parris suspects the girls of practising witchcraft and interrogates Abigail who confesses the crime knowing that she will be spared punishment by doing so.

She becomes chief accuser in a witch hunt, and singles out the innocent Elizabeth Proctor in the hope of supplanting her as Proctor's wife. Instead, Proctor himself, along with many of his neighbours, becomes a victim of the witch hunt, and Abigail flees the town never to be seen again.

Revd Matthew Parris	Deputy Governor Danforth
Betty Parris	Mercy Lewis
Tituba, Revd Parris's	Mary Warren
slave	Rebecca Nurse
Abigail Williams, Revd	Giles Corey
Parris's niece	Francis Nurse
Susanna Walcott	Ezekiel Cheever
Mrs Ann Putnam	Sarah Good
Thomas Putnam	Hopkins
John Proctor	
Elizabeth Proctor	
Revd John Hale	
Marshal Herrick	
Judge Hathorne	

Curious Savage, The
John Patrick
Comedy 3 Acts
New York 1950

The 'guests' at the Cloisters, a tasteful private home for the mentally disturbed, are awaiting a new arrival, Mrs Ethel Savage. They are gentle and dignified, funny and insightful, each with their particular quirks. All are psychologically wounded to a greater or lesser degree. Ethel arrives with her three stepchildren, Senator Titus, Judge Samuel and oft-married Lily Belle. Ethel and the stepchildren do not get on and her plan to establish a memorial fund dedicated to her husband - to enable people to do all the foolish things they missed out on - has spurred the horrid stepchildren into certifying Ethel to stop her spending the family fortune. She soon makes friends with the guests; handsome, war-shocked Jeff; delicately beautiful but 'inventive' and emotionally-withdrawn Fairy May; child-obsessed Florence; would-

be musician Hannibal, and would-be painter Mrs Paddy who hates everything. Nurse Miss Willie is actually Jeff's wife awaiting his return to health and the place is overseen by good young Dr Emmett.

The stepchildren discover Ethel has converted the money into bonds, but she will not reveal their hiding place until the threat of sodium pentothal makes her bring them out. But Mrs Paddy, saving electricity for Lent, turns out the lights and the bonds vanish, later to appear in ashes. The stepchildren give up after various other humiliations, but Dr Emmett releases Ethel who is obviously quite sane and must, therefore, leave the Cloisters. In fact, Miss Willie had snatched the bonds and she returns them to Ethel who, as she turns to say goodbye to the residents, sees them transformed in her mind into talented, beautiful and complete human beings.

Florence
Hannibal
Fairy May
Jeffrey
Mrs Paddy
Titus
Samuel
Lily Belle
Ethel
Miss Wilhelmina
Dr Emmett

Curtmantle
Christopher Fry
Drama 2 Acts
Tilburg 1961

Poetic historical epic of the great Henry Plantagenet (Henry II) and the major events of his reign, centred upon his greatest achievement, the establishment of an English Common Law. A thirty-year timespan is conveyed in uninterrupted action and begins with young Henry married to beautiful Eleanor of Acquitaine, ex-wife of King Louis of France. Henry persuades his friend and Chancellor Thomas Becket to reluctantly become Archbishop of Canterbury but the men immediately quarrel, God's law versus Henry's law, and eventually Henry is forced to exile Becket.

Helped by his faithful servant William Marshall, Henry discovers and grooms his bastard son Roger with an eye towards making him Chancellor, and at the same time prepares his four legitimate sons - Henry Jr, Geoffrey, Richard and John - for their places in the Plantagenet dynasty. He recalls Becket but still they fight; both are intransigent, and at Henry's unwitting instigation Becket is murdered at Canterbury Cathedral. During Henry's three-year sackcloth-and-scourging penance, his wife and sons grow tired of his domination and frolic around at Poitou, where Henry arrives and arrests Eleanor for treason. Soon after, Henry Jr and Geoffrey fall sick and die.

Richard, now the eldest son, allies with Philip, the new French king against his father and John, and when John also turns traitor they succeed in driving Henry out of most of his French dominions. Henry is forced to concede to their demands and dies in the mud by his birthplace, Le Mans, which he has just torched. Only his bastard Roger and William Marshall remain faithful.

Barber	Richard
Wife	Geoffrey
Juggler	John
Huckster	Messenger
Blae	Becket's cross-bearer
Anesty	Constance, Geoffrey's
Eleanor	wife
William Marshall	Margaret, young Henry's
Henry II	wife
Becket	Philip of France
Cleric	Old woman
Gilbert Foliot	Four refugees
Earl of Leicester	Bishops, courtiers
Young Henry	Soldiers

Cymbeline
William Shakespeare
Drama 5 Acts
London 1609

Cymbeline, King of Britain during the reign of Roman Emperor Augustus, has a daughter Imogen to whom his second wife is a wicked stepmother; her plots include marrying Imogen to her own son Cloten to secure the succession. Cymbeline also has two sons, Guiderius and Arviragus, but they were stolen by banished Lord Belarius. Imogen secretely marries her sweetheart Posthumus (his father died before he was born), and when Cymbeline hears of their marriage he exiles Posthumus. The couple exchange love tokens at his departure, Posthumus giving Imogen a bracelet, she giving him a ring.

Posthumus goes to Rome where his tales of Imogen's loveliness and fidelity result in a bet between him and rascally Iachimo who comes to Britain, steals Imogen's bracelet and notices a mole on her neck while she is sleeping. He returns to Rome, convinces Posthumus of Imogen's perfidy, and wins from Posthumus her ring. Enraged Posthumus sends his faithful retainer Pisanio to Britain to kill Imogen, but Pisanio tells Imogen the truth and advises her to bide her time until Posthumus learns the truth too. Imogen decides to flee her father's court and disguises herself as a boy. After various adventures involving Belarius and her lost brothers, (now renamed Polydore and Cadwal) she is captured by the invading Roman army and made page to Gen. Lucius.

Sick of Rome and burdened with the (supposed) death of Imogen on his conscience, Posthumus returns home to face her father. Cymbeline's army meets and fights with Lucius's army, and during the battle Cymbeline's life is saved by the combined bravery of Posthumous, Polydore and Cadwal (alias Guiderius and Arviragus). The Romans, including Iachimo, are defeated. Finally, all meet up; Imogen demands to know why Iachimo has her ring. He confesses all, Posthumus and Imogen are reconciled, and so is Cymbeline with his sons. Belarius is forgiven, Iachimo dismissed without punishment, and a long-standing peace treaty concluded between Cymbeline and Lucius. Meanwhile, the wicked queen has died of despair and a guilty conscience.

Cymbeline, King of Britain
Cloten, son of the Queen by a former husband
Leonatus Posthumus, husband of Imogen
Belarius, a banished Lord, alias Morgan
Guiderius, alias Polydore, son of the King
Arviragus, alias Cadwal, son of the King
Philario, a Roman, friend to Posthumus
Iachimo, a Roman, friend to Philario
A French Gentleman, friend to Philario
Caius Lucius, general of the Roman forces
A Roman Captain
Two British Captains
Pisanio, gentleman to Posthumus
Cornelius, a physician
Two gentlemen of Cymbeline's court
Two goalers
Queen, wife to Cymbeline
Imogen, daughter of Cymbeline by a former Queen
Helen, woman to Imogen
Lords
Ladies
Apparitions
Soothsayer, musicians, officers, captains, soldiers, messengers and other attendants

Cyrano de Bergerac
Edmond Rostand
Comedy 5 Acts
Paris 1897

Poet, swordsman, musician, philosopher, heroic Cyrano de Bergerac has gone through life with an enormous nose which has given him great strength of character. But, it has also made him reluctant to declare his love for his cousin, the beautiful Roxane, who loves the handsome Baron Christian de Neuvillette. Cyrano befriends the inexperienced Christian when he becomes a cadet cavalier and his magnanimity even extends to helping him woo Roxane and write her the most tender of love letters. She makes Cyrano promise to look after her lover when they go to battle, which he does heroically and when Roxane turns up on the battlefield, dispensing provisions, Christian is about to reveal the authorship of the letters when he is killed. Heartbroken, Roxane retires to a convent where Cyrano faithfully visits her every week for fifteen years until he is mortally wounded and she discovers, too late, who her real lover has been.

Cyrano de Bergerac	The poets
Christian de Neuvillette	The pastrycooks
Comte de Guiche	The pages
Ragueneau	Roxane
Le Bret	Her duenna
Carbon de Castel-Jaloux	Lise
The cadets	The orange girl
Ligniere	Mother Marguerite de
Vicomte de Valvert	Jesus
Three marquis	Sister Marthe
Montfleury	Sister Claire
Bellerose	An actress
Jodelet	A comedienne
Cuigy	The flower girl
Brissaille	The crowd
A meddler	Citizens
Two musketeers	Marquis
A Spanish officer	Musketeers
A cavalier	Thieves
The porter	Cadets of Gascoyne
A citizen	Actors
His son	Violinists
A cut-purse	Children
A spectator	Spanish soldiers
A sentry	Spectators
Bertrandou the Fifer	Intellectuals
A capuchin	Academicians
Two musicians	Nuns

Da

Hugh Leonard
Drama 2 Acts
Dublin 1973

Charlie, now in his forties, returns from London for the funeral in Dublin of his foster-father, the Da. As he sorts through the old man's things, the ghost of the Da visits him and they relive the central incidents in their relationship. The old man was a gardener, a rose-grower, and his earthy simplicity, his cunning, his ignorance and his warm-heartedness arouse both Charlie's resentment and his deep, almost subconscious admiration.

Other ghosts include Charlie's strong willed foster-mother, himself as a young man and his first girlfriend. Real-life visitors also arrive, including his boyhood friend Oliver, still a local lad, and mellowed by years, who gives Charlie his Da's will; his father saved all the money Charlie sent him and has now bequeathed it back. Finally Charlie leaves the house to return to London, his frustration at his father's stubborness still rankling, but try as he may he cannot shake off Da's much-loved but unwanted presence.

Charlie	Drumm
Oliver	Mary Tate
Da	Mrs Prynne, Da's
Mother	employer
Young Charlie	

Dame of Sark, The

William Douglas Home
Drama 6 Scenes
London 1974

It is 1940 and Sybil Hathaway is the hereditary Dame of Sark, ruling the tiny Channel Island equally with American husband Bob, who is Seigneur of Sark by dint of marriage. This is explained to invading German Commandant Maj. Lanz and his rather more sinister interpreter, Dr Braun of the SS. The occupation progresses, and after a Commando raid from the UK, the German reins grow tighter, mines are laid and property requisitioned. News arrives of the death of Sybil's son, and after an initial moment of rudeness, she finds mutual respect with German Commandant of the Channel Island, the civilized (and possibly anti-Nazi) Col von Schmettau, who offers her his genuine sympathies. She also strikes up a friendship with young German soldier Muller and takes an interest in his family.

When America enters the war Bob is deported to mainland Europe and Sybil carries on doing her best to guard and protect the interests of the people of Sark against mounting German strictures and demands. She is able to repay von Schmettau's sympathy when his youngest son is killed on the Eastern front, and he helps her foil a German search party looking for some letters. He also realizes she must have a hidden radio, but he says nothing. After the surrender of Germany, Sybil brusquely orders Lanz to now remove the German mines, but unfortunately Muller is killed while doing so and Sybil realizes that the tragedy of war affects friend and foe alike.

Bob Hathaway
Sybil Hathaway
Cecile
Maj. Lanz
Dr Braun
Col von Schmettau
Wilhelm Muller
Col Graham
Jim Robinson
Mr Bishop
Mrs Bishop
The cowman

Damn Yankees

Richard Adler and Jerry Ross
Musical
New York 1955

Set in 1950s America, this is another variation on the Faust theme. Joe, a middle-aged baseball fanatic, is approached by the Devil and offered his lost youth in exchange for his soul. He accepts the offer with a get-out clause and the now youthful Joe goes off to join the failing Washington Senators baseball team, where, managed by Mr Applegate (the Devil), he becomes a champion striker and takes the team to the top of the league. However, he yearns for the old life and the love of his faithful wife, Meg, despite the temptation put before him by the Devil's assistant, seductive Lola. He takes lodgings at his own home, unrecognized by Meg, and the Devil sets about keeping him to his bargain by various tricks including getting him discredited with his team mates. Good, of course, prevails in the end; the team win the championship and Joe wins back his wife. Songs include: 'You've Got to Have Heart'; 'Whatever Lola Wants'; 'Shoeless Joe from Hannibal Mo'.

Joe, a middle-aged baseball fan
Meg, Joe's wife
Applegate, the Devil
Sister
Doris, Meg's friend
Gloria, a newspaper reporter
Lola, a female devil
Welch
Van Buren
Rocky
Smokey
Vernon
Sohovik
Mickey
Eddie
Miss Weston
Aged Lola
Commissioner

Dance of Death, The (Part I)
August Strindberg
Tragedy 2 Acts
Berlin 1905

On an island outpost off the coast of Sweden, Edgar, a captain in the Coastal Artillery and Alice his wife of twenty-five years, languish in an appalling marriage. Edgar, gripped by a persecution mania, has so distorted his scheming irascible past that he paints himself as the innocent victim of his wife's non-existent machinations.

They are joined by Kurt, Alice's cousin, who has been sent to run the outpost quarantine station. In desperation at her husband's distorted view of their past, Alice turns to Kurt for comfort, and they rekindle a past and secret attraction. At the same time Edgar begins to suffer a series of minor strokes and apparently in repentance, reveals that he has brought about Kurt's divorce. They are reconciled until Edgar announces that he has arranged for Kurt's estranged son to be seconded to the post. It is his purpose to win the boy's affection and turn him against his father. In a fit of revulsion Alice sets out to expose Edgar to his superiors as an embezzler. Kurt, meanwhile, unable to tolerate either of them any longer, leaves.

With characteristic cunning Edgar has anticipated Alice's ploy and avoided exposure. They are left alone to contemplate the celebration of their approaching anniversary.

Edgar
Alice
Kurt
Jenny
Old woman
Sentry

Dance of Death, The (Part II)
August Strindberg
Tragedy 2 Acts
Berlin 1905

The second part of this piece finds Edgar recovered from ill health and involved in a plot to ruin Kurt.

Kurt's son, Allan, has come to the island and fallen in love with Edgar's daughter, Judith. At the same time the young man and his father are just becoming reconciled after years of estrangement. Assiduous toadying to the Colonel who runs the island, which goes as far as offering the old soldier his daughter's hand in marriage, has given Edgar near total command of the isolated community. He sets out to ruin Kurt by firstly virtually forcing him into suicidal investments and later taking the credit for advances in quarantine methods which Kurt has pioneered.

Edgar's plans come unstuck when Judith, in love with Allan, insults the Colonel, who breaks off their engagement. Edgar dies of a stroke.

Allan, due to Edgar's earlier plotting, is posted to the mainland and has to leave behind a heartbroken Judith, who with her mother and Kurt contemplate the terrible effect Edgar has had on their lives.

Edgar
Alice
Kurt
Allan
Judith
The Lieutenant

Dancing Years, The
Ivor Novello and Christopher Hassal
Musical 2 Acts
London 1939

Penniless young composer Rudi Kleber has only fifteen-year-old Grete to appreciate his wonderful music, and even his grand piano is threatened by his landlady to whom he owes six months' rent. But this is Vienna in 1911, and not for long does Rudi's talent remain undiscovered. He is saved by attractive opera singer Maria Ziegler, whose influential lover is nice Prince Charles Metterling. Grete goes off to study, but not before she begs Rudi to promise her he won't ask anyone else to marry him unless he gives her first refusal. Maria and Rudi fall in love, Rudi becomes immensely successful, and although Maria eventually leaves Charles, Rudi won't mention marriage.

Several years later Grete returns and realizing Rudi loves Maria, asks him to propose to her so she can refuse him, and then wed Maria. Unfortunately Maria overhears the proposal part but doesn't wait for the refusal. She runs off and marries Charles. Twelve years later they meet again and Rudi begs her to leave Charles and marry him. She has brought along their son Carl, raised by Charles as his own, and although Maria still loves Rudi, he realizes he cannot break up the family and perhaps ruin Charles and Carl's happiness.

Songs include: 'My Dearest Dear'; 'I Can Give You the Starlight'; 'When It's Spring in Vienna'

Rudi Kleber	Countess Lotte
Grete	Maria's dresser
Hattie, a housekeeper	Hans
Franzel, a young officer	Oscar
Lilli	Carl
Elizabeth	Goetzer, an SS Officer
Hilde	A postman
Wanda	A milkmaid
Four young men	Ladies and gentlemen-
Maria Ziegler	about-town
Prince Charles Metterling	Singers and dancers
Cacille Kurt, a music	Guests at the Gala
teacher	Footmen
Ballet mistress	Guests in Locher's
Otto Breitkopf, a	restaurant
composer	Waiters
Ceruti, a tenor	

Dandy Dick
Arthur Wing Pinero
Farce 3 Acts
London 1887

Slightly pompous Very Revd Augustus Jedd (the Dean) has two naughty daughters, Salome and Sheba, and their latest extravagance, unbeknown to their father, is a pair of fancy-dress costumes to enable them to accompany their beaux, sickly Maj. Tarver and very pompous Mr Darbey, to the regimental ball. The Dean announces he will not pick up any more of the spendthrift pair's bills, and urges them to economize; he himself must now raise much money for the renovation of the church spire. The despairing pair are saved by the arrival of the Dean's sister, wayward Georgiana (George) Tidman, who has come to live with them. A horse fanatic and ex-bookie, George's talk is peppered with horse-and-track metaphors and she agrees to place the girls' savings on her horse Dandy Dick, a dead cert for the next day's race. George also meets her and the Dean's old friend Sir Tristram Mardon, another racing enthusiast type, down for the races.

The action heats up to farce-like velocity as the Dean himself succumbs to temptation and gets butler Blore to back Dandy Dick; the Dean is then arrested while tending to Dandy Dick - now resting in his stables - and accused of trying to nobble him. Unknown to the Dean, Blore - whose money is on another horse - slipped strychnine into the Dean's lotion for Dandy Dick. Helped by Tristram, the Dean escapes custody and fools Constable Noah, but then learns Blore did not put his money on Dandy Dick - which won - but on the other horse. Fortunately George and Tristram decide to

wed, and Tristram lends the Dean the money for the spire. Salome and Sheba pay off their bills with their winnings and go off to wed their awful soldier boyfriends. Only the Dean's pride is hurt, and as his sister explains to him - that is no bad thing.

The Very Revd Augustus Jedd DD
Salome
Sheba
Georgiana (George) Tidman
Blore
Hatcham
Maj. Tarver
Mr Darbey
Noah Topping
Hannah Topping
Sir Tristram Mardon

Dangerous Corner
J. B. Priestley
Drama 3 Acts
London, 1932

At an after-dinner gathering at the Caplans, Freda Caplan, Olwen Peel, Betty Whitehouse and lady novelist Maud Mockridge catch the final snatch of a radio play called *The Sleeping Dog* in which the husband shoots himself. In come the men from cigars and brandy: Robert Caplan, Gordon Whitehouse, and cynical Charles Stanton. They discuss the fragment of the play and what it might mean, and opinions differ as to the wisdom of revealing the absolute truth. Gordon abandons his attempts to get some dance music on the radio and the conversation deepens and turns to the recent suicide of Robert's clever but reckless brother Martin. Olwen makes a slip and reveals it was she and not Gordon who last saw Martin alive. Against the wishes of some of the others, Robert is insistent that the whole truth be told, and the revelations begin to snowball.

Martin's suicide was assumed to have been because he stole money from the firm where he worked with Robert and Stanton. In fact Stanton stole the money to spend on his mistress Betty, neglected by boyish husband Gordon who had a crush on Martin. Freda and Robert's marriage is also revealed as unhappy; she was having an affair with Martin, while Robert was sweet on Betty whom he held to be purity incarnate. Finally Olwen, who loves Robert, reveals that Martin's death was not suicide - he was accidentally shot when, drug-crazed, he attempted to rape her and they struggled with a gun.

Shattered, the others leave except for Olwen, Freda and Robert, who becomes so overwhelmed with disillusion he runs upstairs and shoots himself. The lights fade, then come up as in the beginning of the play with the women in the room listening to the end of a radio play in which the husband shoots himself. In come the men and the talk proceeds as before. Then Gordon finds a dance tune on the radio, the couples begin dancing and their lives take a different turn into an alternative dimension of reality.

Robert Caplan
Freda Caplan
Betty Whitehouse
Gordon Whitehouse
Olwen Peel
Charles Trevor Stanton
Maud Mockridge

Dark at the Top of the Stairs, The
William Inge
Drama 3 Acts
New York 1957

Rubin and Cora Flood live in a pleasant house in a small town near Oklahoma City. It is the 1920s and Rubin's work selling harnesses is falling off. He is from pioneer stock and has not quite been tamed by his pretty, neat wife. She complains that he is away from home too much and that their children, Reenie, sixteen, and Sonny, ten, need a father. He counters that she has pampered and coddled the children. Indeed, Reenie is shy and introverted, Sonny is sensitive and gets teased, and they hate each other. Rubin leaves but returns after discovering Cora has spent precious money on a dress for Reenie for a big local party. He hits Cora and leaves and she tells him not to come back.

Reenie's 'fast' friend Flirt has arranged a blind date for her and that evening Flirt and boyfriend Punky appear with Sammy Goldenbaum, a handsome, likeable Jewish boy, neglected by his film-star mother. He gets on well with Reenie and Sonny, and also with Cora's elder sister Lottie and her timid husband Morris, who have arrived to keep Cora company. But Lottie reveals that she has her own problems - Morris has not touched her for three years, and he is a depressive. She advises Cora to make up with virile Rubin and be thankful.

Next day Flirt arrives distraught and tells them that Sammy has killed himself. It seems that after dancing with Reenie, she introduced him to a girl whose mother insulted him because he was Jewish. Sammy looked for shy Reenie, but she was hiding in the girls' room. He could not find her so he went to Oklahoma City and jumped from a hotel window. Cora tells Reenie she is disgusted with her self-obsession and Reenie understands and agrees. Rubin returns and apologizes, and goes upstairs to wait for Cora. Sonny sympathizes with Reenie and invites her to the movies.

Cora Flood
Rubin Flood
Sonny Flood
Reenie Flood
Flirt Conroy
Morris Lacey
Lottie Lacey
Punky Givens
Sammy Goldenbaum
Chauffeur
Boy outside

Dark of the Moon
Howard Richardson and William Berney
Drama/Musical 2 Acts
London 1949

This spooky fable based on *The Ballad of Barbara Allen* is set among the hillbillies of the Smoky Mountains in whom religion and superstition exist in fairly evenly balanced parts. Hero John is a witch who has been happily digging up graveyards and flying beneath the moon with his eagle when he spots lovely Barbara Allen. He falls in love and begs the Conjur Man to make him human. He does not find it too difficult to get to know Barbara, the local good-time gal who is always 'pleasuring herself' with the local young men.

The Conjur Man refuses John's request, but the Conjur Woman sees that John and Barbara are truly in love and she agrees to his request. She tells him he can indeed be a human - but he will only stay that way if Barbara is faithful for a whole year. Barbara does her best despite being pursued by hulking ex-boyfriend Marvin Hudgens and also giving birth to a horrid witch-child that locals burn in the garden. Eventually, in their anxiety to get rid of John, the locals force Barbara into the church (where John cannot go) and allow Marvin to have his way with her. That is it for John and also for Barbara. She runs back to John to tell him what happened - she still loves him - but she dies in his arms and he turns back into a witch.

John	*Mrs Bergen*
Conjur Man	*Mr Summey*
The Dark Witch	*Marvin Hudgens*
The Fair Witch	*Barbara Allen*
Conjur Woman	*Floyd Allen*
Hank Gudger	*Mrs Allen*
Miss Metcalf	*Mr Allen*
Uncle Smelicue	*Preacher Haggler*
Mrs Summey	*Green Gorman*
Edna Summey	*Witches*
Mr Atkins	

Darkness at Noon
Sidney Kingsley from the book by Arthur Koestler
Drama 3 Acts
New York 1951

Pioneer Soviet revolutionary Rubashov has been arrested in 1937 and hauled into prison, to languish in a dank granite underground cell. His fellow-prisoners - including an old Tzarist - are delighted at his downfall ... 'the wolves are tearing themselves to pieces'. Enter Gletkin, a menacing young officer and fanatical Stalinist. He wants to torture Rubashov to extract a confession, but is prevented by his boss Ivanoff, an old friend of Rubashov's. Ivanoff offers a deal; a show trial, trumped-up confessions, a long prison sentence to be commuted to three or four years.

At first Rubashov declines the offer, as he realizes how the original ideals of the revolution have become perverted and evil. In a series of flashbacks he also remembers how his own uncompromising fervour has inevitably led to this kind of situation; his trip to a Communist leader in Nazi Germany; his affair with his beloved - and now dead - secretary Leda; his manipulation and betrayal of Italian union leaders. Rubashov is interrogated mercilessly by Gletkin and begins to waver, and is 'betrayed' by another prisoner, the tortured son of an old friend, his supposed accomplice in an assassination plot. The interrogation breaks Rubashov physically, but he does not compromise. His fellow inmates have been urging him not to confess, and finally he does not. He goes to his death calling Gletkin 'my son' - meaning the child of his mistaken ideal that the end justifies the means.

Rubashov	Young girl
Guard	Second Storm Trooper
402	Ivanoff
302	Bogrov
202	Hrutch
Luba	Albert
Gletkin	Luigi
First Storm Trooper	Pablo
Richard	

Daughter-in-Law, The
D. H. Lawrence
Drama 4 Acts
London 1968

The seven-week marriage of young Nottingham miner Luther Gascoigne and wife Minnie is already rocky when Mrs Purdy tells Luther's mother and brother Joe (who has just broken his arm playing around in the pit) that her daughter is expecting Luther's child. Mrs Purdy is very reasonable and does not want Luther's marriage to suffer, but she does need money for her daughter. Joe goes and tells Luther but advises him not to tell strong-willed Minnie. Later, during an argument, tipsy Luther blurts it out to Minnie and she offers him her savings. Their problem is that Luther has low self-esteem and believes that Minnie, who was in domestic service, thinks she is too good for him. She in turn believes that Luther is still tied to his mother's apron strings and has no real feeling left over for her.

There is a family confrontation and Minnie tells Mrs Gascoigne that she has not let her sons grow up to become men - and Joe agrees. Minnie leaves for Manchester, and Luther and Joe become involved in the local pit strike. When Minnie returns two weeks later having spent her savings in order to get on equal terms with Luther - and force him to be a man and support her - she meets Mrs Gascoigne and they discover both sons are missing. They hear shots from the pit and fear the worst, but Luther returns slightly hurt and tells them Joe is all right. They have fought the blacklegs and won. Mrs Gascoigne goes out after Joe, and Luther and Minnie realize they need each other - and need to allow themselves to love and be loved.

Mrs Gascoigne
Joe
Mrs Purdy
Minnie
Luther

Day in Hollywood, a Night in the Ukraine, A
Lyrics by Dick Vosburgh
Music by Frank Lazarus
Musical Comedy 2 Acts
New York 1984

Act One is a musical celebration of Hollywood, with celebrated numbers performed by theatre ushers who do impersonations of such stars as the Marx Brothers, Sonja Henie, Tom Mix, Judy Garland, Al Jolson, Mickey and Minnie Mouse, Nelson Eddy, Marlene Dietrich, Dorothy Lamour and Charlie Chaplin. Accurate impressions are not required; the right clothes will suffice. Nor is Astaire-type dancing required because with the aid of a strip of stage in the shape of a very large mail-slot (the 'ankle-stage') only the dancers' legs are seen and the performers can steady themselves and achieve airborne effects by using an unseen bar to raise themselves.

Act Two (A Night in the Ukraine) can be presented separately as a little farce, based so loosely as to be unhinged, on Chekhov's The Bear, with characters played as if they were the Marx Brothers and Margaret Dumont; the Groucho character is a lawyer, Serge B. Samover whose father called him Serge because what he really wanted was a new blue suit. Carlo (Chico) talks in phony Wop, and Gino (Harpo) mimes, honks a horn and performs a harp solo on a bicycle wheel.

Eight performers for both halves:
Mrs Pavlenko, a rich widow
Carlo, her Italian footman
Gino, her gardener
Serge B. Samover, a Moscow lawyer
Nina, Mrs Pavelnko's daughter
Constantine, a coachman
Masha, the maid
Sascha, a manservant

Day in the Death of Joe Egg, A
Peter Nichols
Comedy 2 Acts
Glasgow 1967

Bri is a teacher, a youngish thirty-three, married to ample and attractive Sheila, thirty-five. Their daughter Joe is ten and because of a damaged cerebral cortex is a 'vegetable'. The couple play fantasy games with each other and Joe, treating her like a two-year-old and commenting on her (make-believe) reactions to the events of the day. Their mutual tenderness, however, is beginning to dissolve. The strain of Joe is telling on their marriage; Bri believes he is just another of earth-mother Sheila's creatures that she breeds, grows and cultivates, while suspecting her of an affair with fellow amateur actor Freddie. His cynicism upsets Sheila who is fed up with his attention-seeking self-pitying depressions which she blames on his mother, Grace.

One evening after dramatics, Sheila returns home with Freddie and his wife Pam; Freddie, a hearty socialist, has inherited wealth and Pam has airs and graces. The couple's advice, though meant well, seems somehow flimsy in the face of the terrible burden borne by Bri and Sheila. That evening Bri cracks and half-heartedly attempts to let Joe die of exposure. Sheila, realizing the depths of Bri's despair, promises to try to find a 'home' for Joe where she will not pine - as she always has before - and then she gives to Bri the love and comfort he needs, whispering to Joe how lucky she is have such a good daddy.

Bri
Sheila
Joe
Pam
Freddie
Grace

Dead End
Sidney Kingsley
Drama 3 Acts
New York 1935
As a gang of streetwise boys joke and argue in the squalor of a New York East Side dock they are passed and largely ignored by their affluent neighbours. A crippled architect, Gimpty, who grew up on this 'dead end' returns to the slums hoping to do some good, but the kids prefer the advice of his old friend, who is now a successful gangster. They rob a local rich kid and their leader, Tommy McGrath, stabs the boy's father.

For a reward Gimpty, who needs money to marry his rich girlfriend, informs on the gangster and the G men gun him down. One of the gang also informs on Tommy, who tries to 'carve him up' and is sent to reform school despite the pleas of his sister who knows that while there he will just learn more about 'the rackets'. Gimpty's girlfriend, who cannot bear poverty, has left him and Gimpty promises to find Tommy a good lawyer as the gang tell reform school anecdotes.

Gimpty	*Milty*
T. B.	*Drina*
Tommy	*Mr Griswald*
Dippy	*Mr Jones*
Angel	*Kay*
Spit	*Jack Hilton*
Doorman	*Lady with dog*
Old lady	*Three small boys*
Old gentleman	*Second Chauffeur*
First chauffeur	*Second Avenue boys*
'Baby-Face' Martin	*Mrs Martin*
Hunk	*Patrolman Mulligan*
Philip Griswald	*Francey*
Governess	

Dear Brutus
J. M. Barrie
Fantasy 3 Acts
London 1917
Strange old Mr Lob (a character based on Puck) invites several guests to his country home where, on entering, they are warned by the butler to beware of Lob's mysterious forest.

All the guests have problems related to the past, so they find Lob's invitation to the magic woods irresistible when they are informed that, when there, they can have a second chance in life. Once there, however, they all make the same mistakes over again, the crook still steals, the philanderer still has affairs, the miserable are still unhappy. All are disappointed except an artist, who meets the daughter he had always yearned for but never had.

Returning to the real world they awaken to realize the futility of their original longings but are beginning to come to terms with their situations. The artist, grateful for his experience is now happy to return to the empty life he has with his wife.

Mr Dearth
Mrs Dearth
Mr Purdie
Mrs Purdie
Mr Coade
Mrs Coade
Lob
Joanna Trout
Lady Caroline Laney
Margaret

Dear Octopus
Dodie Smith
Comedy 3 Acts
London 1938
At their big country house in Essex, Dora and Charles Randolph are celebrating their diamond wedding anniversary, together with assorted children and grandchildren. It is a time of gratitude, nostalgia and concern, and of course contrasts; daughter Margery and her husband Kenneth, both plump and easygoing, happy with their children Flouncy and Bill (engaged in continual sibling rivalry); daughter Hilda, getting more neurotic and more successful; son Nicholas, unmarried and secretly loved by Dora's quietly attractive companion Fenny. Back from Paris after seven years absence is self-styled black sheep Cynthia, afraid to tell her parents of her now-shattered affair with a married man. But Dora has mellowed and mother and daughter are reconciled - Dora would now sooner lose a principle than a daughter.

Life at the house is quite ordinary but always interesting, with everyone's quirks and feuds being exposed and resolved until finally, delightfully and clumsily, Nicholas realizes he has always loved Fenny. They will marry, bringing Fenny officially into the 'dear Octopus' that is the family, from whose tentacles the members can never quite escape, or wish to.

Charles Randolph
Dora Randolph
Their children:
Hilda Randolph
Margery Harvey
Cynthia Randolph
Nicholas Randolph
Their grandchildren:
Hugh Randolph
Gwen (Flouncy) Harvey
William (Bill) Harvey
Kathleen (Scrap) Kenton
Belle Schlessinger, their sister-in-law
Edna Randolph, Hugh's mother
Laurel Randolph, Hugh's wife
Kenneth Harvey, Margery's husband
Grace Fenning (Fenny), Dora's companion
Nanny Patching, a nurse
Gertrude, a parlourmaid

Dear Ruth

Norman Krasna
Comedy 2 Acts
New York 1944

Judge Henry Wilkins lives in Long Island with wife Edith, grown-up daughter Ruth, and precocious teenage daughter Miriam. Bank clerk Ruth is engaged to dull old Albert Kummer, and one day while she is working, handsome airman Bill Seawright appears at the door. It's 1944 and he's been sustained through tough active service by a constant stream of letters and poems from pen-pal Ruth, plus her photo - he's deeply in love and wants to wed. He leaves and when later upon her return Ruth denies all knowledge of him, socially-aware Miriam proves to be the letter-writing 'culprit', intent on supporting one of America's finest. Dad's hopping mad, but as Bill's only got two days leave, Ruth decides to play along when he comes back that evening.

Much to Albert's displeasure they have a great time, aided by Bill's sister Martha who gets the Judge to marry her to fiancé Chuck, Bill's buddy. But when the guys hear they will not be returning to combat but are posted to Florida, Bill wants Ruth right now, and she has to tell him she does not want to marry him.

Then Miriam spills the beans about the letters and Bill, feeling completely idiotic, goes to leave - but at the last moment Ruth admits her true feelings - she's fallen for Bill and wants to go with him to Florida. Dad tosses off a quickie ceremony and off they rush, just as another Miriam pen-pal, sailor Klobbermayer, arrives at the door, asking for Ruth.

Dora
Mrs Edith Wilkins
Miriam Wilkins
Judge Harry Wilkins
Ruth Wilkins
Lieut William Seawright
Albert Kummer
Martha Seawright
Sergeant Chuck Vincent
Harold Klobbermayer

Death of a Miner, The

Paula Cizmar
Drama 2 Acts
New York 1982

Set in the coal mining hills of Appalachia, this play details the struggles of Mary Alice Hager, a female coal miner in a world of men, and the legacy she leaves. Mary Alice faces constant prejudice from her fellow workers and pressure from her husband Jack, who finds it hard to take the ridicule he receives in his role as house-husband.

When Mary Alice dies in a coal face accident, Jack and their daughter Sallie not only have to face up to her death, but also to the existence of a law which denies survivor's benefits to families of female workers. Despite Jack's struggle for compensation, and the support of a few of Mary Alice's fellow workers, all claims are denied.

Jack and Sallie are left in a world that has changed too late for them, and face a struggle to reconcile Mary Alice's love of the land and the coal industry, with their own bitterness and regret.

Mary Alice Hager
Jack Hager
Sallie Hager
Winina
Pete
Chester
Bonnie Jean
Barney
Dale
Joseph

Death of a Salesman

Arthur Miller
Tragedy 2 Acts
New York 1949

At sixty, Willy Loman is bewildered by his failure in life. After thirty years as a salesman his company in effect demotes him; many of his old and faithful clients are dying off. Willy looks at his successful neighbours and can only draw unfavourable comparisons. In an attempt to isolate himself from the realities of his failures he has delusions about himself and his family.

Although obviously a victim of the capitalist system Willy is still an ardent supporter and believer in 'The American Dream', and in this he is solidly supported by his faithful wife, Linda. Biff, his younger son, sees through his father's weaknesses but does not stop loving him, while his elder son, Happy, successfully deceives himself with dreams of the future and despises Willy's inadequacies and failure. Flashbacks show some of Willy's glorious past successes and he goes to his death still bravely deceiving himself.

Willy Loman
Linda
Biff
Happy
Bernard
Letts
Charley
Uncle Ben

Howard Wagner	Miss Forsyth
Jenny	The woman
Stanley	Waiter

Deathtrap
Ira Levin
Drama 2 Acts
New York 1958

Thriller playwright Sidney Bruhl has hit a dry creative patch when he receives a cracking good manuscript for perusal from protégé Clifford Anderson. Nervy wife Myra gets worried when Sid's joking about inviting Anderson over, killing him and stealing the story, seems just a little too near the knuckle. Anderson arrives and in due course Sidney does kill him, garrotting him on the living room carpet. Myra's weak heart is not helped by all this. Sidney goes and buries Clifford, but when the corpse, all dirt and blood, returns from the grave and bludgeons Sidney, Myra has a heart attack and dies. Of course, it is all a ploy pre-arranged by the two guys, 'closet gay' Sid and gay Cliff. Spice is added when famed Dutch medium crimebuster Helga ten Dorp arrives after picking up the 'vibes' and making some uncanny predictions. Unfortunately for Sidney, Cliff is a mystery buff and thinks the whole true story would make a marvellous 'whodunnit', and so what if the gossip flowed; nothing could be proved anyway.

Conservative Sidney is not impressed and plots to murder Cliff for real; they turn the tables on each other several times before both ending up dead and are found by Helga and Sidney's lawyer, closet phone-pest Porter.

Sidney Bruhl	Helga ten Dorp
Myra Bruhl	Porter Milgrim
Clifford Anderson	

Deep Blue Sea, The
Terence Rattigan
Drama 3 Acts
London 1952

Hester Collyer is rescued by a neighbour after attempting suicide in the furnished flat she shares with her younger lover, ex-RAF pilot Freddie Page. He too is aware that their relationship is doomed and accepts a job abroad as a test pilot, despite a drink problem which may affect his judgement. He does not intend to take Hester with him although she clings obsessively to him begging him to stay. Later she is visited by her husband, judge Sir William Collyer, who wants her to come back to him, but she refuses; even the shaky relationship with Freddie contained more than her stolid marriage. Sir William leaves and Hester decides on suicide again but this attempt is interrupted by her upstairs neighbour Miller, a struck-off doctor. He convinces her that it is possible to live without hope, as he indeed has to. When Freddie unexpectedly returns to say farewell, Hester has come to terms with herself and his departure.

Hester Collyer

Mrs Elton, the landlady
Philip Welch, a neighbour
Ann Welch, his wife
Mr Miller, a struck-off doctor
Sir William Collyer
Freddie Page
Jackie Jackson, Freddie's friend

Delicate Balance, A
Edward Albee
Drama 3 Acts
New York 1966

Agnes and Tobias (Mommy and Daddy) are a comfortably well-off, retired couple living in suburban America in the sixties. She is intelligent but talkative, and boredom makes her contemplate the attractions of being mad. She accuses the taciturn Tobias of having an affair with her alcoholic sister but after a few drinks he begins to talk about how he killed his pet cat because it did not love him.

Quite suddenly their best friends arrive; they have an irrational fear of going home to their house and ask if they can stay for the night. This causes a family conflict for their daughter, who has just divorced her fourth husband, and demands to stay too.

Tobias has to try to maintain a balance between his family obligations and loyalty to his panic-stricken unreasoning friends, and although he has reservations about his friends he insists that they stay.

When they do finally leave, Mommy again ponders on how easily she might go mad.

Agnes (Mommy)
Tobias (Daddy)
Claire
Edna
Harry
Julia

Desert Song, The
Otto Harbach, Oscar Hammerstein and Frank Mandel
Music by Sigmund Romberg
Musical Play 2 Acts
New York 1926

The Red Shadow, a Frenchman, disgusted by the way his country has treated the people of Morocco, has become leader of the Riffs and fights against the French forces of which he is a member, masquerading as a fool, Pierre Birabeau, son of the commanding general.

He loves beautiful Margot Bonvalet, who is pursued by Capt. Paul Fontaine, and in his guise of the Red Shadow he abducts Margot and takes her off to the desert. She is both fascinated and frightened of the mystery man, whom Fontaine is out to capture. A treacherous Arab girl, Azuri, betrays the Shadow's hideout to Baribeau Senr and the brave general comes alone to challenge the Red Shadow to a duel, but of course Pierre cannot fight his own father, so he backs down to the dismay of his faithful followers. They condemn him to be cast alone into the desert, shortly to be followed by Fontaine who, finding only the dim-witted Pierre, imagines that he has disposed of the Red Shadow. Margot, now realizing that she loves the man of the desert, is stunned by the news, but not for long; when they are alone Pierre resurrects him.

Songs include: 'All Alone, to be My Own'; 'Ho, So We Sing as We Go Riding, Ho'; 'Desert Song'; 'Eastern and Western Love'

Sid El Kar	*Mindar*
Hadji	*Hassi*
Neri	*Lieut La Vergne*
Benjamin Kidd	*Sgt De Boussac*
Capt. Paul Fontaine	*Riffs*
Margot Bonvalet	*Soldiers*
Gen. Birabeau	*Spanish girls*
Pierre Birabeau	
Susan	
Edith	
Azuri	
Ali Ben Ali	
Clementina	

Desire Under the Elms
Eugene O'Neill
Tragedy 3 Acts
New York 1924

This domestic tragedy is set in the rocky New England farm country of the 1850s.

Eben Cabot nurses utter hatred for his domineering father, Ephraim, based on the conviction that the old man has swindled ownership of the family farm from Eben's dead mother, to whom it once belonged.

When old Ephraim returns to the farm with a new young wife, Abbie Putnam, Eben takes an immediate dislike to her too, but he soon falls under her spell and becomes her secret lover. When a baby is born the lovers are obliged to pretend that Ephraim is the father.

At a party to celebrate the birth, Ephraim goads Eben by revealing that the farm will now be passed on to the baby under an agreement he has made with Abbie. Eben, convinced that he has again been duped, rejects Abbie and their child and prepares to leave for California. To prove her love and loyalty to Eben, Abbie smothers the child to death. The lovers are arrested for the crime and Ephraim abandons the farm to the encroaching wilderness.

Ephraim Cabot
Simeon and Peter, his sons by his second wife
Eben
Abbie Putnam
Young girl
Two farmers
The fiddler
A sheriff
Farmers

Detective Story
Sidney Kingsley
Drama 3 Acts
New York 1949

An eventful and eventually tragic evening at the detective squad room of a New York precinct police station begins ordinarily enough with the arrival of a nervous woman shoplifter and a paranoid old woman. The detectives take it all in their stride, all except fanatical McLeod who has a psychotic hatred of criminals and particularly of abortionist Dr Schneider, brought in voluntarily by lawyer Sims who warns McLeod against brutalizing his clients. McLeod is also fervent in his compulsion to prosecute young war-hero Arthur, who stole money from his boss Mr Pritchett, hoping to win back his haughty girlfriend. Despite the efforts of Susan, the girlfriend's much nicer sister, and the willingness of Pritchett to drop charges, McLeod is determined to get Arthur jailed. Thieves Charlie and Lewis arrive, and Lewis, realizing he's been duped by crazy Charlie reveals the whereabouts of their loot while Charlie gets more and more edgy. When news arrives that a girl Schneider operated on (and due to be a witness) has died, McLeod beats up Schneider, but Sims then insinuates to Lieut Monoghan, McLeod's superior, that McLeod has a personal reason for harassing Schneider. Mary McLeod is brought in and to her husband's disgust reveals she had an abortion by Schneider before she met McLeod. Her husband, however, never knew. Mary's ex-boyfried Tami Giacoppetti is also present. McLeod is sickened and devastated but despite his love for Mary it is too much for him. His neurotic disgust is so intense that Mary leaves him. Then Charlie manages to get a gun, and with nothing to live for, McLeod boldly disarms him and is shot several times. As he lies dying he finally relents and lets Arthur off the hook.

Joe Feinson	*Miss Hatch*
Detective Drake	*Mrs Feeny*
Shoplifter	*Crumb-bum*
Detective Gallager	*Mr Gallantz*
Mrs Farragut	*Mr Pritchett*
Detective Callahan	*Mary McLeod*
Detective O'Brian	*Tami Giacoppetti*
Detective Brody	*Mr Bagatelle*
Endicott Sims	*Photographer*
Detective McLeod	*Lady*
Arthur Kindred	*Gentleman*
Patrolman Barnes	*Indignant citizen*
First Burglar (Charlie)	
Second Burglar (Lewis)	
Mrs Bagatelle	
Dr Schneider	
Lieut Monoghan	
Susan Carmichael	
Patrolman Keogh	
Patrolman Baker	
Willy	

Devil's Disciple, The
George Bernard Shaw
Melodrama 3 Acts
New York 1897

Dick Dudgeon, an arrogant womanizer, returns home to New Hampshire in 1777 to hear his father's will read. His pious, sanctimonious mother is outraged when it transpires that he, a self-confessed 'devil's disciple', is to be the heir.

The local minister, sympathetic Anthony Anderson, invites Dick to his house, and so great is the impression that he makes on the profligate, that when British troops come to arrest Anderson in his absence, Dick willingly takes his place. This act of heroism makes Judith, the minister's wife, fall in love with Dick, but when he is sentenced to death for her husband's revolutionary activities, she has to reveal his identity. This makes no difference to the verdict and as Dick is about to be hanged, Anderson, now a dedicated soldier and man of action, appears to rescue him.

Dick, destined for the church, promises Judith, who is reunited with the hero Anderson, that he will never reveal the secret of their romance.

Anthony Anderson
Judith Anderson
Richard Dudgeon
Mrs Timothy (Annie) Dudgeon
Christopher Dudgeon
Uncle William Dudgeon
Uncle Titus Dudgeon
Essie
Lawyer Hawkins
Gen. John Burgoyne
Maj. Swindon
Revd Mr Brudenell
A sergeant
Mrs William Dudgeon
Mrs Titus Dudgeon
Soldiers
Officers, townspeople

Devils, The
John Whiting adapted from the book
by Aldous Huxley
Drama 3 Acts
London 1961

In seventeenth-century France, a handsome, urbane and sensuous priest, Urbain Grandier, has found God through his own deliberate self-destruction in lust, hate and vanity.

He is invited by prioress Sister Jeanne to become spiritual adviser to a convent and when he declines, the hunchbacked prioress and the nuns, who all have carnal desires for him, become possessed by devils. Their exorcism is followed by Grandier being implicated. He has many enemies in and outside the church, and he is condemned and sentenced for introducing the devils. After horrible torture and mutilation he is dragged off

to the stake where Jeanne sees for the first time the man that the lustful nuns have always talked about. As his beautiful body is torn apart by the mob to use as love charms, Jeanne can only cry out for him.

Mannoury, a surgeon
Adam, a chemist
Louis Trincant, the public prosecutor
Phillipe Trincant
Jean D'Armagnac, Governor of Loudon
Guillaume de Cerisay, the chief magistrate
A sewerman
Urbain Grandier, vicar of St Peter's Church
Ninon, a widow
De La Rochepozay, bishop of Poitiers
Father Rangier
Father Barré
Sister Jeanne of the Angels, prioress of St Ursula's Convent
Sister Claire
Sister Louise
De Laubardemont, the King's special commissioner
Father Mignon
Sister Gabrielle
Prince Henri de Condé
Richelieu
Louis XIII, king of France
Bontemps, a gaoler
Father Ambrose
A clerk
Townspeople
People from the country
Capuchins
Carmelites
Jesuits
Soldiers

Dial M for Murder
Frederick Knott
Melodrama 3 Acts
London and New York 1952

In London 1952, Sheila is married to ex-tennis-star Tony, now a sporting goods salesman. She is visited by former lover Max who has been away for a year in New York writing TV murder mysteries. The threesome are going to the theatre but Tony, who is thought to know nothing of the affair, says they will have to go without him because he has a business report to write.

When they have gone, Tony calls 'Captain' Lesgate, once a thieving schoolfellow and now a fully-fledged conman, on the pretext of buying a car, but goes on to explain that he really wants Sheila killed. He knows all about her affair because he found a letter from Max in Sheila's handbag. Besides, her will is in his favour and that is why he married her.

With a combination of offered payment and threatened blackmail, Lesgate is persuaded to break in, while Tony is out with Max with a cast-iron alibi, and strangle Sheila. The plan goes wrong and Sheila stabs

Lesgate to death. Fairly ingeniously, Tony attempts to turn this to advantage by making it look as though Sheila had murdered a blackmailer and so Sheila is condemned to hang. However, thanks to the dogged cunning of Inspector Hubbard, and murder story experience of Max, justice prevails.

Sheila Wendice
Max Halliday
Tony Wendice
Capt. Lesgate
Inspector Hubbard
(A walk-on and voice-off detective)

Diary of Anne Frank, The
Frances Goodritch and Albert Hackett
Drama 2 Acts
London 1956

Jewish refugees Anne Frank and her family, the Van Daan family and dentist Dussel are in hiding from the Germans who have just invaded Holland. They all live in three cramped rooms and a tiny attic and every day Miep and Kraler (who own the office downstairs) visit them with news and food. Lots of arguments occur, especially between Mr and Mrs Van Daan and Anne and her mother. The arguments always end with Mr Frank calming everyone down. Members of the hideaway household react differently to their individual sufferings; Margot Frank and Dussel retreat into themselves, while Anne and Mr Frank still need to feel very much alive, and later Anne and Peter Van Daan (the son) become very close.

Finally the Germans find them. They have been betrayed by a thief who thought he could avoid prosecution if he told the soldiers where the Jews were hiding. The ending is a meeting between Miep, Kraler and Mr Frank a year later. Mr Frank is the only member of the families to have survived.

Mr Frank
Miep Giles
Mrs Van Daan
Mr Van Daan
Mrs Frank
Margot Frank
Anne Frank
Mr Kraler
Mr Dussel
Peter Van Daan

Dining Room, The
A. R. Gurney Jnr
Play 2 Acts
New York 1981

A large dining room (representing many dining rooms) is the set for a series of around twenty disconnected vignettes flowing one into another, mercilessly exposing the foibles of the characters and the ironies of each situation. The various slices of life are affected by the dining room itself - its shape, function, history - and the very brevity of each scene is tantalizing.

Parents bully, scold, blackmail and patronize their children, affairs are arranged or disarranged, old people go sadly mad or distribute welcome largesse, relatives squabble, teenagers take advantage, fathers defend the family honour, and so on.

The play is designed to be performed by three actors and three actresses each playing about ten characters and the action takes place during the course of a day.

Dinner at Eight
George S. Kaufman and Edna Ferber
Drama 3 Acts
New York 1933

Vapid New York socialite Millicent Jordan is planning a small (ten-strong) dinner party with guest attractions Lord and Lady Ferncliffe. She asks her husband, nice (but secretly ill) shipping line owner Oliver to invite his old flame, flamboyant actress star Carlotta Vance, but he then insists they also invite hard-nosed tycoon Dan Packard and his fluffy wife Kitty. Oliver is hoping Packard will bail him out of temporary problems, but the unscrupulous Dan plans to take over Oliver's firm.

Other guests include Millicent's 'poor' elder sister, sensible Hattie and her husband Ed, and also capable but philandering Dr Talbot (who is having an affair with Kitty Packard) and his long-suffering wife Lucy. There is an odd man to balance Carlotta, handsome has-been movie star Larry Renault, who is having a secret affair with Oliver and Millie's daughter Paula, engaged to (unseen) Ernest.

On party night, things go wrong. Severe disturbances among jealous domestics lead to a change in the menu; then the Ferncliffes decide not to come, forsaking the Jordans for Florida. Packard and Kitty meanwhile have had a horrific row and she threatened to scupper his political ambitions by revealing his dirty business tricks - nevertheless they go to the party. Back at his hotel, drunk and humiliated, Larry hits rock bottom and gasses himself. Paula stops off at the party on the way out to a date with Ernest, hoping to glimpse Larry, but in vain. Unknown to everyone except Dr Talbot, Oliver has a serious heart condition and will shortly die.

Millicent Jordan　　*The waiter*
Dora　　　　　　　*Max Kane*
Gustave　　　　　 *Mr Hatfield*
Oliver Jordan　　　*Miss Alden*
Paula Jordan　　　*Lucy Talbot*
Ricci　　　　　　 *Mrs Wendel*
Hattie Loomis　　 *Jo Stengel*
Miss Copeland　　 *Mr Fitch*
Carlotta Vance　　*Ed Loomis*
Dan Packard
Kitty Packard
Tina
Dr J. Wayne Talbot
Larry Renault
The bell boy

Dirty Hands or Crime Passionel
Jean-Paul Sartre
Drama 7 Scenes
Paris 1948

In the imaginary Balkan State of Illyria, political gunmen come looking for Hugo Barine, a young intellectual, just released from prison, but his former girlfriend, Olga, pleads for time to find out his motives for having assassinated a party leader.

Two years earlier, Hugo has become involved in a plot to kill the politician, Hoederer, and has infiltrated his office by becoming his secretary. Jessica, his wife, doubts his capacity for killing and flirts with Hoederer. Hugo's first attempt to kill Hoederer is foiled by a bomb being thrown into the office, which Hoederer survives, and gradually the politician's polemic begins to make Hugo question his ideas about political compromise. He tries assassination again, but fails, and only succeeds when he finds his wife in the arms of the man he now admires and shoots him. Hoederer saves him by telling the guards that it was a 'crime passionnel', and two years later Hugo is still unsure of his motives for killing him, in spite of the Party having discredited Hoederer and claiming that they executed him.

Hugo
Jessica, his wife
Hoederer, Party leader
Georges, Leon, Slick, his bodyguards
Members of Proletarian Party: *Louis, Franz,*
  Charles, Ivan, Olga, Prince Paul and
  Karsky

Dirty Linen and New-Found-Land
Tom Stoppard
Comedy 3 Scenes
London 1976

In a House of Commons meeting room in the tower of Big Ben a Parliamentary Committee is discussing Moral Standards in Public Life. The dignitaries are mostly concerned with the many fancy eating-places they frequent and the voluptuous company they keep and with the salacious prying of the popular press. Taking notes for them is Maddie Gotobed, who has difficulty keeping her clothes on and is herself not only a glamorous 'Page 3' girl and courtesan but rather smarter than the absurdly waffling MPs. It is she who tries to wise them up about the antics of journalists and the attitude of the public. In the end the committee finds no evidence of laws broken or harm done and winds itself up.

Dirty Linen started as Tom Stoppard's celebration of the British naturalization of Ed Berman (an American theatre writer, director, performer and organizer of projects) but the play took a different direction so Stoppard inserted a scene, set in the same room as *Dirty Linen* while the others are temporarily absent, in which two Home Office officials discuss an American's application for citizenship. One tells an old joke about how he won a bet with Lloyd George; the other delivers a eulogy on the United States.

Maddie
Cocklebury-Smythe MP
McTeazle MP
Chamberlain MP
Withenshaw MP, Chairman
Mrs Ebury MP
French MP
Home Secretary
Arthur, Junior Home Office Official
Bernard, Senior Home Office Official

Dock Brief, The
John Mortimer
Comedy 2 Acts
London 1958

Hard-up, bumbling, elderly barrister Morgenhall is selected at random from the dock by accused wife-murderer Fowle to represent him. In Fowle's cell the two fools have a series of laughable but plausible misunderstandings about how to defend Fowle from a charge to which he cheerfully seems to want to plead guilty. It takes time for Morgenhall to grasp Fowle's murder motive, which was not because of his wife's infidelity with the lodger but because she has turfed the amorous man out for trying to get too physically intimate. Fowle had wanted his relentlessly cheerful wife taken off his hands.

Morgenhall is mortified when his bungling loses the case, yet the tactic is a success because the sentence is quashed on the grounds of inadequate defence. Fowle is a free man and the relieved Morgenhall, having pointed out that his client, as a man of low education and intellect and high criminal profile, is bound to get into more scrapes, tags along as permanent legal adviser.

Morgenhall
Fowle

Doctor Faustus
Christopher Marlowe
Tragedy 5 Acts
London 1592

Magic, declares Faustus, has ravished him, and by using magic he sets out to fulfil his every longing. His blaspheming summons up Mephistopheles, Lucifer's henchman, and they contract a pact in blood stating that for four-and-twenty years Faustus shall be granted his every desire. At the end of that time, his body and soul will be Lucifer's for all eternity.

Faustus, ever the proud intellectual, first satisfies his cravings for knowledge, seeing from great heights the wonders and workings of the universe. He then plays unholy pranks teasing and tormenting the Pope, freeing heretic pope Bruno and returning with him to Germany.

There he is fêted by Emperor Charles V, and with a terrible vengeance defeats a plot against his life. Various hangers-on suffer or are rewarded by Faustus for their appropriate deeds, and always he is urged to repent, either by angels, or an old man. Always he refuses.

When his time is nearly done, Faustus begins to realize what a terrifying bargain he has made; he conjures up Helen of Troy, the most beautiful woman in the world, and in her arms tries to forget his fate. But the pact cannot be denied and Lucifer finally comes to claim Faustus, first tearing his body limb from limb and then casting his soul into eternal damnation.

Chorus
Dr John Faustus
Wagner, his servant, a student
Valdes, his friend, magician
Cornelius, his friend, magician
Three scholars, students under Faustus
An old man
Pope Adrian
Raymond, the King of Hungary
Bruno, the rival Pope
Cardinals of France and Padua
Archbishop of Rheims
Charles V, Emperor of Germany
Martino, Frederick, Benvolio, knights at the
Emperor's court
Duke of Saxony
Duke of Vanholt
Duchess of Vanholt
Robin, also called the Clown
Dick
A vintner
Carter
A Horse-courser
The hostess at an inn
The good angel
The bad angel
Mephistopheles
Lucifer
Belzebub
Spirits representing: The Seven Deadly Sins,
 Alexander The Great, Alexander's Paramour,
 Darius King of Persia, Helen of Troy,
 Devils, Bishops, Monks, Soldiers and Attendants

Doctor in the House
Ted Willis adapted from the book
by Richard Gordon
Comedy 3 Acts
London 1956
Callow medical student Simon arrives for a night at temporary lodgings, but when his uncle arrives (bluff and fearsome Sir Lancelot, head of the medical school), he insists that the other students shuffle around to make permanent room for his nephew. Simon is soon initiated into zany student ways by wildly demonstrative fellow-student Tony and his friend John. Vera, Tony's spirited

and beautiful girlfriend, adds spice to the proceedings and before long Simon's priorities begin to include getting drunk, the obligatory rugger (for the medical school team) and, of course, pulling the birds.

Various zany pranks are aided and abetted by hospital porter Bromley and nurse Riggie (Rigor Mortis), while battleaxe Matron lurks to prevent liaisons with her nurses. But when Matron's niece, nurse Janet, railroads Simon into prospective wedlock and Matron begins taking over Simon's life, the others realize something must be done. With the help of Sir Lancelot (who dreads the prospect of Matron in the family), the boys, Bromley and Vera gang up and cunningly blacken poor Janet's reputation, thus getting Simon off the hook. They then finally settle down to study for their forthcoming exams.

Tony Grimsdyke	Sir Lancelot Spratt
Simon Sparrow	Miss Winslow (Riggie)
John Evans	The Matron
Vera	Janet
Bromley	

Doctor Knock
Jules Romains
Comedy 3 Acts
Paris 1923
Ambitious and assertive young Dr Knock arrives in a small mountain town in France in the early 1920s to buy the practice of the easy-going Dr Parpalaid. He is anxious to know the state of health of the local populace and is dismayed to learn that they are all in good health; his experiences travelling as a ship's doctor have made him acutely aware of the hidden dangers of disease.

Knock soon sets about enlisting the aid of the local pharmacist, whose trade is slow, and the schoolmaster, to make the townspeople aware that they are suffering from a galaxy of hidden complaints for which he has the cures. He advertises his services via the town crier and soon patients are queuing up for his help, so much so that he has to convert the local hotel into a clinic. The town is now a haven for every hypochondriac for miles around. Dr Knock is a rich and influential saviour.

Dr Parpalaid returns to the town, highly suspicious of the situation, but he soon defers to the silk-tongued Knock and himself becomes a patient in the ever expanding clinic.

Dr Knock	Mme Pons, landowner
Dr Parpalaid	Farmer's wife
Mme Parpalaid	Nurse
M . Mosquet, a	Jean
pharmacist	Locals
M Bernard, a	
schoolmaster	
Town crier	
Scipio, hotel clerk	
Mme Remy, hotel	
keeper	

Doctor's Dilemma, The
George Bernard Shaw
Drama 5 Acts
London 1906

In London, 1903, Jennifer Dubedat's husband Louis, a talented artist, is dying of consumption but she succeeds in convincing prominent medical researcher Sir Colenso Ridgeon to see him.

Although possessing great personal charm, Dubedat is discovered to be a scoundrel, having had affairs and borrowed money from several innocent victims. Ridgeon, who is more than interested in the beautiful Jennifer, declines to take Louis as a patient, preferring to treat a fellow doctor, worthy Blenkinsop, and so he hands the case over to a colleague, Sir Ralph Bloomfield Bonnington.

Improper administration of a new inoculation results in Louis' demise in his studio where he declaims his views on beauty and art. Blenkinsop meanwhile, recovers under Ridgeon's care.

Jennifer writes a biography of Louis and an exhibition of his work is organized at which Ridgeon admits to her that he deliberately neglected Dubedat because he loves, and wants to marry her. She chastizes him for such heartless behaviour and informs him that she has already remarried in accordance with Louis' last wishes.

Redpenny	Dr Blenkinsop
Emmy	Jennifer Dubedat
Sir Colenso Ridgeon	Louis Dubedat
Leo Schutzmacher	Minnie Tinwell
Sir Patrick Cullen	A waiter
Cutler Walpole	Newspaper man
Sir Ralph Bloomfield	Mr Danby
Bonnington	

Doll's House, A
Henrik Ibsen
Drama 3 Acts
Copenhagen 1879

In the Norway of the late 1870s Nora Helmer, a beautiful young mother of two, is a precious unworldly plaything for her lawyer husband, Torvald. Childish and immature, she has in the past been foolish enough to sign her father's name on a note to obtain money for Torvald to take a trip to Italy for his health. Although she works secretly to pay off the debt, the incriminating note is held by Nils Krogstad, who has just been sacked by her husband as dishonest. Krogstad threatens to expose her unless she uses her influence to have him reinstated. Nora is under the delusion that her husband will understand her 'crime' was an act of love for his welfare, but upon hearing about the deed he reacts with panic stricken selfishness and only relents his attitude to her when Krogstad has a change of heart and returns the forged IOU.

Totally disheartened by her husband's cowardly and hypocritical stance she refuses to forgive him, realizing that she has been no more than an amusing doll in his house. She takes her children and leaves to find her own way to maturity.

Torvald Helmer
Nora Helmer
Dr Rank
Nils Krogstad
Mrs Linde
Helmer's children
Anna Maria
Housemaid
Porter

Don Juan
Molière
Drama 5 Acts
Paris 1665

Womanizer Don Juan is a walking scandal, having just forsaken his wife Elvira (whom he recently lured from a convent) is in pursuit of a girl he intends to kidnap. This adventure misfires, but gives him the opportunity to try to seduce peasant girl Charlotte. His valet Sganarelle constantly upbraids his master and warns him of divine retribution, but shameless Don Juan ignores him; he is a man who gratifies his sensual appetites to the exclusion of all else.

Further adventures include playing off fiancées Charlotte and Mathurine against each other, and avoiding Elvira's family who are out for revenge. This is eased when Don Juan, superficially ever a gentleman, saves Elvira's brother Don Carlos from a band of robbers. Don Carlos must, of course, repay the debt. Don Juan decides the answer to his problems is to pretend to reform in order to pursue his schemes under a cloak of respectability, horrifying Sganarelle even more.

Finally, the statue of the Commander, a man Don Juan killed, comes to life and asks him to dinner, giving him a last chance to repent. Don Juan refuses, the earth opens up and he goes to Hell, leaving Sganarelle moaning that now everyone, God, husbands, women, family and parents, are satisfied. All except for him: 'My wages, my wages', he cries.

Don Juan	Ragotin, Don Juan's
Sganarelle	servant
Elvira	Mr Dimanche, a
Guzman, Elvira's squire	tradesman
Don Carlos, Elvira's	La Ramee, a swordsman
brother	A beggar
Don Alonso, Elvira's	A ghost
brother	Followers
Don Louis, Don Juan's	
father	
Charlotte	
Mathurine	
Pierrot	
The statue	
La Violette, Don Juan's	
servant	

Don't Drink the Water
Woody Allen
Comedy 2 Acts
New York 1966

An American embassy somewhere behind the Iron Curtain. Father Drobney - an eccentric priest and amateur magician - sets the scene, explaining that six years ago he sought sanctuary there from the four million or so communists who wouldn't mind killing him. He is safe in the embassy but outside, to survive, he'd have to attempt the biggest mass conversion in history. The wise and incisive ambassador James F. Magee enters, looks out the window and sums up the situation brilliantly; 'Jesus, look at all those communists!' Kilroy is his efficient assistant but there is also another assistant - his son Alex Magee who has left a trail of diplomatic disasters around the world. The ambassador wants to go home for a while to discuss the possibility of becoming a State governor and is apprehensive about leaving young Magee in charge, especially as an important guest, the Sultan of Bashir, is due to come and negotiate an important oil deal.

As soon as the ambassador has gone, three tourists come running into the Embassy hotly pursued by the brutal secret police head Krojack and his henchmen. Loudly dressed Walter Hollander is a caterer - the first to make bridegroom-shaped potato salad - from Newark, New Jersey. He'd wanted to vacation as usual at Atlantic Beach, but no, wife Marion's brother had recommended this 'commie hell'. With them is their lovely daughter Susan and Embassy Assistant Kilroy wants them for spying - taking tourist snaps. Actually the communists want them as hostages to get back one of their men, arrested in the States as a real spy, The Gray Fox. Krojack has to take over and try to restore order especially after the Sultan (with one wife) turns up and is systematically insulted by Walter. Susan and Magee fall in love. It turns out that the Gray Fox has committed suicide. Father Drobney tries to cheer them up with conjuring tricks and only just manages to rescue one of his props - a pet rabbit - from the embassy chef. The tourists disguise themselves as Arabs and Walter is foolishly entrusted with a gun and starts talking of Allah, the desert and camels. The priest marries the lovers and the Hollanders make it back to Newark.

Father Drobney
Ambassador James F.
  Magee
Kilroy
Axel Magee
Marion Hollander
Walter Hollander
Susan Hollander
Krojack
Burns
Chef
The Sultan of Bashir
Sultan's first wife

Kasnar
Countess Bordoni
Novotny

Don't Just Lie There, Say Something
Michael Pertwee
Farce 2 Acts
London 1971

Sir William Mainwaring-Brown MP, Minister of State for Home Affairs, is the reluctant standard-bearer of the latest campaign against permissiveness. Naturally his own life must be unblemished, and he is being dogged by old duffer Wilfred Potts MP, Father of the House, hoping to discredit him and the government. When Sir William's aide Barry Ovis disappears, Potts smells scandal and arrives at Sir William's London flat. So do many others. Ovis reappears, pursued by the police who are unaware of his identity. He was drugged and abducted by hippies and taken to an orgy. He is now with hippie Davina who aims to take photos of the Minister's indiscretions. Sir William has a mistress, Wendy, who comes and goes and comes again, and he also makes a play for his formerly frosty secretary Miss Parkyn, who turns out to be quite a dish. Also in the house is his secretary Jean Fenton, and bemused Inspector Ruff. Everyone becomes variously involved in a series of false identities, hiding in or under the bed in various combinations, zipped to one another, and with the usual quota of misunderstandings and innuendos lubricating the high-speed action. Eventually Barry Ovis is cleared of misbehaviour, naughty Davina turns out to be Potts' granddaughter (so he has to shut up), but just as everything is sorting itself out, Sir William's wife arrives and everybody hides in the bed.

Barry Ovis MP
Rt Hon. Wilfred Potts MP
Jean Fenton
Sir William Mainwaring-Brown
Gisele Parkyn
Inspector Ruff
Davina
Wendy
A caretaker

Donkey's Years
Michael Frayn
Comedy 3 Acts
London 1976

Everything is set for a convivial old boys' reunion in one of the lesser colleges in one of the older universities. Now in their forties, the gang includes government minister Headingly, top surgeon Buckley, and notoriously camp Sainsbury, now a Reverend. They are greeted by young lecturer Taylor and magistrate Lady Driver, the Master's wife, who once attended the college and consorted with some of the old boys. She, however, is looking for her lost love, the absent wild man Roddy Moore. When she shortsightedly enters his old room expecting him there, she finds it occupied by Snell, a nondescript old boy who always boarded out and is now determined to revenge himself for missing out on the japes, pranks and general undergraduate flavour of university life.

The men become increasingly drunk and disorderly and Snell becomes increasingly crazy, even asking Taylor for a mature studentship, which the others urge him to grant in order to quieten Snell. Eventually Snell goes berserk and has to be calmed down and led away to a mental hospital. The other old boys pick up their pieces and leave, Buckley even managing to arrange a tryst with Lady Driver.

Mr S. Birkett
C. D. P. B. Headingly MA MP
D. J. Buckle MB FRCS
K. Snell MA
A. V. Quine BA
The Revd R. D. Sainsbury MA
N. O. P. Tate MA
W. R. Taylor MA PhD
Lady Driver MA

Double Exposure
Jack Sharkey
Comedy 3 Acts
New York 1978

At the swank Los Angeles home of Jed Jericho, Hollywood's greatest tough-guy actor, his day starts in the usual way - trying to recover from a hangover - but that evening, it is Academy Award time and Jed has been nominated for an Oscar for his starring role in *The Invincible Man*. His agent Archie calls round to make sure Jed will be in shape for the ceremony. But the pair have a secret: Jed is also the nation's top writer for young children, Jamie Weems. What is alarming is that Dolly Holiday, Jamie's publisher who has never met Jamie/Jed but used to adore Jed's early films (until he became such a foul-mouthed brute), is flying in from New York to get him to sign a contract with the Disney studio for an animated version of *Melvin the Moose*. Jed's macho image will be destroyed if his public discovers he writes children's books. Dolly will be outraged if she finds out that her author is the hideous killer/seducer of Tinsel Town. Archie is the agent of both Jed and Jamie.

Bessie, Jed's competent housekeeper, is a Jamie Weems reader but is not in on the secret. Valery, Jed's gorgeous dumb blonde actress fiancée, has been since childhood (not yet ended at twenty-five) a Jamie Weems devotee but it is Jed she loves.

Sidney is a messenger for Palatial Pictures and he arrives with a renewal contract for Jed to sign. They persuade Sidney to pretend to be Jamie, and Val pretends to believe that he is, although secretly she knows him from the studio.

Studio head Morgan Kreisler turns up on the way to the Academy Awards and tells Archie he will top Disney's offer. Jed fears he has lost Valery to 'Jamie' (Sidney) and she goes off to the Awards in Sidney's newly acquired hearse. He confesses to her and Bessie that he is Jamie Weems. Since Valery and Sidney are

getting on so well together, Jed is off the hook and he and Dolly are free to tumble into the sack.

Jed Jericho
Archy Feldon
Dolly Holiday
Valery Castle
Bessie Clark
Sidney Bascomb
Morgan Kreisler

Dr Jekyll and Mr Hyde
Thomas Russell Sullivan from the book by Robert Louis Stevenson
Drama 3 Acts
London 1888

In Victorian London a mysterious and brutal Mr Edward Hyde seems to have a hold over respectable Dr Henry Jekyll, who has lately been involved with some strange research. Jekyll assures his friends that he can handle Hyde until the brute murders the vicar father of his admirer Alice. Hyde is, of course, the evil other half of Jekyll and the gentle doctor now has a desperate struggle to rid himself of his satanic alter ego, which is proving difficult because of a fault in his scientific experiments.

Jekyll reveals his dilemma to colleague Dr Lanyon, who dies of shock after a demonstration of 'transcendental medicine', but he leaves a letter for Utterson, a lawyer friend, to be opened only in the event of Jekyll's demise.

Alice and Utterson go to Jekyll's laboratory on an urgent call from Poole, his faithful servant, and from behind a closed door they hear the desperate struggle for survival which only Jekyll or Hyde can win.

Dr Henry Jekyll
Edward Hyde
Revd Edward Leigh
Alice Leigh, his daughter
Dr Lanyon, a friend of Dr Jekyll
Mr Utterson, a lawyer
Pauline, Dr Jekyll's housekeeper
Bridget, his cook
Connie, a maid-servant
Richard Enfield, Utterson's cousin
Inspector Newcomen, a Scotland Yard policeman

Dream Play, A
August Strindberg
Fantasy
Stockholm 1907

Against a cosmic background of the constellations of Leo, Virgo and Libra and the shining planet Jupiter, Indra is explaining to her daughter that she has lost her way, has left the second world and entered the third among banks of clouds, ruined castles and fortresses. Then there is a forest of giant hollyhocks in bloom and above them the gilded roof of a castle which is rising from the earth. An officer sits in a room wearing a modern uniform. A woman, the mother, is also there, and ill. The backcloth is raised to reveal a stage door keeper and a bill-poster. There is a door with clover-shaped holes. The officer does not know where it leads. The officer ages, with grey hair and dilapidated clothes. A lady ballet dancer enters, a locksmith is sent for to open the door but a glazier comes instead. A policeman comes to forbid the opening of the door. The officer goes to an advocate's office to see how the law stands on this. The advocate's office turns into a church where doctors' degrees are being conferred. The church organ turns into Fingal's Cave. The scene changes to a beach where the Quarantine Master is walking dressed as a blackamoor. The officer had hoped they had arrived at Fairhaven but no, this is Foulstrand. An old dandy is wheeled on by a sixty-year-old coquette and her male 'friend'. There is cholera about. A white boat shaped like a dragon with a sail of light blue silk on a golden yard and a gilded mast with a rose-red pennant glides across the water and is greeted by the flags and jetties of Fairhaven where white handkerchiefs wave from the villas and beaches and harps and violins are heard across the water. The landscape turns to winter with snow on the ground and leafless trees. There is dancing and comical instruction from a schoolmaster. A much-envied blind man who owns the whole area is led on. The ship glides away. The daughter thinks she has been dreaming but a poet tells her he scripted it.

At the end, the castle burns showing a wall of human faces, enquiring, grieving, despairing. A big bud on the roof bursts open into a giant chrysanthemum.

Indra	A newly-married husband
Indra's daughter	A newly-married wife
Agnes	The blind man
The glazier	First coal-carrier
The officer	Second coal-carrier
His father	A gentleman
His mother	His wife
Lina	The Chancellor
The stagedoor keeper	Dean of Theology
A ballet dancer	Dean of Philosophy
A singer	Dean of Medicine
A prompter	Dean of Law
A policeman	Dancers
The advocate	Singers
Kristin	Clerks
The quarantine master	Children
A dandy	Schoolboys
A coquette	Sailors
Her 'friend'	
The poet	
He	
She	
A pensioner	
Edith	
Edith's mother	
A naval officer	
Alice	
The schoolmaster	

Dresser, The
Ronald Harwood
Drama 2 Acts
Manchester 1980

When exhausted actor-manager 'Sir' has a nervous breakdown in the street of an English provincial town during wartime, his camp dresser Norman leads him to hospital. That evening her Ladyship - Sir's wife - and faithful company stage-manager Madge prepare to cancel the performance, but Sir returns and Norman has to prepare him for *Lear* in thirty minutes. As Norman coaxes, cajoles, strokes and whines, their relationship is revealed as complex, affectionate and symbolic. Sir, paranoid, forgetful but still masterful, eventually goes on after inventive ad-libbing by the cast and gives a breathtakingly dynamic performance, followed by a movingly patriotic invocation. Back in the dressing room he shows Norman the dedications prefacing his unwritten autobiography, and as Norman reads it, upset that he has been left out, Sir dies. Norman, bitter and devasted after years of selfless service to the man he loved, finally asks, 'What about me?'

Norman
Her Ladyship
Madge
Sir
Irene
Geoffrey Thornton
Mr Oxenby

Dry Rot
John Chapman
Farce 3 Acts
London 1954

Having just taken over the Bull and Cow, a country hotel, Col and Mrs Wagstaff and daughter Susan are awaiting their first guests, impeded somewhat by tetchy hotel maid Beth who came with the property. When ex-public schoolboy John Danby arrives to await his future employer Alf Tubbe (to whom he has been hired as secretary) there is immediate mutual attraction between him and Susan. Tubbe soon arrives with 'valet' Fred Phipps; in fact 'Honest Alf' is a crooked bookmaker and Fred is his runner. The 'valet' pose and the hiring of (innocent) secretary Danby is a feeble attempt at putting up a respectable front to conceal Tubbe's plan to fix the nearby Selsdon Cup horse race the following day. He plans to swap the favourite Cardinal for a doped nag.

Accomplice Flash Harry arrives with the substitute horse Sweet Lavender, and the crooks find a secret panel in the hotel enabling them to keep in contact with Harry while he stays with the horse in the vaults below. Subterfuges, misunderstandings, drunken and romantic encounters proliferate, the dry rot on the stairs being a constant danger to life and limb. When Harry gives Sweet Lavender so much dope it can hardly stand, a new plan is hatched involving recently arrived hotel guest French jockey Polignac, due to ride Cardinal in the big race. Next morning Polignac is clobbered and Fred substituted as Cardinal's jockey. Unfortunately for Tubbe, Cardinal still wins and helpless Fred gallops back to the hotel chased by the police. The crooks quickly substitute still-dazed Polignac and hand him over to the police. They then begin to cook up another scheme - involving Fred and a rigged boxing match.

Col Wagstaff
Mrs Wagstaff
Beth
Susan Wagstaff
John Danby
Fred Phipps
Alfred Tubbe
Flash Harry
Albert Polignac
Sergeant Fire

Duchess of Malfi, The
John Webster
Tragedy 5 Acts
London 1612

Evil Ferdinand, Duke of Calabria, and his corrupt brother the Cardinal, are intent - for diverse reasons - on their beautiful young widowed sister the Duchess of Malfi remaining chaste. Ferdinand plants Bosola, a soldier once imprisoned for murder, into her household as an informer. The Duchess falls in love with her steward Antonio and they secretly wed, and later Bosola realizes that the Duchess is pregnant. He ingratiates himself with her and she reveals her secrets, and when he informs her brothers, Ferdinand flies into a frenzy.

The Duchess decides to flee, pretending she is going on a pilgrimage, but is arrested by Ferdinand who imprisons and torments her before having her and two of her children murdered. When Bosola does not receive his due reward he turns against the brothers and vows to aid Antonio; meanwhile Ferdinand has turned into a werewolf, and the Cardinal's mistress has fallen in love with Bosola. Agony piles upon agony as the Cardinal poisons Julia, Bosola accidentally kills Antonio and is himself killed after slaying the Cardinal and werewolf Ferdinand. Only the Duchess' eldest son survives, now in the care of Antonio's faithful friend Delio.

Bosola, a gentleman of	*The Duchess of Malfi*
the horse	*Cariola, her woman*
Ferdinand	*Julia, wife to Castruchio*
Cardinal	*The doctor*
Antonio	*Court officers*
Delio	***The several mad men***
Forobosco	***including:*** *astrologer,*
Malateste, a count	*tailor, priest, doctor*
The Marquis of Pescara	*Old lady*
Silvio, a lord	*Three young children*
Castruchio, an old lord	*Two pilgrims*
Roderigo, a lord	*Attendants*
Grisolan, a lord	*Ladies, executioners*

Duet for One
Tom Kempinski
Drama 2 Acts
London 1980

This paean to psychiatry takes place in Dr Feldmann's consulting room in London where he is visited by Stephanie Abrahams, an eminent violinist being progressively disabled by multiple sclerosis. She is there somewhat reluctantly at the suggestion of her husband David, a musician and composer, and she tells Feldmann she believes there is little he can do. She more or less implies she is there under sufferance and already knows what is best for herself. Her plans have already been made - she intends to teach and to become her husband's secretary. She does admit to feeling low, and Feldmann prescribes her a course of anti-depressants. As their meetings progress, Feldmann's quiet, patient questioning and probing begin to reveal the hidden despair being masked by Stephanie's 'sensible' plans.

The disease and the sessions continue and inexorably everything of value to Stephanie is destroyed or threatened. Her music, the source of her great strength, is taken away, and her marriage becomes threatened. As she deteriorates, her attacks on Feldmann become more and more vitriolic. She is increasingly self-destructive and the psychiatrist is forced to use a variety of tactics to help save her. Her terrible anger and self-pity lead her in the final session to complete abandonment, and she tells Feldmann that he has her thanks, but it is useless and she is giving up treatment. His support is total and unconditional, though; he asks if the same time next week will be convenient.

Stephanie Abrahams
Dr Alfred Feldmann

Dumb Waiter, The
Harold Pinter
Comedy Mystery
London 1960

A dingy basement room with (off) a kitchen and a toilet with a deficient cistern that rarely flushes. There is a closed serving hatch between two beds. Dimwit Ben is on one, oaf Gus is on the other. They are killing time, Ben reading odd bits out of the newspaper. They make small talk about tea, food and soccer, speculate about the place they're in, what the 'upcoming assignment' is, and when - if at all - Wilson will be along to fill them in. An envelope is slid under the door but there is nothing in it. Gus gets a revolver from under a pillow, opens the door and looks out. Nobody there.

After a while there is a clattering behind the serving hatch. Gus and Ben grab their revolvers but it is only a 'dumb waiter', a box held by pulleys. There is a piece of paper ordering two braised steak and chips, two sago puddings, and two teas without sugar. A succession of orders requiring various dishes, none of which they can provide, so they send what they can, such as crisps, biscuits and an Eccles cake.

Gus discovers a speaking tube which he uses to apologize to whoever is upstairs that they haven't anything left. He listens and then apologizes for the food they'd sent up being defective.

They rehearse how they're going to handle the job: they are hit men. They quarrel. The whistle blows in the speaking tube. Ben answers and receives some instruction about a man about to come in; the normal method to be employed. But Gus has gone outside to get a glass of water. Ben calls for Gus who staggers back into the room stripped of his jacket, waistcoat, tie, holster and revolver. He raises his head and they stare at each other for a long time in silence.

Ben
Gus

Dybbuk, The
S. Ansky
Drama 4 Acts
Warsaw 1920

In a Jewish Chassidic community in Eastern Europe around the turn of the century, old and young scholars pray, chant and debate, but young Channon's aesthetic fire burns higher and brighter. He despises the 'cold and dry' Talmud and studies the Kabala with its dangerous flights into the highest realms. His love is Leah, Sender's daughter, and Channon's agitation increases when she enters the Synagogue and kisses the Holy Scrolls. He sings the Song of Songs and determines ever more spiritual purification, but when he hears that Sender has betrothed Leah to another he falls down and dies.

At Leah's wedding she becomes possessed of a dybbuk - a spirit of the discontented dead inhabiting a living body. It is the spirit of Channon. Rabbi Azrael discovers that Channon's dead father Nissin ben Rifke has a grudge against Sender, and a trial between the living and the dead father is arranged. The dead man is summoned back and his grievance heard. It seems that he and Sender promised their children to one another in marriage and Sender went back on the promise. The dybbuk refuses to leave Leah and has to be exorcized, but upon leaving her body, Channon returns to her soul. Leah joins her predestined bridegroom to be united with Channon forever, soaring upward together higher and higher.

Scholars in the Synagogue
Three Batlonim
The messenger
Meyer the Shamas, Beadle of the Synagogue
An elderly woman with two children
Channon, a young scholar
Chennoch, a young scholar
Leah
Frade, her old nurse
Gittel, her companion
Asher
Sender

A wedding guest
A beggar woman with a child
A lame beggar
A hunchback
Bassia, a friend of Leah's
Nachmon, the bridegroom's father
Rabbi Mendel, of the bridegroom's party
Menashe, the bridegroom
A beggar man on crutches
A blind beggar
A tall pale beggar woman
First Chassid
Second Chassid
Third Chassid
Rabbi Azrael
The Rabbi of Miropol
Michoel, the Rabbi of Miropol's attendant
A Minyen
Rabbi Samson, the city rabbi

Eagle Has Two Heads, The
Jean Cocteau
Tragedy 2 Acts
Paris 1946

Inspired by the death of Ludwig II of Bavaria, Cocteau follows in this play the last night and day in the lives of a Queen and her assassin, a poet, Stanislas.

Under the pseudonym of Azrael, or the Angel of Death, Stanislas has published a vicious satire on his Queen, which inspires a group of revolutionaries to appoint Stanislas to murder her. He agrees, although his satire arose, in fact, from a thwarted passion for its subject.

He finds her alone in a room set for an imaginary dinner with the ghost of her dead husband who had been assassinated ten years earlier. When Stanislas enters the room, wounded and on the run from the traitorous Chief of Police, Baron Foehn, the Queen is astonished by his bravery and his resemblance to the dead king. She falls in love with the poet, who persuades her to abandon a decade of reclusive mourning, and to wrest back control of the government from Baron Foehn and her mother-in-law the Archduchess. To break her resolve Foehn arrests the poet, but he, determined not to be the cause of her undoing, swallows poison. The Queen cannot now face life without him, and she goads him into completing his original mission by declaring that she hates him.

The Queen
Edith de Berg, the Queen's reader
Stanislas
The Duke of Willenstein, lord-in-waiting
Baron Foehn, Chief of Police
Tony, the Queen's black servant

East Lynne
Mrs Henry Wood
Melodrama 3 Acts
London 1864

This tale of passion and jealousy is set in the rural England of the mid-nineteenth century. Archibald Carlyle marries and brings home to East Lynne Lady Isabel, who is despised by Carlyle's half-sister and Barbara Hare, a neighbour.

Isabel, fuelled by gossip from a servant, suspects her husband of renewing an old association with Barbara and when she witnesses a secret meeting between them, in fact to discuss an alleged crime of Barbara's brother Richard, she leaves Carlyle and her two children and goes to live in Paris with scoundrel Francis Levison.

Carlyle and Barbara marry and when Levison leaves Isabel stranded and alone, she returns to England and cleverly disguised she obtains a position as a governess in her old house tending her own children.

Levison is eventually exposed for Richard Hare's crime but by now Isabel is herself failing in health after the death of her son William. Only on her deathbed does Carlyle recognize and forgive his first and true love.

Archibald Carlyle, the master of East Lynne
Isabel Carlyle, his wife
Cornelia Carlyle, his unmarried sister
Lord Mountsevern, Isabel's only living relative
Barbara Hare, secretly in love with Archibald
Richard Hare, her brother, a fugitive from justice
Francis Levison, an unscrupulous rogue with designs
 on Isabel
Joyce Hallijohn, an upper-maid at East Lynne
Wilson, a maidservant

Educating Rita
Willy Russell
Comedy 2 Acts
London 1980

Failed poet Frank is a tutor in English literature at a university in the north of England. He's fifty, he drinks, his wife has left him and he lives, not too joyously, with a younger woman. He is cynical and unhappy.

Then Rita, an Open University student, arrives for her tutorial with him; a tough little hairdresser, sick of the confines of her marriage and horizons limited to crass working-class materialism, she has a fierce yearning to 'know everything'. She and Frank get along well - she respects his wisdom and lack of pretension, and he finds her 'a breath of fresh air'.

A quick learner, Rita delights Frank with her direct manner and wit, and they embark on a series of literary adventures. In the process of education, Rita leaves her husband, makes friends with a gang of younger full-time students and leaves the hairdressers for a job in a bistro. As she inevitably becomes more independent of Frank, he becomes bitter as he sees her originality disappear under academic conventions. His drinking and less-than-model behaviour increases and he is

'sentenced' by the faculty to be banished to a teaching post in Australia for two years. Rita returns to tell him what a good teacher he is, and he tells her he has entered her paper with confidence for the exam. Before they part she wants to do something for him so she takes out her scissors and begins to snip his unruly mop...

Rita
Frank

Edward the Second
Christopher Marlowe
Tragedy 5 Acts
London 1592

Edward has a passion for Gaveston, a skilled flatterer hated by the other Lords. At first Edward is minded to let the Barons carve up the Kingdom among themselves so long as he is left a portion of England where he can frolic with his favourite, upon whom he has bestowed the titles Earl of Cornwall, Lord High Chamberlain, Chief Secretary to the State, King and Lord of Man.

After much argument with the Barons and the Archbishop, he is persuaded to exile his beloved Gaveston, so he makes him Governor of Ireland.

His pining Queen Isabella now hopes to have her love requited but Edward makes it clear he will not allow her near him if he cannot have Gaveston around and she should therefore reconcile the Lords, especially Mortimer Jr, with whom she, Edward thinks, is intimate. She does as bidden, Gaveston returns but is killed. Edward quickly bestows his affections on Spencer Jr, making him Earl of Gloucester and Lord Chamberlain, which infuriates the Barons. After alarms, excursions and a battle (offstage) Edward captures the Barons. Mortimer Jr and the Queen plan a revolt from France. The Earl of Kent is beheaded. Edward is captured, humiliated, and murdered. Prince Edward becomes King Edward the Third and Mortimer Jr thinks he can manipulate him but is mistaken. The young King orders Mortimer's execution and, after the Queen, his mother, has pleaded for her lover to be spared, she is sent to the Tower. The Lords, having lost all taste for rebellion, present Mortimer's head to the King, who 'offers it up' to his father's hearse.

King Edward the Second
Prince Edward, his son
Edmund Earl of Kent, his brother
Pierce De Gaveston, Earl of Cornwall
Guy, Earl of Warwick
Thomas, Earl of Lancaster
Aymer de Valence, Earl of Pembroke
Edmund Fitzalan, Earl of Arundel
Henry, Earl of Leicester, Lancaster's brother
Sir Thomas Berkeley
Roger Mortimer of Chirk (Mortimer Senr)
Roger Mortimer of Wigmore (Mortimer Jr), his
 nephew
Hugh le Despenser (Spencer Senr)
Hugh le Despenser (Spencer Jr), his son

Robert Winchelsey, Archbishop of Canterbury
Walter Langton, Bishop of Coventry
John Stratford, Bishop of Winchester
Robert Baldock
Henry de Beaumont
Sir William Trussel
Thomas Gurney
Lightborn
Sir John of Hainault
Levune
Rice Ap Howell
The Abbot of Neath
Queen Isabella
Lady Margaret De Clare
Lords, ladies, attendants, messengers, soldiers,
monks and poor men

Edward, My Son
Robert Morley and Noel Langley
Drama 3 Acts
London 1947

Arnold Holt may have been (according to his mother) 'happy-go-lucky' to begin with, but marriage and particularly the birth of son Edward turns him into a kind of monster. He spoils poor Edward (who never appears) something rotten, and becomes rich and powerful and more unscrupulous in the process. Suffering wife Evelyn puts up with it all until Edward, now a teenager, is obviously a real brat. Too late, she decides to put her foot down. Arnold has already blackmailed Edward's prep school, swindled the insurance company, betrayed his old mate Soames and got knighted in the process. He's also having an affair with secretary Eileen, but when Evelyn sets a private dick on him and threatens divorce - and to take away beloved Edward - Arnold gets even nastier and Evelyn is forced to stay, rapidly becoming a cynical alcoholic.

Throughout, Evelyn is pursued by Arnold's buddy and her unrequited lover Dr Larry Parker, who first brought Edward into the world, but now even he's fed up with Arnold. Edward marries gorgeous upper-crust Phyllis after Arnold buys off pregnant Betty, Edward's shopgirl fling, and when Edward is killed in World War Two - a fighter pilot - Arnold swallows the line about him being the finest pilot in the squadron, born leader of men, etc.

After the war the Labour government squeeze Arnold so tight he decides to leave for the USA, intending to take with him Phyllis and Edward II, as t'were, but helped by Larry, Phyllis has seen the light. She doesn't want the son to be like the father - or grandfather - and dodges Arnold, leaving him to exploit the New World all alone.

Arnold Holt
Evelyn Holt
Dr Larry Parker
Harry Soames
Dr Waxman

Cunningham, Ellerby, assistant masters at
  Graingerry
Hanray, headmaster at Graingerry
Eileen Perry, personal secretary to Sir Arnold
Walter Prothero, private enquiry agent
Montegue Burton, personal secretary to Lord Holt
Phyllis Maxwell
Summers, butler to Lord Holt
Betty Fowler

Effect of Gamma Rays on Man-in-the-Moon Marigolds, The
Paul Zindel
Drama 2 Acts
New York 1970

Beatrice is an eccentric boor and sloven living in a ramshackle old house together with her two strange daughters Tillie and Ruth. She has vague plans to convert the place into a tea shop and she makes money by looking after discarded old and sick people, her latest charge being old Nanny, almost a shuffling corpse.

Both daughters are awkward and dress badly and Tillie especially is the butt of jokes from kids at school. Ruth has fits and has had psychiatric treatment, while Tillie has gone cosmic and is obsessed with The Atom, and thus the Sun, the Stars and the Universe. Her school science project 'The Effect of Gamma Rays on Man-in-the-Moon Marigolds' involves growing seeds subjected to varying amounts of radiation, and discussing the subsequent mutations and other implications. The project reaches the school finals and Beatrice is invited to sit up on the stage with the parents of the other four finalists. She is reluctant because in her day at the same school she was also laughed at; she makes a brave effort to get ready but a last-minute row with Ruth - who reminds Beatrice how she was nicknamed 'Betty the Loon' at school - results in distraught Beatrice staying home and murdering Ruth's pet rabbit.

Tillie wins and Ruth is jubilant until she returns and finds her rabbit dead. She has a fit and Beatrice reiterates how much she hates the world. But for Tillie, the world of The Atom, her experiment, her success and her cosmic revelations, all make the world beautiful.

Tillie
Beatrice
Ruth
Nanny
Janice Vickerby

Eh?
Henry Livings
Farce 2 Acts
London 1964

Valentine Brose is obviously mad, not exactly just stupid, but peculiar and unpredictable in his responses and exceptionally irritating. For no discernible reason, he is hired by personnel officer Mrs Murray as the boilerman at a dye factory where one of the workers is a gentle Pakistani, Aly, and the works manager is a sorely-tried tough guy, Price. A preacher, the Revd Mort, likes to drop in. Valentine manages to annoy everybody except his fiancée Betty, whom he marries, but who soon takes a shine to Aly.

Val has brought with him some psychedelic mushrooms to grow in the boiler room . He 'turns on' Price and Mort with them, then lets the boiler blow up.

Price
Aly
Mrs Murray
Valentine Brose
Reverend Mort
Betty Dorrick
A chattering tannoy

84 Charing Cross Road
James Roose-Evans adapted from a novel by Helen Hanff
Drama 2 Acts
London 198l

Real-life story of hard-up New York book-lover Helene Hanff and her celebrated literary love-affair with Marks & Co., a London bookshop. Helene, who writes for TV, answers Marks' ad offering out-of-print books in *The Saturday Review* and thus begins a unique correspondence with manager Frank Doel and his collegues at the dusty antiquarian Charing Cross Road bookshop. She is delighted with their service and they are equally delighted with her pithily friendly requests and humorous comments.

As the relationship becomes warmer, it also gets more poignant. Helene determines to visit Marks, but various crises, mostly financial, deter her for almost twenty years until her book chronicling the correspondence is published and she is brought over to promote it. By that time it is too late to meet Frank - he died three years previously and the shop shut down. As the play progresses, we are treated to a series of fascinating extracts which bring to life the love of books and literature, helped by the imaginative stage set - Helene's Manhattan apartment, and a few yards distant, the interior of Marks & Co. in London.

Helene Hanff
Frank Doel
Cecily Farr
Megan Wells
Mr Martin
William Humphries
Maxine Stuart
Joan Todd

Electra
Euripides
Tragedy 1 Act
Athens c.413BC

Clytemnestra and Aegisthus, usurper King of Mycenae, have murdered the rightful king, Agamemnon,

Clytemnestra's husband. Fearing revenge from Orestes and Electra, Agamemnon's son and daughter, Aegisthus has tried to have both killed. Orestes has been rescued, reared to manhood in Argos, and now returns to find Electra and, with her, avenge Agamemnon's death.

Electra has been married to a peasant farmer and exiled from the City of Mycenae. Out of respect, though, the peasant has not consummated the marriage; so she is untainted. Orestes first meets her in disguise to sound out her loyalty, and he spurs him into killing both Aegisthus and their mother. Orestes finds Aegisthus at sacrifice, and kills him with a ritual axe as he had been ordered to do by the god Apollo; but he shrinks from killing his mother.

Electra denounces Clytemnestra, supported by the Chorus, and again goads Orestes to action. Together they kill Clytemnestra, but then sink into remorse. Electra is betrothed to Pylades, Orestes' brother-in-arms, never to return to Mycenae, nor ever to see Orestes, who is banished to a life of wandering by Zeus.

Peasant, narrator and Electra's husband
Electra, Agamemnon's daughter
Orestes, Electra's brother
Old Man, Agamemnon's tormentor
Clytemnestra, Electra's mother
Castor and Pollux, Gods, Clytemnestra's brothers
Chorus

Elephant Man, The
Bernard Pomerance
Drama 21 Scenes
London 1979

Surgeon and teacher Frederick Treves, who considers himself to be well favoured by fortune, joins the staff of the London Hospital, Whitechapel Road in 1884. In the same road, the horrendously deformed John Merrick is being exhibited as a freak by his rough and grasping manager Ross who treats him with contempt. Treves sees Merrick and arranges to hire him for a day in order to lecture on his condition.

Ross takes Merrick to briefly visit Belgium for a fair but the police and some freakish pinheads refuse to allow Merrick to appear so Ross sends him back to London where Treves rescues him and takes him to live at the London Hospital. Porters gawp at him, nurses refuse to deal with him but slowly 'The Elephant Man', whose mind is perfectly sound, becomes well-educated and acquires some celebrity. The public pays for his welfare, a bishop takes an interest and Merrick starts making a model of St Phillip's Church. Mrs Kendal, a beautiful actress, befriends him and because he has never seen a naked woman she disrobes for him - and is caught in the act by a displeased Treves.

As his physical condition steadily deteriorates, Merrick's fame increases and he is visited by titled women, including Princess Alexandra. Lord John, a shameless swindler, gambles away funds intended for the hospital and Merrick, and Ross tries to make a comeback as the 'freak's' manager. Treves has a strange dream in which he has become the curiosity and Merrick lectures on the surgeon's terrifying normality. After finishing the model of the church, Merrick dies and Gomm, the hospital administrator, composes a letter to *The Times*.

Frederick Treves, surgeon
Carr Gomm, hospital administrator
Ross, the Elephant Man's manager
John Merrick, the Elephant Man
Three pinheads, women freaks with pointed heads
Belgian policeman
London policeman
Man at Brussels fairground
Conductor of Ostend boat train
Bishop Walsham How
Two porters
Mrs Kendal, actress
Duchess
Countess
Princess Alexandra
Lord John
Miss Sandwich, nurse

Emperor Jones, The
Eugene O'Neill
Drama 1 Act
New York 1920

In the 1920s Brutus Jones, a black American convict and former Pullman car attendant, has managed to seize control of a small island in the West Indies and within two years he has become its emperor.

With the assistance of a venal English trader, Henry Smithers, Jones is in the final stages of stripping the island and its inhabitants of their wealth. As part of his programme of exploitation, Jones has prepared an emergency escape route through the island's rainforest, in case the islanders should rebel. He has no fear of being shot, for he is convinced that only a silver bullet can kill him. The hard pressed populace eventually revolt and Jones makes his way into the jungle to escape to Martinique, but there he meets a number of phantoms and spectres from his violent past which throw him into so much panic that he loses his way, goes in circles and ends up back where he started. Four silver bullets find their target and Jones is carried back for Smithers to contemplate.

Brutus Jones   *Congo witch-doctor*
Henry Smithers   *Crocodile God*
Old native woman
Native chief
Spectres
Jeff
Convicts
Prison guards
Planters
Auctioneer
Slaves

Endgame
Samuel Beckett
Play 1 Act
London 1957

Four characters inhabit a bleak cell, while outside the world is coming to an end, cold and immobile. Time stands at zero.

Hamm, blind and paralysed, is attended in his wheelchair by his son-cum-slave, Clov, and spends his time tyrannizing his parents, Nagg and Nell, who vegetate in dustbins, reminisce and gabble idiotically until they eventually disintegrate. The past is worn out and the future is a hollow void. Hamm constantly announces his departure but he cannot escape the influence of his father, so he seeks to find some meaning to his life in pseudo-psychological dialogue but ends up in total despair and rambling meaningless soliloquy.

There is a faint glimmer of hope in the form of a small child, but this barely alleviates the oppressive mood of impending doom.

Hamm
Clov
Nagg
Nell

Enemies
Maxim Gorky
Drama 3 Acts
Ukraine 1912

Revolution is in the air during the summer of 1905 in provincial Russia. Textile factory owner Zakhar Bardin has infuriated his hard-line partner Mikhail Skrobotov with his 'liberal' attitudes which have encouraged the workers to make more and more demands. Zakhar's cynical brother Yakov drinks to escape from the situation, while Yakov's beautiful estranged wife, Tatiana, sides with young Nadya, cousin of Zakhar's stupid wife Paulina, in her sympathy for the workers. When Mikhail is shot and killed at the factory, his wife Kleopatra blames Zakhar, and Capt. Boboyedov of the Intelligence Corps arrives to deal with the situation. Aided by Cpl Kvach and Mikhail's brother, assistant public prosecutor Nikolai, the investigations proceed.

The peasants and workers are organized by factory clerk Sintsov, a clever and dedicated revolutionary, but although young Ryabtsov owns up to the murder, the actual culprit, married man Yakimov, eventually confesses. Sintsov is recognized as an escaped political prisoner by his old enemy Kvach, and the entire proceedings are watched with horror by Nadya who finds the whole repressive system repugnant and blames the greed and cowardice of the establishment for the tragedy.

Zakhar Bardin   *Gen. Pechenegov,*
Paulina   *Bardins' uncle*
Yakov Bardin   *Kon, his batman*
Tatiana   *Mikhail Skrobotov*
Nadya   *Kleopatra*

Nikolai Skrobotov   *First worker*
Agrafena, a housekeeper   *Second worker*
Pologgy, a clerk   *Vripaev*
Sintsov, a clerk   *Capt. Boboyedov*
Gregov   *Kvach*
Levshin   *Peasant woman*
Yagodin
Ryabtsov
Yakimov

Enemy of the People, An
Henrik Ibsen
Drama 5 Acts
Christiania 1883

Dr Thomas Stockmann lives with his wife, schoolteacher daughter Petra and two young sons, in a small resort where he is the medical officer at the Baths and his elder brother Peter is Mayor, Chief Constable and Chairman of the Baths' Committee. All the local businessmen and workers are confident that the new Baths are going to put the place on the map and bring them prosperity. Hovstad, Editor of the *People's Tribune*, and his colleague Billing, are looking forward to publishing a Baths-boosting article by the Doctor. But there is a snag. Stockmann has discovered, for sure, what he had long suspected; there is sewage pollution in the Baths and on the beach, and the chief source is a tannery owned by Morten Kiil, foster father to Mrs Stockmann. The Doctor, who is self-important and righteous, is not displeased because he had warned that the (economy) water pipes system was likely to be inadequate and now brother Peter and the Council will have to take notice and act, otherwise the invalid trade they were hoping to attract will only get sicker.

At first Hovstad is delighted to have a hard-hitting, populist story to replace the previously intended promotional one but Aslaksen, the printer (also Chairman of the Property Owners' Association and the Council of the Temperance Society) counsels caution and quickly switches sides when Mayor Peter wants to suppress any bad-for-business publicity, fudge the whole issue and substitute a fraudulently reassuring story. Hovstad and Billing 'see sense' because for all their ostensibly crusading fervour, they cannot afford to affront the subscribers and lose backing. Denied publication of the truth, Dr Stockmann takes his case to a public meeting. Shouted down by all the citizens for obvious reasons of greedy expediency and short-term self-interest, the Doctor abandons the argument about pollution and widens his comments to point out that local democracy enables fools and knaves to govern themselves, that liberals are the most insidious enemies of freedom and, in effect, only a paternalistic aristocratic form of government can be trusted.

He is branded an enemy of the people and decides to sail with Captain Horster to a (potentially) new life in America but the owner of the boat, outraged that Horster lent his house for the public meeting, sacks

Horster. Petra is sacked, Dr Stockmann is sacked. Morten Kiil, who had initially approved of any action that would embarrass the Council he hates, now buys up shares in the Baths and exerts financial 'blackmail', announcing he will cut Mrs Stockmann out of his will unless the Doctor recants about the pollution. Hovstad and Aslaksen come round to the Doctor's house to congratulate him on his crafty scheme enabling the family to buy shares cheaply. That does it: Dr Stockmann drives them away and resolves to stay and fight for right. He feels strong enough to face the corrupt rabble because 'the strongest man in the world is he who stands most alone'.
Dr Stockmann
Mrs Stockmann
Mayor
Hovstad
Billing
Aslaksen
Horster
Petra
Eilif Stockmann
Morten Stockmann
Morten Kiil

Entertainer, The
John Osborne
Comedy 13 Parts
London 1957

It is 1956 and the Rice family live in the backstreets of an English coastal resort. Archie Rice staggers along as a bad music-hall comedian in the shadow of his more successful father, Billy, and wilfully refuses to move with the times. There is an air of bitterness and cynicism about the Rice family. Archie's son, Mick, is killed at Suez, father Billy dies after preventing the philandering Archie from leaving his wife, Phoebe, and daughter Jean decides not to marry her dull solicitor boyfriend, preferring the eccentricities of Archie's outlook to that of his more successful brother, distinguished lawyer William. Music-hall techniques are used in this metaphor on the death of the British Imperial era and the subsequent rise of pop culture and radical politics.
Archie Rice, a middle-aged music-hall comedian
Billy Rice, his father
Jean Rice, his daughter
Phoebe Rice, his wife
Frank Rice, his son
William Rice, his brother
Graham Dodd, Jean's fiancé

Entertaining Mr Sloane
Joe Orton
Comedy 3 Acts
London 1963

Sloane, an amoral and bisexual nineteen-year-old, comes to lodge in a house built in the middle of a rubbish dump. He immediately becomes the object of desire of both the middle-aged Kath and her brother Ed, but is resented by their father, the puritanical Kemp. Sloane allows Kath to seduce him and plays at being both her son and lover; meanwhile, he keeps Ed at arm's length, pretending virginity in order to extract full capital from the situation. Ed soon catches on to Sloane's predatory game, but not before Kemp recognizes Sloane as the killer of his former boss, a photographer interested in Sloane for pornographic purposes.

Kemp refuses to shut up so Sloane kills him, thus giving Ed and the now-pregnant Kath the opportunity of blackmailing him. The tables are turned and Sloane is now in their power; they agree to share, each having him for six months per year.

Sloane
Kath
Ed
Kemp

Equus
Peter Shaffer
Tragedy 2 Acts
London 1973

Martin Dysart, a middle-aged English psychiatrist and lover of classical Greece, tells, in flashback, the story of an intensely disturbed adolescent boy, Alan Strang, whose rehabilitation from madness Dysart has attempted.

Alan is the only son of Frank Strang, a secretly libidinous working-class atheist and self-improvement fanatic, and his dotty, religion-obsessed wife, Dora. In the course of psychoanalyzing Alan, who has been apprehended blinding six horses without any apparent reasons, Dysart slowly teases out the tangled causes of an overwhelming obsession. At once, goaded and relieved by Dysart's probing questions, Alan confronts the memory of those events in his childhood which led him first to secretly worship and adore horses, and then to mutilate them. Dora's secretive and fevered Christian proselytizing, Frank's equally secretive voyeurism and Alan's own passionate but thwarted first love affair, provide a mosaic of unresolved conflict which impels the youngster to explode into barbarity.

As the young man discovers and confronts the roots of his wild confusion, the conflict within him begins to abate. Dysart is left to regret that his patient's increasing stability will inevitably be bought at the expense of the vitality and grandeur of what was, in effect, the boy's personal recreation of the Centaur myth.

Martin Dysart, psychiatrist
Alan Strang, his patient
Frank Strang
Dora Strang
Hesther Salomon
Harry Dalton
Young horseman
Nurse
Six actors playing horses

Erpingham Camp, The
Joe Orton
Farce 11 Scenes
London 1966

A microcosm of a dictatorship, Erpingham's holiday camp is run with would-be no-nonsense efficiency and regimentation. Erpingham is irked by Redcoat Riley's evident lack of organizational skill and wants him to consult the manual more diligently. The Entertainments Officer dies and Riley gets his chance to run a night's entertainment. It soon goes horribly wrong with one of the campers, Eileen, (who keeps on pointing out that she is pregnant) claiming to have been struck and insulted by Riley. Her Kenny knocks Riley down.

As the misunderstanding gets uglier, an infuriated Erpingham decides to teach the campers a lesson by locking away the food and sealing off the chalets. Kenny addresses the campers saying that after the children have been denied bread, the womenfolk insulted and shelter denied them, they will have to take the law into their own hands. Other campers counsel caution, especially Ted whose Lou supports him, so she is attacked by Eileen. The campers march on the stores and the revolution gathers intensity. Kenny beats up Erpingham who falls through the floor and dies. The Padre, who has had his own problems as a result of a taste for creeping into teenage girls' chalets, conducts a makeshift service at which Riley delivers an eloquent eulogy of his late, great employer. A Class A (Higher Employee) wreath is ordered.

Erpingham
Riley
Lou
Ted
Eileen
Kenny
Padre
W. E. Harrison
Jessie Mason
Redcoats
Campers

Escapade
Roger MacDougall
Comedy 3 Acts
London 1953

Writer and peace campaigner John Hampden is having trouble getting prestigious signatures for his latest peace petition, while his wife Stella is being 'chatted up' by old flame Peter Henderson who is telling her what an ogre John is. For a man of peace, John is certainly aggressive, opinionated and a thorough bore - but Stella still loves him. She is not so happy about their three sons being away from home at boarding school, and matters reach a climax when headmaster Dr Skillingworth arrives threatening to expel them. The three boys have run away from school and one of them, 'Battling Max', has shot a teacher in the leg with a home-made ball-bearing gun. There is more to it than mere rebellion or high spirits, however. Schoolfriend Daventry tells the Hampdens an astonishing story; in fact the whole school was behind the escapade, led by sixteen-year-old Icarus Hampden, the eldest son who is revered by the other boys. The plan was for Icarus to steal a plane and fly to Venice for a United Nations conference to present the school's own peace petition. There is no word from Icarus, a good flier, and despite help from newspaperman Deeson, he is presumed dead - except, of course, by John's mother Mrs Hampden, who is convinced of Icarus's common-sense. The whole escapade teaches John a lesson and punctures his self-importance, reconciling him with Stella. The phone rings and it is Icarus, alive and well.

Stella Hampden	Dr Skillingworth
Mrs Hampden	Miss Betts
Peter Henderson	Paton
William Saxon	Daventry
Sir Harold Cookham	Andrew Deeson
John Hampden	Mollie
Walters	George

Eumenides (Oresteia, Part III)
Aeschylus
Drama 1 Act
Athens 458BC

Orestes is under threat of revenge from the Furies for murdering Clytemnestra, so he goes to worship Apollo at Delphi to entreat the god's protection. Apollo promises his guidance and orders Orestes to seek Pallas Athene's forgiving justice at her temple in Athens. The goddess listens to both Orestes and the Furies and refers judgement to a court of Athenian jurists.

They vote and return a hung verdict, but Athene's casting vote is for mercy and Orestes is set free. The Furies' rank indignation over the verdict is placated when Athene offers them a permanent home and honour in her own lands.

The Pythian priestess
Apollo, Hermes
Orestes, son of Agamemnon of Argos
The ghost of Clytemnestra, wife of Agamemnon
Chorus of Furies
Pallas Athene, goddess of justice
Citizens of Athens
Athenian women and girls
The Eumenides, Chorus

Every Good Boy Deserves Favour
Tom Stoppard
Music by Andre Previn
Comedy Drama for Actors and Orchestra 1 Act
London 1977

The orchestra surrounds three separate acting areas, each approachable from the others. They are a cell with two beds, an office with table and two chairs, and a schoolroom with a desk. In the cell are Alexander, a

political prisoner classified as crazy and in a hospital, not a prison, and Ivanov, a genuine mental patient. Ivanov has a triangle and when he plays it he imagines he is sitting in with an orchestra. The audience and Ivanov can hear the imaginary orchestra, Alexander and the Doctor can't. It is part of Ivanov's delusion that Alexander must be a fellow 'musician'. In the school, a lady teacher, who also has a triangle, is teaching Sacha (Alexander's son).

Ivanov goes to the office, one of the violinists leaves the orchestra platform and enters the office as Doctor. He tries to convince Ivanov there is no orchestra, although Doctor admits to playing in one as a hobby. Back in the cell Alexander tells Ivanov, partly accompanied by a children's percussion band, about the arrests of his writer friends for reading the wrong books and protesting in Red Square about Czechoslovakia. Alexander had been in Leningrad Special Psychiatric Hospital for thirty months before being transferred to this place.

Back in the office, Doctor advises Alexander to admit to everything and say sorry for alleging he'd been badly treated. Alexander says he was never mad and his treatment was barbaric and the Doctor replies that stupidity is one thing he can't cure. There is much confusion over terms, such as whether Alexander has been dealt with by medical staff or brutal thieving criminals and KGB thugs. Doctor tells him he is a paranoid schizophrenic, Alexander insists he has no symptoms, he has opinions. Doctor: 'Your opinions are your symptoms, Your disease is dissent.' It is the official line that any patient (prisoner) who says that sane people are locked up in asylums must be crazy.

A Colonel (alias Head Doctor) arrives to examine the two men, muddling them up, and says there is nothing wrong with them - 'get them out of here'. The teacher, Doctor and Ivanov join the orchestra while, to music, Alexander and Sacha move through an aisle in the middle of the orchestra.

Alexander
Ivanov
Sacha
Doctor
Teacher
Colonel
Symphony orchestra

Every Man in His Humour
Ben Jonson
Comedy 5 Acts
London 1598

Fearing the worst, kindly but serious old master Knowell follows his son Edward, the play's hero, into town after reading a note from roisterous friend Wellbred inviting Edward for japes. Servant Brainworm disguises himself and becomes Edward's ally and together with rustic-fop cousin Stephen they all become involved in a series of encounters with diverse London characters: Master

Matthew, the would-be versifier who steals poetry; Capt. Bobadill, the cowardly braggart soldier; water-carrier Cob and wife Tib; surly squire George Downright; and the family of city merchant Thomas Kitely, whose wife is Wellbred's sister. Kitely's own sister Mistress Bridget and Edward are enamoured of one another and eventually wed, but not before a series of pranks, fights, and Kitely's near-insane jealousy lead them all before cranky old Justice Clement, who effects reconciliation in the name of wit and general goodwill.

Master Edward Knowell
Brainworm
Master Stephen
A servant to Wellbred
Young Master Edward
Master Matthew
Oliver Cob
Tib, his wife
Capt. Bobadill
Master Thomas Kitely
Master George Downright, a country squire
Thomas Cash, Kitely's cashier
Dame Kitely
Mistress Bridget, Kitely's sister
Master Wellbred
Justice Clement
Roger Formal, Clement's clerk
Servants

Evita
Tim Rice
Music by Andrew Lloyd Webber
Musical 2 Acts
London 1978

Musical biography of Argentina's charismatic post-war first lady Eva Peron opens with a cinema screen in 1952 and the announcement of her death. The action then proceeds through flashback from Eva at fifteen in her little home town where she works her wiles to make tango singer Magaldi bring her to Buenos Aires. Charming and scratching, she then works her way up through ever-increasingly influential beds.

Throughout, Eva indulges in a virtual dialogue with a usually-mocking Che Guevara on the sidelines, and soon she manages to fix a meeting with General Juan Peron himself, Argentina's dictator. Peron's mistress is soon thrown out and Eva moves in, eventually marrying Peron. Her background and her flamboyant success endear her to the peasants and the working-class and after Peron's election victory it is the moment of Eva's shining triumph. There is a European propaganda tour, but confrontation with Peron sets in when she aspires to the Vice-Presidency. She sets up the charitable Eva Peron Foundation and shortly afterwards falls ill, refusing the (unoffered) Vice-Presidency. She dies, and a nation mourns.

Songs include: 'Don't Cry for Me Argentina'; 'Another Suitcase in Another Hall'

Che
Eva
Peron
Peron's mistress
Magaldi
Singers
Dancers

Exiles
James Joyce
Drama 3 Acts
Munich 1919

In 1912, after a nine-year exile, Richard Rowan, a writer of genius, has returned to his native Dublin with his common-law wife, Bertha, and young son, Archie.

During their exile, Richard has written often and with passion to Beatrice Justice, a Dublin woman of wit and education who, upon their return, becomes music teacher to Archie. Bertha, a plain but clever country girl, finds Beatrice both intriguing and threatening. At the same time, the Rowans re-kindle their joint friendship with Robert Hand, a Dublin journalist whose envious admiration for Richard's work sits uneasily with his long-suppressed love for Bertha.

Richard's determination to live unshackled by convention leads him not just to tolerate Robert's interest in Bertha, but to insist that she confront it openly. For the same reason, he refuses to be discreet with Beatrice. Caught between Richard's extreme frankness, Robert's growing passion and her own loneliness and sense of inadequacy, Bertha almost has an affair with Robert, but pulls back at the last moment. She is, however, enriched by the experience, and returns to Richard with a new maturity.

Richard Rowan
Bertha, his wife
Archie, their son
Robert Hand
Beatrice Justice
Brigid, servant
A fisherwoman

Fallen Angels
Noël Coward
Comedy 3 Acts
London 1925

Two longtime and very close friends, Julia Sterroll and Jane Banbury, both settled in companionable but staid marriages, hear that Maurice Duclos, a lover to both women before they married, is about to visit them in London.

The women are caught between a thirst for the passions Duclos represents, fear that his reappearance could jeopardize their marriages and jealousy of each other over Duclos' possible attentions. Each believes that the other is scheming to see him secretly, and both behave so erratically that even their husbands are drawn into discovering the old affairs.

Order is restored by Duclos' eventual arrival and his quick thinking in pretending to both husbands that the affairs were invented to jolt them out of their marital complacency.

Julia Sterroll
Frederick Sterroll
Jane Banbury
William Banbury
Maurice Duclos
Saunders

Family Album
Noël Coward
Play 1 Act
London 1935
See: *Tonight at 8.30*

Family Reunion, The
T.S. Eliot
Drama 2 Acts
London 1939

Lord Harry Monchensey returns to his family home in the north of England, which is full of his semi-dependent relatives and dominated by his mother, Amy, the Dowager Lady Monchensey. For eight years, Harry has been travelling abroad, largely to escape his family's influence. During that time, his young wife, whom his mother had never accepted, was drowned on a cruise, leaving Harry obsessed with guilt.

The whole Monchensey family is assembling to celebrate both Harry's return and Amy's birthday. Harry finds, as he had expected, that Amy has kept the estate obsessively preserved as he had left it. He is expected and partly expects himself, to settle again in the family home and take charge of the estate. He considers this expectation, refuses to live up to it and decides instead to resume his travels. But, having confronted the familial pressure, he also finds himself released from the guilt he suffered, free to search for the 'bright angels'.

Amy, Dowager Lady Monchensey
Ivy, Violet, Agatha, her sisters
Col the Hon. Gerald Piper and the Hon. Charles
* Piper, her brothers*
Mary, young relation/housekeeper
Denman, parlourmaid
Harry, Lord Monchensey
Downing, Harry's servant
Dr Warburton
Sergeant Winchell

Fantasticks, The
Tom Jones
Music by Harvey Schmidt
Musical 2 Acts
New York 1960

Based on Edmond Rostand's *Les Romanesques*. This is a camp celebration - of the seasons ('the necessity of winter to ensure the rebirth of spring'), the weather, vegetation, gardening, boy and girl lovers, swashbuckling - song and dance with minimal scenery. Luisa and Matt are separated by a wall erected by their respective fathers who believe parental opposition is the way to bring children together. The two fathers also hire bandit El Gallo to attempt to rape Luisa. The plan, of course, is for Matt to come to the rescue. He does, and the couple grow even closer. But then they discover the parental plot and love turns sour. Matt decides he wants to see the world and Luisa is off with El Gallo. The disillusioned fathers rebuild the wall, but then the children, fed up with life alone, reunite - 'without a hurt, the heart is hollow'.

Included is a song and ballet about rape (it depends on what you pay) and other peculiarities. The show is part poetic, part burlesque.

Songs include: 'Try to Remember'; 'Soon It's Gonna Rain'; 'Much More'

The Mute
El Gallo
Luisa
Matt
Hucklebee
Bellamy
Henry
Mortimer
The Handyman
Pianist
Harpist

Far Country, A
Henry Denker
Drama 3 Acts
New York 1961

It is 1938 and Sigmund Freud, father of psychoanalysis, is finally able to leave Nazi Vienna for exile in London after Mme Bonaparte has paid a huge ransom to the government. While packing, Freud comes across an old file - that of Elizabeth Von R. - and the scene flashes back to 1903 when the younger Freud was still fumbling his way towards a theory of the unconscious, and his methods, including hypnotism, were earning him the disapproval of both the medical establishment and his mother Amalie.

Young widower Frederick Wohlmuth arrives at his house asking Freud to help his crippled sister-in-law Elizabeth. Every other doctor in Vienna has failed, and, unwilling to upset the establishment even more, Freud refuses to see her. Frederick is insistent and eventually Freud relents. Elizabeth's problems are psychosomatic in origin and he begins treatment along an uncharted path, using a combination of untried methods and insights gained from his friend Dr Joseph Breuer - who has been reluctant to disclose his findings, also fearing the anti-semitic medical establishment. Freud and Elizabeth grow close, to the distress of his pregnant wife Martha, but eventually Freud discovers Elizabeth's pains and paralysis are caused by guilt connected with wishing for the death of her beloved father whom she nursed, and guilt at her feelings of gladness that when her sister Charlotte died, the way was open for her to wed Frederick whom she secretly loves. Freud compares this revelation with the myth of unwinding the ball of wool in the labyrinth before confronting the Minotaur, and eventually his compassion for Elizabeth helps her to take her first unaided steps towards Frederick.

At the end the scene changes back to 1938 and the Nazi tyranny, and the play ends with Freud declaring that a human being free within himself is free everywhere.

Sigmund Freud
Martha Bernays Freud, his wife
A Nazi
Gordon Douglas, attaché, British consulate, Vienna
Kathy, the Freud's maid of all work
Frederick Wohlmuth
Dolfi Freud, Freud's younger sister
Amalie Freud
Elizabeth Von Ritter
Dr Joseph Breuer

Farmer's Wife, The
Eden Phillpotts
Comedy 3 Acts
Birmingham 1916

Marriage is in the air at Applegarth Farm in the village of Little Silver early this century. Widower farmer Samuel Sweetland, helped by his sensible cook/housekeeper Araminta Dench, plans to take a new wife. The trouble is, nice but pompous Sweetland takes himself too seriously, and his hopes are dashed when his three matrimonial choices, Thirza Tapper, Louisa Windeatt, and Mary Hearn, all refuse him. Meanwhile his smart daughter Petronell is being chased by determined George Smerdon, newly-rich and none too bright, but she loves Richard Coaker, who in turn secretly loves Petronell's sister Sibley.

Sweetland at last realizes that the best woman for him is on his own doorstep - Araminta - and she accepts his proposal. Then Thirza, Louisa and Mary change their minds and come running back after Samuel, but he sticks to Araminta. Richard (whom everyone imagines is after Petronell) finally reveals his feelings to Sibley, and as she also secretly loves him, that sorts them out. Petronell too sees sense and, impressed by George's devotion, accepts him.

Samuel Sweetland *Mr Gregson*
Henry Coaker *Teddy Smerdon*
Richard Coaker *Araminta Dench*
George Smerdon *Thirza Tapper*
Valiant Dunnybrig *Petronell Sweetland*
Revd Septimus Tudor *Sibley Sweetland*
Dr Rundle *Louisa Windeatt*
Churdles Ash *Mary Hearn*

Sarah Smerdon *Mrs Tudor*
Susan Maine *Mrs Rundle*
Sophie Smerdon

Fatal Attraction
Bernard Slade
Thriller 2 Acts
Toronto 1984

Paparazzi Tony Lombardi is obsessed with film star Blair Griffin and one night enters her house and kills her husband, painter Morgan Richards. Sgt Doris Aylesworth and likeably-flawed middle-aged Lieut Gus Braden, a successful crime author investigate, but when they leave Lombardi returns and rapes Blair who stabs him to death. Gus smells a rat. Blair tells him Morgan was leaving her and was having an affair with her agent, beautiful Maggie, but Gus discovers Morgan was in fact involved with a woman called Ruth, intending to marry her and take the children away from Blair.

Gus knows Blair plotted the whole thing but has no evidence, and Blair, cool, collected and murderous, takes a shine to him and admits to a lesbian affair with Maggie. She then plots with Gus to kill Maggie, but when Gus double-crosses her she tries to kill him instead. He survives her attempts to drown him in the jacuzzi and then to shoot him, and disillusioned Maggie agrees to be a witness against her. Blair is led away, but not before propositioning Gus with an idea for a best-seller titled *Fatal Attraction* based on their relationship.

Blair Griffin
Morgan Richards
Tony Lombardi
Sgt Doris Aylesworth
Lieut Gus Braden
Maggie Stratten

Father, The
August Strindberg
Tragedy 3 Acts
Copenhagen 1887

A vicious and cunning Swedish bourgeois wife, Laura, sets out to wrest control over the upbringing of her daughter from her husband, the amiable Capt. Adolph. By planting in the Captain's mind the notion that he is not the child's father and by deft innuendo amongst their mutual friends and relations, Laura goads her husband into a display of violent temper in order to justify her accusation that he is insane.

With the help of a credulous doctor and an old and trusted family nurse, she inveigles the Captain into a straitjacket. Thus restrained and overwhelmed by her betrayal, the Captain suffers a stroke and Laura wins sole control over their daughter.

The intensity of the relations between husband and wife is so narrowly the focus of the play's action that it may be set in any typical bourgeois home.

Capt. Adolph
Laura

Bertha, their daughter
Margaret, family nurse
Dr Oestermark
Pastor Jonas, Laura's half brother
Corporal Noyd, an orderly
Svaird, another orderly

Fences
August Wilson
Drama 2 Acts
New Haven 1985

Troy Maxson and his friend Bono get together for their routine Friday night drink on Troy's porch, and the interruptions by Troy's wife Rose, and would-be-hipster son Lyons provide Troy an opportunity to air his hard-earned wisdom ... and also wonder if he will keep his garbage job after complaining to the union that black men were never allowed to drive the truck.

Troy's brother Gabe suffered a massive war-wound to the head and now believes he is the Archangel Gabriel; his compensation helped Troy build his house, but although he is now moved and lives across the street, Troy still has to bail him out from jail.

Reformed ex-con Troy, son of a violent failed sharecropper, killed a man during a robbery and served fifteen years; he was also a fine baseball player whose experience of prejudice in sport brings him into conflict with son Cory, who has an opportunity in pro football. Troy's life and dedication to his responsibilities have imbued him with a kind of nobility, but his family turn against him when he seizes a chance of carefree happiness with young Alberta. She dies in childbirth and Rose will look after the baby - but no longer be a wife to Troy.

Troy finally finishes building the wooden fence around his property - to keep death out and loved ones in - but seven years later is dead, mourned by all - even son Cory, now in the Marines - and he is given an appropriate send-off by 'Archangel' Gabe.

Troy Maxson
Jim Bono
Rose
Lyons, Troys' eldest son by a previous marriage
Gabriel
Cory, Troy and Rose's son
Raynell, Troy's daughter by Alberta

Fiddler on the Roof
Joseph Stein based on stories
by Sholom Aleichem
Music by Jerry Bock
Lyrics by Sheldon Harnick
Musical 2 Acts
New York 1964

Anatevka is a ramshackle Jewish village in Tzarist Russia, and Tevye, the milkman, is the local 'Papa', the upholder of traditions that for centuries have ensured the survival of these simple, religious, complicated and humorous people. He has five daughters who, according to tradition, would be found husbands by Yente, the local matchmaker, together with the approval of Tevye's wife Golde. But this is 1905 and it is a time of disintegration for the community; the girls wish to choose for themselves and one by one they do so. Tevye is torn between consenting to his daughters' wishes and clinging to centuries-old traditions. The community breakdown is completed by the pogroms, the persecution of the Jews by Cossacks, and the families are forced to start new lives in Poland, the Holy Land and America. Songs include: 'Matchmaker, Matchmaker'; 'If I Were A Rich Man'; 'Sunrise Sunset'; 'Far from the Home I Love'.

Tevye, the milkman	*Mordcha, the innkeeper*
Golde, his wife	*Rabbi*
Tzeitel	*Mendel, his son*
Hodel	*Avram, the bookseller*
Chava, Shprintze,	*Machum, the beggar*
Mielka, his daughters	*Grandma Tzeitel*
Yente, the matchmaker	*Fruma-Sarah*
Motel, the tailor	*Constable*
Perchik, the student	*Fyedka*
Lazar Wolf, the	*Shandel, Motel's mother*
butcher	*The Fiddler*

Fifth Column, The
Ernest Hemingway
Drama 3 Acts
New York 1939

Philip is in Republican Madrid, on which Franco's rebels are converging, working as a counter-espionage operative for the Republican cause as part of the International Brigade. He works undercover from the Florida Hotel bringing in reports from behind enemy lines. Also at the hotel is the beautiful and cosmopolitan journalist, Dorothy Bridges, with whom Philip falls reluctantly and bitterly in love. Whereas Philip is committed first to his secret work, and his cover as a dissipated adventurer, Dorothy is interested only in love, luxury and eventual marriage.

The tensions in their affair come to a head when Philip realizes that his love for Dorothy is starting to interfere with the ruthlessness his work demands. With his colleague, Max, he captures a German general seconded to Franco, and a civilian informer from Madrid who had worked as part of a team of fifth column assassins who shot Republicans in Madrid under cover of pre-arranged barrages from Franco's surrounding forces. Philip's resolve fails him when the captives are interrogated and shot and he brutally and coldly breaks with Dorothy to regain the hardness of purpose he feels being undermined by his love.

Preston	*Philip*
Dorothy Bridges	*Electrician*
Manager of the Florida	*Moorish tart/Anita*
Hotel	*Two comrades*

Comrade Wilkinson
Petra, hotel maid
Antonio, Philip's Colonel
Three comrades
Max, Philip's colleague
Sentry

Two signallers
Large Officer/General
His aide
A civilian
Assault guards
Comrades

Fifth Season, The
Sylvia Regan
Comedy 3 Acts
New York 1953
In the rag trade there are five seasons - Spring, Summer, Fall, Winter ... and Slack. In the centre of Manhattan's garment district, the combination office/model's dressing room of Goodwin-Pincus may be lush and showy, but the order book isn't. Partners Johnny Goodwin and Max Pincus are nearly broke when their top model Lorraine McKay brings along chain-store owner Miles Lewis who orders up a bonanza of their classy ladies' garments, designed by firm's wonder boy Ferelli.

For a while everything goes swingingly, enabling Johnny to pay for his and his family's extravagant lifestyle. His son Marty enters the business, but soon everything goes wrong. Johnny begins an affair with Lorraine and is discovered by wife Fran, while Lewis stops paying and the firm can't fill their orders. The problems are resolved partly by Pincus's naive cleverness and partly by the break-up of Johnny and Lorraine. Generous Lorraine then dates Lewis and later threatens to reveal all to his wife; he is forced to pay up and make friends again with Johnny, and Pinkie finds romance with book-keeper Miriam, who now appreciates good qualities over looks. To cap it all, the South's biggest buyer is on his way up the stairs ...
Ruby D. Prince
Shelly
Lorraine McKay
Ferelli
Max Pincus
Johnny Goodwin
Frances Goodwin
Marty Goodwin
Miriam Oppenheim
Dolores
Midge, a redhead model
Carole, a brunette model
Miles Lewis

Filumena Marturano
Eduardo de Filippo
Comedy 3 Acts
Naples 1946
For twenty-five years, wealthy Neopolitan Domenico Soriano has been faithfully served by Filumena as mistress, housekeeper and comforter. Although he had promised to marry her years before, he does not do so until she is on her deathbed. The marriage produces a miraculous recovery and she takes on her new wifely role vigorously and throws Domenico's current mistress, Diana, out of the house. Domenico now realizes he has been fooled into marriage and tries to get an annulment, but Filumena brings her three grown sons to the house and tells Domenico that one of them is his, but she will not reveal which.

Try as he may, she will not tell him the secret and gradually he begins to realize how great the love is that Filumena has for him and he happily offers to adopt all three boys as his own.
Filumena Marturano
Domenico Soriano
Alfredo Amoroso
Rosalia Solimene
Diana
Lucia
Umberto
Riccardo
Michele
Nocella
Teresina
Waiters

Fings Ain't Wot They Used T'be
Frank Norman
Music and lyrics by Lionel Bart
Musical 2 Acts
London 1959
Scar-faced gangster Fred Cochran, now past his prime, runs a run-down shpieler (illegal gambling den) in Soho during the late fifties. He is assisted by ladyfriend and ex-tart Lil, and they are almost broke. So are most of the hangers-on who include: mouthy ponce Tosher and his two cheeky girls Betty and Rosey, good-natured Paddy, and newly-released burglar Redhot (perpetually chilled through long spells in damp cells). Their wheelings and dealings, conducted in authentic Cockney-underworld lingo, are perpetually interrupted by local cop, Sergeant Collins, who is paid off by Fred.

When Fred wins a considerable sum of money on the horses, he gets the club redecorated, courtesy of camp Horace Seaton, and intends getting back into the big time. Opening night is attended by 'Orrible (Honourable) Percy Fortesque, an old gambling friend of Fred's, and plummy girlfriend Myrtle. Percy, of course, is also broke, but that is the least of Fred's problems. He has incurred the wrath of upmarket rival French 'Erbert, who sends along vicious heavy Meathead and boys to carve up Fred. But there is life in the old dog yet - Fred disposes of the opposition and then decides it is time to go straight. Paddy drags along a bribable priest to marry Lil and Fred, and Sergeant Collins, threatened with being booted out of the Soho police, realizes his ambition to go crooked by leaving the force and taking over Fred's shpieler.
Songs include: 'Fings Ain't Wot They Used T'Be'; 'Big Time'; 'Contemporary'

Frederick Cochran	*The Brass Upstairs*
Lily Smith	*Horace Seaton*
Paddy	*Gamblers*
Sergeant Collins	*Builders*
Policewoman	*Percy Fortesque*
Police Constable	*Myrtle*
Betty	*Busker*
Rosey	*Teddy girls and boys*
Tosher	*A 'Mystery'*
Redhot	*A priest*

Fiorello!
Jerome Weidman
Book by George Abbott
Music by Jerry Bock
Lyrics by Sheldon Harnick
Musical 2 Acts
New York 1959

In New York City shortly before the First World War, the Fourteenth District, like most of the town, is under the political control of the Democratic Party's Tammany Hall machine. The flamboyant little Fiorello La Guardia is an oddball: half Jewish, Italian, and not a Catholic, he fights for harassed and exploited workers; such as the ladies of the Nifty Shirt Waist Factory, he is incorruptible and he wants to be a Republican Congressman. He succeeds and goes to Washington where he creates a lot of hostility by trying to get Uncle Sam into the European war. Though the Draft Act did not apply to Congressmen he enlists, pausing only to marry Catholic Thea.

On a movie screen we see the *Pathé News* showing basic training and La Guardia in Europe making sure the Allies win the war. Ten years later war hero Maj. La Guardia is back at his law practice and wanting to become Mayor of New York City. But his campaign against the powerful Jimmy Walker is doomed; his opponents are too unscrupulous and violent. Also, his wife dies.

However, many big-hearted folk want to see him serve the city he loves. He marries his assistant Marie who has loved him for years, again accepts the nomination and this time he is destined to win.

Songs include:'On the Side of the Angels'; 'Politics and Poker'; Little Tin Box'

Announcer	*Floyd*
Fiorello	*Sophie*
Neil	*Four Hecklers*
Morris	*Thea*
Mrs Pomerantz	*Senator*
Mr Lopez	*Judge Carter*
Mr Zappatella	*Commissioner*
Dora	
Marie	
Ben	
Six hack policitians	
Seedy man	
Nina	

Fire Raisers, The
Max Frisch
Play 6 Scenes
Zurich 1958

This piece is simultaneously presented in a living room and attic setting, watched over by a chorus of firemen.

Biedermann, a benevolent factory owner, is disturbed by newspaper reports of an arsonist at large, who sets fire to attics, but is easily persuaded to let his own attic to an insolent ex-wrestler Joseph Schmitz, who laughs off ideas that he might be a firebug. Biedermann's wife, however, is not impressed by Schmitz's bad manners and is deeply disturbed when he has a friend Eisenring to share his room and starts rolling in barrels of gasoline. The gullible and guilt-ridden Biedermann assures the police that the barrels contain only hair tonic, and he invites his lodgers to dinner, enjoys their jokes about being arsonists and even helps them to measure up detonating fuses. A third accomplice appears, an idealistic philosopher, but he dissociates himself from the impending disaster as the foolish Biedermann supplies his guests with matches.

Gottlieb Biedermann	*Policeman*
Anna	*Widow Knechtling*
Schmitz	*Doctor of philosophy*
Babette Biedermann	*Chief fireman*
Eisenring	*Firemen*

Five Finger Exercise
Peter Shaffer
Tragedy 2 Acts
London 1958

A young highly educated German orphan, Walter Langer, recently hired as tutor to Pamela Harrington, arrives with the family for a weekend at their cottage in Suffolk. He is the favourite of Louise Harrington, Pamela's neurotic, affected and arty mother, whose patronage he has received despite the resistance of Pamela's father, a bluff self-made businessman, Stanley.

Their son, Clive, is emotionally stranded in the confusion of late adolescence; alienated from his father, he is beginning to view with irony his mother's cultural pretensions, and waiting anxiously to go off to university. Pamela, a rather horsey, commonsensical girl, fails to notice Walter's growing attachment to her and the rest of the family. Clive, however, is pricked by jealousy of Walter's closeness to his mother, and sets out to destroy their attachment by indicating to his father that his mother and Walter are having an affair.

The tensions created by Stanley's jealousy and Clive's bad faith spill over into estrangement of all the family members for one another, and the German orphan loses all hope of being adopted by them. Indeed, Walter's confession that he sees Louise as an ideal adoptive mother so offends her vanity that she insists that Stanley dismiss him on the entirely false grounds that Walter is romancing Pamela. In despair, Walter attempts suicide.

Louise Harrington
Stanley Harrington
Pamela Harrington
Clive Harrington
Walter Langer

Flare Path
Terence Rattigan
Drama 3 Acts
London 1942

Life at the Falcon Hotel in Milchester, Lincs, revolves around the nearby airfield. It is wartime and the hotel is home for Doris, Countess Skriczevinsky, a likeable former barmaid married to Polish flier Johnny (the Count), and several other RAF bods. Fading movie star Peter Kyle arrives to surprise former lover, actress Patricia, now married to Flight-Lieut. Teddy Graham; the plan is that Patricia will be leaving Teddy for Peter. Also present is Sgt (Dusty) Miller and his wife Maudie, who's staying just for the one night before she has to return to London for her job in a laundry. But before Peter and Patricia get a chance to tell Teddy it's all over, there's an emergency bombing raid. When Teddy returns and confesses to Patricia his fears (after saving his aircraft and crew when the plane has been shot up), Patricia changes her mind and decides her place is with her husband. Meanwhile Johnny's plane has disappeared and Doris gets Peter to translate a letter Johnny left for her, written in French. It's moving and loving and makes nonsense of Doris's (and the others) fears that Johnny might ditch her when the war is over. But all her fears are premature; Johnny returns and tells everyone the tale of his watery adventures after being shot down, and at the end Patricia decides to give up acting to stay with Teddy. They gather round the piano and sing, and Peter leaves.

Countess Skriczevinsky	*Flight-Lieut Graham*
Peter Kyle	*Patricia Graham*
Mrs Oakes	*Mrs Miller*
Sgt Miller	*Sqn-Leader Swanson*
Percy	*Cpl Jones*
Count Skriczevinksy	

Flea in Her Ear, A
Georges Feydeau
Translated by John Mortimer
Farce 3 Acts
London 1966

Antoinette, the cook at the Paris home of insurance agent Victor Emmanuel Chandebise, is obviously amorously interested in Camille, Chandebise's nephew, behind the back of her husband the butler Etienne. Camille is a clerk who has a cleft palate and can hardly be understood. Dr Finache, who examines insurance customers, calls to report on the health of Spanish gentleman Homenides who had been examined that morning though the doctor would later discover that he should have examined Homenides' wife Lucienne. Chandebise's wife Raymonde is scheming with Lucienne to trap Chandebise who, Raymonde is convinced, is being unfaithful though actually, as Chandebise confides to the doctor, the problem is one of sudden impotence. Lucienne, whose handwriting is unknown to Chandebise, writes a passionate letter saying she had spotted him at the theatre and fallen in love at first sight so she is expecting him to meet him for a fling in the Hotel Coq d'Or in Montretout, an establishment frequented by the doctor for his numerous assignations and who recommends its amenities to young Camille whom he fixes up with a silver palate so that he can talk normally. When Chandebise gets the note, he cannot believe any sexy woman could be interested in a man of his unfortunate appearance; it must be a case of mistaken identity and the true target of the unknown lady's desire must be his friend Tournel who was with him at the theatre. Tournel is persuaded to keep the assignation and leaves . Homenides sees the note and recognizes Lucienne's writing, produces his revolver and says he will go to the hotel and kill Tournel. Chandebise will have to try to warn Tournel.

The hotel is run with would-be military precision by ex-Sgt Maj. Feraillon with his ex-courtesan wife Olympe, maid Eugénie, Feraillon's malingering uncle Baptistin and hotel porter Poche who drank himself out of the Army and was found by Feraillon selling matches on the Champs Elysées. Though scruffy and battered, Poche looks very like the dignified Chandebise. Among the guests is the Prussian Schwarz who is expecting a woman to be provided and keeps approaching most of the above female characters. Antoinette is there for a tryst with Camille, who soon loses his silver palate, and Etienne comes to catch his wife. Raymonde is there to catch her husband at it. She and Tournel, found together, think Poche is Chandebise and Feraillon mistakes Chandebise for Poche and kicks him to get into uniform. Lucienne, there as a witness, tangles with a confused Chandebise and then thinks it is she that Homenides has comes to kill. A revolving bed, turned with a button to enable adulterous guests to hide, keeps removing people or bringing them on to ever-increasing embarrassment and chaos. Homenides starts firing and has to be overpowered.

Back *chez* Chandebise, Antoinette denies to Etienne that he had seen her at the hotel. A drunken Poche turns up to try to get his uniform back and is thought by the doctor to be Chandebise become alcoholic. Feraillon turns up, having found Camille's palate, and starts again kicking the real Chandebise around. At the end the lookalike phenomenon is realized by all and the Chandebises are reconciled.

Camille
Antoinette
Etienne
Dr Finache
Lucienne Homenides de Histangua

Raymonde Chandebise
Victor Emmanuel Chandebise
Romain Tournel
Carlos Homenides de Histangua
Eugénie
Augustin Feraillon
Olympe
Baptistin
Herr Schwarz
Poche (played by the Chandebise actor)

Fool for Love
Sam Shepard
Tragedy
San Francisco 1983

A character who is identified only as the Old Man, sits rocking in a chair explaining and describing the tortured love of May and Eddie. As May and Eddie (who has just returned to May from touring the Western USA with a rodeo show) vacillate between a devouring mutual need and hysterical mutual rejection, the Old Man interjects the history of the two into the action. Bit by bit he reveals, mixed with much self-justification, the fact that both are his children, each by a different wife; and that he spent several years trying, ultimately without success, to prevent the two families from meeting.

A limousine arrives, incongruously, outside the caravan in which May has been living, and several shots are fired at the caravan. The limousine, it appears, belongs to a Countess with whom Eddie has had an affair. Spurred by jealousy, she has followed Eddie to May's. Herself now infuriated with jealousy, May taunts Eddie with the impending arrival of Martin, with whom she has a date.

When Martin arrives, he finds both Eddie and May drunk on tequila. To dissuade Martin from serious interest in May, Eddie reveals that she is both his half-sister and his lover. May reveals that her mother committed suicide because the Old Man abandoned them both, when they had only just found him again after years of searching. The Countess returns, sets fire to Eddie's pickup truck and horse trailer and stampedes his horses. Eddie leaves the caravan to survey the damage but May, believing he has left for good, packs a bag and follows him. The Old Man is left alone, still rocking in his chair.

May
Eddie
Martin
The Old Man

Fools Rush In
Kenneth Horne
Comedy 3 Acts
London 1947

Pam is a pretty and scatty ditherer, but she's already dressed and ready for her wedding with Joe, while everyone else is still rushing around. So she reads through the prayer book and to her consternation realizes those matrimonial vows are serious, solemn and lifelong. Who should turn up out of the blue but Paul, her long-lost father, divorced from her scatty mother Angela since before Pam can remember. Contrary to myth, he isn't an ogre but a thoroughly pleasant chap, which sets Pam thinking: if Mum didn't know with Paul, how is she to know with Joe? After all, Joe's a thoroughly pleasant chap too. So she postpones the wedding until she can get to know Joe better. Everyone, including her mother, housekeeper Mrs Mandrake, daily help Mrs Coot and her mother's pompously hearty fiancé Charles are thunderstruck. Actress bridesmaid Millicent tries a ploy involving showing up Paul as a philandering rogue, but her silly seduction routine falls flat.

Fresh complications occur when Joe and Charles, naturally enough, begin to have doubts about marrying into this family. Events are resolved when Joe masterfully gets Pam to elope and Charles realizes he's probably better off going alone to his new posting in Peru. The way is clear for a reconciliation between Paul and Angela and they appear to be getting on well ... until Angela, eminently unreasonable, provokes a fight.

Millicent
Mrs Coot
Mrs Mandrake
Angela
Pam
Charles
Paul
Joe

For Better, for Worse
Arthur Watkyn
Comedy 3 Acts
London 1952

Tony is broke and jobless but a pleasant chap, and when he asks Mr Purves for his daughter Anne's hand, Mr Purves tells him first find a job and a flat. He does so and permission is granted. The trouble is, the job is not very well paid and the flat very small and they start out on the wrong foot by filling it with a lot of furniture. Due to a misunderstanding, they do not get on with upstairs neighbours Peter and Jane Debenham, and then there are all sorts of problems with gossipy cleaning ladies, comic plumbers and nosy spinster neighbours.

The marriage stays happy though, and there is a reconciliation with the Debenhams (a pleasant couple really), but sadly the young couple's expenditure outstrips their income. When the men come to repossess the furniture, Tony and Anne hide upstairs with the Debenhams, but then Mr and Mrs Purves arrive. Mr Purves pays off the men, Anne and Tony reappear and to everyone's satisfaction father-in-law tells Tony he has an opening at his own firm at a better wage. Everyone is happy, especially the Purves - who were afraid that Tony and Anne might want to come back and live at their home.

Forty Carats

Anne	*Fred*
Tony	*Alf*
Mrs Purves	*Mrs Doyle*
Mr Purves	*Medlicott*
Peter Debenham	*Miss Mainbrace*
Jane Debenham	*Furniture man*

Forty Carats
Pierre Barillet and Jean Pierre Gredy
Comedy 2 Acts
New York 1969
Estate agent Ann Stanley, just past her fortieth birthday, feels life has passed her by. She has an eighteen-year-old daughter, Trina, an eccentric mother and a constantly broke ex-husband, Billy, who continually pesters her for money. Despite the attentions of Eddy Edwards, a client, she cannot help but reminisce on a brief affair in Greece the previous summer with twenty-two-year-old Peter Latham, heir to a fortune.

When Peter re-enters her life, her feelings are confused; she is flattered, but intensely worried about the age difference and what her family will think. When Peter proposes, her family (and his) are definitely opposed, but his maturity and self-assurance shine through, and Ann's doubts and the opposition of the families are overcome by the end of the play.

Ann Stanley	*Trina Stanley*
Peter Latham	*Mrs Latham*
Mrs Adams	*Mr Latham*
Mrs Margolin	*Pat*
Billy Boylan	
Eddy Edwards	
Maud Hayes	

42nd Street
Michael Stewart and Mark Bramble
Songs by Harry Warren and Al Dubin
Musical 2 Acts
New York 1981
Down-and-out producer/director Julian Marsh needs to make a comeback; his vehicle is a show titled *Pretty Polly* that is currently in New York rehearsal and aiming towards a tryout in Philadelphia - and thenceforth to a Broadway opening night at the prestigious Forty Second Street Theatre. Problems beset the production all the way along the line, not least of which are the economic strictures of the Depression era in which the story is set. The temperament of the show's star Dorothy Brock does not help either, and she has Julian over a barrel because she is the one who has persuaded an admirer of hers to back the show.

When Dorothy sprains an ankle it looks like the end for Julian and *Pretty Polly*. The sets are struck, everybody is out of work and the Philadelphia train is headed back to New York. Then somebody remembers that little chorus girl who was sacked the other day. Her name is Peggy Sawyer and she knows all the star's numbers, she can sing and she can dance and ... but Julian has now got to persuade her to rejoin the show. Well, he does, and of course Peggy triumphs mightily, taking over the leading role with masterly aplomb. A star is born yet again.

Andy Lee	*Lorraine*
Oscar	*Phyllis*
Mac	*Julian Marsh*
Annie	*Dorothy Brock*
Maggie Jones	*Abner Dillon*
Bert Barry	*Pat Denning*
Billy Lawlor	*Thugs*
Peggy Sawyer	*Doctor*

Forty Years On
Alan Bennett
Comedy Drama 2 Acts
London 1968
The schoolboys and teachers of Albion House are presenting *Speak for England, Arthur*, a play about the past century, mostly concerning war, literary gossip and reminiscences. It is an ambitious production, involving back-projection slides, excerpts from radio broadcasts - Chamberlain, Hippodrome, Robb Wilton - with many sound effects, music and excerpts from the memoirs of Harold Nicolson, Osbert Sitwell and Leonard Woolf. Things do not go well. There are deviations from the script, dirty jokes and interruptions from boys in the audience including obscene songs from the rugger team.

After the school play, this play ends on a serious note of nostalgia for a lost romantic and old-fashioned concept of honour, patriotism, chivalry and duty. The headmaster muses that the modern crowd 'has found the door into the secret garden. Now they will tear up the flowers by the roots, strip the borders and strew them with paper and broken bottles.'

The headmaster
Franklin, housemaster
Tempest, junior master
Matron
Miss Nisbitt, bursar's secretary
Head boy and lectern reader
The organist
Twenty schoolboys

Frankenstein
Tim Kelly adapted from the story by Mary Shelley
Drama 2 Acts
New York 1974
Victor Frankenstein is a brilliant young scientist who is troubled because his young brother was recently murdered. When police officer Ernst visits and tells Victor that a young girl was given the cross his brother was wearing when he died by a 'large man stitched together', Victor is almost violent and his reaction

shocks his mother and best friend Henry.

Henry demands an explanation for Victor's behaviour and Victor tells him that when he was at university he created a monster using different parts of dead human bodies stitched together - this means that his monster has killed his brother. Henry cannot believe what he has heard, but at this moment the monster walks in wanting help - he wants to die.

Victor feels no sympathy for the monster but decides to reverse the transplantation. However, the monster changes his mind and decides he wants a wife after listening to Victor and fiancée Elizabeth. But the monster never gets a wife; just more despair as he causes the deaths of three other people including Victor's mother and Henry. The monster leaves but returns as promised on the wedding night of Victor and Elizabeth. He is shot and drowned and it is only then that Victor Frankenstein feels a little compassion for his dead creation.

Ernst
Sophie, housekeeper
Victor Frankenstein
Elizabeth
Henry, scientist and Victor's friend
Frau Frankenstein, Victor's mother
The creature
Justine, a gypsy girl

French Without Tears
Terence Rattigan
Comedy 3 Acts
London 1936

At M.Maingot's villa Miramar a group of young Britons are learning French, hoping for entry into the Diplomatic Corps. M. Maingot insists they speak only French in his presence, and much mirth ensues. Young Kenneth 'Babe' Lake is doing dismally, but his beautiful sister Diana is brilliant - at flirting. She has stolen Kit Neilan's heart and so he is oblivious to Maingot's attractive daughter Jacqueline who dotes on him. These proceedings are watched with cynicism by would-be writer Hon. Alan Howard and hearty Brian Curtis, but when unpopular new arrival Lieut-Com. Rogers appears, Diana switches her affections to him.

Fights, threats, and a drunken evening at the local fancy dress ball ensue, and the two contenders become friends united against Diana's wiles. When Diana admits to Alan that her scheming was intended all along to catch him, he, like the others, finds her hard to resist and enlists their help in thwarting her. They are hoping that the arrival of one Lord Heybrook will divert Diana, and Alan determines to leave immediately and against his parents' wishes become a writer. When Lord Heybrook turns out to be a fifteen-year-old boy, Diana also starts to pack, and Alan realizes he is done for.

Kenneth Lake
Brian Curtis
Hon. Alan Howard
Marianne
M . Maingot
Lieut-Com. Rogers
Diana Lake
Kit Neilan
Jacqueline Maingot
Lord Heybrook

Friends, The
Arnold Wesker
Drama 2 Acts
Stockholm 1970

In a room in Leeds middle-aged Esther is ill and in pain in bed, probably dying. Her lover Roland who does not feel too good himself, holds peculiar views on the non-existence of death, and appears to relish pain because he likes to slash himself with a razor. Her brother Manfred is a voracious reader, notemaker and philosophical ruminator who feels he is turning into an aesthete. Their friend and partner (in their shops' business), Crispin, is sexually ambiguous and earns money servicing old ladies.

Friends Tessa and Simone call and with them comes Macey who has been the manager of their main shop. He is the most down-to-earth in that he is concerned about their finances as they are going bankrupt. The others are not much bothered about the money except that they will not be able to contribute to violent revolutionary socialist causes, one of the subjects they love to dwell on, along with youth, death and the meanings of words.

Esther dies and Roland, Manfred, Simone, Tessa and Crispin manipulate the corpse into such gestures as blowing a kiss and making a clenched fist salute. This appears macabre but is done with love. The watching Macey kisses Esther before leaving.

Esther
Manfred
Crispin
Tessa
Simone
Macey
Roland

Frogs, The
Aristophanes
Comedy 1 Act
Athens c. 405BC

Dionysus, in whose honour all Athenian tragedy was written, has become appalled at the low standards of recent drama. He decides to journey to Hades to bring back Euripedes so that the great tragedian can inspire higher standards.

Disguised as Hercules, who had once brought Cerberus back from Hades, Dionysus, with his slave, Xanthias, is ferried across the Styx to Hades. In the underworld, they find some who had welcomed Hercules' visit, others who had attacked it. To the former, Dionysus impersonates Hercules but forces

Xanthias to do so when they encounter opposition to their visit.

Although Dionysus intends to return to Athens with Euripedes, Aeschylus insists that his own achievements entitle him to go instead. There ensues a series of slightly absurd poetic contests by means of which Dionysus hopes that Euripedes' claims to superiority will be established. Instead, the greater majesty and authority of Aeschylus's work becomes clear and he and Dionysus bid farewell to Pluto, God of the Underworld and set off for Athens.

Dionysus, patron of Drama
Xanthias, Dionysus's slave
Hercules
Charon, ferryman of the Styx
Aeacus, gatekeeper of Hades
Euripedes, dramatist
Aeschylus, dramatist
Pluto, god of the underworld
Chorus
Chorus of frogs
Slaves
Shades of dancing girls

Front Page, The
Ben Hecht and Charles MacArthur
Farce 3 Acts
New York 1928

In the press room of the Criminal Courts Building in Chicago, a group of cynical and hard-bitten reporters await the hanging of Earl Williams, a 'Bolshevik' who shot and killed a black policeman. The Mayor and bungling Sheriff are desperate for Williams to hang in order to secure the Negro vote in the forthcoming election. When Williams escapes due to the Sheriff's stupidity, they even bribe and send Pincus, a messenger, with a reprieve for Williams. They plan for Williams to be shot by deputies.

Hildy Johnson of the *Herald Examiner* arrives to say goodbye to his buddies. He is getting married to Peggy, who has persuaded him to quit his job and move to New York. He is being continually pestered to stay by his unscrupulous editor Walter Burns who resorts to all kinds of dirty tricks to get his way, including having Peggy's mother 'kidnapped'.

When everyone rushes out after a report comes in of Williams being found and cornered, Hildy is left alone. The exhausted Williams comes in through the window and gives himself up. Hildy hides him in a big desk and phones Burns with the scoop of his life. The others arrive back and taunt Williams' friend Mollie, a gold-hearted prostitute, until she jumps from the window. Burns arrives, but soon Williams is found and Hildy and Burns are arrested for harbouring the felon. But when Pincus returns with the reprieve and refuses to be bribed, the two newspapermen are released in the hope they will keep quiet. Peggy and her mother return and Burns magnanimously changes his mind about the

marriage and sends the couple off with his blessing, even giving Hildy a wedding present - his own watch. Shortly after the couple leave, Burns almost reluctantly pulls yet another trick on Hildy.

Wilson, American	*Mollie Malloy*
Endicott, Post	*Sheriff Hartman*
Murphy, Journal	*Peggy Grant*
McCue, City Press	*Mrs Grant*
Shwartz, Daily News	*The Mayor*
Kruger, Journal of Commerce	*Mr Pincus*
	Earl Williams
Bensinger, Tribune	*Walter Burns*
Mrs Schlosser	*Carl, a deputy*
Woodenshoes Eichorn	*Frank, a deputy*
Diamond Louis	*Two policemen*
Hildy Johnson, Herald Examiner	
Jennie	

Fumed Oak
Noël Coward
Play 1 Act
London 1935
See: *Tonight at 8.30*

Funeral Games
Joe Orton
Comedy 8 Scenes
Yorkshire TV 1968

Pringle, a 'religious' conman, is visited by young rascal Caulfield who is shown an anonymous letter branding Tessa, Mrs Pringle, as an adulteress. Caulfield is hired to investigate. He finds Tessa with unfrocked priest McCorquodale to whom she administers odd therapies. McCorquodale has murdered his wife, whose corpse is in the cellar under coal.

Caulfield reports back to Pringle who gets a gun and resolves to murder Tessa on the grounds that if she can break the seventh commandment, he can break the sixth. But in the confrontation at McCorquodale's he is persuaded only to pretend, to say she has gone away, so that she can stay with McCorquodale.

Rumours get around that Pringle is a murderer but then a reporter writes demanding proof, alleging that Pringle's trendy reputation as a killer is fraudulent. Caulfield is asked to provide as proof some part of a body, preferably a head. Caulfield goes to McCorquodale's cellar but, unable to get the head off, severs a hand instead. Tessa protests, so Caulfield and McCorquodale tie her up.

Pringle shows the 'proof' to the press. Caulfield advises him that Tessa is acting up and must be killed (again). They go to McCorquodale's room. There is a fight during which Caulfield tries to shoot Tessa but the gun is empty. McCorquodale reveals that Pringle was making a breach in the seventh commandment and Mrs McCorquodale. It is discovered that the real hand has been taken by the reporter and a fake hand substituted.

The press now have evidence. Police officers arrive with a warrant. Pringle says the remains in the cellar are of his wife. They are all arrested with Pringle confident that some angel will release them, as everything works out in accordance with the Divine Will.

Pringle
Tessa
Caulfield
McCorquodale
First man
Police officers

Funny Girl
Isobel Lennart
Lyrics by Bob Merrill
Music by Jule Styne
Musical 2 Acts
New York 1964

Based on the career of Fanny Brice, Queen of the Ziegfield Follies (c.1912), this musical opens with Fanny in her dressing room waiting for husband Nick Arnstein, shortly to be released from jail. As she wonders and worries about the future, she flashes back to the past; to her gawky stagestruck teenager years when, to her mother's disapproval, she auditions for Keeney's music hall and is rejected. Then she's befriended and coached by vaudeville dancer Eddie Ryan and triumphs at Keeney's with the song 'Cornet Man'. Backstage she meets gambler Nick. She later gets a telegram from the great Ziegfield himself, and goes on to conquer the Follies, and at a party thrown by her mother she and Nick realize they are falling in love. Fanny goes on tour with the Follies and Nick buys a horse farm in Kentucky, but when they meet again, Fanny is so smitten she gives up touring to be with Nick.

They marry and their friends throw a surprise party, but later she loses all her savings on Nick's Florida Casino enterprise which flops. Nick refuses to accept any more financial help from Fanny, and after involvement in a crooked deal he is jailed.

Back in her dressing room, Nick arrives but it is obvious their marriage is at an end; there are sad farewells and for Fanny it is back to the Follies.

Songs include: 'People'; 'Don't Rain On My Parade'; 'His Love Makes Me Beautiful'

Fanny Brice	*Trombone Soloist*
John	*Bubbles*
Emma	*Polly*
Mrs Brice	*Maude*
Mrs Strakosh	*Nick Arnstein*
Mrs Meeker	*Stage Director*
Mrs O'Malley	*Florenz Ziegfield Jr*
Tom Keeney	*Mimsey*
Eddie Ryan	*Ziegfield Tenor*
Heckie	*Ziegfield Lead Dancer*
Snub Taylor	*Adolph*
Trombone Smitty	*Mrs Nadler*
Five Finger Finney	*Paul*
Cathy	*Mr Renaldi*
Vera	*Mike Halsey*
Jenny	*Two showgirls*
Ben	*Two workmen*

Funny Peculiar
Mike Stott
Comedy
Liverpool 1975

Young married couple Trevor and Irene run the local shop in a small Pennine village, but to Irene's dismay, Trevor is obsessed with 'self-expression' and free love. Irene is nice and ordinary but unadventurous in bed and she reckons that is affecting Trevor. For all his preaching and earnest philosophizing, Trevor doesn't have the basic commonsense of most of the other villagers, including down-to-earth police Sergeant Harry Asquith or even simpleton Stanley, son of local gossip Mrs Baldry. And when Trevor's letter of support to their homosexual local Revd Thwaite brings him round to express thanks, Trevor's heavy-handed candidness is the last straw towards Thwaite's suicide.

Trevor's frustration is appeased somewhat when attractive new villager Shirley practises what Trevor preaches and they have a night together; to Trevor's astonishment, husband Eric returns and doesn't seem to mind. And when Mrs Baldry lets her hair down and propositions Trevor, he backs off, falls downstairs and breaks almost everything. Shirley and Eric turn up to visit him, strapped up in hospital, together with Irene who's been sexually liberated by the new duo, and proceeds to prove it to Trevor, enthusiastically fellating him under the covers until he agrees to go into business and who knows what else with their new friends.

Trevor Tinsley	*Stanley Baldry*
Irene Tinsley	*Shirley Smith*
Revd A. J. Thwaite	*Eric Smith*
Sergeant Harry Asquith	*Desmond Ainsley*
Mrs Baldry	*Shane Pritchard*

Funny Thing Happened on the Way to the Forum, A
Burt Shevelove and Larry Gelbart
Music by Stephen Sondheim
Musical Comedy 2 Acts
New York 1962

Based loosely on the plays of Plautus, this Marx Brothers'-style comedy has as its central character Pseudolus, a slave desperate to get his freedom. To do so he bargains with his master's son, Hero, to obtain for him a beautiful courtesan Philia, who has been sold to a soldier, Miles Gloriosus, by Lycus. Senex, Hero's father, also fancies the girl but he is under the eye of his wife, Domina, who, hoping to catch him, out disguises herself and is confused as a 'madame' by Miles Gloriosus. Pseudolus, to save Philia, spreads a rumour that she has died of plague and provides a corpse in the shape of another slave, Hysterium, appropriately dressed. General confusion and mayhem ensue before Miles learns that he is Philia's brother, Hero gets his girl and cunning Pseudolus gets his freedom.

Songs include: 'Lovely'; 'Comedy Tonight'; 'Love, I Hear'; 'Everybody Ought to Have a Maid'

Prologus, an actor	Lycus, a trader in
Senex, an old man	courtesans
Domina, his wife	**Courtesans:** Tintinabula,
Hero, his son	Panacea, The Geminae,
Hysterium, Senex' slave	Vibrata and Gymnasia
Pseudolus, Hero's slave	Philia, a virgin
Erronius, an old man	The Proteans
Miles Gloriosus,	
a warrior	

Fur Coat and No Knickers
Mike Harding
Comedy 2 Acts
London 1980

It is the eve of Mark Greenhalgh's wedding to Deirdre Ollerenshawe. Mark is having a stag-night and after going with his friends to every pub in the neighbourhood, they end up at a nightclub. When they leave, Mark's friends, always ready for a laugh, chain him to a lamp-post with a pump-up rubber doll purloined from the club. Mark is almost arrested but as he is the son of local Councillor Greenhalgh, the police let him off.

The next day all the men have ghastly hangovers and Deirdre and her mother Edith are in a panic. The wedding goes well, but afterwards everyone ends up drunk again including Father Molloy who has found the rubber doll. Molloy quickly explains that the doll is Mark's and a row breaks out.

Edith Ollerenshawe	Ronald Greenhalgh
Barmaid	Man
Harry Ollerenshawe	Policeman
Kevin Ollerenshawe	Mark Greenhalgh
Deirdre Ollerenshawe	Father Finbar Molloy
Evette	Hamish
Peter Ollerenshawe	Jimmy
Nip (George Albert)	Bouncer
Muriel Greenhalgh	Waiter
Barmaid	Kirstene
Policewoman	Wendy

Gang's All Here, The
Jerome Lawrence and Robert E. Lee
Drama 3 Acts
New York 1959

Griffith P. Hastings, a relatively unknown senator, has been elected President of the United States. This he has achieved through the strength and influence of his powerful friends. Once in office he is bewildered by both power and duty. He foolishly divides his cabinet posts among those very friends - which had been their plan all along.

With the President's blind faith firmly invested in

them, they systematically abuse their positions for financial gain until the Presidency itself comes under independent inquiry. When realization finally dawns on Hastings, he acts for the first time with true assertion, sacking the Attorney-General and shifting the blame away from the Presidency, finally taking his own life.

Walter Rafferty	Cobb
Joshua Loomis	Maid
Charles Webster	Bruce Bellingham
Tad	Arthur Anderson
Higgy	Axel Maley
Judge Corriglione	LaVerne
Doc Kirkaby	Renee
Frances Greeley Hastings	Piano Player
Griffith P. Hastings	John Boyd

Gaslight
Patrick Hamilton
Melodrama 3 Acts
Richmond 1938

In the slightly seedy living room of a four-storied house in an unfashionable part of Victorian London, Mr (Jack) Manningham is cunningly, odiously trying to drive his nervous, timid and insecure wife Betty mad. He alternates between fake solicitousness, such as promising a visit to the theatre, and brutal accusations that she has hidden or lost things, so she must be punished and humiliated in front of the housekeeper, Elizabeth, and the pretty, impudent maid Nancy who turns out to be promiscuous and fancied by Manningham.

After Manningham goes out, ostensibly for a night on the town, the elderly, friendly but domineering ex-detective Rough calls and convinces Mrs Manningham that her husband is Sydney Power, already married, who murdered an old woman for her rubies in this very house twenty years ago and who is at that moment back in the house on the forbidden top floor, searching for the jewellery he never found. His presence upstairs is always detectable because when he lights the gas there, the gaslight downstairs dims. When the light goes back up they know Manningham's return is imminent, so Rough hides and Mrs Manningham goes up to bed. Manningham returns briefly and invites Elizabeth to sympathize with him because his wife takes after her mother who died insane. He goes out in search of new entertainment and Rough and Mrs Manningham re-emerge and go through his bureau where all the things she has lost or 'hidden' are found, including a brooch which, unbeknownst to Manningham, contains the rubies. Rough goes off to get the police, Mrs Manningham goes to her bedroom. Manningham returns, he and Nancy - who expects to take over as mistress - kiss. Mrs Manningham is persuaded to come down by a note threatening to harm their dog. Manningham, having discovered that his bureau has been forced open, resumes his persecution more menacingly than ever but is stopped by the reappearance of Rough who explains at teasing length that the game is up. Mrs Manningham asks for a last private word with Manningham/Power so policemen tie him to a chair and leave them. Now she enjoys tormenting him by pretending to help him escape, then feigning madness and incompetence. As he is taken away, destination gallows, she is gloriously happy.

Mrs Manningham
Mr Manningham
Rough
Elizabeth
Nancy
Policemen

Gay Lord Quex, The
Arthur Wing Pinero
Comedy 4 Acts
London 1899

Society manicurist Sophy Fullgarney believes her friend Muriel Eden is being forced by ambitious relatives into marriage with middle-aged roué Lord Quex. Sophy attempts to stop the marriage by arranging liaisons between Muriel and her sweetheart Capt. Bastling, then during an evening at Lady Owbridge's home, Sophy first attempts to compromise Quex with his old flame Duchess Strood, and then with herself. Both attempts fail, for Quex has truly reformed and loves Muriel, but is nevertheless impressed by Sophy's misguided devotion to her friend ... especially considering she was willing to put at risk her own engagement to jealous palmist Valma.

Back at her manicure establishment, Sophy is now ashamed of her mistrust of Quex, but realizes her suspicions of him have persuaded Muriel to attempt elopement with Bastling. So in fairness she subjects Bastling to the same temptation as she did Lord Quex - and Bastling kisses her while being observed by Muriel. Bastling leaves alone, Quex returns and leaves with Muriel, who then returns to thank Sophy, now collapsed in Valma's arms after her frantic maneuverings.

The Marquis of Quex	*Sophy Fullgarney*
Sir Chichester Frayne	*Miss Moon*
Capt. Bastling	*Miss Huddle*
'Valma', otherwise	*Miss Claridge*
Frank Pollitt	*Miss Limbird*
The Duchess of Strood	*Patrons of Miss*
Julia, Countess of	*Fullgarney*
Owbridge	*Servants at Fauncey*
Mrs Jack Eden	*Court*
Muriel Eden	*Governor of Uumbos*

Gazebo, The
Alec Coppel
Comedy 3 Acts
New York 1958

There is a lovely sylvan view from the living-room of TV crime writer Elliott Nash's house on Long Island and his actress wife Nell intends gilding the lily by erecting a genuine gazebo - an ornamental eighteenth-century summerhouse - on the lawn. Elliott secretly wants to move back to Manhattan and the Algonquin, but his ears prick up when Nell mentions that cement-filled foundations must be dug. This is the final piece in Elliott's plot to kill blackmailer Shelby, and he has even discussed it theoretically with his detective pal Harlow Edison - who can always spot the flaw in Elliott's plots. That night Shelby arrives and in the darkness Elliott shoots him, wraps him up and buries him. Next day Harlow arrives and tells them Nell's name was on Shelby's blackmail list (for a minor reefer offence) and that Shelby has been found dead in New York.

Flummoxed Elliott wonders who exactly he has killed, then is visited by The Dook and Louie, two villains looking for Joe the Black whom they dropped off at this address last night. Joe was Shelby's heavy and Elliott realizes it was Joe he killed. The villains want a key Joe had on him and Elliott tells them where the body is. They get the key and leave. Next day Harlow and tough cop Ryan appear; they have picked up The Dook and Louie who have informed on him. Elliott denies everything but when the police find and examine Joe's body they discover he was not shot - he died of a heart attack. Elliott is in the clear, Ryan leaves and Harlow returns, digs the bullet from the woodwork and tells Elliott how lucky he was. The gazebo falls over and Elliott and Nell plan to return to New York.

Elliott Nash	*Mr Thorpe*
Harlow Edison	*The Dook*
Matilda	*Louie*
Nell Nash	*Dr Wyner*
Mrs Chandler	*Ryan*
The visitor	*Druker*

Gentlemen Prefer Blondes
Joseph Fields based on the play and novel by Anita Loos
Music by Leo Robin and Jule Styne
Musical Comedy 2 Acts
New York 1949

Blonde bombshell flapper Lorelei Lee (a little girl from Little Rock) is aboard the liner *Ile de France* and bound for gay Paree with her brunette pal Dorothy who is escaping from Prohibition. Lorelei's fiancé, button tycoon Gus, bids them 'bon voyage', but before they have been in Paris very long, complications arise. Dorothy meets and falls for wealthy Henry Spoffard, but Lorelei flirts with old Sir Francis Beekman and borrows 5,000 dollars to buy a tiara.

Lady Beekman discovers what's going on and a posse of lawyers pounce on Lorelei, who has further complicated her life by excessive flirting with zipper manufacturer Josephus Gage. The pair are caught together by Gus, who has followed Lorelei to Europe, and their engagement is off. However, after Lorelei's terrific debut at a Paris nightclub, Gus relents; he and

Lorelei make up and he pays back Sir Francis. The lovers decide to return to the States and get married. Songs include: 'Diamonds are a Girl's Best Friend'; 'Coquette'; 'A Little Girl from Little Rock'

Dorothy Shaw	Sam
Lorelei Lee	Charlie
Gus Esmond	Taxi driver
Frank	Leon
George	Robert Lemanteur
Lady Phillis Beekman	Louis Lemanteur
Sir Francis Beekman	A flower girl
Mrs Ella Spoffard	Maître d'Hôtel
Deck stewards (2)	Mimi
Henry Spoffard	Fifi
Josephus Gage	Headwaiter
Pierre	Policemen
Gloria Stark	Mr Esmond
Bill	Entertainers
Joe	

Geography of a Horse Dreamer
Sam Shepard
Mystery 2 Acts
London 1974

In this absurdist piece, a man known simply as Cody, whose only talent is to be able to predict from dreams the winners of horse races, lies manacled to the bed in a sleazy hotel room somewhere in America.

Two sinister guards, Santee and Beaujo, have been charged with watching him and with getting him back to the highly accurate qualities of prediction which seem to have deserted him. All three men are waiting in fear of an impending visit from their criminal boss, Fingers, who will be in a murderous fury if Cody's predictions do not improve. Cody swallows sleeping tablets and manages to dream the winners of seven English dog races, thus bringing the men to believe Fingers will reprieve them.

Fingers arrives with a doctor, having decided that Cody is expendable, even given his recent improvement. The doctor announces that he will operate on Cody's neck to remove the 'dreamer's magic' which has accumulated there. Just as the doctor is about to sink the scalpel into Cody's neck, two immense Wyoming cowboys, who turn out to be Cody's brothers, blast their way into the hotel room to rescue him.

Cody, the dreamer
Santee, Beaujo, Cody's captors
Fingers, Cody's boss
Doctor
Waiter
Jasper and Jason, Cody's brothers

George and Margaret
Gerald Savory
Comedy 3 Acts
London 1937

Nobody really wants to see George and Margaret at the Garth-Banders home in Hampstead, but somehow Alice feels it is her duty to keep inviting them. They seldom arrive, and a good job too, because one February brings a host of domestic adventures. Youngest son Dudley, a musical prodigy and delightful young man, brings home his friend Roger, another delightful chap, and romance is in the air between Roger and Dudley's sister Frankie, who imagines herself rather avant-garde and an expert on all things romantic/sexual. They don't tell each other of their feelings right away. This leads to Roger nearly running off, before coming clean with Frankie and promising to marry her. Meanwhile eldest son Claude, a stolid architect, is in love with the family's maid Gladys, an attractive girl, but Alice, his mother, is upset as she feels Claude is marrying below his station. Sensible Gladys soon brings her round though, and the various intrigues and comings-and-goings are watched with equanimity by Alice's husband, sensible Malcolm. Finally, after Gladys has been replaced by old maid Beer, at whom everybody laughs, George and Margaret turn up amidst a hail of chortles.

Gladys
Malcolm Garth-Bander
Alice Garth-Bander
Dudley
Frankie
Claude
Roger
Beer

Getting Married
George Bernard Shaw
Drama 1 Act
London 1908

The family are gathered for the wedding of the Bishop of Chelsea's fifth daughter Edith to Cecil Sykes. It is a matrimonial occasion and matrimonial problems arise. The Bishop's brother Boxer (Gen. Bridgenorth) has always loved Lesbia, younger sister of the Bishop's wife. Lesbia, however, is determined to remain single. Their other brother Reginald, married to silly-clever young thing Leo, is upset because Leo has fallen for young Hotchkiss - 'mushroom face'. And typically, both bride and groom have begun to have second thoughts about their commitment. An attempt is then made to draw up a partnership contract in the fashion of the ancient Romans, but it fails miserably; marriage, it seems, is the lesser of the alternative evils. The problem of Leo, Reginald and Hotchkiss is solved by the appearance of Mayoress Mrs George, brought along by eminently sensible greengrocer Alderman Collins. She is a secret admirer of the Bishop and she has also been worshipped from afar by snobby Hotchkiss, a slave to her common but sensible charms. All this is aided by the Bishop's chaplain Soames, a former solicitor and total celibate who nevertheless has some idea of what women want.

Mrs Bridgenorth   William Collins

Gen. Bridgenorth
Lesbia Grantham
Reginald Bridgenorth
Leo Bridgenorth
The Bishop of Chelsea
St John Hotchkiss

Cecil Sykes
Edith Bridgenorth
Soames
Mrs George
Beadle

Getting On
Alan Bennett
Drama 2 Acts
London 1971

Self-absorbed George, a Labour MP is 'getting on' - he's a middle-aged and disillusioned idealist and fails to notice when his ever-busy attractive wife Polly falls mildly for young handyman Geoff and they have an affair. Geoff also has an affair with George's Tory 'double', his friend Brian, a homosexual who is in the process of quietly leaving Parliament, threatened by anonymous exposure. George's contempt for the modern 'hippie' attitudes of Andy, his discontented seventeen-year-old son from his first marriage is echoed in the boy's venom towards his father, but nevertheless George shows more interest in Andy's progress than that of his younger son and daughter by Polly.

Popular Geoff finally decides to leave for Torremolinos, and how long Andy will remain living at home in mutual bitterness is doubtful. George is also too busy with his obsessive self-analysis to notice his beloved mother-in-law Edith is probably dying, and his advice to Brian about the blackmailer is both foolish and naive. Geoff goes, Brian leaves, and George and Polly just have to get on with it.

George Oliver, MP
Polly Oliver
Brian Lowther, MP
Edith Baker

Geoff Price
Andy Oliver
Mrs Brodribb

Ghost Sonata, The
August Strindberg
Grotesque 1 Act
Stockholm 1907

As with many other of Strindberg's plays, *The Ghost Sonata* may be set almost anywhere in modern Europe.

A sinister, crippled, rich and deeply embittered old man, Director Hummel, sets out to destroy a Colonel who, when both men were still young, had won the hand of a woman he loved. The Director's hatred has been magnified by the fact, known only to himself and the Colonel's wife, that the daughter the Colonel dotes on is really Hummel's natural child.

Hummel insinuates himself into a supper party at the Colonel's home and, in front of the other guests, reveals that everything about the old soldier - even his rank, is a sham. At the same time, the Director has managed to precipitate a friendship between his natural daughter and a promising young student, Arkenholz, in the hope that the two young people will escape the morbidity of life with the Colonel and his wife. Instead,

the Colonel's wife exposes Hummel's own foul nature and drives him to suicide, while their daughter, spiritually poisoned by her upbringing, is placed behind a macabre 'death screen' and left to wither away.

The Old Man (Director Hummel)
The Student (Arkenholz)
The Milkmaid, an apparition
The Superintendent
The Dead Man
The Lady in Black
The Colonel
The Young Lady, the Colonel's daughter/ Hummel's natural daughter

The Mummy, the Colonel's wife
Baron Skanskorg
Johansson, Hummel's servant
Bengtsson, the Colonel's servant
The Fiancée
The Cook
Beggars
A maid

Ghost Train, The
Arnold Ridley
Drama 3 Acts
London 1925

Young honeymooners Charles and Peggy Murdock are naturally disappointed when, due to silly fool Teddie Deakin pulling the communication cord to retrieve his lost hat, they miss their train connection and have to spend the night in the waiting room at Fal Vale, a little station in Cornwall. Also stuck are slightly older couple Richard and Elsie Winthrop who are not getting on and planning a separation, and elderly Miss Bourne. Grumpy stationmaster Saul Hodgkin advises them not to spend the night at the station - it is haunted, he warns, and tells them a chilling story of wrecked trains, dead passengers, and ghostly trains and railwaymen. He leaves, but then collapses, apparently dead. After he is moved to the ticket office, a mad young girl Julia appears who claims to be fascinated with the ghostly train. Two men with her are trying to calm her down, but sure enough the 'ghost train' is heard, and Julia jumps on a table to see it. The others cannot get out to see it because the doors have been mysteriously locked. Julia collapses, there are more ghostly goings-on, and eventually the two men with Julia insist that the stranded passengers must leave the waiting room for their own good. Teddie refuses point-blank as the ghostly train returns. He produces a revolver, dashes out and shunts the train on to the siding. Policemen appear, and it is revealed Teddie is a secret agent and has foiled a Bolshevik plan to bring weapons into Britain. Julia is revealed as a hard-bitten criminal, and after their ordeal the Winthrops make up, and Charles and Peggy can continue their honeymoon.

Saul Hodgkin
Richard Winthrop
Elsie Winthrop
Charles Murdock
Peggy Murdock
Miss Bourne

Teddie Deakin
Julia Price
Herbert Price
John Sterling
Jackson
Smith

Ghosts

Henrik Ibsen
Drama 3 Acts
Helsingborg 1883

Self-righteous pastor Manders visits widowed Helen Alving who has built an orphanage in her husband's memory. Her son Oswald has just returned from living away in Paris, and Manders is shocked to learn that he has been living with an unmarried family of which Helen approves. Her own marriage has been a sham, her husband having been debauched all his life; she left him once and Manders persuaded her to return. A child Alving had by a maid has been brought up by a local carpenter Engstrand as his own, for a fee, and Helen is haunted by the past when her son has an affair with the now grown-up illegitimate girl, Regine, in fact his half-sister. Helen is about to reveal the truth about his father to her son, who has a congenital disease, when a fire breaks out at the orphanage. Engstrand offers to take the blame for the fire in return for a favour from Manders.

Regine learns of her parentage and decides to leave Oswald who is now having severe attacks which affect his brain. The agony continues as he pleads with his mother to give him a fatal dose of pills.

Mrs Alving
Oswald Alving
Pastor Manders
Engstrand
Regine Engstrand

Gift, The

Mary Lumsden
Drama 2 Acts
London 1953

Julie Dennison, a mature student training for medicine, has blinded herself in a laboratory experiment. She makes her way to the Harley Street consulting room of her brother-in-law Sir David Crossley, Britain's top ophthalmic surgeon. She has always been in love with David but he married her elder sister Elizabeth; now, David's assistant Justin wants to marry her. David examines Julie and tells her that her sight can be restored with corneal grafts, but it is a new operation and donors are rare. Eyes can be donated from a dead person - or a living one - and Elizabeth insists she will donate one of her eyes so that Julie can see and finish her medical studies.

David is very reluctant to operate but Elizabeth becomes insistent. Eventually she confesses that before their marriage when both sisters were in love with David, she arranged for Julie (then in the services) to be transferred abroad, leaving the field clear for her with David. Her guilt has mounted over the years into an obsession. Unknown to everyone, Elizabeth has a weak heart and after the anaesthetic has a heart attack and dies. David loses his nerve to operate but Julie insists, and the graft is successful. When Julie's eyesight is finally restored, it is revealed that Elizabeth left a note

saying that if anything happened, Julie was to benefit from both her eyes. David now has his nerve back but must learn to live without Elizabeth. Julie decides to marry Justin, about to take up a post in South Africa.

Miss Hooper, secretary to Sir David
Mrs Saunders, the housekeeper
Justin Allister, assistant to Sir David
Julie Dennison
Lady Elizabeth Crossley
Sir David Crossley

Gigi

Anita Loos
Comedy 6 Scenes
Paris 1954

Based on the novel by Colette this light comedy has as its heroine the lively and carefree sixteen-year-old Gigi.

Her grandmother Mme Alvarez and her mother Andrée have both been great beauties but never really successful, and they plan that Gigi will find her way into the society that has eluded them. They train her for a life of luxury and high living where she will be courted by the rich and famous, but Gigi is still a little girl at heart and cannot refrain from outbursts of childish behaviour. However, she has won the attentions of man of the world, Lachaille, and he offers to introduce her into the smart society set by suggesting a little 'scandal'. Naive child that she is, she reacts with outrage at this idea and predictably this has the effect of making an honourable gentleman out of Lachaille and a suitable husband for Gigi.

Gigi
Mme Alvarez
Andrée
Gaston Lachaille (Tonton)
Victor
Alicia de St Ephlam
Sidonie

Gimme Shelter

Barrie Keeffe
Drama Trilogy
London 1975-1977

Gem: At the insurance firm's August Bank Holiday outing cricket match, rebels Kev and Gary lounge around at the edge of the pitch taking the mickey out of the players. Janet, whom Kev desires, is there too, though later it is Gary she goes with. Gary is a talented musician and footballer, but like Kev is confined to a life-time of paper-shuffling. When Gary is persuaded to bat and makes fifty-six, Kev feels betrayed.

Gotcha: Teachers Lynn and married sports master Ton are finishing off their affair in a school stockroom where a pupil's motorbike has been parked. In comes the boy, a no-hoper, and with a lighted cigarette poised over the lidless petrol tank exploits his position. The boy is a desperate nobody - none of the teachers can even remember his name, his report is bad, he feels he has no future. Now, however, he has power and can insult the teachers (and the headmaster who comes in), air his grievances, be an individual. The police arrive and there is a siege. Only Lynn has any real sympathy for him, but eventually he loses his perch and gets kicked around by Ton.

Getaway: A year later, at the firm's cricket match, Janet is married and pregnant, and even rebel Kev is now in whites waiting for his innings. He disparages Gary's impressive innings because of 'lack of artistry', then gets talking to the boy, now a groundsman, and finds out who he is (the siege was much-publicized). Kev is impressed and tells him not to lose his rage and rebellion but the boy has now found satisfaction in his work and does not want to know. Kev has not lost his rage but is sucked deeper into the system he abhors, neither on one side nor the other - and as his team wins again, he is not even needed for the game.

Gem: Kev, Gary, Baill, Janet
Gotcha: Ton, Lynn, Kid, Head
Getaway: Kev, Janet, Gary, Kid

Gin Game, The
D. L. Coburn
Tragic Comedy 2 Acts
New York 1977

Fonsia Dorsey and Weller Martin are stuck in an old folks' home. They are resentful and bored and nobody visits them, though they pretend this and that to each other. They play gin rummy and Weller reckons he is the expert but somehow Fonsia keeps winning. This infuriates him, and he gets even madder when she tries to lose. Eventually they get untypically foul-mouthed and their friendship is destroyed by a silly game of cards.

Fonsia Dorsey
Weller Martin

Ginger Man, The
J. P. Donleavy
Comedy 2 Acts
London 1959

Sebastian Balfe Dangerfield is the Ginger Man, an American law student living in debt and squalor in a rented house in Dublin. His friend, pathetic Irish-American Kenneth O'Keefe visits, they drink, and O'Keefe complains about his lack of a sex life. Sebastian's English wife Marion returns and is at her wits' end at her husband's irresponsibility and self-destructiveness. Nevertheless Sebastian's awfulness is not without a certain insightful charm, and his love-hate affair with Ireland is reflected in his bawdy blarney. Marion and baby run off and move to a nicer house but Sebastian finds her and moves in again. He flatters and seduces lodger Miss Lilly Frost, a good Catholic girl who suffers the usual agonies of potential damnation, not to mention local gossip. O'Keefe returns to say

goodbye to Sebastian - he is going back to America after further failures; he leaves, Miss Frost leaves and Sebastian now alone gets even more mystical and poetic.

Sebastian Balfe Dangerfield
Marion Dangerfield
Miss Lilly Frost
Kenneth O'Keefe

Gingerbread Man, The
David Wood
Children's Musical 2 Acts
Basildon 1976

Ingenious children's play (with plenty of opportunities for audience participation) takes place on two shelves of a kitchen dresser. Poor Herr Von Cuckoo of the cuckoo clock loses his voice and his pathetic croaks put him in danger of being dumped in the dreaded dustbin by the Big Ones (the humans). He is saved by the newly-minted Gingerbread Man with the help of Salt and Pepper. The Gingerbread Man climbs on to the next shelf, braving the wrath of the grumpy and witchy Old (tea) Bag and returns with the precious honey for Herr Von Cuckoo's throat.

Unfortunately the Big Ones poison the honey, intending to kill Sleek the mouse, and poor Herr Von Cuckoo falls ill. But the Old Bag saves him with her herbal remedies, and after thwarting the cowardly bully Sleek, all are safe and well, with the Old Bag now a firm friend. The Gingerbread Man is reprieved from being eaten by the Big Ones, and will henceforth be an ornament on the shelf.

Songs include: 'Toad in the Throat'; 'The Gingerbread Man'; 'Heave-Ho, a-Rolling Go'
Herr Von Cuckoo
Salt
Pepper
The Gingerbread Man
The Old Bag
Sleek
The voices of the Big Ones

Girl of the Golden West, The
David Belasco
Drama 4 Acts
New York 1905

Minnie, 'The Girl', is lovely, pure and brave; she is the saloon keeper and local schoolmistress in a mining town and the rough miners worship her. She falls in love with a strange gentleman, little knowing that he is the notorious bandit Dick Johnson, alias Ramerrez the road agent. He falls in love with her, but their idyll is ended by a blizzard trapping Johnson. He tries to escape but is wounded and Minnie hides him in the loft of her cabin. The sheriff arrives and Minnie almost succeeds in convincing him she has not seen Johnson. Then the blood from the wounded outlaw drips down from above on to the sheriff's white handkerchief.

Throwing caution to the wind, Minnie challenges the sheriff to a game of poker. If he wins, he gets Johnson - and Minnie, whom he has long desired. If he loses, then Minnie gets Johnson. A typical western gambling man, the sheriff takes up the challenge and loses, although Minnie has had to cheat to win. The sheriff leaves but Johnson is caught again and about to be hanged. He is released by the miners when they realise how much their adored Minnie loves him, and the pair must now go to another part of the country, leaving behind their beloved Golden West.

The Girl	*Jack Rance*
Dick Johnson	*Trinidad Joe*
Sonora Slim	*The Sidney Duck*
Nick	*'Happy' Haliday*
Jim Larkens	*Sheriff*
'Handsome' Charlie	*Deputy Sheriff*
Billy Jackrabbit	*Ashby*
Jose Castro	*Jake Wallace*
Bucking Billy	*The lookout*
A Faro dealer	*The Ridge Boy*
Concertina player	*Joe*
Worokle	*Rider of the Pony Express*

Glass Menagerie, The
Tennessee Williams
Drama 1 Act
New York 1945
Williams described this semi-autobiographical piece as a 'memory play'. In it, he recreates the essentials of his own relations with his mother and sister as he was coming to manhood.

By dint of perpetual labour, Amanda Wingfield has managed, although abandoned by her husband, to raise her children to adulthood and to see Tom into his first job. Her one remaining aim is to see Laura well married, but Laura, who is badly crippled, retreats into madness under the pressure of her mother's hope. At Amanda's urging, Tom brings home a workmate whom she thrusts at Laura, precipitating the girl's final collapse.
Amanda Wingfield
Laura Wingfield
Tom Wingfield
Jim O'Connor

Glengarry Glen Ross
David Mamet
Drama 2 Acts
New York 1984
Shelley Levene, a salesman for a Chicago real estate firm which sells Florida scrubland under glamorous names like Glengarry and Glen Ross, faces the sack because his recent performance has been so inadequate. A much younger man, Richard Roma, is, by contrast, so successful that Levene is made even more aware of his own failures. The two men define the two poles of achievement in the ruthless world of American salesmanship.

Two of their colleagues, whose achievements are mid-way between Levene's and Roma's, decide to steal the firm's list of contracts, sell it to a competitor, and split the profits. One of them, Dave Moss, sets up the deal, while the other, George Aaronow, is to carry out the actual theft. The morning after the theft, the manager of the firm, John Williamson, faces an irate Roma, who is furious that contracts proving his recent sales have been taken by the burglars. At the same time, though, Williamson hears from Levene that the erstwhile failure has made a big, and unexpected, sale.

As the detective investigating the burglary interviews each of the employees, it becomes clear that the theft was not the work of Moss and Aaronow, but the real culprit appears to have covered his trail. Buoyed up by his return to sales form, Levene is now behaving with the same wild aggression characteristic of Roma but he overreaches himself in discussing a sale with Williamson, lets out that he knows details of the stolen contracts which suggests he is the thief, and is obliged to submit to interrogation and the certainty of being found out. His return to form, of course, was possible only because he had stolen the name of the contact to whom he made the big sale.
Shelley Levene, a salesman
John Williamson, his manager
Dave Moss, George Aaronow, Richard Roma,
Levene's colleagues
James Lingk, a client
Baylen, a detective

Godspell
John Michael Tebelak
Music by Stephen Schwartz
Musical 2 Acts
New York 1971
This loosely structured piece is based on the Gospel according to St Matthew and is presented by John the Baptist who interrupts a meeting of great figures from history to announce the coming of Jesus Christ. Our Saviour appears wearing a Superman T-shirt and a red plastic nose and His story is played out in a series of scenes in a naive style that uses the techniques of circus, cartoons and television. The small cast are dressed in various costumes and frequently interchange roles.
Principal song: 'Day by Day'
Cast of six

Golden Boy
Clifford Odets
Drama 3 Acts
New York 1937
Joe Bonaparte, a brash confident young boxer in pre-war New York, is so keen to get into the ring professionally that he breaks a fighter's hand during a sparring session to get the fight for himself. But he has a dilemma; he is also a talented violinist and so holds back from throwing big punches for fear of ruining his

hands. Despite his father's pleading, Joe continues fighting and several matches later he is enjoying the money and prestige that winning brings. His devious manager gets his girl, Lorna, to reassure Joe that he is better suited to boxing than fiddling. A romance develops between the 'golden boy' and Lorna, but she has promised to marry the manager and so Joe vents his wrath by viciously beating his opponents in the ring. He becomes involved with gangsters and only when he ends up killing an opponent does he realize that he has gone too far and Lorna, who now no longer doubts her love for him, convinces him to give up boxing and return to his musical career. But it is too late for the starry-eyed lovers; they are both killed in a car crash.

Tom Moody	Pepper White
Lorna Moon	Mickey
Joe Bonaparte	Call boy
Tokio	Sam
Mr Carp	Lewis
Siggie	Drake
Mr Bonaparte	Driscoll
Anna	Barker
Frank Bonaparte	
Roxy Gottlieb	
Eddie Fuseli	

Golden Pathway Annual, The
John Harding and John Burrows
Drama 2 Acts
London 1974

Archetypal 'bulge baby' Michael Peters is the focus of the aspirations of his decent working-class parents George and Enid. He progresses from 1945 baby to 1967 university graduate, and in a series of short scenes his life - inner and outer - is poignantly mapped out; his schools and teachers, his friendships and rivalries, his fantasies, and his academic triumphs. Finally there is the disillusion of both Michael and his parents, not only towards each other but to the society and culture in which they live, symbolized by *The Golden Pathway Annual*. This is an encyclopedia, sent to Michael each year on his birthday, that the Peters have subscribed to since Michael was at infant school and whose stories, legends, adventures and learning programmes have inspired Michael's life and fantasies but proved to be a cruel and impossible ideal in the face of the real conflicts of a superficially changing Britain where the entrenchments of privilege are as real as ever.

This piece can be performed by three men and one woman.

George Peters	Girlfriend
Michael Peters	The officer
Enid Peters	Collins
June	A chicken
Miss Jones	Vadia
William	Owen
Lady	Seth
Mademoiselle	Roger

The head	Magistrate
Irishman	Doorman

Gondoliers, The
W.S. Gilbert and Arthur Sullivan
Comic Opera 2 Acts
London 1889

Subtitled *The King of Barataria* this takes place in 1750 when two handsome Venetian gondoliers, Marco and Giuseppe, have recently married. Their weddings coincide with the visit to Venice of the Duke of Plaza-Toro, his daughter Casilda and her attendant Luiz, who is in love with her. The Duke reveals to his daughter a dark secret; twenty years ago she was married by proxy to the infant son of the immensely wealthy King of Barataria, who was subsequently killed in an insurrection. The prince disappeared and now lives somewhere in Venice. It transpires that either Giuseppe or Marco is the King of Barataria and the two gondoliers jointly take the throne of that country, and being republicans, run it on very democratic lines.

Casilda is to marry one of the two when an old nurse, mother of Luiz, can identify the real prince. She, of course, reveals that neither is the heir; she substituted her own child and Luiz is the real King and husband to Casilda, so the gondoliers can happily go back to their wives in Venice.

Songs include:'We're Called Gondolieri'; 'O Rapture When Alone Together'; 'When a Merry Maiden Marries'; 'Take a Pair of Sparkling Eyes'; 'In a Contemplative Fashion'

The Duke of Plaza- Toro, a grandee of Spain	Tessa Fiametta Contadine
Luiz, his attendant	Vittoria
Don Alhambra Del Bolero, the Grand Inquisitor	Giulia Inez, former foster-mother of the King
Gondoliers: Marco Palmieri, Giuseppe Palmieri, Antonio, Francesco, Giorgio and Annibale	Gondoliers Contadine Men-at-arms Heralds Pages
The Duchess of Plaza- Toro	
Casilda, her daughter	
Gianetta	

Good
C. P. Taylor
Tragedy 2 Acts
London 1981

During the early years of the Third Reich, Halder, a lecturer in German literature, becomes caught up in the Nazi juggernaut. His pro-euthanasia novel, written as a cathartic reaction to his blind and senile mother's moving predicament, is approved by the Nazi hierarchy and even praised by Hitler himself - 'written from the heart'. Yet Halder is no Nazi. His best friend Maurice is a Jewish analyst whose situation in Berlin grows worse and worse as Halder's gets better and better, and when Halder leaves his difficult wife Helen and his two young children for young student Anne, his personal problems overshadow or even make him overlook book-burning and racial persecution. Even his trip to Auschwitz to help set up an extermination centre seems hardly to affect him. He loves band music and jazz, also forbidden by the regime (although the Nazi brass have their own private supply), and the play is punctuated by appropriate tunes, as well as appearances by historical figures such as Eichmann, Hitler and Höss. Halder, a fundamentally decent man who has been insidiously corrupted (mainly through taking the line of least resistance) is revealed as a metaphor for Germany.

Halder	Doctor
Helen	Nurses
Anne	Bouller
Maurice	Eichmann
Bok, SS NCO	Höss
Freddie, SS Major	Hitler
Elisabeth, his wife	Musicians

Good and Faithful Servant
Joe Orton
Comedy 19 Scenes
Rediffusion TV 1967

Commissionaire Buchanan is retiring from the firm he has served long and well. On the way to the personnel department he meets cleaner Edith and feels they have met before, even though they worked in different areas. It turns out that as youngsters they had a brief affair which, unknown to Buchanan, had resulted in twins, killed in wartime Italy. They arrange to meet again. In personnel Mrs Vealfoy interrogates Buchanan to make sure he is taking nothing of value with him. He lets slip that he has a grandson (fathered in Italy by one of his sons) and she is bothered because Records have no record of living descendants. She asks him to send the grandson's address so she can forward some of the company's literature. At the leaving ceremony Buchanan is presented with an electric toaster and a clock.

Mrs Vealfoy is visited by Debbie, a typist, seeking advice because she is pregnant by one Ray whom she hardly knows. Mrs Vealfoy says not to worry; she'll soon fix it that she will be married.

Buchanan moves in with Edith, meets unemployed son Ray, and while up in Ray's bedroom convincing Ray that he ought to seek a job with the company, finds Debbie under the bed. Mrs Vealfoy, armed with Ray's address, visits Edith and asks for Ray to visit her - he says he intends to marry Debbie.

There is an embarrassing get-together of ex-employees at the firm's recreation centre, and while Edith is later examining Ray and Debbie's wedding photos, Buchanan dies. At the next get-together Mrs Vealfoy announces Buchanan's death after which the band plays 'On the Sunny Side of the Street' and the employees sing and dance.

Buchanan	Debbie
Edith	Ray
Mrs Vealfoy	An old man

Good Companions, The
J. B. Priestley and Edward Knoblock
Comedy 3 Acts
London 1931

Yorkshireman Jess Oakroyd, a joiner and carpenter, gets the sack during the Depression and after a family quarrel hits the road. He meets young Elizabeth Trant, motoring in search of adventure, and together they deliver a crate of clothes she promised barmaid Effie to get to Elsie, her actress sister. Elsie's troupe, the Dinky Doos, have meanwhile picked up a young runaway schoolteacher Inigo Jollifant, a fabulous pianist and songwriter who is smitten with Dinky's singer Susie Dean. Unfortunately the troupe are on their last financial legs but the infusion of new talent plus Oakroyd as handyman convinces Miss Trant to back the outfit which she renames The Good Companions.

They go from success to success, but Inigo's efforts to sell Susie to a big London agency are thwarted when a gang of toughs employed by a rival break up the act and knock out the agent. Luckily, rich Lady Partlett falls for Good Companion Jerry - they wed, and Lady P's influences secure a promise of fame and fortune for all in London.

Oakroyd hears his wife is ill, returns North and after making up their quarrel, she dies. Left alone, he gets a letter from Miss Trant enclosing a hundred pounds followed by a telegram from daughter Lily in Canada - there is a home for him there, and plenty of work.

Mrs Oakroyd	Jimmy Nunn
Sam Oglethorpe	Elsie Longstaff
Jess Oakroyd	Joe Brundit
Leonard Oakroyd	Mrs Joe Brundit
Albert Tuggeridge	Mrs Maunders
Elizabeth Trant	Jerry Jerningham
Landlord at Tumbleby	Lady Partlit
Effie	Mr Dulver
Roughs	Waiter at the 'Royal
Inigo Jollifantz	Standard'
Mr Fauntley	Photographer at Gatford
Susie Dean	Landlord of 'The Crown',
Morton Mitcham	Gatford
Mrs Tarvin	Mr Pitsner
Mr Tarvin	Ethel Georgia
Joby Jackson	Monte Mortimer
Professor Miro	Mr Gooch
Linoleum man	Market people
Envelope man	Guests
Summers	Audience
Policeman at Ribsden	

Good Woman of Setzuan, The
Bertolt Brecht
Play 10 Scenes, Verse and Prose
Zurich 1943

Three gods come to the modern city of Setzuan seeking a good person to give them shelter, but find no help from the local population, except from a young prostitute, Shen Te, whom they reward for her kindness by providing money for her to set up a tobacco factory. Scoundrels and debtors, however, force her to assume another identity as a man, her cousin, Shui Ta, and 'he' ruthlessly sets the business in order.

Later, Shen Te meets a young flyer, with whom she falls desperately in love, but he brags to her 'cousin' Shui Ta, that he is only after her money and although she still wants to marry him, he refuses when she becomes pregnant. Her 'cousin' now blackmails the aviator into working in the factory as a foreman, but because Shen Te has disappeared, the aviator suspects foul play and has Shui Ta arrested.

When the split personality Shen Te has to reveal her true identity to the three gods and plead her case for the dual roles, they are blind to her dilemma and urge her to 'continue to be good'.

Wong, water seller	Pilot
Three gods	Old whore
Shen Te, prostitute	Policeman
Mrs Shin, shop owner	Old man
A family of eight	Old woman
An unemployed man	Mr Shu Fu, barber
A carpenter	Mrs Yang, pilot's mother
Mrs Mitzu, Shen Te's	Gentlemen
landlady	Voices
Yang Sun, unemployed	Children

Goodbye Charlie
George Axelrod
Comedy 2 Acts
New York 1959

At a small memorial service for late screenwriter Charlie Sorel at his beach house in Malibu, only his lawyer, his accountant, his agent, the wife of his head of studio and friend George, over from France, are present. Charlie, thirty-eight, was shot dead by another friend, the husband of Rusty Mayerling with whom Charlie was having an affair. The only nice thing anyone present can seem to say about Charlie is that he was full of life. He was a womanizer and died in debt, and only old buddy George - executor of his will - seems upset.

George is left alone in the house after the service and in comes a girl, very attractive but dressed just in Charlie's mac. The girl is in fact a bewildered Charlie, reincarnated in female form. George is astonished but gradually begins to accept this miracle, and Charlie too begins getting used to - and enjoying - being a woman. Next day Charlie goes into town to the beauty salon and ends up blackmailing his ex-girlfriends; he/she pretending he/she is Charlie's widow over from Europe,

and has Charlie's diary. But at the same time, he/she learns what a heel he has been, making his women friends fall in love with him without once falling in love with them. Now, however, the boot is on the other foot. Charlie drops the blackmail because he is falling in love with unwilling George who becomes horrified, even though Charlie is now a good-looking woman.

Poor Charlie realizes his karma has come home to roost. He/she gets drunk and goes to bed and prays, saying she knows everything could work out wonderfully between her and George, and please, please let it happen. The lights dim and it is back to George ... he has miraculously forgotten all that has happened and once more the girl appears, but this time does not let on, telling George she is an old friend of Charlie's. Things start to look good between them...

Greg Morris
George Tracy
Franny Saltzman
Irving
Mr Shreiber
Rusty Mayerling
Charlie

Goose Pimples
Devised by Mike Leigh
Drama 2 Acts
London 1981

Vernon, a car salesman, has Jackie, a girl croupier, as a lodger in his flat. They get on well and respect each other's privacy. While Jackie is at work, Vernon is visited by a young couple, Frankie and Irving. They drink and exchange small-talk with a touch of ribaldry. Vernon and Irving work for the same company but are only friendly on the surface: it becomes clear that Vernon is having something of an affair with Frankie. The meat Vernon has bought for their meal is off so they go out to dine.

Jackie comes home with Muhammed who speaks hardly any English. They can barely communicate but it becomes obvious that he has sex in mind and does not mind paying. The others come back and there is more drinking which makes Muhammed sick. Things get steadily nastier. Muhammed gets assaulted by Irving who obviously fancies Jackie and is accused by Vernon of trying to feel her up. It turns out that Irving knows full well that Vernon has been 'having it off' with Frankie. Vernon tells Irving and Frankie to leave.

After they have gone and Muhammed is asleep on the floor Vernon denies to Jackie that he fancies Frankie. They kiss enthusiastically and Vernon suggests she sleep with him. She is hesitant ...

Vernon
Jackie
Irving
Frankie
Muhammed

Government Inspector, The
Nikolai Gogol
Comedy 2 Acts
Moscow 1836

Corruption and inefficiency are running rife in a small Russian provincial town when the Governor reveals to his cronies - the Judge, the Charity Commissioner, the School's Superintendent, the Doctor and the Postmaster - that they are to be investigated by a government inspector who may be travelling incognito. When landowners Bobchinsky and Dobchinsky say they have seen the Inspector staying at the local inn, the officials panic and plan to clean up the town, at least cosmetically. The visitor is actually foolish young wastrel clerk Khlestakov from St Petersburg, on gambling travels with servant Osip. Khlestakov is fêted, bribed, taken to the Governor's house where he gets completely drunk, and treated with every deference by the cowering officials. Oafish Khlestakov insists on marrying the Governor's daughter Marya, much to her father's delight.

Khlestakov and Osip then commandeer the fastest troika in town, and laden with gifts and bribes, speed away purportedly to tell Khlestakov's influential uncle about the wedding and then return. Meanwhile, the Postmaster is up to his old tricks and steams open a letter from Khlestakov, thus discovering that not only is he not the Inspector, but that he is reporting the joke to a Petersburg journalist friend.

The horrified and humiliated officials realize Khlestakov will not return, whereupon a city gendarme enters, commanding that they all report to the real Inspector - immediately.

Anton Skvoznik-Dmuchanovsky, Governor
Anna, Governor's wife
Marya, Governor's daughter
Luka Khlopov, Schools' Superintendent
Super's wife
Ammos Lyapkin-Tyapkin, Judge
Ivan Shpekin, Postmaster
Petr Dobchinsky, landowner
Petr Bobchinsky, landowner
Artemy Zemlyanika, charity commissioner
Dr Khristian (Gibner), district doctor
Police inspector
Svistunov, Pugovitizin and Derzhimorda, police
  constables
Ivan Khlestiakov, government clerk from St
  Petersburg
Osip, his servant
Ivan Rastakovsky, retired official
Stepan Korobkin, retired official
Korobin's wife
Mishka, Governor's servant
Waiter
Poshlepkinka, locksmith's wife
Sergeant's widow
First merchant
Second merchant
Third merchant
Guests, townspeople, merchants, petitioners, serfs,
  town band

Grass Harp, The
Truman Capote
Drama 2 Acts
New York 1952

Verena Talbo rules the roost at the Talbo household on the edge of town. The house is looked after by whimsical sister Dolly and chunky Negress Catherine Creek, while Collin, their late cousin Mary's fifteen-year-old son, also lives with them. When Dolly was small, a kindness to the gypsies resulted in them giving her a secret formula for curing dropsy. Now it's their cottage industry, but one day Verena brings home shifty Dr Morris Ritz, announcing she's sunk a lot of money into a factory, and with the doctor's help they intend to mass-market the cure. The others protest and Verena loses her temper, so Dolly, Catherine and Collin run away to their forest tree-house, where they're pursued by half the town for varying reasons.

The elderly judge is their ally, and that night proposes to Dolly, but after various adventures involving Collin, his girlfriend Maude, eccentric beautician Miss Baby Love Dallas, and phony shyster Dr Ritz absconding with Verena's money, the sheriff and his men arrive and a blundering deputy shoots and wounds Collin. They all go home, and Verena opens her heart and confesses her envy of Dolly, who is happy that they can once more be close. She turns down the disappointed old judge, but resolves to make him a partner in the dropsy cure business, and let Verena also be involved.

Catherine Creek *The postmaster*
Collin Talbo *The sheriff*
Dolly Talbo *Judge Charlie Cool*
Verena Talbo *The choir mistress*
Dr Morris Ritz *Big Eddie Stover*
The Reverend's wife *Brophy*
The Reverend *Sam*
The barber *Maude Riordan*
The baker's wife *Miss Baby Love Dallas*

Grease
Jim Jacobs and Warren Casey
Musical 2 Acts
New York 1972

A group of former high school students gather at Rydell High School for a reunion of the Class of '59.

The old English teacher introduces various now-successful, and unsuccessful ex-students and together they recall their High School days and particularly the romances that developed between the Burger Palace Boys and the Pink Ladies, their girlfriends.

Through a series of scenes at a pajama party, at a picnic, at the Burger Palace and at the ever-popular High School Hop, in which most of the cast participate, a central romance dominates between Danny Zuko and newcomer Sandy who turns from a wholesome, naive cute teenager into a raunchy, mature sex bomb.

Songs include: 'Look at Me, I'm Sandra Dee'; 'Summer Nights'; 'Born to Hand Jive'; 'Shakin' at the High School Hop'

Miss Lynch	Frenchy
Patty Simcox	Sandy Dumbrowski
Eugene Florczyk	Danny Zuko
Jan	Vince Fontaine
Marty	Johnny Casino
Betty Rizzo	Cha-Cha DiGregorio
Doody	Teen Angel
Roger	
Kenickie	
Sonny LaTierri	

Great Divide, The
William Vaughn Moody
Melodrama 3 Acts
New York 1906

A frontier cabin in the wilds of Arizona around the turn of the century. The Jordans, a New England family, have moved there with a plan to enrich themselves by marketing cactus fibre. It is the project of thirty-year-old Philip and his nineteen-year-old sister Ruth who absolutely adores the life and the area. Philip's blonde wife Polly hates it and so Philip is taking her for a vacation to San Francisco.

Ruth is visited at night by; Mexican, Dutch and Stephen Ghent, unsavoury characters, drunk and lustful. They start to play dice over who gets Ruth. She pleads with Ghent to rescue her from gang rape, in return for which she will give herself to him, for life. He bribes the others to go. She prepares to leave with Ghent, packs a few things and leaves a note for her brother, and as she does so, Ghent starts to sober up and reveal glimmerings of decency.

About a year later Ghent is now co-owner of a gold mine in Cordilleras and bent on pleasing his coldly remote wife. He discusses, in her absence, a new and splendid home with an architect and contractor. Ruth has what he thinks is a hobby - making blankets and Indian baskets - but actually she is selling them in the nearby town, saving up to humiliate Ghent by eventually paying him back all that he paid his ex-cronies 'for' her. She has already got a necklace back from the Mexican.

Philip and Polly eventually discover her new home and visit her. Ruth pretends to be happy - fulfilling her bargain with Ghent - but a hostile Philip sneaks back and overhears conversation revealing the real relationship. He takes Ruth away.

In Mother Jordan's Massachusetts house, Philip and Ruth (with baby Ghent) are now living in poverty, the cactus fibre business having gone broke because of Ruth's 'elopement' with Ghent. She is withdrawn and miserable. To Philip's fury, Polly says Ruth is missing

her husband and ought to go back to Arizona.

It turns out that Ghent had followed the family to New England, had bought the house for them (letting them believe it was an English relative who was the philanthropist). On top of that, he'd bought the Jordan's farm and the cactus fibre business is now prosperous. Ghent comes to the house to plead for Ruth's return and to confess his deep love and remorse but says he understands - the divide is too great and they should remain apart. As he makes to leave she decides that their suffering has cleansed them and they and their son can build a joyful life for themselves.

Philip Jordan	Lon Anderson
Polly Jordan	Burt Williams
Mrs Jordan	Dutch
Ruth Jordan	Mexican
Winthrop Newbury	Contractor
Dr Newbury	Architect
Stephen Ghent	Boy

Great God Brown, The
Eugene O'Neill
Tragedy 4 Acts
New York 1926

Billy Brown and Dion Anthony are the sons of two partners in a small town firm of building contractors in twenties America.

Billy has fallen in love with Margaret, but she prefers and eventually marries Dion. Following the deaths of the two old partners, Billy transforms the firm into a thriving architectural practice. The young Anthony sells his share of the business to Billy, carouses his way through Europe in a vain attempt to become a painter, and returns home with Margaret, broke and bitter.

To help Margaret, whom he still loves, Billy gives Dion a job in the practice. Despite his love of drink, Dion proves to be an inspired architect, and his designs win the firm its most important commissions. Vanity prevents Billy from giving Dion due credit, and when Dion dies from the effects of drink, Billy even tries to take Dion's place as husband to Margaret and father to the Anthony children. Instead he becomes suspected of causing Dion's death and is shot by the police while trying to evade arrest.

William A. Brown (Billy)	Margaret
His father	Her three sons
His mother	Cybel
Dion Anthony	Two draughtsmen
His father	A stenographer
His mother	

Great White Hope, The
Howard Sackler
Drama 2 Acts
New York 1968

Based on the career of Jack Johnson who in 1908 became the first Negro heavyweight boxing champion of the world, this is the story of the rise and fall of Jack Jefferson. Retired (white) champion Brady is reluctantly forced to be the 'White Hope' and stand up to barnstorming black challenger Jefferson. To the dismay of the boxing establishment (and other white power interests) Jefferson wins easily and is now in possession of the coveted belt. To make matters worse he has a white girlfriend, Ellie Bachman, whom he met on a boat coming home from a fight in Australia. A divorcée, she is a decent girl and Jack and she are in love, much to the disgust of his fiery black ex-girlfriend Clara.

No new white hope emerges, Jefferson is subsequently framed on a morals charge, and with the help of his family has to flee with Ellie to Europe. Things there go from bad to worse; he is not allowed to fight in Britain, and in France he only gets fifth-rate challengers. He and Ellie are eventually reduced to participate in a humiliating Uncle Tom-type cabaret act in Hungary. All the while the American boxing establishment are pleading with him to return and 'take a fall' to a white challenger - he would then have money and his sentence would be quashed. He refuses, and grows more and more bitter with Ellie, eventually telling her to leave. She does, and kills herself. With nothing to live for, Jack returns and fights The Kid, the new White Hope, who wins in ten rounds, bloody and battered and not knowing Jack had taken a fall.

Frank Brady, the retired champion
Fred, his manager
Cap'n Dan, a champion of early days
Smitty, a famous sports' writer
Goldie, Jack's manager
Jack Jefferson
Tick, his trainer
Ellie Bachman
Clara
Blackface, an entertainer
Col Cox
Deacon
Donnelly, Mrs Bachman's attorney
Mrs Bachman, Ellie's mother
Cameron, Chicago District Attorney
Dixon, a Federal agent
Scipio, a street philosopher
Mrs Jefferson, Jack's mother
Pastor
Rudy, a baseball player
Treacher, Jack's solicitor
Sir William Griswold, Home Office undersecretary
Eubanks, his aide
Coates, Chairman of the British Vigilance Board
Mrs Kimball, a landlady
Inspector Wainwright, Metropolitan Police
Bratby, Olympic Sporting Club officer
Farlow, London County Council
Klossowski, a Polish heavyweight
Pop Weaver, a promoter
Ragosy, a Hungarian impresario

Negro, an African student
Paco, a Mexican boy
El Jefe, a Mexican politico
A young Federal agent
The Kid
Reporters
Photographers
Trainers
Handlers
Fight fans
Gamblers
Nevada Rangers
Weighers-in
Barker
Chicago police

Temperance marchers
Civic leaders
Musicians
Revellers
Mourners
Brothers and sisters of the congregation
French crowd
German officers
Hungarian audience
Stagehands
Mexicans
Pinkerton men
Cuban boys

Green Pastures, The
Mark Connelly
Folk Drama 2 Parts
New York 1930

This fable play, set in a black Louisiana church, retells Bible stories as interpreted by the simple Negro congregation in words and spiritual songs.

The preacher explains to the children in Sunday school the stories of the Creation, Adam and Eve and Cain and Abel using contemporary references to which they can relate. In Heaven, God, who is a tall Negro, smokes cigars and encourages people to enjoy themselves; when He becomes concerned about all the sinning on Earth He comes down to command Noah to make an ark - and take a barrel of liquor on board.

Later from his office in Heaven, He sees the plight of the Jews and tells Moses to lead his people to 'de choice piece of property' in Canaan.

After seeing the debauchery in a Babylon (a black nightclub) He again visits Earth and is impressed by Hosea, who has found mercy through suffering, and speculates 'dat even God must suffer'. The prospect of the Crucifixion is greeted by the angels who sing 'Hallelujah, King Jesus'.

Mr Deshee
Myrtle
First boy
Second boy
Third boy
Randolph
A cook
Custard maker
First mammy angel
A stout angel
A slender angel
Archangel
Gabriel
The Lord
Choir leader
Adam

Eve
Cain
Cain's girl
Zeba
Cain the sixth
Boy gambler
First gambler
Second gambler
Voice in shanty
Noah
Noah's wife
Shem
First woman
Second woman
Third woman
First man

Flatfoot	*Joshua*
Ham	*First scout*
Japheth	*MC*
First cleaner	*King of Babylon*
Second cleaner	*Prophet*
Abraham	*High priest*
Isaac	*The king's favourites*
Moses	*Officer*
Zipporah	*Hezdrel*
Aaron	*Another officer*
Magician	*Children*
Pharaoh	*Angels*
The general	*Townspeople*
First wizard	*Babylonian band*
Head magician	*The choir*

Guys and Dolls

Music and lyrics by Frank Loesser from the
book by Abe Burrows and Jo Swerling, based
on stories by Damon Runyon
Musical 2 Acts
New York 1950

Among the various shady characters of Manhattan's
underworld, a young Salvation Army girl, Sister Sarah,
tries vainly to bring a message of hope, but she makes
little impression on the likes of Nathan Detroit and his
gambling colleagues. He is busy trying to organize a
big floating crap game with handsome young Sky
Masterson, the highest player of them all. Nathan, who
has been engaged to Adelaide for fourteen years, taunts
Sky about his abilities with women and bets him that he
cannot take the innocent Sister Sarah on a date to
Havana. Sky cannot refuse a bet, so he goes to the
mission and offers Sarah 'a dozen genuine sinners' if
she will go on a date with him. She first declines, but
when she learns that the mission may close, accepts.
Little does she realize that the sinners are gamblers
looking for somewhere to hold a game, but at the
mission they are all reformed, as is Sky, who joins the
Army and marries Sarah while Nathan weds Adelaide.
Songs include: 'Bushel and a Peck'; 'I've Never Been in
Love Before'; 'If I Were a Bell'; 'Luck be a Lady'; 'Sit
Down, You're Rocking the Boat'

Benny Southstreet	*Regret, Society Max,*
Nicely-Nicely Johnson	*Liverlips Louis, Hot*
Rusty Charlie	*Horse Herbie, Sky*
Sarah	*Rocket*
Arvide Abernathy	*Miss Adelaide*
Agatha, Calvin , Martha,	*Hot Box Girls*
the Mission band	*Sky Masterson*
Harry the Horse	*Voice of Joey Biltmore*
Lieut Brannigan	*Master of Ceremonies*
Nathan Detroit	*Mimi*
The Crap Shooters:	*Gen. Cartwright*
Angie the Ox, Brandy	*Big Julie*
Bottle Bates, Scranton	*Drunk*
Slim, Joey Perhaps,	*Waiter*

Habeas Corpus

Alan Bennett
Farce 2 Acts
London 1973

This lusty modern farce is played with a minimum of
props and maximum amount of sexual encounters,
mistaken identities, etc.

The cleaning lady at Dr Wicksteed's house is Mrs
Swabb and she is the narrator/chorus, explaining the
various to-ings and fro-ings; Wicksteed is after almost
everybody, but his hypochondriac son Dennis beats
him to lovely young Felicity, daughter of white settler
Lady Rumpers. Meanwhile neglected Mrs Wicksteed
throws herself at sales rep. Shanks, then meets old
flame Sir Percy Shorter, diminutive medical giant, and
trysts are planned. Bustless sister Connie Wicksteed
puffs up and attracts Canon Throbbing for an on-off
relationship, and jealous Sir Percy's attempts to get
rival Wicksteed struck off are thwarted when he turns
out to be Felicity's father from a war-time one-night
stand at Liverpool Docks with Lady R. just as she was
departing for the colonies. Poor Dennis finds he really
is dying, but that's OK with fiancée Felicity who
couldn't take much more than three months of him
anyway; Shanks leaves with Connie, Mr and Mrs
Wicksteed get back together vowing extra intimacy,
lonely Sir Percy and Lady R. decide to make a go of it,
and with a bit of philosophy Wicksteed does a little
dance in the spotlight, ending with the words '... whatever
right or wrong is, He whose lust lasts, lasts longest'.

Arthur Wicksteed	*Lady Rumpers*
Muriel Wicksteed	*Felicity Rumpers*
Dennis Wicksteed	*Mr Shanks*
Constance Wicksteed	*Sir Percy Shorter*
Mrs Swabb	*Mr Purdue*
Canon Throbbing	

Hadrian the Seventh

Peter Luke, based on works by Frederick Rolfe
Drama 2 Acts
London 1968

It is 1903 and William Rolfe, a fastidious and austere
Roman Catholic fanatic, lives alone in a shabby bed-sit,
unloving and unloved, but longing to serve the Church.
Two bailiffs arrive to warn him his prickliness has lost
him a law suit and he must pay costs and damages. They
leave but threaten to return, and his landlady Mrs
Crowe then threatens him with eviction; she wants to
move in his arch-enemy, Protestant fanatic Jeremiah
Sant. Rolfe's only friend, charwoman Agnes, arrives
and they discuss the recent death of the Pope. She
leaves, the room begins to glow with warmth and then
Dr Talacryn, Bishop of Caerleon and Dr Courtleigh,
Cardinal-Archbishop of Pimlico arrive. They explain
that the Church has relented, and Rolfe is summoned to
Holy Orders and asked to accompany Courtleigh to
Rome immediately.

Political machinations in the Papal voting process lead to Rolfe being declared Pope. His incorruptible convictions, his honesty and his extraordinary dignified presence win over his many enemies in the Vatican. His wildest dreams come true as he plans to liberate the Church from secular affairs and give away its hoarded millions to the poor and needy. He personally takes an interest in young seminarist George Rose whose cynicism and vulnerability are similar to his own, and in doing so finds the love of neighbour, leading to love of God, which has for so long been missing in his life.

Sant and Mrs Crowe arrive in Rome intending to blackmail him with a pack of lies, and when Rolfe/Hadrian offers Sant not money but the opportunity to save his soul, Sant goes beserk and shoots Rolfe/Hadrian, who dies forgiving his murderer. Rose's moving eulogy to Hadrian implies that here is the new martyr so badly needed by the Church.

Fade-out to Rolfe's bed-sit. He is clutching a bundle of manuscripts when Mrs Crowe announces two men are coming up to see him. Rolfe expects the Bishops, but the bailiffs appear. They take away his possessions, including the manuscript of *Hadrian the Seventh*, his wonderful Catholic daydream. He is left alone in the bare room.

Fr William Rolfe	Cardinal Berstein
Mrs Crowe	Cardinal Ragna
First bailiff, Bishop of Caerleon	Rector of St Andrews College
Second bailiff, Cardinal-Archbishop of Pimlico	George Arthur Rose Papal Chamberlain
Agnes	Cardinals
Jeremiah Sant	Seminarists
Father St Albans, Prepositor-General of the Jesuits	Papal guards Swiss guards Acolytes

Hair

Gerome Ragni and James Rado
Music by Galt MacDermot
Musical 2 Acts
New York 1968

Psychedelic tribal love-rock musical is a loose 'happening', virtually plotless and anarchistic, pro-pot and anti-establishment. Story as such begins with the dawning of the new Age of Aquarius with an explanation of just what this means - love and peace will reign.

Hippie Claude leaves his home in Flatbush, and, pretending to be from Manchester, England, moves in with his buddy Berger forming a ménage à trois with Berger and girlfriend Sheila in the East Village. His flower-children pals, especially pregnant Jeannie, are upset when he tells them he's up for the draft, and after chasing after a poster-painting hippie girl who isn't too turned on by sex, Claude is drafted. His friends mourn the death of his spirit.

Songs include: 'The Age of Aquarius'; 'Let the Sunshine In'; 'Good Morning Star Shine'; 'Easy to be Hard'; 'Frank Mills'

Claude	Father
Berger	Three principals
Woof	Tourist couple
Hud	Gen. Grant
Sheila	Abraham Lincoln
Jeannie	Coolidge
Crissy	Franklyn
Mother	Scarlet

Hairy Ape, The

Eugene O'Neill
'Comedy' 8 Scenes
New York 1922

In the boiler room of a transatlantic liner, Yank is the top man. Strong, brutal and macho he despises everyone and everything, Left and Right, old and new, rich and poor. He knows where he belongs and enjoys his lifestyle.

When a decadent millionaire's daughter, Mildred Douglas, indulges herself in a little social work and descends to the bowels of the ship to see the workers she is horror struck and repulsed by the 'hairy ape' Yank and his filthy companions. Her looks and comments enrage Yank and he swears to get even with her.

On land in New York, Yank and his well-meaning mate Long, become involved in a brawl outside a church and the 'ape' ends up in jail where he joins up with a revolutionary group, but they cannot handle his mindless schemes which include blowing up Mildred's father's factory. He finally ends up in a zoo park, where he at last finds someone who will listen to his primitive philosophical rantings, a gorilla. When he naively opens up the cage door for his new-found friend he too finds out what it is like to be the victim of mindless violence.

Robert 'Yank' Smith	A guard
Paddy	A secretary of an organization
Long	
Mildred Douglas	Stokers
Her aunt	Ladies
Second engineer	Gentlemen

Half a Sixpence

Beverley Cross adapted from H. G. Wells' *Kipps*
Songs by David Heneker
Musical Comedy 2 Acts
London 1963

Ambitious draper's apprentice Arthur Kipps works at Shalford's Drapery Emporium at Folkestone at the turn of the century. He is engaged to childhood sweetheart Ann Pornick and gives her half a sixpence as a love token; he keeps the other half. However, when he is enriched by an inheritance, he gets uppity and pursues the more socially elevated Helen Walsingham, who, with an eye towards his money, accepts his proposal of marriage. Arthur, though, loses his money, and in the process loses Helen. However, still-faithful Ann is willing to forgive, and eventually he finds true happiness with her.

Songs include: 'Flash Bang Wallop'; 'She's too Far Above Me'; 'Money to Burn'

Arthur Kipps	Chitterlow
Sid Pornick	Laura
Buggins	Girl student
Pearce	Boy student
Carshot	Photographer
Flo	Photographer's assistant
Emma	First reporter
Kate	Second reporter
Victoria	Gwendolin
Mr Shalford	Dancers
Mrs Walsingham	Singers
Mrs Botting	
Ann Pornick	
Young Walsingham	
Helen Walsingham	

Halfway up the Tree
Peter Ustinov
Comedy 3 Acts
London 1967

Gen. Sir Mallalieu Fitzbutress returns home to his cottage in Hampshire, retired from fighting the communists in Malaya. Lady Fitzbutress's homecoming greetings are muted; their son Robert has become an irritatingly righteous hipie, daughter Judy is pregnant, by whom she does not know, and lovely Norwegian *au pair* Helga is just plain useless. Confronted by his 'rebel' offspring and their various sixties-ish philosophies, the General takes a leaf from Robert's book and drops out himself. To everyone's horror, he becomes a national celebrity, wandering hither and thither, thoroughly enjoying his new-found freedom, and ending up living in a tree in his garden from where he can watch the double-marriage of shorn-haired son Robert with now-pregnant Helga, and daughter Judy with spartan runner Basil Utterwood. His friend Brig. Tiny Gilliatt-Brown, thwarted in his attempts to woo Lady Fitzbutress from Sir Mallalieu, decides to find a tree of his own - a pastime now becoming a national craze. However, there are reservations to the tree life, explains the General to Tiny, who retorts that even though the General says he is mentally only half way up the tree, as leader he must pretend to be at the top.

Lady Fitzbutress
Helga
Gen. Sir Mallalieu Fitzbutress
Robert
Lesley
Judy
Basil Utterwood
Brig. (Tiny) Gilliatt-Brown
Vicar

Hamlet of Stepney Green, The
Bernard Kops
Comedy 3 Acts
London 1958

The Levy family live in Stepney Green in the blitz-torn heart of London's East End Jewish community. Sam Levy, who runs a herring stall, is dying and bemoaning his life, especially his now-loveless marriage to Bessie, and the impractical ambitions of his handsome son David, a dreamer with visions of himself as a great crooner. David is too self-obsessed to notice that neighbour Solly Segal's lovely daughter Hava is crazy about him.

When Sam dies, his final words to David are that he has been poisoned; he means by his life in general but David takes this literally and plots revenge against widower Solly who now wants to marry Bessie. Everyone thinks David is deranged because he sees and speaks to Sam's ghost (no one else can see or hear him), and broods moodily like a Teddy Boy Hamlet. Eventually David is tricked by ghostly Sam into noticing and falling in love with Hava. Now Sam can at last go happily to the hereafter. Solly and Bessie can marry, and so can David and Hava. He decides to become the first singing herring salesman in history. This lively play includes a number of Jewish and children's songs.

Sam Levy	Mr Green
Bessie Levy	Mr Black
David Levy	Mr White
Solly Segal	Children
Hava Segal	
Mr Stone	
Mrs Stone	

Hamlet, Prince of Denmark
William Shakespeare
Tragedy 5 Acts
London 1601

The ghost of recently-dead old King Hamlet haunts the battlements of Castle Elsinore and appears to his son demanding revenge for his murder by poisoning, on Claudius, now king and husband to Hamlet's mother, Gertrude. Hamlet, deeply shocked at his mother's marriage, feigns madness which greatly distresses his love Ophelia, the daughter of Claudius's Lord Chamberlain, Polonius.

Hamlet asks a company of actors to perform a play with a plot similar to the way that his father was murdered so that he can gauge Claudius's reaction to it. Hamlet decides that Claudius is guilty but he cannot bring himself to kill his uncle. Hamlet goes to his mother to chide her for yielding to Claudius, and mistakenly kills Polonius who is hiding in her chamber. Claudius orders Hamlet to go to England for his own safety, but he has plotted for the Prince to be killed there. Laertes, son of Polonius, when he hears of his father's death and the subsequent madness of his sister Ophelia, swears to kill Hamlet who is returning to

Elsinore after a sea fight. Distraught Ophelia drowns herself.

Later, at a supposedly friendly fencing match between Hamlet and Laertes, Claudius tips Laertes's sword with poison but both men are wounded in the fight and Laertes confesses the king's treachery. Hamlet kills Claudius but unfortunately his mother has mistakenly taken poison intended for Hamlet.

As Hamlet lies dying news arrives that Fortinbras, Prince of Norway, has arrived to claim the throne that Hamlet has bequeathed to him with his dying breath.

Claudius, King of Denmark	Cornelius
	Voltemand
Hamlet, Prince of Denmark	A gentleman
	A priest
Polonius, Lord Chamberlain	Marcellus and Bernardo, officers
Horatio, Hamlet's friend	Francisco, soldier
	Reynaldo, servant to Polonius
Laertes, son of Polonius	
Ophelia, daughter of Polonius	Three players
	Two gravediggers
Fortinbras, Prince of Norway	Norwegian captain
	English ambassador
Gertrude, Queen of Denmark	Lords
	Ladies
Ghost of Hamlet's father	Soldiers
	Sailors
Courtiers:	Messengers
Rosencrantz	
Guildenstern	
Osric	

Hamp
John Wilson
Drama 3 Acts
London 1964

On the Western Front during the Battle of Passchendale in 1917, Pte Arthur Hamp from a Lancashire mill town is being court-martialled for desertion. Hamp is gormless, inarticulate and likeable. He has survived with 'A' Company longer than anyone and has been through the horrors. One day he was sucked into a muddy shell-hole and it terrified him more than the enemy fire. Ten days later he walked away, jumped a train, and was soon caught. His single-mindedness and honesty is no help to defending officer Lieut Hargreaves or his friend Lieut Webb, who covers his own distaste for the proceedings with cynicism. Hamp himself believes he is too insignificant for the authorities to go to the trouble of carrying out the death sentence. He also has a pathetic faith in the power of Hargreaves' rhetoric, and all the efforts of Hargreaves, Webb and the Padre fail to convince Hamp of the seriousness of his situation.

He is found guilty but not until the evening prior to the execution does the penny drop. He is being executed to 'stop the rot setting in'; the principle is being maintained, but in reality an innocent is being sacrificed.

Hargreaves, the Padre and Webb - who must lead the firing squad - do what they can in their various ways. Webb gives Hamp brandy and morphia so he is insensible, and then has to administer the final shot after a ragged round from the reluctant firing squad.

Pte Arthur Hamp	Members of the Court
Cpl of Guard	Lieut Prescott
Guard Privates	Prosecuting Officer
Lieut William Hargreaves	(Midgley)
	Padre
Lieut Tom Webb	MO (Sullivan)
President of the Court	Orderly Officer

Hands Across the Sea
Noël Coward
Play 1 Act
London 1935
See: Tonight at 8.30

Happiest Days of Your Life, The
John Dighton
Farce 3 Acts
London 1948

The teachers of Hilary Hall School for Boys have just settled into a new term after wartime evacuation, when they are informed that another school, St Swithins, will be billeted with them. To their horror, this turns out to be a girls' school, and the matriarchal principal, Miss Whitchurch, makes certain that both her staff and pupils secure the best rooms. To compound the problem, parents start arriving to see their children, with the harassed staff attempting to conceal the fact that boys and girls are together. They fail in this and the furious parents decide to take their children home. A message arrives, however, stating that yet a third school is to be billeted with them. Uniting finally against a common enemy, staff and parents barricade the gates.

Dick Tassell, assistant master at Hilary School
Rainbow, school porter and groundsman
Rupert Billings, senior assistant master
Godfrey Pond, headmaster
Miss Evelyn Whitchurch, principal of St Swithins
Miss Gossage, senior assistant mistress
Hopcroft, pupil at Hilary Hall
Barbara Cahoun, pupil at St Swithins
Joyce Harper, assistant mistress
The Revd Edward Peck
Mrs Peck
Edgar Sowter
Mrs Sowter

Happy Birthday
Marc Camoletti
Adapted by Beverley Cross
Comedy 2 Acts
London 1979

Jacqueline is delighted when her husband Bernard's best friend Robert arrives to stay for the weekend at their country house; the pair are having a secret affair. Robert is not so happy when Bernard slyly tells him that he must pretend to Jacqueline that he is bringing his mistress Brigit along, who will be arriving later. In fact Brigit is Bernard's mistress and he optimistically hopes her presence will spice up the weekend. Robert, naturally, is most reluctant, and things begin to go awry when the temporary maid arrives while Bernard is out. Her name is also Brigit, and Robert believes it is she who is Bernard's mistress. From this point on the complications of the situation proliferate with bewildering rapidity. The real Brigit arrives and must now pretend to be the maid, the maid Brigit has to pretend to be Robert's mistress, then his niece. Confusions abound until in the end Bernard and Jacqueline are reconciled (though she never learns of Bernard's low ploys), and beautiful Brigit and Robert leave together. Maid Brigit also does well from her temporary post - she leaves with a new mink coat and a fistful of money.

Jacqueline
Robert
Bernard
Brigit 1
Brigit 2

Happy Days
Samuel Beckett
Tragicomedy 2 Acts
New York 1961

In a tropical desert setting Winnie, an optimistic middle-class lady, up to her waist in sand, is asleep. Behind her lies her husband Willie. A bell rings out and she wakes up to go through her morning toilet routine before waking up Willie. He reads the notices in an old newspaper and she listens to love songs from a music box as she waits for the signal to go back to sleep. Nearby a pistol is stuck prominently in the sand.

Later, when she again wakens, she is now up to her neck in sand and immobile, but this does not deter her enjoyment of life. She calls Willie, who does not appear until she has told a story about a little girl who is frightened by a mouse; when he does, he is very smartly attired. Winnie is overjoyed by this 'happy day.' She sings to the music box, they look at each other and smile. When she stops smiling there is a long pause before the curtain falls.

Winnie
Willie

Harold and Maude
Colin Higgins
Comedy 3 Acts
New York 1983

Harold is nineteen and morbidly eccentric, shocking everyone except his wealthy widowed mother with his elaborate fake suicides. His mother, naturally disturbed about this, sends him to a 'shrink' and also decides a

dating agency might help; several silly girls subsequently come and go. Harold also likes to attend funerals, and on one jaunt he meets Maude, busy replanting an unhappy shrub. She's almost eighty, very 'together' and semi-mystical, natural and non-materialistic. Her vivacity and openness to new experiences enchants Harold who is gradually drawn to her, sharing her adventures and run-ins with the Priest and Inspector Bernard, whom she always manages to outwit.

Maude's example teaches Harold to enjoy life, and he determines to marry her. He tells his mother he now has a fiancée, but when relieved Ma goes to meet Maude she is, of course, horrified. Harold is undeterred and throws an exuberant eightieth birthday party for Maude, in the middle of which she announces she's going away. Horrified Harold gets the picture and tries to stop her but it is too late. Maude comforts him, then dies. Next day, despite his grief, Harold finds life still worth living, even more so when he discovers Maude's goodbye present to him - her magic Chinese gong.

Harold	*Chief Gardener*
Mrs Chasen	*Sylvie Gazel*
Maid	*Inspector Bernard*
Dr Matthews	*Nancy Mersch*
Maude	*Sunshine Dore*
Priest	*Removal Men*
Gardener	

Harvey
Mary Chase
Comedy 3 Acts
New York 1943

Veta Louise Simmons and her daughter Myrtle Mae are at their wits' end at their home in the Dowd family mansion where they live courtesy of Veta's brother, Elwood P. Dowd. He is a wise and likeable middle-aged man, but his constant attentions to his invisible/imaginary companion Harvey, a six-foot white rabbit, are proving a constant social embarrassment to mother and especially daughter. Veta schemes to get Elwood committed to a sanitorium but the plan backfires when assistant head doctor Sanderson commits her instead. Head doctor Chumley agrees to meet Elwood for a drink and ends up meeting, and to his horror believing in, Harvey. Veta has also seen Harvey and it is this threat to their own sanity that disturbs them as much as Elwood's behaviour. In fact Harvey is a pookah, a mischievous (but clever) fairy spirit in animal form. Eventually Elwood agrees to be committed for the sake of his sister's peace of mind, but at the last moment Veta relents after hearing how the 'treatment' changes the personality. She likes Elwood the way he is.

Myrtle Mae Simmons	*Marvin Wilson*
Veta Louise Simmons	*Lyman Sanderson MD*
Elwood P Dowd	*William R. Chumley MD*
Miss Johnson	*Betty Chumley*
Mrs Ethel Chauvenet	*Judge Omar Gaffney*
Ruth Kelly	*E. J. Lofgren*

Hatful of Rain, A
Michael V. Gazzo
Drama 3 Acts
New York 1955

Father is visiting war-hero son Johnny and pregnant wife Celia at their tiny apartment on New York's Lower East Side. He is mad that son Polo, who lodges with Johnny and Celia, promised him a loan but did not deliver. Johnny then answers the door and has to go out into the hall to talk to Apples and Mother, two drug dealers. He owes them money and has a day to pay. He tells his wife and father that they are gambling pals. Dad leaves and Johnny squirms at Celia's accusations about their marriage; he will not touch her, will not talk about the baby and goes out night after night. She wrongly suspects him of having another woman, but even after declaring his love for her, Johnny once again must go out to buy drugs.

Polo, Johnny's simple and devoted brother returns; he loves Celia and she is beginning to get so fond of him that she asks him to leave and find somewhere else to live. He is drunk and things almost go too far between them.

Next morning, Johnny returns and begs Polo for enough money for a final fix. Polo spends all his money on Johnny's habit, and he tries to persuade Johnny to take the cure. He leaves and the dealers return. Johnny is saved only by Polo's return - he has sold his last possession, his car. When Celia gets back from work Johnny is determined to reform and with Polo's urging he tells the truth to her and his father. Dad is horrified that his favourite son is an addict and disgusted with Polo for helping him. When he sees Johnny's distress as he suffers withdrawal symptoms, both he and Celia begin to understand the mutual predicament of the brothers. Father and Polo leave, and Celia phones the police, who will take Johnny to hospital - he is willing to take the cure.

Johnny Pope Snr	Chuch
Johnny Pope	Polo Pope
Celia Pope	A man
Mother	Putski
Apples	

Haunted, The (Mourning Becomes Electra III)
Eugene O'Neill
Tragedy 4 Acts
New York 1932

Orin Mannon and his sister Lavinia return to their New England home after a cruise to the South Sea islands, where they had gone when Orin suffered a nervous collapse brought on by guilt over their mother's suicide. Though they had both engineered the suicide, only Orin feels any remorse. Lavinia feels her mother's death only as a liberation, and has changed from a rather pinched, prissy girl into a strong sensual woman.

To soothe Orin, Lavinia attempts to arrange his marriage to Hazel Niles, his boyhood sweetheart, and herself plans to wed Hazel's brother Peter, a longstanding admirer. Orin is too tainted by guilt to carry through with the marriage and determines that Lavinia is unfit for Peter as well. Orin reveals to Hazel both his own and Lavinia's hand in driving their mother to suicide, extracts Hazel's promise to prevent Peter marrying Lavinia, and kills himself in despair. Peter appears likely to press ahead with the marriage at all costs, until Lavinia herself admits to an affair with a native during her stay in the South Seas. Peter abandons her to a life bound to the memory of her dead family.

Lavinia Mannon
Orin Mannon, her brother
Peter Niles
Hazel Niles, Peter's sister
Seth, the Mannon's handyman
Amos Ames
Ira Mackel
Joe Silva
Abner Small

Having a Ball
Alan Bleasdale
Comedy 2 Acts
Oldham 1981

There is much trepidation among the men awaiting vasectomies at a private clinic, the action taking place in three rooms onstage - the waiting room, the preparation room and the operating theatre. The cool woman surgeon is trying to pursuade her efficient male nurse to stay on, but he objects to abortion and is set to quit and she cannot get a replacement. Pandemonium ensues when patient Lenny recognizes patient Ritchie as his hated tormentor ('Big Jobs') from his school days. Although both men have changed considerably, anarchic Lenny seizes every opportunity to bait nervous Ritchie. Attractive Doreen Thomas wanders around with a bottle of vodka getting drunker and drunker and gloating at her pompous husband Malcolm, chief executive of the local county council, also there for the snip. Malcolm tries to take away Doreen's vodka, but she fools him and then shares a drink and some kind words with Lenny.

Elderly George, rich and still-virile, arrives with younger wife Jean, and he starts philosophizing at the younger men ... his marriage seems better than theirs. Malcolm gets 'done', the surgeon gets fed up with Lenny and Ritchie and their mutual chaos, but Lenny does summon up a final effort to be snipped. He enters the theatre, lays down, and screams, long and real.

Nurse (John Gilbert)	George Hill
Surgeon	Jean Hill
Lenny Anderson	
Ritchie Burrows	
Three female patients	
Anaesthetist (Mr Martin)	
Malcolm Thomas	
Doreen Thomas	

Hay Fever
Noël Coward
Comedy 3 Acts
London 1925

A summer weekend at the Thames-side home of David Bliss, popular writer of gaudy romantic novels, his madly theatrical wife Judith, recently retired from the West End stage and worried about ageing and the loss of her public, their nineteen-year-old daughter Sorel and artist son Simon. It emerges that, unknown to the others, each has invited someone for the weekend. The maid is off with toothache and housekeeper Clara - formerly Judith's dresser - is grumbling about the extra work. David is upstairs trying to finish his latest book, *The Sinful Woman* and Judith is thinking of making another comeback, in *Love's Whirlwind*.

First to arrive are a diplomat, grey-haired Richard, to see Sorel, and Jackie, a flapper daft enough to think David is a great writer. Next is manly young Sandy, devoted to Judith's image, and Mrs Myra Arundel, a woman of a certain age who is disapproved of by Judith (who says Myra goes about using sex like a shrimping net and currently has Simon in it).

With high drama, mostly created by Judith but connived at by all the Blisses, they switch alliances around. Richard and Judith get together and so her marriage to David is finished, especially as he is taking up with Myra. Sorel and Sandy start smooching and Simon announces his engagement to Jackie. But it is all play-acting, much of it out of *Love's Whirlwind*, for egotistic kicks and the opportunity to make biting, bitchy and sparklingly witty cracks. On Sunday morning, the guests creep out and drive off in Sandy's car. Them forgotten, David starts to read his last chapter to the family over breakfast.

Judith Bliss	*Richard Greatham*
David Bliss	*Jackie Coryton*
Sorel Bliss	*Sandy Tyrell*
Simon Bliss	*Clara*
Myra Arundel	

Heartbreak House
George Bernard Shaw
Play 3 Acts
New York 1920

At the outbreak of World War One a number of family and friends gather at the ship-like house of the eccentric eighty-eight-year-old Capt. Shotover. Hesione, his daughter, brings her young friend, Ellie Dunn and Ellie's intended Alfred Mangan, an industrialist. Hesoine is unhappy about this match but even more so when she learns that Ellie is in love with her liar of a husband Hector, who is in turn flirting with her sister, Lady Ariadne Utterword, a colonial. Mangan becomes infatuated with Hesione and wants to end his association with Ellie, who has now fallen under the influence of the crazy old Shotover, who is working on even more effective means of exterminating the human race. A burglar comes into this complicated, morally vacuous 'heartbreak house' and only he and Mangan have the common sense to protect Shotover's store of dynamite, as the women get excited at the prospect of an imminent air raid.

Ellie Dunn	*Mazzini Dunn*
Nurse Guinness	*Hector Hushabye*
Capt. Shotover	*Alfred 'Boss' Mangan*
Lady Utterword	*Randall Utterword*
Hesione Hushabye	*Billy Dunn, the burglar*

Hedda Gabler
Henrik Ibsen
Play 4 Acts
Munich 1891

Hedda, recently married to Jorgen Tesman, is exasperated and contemptuous of her husband's smug middle-class attitudes. She admires, but resents, the brilliant scholar Loevborg who has come to town with her old school friend Thea Elvsted; he is in competition with Jorgen for a professional appointment. She amuses herself by flirting with Judge Brack who invites Jorgen and Loevborg to a stag party, where in a drunken stupor Loevborg loses the manuscript of his important new book. Jorgen finds the document and Hedda, secretly enjoying the power of influencing destiny, destroys it.

Loevborg is distraught over the loss and Hedda gives him one of her father's pistols and suggests he does away with himself - beautifully.

Thea is devastated by the suicide attempt, but she has recovered the original notes of his book and scholar Tesman offers to help reconstruct the manuscript. Brack, who has discovered where Loevborg got the gun, now has Hedda in his grasp, and Tesman is too busy to be concerned. Hedda makes a grave decision.

Jorgen (George) Tesman, an academic
Hedda Tesman, née Gabler, his wife
Miss Juliana Tesman, his aunt
Mrs Elvsted
Judge Brack
Eilert Loevborg
Bertha, elderly maid

Heiress, The
Ruth and Augustus Goetz
Drama 2 Acts
London 1949

Catherine Sloper is not unattractive, but constant unfavourable comparisons by her father, Dr Sloper, to her beautiful talented mother (who died in childbirth) have not given Catherine much confidence. They live in a fine house in Washington Square, Greenwich Village in 1850 together with her widowed aunt, Mrs Penniman. When cousin Maria visits with fiancé Arthur Townshend and his handsome cousin Morris, everyone is shocked when charming Morris pays ardent court to Catherine. Morris, however, is a rake and an adventurer, and Dr Sloper is convinced he only wants Catherine for her inheritance. Mrs Penniman encourages Catherine with the match, more or less regardless of Morris's motives, but events come to a head when the doctor threatens to disinherit Catherine and she is jilted by Morris. Catherine never forgives her dying father for disillusioning her of Morris, whom she loved dearly, and she settles down to a quiet spinsterly life.

Two years later Morris returns broke from California and his unsuccessful gold panning - he now intends to pan for gold in New York. Catherine has matured and become more attractive and Morris is impressed; they meet and agree to elope, as before. But when the appointed hour arrives and Morris knocks at the door, it is Catherine's turn to reject him. Ordering her maid to bolt the door, she ignores Morris and goes to bed.

Dr Sloper
Catherine
Morris Townshend
Lavinia Penniman
Elizabeth Almond
Marian Almond
Arthur Townshend
Maria

Helen
Euripides
Drama 1 Act
Athens 412BC

This play is based on a legend that the Queen Helen who left King Menelaus for Paris of Troy was, in fact, merely the wraith (double) of the real Queen Helen, who had been spirited to Egypt by the god Hermes.

The Egyptian king, Proteus, who was Helen's protector, has died and been succeeded by his son Theoclymenus, who is trying to force Helen to marry him. To forestall his attentions, Helen has taken refuge in the sacred precincts of Proteus's tomb, where she is brought the news that Troy was destroyed years ago and Menelaus probably killed during its fall.

While she mourns his death, Menelaus arrives, having been shipwrecked on the Egyptian coast along with the wraith Helen, whom he has left hiding in a coastal cave. Menelaus is thrown into confusion, but is finally satisfied that he had found the real Helen when he learns that the wraith has vanished, after admitting it was a counterfeit.

Helen and Menelaus escape both Egypt and Theoclymenus, on a bogus funeral ship which feigns a service in honour of Menelaus' supposed death.

Helen, daughter of Zeus and Leda
Tencer, brother of Ajax
Menelaus, Helen's husband
Old woman
Messenger
Thenoe
Theoclymenus, king of Egypt
The Discori, Helen's deified brothers
Chorus

Hello, Dolly!
Music by Michael Stewart and Jerry Herman
Musical 2 Acts
New York 1964
See: *Matchmaker, The*
Songs include: 'Before the Parade Passes Me By'; 'It Only Takes a Moment'; 'Hello, Dolly!'

Henry IV
Luigi Pirandello
Tragedy 3 Acts
Rome 1922

At a villa in Italy in the present day, Berthold has been recruited to be a 'secret counsellor', to join with Harold, Landolph and Ordulph at the make-believe (but historically accurate) 'court' of eleventh-century German Emperor Henry IV. The charade is to humour Henry, a rich madman. Enter beautiful middle-aged widow Marchioness Donna Matilda Spina, her lover Baron Tito Belcredi, her lovely sad daughter Frida with fiancé Marquis Charles Di Nolli, and Dr Genoni. They have arrived at the dying request of Di Nolli's mother - and Henry's sister - who believed her brother was about to be cured. Donna Matilda was Henry's lover before an accident twenty years ago when, during an historical pageant, Henry fell off his horse, knocked his head and awoke believing himself to be the character he had chosen to play.

Donna Matilda, the Doctor and Belcredi dress up in appropriate costume and Henry enters the throne room. He is a strange and tragic figure, totally involved with the exactitudes of the character. Two portraits in the throne room painted at the time of the pageant depict the younger Henry and Matilda, painted as the historical Bertha, whom the historical Henry wished to wed. Matilda now intends using her daughter Frida to wake Henry from his delusion. Henry seems to dislike Belcredi, and when the guests leave the throne room, he reveals to his secret counsellors that he knows what is happening and that Belcredi is Matilda's lover. He is not mad and is enjoying manipulating the situation.

The counsellors reveal the truth to the relatives who nevertheless surprise Henry with Frida, who looks more like his original Bertha than does Matilda now. Poor Frida is terrified of all this, and as the explanations get deeper and more emotional, no one is quite sure of Henry's - or their own - sanity. Henry grabs Frida, his dream embodied, and when Belcredi tries to stop him, Henry runs him through with a sword. Belcredi is taken away and dies, with Henry calling for his counsellors and attempting to sink even deeper into his masquerade.

Henry IV
The Marchioness Donna
* Matilda Spina*
Frida
Marquis Charles Di Nolli
* Baron Tito Belcredi*
Dr Dionysius Genoni
Harold (Frank)
Landolph (Lolo)
Ordulph (Momo)
Berthold (Fino)
John, the old waiter
Two valets

Henry IV Part 1
William Shakespeare
Drama 5 Acts
London 1597

Rebellion looms for Henry IV; the Percy family (Earl of Worcester, Earl of Northumberland and fiery son Harry Hotspur) are aggrieved at Henry's high-handed treatment of them after they helped put him on the throne. Hotspur refuses to yield to the King his prisoners after a victory over Scottish Earl Douglas, and Henry bemoans the fact that his own elder son Henry (Prince Hal) is a dissolute wastrel, while Hotspur is gloriously martial. Meanwhile, Prince Hal spends his time in taverns, plotting muggings and generally engaging in pranks and witty riposte with his gross pal Sir John Falstaff, whose appetite for food and drink are matched only by his capacity for lies and exaggerations.

The plotters include not only the Percys, but also Welsh mystic Owen Glendower whom the King has never succeeded in defeating, plus mighty Earl Douglas, Sir Richard Vernon, and Scroop, Archbishop of York. When the final battle approaches, the rebels' position is undermined by the absence of Northumberland, who is sick, and Glendower, who is delayed. Undaunted, Hotspur leads the fray. King Henry offers to negotiate for peace, and Prince Hal casts off his debauchery and showing true Bolingbroke spirit offers to fight Hotspur man-to-man to save the lives of those assembled. But Worcester does not tell Hotspur of the offer; the battle proceeds and the rebels lose. Prince Hal saves the life of his father and slays valiant Hotspur (with some regret), and Falstaff, cunning as ever, attempts to take credit for the deed (with Hal's connivance).

King Henry IV
Henry, Prince of Wales and Prince John of
  Lancaster, sons of the King
Earl of Westmoreland
Sir Walter Blunt
Thomas Percy, Earl of Worcester
Henry Percy, Earl of Northumberland
Henry Percy surnamed Hotspur, his son
Edmund Mortimer, Earl of March
Archibald, Earl of Douglas
Owen Glendower
Sir Richard Vernon
Richard Scroop, Archbishop of York
Sir Michael, a friend of the Archbishop of York
Sir John Falstaff
Poins
Peto
Bardolph
Gadshill
Lady Percy, Hotspur's wife and Mortimer's sister
Lady Mortimer, Glendower's daughter and
  Mortimer's wife
Mistress Quickly, Hostess of the Boar's Head in
  Eastcheap
Lords

Officers
Sheriff
Vintner
Chamberlain
Drawers
Two carriers
Ostler, messengers, attendants

Henry IV Part 2
William Shakespeare
Drama 5 Acts
London 1598

The rebellion against Henry continues, and three years after Hotspur's defeat at Shrewsbury, a new insurrection led by Scroop, Archbishop of York, threatens the throne. The plotters include Lord Hastings, Lord Mowbray and Lord Bardolph who are relying on the support of Hotspur's father Northumberland. But, unknown to them, Northumberland is dissuaded from the fray by daughter-in-law Lady Percy, still grieving for Hotspur, and he decides to retreat to Scotland out of harm's way. Meanwhile in London, Falstaff and his cronies Bardolph and Pistol continue their antics with Hostess Quickly and whore Doll Tear-Sheet, while mischievous Prince Hal disguises himself, and chief attendant Poins, in order to spy on and surprise them.

News then arrives of the rebellion and Falstaff is required to recruit soldiers, and en route to the encounter stays in Gloucestershire with his old friend Justice Shallow from the Inns of Court. Nostalgic Shallow is taken advantage of in every possible way by unscrupulous Falstaff, who borrows large sums of money, eats and drinks off him, and stores up a fund of cruel anecdotes to retell to Prince Hal. Hal's brother Prince John of Lancaster tricks the rebels and captures the leaders without a fight, but when the victorious Bolingbrokes return to London the King is dying. Prince Hal convinces the King he will cast off his low friends and low ways, and after his father's death one of Henry V's first acts is to order Falstaff not to come within ten miles of him. He will reconsider his decision if and when Falstaff behaves himself.

King Henry IV
Henry, Prince of Wales
Thomas, Duke of Clarence
Prince John of Lancaster
Prince Humphrey of Gloucester
Earl of Warwick
Earl of Westmoreland
Gower
Harcourt
Lord Chief Justice
A gentleman attendant
Earl of Northumberland
Scroop, Archbishop of York
Lord Mowbray
Lord Hastings
Lord Bardolph

Sir John Colville
Morton/Travers, domestics of Northumberland
Falstaff
Bardolph
Pistol
Page
Poins, Peto, attendants on Prince Henry
Shallow, Silence, country justices
Davy, servant to Shallow
Mouldy, Shadow, Wart, Feeble, Bull-Calf, recruits
Fang, Snare, sheriff's officers
A dancer, speaker of the epilogue
A porter
Lady Northumberland
Lady Percy
Hostess Quickly
Doll Tear-Sheet

Henry V
William Shakespeare
Drama 5 Acts
London 1599

Fearful of a bill passed at the end of the reign of Henry IV, which would strip the church of most of its wealth, the Archbishop of Canterbury encourages and supports Henry V's claim to the throne of France and offers him much assistance. Henry is encouraged thus to proceed with his ambitions and challenges the French, who then insult him. Still anxious about the rebellious factors in his kingdom that warred against his father, Henry goes to France with a small army, leaving the bulk of his forces to deal with potential insurrection by the Welsh, the Scots, and rebellious barons.

Although Falstaff has since died, purportedly from a broken heart after former friend Henry's turncoat treatment of him, his servants Nym, Bardolph and Pistol join Henry's army. Nym and Bardolph are hanged for looting, while braggart Pistol gets into trouble with verbose but brave Fluellen for mocking the Welsh. Henry himself mingles with common soldiers to hear not a lot of good of himself, and in doing so is almost beaten up by common soldier William, who, when all is unmasked, is forgiven and rewarded for his loyalty.

Despite smirking and boasting about their superior numbers and better army the French are humiliated and soundly beaten at Agincourt. Henry ends up getting everything he wants, including peace and the hand of French Princess Katherine, daughter of the King and Queen of France. The chorus, however, predicts the early death of Henry and the fall of his empire.

King Henry V
Duke of Gloucester, Duke of Bedford, brothers to the King
Duke of Exeter, uncle to the King
Duke of York, cousin to the King
Earl of Salisbury
Earl of Warwick
Earl of Westmoreland

Archbishop of Canterbury
Bishop of Ely
Conspirators against the King: Earl of Cambridge, Lord Scroop, Sir Thomas Grey
Officers in King Henry's army: Sir Thomas Erpingham, Gower, Fluellen, Macmorris, Jamy
Soldiers in King Henry's army: Court, Bates, Williams
Nym, Bardolph, Pistol, formerly servants to Falstaff
Boy
A herald
Chorus
Charles VI, King of France
Lewis, the Dauphin
Duke of Burgundy
Duke of Orleans
Duke of Britaine
Duke of Bourbon
The Constable of France
Rambures, Grandpré, French lords
Governor of Harfleur
Montjoy, a French herald
Ambassadors to the King of England
Isabel, Queen of France
Katherine, daughter to Charles and Isabel
Alice, a lady attending her
Hostess of the Boar's Head, Eastcheap, formerly Mistress Nell Quickly
Lords, ladies, officers, soldiers in attendance

Henry VI Part 1
William Shakespeare
Drama 5 Acts
London 1593

Even before Henry V is buried, news arrives of a great French rebellion. The Dauphin now has the mystic power of Joan La Pucelle (Joan of Arc) behind him and he is smitten with her. She, however, must remain pure. Even warlike Lord Talbot, much feared by the French, is thwarted by Joan's power and the battles and sieges ebb and flow first one way then another, generally favouring the French. In Britain, Richard Plantagenet, later Duke of York, and Beaufort, Earl of Somerset, quarrel and the seeds of the Wars of the Roses are sown - but these baronial conflicts in fact stretch back to Henry IV's usurpation of the throne from Richard II. Feeble young King Henry VI tries to make peace all round, but is generally deceived.

In France, Talbot's forces begin to recapture lost territory, but when Joan persuades turncoat Duke of Burgundy to fight for the French, Talbot is surrounded. York and Somerset are too busy arguing among themselves to help Talbot, and together with his son they are slaughtered. York finally joins in the combat and Joan is defeated, taken prisoner and burnt at the stake, her inspiration revealed to be diabolical. King Henry VI foolishly signs a truce with the French and Suffolk brings back French Princess Margaret to be

Henry's bride while secretly intending to rule her and the King himself.

King Henry VI

Duke of Gloucester, uncle to the King and Protector

Duke of Bedford, uncle to the King and Regent of France

Thomas Beaufort, duke of Exeter, great uncle to the King

Henry Beaufort, great-uncle to the King, Bishop of Winchester and afterwards Cardinal

John Beaufort, Earl of Somerset, afterwards Duke

Richard Plantagenet, eldest son of Richard, late Earl of Cambridge, afterwards Duke of York

Earl of Warwick

Earl of Salisbury

Earl of Suffolk

Lord Talbot, afterwards Earl of Shrewsbury

John Talbot, his son

Edmund Mortimer, Earl of March

Mortimer's keeper

A lawyer

Sir John Fastolfe

Sir William Lucy

Sir William Glansdale

Sir Thomas Gargreve

Mayor of London

Woodville, Lieutenant of the Tower

Vernon, of the White Rose or York faction

Bassett, of the Red Rose or Lancaster faction

Charles, Dauphin and afterwards King of France

Reignier, Duke of Anjou and titular King of Naples

Duke of Burgundy

Duke of Alençon

Governor of Paris

Bastard of Orleans

Master-gunner of Orleans

His son

General of the French forces in Bordeaux

A French sergeant

A porter

An old shepherd, father to Joan La Pucelle

Margaret, daughter to Reignier, afterwards married to King Henry

Countess of Auvergne

Joan la Pucelle, Joan of Arc

Fiends to la Pucelle

Lords

Warders of the Tower

Heralds, officers, soldiers, messengers, attendants

Henry VI Part 2
William Shakespeare
Drama 5 Acts
London 1593

The realm is further fractured under reluctant sovereign Henry, who is pious but weak and meek. His ambitious wife Margaret schemes with her lover Suffolk to discredit with witchcraft the Duchess of Gloucester,

wife of the King's loyal protector; they succeed, and later Suffolk has Gloucester murdered, much to Henry's grief. Suffolk is arrested by public demand and later killed, leaving the way clear for ambitious York (Richard Plantagenet) to pursue his claims to the throne. York needs men, and when given an opportunity by Henry to raise an army to quell an Ulster revolt, he does so and secretly plots with Kentish fanatic John Cade to start a peasant's revolt in his absence.

Bloodthirsty Cade is spectacularly successful and reaches London, but when his followers are offered unconditional pardons by Lord Clifford, they desert Cade. The leader flees back to Kent, and, weakened by hunger, is killed by Alexander Iden. York returns with his army, purportedly to quell Cade, but then refuses to disband the army until Somerset of the House of Lancaster is arrested. Somerset is arrested but then freed and this gives York a pretext to assert his own claim to the throne. The two sides meet at St Albans, the first great battle of the Wars of the Roses. York, with his sons Edward and Richard, and their allies Warwick and Salisbury gain the day. The King and Queen flee to London, Lord Clifford and Somerset are slain, and Clifford's son swears revenge. The victors then pursue the King to London.

King Henry VI

Humphrey, Duke of Gloucester, his uncle

Cardinal Beaufort, Bishop of Winchester

Richard Plantagenet, Duke of York

Edward and Richard, his sons

Duke of Somerset

Duke of Suffolk

Duke of Buckingham

Lord Clifford

Young Clifford, his son

Earl of Salisbury

Earl of Warwick, his son

Lord Scales

Lord Say

Sir Humphrey Stafford

William Stafford, his brother

Sir John Stanley

Vaux

Matthew Goffe

Walter Whitmore

Lieutenant

Master

Master's mate

Two gentlemen

Prisoners with Suffolk

John Hume, John Southwell, priests

Roger Bolingbroke, conjuror

Thomas Horner, armourer

Peter, his man

The Clerk of Chartham

The Mayor of St Albans

Simpcox, imposter

Jack (John) Cade, rebel

Followers of Cade:
Bevis
John Holland
Dick the Butcher
Smith the Weaver
Michael
Alexander Iden, Kentish gentleman
Two murderers
Margaret, Queen to King Henry
Eleanor Cobham, Duchess of Gloucester
Margery Jourdain, witch
Wife of Simpcox
Lords
Ladies
Attendants
Heralds
Petitioners
Aldermen
Beadle
Sheriff
Officers
Citizens
Prentices
Falconers
Guards
Soldiers
Messengers
A spirit

Henry VI Part 3
William Shakespeare
Drama 5 Acts
London 1593

Reluctant ruler Henry of the House of Lancaster is losing the Wars of the Roses. Pressed by the claims of the Duke of York to the throne, Henry agrees that York and his family shall succeed to the throne after his death. This enrages Queen Margaret and her son Edward, Prince of Wales, and in a battle at Sandal Castle the Yorkist forces are temporarily beaten. York is slain, and his youngest son Rutland murdered by vengeful Lord Clifford. However, at the next battle between Towton and Saxton, the Yorkist forces rally and defeat the Lancastrians. Clifford is killed and King Henry flees to Scotland, where he is captured and brought back to London and the Tower. Meanwhile, hunchbacked Richard, York's third son, begins his ambitious scheming for the throne. First he must get rid of the remaining Lancastrians, then his two elder brothers Edward and George.

Queen Margaret and the Prince of Wales go to France to petition King Louis, but Yorkist kingmaker Warwick also arrives seeking Louis' sister Bona's hand for Edward, thus cementing Anglo-French relations. Meanwhile Edward, now King of England, has taken a fancy to lovely widow Lady Elizabeth Grey and they wed in haste. When the news arrives at the French court, Warwick is enraged, feeling his mission has been betrayed. He joins forces with Margaret and Bona, and together with a French army returns to England and fights along with turncoat George, Duke of Clarence. Battles follow at Barnet and Tewkesbury, but George turns again, and the Yorkists triumph. Richard kills Edward, Prince of Wales, and his father King Henry, and Margaret is returned to France.

Edward now seems secure on the throne with his son set for the succession. Heartless Richard, though, is lurking and plotting, and his kiss of fealty is a Judas's kiss.

King Henry VI
Edward, Prince of Wales, his son
Louis XI, King of France
Of King Henry's party:
Duke of Somerset
Duke of Exeter
Earl of Oxford
Earl of Northumberland
Earl of Westmoreland
Lord Clifford
Richard Plantagenet, Duke of York
His sons:
Edward, Earl of March, afterwards King Edward IV
George, afterwards Duke of Clarence
Richard, afterwards Duke of Gloucester
Edmund, Earl of Rutland
Of the Duke of York's party:
Duke of Norfolk
Marquess of Montague
Earl of Warwick
Earl of Pembroke
Lord Falconbridge
Lord Hastings
Lord Stafford
Sir John Mortimer
Sir Hugh Mortimer
Henry, Earl of Richmond, a youth
Earl Rivers, brother of Lady Grey
Sir William Stanley
Sir John Montgomery
Sir John Somerville
Tutor of Rutland
Mayor of York
Lieutenant of the Tower
A nobleman
Two keepers
A huntsman
A son that has killed his father
A father that has killed his son
Queen Margaret
Lady Elizabeth Grey, afterwards Queen to Edward IV
Bona, sister to the French Queen
Soldiers
Attendants
Messengers
Watchmen

Henry VIII
William Shakespeare
Drama 5 Acts
London 1613

Shakespeare's (probably) final play is a history opening with the Duke of Norfolk and Lord Abergavenny unable to prevent the arrest and trial of the innocent Duke of Buckingham for treason, instigated by King Henry's favourite, Cardinal Wolsey. The Cardinal is then condemed by Queen Katherine for his injurious taxations, but at a party thrown by the Cardinal, Henry meets and is smitten with Lady Anne Bullen, one of Katherine's ladies-in-waiting. Buckingham is executed, and the Lord Chamberlain, Norfolk and the Dukes of Suffolk and Surrey lament Wolsey's pre-eminence with the King and their own lack of influence.

In order that the King may leave Katherine, Wolsey negotiates with Rome so that Henry's marriage is declared invalid (being married to the widow of his brother). Katherine refuses to stay at the court to plead her case and Henry becomes impatient. Then Wolsey himself falls from the King's grace when Henry discovers a document written by Wolsey to the Pope asking him to stay judgement on the divorce, otherwise Henry will wed the unsuitable Bullen. Later, Henry secretly marries Anne and virtuous Katherine falls ill, shortly before her death having a beatific vision.

Archbishop Cranmer, the new Archbishop of Canterbury, is then condemned by the barons, but is under Henry's protection. The baby Elizabeth is born and Cranmer officiates at the christening, prophesying a glorious reign for the new princess.

King Henry VIII
Cardinal Wolsey
Cardinal Campeius
Cranmer, Archbishop of Canterbury
Gardiner, Bishop of Winchester
Bishop of Lincoln
Duke of Buckingham
Duke of Norfolk
Duke of Suffolk
Earl of Surrey
Lord Abergavenny
Lord Sands (Sir Walter Sands)
Lord Chancellor
Lord Chamberlain
Sir Henry Guilford
Sir Thomas Lovell
Sir Nicholas Vaux
Sir Anthony Denny
Brandon
Cromwell, Wolsey's servant
Dr Butts
Griffiths, gentleman-usher to Queen Katherine
Capuchius, ambassador from Emperor Charles V
First, second and third gentlemen
Garter King-at-Arms
Sergeant-at-Arms
Door-keeper to the council chamber
Secretary to Wolsey
Page to Gardiner
A crier
A messenger
A servant
Queen Katherine, King Henry's wife, afterwards divorced
Anne Bullen, her maid of honour, afterwards Queen
Old lady, Anne Bullen's friend
Patience, Queen Katherine's woman
Lords
Ladies
Bishops
Judges
Gentlemen
Priests
Lord Mayor of London
Aldermen
Vergers
Scribes
Guards
Attendants, servants and common people
Women attendant upon Queen Katherine
Spirits

Hiawatha
Henry Wadsworth Longfellow
Adapted by Michael Bogdanov
Drama 2 Acts
London 1980

Set in a giant teepee with a padded canvas floor painted with a Red Indian motif and a circular white disc in the background to represent sun/moon, this adaptation of Longfellow's masterpiece is filled with chanting and percussion against which the storyteller relates the legend of the mighty Hiawatha. Told in that distinctly hypnotic metre (borrowed by Longfellow from a Finnish collection of poems), the tale reveals the Iroquois' animistic existence in all its dignity. The birth of Hiawatha to Wenonah and the faithless Mudjekeewis (the West Wind), Hiawatha's friendship with Iagoo the great boaster and storyteller, his confrontation with his father, his building of the canoe and slaying the giant sturgeon, and his romance and wedding to Minnehaha are all described and enacted.

Trouble comes when handsome mischief-maker Pau-Puk-Keewis cunningly cheats the villagers and strangles Kahgahgee, the raven, as a calculated insult to Hiawatha. He is pursued by a vengeful Hiawatha who catches him and changes him to Keneu, the great War Eagle. Minnehaha dies in the great famine and the tale ends with the return of Iagoo who tells of the coming of the white man. The villagers do not believe his story, but Hiawatha has seen the coming in a vision. The forthcoming destruction of the Indian nation is thus predicted.

Nawadaha

Gitche Manito
Nokomis
Mudjekeewis
Hiawatha
Iagoo
Chibiabos
Kwasind
Kwasind's mother
Minnehaha
Pau-Puk-Keewis

Hindle Wakes
Stanley Houghton
Drama 3 Acts
Manchester 1912

It's a nasty shock for respectable working-class Mr and Mrs Hawthorne when they find headstrong daughter Fanny has been off for a 'dirty weekend' with mill boss Jeffcote's handsome but weak son Alan. Morality demands nuptials, and when Chris Hawthorne confronts his old friend and employer Jeffcote, the staid but honest old capitalist reluctantly agrees. However, Mrs Jeffcote and Alan (who's engaged to Mayor Sir Timothy's lovely daughter Beatrice) are all for trying to buy off the Hawthornes but Jeffcote will have none of it. He even threatens to disinherit Alan if he defies him, and Beatrice too tells Alan he must marry Fanny.

No one has bothered to ask Fanny, and beneath her weaver's shawl she's a liberated girl. She doesn't love Alan - she only likes him and certainly doesn't respect him. She explains to him that just as she was merely a fling for him so he was merely the same for her. She certainly doesn't intend to marry him. Alan is dumbfounded, and when both families meet he has to confess Fanny won't have him. The Jeffcotes end up admiring Fanny but Mrs Hawthorne is furious and doesn't want her to darken the doorstep again. That suits Fanny - she's old enough and experienced enough to make her own way in the world. After she leaves, Alan rushes over to repropose to Beatrice.

Mrs Hawthorne
Christopher Hawthorne
Fanny Hawthorne
Mrs Jeffcote
Nathaniel Jeffcote
Alan Jeffcote
Sir Timothy Farras
Ada

Hippolytus
Euripides
Tragedy 1 Act
Athens 428 BC

Hippolytus, bastard son of King Theseus, is an utterly chaste devotee of the goddess Artemis, and of her main love, the hunt. The love goddess Aphrodite, jealous of Hippolytus's commitment to her rival, inspires a passionate love for him in his stepmother, Phaedra.

Although Phaedra fights her passion, her old nurse reveals it to Hippolytus, who is both revolted and enraged by the news.

In despair, Phaedra hangs herself, but not before leaving her husband a message that Hippolytus has violated her. Enraged in his turn, Theseus banishes his son, and pronounces a curse on him, only to discover from Artemis, after Hippolytus dies, that his son and wife had never been intimate at all.

Aphrodite, Love goddess
Hippolytus, King Theseus's son
Phaedra, Theseus's wife
Nurse, Phaedra's confidante
Theseus, King of Athens
Artemis, Goddess of the hunt
Servant to Hippolytus
Messenger
Chorus
Attendants
Huntsmen
Maids

HMS Pinafore
W. S. Gilbert and Arthur Sullivan
Comic Opera 2 Acts
London 1878

Subtitled *The Lass that Loved the Sailor* this finds Little Buttercup, a vendor of cakes, aboard *HMS Pinafore* which is anchored off Portsmouth. This ship is a model of how a British naval vessel should be; the Captain and the crew are one in complete harmony and peace. There is only one dissenting voice, that of Dick Deadeye, but the crew distrust and ignore him.

The ship's commander, Capt. Corcoran, has a beautiful daughter, Josephine, who has been promised to Adm. Sir Joseph Porter, but she secretly loves a humble sailor, Ralph Rackstraw, and the pair plan to elope. Dastardly Dick Deadeye divulges their plan to the Captain, who throws Ralph in jail, but when the Captain utters a curse word (unforgiveable on the good ship *Pinafore*), he himself is thrown in jail.

Little Buttercup can however sort out the mess. She tells the Admiral how, as children, Corcoran and Rackstraw were mixed up and their roles should be reversed. The Captain's daughter, now being common, can marry Rackstraw, who is now a Captain, while Corcoran marries the happy Buttercup.

Songs include: 'For I'm Called Little Buttercup - Dear Little Buttercup'; 'I am the Captain of the *Pinafore*'; 'I am the Monarch of the Sea'; 'When I was a Lad I Served a Term'

The Rt Hon. Sir Joseph Porter
Capt. Corcoran
Tom Tucker, midshipmite
Ralph Rackstraw
Dick Deadeye
Bill Bobstay, boatswain's mate
Bob Becket, carpenter's mate

Josephine, Captain's daughter
Hebe, Sir Joseph's first cousin
Little Buttercup
Mrs Cripps, a bumboat woman
First Lord's sisters, cousins
Sailors
Marines

Hobson's Choice
Harold Brighouse
Comedy 4 Acts
New York 1916

It is 1880 and domineering widower Horatio Hobson, florid and self-satisfied, runs Hobson's Boot Shop in Salford. He's helped by daughters Alice and Vicky, both in their early twenties, but mostly by daughter Maggie who is thirty and considered by Hobson to be an old maid. But Maggie's the shrewd one and sees potential in Hobson's chief bootmaker Willie Mossup, a likeable craftsman who makes superb boots. She half-bullies Willie into agreeing to marriage with her, and when Hobson objects, Willie stands up for himself against his boss and he and Maggie leave to set up in business together. Hobson is upset and on a drunken binge falls down a corn-merchant's cellar, damaging property.

Maggie and Willie's business prospers and with Maggie's support Willie finds new confidence and manliness. When Hobson is sued for damages, Maggie helps him to settle out of court and at the same time helps her sisters to marry the men of their choice, Fred Beenstock, son of the man suing Hobson, and Albert Prosser, solicitor representing Beenstock. Hobson, however, is drinking himself to death and is ordered to stop by Dr MacFarlane. Neither Alice nor Vicky will return home to nurse him, but Maggie says she will, providing Willie agrees. He does, but only on his terms - that he is made a full partner in the company and can merge his own now-successful business with Hobson's, which is falling away since he left. Hobson is reluctantly forced to agree, and Willie is amazed by his success in business and marriage, for now he not only respects Maggie, but also loves her.

Alice Hobson   *Timothy Wadlow (Tubby)*
Maggie Hobson   *William Mossop*
Vicky Hobson   *Jim Heeler*
Albert Prosser   *Ada Higgins*
Henry Horatio Hobson *Fred Beenstock*
Mrs Hepworth   *Dr MacFarlane*

Hollow, The
Agatha Christie
Drama 3 Acts
London 1951

Weekend guests at The Hollow, country home of former diplomat Sir Henry Angkatell and eccentric wife Lucy, are bookish cousin Edward, attractively dynamic Dr John Cristow and stupid wife Gerda, and warm-hearted half-cousin Midge. Another cousin, young sculptress Henrietta, also lives at The Hollow and is having a secret affair with Cristow...but Edward loves Henrietta (or so he thinks) and wants to take her back to Ainswick, the Angkatell's beloved ancestral home which he inherited. Just before dinner there is a surprise visitor - Cristow's first love and now-famous film star Veronica Craye, recently moved into the area and 'run out of matches'. That night Cristow slinks off to be with her, but next day ignores her note and while the others are off on shooting practice, she returns and he rejects her further advances. Scorned, she leaves.

Shortly afterwards Cristow is shot dead in the study and Gerda is found over him, holding a gun. But Inspector Colquhoun CID and Detective Sergeant Penny discover that gun wasn't the murder weapon, which is found in Veronica's bag. Intensive questioning leads nowhere, for there is no proof - even though there are several suspects with motives: Edward (jealousy), Henrietta (jealous of Veronica), Gerda (jealous of Henrietta and Veronica), butler Gudgeon (helping out the family) and Veronica (scorned). The culprit is finally revealed and disposed of with typical Christie ingenuity, but not before innocent Edward sees the light and proposes to Midge - who is deliriously happy, not least because she won't have to go back and work in a horrid dress shop.

Henrietta Angkatell   *Edward Angkatell*
Sir Henry Angkatell KCB *Doris*
Lady Angkatell   *Gerda Christow*
Midge Harvey   *John Christow MD FRCP*
Gudgeon   *Veronica Craye*
Inspector Colquhoun CID *Detective Sergeant Penny*

Home
David Storey
Play 2 Acts
London 1970

On the terrace of a house there is a metalwork table and a couple of chairs. Two elderly gentlemen, Harry and Jack, meet and converse. Their talk is sparse and somewhat disconnected, yet warm, courteous and mildly amusing. They seem to understand each other. Kathleen and Marjorie, two middle-aged working-class women enter and fall into conversation with Harry and Jack. Alfred, a strong but simple young man comes and goes, performing tricks with the chairs like a weightlifter before taking them inside the house. There is mild bickering between the women, and it is now apparent this is a mental institution.

At the end of the afternoon the women and Alfred have gone inside and Harry weeps a lot and Jack weeps a little. Their shared humanity and matter-of-factness in this, their shared home, is somehow a triumph in the face of their tragedies.

Harry   *Marjorie*
Jack   *Kathleen*
Alfred

Home at Seven
R. C. Sherriff
Drama 3 Acts
London 1950

When banker David Preston comes home after work he finds wife Janet sobbing. She tells him he has been missing for twenty-four hours. It is Tuesday and he thinks it is Monday and cannot remember what happened. Apart from the missing day, the bank manager has told Janet that David always leaves at five o'clock; but he always told Janet he leaves at six.

Later David confesses to the doctor he goes for a secret drink after work at a City pub, The Feathers. It relaxes him to be in the company of the Dobson family, particularly young Peggy - but nothing is 'going on'. Things take a sinister turn when Maj. Watson of the local social club tells David that Club Steward Robinson told him that last night David came and took the money from the kitty - several hundred pounds. David denies this, and later Robinson is found dead. David unwisely fixes up a fake alibi and suspicion falls upon him - he admits he never liked Robinson, and it is also revealed that he is in debt to moneylenders. His solicitor advises him to be completely honest, but even David is beginning to have doubts about what happened during the missing twenty-four hours. All is made clear when Peggy turns up. It seems that David had a bad turn at the pub after hearing a loud noise, reverted back to war-time, collapsed and slept, and was shaved and washed on the premises. He is now in the clear, and the police discover that Robinson and a colleague plotted to steal the money and blame David. The fact that David was missing helped them even more - but later the thieves fell out and Robinson was murdered.

Mrs Preston
David Preston
Dr Sparling
Maj. Watson
Inspector Hemingway
Mr Petherbridge
Peggy Dobson

Home is the Hunter
Helen MacInnes
Comedy 2 Acts
New York 1964

After ten years at the Trojan Wars and another seven wandering slowly home, Ulysses finally arrives in Ithaca. Before making his way up to the big house where he imagines wife Penelope and son Telemachus are peacefully awaiting him, Ulysses sees swineherd Eumaeus, an old warrior friend, who tells him that Penelope is a virtual prisoner in the house, held by a gang of thugs led by rivals Melas and Eryx, who are contesting for Penelope's hand - and the house and land that go with it. Ulysses, of course, is presumed dead. Penelope herself has been fending off Melas and Eryx for nearly four years and cannot do so much longer but

when she hears Ulysses has returned, she arranges an archery contest for her hand which she is sure the disguised Ulysses will win. All is not so simple but, with the aid of Telemachus, Eumaeus and stableman-warrior Philetius, Ulysses organizes a mini-military campaign and eventually slaughters all eleven intruders. The proceedings are watched with alternate delight and horror by a (sighted) Homer - delight at the return of Ulysses so that he can complete his *Odyssey*, and dismay that some of the details may not be quite as poetic as he would wish.

Ulysses	*Homer*
Eumaeus	*Philetius*
Clia, Ulysses' old nurse	*Other suitors*
Amaryllis, maidservant	
Penelope	
Telemachus	
Melas	
Eryx	
Athena, Goddess of	
Reason	

Homecoming (Mourning Becomes Electra)
Eugene O'Neill
Tragedy 4 Acts
New York 1932

The American civil war is just drawing to a close as Christine Mannon, the disillusioned wife of General Ezra Mannon, is discovered by their daughter Lavinia having an affair with the family's disgraced cousin Capt. Adam Brant, commander of a clipper ship.

Lavinia and her mother have always hated one another and Christine is forced to agree to give up her lover on pain of exposure by her daughter. Christine sends Brant away, but decides to murder her husband as soon as the General returns from the war, leaving her free to rejoin the young captain. When the General does return, he has been changed by the horror of war into a much more loving, open character, and his once overpowering vigour has been undermined by a heart condition.

Just as he and Christine retire to bed on the evening of his return, she admits her affair, in a successful attempt to induce a heart attack. When the attack comes, Christine ensures it will be fatal by substituting a sleeping draught for the medicine he should be given.

Her treachery is discovered by Lavinia, who decides to avoid scandal by murdering her mother in turn.

Brig. Gen. Ezra Mannon
Christine, his wife
Lavinia, his daughter
Capt. Adam Brant, Christine's lover
Capt. Peter Niles
Hazel Niles
Seth Beckwith, his handyman
Amos Ames
Louisa, Amos's wife
Minnie, Louisa's cousin

Homecoming, The

Harold Pinter
Drama 2 Acts
London 1965

In an old house in North London live Max, his unmarried chauffeur brother Sam and his two sons Lenny and Joey, a prospective boxer. There is an undercurrent of vicious degeneracy in the all-male household, and into this situation arrives Max's eldest son Ted and his wife Ruth. Ted has 'done good' and is a Professor of Philosophy at an American university. He is bringing Ruth home to meet his family on their way back to the States from a holiday in Italy. Ruth is enigmatic with a dubious past, and she finds an attraction in Ted's family. They invite her to stay and she accepts; Lenny is a pimp and they agree Ruth should work from a flat in Soho. The atmosphere is one of mutual exploitation. Ted leaves for America and jealousy over Ruth's favours begins immediately.

Max
Lenny, his son
Sam, his brother
Joey, his son
Ted, his son
Ruth, Ted's wife

Hostage, The

Brendan Behan
Play with Music 3 Acts
London 1958

It is the late fifties in a Dublin 'brockel' (brothel) and the proprietor, Monsewer, entertains with music and songs his whores, their gay friends, his staff, and a social worker Miss Gilchrist.

Into this ménage come the IRA who have taken hostage a British soldier who they hope to exchange for one of their assassins due for execution. Leslie, the soldier, is initially not too concerned about his captivity and has an affair with Teresa, a maid but he begins to worry at the constant tirade of anti-British sentiments as the execution of the IRA man approaches. Miss Gilchrist pleads for his life with the other inmates of the brockel and they begin to have their doubts as the place is raided by the British police. Leslie is shot by mistake in the ensuing confusion. Monsewer and his cronies are arrested and Teresa returns to find Leslie dead, but miraculously he is still capable of singing a song.

Pat, the caretaker	*Leslie, the British soldier*
Meg Dillon	*Teresa, a country girl*
Monsewer, the brockel	*IRA officer*
owner	*Volunteer*
Colette	*Sailors*
Bobo	*Whores*
Princess Grace	*Policeman*
Rio Rita	
Mrs Mulleady	
Miss Gilchrist, a social	
worker	

Hotel Paradiso

Georges Feydeau
Farce 3 Acts
London 1956

M. Boniface, a mild-mannered builder, has a large and overbearing wife, Angelique. His pompous architect friend Cot has a beautiful, sexually frustrated wife, Marcelle, and on being told of her dissatisfaction, Boniface offers her a night of clandestine bliss at the notorious Hotel Paradiso. His highly-sexed maid Victoire is after Cot's studious nephew Maxime whose knowledge of passion is strictly theoretical and derived from the philosophical opinions of Spinoza. A friend of the Bonifaces, Martin, arrives in Paris from Valence with his four young daughters and wants to stay a couple of months, which is out of the question.

By accident, Martin and daughters seek accommodation at Hotel Paradiso on the same night as it is visited by Boniface and Marcelle, and Victoire and Maxime, and by Cot who is there on his own to check the plumbing which makes ghostly noises, leading the management to think that the place is haunted. In the late-night darkness Cot mistakes the daughters, singing a witches' song, for phantoms. The girls are terrified, just about everybody gets into the wrong room, the police are sent for and, naturally, Boniface gives his name as Cot and Marcelle says she is Mme Boniface. The whole hotelful (everybody save the real Mme Boniface who is out of town) is arrested. The next morning the Boniface home is visited by Police Inspector Bouchard and though misunderstandings still abound, everything is straightened out to almost everybody's satisfaction.

Boniface, a builder	*Paquerette*
Angelique, his wife	*Pervenche*
Cot, an architect	*Anniello, hotel manager*
Marcelle, his wife	*George, a page*
Maxime, his nephew	*A lady*
Victoire, the maid	*A duke*
Martin, a barrister	*Tabu, a Turkish professor*
Violette and	*Police Inspector Bouchard*
Marguerite, his	*Policeman*
daughters	*Porters*

Hothouse, The

Harold Pinter
Drama 2 Acts
Hampstead 1980

Ex-military man Col Archie Roote is in charge of a secure 'hospital' establishment somewhere in rural England and on Christmas Day all is not well. Patients are dying and having babies without his knowledge, or has he forgotten? He is a man who constantly contradicts himself and is given to tautology, and his staff have to endure the results of his lack of direction. His assistant, Charlie Gibbs, has to bear the brunt of Roote's inefficiency, which he does stoically while he has an affair with Roote's mistress, Miss Cutts. She and Gibbs are conducting a series of psychological tests on new staff member, Lamb. Gibbs also has problems with Lush, a bitter cynical member of staff, who enjoys baiting the Colonel.

When Roote, Lush and Gibbs share a Christmas drink, strange noises disturb the celebration, and the three suspect trouble is afoot. They are justified in their suspicions for later that evening, after the Colonel has delivered his clichéd Christmas address over the tannoy, the patients escape (or are freed) from their rooms and proceed to assassinate the whole staff, except for Charlie Gibbs.

When he is appointed as the new director, Gibbs explains to ministry official Lobb that Roote was very unpopular with the staff and patients and that Lamb may have neglected his job of locking up the patients.

Col Archie Roote
Charlie Gibbs
Miss Cutts
Lush
Lamb
Tubb
Mr Lobb

House Guest
Francis Durbridge
Thriller 2 Acts
Guildford 1981

Actress Stella Drury is content to be a wife and mother while successful actor husband Robert carries on with his career. She thinks he's in Italy with young son Mike, but while being interviewed by a Vivien Norwood for a woman's magazine, distraught Robert returns and reveals Mike has been kidnapped. Shortly afterwards, sinister Crozier appears and tells them that if he can stay at their house for forty-eight hours, Mike will be released unharmed. Vivien proves to be his accomplice, but after the Drurys agree to their terms, an Inspector Burford and a Sergeant Clayton arrive...but they are not what they seem. They kill Crozier and Vivien and announce they now hold Mike, and that they are to be the new house guests. Their plan, stolen from Crozier, is to send Robert look-alike Philip Henderson to trade drugs for diamonds in New York, accompanied by Stella for authenticity. But Robert manages to foil their plans with a clever ruse involving a radio transmitter in a toy that enables the real police to find Mike. After further scuffles and another murder, Stella and Robert get the gun and the police arrive.

Vivien Norwood
Jane Mercer
Stella Drury
Robert Drury
Crozier
Inspector Burford
Sergeant Clayton
Dorothy Medway
Philip Henderson

House of Bernarda Alba, The
Federico Garcia Lorca
Tragedy 3 Acts
Granada 1936

Set in a remote Spanish farm village during the early years of this century, this tragedy traces the course of the destruction of Bernarda Alba's family after the death of her husband.

Living, as they have, in an atmosphere of tensely suppressed emotion, the Alba women, Bernarda, her aged mad mother and five spinster daughters are ill-equipped to handle the strain of losing the head of the household. Angustias, the eldest daughter, is set to inherit her father's wealth, and so attracts a proposal of marriage even though she is thirty-nine-years old and far from pretty. Her sisters immediately succumb to overwhelming jealousy and the youngest, Adela, begins a clandestine affair with Angustias's fiancé. Bernarda pretends to have him killed in order to shock Adela, but the ploy miscarries when Adela commits suicide.

Bernarda
Maria Josefa, her mother
Angustias, her eldest daughter
Magdalena, Amelia, Martirio and Adela, her other
  daughters
A maid
La Poncia, her maid and confidante
Prudencia
Women in mourning

How the Other Half Loves
Alan Ayckbourn
Comedy 2 Acts
London 1970

On a complex set which mixes two couples' living rooms, philandering employee Bob Phillips and his scatterbrained wife Teresa are invited to dinner by Bob's boss Frank Foster with whose wife, Fiona, Bob is having a fling. The next night Bob and Teresa are having dinner with company accountant William Featherstone and his wife Mary.

The play shows the two nights simultaneously which means that Bob and Teresa have to sit front and centre in swivel chairs and be coping with one night one moment, the next night the next. With the marginal exception of the elegant adulteress Fiona, all are dim and talk like anthologies of middle-class cliché, jargon and utter trivia. Frank, in particular, is a bossy meddler, and Teresa and Mary are would-be do-gooders. Consequently, who is going to bed with whom gets constantly confused and all accusations are false. Fiona thinks she has been caught out but the bumbling Frank never catches on. However, as the curtain falls it is hinted that Frank and Teresa are in for a mutual treat.

Frank Foster   William Featherstone
Fiona Foster   Mary Featherstone
Bob Phillips
Teresa Phillips

How to Succeed in Business Without Really Trying

Abe Burrows, Jack Weinstock and Willie Gilbert
Music by Frank Loesser
Musical 2 Acts
New York 1961

Young J. Pierrepoint Finch (Ponty) is cleaning the windows of the World Wide Wicket Company while reading the *How to Succeed in Business...* manual. Following its cynically humorous advice, he gets himself a junior job in the company's mail room, where he earns the emnity of Bud (nephew of company president Mr Biggley) and the love of pretty secretary Rosemary, who entertains dreams of marriage to upwardly-mobile Ponty. By a shrewd mix of flattery and 'accident', Ponty graduates from the mail room to a junior executive post in Mr Gatch's department, while recommending Bud for head of the mail room.

Ponty continually stands Rosemary up as various opportunities present themselves, and when he is assigned Biggley's glamorous but dumb mistress Hedy La Rue as his secretary, he sends her off with a memo to Gatch, who, unaware of her involvement with the boss, tries to date her.

Later, Gatch has left and Ponty has taken over his job. Bud then tries to compromise Ponty with Hedy, but the tables are turned and Biggley catches Ponty with Rosemary instead - which is all right. Ponty's unashamed ambition also involves swatting up on Biggley's old school and their football team the Groundhogs, and this pays dividends when ad manager Ovington is discovered to be a hated rival, a Chipmunk. Ponty is soon vice-president of advertising. Unfortunately, this post has a quick staff turnover and Ponty must get a bright idea immediately; he borrows Bud's oft-rejected idea of a TV Treasure Hunt (for company stock), but Biggley insists Hedy be the game show hostess. She makes a mess of it, and Ponty is made the scapegoat.

Biggley tells Chairman of the Board, Wally Womper, it is all Ponty's fault, but when Ponty confesses all, he manages to ingratiate himself with Wally, who also started as a window cleaner. Poor Bud once again takes the rap as it was his original idea, and there is another company shake-up. Biggley remains as President, but Ponty is now Chairman of the Board; Wally has married Hedy and is going on a world cruise. Bud is washing the windows and reading *How to Succeed in Business ...*
Songs include: 'I Believe In You'; 'Happy To Keep His Dinner Warm'; 'Brotherhood of Man'

Finch	Miss Jones
Gatch	Mr Twimble
Jenkins	Hedy
Tackaberry	Scrubwoman
J. B. Biggley	Miss Krumholtz
Rosemary	Toynbee
Bratt	Ovington
Smitty	Policeman
Frump	Womper

Huis Clos (In Camera or No Exit)

Jean-Paul Sartre
Drama 1 Act
Paris 1944

A valet brings, in turn, three characters into an elegant, windowless, constantly lit room. It transpires that each has recently died and are now apparently condemned to spend eternity together. They relive and recall their experiences on earth and a complex triangle emerges of a cowardly womanizer, a socialite adultress and a jealous lesbian, whose desires are all thwarted and held in check by one of the others.

This is an existentialist examination of the nature of the termination of the living body and the end of free will, and throughout the characters follow a completely predictable pattern of actions which bring them to the interminable realization that people create their own hell in others.

Estelle Rigault
Joseph Garcin
Inez Serrano
Valet

Hunted, The (Mourning Becomes Electra II)

Eugene O'Neill
Tragedy 5 Acts
New York 1932

Orin Mannon returns to his family after the American Civil War to find that his father, Gen. Ezra Mannon, has just died. His mother Christine, who has murdered the General, and his sister Lavinia, who knows their mother's guilt, give conflicting versions of the death. Lavinia attests to the murder, but Christine is able to persuade Orin, for a time, that Lavinia has gone mad with grief.

Eventually, Lavinia entices Christine into re-establishing contact with the latter's lover, Adam Brant, thus satisfying Orin that their father was indeed murdered. Lavinia and Orin lie in wait for Brant, and Orin murders him, to the delight of the implacable Lavinia.

When she hears of Brant's death, Christine commits suicide. Realizing too late that he still loved his mother despite her infidelity, Orin suffers a breakdown, but Lavinia, with cold resolve, tries to calm him with an assurance that she will take care of him.

Christine Mannon, widow of Ezra Mannon
Lavinia Mannon, her daughter
Orin Mannon, her son
Capt. Adam Brant, her lover
Hazel Niles
Peter Niles
Josiah Borden
Emma Borden
Everett Hills, DD
Hill's wife
Dr Joseph Blake
The Chantyman

Hypochondriac, The
Molière
Comedy Ballet 3 Acts
Paris 1673

Argan is obsessed with his ill-health, especially his bowels which are in constant need of enemas, purgatives, pills and potions. This is all very satisfactory to his doctor, Purgon, and apothecary Fleurant but his smart maid Toinette is annoyingly cynical about the way he is being swindled. His second wife Béline is only pretending to pamper, baby and sympathize; it soon becomes clear that she is just after the old fool's money. He has two daughters, the lovely Angélique and the young Louison. Béline wants the girls stuck in a convent. Argan has decided Angélique will conveniently marry into a family of doctors and Diaforus Senr brings his doltish son Thomas over to ask for her hand. Angélique will have none of it because she loves Cléante who is posing as a music teacher and disguising his declaration of love in song.

In the street, Molière and a group of players are putting on a little show in which Scagnarelle plays two parts that are almost (but obviously not quite) seen together; a doctor and his wastrel brother. This playlet gives Toinette an idea.

Béralde, Argan's shrewd brother, comes visiting and he and Toinette hatch a plot. First Béralde pleads for Angélique to marry a man of her choice. Then he drives off Purgon and Fleurant when they come to call. Then Toinette comes on disguised as a doctor (sometimes going out and reappearing briefly as herself) and rubbishes Purgon's advice and knowledge. 'Doctor' Toinette recommends the removal of an arm and an eye, after which Argan will feel much better. 'Doctor' goes, maid Toinette returns and advises Argan to feign death so that he'll see Béline's distress and know how much she cares. But Béline is pleased and relieved whereas Angélique is distraught. Béline gets the boot and Argan says his loving daughter can marry Cléante if he becomes a doctor. If that's what it takes, Cléante agrees but Béralde has a better idea: Argan should become his own doctor so that the physician can heal himself.

Argan	Purgon
Béline	Fleurant
Angélique	Notary
Louison	Toinette
Béralde	Players
Cléante	Aunt
Diaforus Senr	The watch
Thomas Diaforus	Bystanders

I Am a Camera
John Van Druten
Drama 3 Acts
London 1954

Young Christopher (Isherwood) is in Weimar Berlin, teaching English and suffering from writer's block, when his friend Fritz introduces him to Sally Bowles, a self-dramatizing and selfish English girl, fascinatingly half-tart and half-child. They become close platonic friends and Sally moves into his room, while Chris moves next door. Their relationship carries on amidst the stilted romance of hard-up semi-gigolo Fritz and Chris's rich Jewish pupil Natalia, who eventually succumbs to his 'pounce', a ploy suggested by Sally. In and out of the action moves cosy landlady Fraulein Schneider, good-hearted and crude but increasingly susceptible to Nazi propaganda. When Sally discovers she is pregnant by ex-boyfriend Klaus, it is Fraulein Schneider who sends her to an appropriate clinic.

Rich and desperate playboy friend Clive offers to take Chris and Sally on an Eastern adventure; they eagerly pack their bags but he casually and thoughtlessly lets them down at the last moment. Sally's mother Mrs Watson-Courtneidge arrives to 'rescue' her daughter, but Sally finds a ruse to pack her back to the UK. After inspiring Chris to begin a series of short stories about his Berlin experiences, Sally finds yet another exciting lover, a Yugoslav, and she leaves. The camera has taken its photographs and now Chris must develop them.

Christopher Isherwood	Natalia Landauer
Fraulein Schneider	Clive Mortimer
Fritz Wendel	Mrs Watson-Courtneidge
Sally Bowles	

I Have Been Here Before
J. B. Priestley
Drama 3 Acts
London 1937

This down-to-earth exposition of the 'theory of eternal recurrence' takes place at the Black Bull Inn, North Yorkshire, run by contented landlord Sam Shipley and his widowed daughter Sally. When mysterious German Dr Görtler arrives, his pervading sense of déja-vù and theories of time as a continuum begin to upset Sally and the Whitsun weekend guests, young school headmaster Farrant, and hard-working hard-drinking middle-aged tycoon Ormund and his unhappy wife Janet. She and Farrant (whose school depends on Ormund's money) fall in love, and Görtler reveals he is there in an attempt to change this particular path of fate - in a dream he saw devastating consequences of their relationship when Ormund committed suicide and ruined the lives of all those dependent upon him.

Despite their initial scepticism, all but Farrant come around to Görtler's viewpoint, and Janet decides to stay with Ormund. But her husband, inspired by Görtler's theories and now with a fresh untravelled route beckoning, tells Janet to leave with Farrant. With a new maturity he is ready to begin anew.

Sally Pratt
Sam Shipley
Dr Görtler
Oliver Farrant
Janet Ormund
Walter Ormund

I Love My Wife
Michael Stewart
Music by Cy Coleman
Musical 2 Acts
New York 1977

Two married couples, lifelong friends, prepare for the Christmas season in their quiet home town, Trenton, New Jersey. One of the husbands, Wally, imagines himself to be more a man of the world than the other, Alvin, and recommends to him that, with his wife Cleo, Alvin should arrange a sexual threesome involving another woman.

At first Alvin is sceptical, but then decides to heed Wally's advice and so, to Wally's surprise, asks Monica, Wally's wife, to make up the third side of the triangle. After an unsuccessful attempt to accustom Cleo to the idea of sharing him with Monica, Alvin is very nervous indeed when, instead, his wife suggests that Wally should become their third partner. Finally, the couples agree to swap spouses on Christmas Eve, but in the event, Alvin finds himself unable to consummate his intentions. The party ends when Alvin declares that he loves his wife and can desire no one else.

Songs include: 'Hey There, Good Times'; 'I Love My Wife'

Cleo	Quentin
Monica	Harvey
Wally	Norman
Stanley	Alvin

I Remember Mama
John Van Druten
Drama 2 Acts
London 1948

In the poorest part of San Francisco in 1910, an extended family of impecunious Norwegian immigrants are trying to prosper by the American formula of hard work and tough-minded honesty.

The formal head of the family, Uncle Chris, is a blustering property speculator but the real centre of the family's life is the home of his niece, Mama Hanson, and her family. Mama's selfless devotion to her husband, Papa, and their children, Dagmar, Christie, Katrin and Nels, leaves her little time for anything but work. She still manages, however, to mediate in many squabbles between her three Aunts, Trina, Jenny and Sigrid, as well as smoothing their relations with the volatile Uncle Chris.

To give the children a sense of security Mama and Papa pretend that they have an account at the local bank but it is only by the tightest management and constant self-denial that Mama manages to have shoes resoled, buy schoolbooks, provide new clothes and so on, never letting the children see her worry over the future.

When word reaches the family that Uncle Chris is dying, Mama and her aunts rush to his deathbed, the aunts hoping to inherit something from him but Mama content to ease his going. They discover that Uncle

Chris has spent all his money paying medical bills for the children of his family and friends, hiding his generosity behind his terrible temper. All hope of financial help is gone, but Mama still manages to keep the family going, even when their boarder, Mr Hyde, absconds without paying off his arrears of rent.

At this lowest point in the family fortunes, Katrin is about to graduate from secondary school and has chosen as a graduation present, a cheap, gaudy girl's dresser set. To pay for the set Mama sells a fine brooch she had inherited and when Katrin discovers Mama's generosity she manages to get the brooch back by working after school hours herself, and paying the new owner to return it. Later Katrin is downcast by constant rejection slips which follow her every attempt to get her short stories published and Mama takes matters into her own hands and boldly confronts a famous novelist, Florence Moorhead, with a request to help her daughter. The writer agrees and we discover that the play we have been watching is the first fruit of Katrin's success.

Katrin Hanson
Mama, Katrin's mother
Papa, Katrin's father
Dagmar and Christine Hanson, Katrin's sisters
Mr Hyde, the Hansons' boarder
Nels Hanson, Katrin's brother
Aunt Trina, Aunt Jenny, Aunt Sigrid, Mama's aunts
Uncle Chris, Mama's uncle
A woman
Dr Johnson
Mr Thorkelson
A nurse
A charwoman
A doctor
An orderly
Elevator boy
Anne
Another nurse
Soda clerk
Madeline
Dorothy Schiller
Florence Dana Morehead
Bell boy

I'm Not Rappaport
Herb Gardner
Comedy 2 Acts
Seattle 1984

On a bench near a path at the edge of the lake in New York's Central Park, sit Nat, an old white man, and Midge, an old black man. Nat is a still-fervent socialist and worker-revolutionary and entertains and infuriates Midge with an astounding compendium of far-fetched escapades and downright lies. Midge is trying to keep his jeopardized boiler-room job till Christmas, but Nat manages to ruin that with his elaborate threats to Danforth, head of the tenants' committee in Midge's building.

Nat's brave and futile stand against young local mugger Gilley only results in the hood increasing his 'protection' rates for the pair, and when Nat's daughter Clara arrives and tries to persuade her dad to adopt a safer lifestyle, he fobs her off with stories of emigrating to Israel with a mysterious illegitimate daughter.

The action hots up even more when a powerful drug-dealer threatens pretty young painter Laurie and the old men attempt to defend her with mixed success, both ending up the worse for wear and tear. Dismayed by his failures, Nat decides to go along with Clara's plans and tells Midge the truth about his dull life. Midge, now hooked on Nat and his lively stories, gets angry and demands to know the 'real truth'. So, to their mutual delight, Nat sits down and begins to spin yet another convincingly outrageous yarn, this time about his period as a movie mogul.

Nat
Midge
Danforth
Laurie
Gilley
Clara
The cowboy

I'm Talking About Jerusalem
Arnold Wesker
Drama 2 Acts
London 1960

This third part of *The Wesker Trilogy*, set in 1946, sees Dave and Ada Simmonds moving into their house in the middle of a Norfolk field with no gas, electricity or running water. Assisted in the move by Ada's high-spirited brother Ronnie Kahn and mother Sarah, the pair find they are constantly having to explain their alienation from city life. When Dave's old army pal Libby Dobson visits, they find him cynical and disillusioned, and that same evening Dave is sacked from his farming job for inadvertently 'stealing' some linoleum. He proceeds with his plan to produce quality hand-made furniture and sets up a workshop with some success; Ada raises a family but by 1959 economic necessity forces them to move back to London. Helped again in the move by Ronnie and Sarah, they find that Ronnie feels more of a sense of failure at their rural experiment than they do.

Ronnie Kahn
Ada Simmonds, his sister
Sarah Kahn, their mother
Dave Simmonds, Ada's husband
First removal man
Second removal man
Libby Dobson, wartime friend of Dave's
Col Dewhurst, Dave's employer
Sammy, Dave's apprentice
Danny Simmonds, Ada and Dave's son
Esther Kahn, Cissie Kahn, aunts of Ronnie and Ada
Postman

Iceman Cometh, The
Eugene O'Neill
Tragedy 4 Acts
New York 1946

A group of dissolute but rather lovable low-life characters, all of them alcoholics, are waiting anxiously in the saloon of Harry Hope's cheap New York City rooming house in the summer of 1912.

They are looking for the arrival of Theodore Hickman, 'Hickey' to them, a drunken but successful travelling salesman who appears each year on this, the eve of Harry Hope's birthday, to sponsor a lavishly alcoholic party. When Hickey arrives though, he has become evangelically teetotal and tries to cajole all his old cronies into joining him. Such is the power of Hickey's salesmanship that several of them make foredoomed attempts to emulate him, but at the same time his fervour spreads nervousness through those who do not.

Harry Hope, proprietor of a rooming house
Larry Slade, disillusioned political activist
Theodore Hickman ('Hickey'), reformed alcoholic
Denizens of Harry Hope's:
 Ed Mosher
 Pat McGloin
 Willie Oban
 Joe Mott
 Piet Wetjoen ('The General')
 Cecil Lewis ('The Captain')
 James Cameron ('Jimmy Tomorrow')
 Hugo Kalmar
Rocky Pioggi, Harry's night barman
Pearl, Maggie, Cora, prostitutes
Moran
Lieb

Ideal Husband, An
Oscar Wilde
Drama 4 Acts
London 1895

Into a fashionable London party of politicians and diplomats comes the mysterious Mrs Cheveley, an ex-fiancée of one of the guests, Lord Goring, a dandy.

She broaches the host, Sir Robert Chiltern, on his attitude to the Argentine Canal company, in which she has an interest, and he declares it to be a swindle. She tells him that he should change his attitude or she will expose him as having sold secret information to a foreign financier. He regretfully agrees to withdraw his objections.

Later, after an incident with a stolen brooch, Lady Chiltern tells her husband that Mrs Cheveley was expelled from school for theft and urges him to withdraw his support for the canal project.

Lord Goring advises Sir Robert to confess his lapse of judgement to his wife, but he refuses, and later Lord Goring offers to help Lady Chiltern if the need arises. She does not understand his offer until Mrs Cheveley calls and reveals all about her husband's transgressions. She goes to Lord Goring for help, but due to a misunderstanding, Mrs Cheveley gains possession of a note which makes it appear that Lady Chiltern is being unfaithful with Lord Goring. Her blackmailing tactics fail in the face of Lady Chiltern's devotion to her husband and the loyalty of their good friend Lord Goring, who has become engaged to their daughter Mabel. Sir Robert brilliantly denounces the canal scheme in Parliament and is offered a Cabinet post.

Sir Robert Chiltern	James, Harold, footmen
Viscount Goring	Lady Chiltern
The Earl of Caversham	Lady Markby
Vicomte de Nanjac	The Countess of Basildon
Mason, butler	Mrs Marchmont
Phipps, Lord Goring's	Miss Mabel Chiltern
servant	Mrs Cheveley

Idiot's Delight
Robert E. Sherwood
Drama 3 Acts
London 1938

On the eve of the declaration of war, a varied group of travellers arrive in the Hotel Loda, near the mountainous border of an unspecified European country. The hotel is an unsuccessful resort run by Mr Pittatek, and the group who stop over, compelled for the most part by a border closure, represent the hotel's first real clients.

All of them - the German Dr Waldersee seeking refuge to pursue cancer research, Mr and Mrs Cherry, a naive pair of newlyweds, Harry Van and his troupe of American exotic dancers, the French arms dealer Achille Weber and his companion, the stateless Irene, and finally Quillery, a radical French socialist - want to be elsewhere, and, with the exception of Weber, who has been pulling strings to start the war, try rather frantically to remain unmoved by its inexorable approach. But when news reaches the hotel that war has been declared, Quillery denounces a local military Captain and is immediately arrested and dragged away, bringing the conflict personally alive for all the guests.

To lighten the mood, Harry's dancers have been giving a show, but it breaks up with the news that Quillery has been executed. Harry, a cynic and romantic, has remembered meeting Irene, who gives out tall tales about her white Russian past, years before in Omaha, Nebraska, where he fell in love with her, and then lost touch. As he tries to piece together his memories, word arrives that the border is now clear. All but Irene, whom the ruthless Weber, now tired of her company and fearful of her intimate knowledge of his intrigues, has betrayed to the local Customs authorities, are granted exit visas. Although he has now become certain that Irene is the woman he once loved, Harry sets out for the train station with the others.

At the last minute, he returns to stay with Irene, and they plan to carry through a notion for a mind reading act they had discussed in Omaha.

Dumpsty, a waiter	Françine
Orchestra leader	Edna
Don Navadel	Elaine
Pittatek	Bebe
Capt. Kirvlin	Four officers
Auguste	Quillery
Dr Waldersee	Mr Preva
Mr Cherry	Mrs Preva
Mrs Cherry	Major
Harry Van	Maid
Shirley	Irene
Beulah	Achille Weber

Idiot, The
Simon Gray
Drama 2 Acts
London 1970

This adaptation of Dostoevsky's novel follows the life of Prince Myshkin from his release from a Swiss mental clinic until, wracked by the pains of a futile attempt to live a saintly life, he relapses into madness.

On the train to Petersburg, Myshkin falls in with Roghozin, the debauched inheritor of a huge fortune, who shows him a picture of Nastasya Fillippovna, a beauty he intends to marry, despite her recent engagement to someone else.

Arriving a bit later at the home of his only living relatives, Gen. Yepanchin and family in Pavlovsk, Myshkin discovers that Nastasya is in fact the ward of the General's close friend Totsky, a decadent aesthete recently engaged to one of the Yepanchin daughters. From her early youth, Nastasya has been used as a mistress by Totsky, who is now trying to marry her off to Ganya, the General's secretary. Nastasya becomes the unwilling prize in a contest between Roghozin and Ganya, to the overpowering dismay of Myshkin, who has a terrified love for the girl himself. She chooses a life of carousing with Roghozin, while hoping that Myshkin will take her for his own. The Prince, though, is torn between her and the General's sardonic but steadfast daughter, Aglaya, his youngest. Believing that Nastasya can escape suicide only if he marries her, Myshkin proposes. At the altar, Roghozin intervenes to take her away, but she soon kills herself in despair, driving both Roghozin and the Prince mad.

Ferdyschenko, the	Keller
narrator	Moneylender
Prince Leo Nikolaievish	Ganya Ivolgin
Myshkin	Nastasya Fillippovna
Parfyon Roghozin	Prince Shulovsky
Lebedev	Radomsky
Totsky	Ippolit
General Yepanchin	Burdovsky
Mrs Yepanchin	Princess Belekonsky
Adelaida Yepanchin	Elder Statesman
Aglaya Yepanchin	General Petrovich
Roghozin's seven	Accordionist
followers	Guitarist

If Winter Comes
B. Macdonald Hastings and A.S.M. Hutchinson
Drama 4 Acts
London 1923

Mark Sabre is in danger of losing his position with his family's publishing company, when he and his partners are saved this embarrassment by his successful application to join the army and go off to the Great War in 1915. Mr Twyning, a junior partner in the firm, is determined to undermine Sabre's position, and has been putting out gossip that his colleague's interest in one of their employees, Sarah Bright, might be improper.

Sabre unwittingly fuels the speculation when he hires Sarah as his wife's companion for the term of his tour of duty. Just before Sabre's return his wife dismisses Sarah who, left on her own, becomes the lover of Twyning's son Harold, by whom she has an illegitimate child. When Sarah arrives at the Sabre home, disgraced, hysterical and with no source of help, Sabre insists on giving her shelter, to the fury of his wife, who pretends to believe the rumours about Sabre and the girl, and leaves him for her secret lover, Maj. Millet.

Sarah refuses to name the father of her child, and it comes to be assumed that Sabre's kindness to her stems from being the responsible party. For her part Sarah is unwilling to see her benefactor ruined and commits suicide. Instead of absolving Sabre, though, her action casts suspicion on him for abetting her end. He is only cleared when a note from Sarah is accidentally discovered, in which the younger Twyning is named.

In fury with the younger man, and aware that by disgracing him he can be exonerated himself, Sabre rushes to confront the elder Twyning, only to be stopped short when his old enemy receives a telegram announcing his son's death at the front. Unable to further hurt even such an adversary Sabre burns the note, and with it his last chance of regaining his lost reputation.

The Revd Sebastian	*A coroner*
Fortune	*A solicitor*
Mr Twyning	*A chemist*
Mark Sabre,	*Coroner's officer*
Sebastian's nephew	*A girl clerk*
Lady Tybar	
Mrs Sabre, Mark's wife	
Maj. Millet	
Mr Bright	
Harold Twyning	
Sarah Bright	
Rebecca Jinks	

Imbecile, The
Luigi Pirandello
Comedy 1 Act
Rome 1922

Luca Fazio waits in the offices of the republican *Sentinel* newspaper to see the editor, Leopoldo Paroni. Fazio overhears Paroni deride the suicide of Lulu Pulino, whom he calls an imbecile for not having murdered the socialist Guido Mazzarini, Paroni's political rival, before doing away with himself.

Fazio, who has been sent by Mazzarini in fact to kill Paroni, and who then intends suicide, decides instead to force Paroni, at gunpoint, to write a letter describing his own cowardice in the face of Fazio's threat. This letter Fazio decides to leave by his own body to disgrace Paroni, and end his political ambitions.

Luca Fazio
Leopoldo Paroni
A travelling salesman
Rosa Lavecchia
Five reporters

Importance of Being Earnest, The
Oscar Wilde
Comedy 3 Acts
London 1895

Jack Worthing is in love with Gwendolen Fairfax, daughter of the redoubtable Lady Bracknell, and cousin of his friend Algernon Moncrieff. They cannot wed until the mystery of his parentage (he was found in a handbag in Victoria Station) has been resolved to Lady Bracknell's satisfaction. When Algy discovers Jack has a pretty young ward, Cecily Cardew, living at Wooten Manor, his country house, Algy visits her pretending to be Jack's fictitious wayward brother Ernest, invented by Jack to justify his frequent jaunts to London. Algy and Cecily fall in love, Jack arrives, and so do Lady Bracknell and Gwendolen. Farcical complications ensue, and with the help of Cecily's governess, Miss Prism, Jack's parentage is discovered and found to be eminently satisfactory to Lady Bracknell. The two pairs of lovers can now wed.

John Worthing, JP	*Lady Bracknell*
Algernon Moncrieff	*Hon. Gwendolen Fairfax*
Revd Canon Chasuble	*Cecily Cardew*
Merriman	*Miss Prism*
Lane	

In Camera
Jean-Paul Sartre
Drama 1 Act
Paris 1944
See: *Huis Clos*

In Praise of Love
Terence Rattigan
Drama 2 Acts
London 1973

Lydia, an Estonian *émigré* married to the famous literary critic Sebastian Cruttwell, returns to her North London flat deeply depressed on learning that she is mortally ill with an incurable disease and has only a short time to live.

Her spirits rise with the arrival of Mark Walters, another Estonian *émigré* and massively popular adventure novelist, who has come from Hong Kong in response to a letter from Lydia. She reveals her condition to Mark, her husband's best friend, who is clearly in love with her, because she feels her husband, a man of colossal egocentricity and selfishness, could not face the news and would provide no comfort if he did. Mark is the soul of patient compassion as he listens to Lydia's description of how she has tricked the true diagnosis out of her unwilling doctor, using techniques acquired in her Second World War work for Estonian intelligence, and goes on to reminisce about her first encounter with Sebastian when she was a prostitute in a Berlin bordello run by the Russians just after the war.

She persuades Mark to take her on a short holiday, and then cajoles her teenage son Joey into taking care of domestic routine for his father during her absence. Joey, who as a young liberal is constantly at odds with his father's drawing-room brand of revolutionary Marxism, reluctantly agrees, but then angrily changes his mind when Sebastian fails to turn up to watch the television première of his son's first play, in sharp contrast to Mark, who makes a special effort to be there.

In the course of acknowledging his insensitivity to Mark, Sebastian reveals that he is fully aware of Lydia's condition, which he has been concealing from her, and that he missed the broadcast only because he was pouring out his worries to a kind sometime lover. Mark then shows Lydia that Sebastian, self-centred though he is, has been trying for her sake to carry on as normal. In what is, for Sebastian, an unprecedented display of feeling, he apologizes to Joey, castigates himself thoroughly, and so gives Lydia the hope that father and son may remain close even after her death.

The play is an expanded version of an earlier, eponymous work usually performed in tandem with Rattigan's *Before Dawn*.

Lydia Cruttwell
Sebastian Cruttwell
Mark Walters
Joey Cruttwell

Inadmissable Evidence
John Osborne
Drama 2 Acts
London 1964

Solicitor Bill Maitland, now nearly forty, came up in the law the hard way. Quick, bright and a bit flashy, he left school at fifteen and eventually took over his law firm, leapfrogging over the older Hudson, the managing clerk. But Bill is now a cynical alcoholic, bitter and biting, and as his dubious business methods and unfulfilling personal relationships catch up with him, his world crumbles. The Law Society is on his tail for his habit of falsifying witnesses, and his colleagues and employees are starting to shun him. Secretary Shirley Jones, once his mistress, walks out of the firm, unable to stand his vituperative comments any longer, and Hudson, fed up with divorce cases, gets a better offer

from another law firm which he eventually accepts. Bill turns to secretary Joy but she soon turns against him, and the running sore that is his relationship with wife Anna, seventeen-year-old daughter Jane and mistress Liz, ends in total alienation.

Despite the manic mess his life is in, there is a thread of real compassion for his clients, whatever their sins; he is too aware of his own predicament not to empathize with other unfortunates. It is this that keeps Bill desperately striving, fighting against his fading powers, but in the end it is not enough to keep him from complete self-immolation.

Jones
Bill Maitland
Hudson
Shirley
Joy
Mrs Garnsen
Jane Maitland
Liz

Infernal Machine, The
Jean Cocteau
Tragedy 4 Acts
Paris 1934

This compressed, elliptical treatment of the Oedipus legend departs much further from its classical sources than did Cocteau's *Antigone*.

Jocasta, Queen of Thebes, has offered to marry any man who solves the riddle of the Sphinx. She is obsessed with her murdered husband, King Laius, and roams through the Theban night with the prophet Tiresias trying to encounter the King's ghost

Without realizing quite what he has done, Oedipus encounters the Sphinx, who takes pity on him and leads him to answer her riddle. In vainglory, and ignoring Tiresias's warning, Oedipus marries Jocasta, with both of them ignorant that he is her son.

After seventeen years of prosperity under their joint rule, Thebes is gripped by the plague and Oedipus's attempts to find the cause of the disease lead first Jocasta, and then Oedipus himself, to discover their kinship. Jocasta commits suicide and Oedipus, maddened by his discovery, blinds himself and leaves Thebes so the plague may be ended and his guilt purged.

The Voice	*A little boy*
Young soldier	*A little girl*
Soldier	*Messenger*
The Captain	*Shepherd*
Jocasta	*Antigone*
Tiresias	
Ghost of King Laius	
The Sphinx	
Oedipus	
Creon	
Anubia	
A Theban mother	

Inherit the Wind
Jerome Lawrence and Robert E. Lee
Drama 3 Acts
New York 1955

The play is based on the notorious 'Scopes monkey-trial' of 1925.

Hillsboro, a Midwestern American town, is in an uproar because a local high school teacher, Bertram Cates, is being tried for teaching Darwin's theory of evolution and thus, in the minds of the townsfolk, undermining the Biblical view of creation. Led by its bigoted Mayor the town has hired a demagogic politician and lawyer, Matthew Brady, to lead the prosecution.

Brady arrives in the town to a rapturous welcome, but his optimism is jolted by the discovery that a Baltimore newspaper has hired Henry Drummond, a famous past adversary of Brady's, to conduct Cates' defence. When the judge rules that no testimony is to be allowed from the scientific experts Drummond wishes to call, and the jury then hears the apparently damaging evidence of Cates' girlfriend, Rachel Brown, it begins to seem that Cates' cause is lost. But Drummond takes the unusual step of bringing Brady himself to the stand, and so entangles his opposite number in contradictions that even when Cates is found guilty, the judge imposes only a derisory fine. Brady, humiliated, dies of a heart attack, while Cates and Rachel leave Hillsboro.

Rachel Brown
Meaker
Bertram Cates, a high school teacher
Mr Goodfellow
Mrs Krebs
Revd Jeremiah Brown, Rachel's father
Corkin
Bollinger
Platt
Mr Bannister
Melinda
Howard
Mrs Loomis
Hot Dog Man
Mrs McLain
Mrs Blair
Elijah
E. K. Hornbeck, a Baltimore newsman
Hurdy Gurdy Man
Timmy
Mayor
Matthew Harrison Brady, the prosecutor
Mrs Brady
Tom Davenport
Henry Drummond, the defence attorney
Judge
Dunlap
Sillers
Reuters man
Harry Y. Esterbrook
Townspeople, hawkers, reporters, jurors, spectators

Inner Voices
Eduardo de Filippo
Comedy 3 Acts
Naples 1948

Two post-war families in the slums of Naples driven by the fearfulness left over from living under fascism, and by the resentments arising from poverty, become involved in denouncing one another to the police in a series of charges and counter-charges.

The conflict begins when Alberto Saporito, whose family business is near ruin, accuses Pasquale Cimmarata of murder, and signs a statement to that effect with the police. Each member of the Cimmarata family tries to convince Alberto, and his brother Carlo, that another member of the clan committed the crime. In fact, Alberto had merely dreamt the details he gave the police, but even when he explains his mistake, he is not believed.

When at last the police are satisfied of Alberto's good faith, he discovers that his brother, fearing Alberto would be arrested for perjury, had been planning to embezzle the family's remaining assets. The re-appearance of Aniello Amitrano, the supposed murder victim, clears all the Cimmaratas of suspicion, and leaves the families to consider the destruction of trust they have all been involved in causing.

The Cimmarata family:
Pasquale
Mathilde, Pasquale's wife
Luigi, their son
Elvira, their daughter
Rosa, Pasquale's sister
Muria, their maid
The Saporito family:
Alberto
Carlo, his brother
Zi Nicola, their uncle
Others:
Michele, hall porter
Aniello Amitrano
Teresa Amitramo, Aniello's wife
Capa C'Angelo
Lieutenant
Five Carabinieri

Insect Play, The (and so on Ad Infinitum or The Life of the Insects)
Karel and Josef Capek
Comedy 3 Acts
Prague 1921

A drunken tramp falls asleep and is woken by a lepidopterist leaping around after butterflies to kill and mount, because, he says, of his great love of nature. This sets the tone for the ironies to follow. The tramp has been thwarted in love but is still interested in what makes the world tick, so he observes the insects around him. Enter the Butterflies; they are a flighty lot, all poetry and romance, love affairs and teasing. But the

Creepers and Crawlers go about their grubby business differently - Mr and Mrs Beetle roll around their precious ball of dung for which they have 'saved, scraped, toiled and moiled'. Now it is finished, they want to bury it and make another. Then it is stolen by a rogue beetle. Oh woe!

A Chrysalis, straining to be born, is convinced her birth will be nothing less than a cosmic convulsion. The horrid Ichneumon Fly murders the nice musical Cricket family just to add to his store of food for his spoilt and pampered daughter who in turn is gobbled by the rascally Parasite, an ingratiating and treacherous Bolshevik.

Disillusioned with these bugs, the tramp declares that man's greatness must be his ability to live and work for the sake of the State; enter then the Ants. Their machine-like organization and self-importance is frightening to behold, and their mad and egotistical justification of a senseless war reminds the tramp only too well of his own military experiences. When the Ant victor declares himself Ruler of the Universe, the tramp angrily grinds him into pieces. He then falls asleep with a fever, and upon awakening sees the Moths, newly born and fluttering straight into their dance of death.

The Chrysalis rends her husk and leaps forth as a moth, and as light, love and ecstasy enter her, she promises to reveal the Great Secret - then falls dead. The tramp, having just learned of life and death and how to live and let live, then feels death pressing down on him. He fights but loses, and a woman passer-by with a new born baby lays a flower on him.

A tramp	The Chief Engineer
A lepidopterist	The Second Engineer
Clytie, Otto, Felix, Iris,	An inventor
Victor, butterflies	A messenger
A Chrysalis	A signal officer
Mr Beetle	A journalist
Mrs Beetle	A philanthropist
Another beetle	The Commander-in-Chief
Ichneumon Fly	of the Yellows
His daughter	Three moths
Mr Cricket	First snail
Mrs Cricket	Second snail
A Parasite	A woodcutter
Other creepers and	A woman
crawlers	Schoolchildren
The Blind Timekeeper	

Inspector Calls, An
J. B. Priestley
Drama 3 Acts
Manchester 1946

Just before World War One, the Birlings are a successful Northern business family. One evening, as they dine and speculate on their fortunes, a police inspector calls to question them collectively and individually about the suicide of a young lady, Daisy Renton, and although they deny being implicated, it transpires that all of them, at some time, have ill-treated the apparently innocent young victim. Their attitudes to the incident change from aloof indifference to involved guilt as the facts of the story are unveiled. Birling becomes increasingly concerned about the effect this is having on his respectable family and checks on the strange inspector to find that he is unknown to the local police. The inspector suddenly disappears and the smug family convince themselves that the whole incident was an elaborate hoax and they revert to their former superior attitudes until a phone call informs them that an inspector will soon call to investigate a suicide.

Arthur Birling
Sheila Birling
Sybil Birling
Eric Birling
Gerald Croft
Edna
Inspector Goole

Intermezzo
Jean Giradoux
Comedy 3 Acts
Paris 1933

A provincial French town has been plunged into turmoil in the thirties by the obsession of its young schoolmistress, Isabelle, with the supernatural, ghosts and the afterlife. Dropping all normal methods of instruction, she takes her class of girl students ever further into magical explanations of the natural world.

To prevent further deterioration of the community, a government inspector has been sent to restore normal teaching practices. With the help of the town's influential citizens, he sets out to demonstrate that Isabelle's beliefs are without foundation, but she however, raises the ghost of a local murderer, and the inspector must find a way of forcing it back to the afterlife. His efforts are a failure, but the superintendent of the local school succeeds by winning Isabelle's love, and leaving the ghost without a living audience.

Isabelle
The superintendent
The ghost
The chemist
The mayor
Armande and Leonide Mangebois, local busybodies
Cambrone and Crapuce, executioners
Local girls:
Luce
Giselle
Daisy
Gilberte
Irene
Nicole
Marie-Louise
Viola

Iolanthe
W. S. Gilbert and Arthur Sullivan
Comic Opera 2 Acts
London 1882

Subtitled *The Peer and the Peri* this finds that Iolanthe, a fairy, has been banished for twenty-five years by the Fairy Queen for having married a mortal by whom she has had a son, Strephon. This half-human, half-fairy boy now wishes to marry Phyllis, a ward in chancery, but the Lord Chancellor wants her to be his own wife. Phyllis has given her heart to Strephon, but when she sees him with his beautiful fairy mother Iolanthe, she thinks he has a lover and offers to marry a lord. The fairies and the lords become involved in the affair and battle lines are drawn up between them. Strephon has meanwhile become a Member of Parliament and Phyllis, becoming disillusioned with her mortal suitors, decides on him.

Iolanthe reveals that the Lord Chancellor was her mortal lover and is, therefore, Strephon's father, and the whole House of Lords decide to marry fairies and immediately sprout wings.

Songs include: 'Tripping Hither, Tripping Thither'; 'Good Morrow, Good Lover'; 'When I Went to the Bar as a Very Young Man'; 'Strephon's a Member of Parliament!'; 'Soon as We May'

The Lord Chancellor	*Celia and Leila, fairies*
Earl of Mountararat	*Fleta*
Earl Tolloller	*Phyllis, a ward in*
Pte Willis, a Grenadier	*chancery*
Guard	*Dukes*
Strephon, an Arcadian	*Marquises*
shepherd	*Earls*
Queen of the Fairies	*Viscounts*
Iolanthe, Strephon's	*Barons*
mother	*Fairies*

Irene
Hugh Wheeler and Joseph Stein
Musical 2 Acts
New York 1919

Irene O'Dare, a poor New York Irish girl who is by trade a piano tuner, is sent to the home of a rich, bachelor socialite, Donald Marshall, in the course of her work. While she is tuning Marshall's piano, his protégé Mme Lucy, an aspiring couturier in whom the young socialite has invested, notices Irene's outstanding beauty and decides to turn her into a fashion model.

So successful is her transition that Irene is even able to pass herself off as a member of a continental royal house, and inevitably Marshall falls madly in love with her. Even when he discovers her true, humble origins, Marshall's love remains true and the pair look set to be married. Songs include: 'Alice Blue Gown'; 'Irene'; 'You Made Me Love You'

Mrs O'Dare, Irene's mother
Jane Burke
Helen McFudd
Jimmy O'Flaherty
Irene O'Dare
Emmeline Marshall
Clarkson
Donald Marshall
Ozzie Babson
Mme Lucy
Arabella Thornsworthy

Irma La Douce
Alexandre Breffori
Musical 2 Acts
Paris 1956

In contemporary Paris, best among the prostitutes is Irma La Douce, and her pimp Polyte Le Mou is not pleased when she falls in love with a poor student, Nestor, and makes him her new protector. The young man, jealous of Irma's clients, adopts a clever plan. He disguises himself as a rich old gent, M. Oscar, who pays Irma 10,000 francs every night for her exclusive services. She gives the money to Nestor, every morning, who spends it again every night as Oscar. Nestor eventually becomes jealous of his other half 'Oscar', and when the older man disappears, Nestor is convicted for his murder and sent to Devil's Island.

Managing to get a job as houseboy to the Governor's wife, Nestor builds a raft, escapes and gets back to Paris where he presents himself to the police as Oscar; therefore, Nestor must be innocent. He finds Irma again, they marry and settle down in modest domestic bliss with their twins, Nestor and Oscar.

Irma La Douce, a	*Passer-by*
'poule'	*Counsel for prosecution*
Nestor Le Fripe, a law	*Counsel for defence*
student	*Honest man*
Bob Le Hotu,	*Usher*
proprietor of the bar	*Three warders*
Mecs: *Polyte Le Mou,*	*Tax inspector*
Jojo Les Yeux Sales,	*Doctor*
Roberto Les Diams,	*Priest*
Frangipane, Persil	*Policemen*
Police Inspector	*Irma's admirers*
M. Bougne	*Prisoners*
Gendarme	*Bar loungers*

Is Your Honeymoon Really Necessary?
E. V. Tidmarsh
Comedy 3 Acts
London 1947

Lawrence Vining returns with his young second wife Rosemary to his Kent country home for a quiet honeymoon. After greeting his staff - Hemming, the butler, Lucy, the parlourmaid, and Marie, his wife's maid - the happy couple prepare to retire, and Rosemary leaves Lawrence in the lounge as she sets about prettying herself in the couple's bedroom.

To Lawrence's utter horror, his first wife, Yvonne,

arrives just as he is about to join Rosemary, claims the divorce he has obtained is invalid, and demands 3,000 pounds in back alimony with the threat that unless she is paid immediately, she will reveal to Rosemary that Lawrence is a bigamist. With the help of his misogynistic butler, Lawrence hides Yvonne away in the spare bedroom and promises to bring his lawyer to settle matters with her in the morning.

The lawyer, Frank Betterton, a confirmed bachelor and Lawrence's oldest friend, duly arrives, but points out that as it is Sunday, he will be unable to raise the sum Yvonne requires. Lawrence, believing a deal has been struck and Yvonne got rid of, brings Rosemary down for breakfast and interrupts the negotiations. To cover up the truth, he pretends that Yvonne is Frank's wife, and tries to hustle them both out. But Rosemary, who has deduced the truth about Yvonne, mischievously asks their guests to stay the night.

Frank is aghast at the prospect of sharing a room with Yvonne, but manages to get through the night in their dressing room. The next day at breakfast Rosemary exploits the situation to create maximum suspense for the other three, but eventually the truth comes out and she and Lawrence watch in some surprise as it emerges that Frank and Yvonne, thrown together so unceremoniously, have fallen in love. Both couples are then relieved when Frank's clerk arrives with the proof that Lawrence's divorce was, after all, perfectly valid.

Fred Thompson
William Hemming, the butler
Marie, Rosemary's maid
Lucy Watkins
Lawrence Vining
Rosemary Vining, his second wife
Yvonne Vining, his first wife
Frank Betterton, his lawyer
James Hicks

It's a Dog's Life
John Patrick
Comedy Three One-act Plays
New York 1980

These three one-act plays are held together by the common theme of the effects a pet dog can have on the relations between human beings in New York City.

The Gift. A young wife receives from the estate of her wealthy aunt nothing but the dead woman's pet lapdog, and its elaborate doghouse. Her husband takes the dog for a walk, gives its dog collar away to a young girl who asks for it, and returns home to find his wife nearly hysterical following her discovery that the collar is inset with diamonds. All ends happily, though, when the collar is returned to them by the young girl, who has found it to be too small for her own pet.

Co-Incidence. The development of a friendship between a young man and woman who meet because they both use violin cases to transport their miniature poodles into and out of an apartment building which prohibits the keeping of pets.

The Divorce. A meeting between a couple whose marriage has broken down leads not to the division of property for which it was called, but rather to their reconciliation when neither of them can bear to part from their pet dog.

The Gift:
Mary Ruskin
Bill Ruskin, Mary's husband
Mr Smythe-Jones, a lawyer
Co-Incidence:
Prudence Allcott
Mister Pincus
Bruce Lacey
The Divorce:
Peggy Bolt
Adam Bolt, her husband
Mark Mellon, Peggy's lawyer

Italian Straw Hat, An
Eugène Labiche
Comedy 3 Acts
Paris 1851

Wealthy young bridegroom Fadinard is returning to Paris on his wedding morning when en route his horse eats most of the straw hat of young Mme Annette Beaujolais, who has hung it up while having a 'tête-à-tête' in a field with a soldier lover, Emile. Emile and Annette follow Fadinard home and she refuses to budge from his bedroom until he replaces the hat, the absence of which will arouse the suspicions of her husband, jealous old M. Beaujolais. Meanwhile, the wedding party have arrived, a motley crew led by bride Helen's obstreperous old father Nonancourt, and Fadinard proceeds to lead them all in a hilarious chase all over Paris while he searches for a matching hat in order to get rid of Annette who is having hysterics.

He cannot tell his guests the truth, so there are a series of tableaux in which the short-sightedness, deafness, and general stupidity of the party assist Fadinard in his quest. He leads them in and out of milliner Clara's salon (he once jilted her), and he is mistaken for an Italian opera singer when he attempts to get a similar hat that Clara sold to society hostess Mme de Champigny. Finally he tracks down the duplicate hat to M. Beaujolais, and realizes he has been chasing the very same hat which has already been eaten. To make matters worse he's also given the game away to M. Beaujolais. But when everyone returns to his house, he finds deaf old Vezinet, Helen's uncle, has given her an identical hat as a wedding present. Annette gets the hat and confounds her husband's suspicions. Fadinard is at last off the hook and enters his now-empty house with his new wife and guests.

Virginia, Mme Beaujolais' maid
Felix, Fadinard's valet
Vezinet, Helen's deaf uncle
Fadinard, bridegroom

Emile Tavernier, a Captain of Zouaves
Annette Beaujolais
Nonancourt, bride's father, nursery gardener
Helen, bride
Boby, bride's cousin
Clara, milliner
Tardiveau, Clara's cashier
La Comtesse de Champigny, society hostess
Achille de Rosalba, the countess's cousin
A footman
La Duchess de Château Gaillard
Mlle Ondine de Château Lapompe
Le Duc de Château Gaillard
Clotilde, the Comtesse's maid
M. Beaujolias, Annette's husband
A Corporal of the National Guard
A man in a night-cap
Guest at the wedding and party
National guards
Neighbours

Jesus Christ Superstar
Music by Andrew Lloyd Webber
Lyrics by Tim Rice
Rock Opera 24 Scenes
Pittsburgh 1971

This piece traces, mainly in song, the life of Jesus Christ from his entry into Jerusalem up to the Crucifixion as seen through the eyes of Judas Iscariot. He reminds Jesus of the past and warns him against letting the movement get out of hand otherwise there will be forces that will suppress it. Jesus responds angrily and falls into the lap of Mary Magdelene to be anointed and comforted, much to Judas's disgust. Jesus seems to be worn out and tired of all that is going on around him and passively advises cripples to heal themselves.

Judas's predictions, of course, come true and the familiar events of the Crucifixion are played against a backdrop of anachronisms and glamour.

Songs include: 'I Don't Know How to Love Him'; 'Everything's All Right'; 'Superstar'.

Judas Iscariot	*Pontius Pilate*
Jesus of Nazareth	*Soldier*
Mary Magdelene	*Tormentor*
Two priests	*Maid by the fire*
Calaphas	*King Herod*
Annas	*Apostles*
Simon Zealotes	*Soul girls*
Peter	*Chorus*

Jew of Malta, The
Christopher Marlowe
Tragedy 5 Acts
London 1590

Turkish Prince Calymath gives the Governor of Malta one month to pay the outstanding tribute, and in order to raise the money the Governor confiscates all of wealthy Jew Barabas's fortune. Well, almost. Barabas has hidden a few bags of diamonds, pearls, gold, etc, under his floorboards, and as the house is now converted into a nunnery, he persuades beautiful daughter Abigail to convert to Christianity for a night or two and get him back the riches. This she does, but Barabas seeks further revenge, and using the unwitting Abigail he forges a challenge between Governor's son Don Lodowick and Abigail's love, Don Mathias. They kill each other and distraught Abigail enters the convent for real. With the connivance of his wicked Turkish slave Ithamore, Barabas then poisons the whole nunnery including his own daughter. Abigail's dying confession is heard by two friars but Barabas and Ithamore kill one and pin the murder on the other, who is then hanged.

When Ithamore is seduced by courtesan Bellamira and betrays Barabas, the Jew poisons them, but not before they betray him to the Governor. Barabas, taking a potion, feigns death and is flung out of the city walls, but recovers and plots with Prince Calymath; he betrays the Christians and the grateful Turks make him Governor. He then decides his general unpopularity must be remedied so he plans with the ex-Governor to destroy Calymath's armies. But he is double-crossed by the Governor and instead of Calymath falling into a pot of boiling oil, it is Barabas who meets this fate. The Governor then takes the Turk hostage and praises not Fate or Fortune, but Heaven.

Machiavel, the prologue
Barabas
Ferneze, Governor of Malta
Selim Calymath, son of the Turkish Grand Signior
Don Lodowick, the Governor's son
Don Mathias
Ithamore
Martin Del Bosco, Spanish Vice Admiral
Jacomo and Barnardino, friars
Pilia Borza, the courtesan's man
Two merchants
Three Jews
Knights
Bashaws
Officers
Reader
Abigail
Katherine (Mater), mother of Mathias
Two nuns
Abbess
Bellamira, a courtesan

John Bull's Other Island
George Bernard Shaw
Play 4 Acts
London 1904

This *Preface for Politicians* dealing in the vagaries of Anglo-Irish political attitudes is set in London and Ireland in the early part of the century.

Larry Doyle, an Irish businessman, successful in England, decides to visit his home town with his partner,

Thomas Broadbent, to see his old sweetheart, Nora Reilly, but he is concerned about seeing his father with whose political and religious views he is now at odds.

Doyle is asked by the local townspeople to run for Parliament but when they hear his progressive and scandalous modern ideas they change their offer very quickly. They are, however, impressed by Broadbent, an amiable but clever fool, with his good natured antics and his pragmatic approach to politics. He is successfully nominated and as a bonus wins the affection of Nora Reilly. Broadbent now has ambitious plans for the town including a golf course and a hotel, which do not coincide with the dreams of a local unfrocked priest and idealist Keegan, who is obviously a 'madman'.

Thomas Broadbent
Larry Doyle
Tim Haffigan
Hodson
Peter Keegan
Patsy Farrell
Father Dempsey
Corney Doyle
Barney Doran
Matthew Haffigan
Aunt Judy
Nora Reilly

John Gabriel Borkman
Henrik Ibsen
Drama 4 Acts
Copenhagen 1897

In late-nineteenth-century Oslo, Borkman, since his release from prison for large scale fraud, has spent the past eight years proudly imagining that his financial genius will again be recognized and he will be grandly reinstated in the banking business. He lives with his long suffering, silent wife and son, Erhart, in the house of his wife's rich twin sister, Ella, who has loved him for years. Borkman credits himself for her fortune; due to his business machinations, she benefited while thousands lost fortunes, but she refuses to forgive him in his ruthless quest for power.

Ella, who has only months to live, offers to leave her fortune to Erhart, while Borkman wants his son to help him resume working; his mother wants him to stay, but the boy rejects them all, wanting his freedom he leaves to get married.

For the first time in years, the self-deluding Borkman leaves the house to go to the wild mountains, which he loves for their hidden, but unexploited, fortune but the cold air kills him. The twin sisters join hands, united over the body of the man they both once loved.

John Gabriel Borkman, a sometime banker
Gunhild, his wife
Erhart Miss Ella Rentheim, Gunhild's
  twin sister
Mrs Fanny Wilton
Vilhelm Foldal, a clerk
Frida Foldal, daughter
Borkman's maid

Johnny Belinda
Elmer Harris
Adapted by Sorrel Carson and John Hanau
Drama 3 Acts
London 1950

Widower Black McDonald ekes a hard living from his small farm and grist mill on bleak Prince Edward Island in the extreme north of Canada. He is helped by dour spinster sister Maggie and his daughter Belinda, a deaf-mute. McDonald treats Belinda -'the dummy'- as a beast of burden until Dr Jack Davidson arrives and strikes up a friendship with her, teaching her sign language. Belinda is warm and responsive and McDonald is impressed and moved and begins truly to communicate with his daughter for the first time, much to their mutual delight.

One day Belinda is cornered in the barn by young farmer Locky McCormick who rapes her. She becomes pregnant but because of a mental block cannot identify the baby's father. When baby Johnny Belinda is born, she experiences strong maternal feelings which lighten her loneliness. Dr Jack offers to marry her, but first must take work in Montreal to help McDonald out of his current financial crisis. Just before he leaves, McDonald is killed by lightning, and immediately following his departure, the local vultures descend to 'look after' Belinda and Johnny.

Childless Locky and wife Stella obtain papers to adopt Johnny but when they come to take the baby, Belinda resists, Locky gets rough, and Belinda shoots and kills him. Dr Jack returns just in time for the official enquiry, and after questioning Stella and discovering the truth about the rape, it is apparent that no charges will be brought against Belinda. She is given back her baby and is free to marry the doctor.

Belinda McDonald
Dr Jack Davidson
Black McDonald
Locky McCormick
Stella
Jimmy Dingwell, the butcher
Maggie McDonald
Mrs McKee
Mrs Lutz
The Revd Edward Tidmarsh
Two villagers

Joking Apart
Alan Ayckbourn
Drama 2 Acts
Scarborough 1978

Four scenes, each set at an occasion (Boxing Day, a birthday, etc) in the garden/tennis court of Richard and Anthea, an attractive couple who are two of life's natural winners. Over the twelve-year span of the play, their magnetism distorts and brings to the brink of disaster the lives of several of their closest and less fortunate friends; Brian loves Anthea but missed his chance just before she met Richard, and his subsequent string of unsuitable - and always similar - girlfriends (who get younger as he gets older) barely disguise his undiminishingly hopeless devotion, rewarded by Anthea's friendship and unconscious contempt. Brian now works for Richard and Sven, a methodical and slightly pompous Finn whose diligence and hard work are always eclipsed by Richard's natural flair and success at business. Sven ends up convalescing after a heart attack, perpetually unable to beat Richard at anything. His wife Olive is being driven to desperation by her husband's frustration, illness and self-pity.

Neighbours Hugh and Louise, the nervous young local vicar and his tense wife, fare just as badly with Hugh ending up nursing a hopeless passion for Anthea, and Louise mentally unstable, high and fanatical on prescription drugs. When Anthea's daughter Debbie has her eighteenth birthday party, she is confronted by the good wishes of her parents' emotionally-mutilated friends and the generation gap looms - she is bewildered and unable to spare even a moment of tenderness for pathetic 'Uncle' Brian.

Richard	*Brian*
Anthea	*Melody*
Hugh	*Mandy*
Louise	*Mo*
Sven	*Debbie*
Olive	

Joseph and the Amazing Technicolour Dreamcoat

Andrew Lloyd Webber and Tim Rice
Musical 2 Acts
London 1973

The play is a series of very loosely connected incidents from the life of the biblical Joseph, son of Jacob and Rachel, who was sold into slavery in Egypt by his brothers only to rise to become Prime Minister to the Pharaoh and, from this position, benefactor of his real people, the Jews, when he saved them from famine by providing Egyptian grain.

Joseph	*Pharaoh*
Reuben	*Asher*
Adam	*Bad angels*
God	*Good angels*
Lucifer	*Noah's sons*
Judah	*Noah's daughter-in-law*
Eve	*Jacob's other sons*
Cain	*Ishmaelites*
Napthali	*Egyptians*
Abel	*Wives*
Simeon	*Harems*
Noah	
Dan	
Noah's wife	
Jacob	
Jacob's wife	
Potiphar's wife	

Joseph Andrews

P. M. Clepper from the novel by Henry Fielding
Comedy 2 Acts
London 1977

This mid-eighteenth-century romp features women as sexual predators and follows the adventures of lusty Lady Booby's innocent young footman, Joseph, and his true love, maid Fanny. A Mrs Wilson eases the tale along with descriptive narration as handsome Joseph is pursued by both her ladyship and her randy housekeeper Mrs Slipslop. His refusal of their advances leads to his dismissal and he sets out on the road, helped by naive Parson Adams. Meanwhile, his scheming sister, lovely tease Pamela, works her wiles on Booby's nephew in order to marry into society and betterment.

On the road, Joseph is robbed and hurt, but Betty, servant at a nearby inn, helps him recover - not without ulterior motive - while Fanny, in pursuit, is saved from rake Didapper's clutches by Adams. Unfortunately Lady Booby eventually gets them jailed with the connivance of corrupt Judge Frolick, but when Pamela finally snares the Nephew and they wed, her Ladyship has to get them released for the sake of family honour (and her designs on Joseph). A further plot to discredit Fanny ends up in a farcical bedroom fiasco between Didapper, Slipslop and Adams.

When an old gypsy arrives, it appears that Joseph and Fanny might actually be brother and sister - further frustration! However, Joseph is proved to be not Mrs Andrew's son, but son of gentlewoman Mrs Wilson, stolen from his cot and swapped with Mrs Andrews for her missing daughter - Fanny. Thus, the way is now clear for the pair of innocents to wed, while Didapper slinks off to fondle Lady Booby.

Joseph Andrews	*Female robber*
Parson Adams	*Male robber*
Lady Booby	*Pigs*
Fanny	
Pamela	
Nephew	
Slipslop	
Betty	
Didapper	
Mrs Tow-Wouse	
Mrs Trulliber	
Mrs Wilson	
Mrs Andrews	
Justice Frolick	
Constable	
Gypsy	

Journey's End

R. C. Sherriff
Drama 3 Acts
London 1928

As a major German attack is awaited, a new young officer, James Raleigh, arrives in the trenches in France in 1918. He is proud to be under the command of Capt. Dennis Stanhope, an ex-school friend, but three years in battle have taken their toll and Stanhope can only bear the horrors of war by drinking vast quantities of whisky.

Confiding in a fellow officer, Stanhope admits that he finds Raleigh's hero worship a problem in that if disillusioned he may inform his sister, who is Stanhope's fiancée.

The officer, Osborne, befriends Raleigh and Stanhope and has the agonizing duty of sending them both on a dangerous mission to capture Germans for interrogation. The young Raleigh is excited by the prospect of action, but the older and wiser Osborne, who has seen it all before, is apprehensive, justifiably as it turns out, for he is killed on the mission. Returning dazed, Raleigh cannot understand Stanhope's drunken attempts to forget the horror of losing a friend. The next day, the young officer is wounded during the German attack and Stanhope tries to comfort him with memories of good times they had together, before he too goes into the fray.

Stanhope
Osborne
Trotter
Hibbert
Raleigh
The Colonel
The Company Sergeant Major
Mason
Hardy
German soldier

Julius Caesar
William Shakespeare
Tragedy 5 Acts
London 1600

Caesar enters Rome to wild popular acclaim, having defeated Pompey's renegade army. The Roman nobility, fearful of Caesar's ambition, conspire against him. Their intrigue is guided by Cassius who, with the help of Casca and Cinna, persuades the virtuous Brutus to join a plot to assassinate the triumphant general.

Although he is warned by both omens and a soothsayer to remain at home, Caesar ventures to the Capitol, where the conspirators stab him to death. The dead hero's friend, Mark Antony then stirs up popular opposition to the assassins, and with Lepidus and Caesar's nephew Octavius, forms an army which defeats the forces of Brutus and Cassius, both of whom commit suicide.

Julius Caesar
Triumvirate after Caesar's murder: *Octavius Caesar, Mark Antony, M. Aemilius Lepidus*
Cicero, Publius, Popilius Lena, senators
Assassins of Caesar: *Marcus Brutus, Cassius, Casca, Trebonius, Caius Ligarius, Decius Brutus, Metellus Cimber, Cinna*

Flavius and Murellus, tribunes
Artemidorus of Cnidos
Soothsayer
Cinna, a poet
Another poet
Friends of Brutus and Cassius: *Lucilius, Titinius, Messala, Young Cato, Volumnius, Flavius*
Brutus's servants: *Varrus, Clitus, Claudio, Strato, Lucius, Dardanius*
Pindarus, Cassius's servant
Calpurnia, Caesar's wife
Portia, Brutus's wife
Senators
Citizens
Guards, attendants

Jumpers
Tom Stoppard
Comedy 2 Acts
London 1972

George, a Professor of Moral Philosophy, and his much younger wife Dorothy, a reluctantly-retired actress of uncertain mental health, are hosts at a party where Archie, George's senior colleague, apparently murders one of his rivals for Dorothy's extra-marital favours.

The crime is investigated by Inspector Bones, a great fan of Dorothy's, whose infatuation with her leads him to dismiss her as a serious suspect in the murder, although the presence of the corpse in her bedroom should arouse his professional concern. Meanwhile Archie, another suspect, as leader of the gymnastic troupe to which the dead man belonged, continues his lechery with Dorothy under George's none too acute nose. George himself is so busy polishing a lecture he is about to give that he inadvertently takes the guilt for the crime on his own shoulders, while remaining quite unaware that he has done so.

The play never establishes who in fact committed the murder, but Archie remains the chief suspect, particularly because it is he who finally contrives the removal of the corpse.

George
Dorothy, George's wife
Archie
Inspector Bones
Crouch
Secretary
Eight jumpers (gymnasts) who also play:
Scott
Clegthorpe
Ushers
Dancers, chaplains

Juno and the Paycock
Sean O'Casey
Tragedy 3 Acts
Dublin 1924

The Boyle family, 'Captain' Jack, his wife Juno, their

son Johnny and daughter Mary, live in the squalor of a two-room Dublin tenement in the twenties. Neither the 'Captain', a drunken malingering former seaman, nor Johnny, horribly wounded fighting for the IRA, do any work at all. This is left to Juno and Mary.

Their lives are considerably brightened up when Charles Bentham, a dapper young schoolmaster, brings news that the 'Captain' has inherited a tidy sum. When Bentham sets out to court Mary, and the tenement is refurbished on credit, Juno believes that their fortunes have at last changed.

Unfortunately, the young Bentham is mainly interested in Mary's prospects, and so when he discovers an error in his own drafting of the will that was to have provided the inheritance, which will mean that the Boyle's are penniless, he flees to London leaving Mary pregnant. Her disgrace is quickly followed by the repossession of the furniture and then, disastrously, by Johnny's execution for betraying the Republican cause.

The 'Captain' reacts to these reverses with his usual drunken self-pity, finally driving Juno to leave him behind as she and Mary leave Dublin to find a new life.

'Captain' Jack Boyle
Juno Boyle
Johnny Boyle
Mary Boyle
'Joxer' Daly
Mrs Maisie Madigan
Charles Bentham
'Needle' Nugent
Mrs Tancred
Jerry Devine
An irregular mobilizer
Two irregulars
A coal vendor
A sewing machine man
Two furniture removers
Two neighbours

Just Between Ourselves
Alan Ayckbourn
Drama 2 Acts
Scarborough 1977

Neil and Pam meet Dennis and Vera on Pam's birthday when they go to see Vera's car which is for sale - a possible present for Pam which she doesn't want anyway. Dennis, as usual, is pottering around unsuccessfully in his messy garage/shed, and as his interfering mother Marjorie (who lives with them) keeps reminding them, he isn't the perfect handyman his father was. Jovial insensitive Dennis is also unable to hear Vera's cries for help; she is being slowly driven mad by mother-in-law Marjorie, and unlike Pam who is going through a different kind of crisis with Neil, she does not have the strength or determination to successfully assert herself.

The two men become pals of a sort, and the four scenes take place successively on the birthdays of each

of the characters. Vera's patience is sorely tried by Marjorie on Dennis's birthday - she hasn't made him his traditional cake - and on Marjorie's birthday Vera finally explodes into violence. Finally, three months later on her own birthday, Vera has become totally withdrawn, unable or unwilling to speak, huddled in the cold out in the garden, and able only to indicate she doesn't want to go into the house where Marjorie now reigns supreme and Dennis is her good little boy again.

Dennis
Vera
Neil
Marjorie
Pam

Justice
John Galsworthy
Tragedy 4 Acts
London 1910

At work in the How Brothers lawyers' office, junior clerk, William Falder is an exemplary employee, but when he becomes involved with a young mother, Ruth Honeywill, the victim of a brutal husband, he foolishly forges a cheque to help her. His crime is discovered and despite efforts by his kindly office manager, Cokeson, and an eloquent defence in court, he receives the maximum prison sentence.

Inhuman solitary confinement is more than he can bear, although the prison governor is convinced it is for his own good. Deprived of visits by Cokeson and Ruth, he finally cracks.

Two years later, shunned by society as an ex-convict, Falder tries to regain his old job, but his former sanctimonious employer imposes the condition that he must give up the now fallen woman, Ruth. He refuses and desperate for work he forges a reference about which he is questioned by the police. Rather than face prison again, he throws himself to his death. The ever-compassionate Cokeson comforts Ruth with the thought that now at least Falder is 'safe with gentle Jesus'.

James How
Walter How
Cokeson
Falder
Ruth Honeywill
Office Boy
Detective
Cashier
Judge
Old Advocate
Young Advocate
Prison Governor
Prison Chaplain
Prison Doctor
Wooder
Moaney
Clipton
O'Cleary

Kean (Disorder and Genius)
Jean-Paul Sartre
Comedy 5 Acts
Paris 1954

In the person of forty-year-old Edmund Kean, the greatest actor of his generation, the actor's traditional foibles are magnified appropriately. For Edmund, the real is sham and the sham is real, and his misplaced sense of drama spills dangerously over into his private life, much to the frustration of his faithful factotum and prompter Solomon, who strives valiantly to make ends meet against Kean's mounting debts.

Kean's affair with Elena, wife of an elderly noble Danish diplomat, lands him in trouble with his friend the Prince of Wales (later William IV), but when beautiful young heiress and would-be actress Anna declares her love for him, Kean is forced to use her as his leading lady with disastrous results. He insults the Prince and waits in his dressing room to be arrested for *lèse-majesté*, but when Elena's husband arrives demanding satisfaction, Anna saves the day. Kean has realized that Elena too is unwilling for their affair to go further and is herself playing a role, and when the Prince arrives and with princely generosity allows Edmund a way out, the actor decides to marry Anna and go with her in exile to New York for a year.

Kean	*Theatre attendants*
The Prince of Wales	*Fireman*
Solomon	
Peter Pott, landlord of the	
Black Horse	
Lord Neville	
A constable	
Darius, a hairdresser	
Stage manager	
Anna Danby	
Elena, Countess de	
Koefeld	
Amy, Countess of Gosville	
Gidsa, Elena's maid	
Major-domo	
Footmen	
Acrobats	
Stage hands	

Key for Two
John Chapman and Dave Freeman
Comedy 2 Acts
London 1982

Harriet, an attractive divorcée, lives in an elegant flat in Brighton where on different days of the week she entertains her two lovers, ad. man Gordon and fishing fleet owner Alec. She freely admits to her friend Anne, who turns up from New Zealand, that she needs the money that these gentlemen provide, and she has invented a demanding boozy mother to justify lots of extra expenses.

When Gordon and Alec suddenly appear on the same day, Harriet, aided by Anne, has to do a lot of quick thinking to keep them apart, passing off Gordon as Anne's husband to Alec, and Alec as her own divorced husband, suddenly returned from Peru, to Gordon. Gordon breaks a leg, which adds further opportunities for comedy when his wife Magda arrives to see him at the flat which has been converted for the occasion into a nursing home with the increasingly confused lovers acting as doctors and nurses.

To complete the ménage Alec's wife Mildred comes looking for her wayward husband but eventually all the partnerships are properly sorted out with the possibility of future liaisons still in the offing.

Harriet
Anne
Alec Bulthorpe
Gordon Farrow
Magda Farrow
Mildred Bulthorpe

Killing of Sister George, The
Frank Marcus
Comedy 3 Acts
Bristol 1965

June Buckridge has come to national fame as the lovable 'Sister George' in the radio serial *Applehurst* as a district nurse who rides round the country lanes doing good and singing hymns. However, she is about to be dropped from the show and her private life begins to suffer, compounded by booze and a strained relationship with her live-in lover, Alice (Childie) McNaught. She is visited by her BBC boss who warns her about her public image after a drunken incident in a taxi with some nuns. Later, as June and Alice prepare to go to a fancy-dress party as Laurel and Hardy, they are visited again by the boss, Mrs Mercy Croft who announces that Sister George is to be killed off in a fatal road accident in two weeks' time. Mercy offers to help Alice find a job. Eventually, George has to listen to her public death on a morning that brings a private catastrophy and the offer of help from a psychic neighbour, Mme Xenia. To add insult to injury Mercy offers June a part in a new series as a cow, and begins to take a more than professional interest in Childie's welfare.

June Buckridge (Sister George), an actress
Alice (Childie) McNaught, her friend
Mrs Mercy Croft, a BBC executive
Mme Xenia, a neighbour

Kind of Alaska, A
Harold Pinter
Drama 1 Act
London 1982

Deborah, a victim of the sleeping sickness epidemic which swept Europe in 1916-1917, awakens in her hospital room from twenty-nine years of semiconsciousness. She has been revived by an injection of L-Dopa administered by her doctor and brother-in-law, Hornby.

As she struggles to reorientate herself, Deborah must somehow face the fact that she is no longer the sixteen-year-old who was struck down, but a mature woman who has missed the whole of her adult life. When she meets her sister Pauline, Hornby's wife, Deborah gradually starts to accept her condition. After a poignant description, from Hornby and Pauline, of her descent into sickness, Deborah just about grasps the length of time she has spent semi-conscious, but her chief desire is to celebrate her own birthday in the way she had done as an adolescent.

Deborah
Hornby
Pauline

King and I, The

Richard Rodgers and Oscar Hammerstein
Musical 2 Acts
New York 1951

Following the death of her husband, a British officer of the mid-nineteenth century Raj, Anna Leonowens and her young son Louis arrive in Bangkok, where Anna has taken a position as tutor to the many children of the King of Siam. Her keen intelligence, sympathy and democratic spirit soon win the love of the King's children and various wives, but though he himself comes rather grudgingly to rely on her for advice in his dealings with the European powers, her independence offends his belief in his own absolute powers.

With the support of Lady Thiang, the King's senior wife, Anna organizes an elaborate dinner party, in European style, to impress a visiting British diplomatic team which includes Anna's long-time admirer, Ambassador Sir Edward Ramsay. The dinner is a success and the King, although prevented by his vanity from giving her fulsome credit for her part in it, rewards her by providing Anna and Louis with a home of their own outside the palace precincts. Even this minimal concession, though, is a major gesture, coming as it does from a man raised to expect unquestioning obedience from everyone he meets, and it seems to signal a new understanding of their mutual strengths between the King and his tutor.

However, the new accord is broken when the King orders that one of his concubines, Tuptim, should be beaten for attempting to elope with her lover. Revolted by this, Anna resigns and prepares to sail for British territory. Just as she is about to depart, though, word arrives that the King is mortally ill. She rushes to his bedside, where they are reconciled just before he dies.

His son and successor, Prince Chulalongkorn, abolishes the duty of his new subjects to prostrate themselves in his presence. He is Anna's star pupil, and Siam looks set for a more egalitarian style of rule.

Songs include: 'I Whistle a Happy Tune'; 'Hello, Young Lovers'; 'We Kiss in a Shadow'; 'Shall We Dance?'

Capt. Orton
Louis Leonowens
Anna Leonowens
The interpreter
The Kralahome
The King
Phra Alack
Tuptim
Lady Thiang
Prince Chulalongkorn
Princess Ying Yaowalak
Lun Tha
Sir Edward Ramsay
Princes
Princesses
Royal dancers
Wives, amazons, priests, slaves

King John

William Shakespeare
Drama 5 Acts
London 1597

King John finds his hold on the English throne threatened by a rival claimant, his nephew Arthur of Bretagne, who is supported by a number of disloyal English barons. John sends an army to Angiers, one of his French territories, to enforce his authority, but neither he nor Arthur can win the loyalty of its inhabitants.

To neutralize the threat from Arthur, John arranges the marriage of his niece Blanch to Lewis, heir to King Philip of France, to whom he also cedes his smaller French possessions. Many of his English subjects abhor this gambit, which they find humiliating, and when the Pope excommunicates John and authorizes a French attack on England, the King's strategy falls apart.

The English army, however, defeats the French under Arthur, who becomes John's prisoner. When Arthur leaps to a suicidal death, suspicion grows that the King was responsible. But before the Pope's efforts to mediate in the war can take effect, John dies, apparently poisoned.

King John of England
Prince Henry, John's son
Arthur, Duke of Bretagne, John's nephew
Earl of Pembroke
Earl of Essex
Earl of Salisbury
Lord Bigot
Hubert de Burgh
Robert Faulconbridge
Philip the Bastard
James Gurney
Peter of Pomfret
Philip, King of France
Lewis, the Dauphin
Lymoges, Archduke of Austria

Cardinal Pandulpho, the Pope's legate
Melune
Chatillion, French ambassador
Queen Elinor, John's mother
Constance, Arthur's mother
Blanch of Spain, John's niece
Lady Faulconbridge
Lords
Ladies
Citizens of Angiers
Sheriff
Heralds
Officers
Soldiers
Executioners
Messengers, attendants

King Lear
William Shakespeare
Tragedy 5 Acts
London 1608

Lear, King of Britain, declining in years, decides to divide his kingdom among his three daughters. Through petty misunderstandings he disinherits his youngest, Cordelia, and she marries the King of France. Lear lives alternately with his two older daughters, Goneril and Regan who soon tire of him and turn him out while plotting against each other for total power with their mutual lover, Edmund, bastard son of Gloucester. Edmund tricks his father into believing that his legitimate heir, Edgar, has been false to him, and with the collusion of Cornwall, Regan's husband, has his father's eyes put out. Edgar, disguised as a half-wit, takes his blinded father to Dover where they encounter Lear and Cordelia who have returned from France, but they are captured by Edmund who instructs his men to kill them. Edgar, however, defeats Edmund in battle, Goneril poisons Regan and commits suicide, while Cordelia is hanged in prison. This is more than poor Lear can bear and he dies with Cordelia's body in his arms closely followed by his faithful servant, Kent.

Lear, King of Britain
Regan, his daughter
Goneril, his daughter
Cordelia, his daughter
Earl of Gloucester
Edgar, Gloucester's son
Edmund, Gloucester's bastard son
Duke of Cornwall, Regan's husband
Duke of Albany, Goneril's husband
Earl of Kent
King of France
Duke of Burgundy
Curran, a courtier
Old man
Doctor
Lear's fool
Oswald, Goneril's steward

A Captain
A gentleman
A herald
Knights, officers, messenger, attendants, servants

King Ubu (Ubu Roi)
Alfred Jarry
Play 5 Acts
Paris 1896

This controversial avant-garde piece is set in a timeless and spaceless Eastern Europe.

'Shit' exclaims the fat and stupid Ubu as he is urged by his wife, Mother Ubu, to kill the Polish king. He invites Capt. Bordure, after a meal at which many die by licking a toilet brush, to support him, and their plot succeeds but Ubu decides to double-cross his fellow conspirator and so Bordure escapes to Russia to counter plot with the Tzar.

Ubu and Mother impose a ruthless regime in Warsaw with heavy taxes and frequent executions; she feels no compunction about swindling Ubu herself.

Prince Bougrelas, son of the dead king, recaptures Warsaw and the Ubus escape to the Ukraine, only to have to flee again in the face of the advancing Russians. Now in Lithuania, the vindictive Ubu, angry at Mother's deceit, throws her to a bear, which begins to tear her apart, and she is only saved by the entry of Bougrelas when the Ubus have to join forces to fight him. They escape yet again and as they sail past Elsinore, the pathetic imbecile, Ubu, looks forward to his new post as Minister of Finance in Paris.

Pa Ubu
Mother Ubu
Capt. Bordure
King Wenceslas
Queen Rosamund
Sons: Boleslas, Ladislas, Bougrelas
Stanislas Leszczynski
John Sobieski III
Nicolas Renski
Tzar Alexis
Palcontents: Gyron, Heads, Tails
Conspirators
Soldiers
People
Michael Feodorovitch
Nobles
Judges
Councillors
Financiers
Lackeys
Peasants
Entire Russian Army
Entire Polish Army
Mother Ubu's guards
A Captain
The Bear
The Phynance Charger

The Debraining Machine
The Crew
The Sea Captain

King's Rhapsody
Ivor Novello
Lyrics by Christopher Hassel
Musical Play 2 Acts
London 1949

At the Summer Palace in Norseland the beautiful Princess Cristiane is delighted when her father, King Peter, tells her that a marriage has been arranged for her with Prince Nicholas (Nikki) of Murania; she has admired him from afar since she was a child. Nikki, however, is not keen to marry her, or assume the mantle of kingship, and would prefer to stay in Paris with his long-time lover Marta.

He does, however, return home where he mistakes Cristiane for a peasant girl and confesses to her that he loves Marta. The marriage takes place, and loving Cristiane turns a blind eye to Nikki's continuing romance with Marta for the sake of the country and their son, the Prince. Nikki's attitudes anger some of the local politicians and eventually a revolution looks possible. Only Cristiane's commonsense averts a tragedy and Nikki, who is beginning to understand how much his wife loves him, realizes that he should abdicate to leave her and their son, the Boy King, to run the country.

Songs include: 'Some Day My Heart Will Awake'; 'If This Were Love'

Princesses Kirsten and Hulda, Cristiane's cousins
Mr Trotzen, dance master
Countess Vera
Lemainken
Princess Cristiane
King Peter of Norseland
Jules, Nikki's valet
Queen Elena of Murania
Vanescu, Prime Minister of Murania
Nikki
Marta Karillos, an actress
Countess Olga Varsov, lady-in-waiting
Flunkey
Madame Koska, a modiste
Major-domo
Count Egon Stanief
Volkoff
Three roughs
Ballet dancers
The Boy King
Archbishop
Servants
Maids
Villagers
Officers
Gipsies
Tartars

Kingfisher, The
William Douglas Home
Comedy 2 Acts
New York 1978

Famous author Sir Cecil Warburton and faithful butler-valet Hawkins live in his lovely house by a stream. Cecil writes and avidly watches the local kingfisher, and one day invites old flame Evelyn to visit on her way home from husband Reggie's funeral. Cecil missed his chance of marriage with Evelyn first time around fifty years ago, and this time intends to propose and be accepted. She arrives, and it is clear they have both always loved each other, but much of the past must be explained and forgiven.

Hawkins, however, is deeply fond of his master and when Cecil announces he and Evelyn - with whom he spends the night - are to wed, the butler gives in his notice. Cecil becomes abusive and insulting, and reconciliation appears impossible. Evelyn tells Cecil that he needs Hawkins more than he needs her, so she persuades Hawkins to stay, convincing him of Cecil's appreciation of him. She goes to leave, but realizing she really wants to stay, changes her mind and joins Cecil in looking for the beautiful kingfisher.

Cecil
Hawkins
Evelyn

Kismet
Robert Wright
Book by Edward Knoblock
Lyrics by George Forrest
Musical
New York 1953

This is an adaptation of the music of Alexander Borodin. Set in the Baghdad of the *Arabian Nights* we find Omar (later Hajj) the beggar poet accused of theft and escaping mutilation by demonstrating his 'magic powers' to the wicked Wazir. They then scheme together to prevent the Caliph's marriage, unaware the chosen bride is Marsinah, Omar's daughter who fell in love with the Caliph, believing him to be a simple gardener. When the Wazir locates Marsinah he plots to dishonour her, but in the nick of time, Omar discovers the truth and reveals the Wazir's perfidy to the Caliph, cunningly killing the Wazir in the process. The Caliph duly weds Marsinah, and Omar wins the affection of the Wazir's chief wife, Lalume.

Songs include: 'Stranger in Paradise', 'And This is My Beloved', 'Baubles Bangles and Beads'

Omar (Hajj), the beggar poet
Marsinah, Omar's daughter
Imam
Bashassi
Jawn
Wazir
Lalume, Wazir's wife
The Chief of Police

Caliph
Princess of Ababu
The widow Yusseff
Zubbediya of Damascus
Samaris of Bangalore
Beggars
Herald
Orange Seller, her Aya

Kiss and Tell
Hugh F. Herbert
Comedy 3 Acts
New York 1943

A family feud has developed between the Archers and the Pringles, friends for a generation, but now at odds because Mildred Pringle, seventeen, has led Corliss Archer, fifteen, into manning a stall selling kisses - innocently enough - to raise money for the American war effort in the forties. The Archers, however, are scandalized and blame the older Mildred for leading Corliss - who is in fact a flirt - somewhat astray. This only annoys the Pringles, but when Mrs Archer compares Mildred to a tart while gossiping with neighbours, and Mildred's mother Dorothy hears of it, a fist fight between the two husbands leads to lawsuits and apparently permanent bitterness.

While the adults behave like children, the children of both families share the fact that the Archers' eldest son, Lieut Lenny Archer, twenty, has secretly married Mildred during leave from service in the US Air Force. The pressure on them all to reveal their secret becomes unbearable - almost - when Corliss is seen leaving an obstetrician, and blames Dexter Franklin, seventeen, the boy next door, with his complicity, for what the adults assume is her pregnancy. In fact, though, Corliss, has been going with Mildred, who is the doctor's real patient, so her secret sister-in-law has some family support.

None of the children will reveal the truth until a telegram arrives for Mildred, at the Pringles, saying her husband is to be awarded a medal for bravery. The feud suddenly evaporates, and the two families celebrate Lenny's bravery and the coming grandchild.

Mr Willard
Louise, the Archers' maid
Corliss Archer, aged fifteen
Raymond Pringle, aged twelve
Mildred Pringle, aged seventeen
Dexter Franklin, aged seventeen
Janet Archer, Corliss's mother
Harry Archer, Corliss's father
Pte Earhart
Lieut Lenny Archer, aged twenty
Mary Franklin, Dexter's mother
Bill Franklin, Dexter's father
Dorothy Pringle, Mildred's mother
Uncle George, Corliss's uncle
Robert Pringle, Mildred's father

Kiss Me Kate
Bella and Samuel Spewack
Music and Lyrics by Cole Porter
Musical Comedy 2 Acts
New York 1948

On the stage of a theatre in contemporary Baltimore a touring company have just had a run-through of a musical version of *The Taming of the Shrew* and everyone's nerves are on edge.

Leading man Fred Graham feuds with his ex-wife and co-star Lilli Vanessi, not only on the stage, but also in the dressing room, and actress Lois Lane and her gambling boyfriend Bill Calhoun are also at each others' throats. Bill has just confessed to losing all his money and foolishly signing an IOU in Fred Graham's name. Lilli, tired of all the fighting, becomes engaged to wealthy Harrison Howell, who also has his eye on Lois. The rough-house action on stage eventually spills over into real life when Fred and Lilli have a punching-match and gangsters turn up to collect on Bill's IOU, but the love tangles are finally sorted out and even the gangsters become fans of the Bard of Avon.

Songs include: 'So in Love'; 'We Open in Venice'; 'Too Damn Hot'; 'Always True to You in My Fashion'; 'Brush Up Your Shakespeare'

Fred Graham (Petruchio)
Harry Trevor (Baptista)
Lois Lane (Bianca)
Ralph (Haberdasher)
Lilli Vanessi (Katherine)
Felix (Gremio)
Virgil (Hortensio)
Stage manager
Wardrobe mistress
Stage doorman
Hattie
Two men
Paul
Cab driver
Bill Calhoun (Lucentio)
Harrison Howell
Dancers
Chorus
Wedding guests
Waiters

Kitchen, The
Arnold Wesker
Drama 2 Parts
London 1959

A day in the tension-packed life of the staff of an ordinary, busy, quite large London restaurant, the Tivoli, owned by a melancholy old man, Mr Marango. They are a mixed lot - German, French, Cypriot, Italian, Jewish, Irish, English. The kitchen workers are mostly visible and engaged in their tasks throughout. The waitresses come and go with orders and rushing out to deliver them to unseen customers.

In the early morning the night porter fires up the noisy ovens, the staff begins to assemble and bicker and joke and flirt. At the centre of the action is a desperate affair going on between young German fish cook Peter and waitress Monique who is hesitating about leaving her husband.

Activity gets more frantic up to and including lunchtime, then there is an afternoon lull. ('The author would prefer there to be no interval but recognizes the wish of theatre bars to make some money.') As evening approaches, the visit of a hungry, cadging tramp causes a dispute, a pregnant waitress has to be taken to hospital, and after a trivial quarrel with a waitress over kitchen procedure, Peter goes berserk, destroying crockery and glass and ripping his hands. Mr Marango wonders why he is so senselessly sabotaged when he provides work, good pay, and the employees eat what they want. The force of the play is in its rhythmic pacing.

Magi	Betty
Max	Jackie
Bertha	Hans
Molly	Monique
Winnie	Alfredo
Mangolis	Michael
Paul	Gaston
Raymond	Kevin
Hettie	Nicholas
Violet	Peter
Anne	Frank
Gwen	Chef
Daphne	Head Waiter
Cynthia	Marango
Dimitri	Tramp

Knack, The
Ann Jellicoe
Comedy 3 Acts
Cambridge 1961

Three young North London men, Tom, Colin and Tolen - who goes by his last name only - are ineptly decorating their rented house in Tottenham in the early sixties.

As the work proceeds, Tom, a somewhat know-all schoolteacher, forces a reluctant Colin, in whose name the house is rented, to help turn the sitting room into a bedroom with no furniture but a mattress. As a result, the common parts of the house are full of piled furniture and in a complete shambles. Through the mess Tolen comes and goes, usually by the window, pursuing his favourite hobby of chatting up every passing female. So great is Tolen's status with the other two that he does none of the work, instead contenting himself with condescending descriptions of his apparently infallible techniques of seduction.

Tolen decides to demonstrate his technique, for Colin's benefit and to annoy Tom, on a young girl called Nancy Jones who stops at the house to ask directions to the YWCA, where, having just arrived in London, she hopes to find a room. With frequent technical asides to Colin, and supercilious jibes at Tom, Tolen sets to work trying to get Nancy into bed. He emphasizes his supposed authority at the knack Colin must develop for success with the ladies, but his approach, far from convincing Nancy, so upsets her that she has a fainting fit from which she emerges convinced that she has been raped.

The young men seem to be in a dangerous position, and their fear becomes clear, though they try to bluff it away, when Nancy starts to scream 'Rape!' Tolen somewhat shakily adopts the opinion that being raped is Nancy's deepest sexual fantasy, a belief which Tom openly derides. While these two argue, though, Colin behaves with genuine if somewhat ludicrous aplomb and falsely admits to Nancy that it was he who raped her. Tolen roundly derides his claim and announces his decision to do the deed himself, both to show up Colin's claim and to win Nancy over. Colin threatens to kill Tolen if he touches Nancy, and so wins her affection.

Tom
Colin
Tolen
Nancy

Knight of the Burning Pestle, The
Francis Beaumont
Comedy 5 Acts
London 1613

The Citizen - a grocer - and his wife settle down to watch the latest play, and in their simple enthusiasm urge their good-hearted grocer's man Rafe onto the stage to take part in the proceedings. Inspired by tales of knight-errants rescuing fair damsels in distress, Rafe declares himself the first grocer-errant, the Knight of the Burning Pestle, determined to heap honour on himself and his company. Accompanied by his squire (apprentice Tim) and his dwarf (apprentice George), Rafe becomes an English Don Quixote, first involving himself in the love triangle of the Merchant's friend Master Humphrey, the Merchant's daughter Luce, and disgraced Merchant's apprentice Jasper. Rafe sides with Humphrey, is bested by Jasper (who eventually wins Luce by devious strategems), but later redeems himself by felling feared barber-surgeon Barberoo and releasing his pitiful captives.

Rafe gives dubious assistance to Jasper's mother Mistress Merrythought, and abroad in Moldavia he captures the heart of Princess Pomponia, but vows to stay true to lucky cobbler's maid Susan, 'as long as life and pestle last'. Meanwhile the Merchant is reconciled to Jasper thanks to tipsy old songster Merrythought, and finally Rafe returns, a forked arrow through his head. After a charming resumé of his gallant achievements he dies, his soul flying to Grocers' Hall. Exit the Citizen with his wife, offering the players wine and tobacco back at his house.

Prologue
A Citizen

Citizen's wife
Rafe, her man, sitting below amidst the spectators
Venturewell, a rich merchant
Jasper, his apprentice
Master Humphrey, a friend to the merchant
Luce, the merchant's daughter
Mistress Merrythought, Jasper's mother
Michael, a second son of Mistress Merrythought
Old Master Merrythought
Tim, a squire
George, a dwarf
A tapser
A boy that danceth and singeth
An host
A barber
(Three captive) knights
A captive woman
A sergeant
Soldiers
William Hamerton, a pewterer
George Greengoose, a poulterer
Pompiona, daughter to the King of Moldavia

Krapp's Last Tape
Samuel Beckett
Play 1 Act
London 1958

Set some time in the future this play takes the form of a monologue in which Krapp, an almost blind and deaf old man, listens to and comments on tapes that he made some thirty years before.

In his study, Krapp goes through a ledger and reads various descriptions of events in his past. He selects a tape made on his thirty-ninth birthday, and puts it into a player. His younger voice describes a failed love affair and after listening he decides to make a new recording.

He reflects critically on his dreary life, his lack of success as an author and particularly his failure as a lover, but is drawn to the conclusion that he would not want those years back now. He sits staring into space.
Krapp, an old man

Laburnum Grove
J. B. Priestley
Drama 3 Acts
London 1933

It is a dull peaceful life for George and Dorothy Radfern and especially teenage daughter Elsie at their home in Laburnum Grove in the pleasant North London suburb of Shooters Green. Peaceful, except for houseguests Mrs Lucy Baxter (Dorothy's sister) and her sponging husband Bernard, who have long outstayed their welcome while 'waiting for something to turn up'. Another nuisance is Elsie's unsuitable boyfriend, flashy spineless Harold, and so George devises a ruse to get rid of them. He lets it slip that he is not as dull as he appears; he is part of a large counterfeiting ring forging bonds and banknotes.

The Baxters are not anxious to be accessories and prepare to move out, and Harold decides Elsie is not worth an engagement ring if her dad is a crook. No one knows whether or not Dad is joking, but after a visit from Inspector Stack it is obvious that Dad is involved; the game is nearly up and Radfern must flee to avoid arrest. He warns partner-in-crime Joe Fletten, purportedly arrived to get some greenhouse tips, and much to Elsie's delight announces that the family will be going abroad for a while.

Whether or not Mrs Radfern knows about her husband's activities, she nevertheless goes along with his plans, playing it cool and keeping mum.

Elsie Radfern	Inspector Stack
George Radfern	Sergeant Morris
Dorothy Radfern	
Bernard Baxter	
Lucy Baxter	
Harold Russ	
Joe Fletten	

Labyrinth, The
Fernando Arrabal
Drama 1 Act
Paris 1961

This Kafkaesque one-act play finds Etienne manacled to sick, dirty Bruno in a latrine in the middle of an immense park which is criss-crossed with blankets hanging out to dry. Etienne files his way free from Bruno, but is confronted with Micaela, daughter of park's owner Justin, who explains the story of the blankets, her father, and the impossibility of escape from the situation which is assuming nightmarish proportions. Justin appears and seems reasonable and tells Etienne that his daughter, now trying obscenely to seduce Bruno, is lying. He leaves, and Micaela tells Etienne her father makes her do these things. When Bruno hangs himself, they hide the body; then Justin appears with the Judge, a nasty old man who tries and condemns to death everyone who gets lost in the park. All Etienne's attempts to prove himself innocent of wrongdoing are thwarted, he is eventually accused and found guilty of Bruno's murder and sentenced to death. Left alone, he goes to escape, but reappears again with Bruno behind him in his death throes. The same scene goes on repeating until Curtain.
Etienne
Bruna
Micaela
Justin
The Judge

Ladder, The
Peter Howard
Drama 1 Act
Switzerland 1960

This highly stylized allegory casts Christ as a peripatetic, lonely man carrying a bag which, though it looks small enough, contains an immensely heavy wooden cross. The man with the bag seeks to convert a hero to the Christian life, but the hero, intent on worldly success, is concerned only to fight his way to the top of a ladder which symbolizes it.

Unfortunately for the hero, his path to eminence is bought by selling himself, body and soul, to his mother's ambition and to the corrupting help of a businessman and a statesman, both of whom use him for their own ends. Even the hero's wife is not his free choice, but a woman picked by his mother to fit her notions of what the hero needs to get ahead.

Although the hero reaches the top of the ladder, he must give it up to the man with the bag, who uses it to mount the cross in glory.

Hero	Businessman
Man with the bag	Mary
Cockney	Hero's wife
Hero's mother	Statesman

Ladies in Waiting
Cyril Campion
Mystery 3 Acts
London 1934

A group of women are gathered in the small Tudor house of Lady Evelyn Spate in a remote part of Yorkshire. One of them, Una Verity, is to be married next day. The other women present are sisters and bridesmaids Pat and Phil Blakeney, Una's old psychic school-chum Janet Garner, Lady Evelyn's great-niece and paid companion Dora Lester, cook Mrs Dawson and maid Maud.

It soon becomes apparent that someone does not want Una to get married. Her precious pearls, a present from her future bridegroom, disappear and so Lady Evelyn reluctantly calls in capable young detective Pamela Dark who soon discovers the pearls and also Una's wedding dress - shredded. Sinister comings-and-goings, hints of the supernatural, superstitious servants and shoals of red herrings all keep the action in this all-female drama menacing and mysterious until the dénouement. Finally the culprit, jealous of Una's happiness and determined to repeat an old legend of a bride's death at the house, is unmasked and herself commits suicide.

Janet Garner	Lady Evelyn Spate
Maud	Dora Lester
Una Verity	Mrs Dawson
Phil Blakeney	Pamela Dark
Pat Blakeney	

Lady Precious Stream
S. I. Hsiung
Drama 4 Acts
London 1934

This traditional folk play contrasts the relentless arrogance of Wang Yun, the Prime Minister of China, and his two elder daughters, with the steadfast loyalty and simplicity of Precious Stream, Yun's youngest daughter.

The two elder daughters have married brutal generals, whose narrow ambitions they too embrace. Precious Stream, however, has chosen, against her father's will, to marry a wise but very humble gardener, Hsieh Ping-Kuei. So poor are the young newlyweds that they can afford nothing better than a cave for a home, and the barest essentials in food and furnishing.

Hsieh joins a military campaign in the Western Regions of China, and asks his wife to await his return. Although he is gone for eighteen years, and word even comes that he has died, Precious Stream refuses to leave their cave and, as her father wishes, marry again. When he does return, Hsieh's military prowess has won him the Kingship of the Western Regions, and he is joyfully reunited with Precious Stream.

His Excellency Wang Yun
Mme Wang, his wife
Su, the Dragon General, his son-in-law
Wei, the Tiger General, his second son-in-law
Golden Stream, his eldest daughter
Silver Stream, his second daughter
Precious Stream, his youngest daughter
Hsieh Ping-Kuei. his gardener
HRH The Princess of the Western Regions
Minister of Foreign Affairs

Lady Windermere's Fan
Oscar Wilde
Comedy 4 Acts
London 1892

The idyllic early married life of Lord and Lady Windermere in turn-of-the-century London is threatened by his lordship's apparent fascination with Mrs Erlynne, 'a lady with a past'. In fact, the lady is Lady Windermere's disgraced mother, who has been presumed dead for over twenty years. The liaison with Windermere is solely for the purpose of reintroducing her to society, under the pseudonym of Erlynne, so that she may befriend her daughter. The plan goes awry when Lady Windermere is told of the scandal her husband has provoked and flees to the home of Lord Darlington, who is passionately in love with her. There, she is almost caught out by Darlington's unexpected return with Windermere and a party of revelling friends.

Mrs Erlynne, who has discovered Lady Windermere's flight and its cause, spirits her daughter away in order to avoid further scandal, but is herself compromised when the men see her instead. She is once more obliged to leave London, but takes with her the satisfaction of having prevented her daughter from following her into disgrace.

Lord Windermere	Mr Dumby
Lord Darlington	Mr Hopper
Lord Augustus	Parker, the Windermere's
Lorton	butler
Mr Cecil Graham	Mrs Erlynne

Lady Windermere   Mrs Cowper-Cowper
Duchess of Berwick,   Rosalie
  Lady Windermere's
  confidante
Lady Agatha Carlisle
Lady Plymdale
Lady Jedburgh
Lady Stutfield

Lady's Not For Burning, The
Christopher Fry
Comedy 3 Acts
London 1948
Wry poetic medieval tale set in the small market town of Cool Clary in 1450 where discharged soldier Thomas Mendip appears at the house of Mayor Tyson demanding to be hanged, confessing to two local murders. Meanwhile, Tyson's nephews, pompous Humphrey and crazy Nicholas, vie for lovely Alizon Ellis, betrothed to Humphrey. Then Jennet Jourdemayne is brought in, accused of witchcraft, while outside the mob bays for her to be burned at the stake. Mendip becomes more and more vociferous, claiming his lust for death springs from disillusion with human existence, but Tyson and local justice Tappercoom merely consider him a nuisance; nevertheless they try to use him to incriminate innocent Jennet.

On the night of Humphrey and Alizon's betrothal celebrations, Mendip and Jennet are allowed to mingle with the partygoers; she looks ravishing in a dress provided by Tyson's sister Margaret Devize, mother of Humphrey and Nicholas, and Jennet's ineffable sweetness persuades tipsy Tyson and Tappercoom of her innocence. Mendip reveals to Jennet that he loves her and his 'confessions' had been a ploy to save her by drawing the attention of the authorities towards himself. They leave quietly together, and Alizon rejects both brothers in favour of Tyson's young clerk Richard.

Richard   Hebble Tyson
Thomas Mendip   Jennet Jourdemayne
Alizon Ellis   The chaplain
Nicholas Devize   Edward Tappercoom
Margaret Devize   Matthew Skipps
Humphrey Devize

Lark Rise to Candleford
Keith Dewhurst
Drama 2 Plays
London 1978 and 1979
The story of Laura, aged ten (alias Flora Thompson), her childhood in the Oxfordshire village of Lark Rise in the 1880s, and her subsequent employment at fourteen at the post office-cum-smithy in the nearby village of Candleford is the narrative thread that enables two fascinating samples of bygone rural life to be celebrated as 'promenade productions', i.e. with no distinction between the stage and the auditorium.

Lark Rise takes place on the first day of harvest,

while Candleford is at a meet of the local hunt in mid-winter. Richly realistic characterizations abound of the many poor and of the few rich - the farm labourers during harvest led by 'King' Boamer; the rigorously-efficient life at the post office run by postmistress Dorcus Lane; the local gentry at the hunt; the travelling cheapjack with his crockery...all are told by Laura (Flora), with a final flash forward to her own unhappy married life, after which the whole company and audience perform the Grand Circle dance.

Laura aged ten   Polly, John Price's girl
Edmund aged eight   Landlord of pub
Emma Timms, Laura's   Algy
  mother   Mr Prideham, band singer
Albert Timms, Laura's   Rector
father   Sam
Farm labourers: Cockie
Blishie   Chad Gubbins
Bill Miller   Laura aged fourteen
Boamer   Edmund
Dick Tuffrey   Emma Timms
Pumpkin   Albert Timms
Tom Gaskin   Mrs Peverill
Old Price   Mrs Andrews
Old David, Boamer's   Landlord
father   Dorcus Lane
Mr Morris, bailiff - Old   Zillah, her maid
Monday morning   Matthew, foreman
Fisher, youth   Bill, Bavour, Soloman,
Stut   apprentice smiths
Mrs Spicer, leader of   Thomas Brown, postman
women's gang   Mrs Gubbins
Mrs Blaby   Mrs Macey
Mrs Peverill   John
Mrs Miller   Robert
Old Sally aged eighty   Mr Chitty
Dick, her husband   Sir Timothy, the Squire
Old Postie, the postman   Sir Austin
Mr Sharman, the Major   Mrs Gascoigne
Doctor   Mr Rowbotham
Carrier   Lavinia
Grandfather, Emma's   Lavinia's mother
father   Lavinia's fiancé
Queenie Macey   Huntsman
Twister, her husband,   Cinderella Doe
gamekeeper   Loony Joe
Jerry Parish, fish/fruit   Cowman Jolliffe
cart   Mr Coulsdon, the Rector
Martha Beamish aged   Mr Wilkins, the carrier
twelve   Minnie Hickman, the
Mrs Beamish   telegram girl
Squire Bracewell   Ben Trollope, old soldier
John Price, son of old   Tom Ashley
Price   Mr Cochrane, the Post
Mrs Andrews   Office Inspector
Garibaldi Jacket   John, Laura's husband
Cheapjack
Tramp

Last of the Red-hot Lovers
Neil Simon
Comedy 3 Acts
New York 1969

Middle-aged fish restauranteur Barney Cashman is a nice solid guy who has been happily married for a long time but wants an affair.

His first tryst, in his absent mother's immaculate apartment, is with Elaine, an attractive but desperate married woman. But Barney is not able to just jump into it; he needs to talk first, and talk he does, and by the time they've finished talking, to Elaine's frustration it's time to go.

Second tryst is with glamorous Bobbi, paranoid would-be starlet and complete kook who can't stop talking about her kinky friends and pathetic ambitions. She finally turns Barney on - but with pot, not sex.

Finally there's Jeanette, the chronically depressed wife of his adulterous friend Mitch, and she sinks deeper and deeper into her despair while Barney valiantly attempts to relieve her doldrums. When she leaves, untouched but hopeful, Barney at last realizes where his treasure lies - and calls loving wife Thelma to the 'love nest'.

Barney Cashman
Elaine Navizio
Bobbi Michele
Jeanette Fisher

Late Edwina Black, The
William Dinner and William Morum
Drama 3 Acts
London 1949

The death of Edwina Black, after a long illness, has left her husband Gregory free to marry his lover, Elizabeth Graham, Edwina's former housekeeper. The lovers are busily planning a long trip to Italy when they are interrupted by Detective Henry Martin with the news that Edwina's doctor is uneasy about the cause of her death, and has asked for an autopsy.

Martin's careful, polite but very thorough investigations reveal that Edwina died from arsenic poisoning. As his questions to Gregory and Elizabeth become more and more pointed, they grow suspicious of one another, until finally each accuses the other, in Martin's presence, of murder.

By the time Martin establishes that Edwina died by her own hand, with the help of her maid Ellen, all love between Gregory and Elizabeth has vanished. They are then left to live with the irony that it was precisely to cause suspicion to fall on them that Edwina had slowly poisoned herself.

Ellen
Elizabeth Graham,
  companion to the late Edwina Black
Detective Henry Martin
Gregory Black,
  Edwina Black's husband

Leaving Home
David French
Drama 2 Acts
Toronto 1972

Billy Mercer, youngest and favourite son of Jacob Mercer, a Toronto working man, is on the point of marrying his pregnant girlfriend, Kathy Jackson, mainly to escape the odium facing unmarried parents in the provincial moral atmosphere of fifties Canada.

Jacob is unaware that his eldest son, Ben, with whom he has never got on, will be leaving home to live with Billy and Kathy, in order to escape Jacob's foul temper and brittle displays of pride. As Kathy's mother, Minnie, and her boyfriend, Harold, arrive at the Mercer's home for a wedding eve celebration, Kathy informs Billy that she has miscarried, leaving him free to break off the wedding. Billy considers his course of action as the celebration turns into a serious drinking spree, during which Jacob constantly jibes at Ben, whom he accuses of being ashamed of his origins.

In exasperation with Jacob's bullying, his long suffering wife, Mary, reveals that without Ben's recent financial contributions, made to her in secret, the family would long have gone bankrupt, and that Ben, too, is leaving home.

Although Jacob, stunned at the prospect of losing both his sons, tries to talk Ben into staying, Mary realizes that it is time for both boys to make their own way. Billy presses on with his marriage, Ben departs, and Mary is left alone with Jacob.

Mary Mercer
Ben Mercer
Billy Mercer
Jacob Mercer
Kathy Jackson
Minnie Jackson
Harold

Lesson, The
Eugene Ionesco
Comedy 1 Act
Paris 1951

A young girl of eighteen arrives for private tuition at the home of a dapper, apparently ineffectual professor, who is in late middle-age. The girl is at first able to dominate the professor with her youth and energy, but gradually, during the course of his incoherent lessons on arithmetic and linguistics, he assumes control of their meeting.

As he rambles deeper and deeper into his wild linguistic theories, the girl develops a raging toothache, which the professor ignores. When his sense of power is at its height, the professor, in the middle of a tirade on the meaning of the word 'knife', stabs and kills his pupil. In a panic, he calls his maid Marie, who scolds him for the murder and reveals that the girl is the professor's fortieth victim during that day alone.

While the professor and Marie prepare to put the

pupil's body in a coffin, another youngster arrives at the door for yet another lesson.

The professor
The girl pupil
Marie

Let's Get a Divorce
Angela and Robert Goldsby
Comedy 3 Acts
London 1966

At the home of Henri des Prunelles in a provincial town in France, everyone, including servants Josepha and Bastien, is abuzz with anticipation of the result of the vote on the new divorce laws. The various discussions take place between Henri, his wife Cyprienne, his friend M. Clavignac, and family friends Mme de Brionne and M. Bafourdin, the only one whose marriage appears to be content. Cyprienne has a special interest - she is infatuated with Adhemar, Henri's younger cousin. She doesn't want to commit adultery, so divorce is the obvious answer.

Adhemar produces a forged telegram saying the bill has been passed, and Henri, now in the know, magnanimously 'gives' his wife to Adhemar, wishing them all the luck in the world. Cyprienne is a bit disconcerted by this and is cunningly manoeuvred by Henri into a tête-à-tête meal where Adhemar arrives in pursuit of her; she hides and overhears some not very flattering remarks about herself. Soon she has changed her mind and now finds Henri wonderful again and becomes contemptuous of poor Adhemar who almost gets arrested as he pesters the couple.

Josepha
Bastien
Henri de Prunelles
M. Clavignac
Cyprienne
M. Bafourdin
Estelle de Brionne
Adhemar de Gratignan
Clarissa de Valfontaine
Joseph, the head waiter
Hercules, an elderly waiter
The police officer
The policeman

Letter from the General, A
Maurice McLoughlin
Drama 3 Acts
Edinburgh 1961

A community of teaching nuns in a Far Eastern country recently taken over by communist revolutionaries prepares to return to England, rightly assuming they will not be welcome under the new regime. Their confessor, Father Schiller, has escaped from a communist prison after torture, and comes to the nuns for refuge.

The oldest of the nuns, Sister Magdalen, was once

guardian to the communist's general, Mei Cheng, so when he suspects that Schiller will make his way to the community, the general is relatively restrained in only surrounding it with a detachment of men under Capt. Lee, an English convert to the communist cause. Suspecting that Schiller is already in the compound, Lee searches vainly for his quarry.

Sister Magdalen, realizing that Schiller will only be able to escape if he takes the place, in appropriate disguise, of one of the nuns, feigns receiving a request from Cheng to stay behind and establish an orphanage. The nuns administer a strong sedative to Lee and make their escape with Schiller in nun's habit. Sister Magdalen stays behind to face Cheng's inevitable revenge.

Sister Henry
Sister Lucy
Sister Bridget
Revd Mother
Sister Magdalen
Arthur Stilton, the British Consul
Ruth Stilton, Stilton's wife
Capt. Lee
Father Schiller

Liaisons Dangereuses, Les
Christopher Hampton based on the novel by
Choderlos de Laclos
Drama 2 Acts
London 1986

Two cynical sensualists, the Marquise de Merteuil and her ex-lover the Viscomte de Valmont, plot together to avenge a mutual slight they have received from M. de Gercount who has just ended an affair with the Marquise in order to run off with Valmont's current lover.

They agree that Valmont shall seduce de Gercount's virgin fiancée, Cécile, to spoil her for their enemy. But Valmont also decides he must have Mme de Tourvel, a married woman noted for the purity of her morals. The Marquise offers Valmont a night of uninhibited love should he succeed in both conquests, but he is unaware that she wants Cécile to be seduced so that her own current lover, M. Danceny, who is also a suitor to Cécile, will throw the young woman over.

Valmont succeeds so well with Cécile that he makes her pregnant, but his progress with Mme de Tourvel is much slower, partly because he has very reluctantly fallen in love with her. When, eventually, he is able to seduce her, Valmont is so infatuated and so repelled by the tenderness he feels that he breaks with her in a particularly brutal manner. Mme de Tourvel retires to a convent, where she wastes slowly away in a fever of unrequited love and regret.

Part of Valmont's bargain with the Marquise is that she must drop her current lover once Valmont has succeeded with his seductions. When she refuses, and reveals that her lover is, in fact, Danceny, their alliance turns to bitter enmity and the Marquise provokes a duel between Valmont and the younger man. Full of self-loathing for his treatment of Mme de Tourvel, Valmont purposely leaves his guard down and is killed by a sword thrust to the heart. In his death throes he asks Danceny to relay to Mme de Tourvel the message that she was the only true love of his life. Hearing the message, she dies happily, and the Marquise is left to gloat over the fullness of her victory over Valmont.

Major domo

Marquise de Merteuil

Mme de Volanges

Cécile Volanges

Viscomte de Valmont

Azolan

La Présidente de Tourvel

Mme de Rosemonde

Emilie

Chevalier Danceny

Liars, The
Henry Arthur Jones
Comedy 4 Acts
London 1897

A British diplomat, Edward Falkner, with a reputation for complete probity, falls hopelessly in love with a married woman, Lady Jessica Nepean, and in so doing is in danger of social ostracism from his upper class 'set' in the England of the 1890s. Lady Jessica, bored by her husband's disinterest in her, flirts with Falkner just enough to maintain his interest.

Falkner's friend and colleague, Col Sir Christopher Deering, repeatedly warns the diplomat of the danger in courting Lady Jessica, but he persists, even more indiscreetly, until her husband discovers the liaison.

To save the situation, Deering persuades her husband to forgive Lady Jessica, just manages to convince her to renounce Falkner, and sets out with the chastened diplomat to fight the slave trade in Africa.

Col Sir Christopher Deering

Edward Falkner

Gilbert Nepean, Lady Jessica's husband

George Nepean, Gilbert's brother

Freddie Tatton

Archibald Coke

Waiter

Gadsby

Taplin, Sir Christopher's servant

Footman

Lady Jessica Nepean

Lady Rosamund Tatton, Lady Jessica's sister

Dolly Coke

Beatrice Ebernoe

Mrs Crespin

Ferris

Liberty Hall
R. C. Carton
Drama 4 Acts
London 1892

The death of their father forces Blanche and Amy Chilworth to abandon their ancestral home in favour of the heir to their father's baronetcy, a distant cousin called Hartley, now Sir Hartley Chilworth. Worse for the girls, their father has left them virtually penniless,

and they are obliged, in Blanche's case haughtily, to live on the hospitality of their uncle, William Todman, a hapless Bloomsbury bookseller who is himself ruinously in debt. They leave their home even though Sir Hartley, a reputed eccentric, sends a Mr Owen, a commercial traveller who met the new baronet while they were both travelling in Turkey, to inform the girls that they are welcome to remain, and that Sir Hartley will be travelling indefinitely in the Himalayas.

The girls install themselves in Todman's rambling home to find that Owen has become a lodger there as well. Though Owen shows a strong interest in Blanche, he is rebuffed and falls from her grace altogether when she finds Owen apparently trying to seduce Amy. In fact, Owen has been trying to persuade Amy not to elope with her lover, Hon. Gerald Harringay, but to marry with family consent, and has sworn to keep Amy's secret.

Believing he has lost Blanche, Owen, with great kindness, writes out a cheque to cover old Todman's debts and prepares to depart. It is then we discover that Owen is, in fact, Sir Hartley, working in disguise because he did not wish Blanche to love him for his new status. When this comes out, though, Blanche has already softened, having been told by Amy of Chilworth/Owen's loyalty, and the two are able to marry for both love and money.

Blanche Chilworth

Amy Chilworth

Mr Owen (Sir Hartley Chilworth)

Hon. Gerald Harringay

William Todman

J. Briginshaw

Mr Pedrick

Mr Hickson

Miss Hickson

Robert Binks

Crafer

Luscombe, Todman's servant

Lie of the Mind, A
Sam Shepard
Drama 3 Acts
New York 1985

Two 'ordinary' American families, spiritually impoverished and internally alienated, are revealed, and their tragic backgrounds examined, in the aftermath of psychopathic Jake beating up and almost killing wife Beth, jealous that her theatrical career is masking infidelity. Jake gets a fever and is 'nursed' by his concerned brother Frankie, his sister Sally and their coarse and bitter mother Lorraine. Brain-damaged Beth goes back with protective tough brother Mike to the home of their parents Baylor and Meg; he's obsessed with hunting, she's dozy and over-protective. Jake is convinced Beth is dead, so Frankie goes to find out what happened but is shot in the leg by Baylor. Mike tracks down Jake and humiliatingly brings him to Beth.

The pair are still 'in love', but Beth has got it into her damaged head that she's going to marry Frankie. She and Jake kiss goodbye and he leaves, amidst injured Frankie's protests. Baylor and Meg carefully fold an American flag that Mike used to bring Jake over, and ignore everything else. They kiss for the first time in twenty years.

Jake	Lorraine
Frankie	Sally
Beth	Baylor
Mike	Meg

Life of Galileo
Bertolt Brecht
History Play 15 Scenes
Berlin 1955

In several versions of this play Brecht gradually modified Galileo's character so that a fairly straightforward anti-hero of science became a complex genius compromised in both his moral and political life.

We are introduced to Galileo in his study teaching his landlady's young son Copernicus' theory of the heavens in an atmosphere more of a painter's studio than a modern laboratory. Beset by financial problems, arising from the meagre stipend he is granted for lecturing at the University of Padua, Galileo unscrupulously copies, and sells as his own invention, a Dutch telescope he is shown. The instrument also allows him to make observations which confirm Copernicus' heliocentric astronomy. Continuing poverty, however, obliges him to leave the intellectual freedom of Venice for the financial rewards of a position as court mathematician to the Duke of Florence.

When he proves that the heliocentric theory is true, the Papal College admits he is right but forbid publication of his findings. For eight years Galileo obeys their injunction to preserve his comforts but eventually publishes when a new, scientifically-trained Pope is elected. He is nonetheless arrested by the Inquisition and repudiates his teachings under threat of torture. Four years later he manages to smuggle a copy of his *Discorsi* to Holland where it can be published without fear of the Inquisition.

Galileo Galilei	Father Christopher
Andrea Sarti, his	Cosimo de Medici, Grand
helper	Duke of Florence
Mrs Sarti, Galileo's	Cardinal Barberi
landlady	Theologians
Ludovico Marsili, a	Philosophers
rich student	Clerics
Sagredo, Galileo's	Monks
friend	Scholars
Virginia, Galileo's	Officials
daughter	Servants
Federzoni, Galileo's	
assistant	
The Doge of Venice	
Clavius, an astronomer	

Life with Father
Howard Lindsay and Russel Crouse
Comedy 3 Acts
New York 1939

In his Madison Avenue residence in the late 1880s Clarence Day Senr blows hot and cold about everything; politics, the state of the household, the servants, and his expenditure.

His clever and affectionate wife, Vinnie, has to deal with his changing moods as she tries vainly to get him to contribute to her church funds, but he shocks her by revealing that he was never baptized thus throwing the validity of their marriage into question.

The eldest of their four sons has fallen in love and father lectures him about women whom he little understands. When, however, Vinnie falls ill due to a slip-up with some patent medicine that her son is selling to make some money, Clarence becomes deeply concerned about her welfare even to the point of promising to be baptized.

Later, he of course changes his mind, claiming the credit for Vinnie's recovery, but she has carefully laid plans to bring her erratic, but lovable, husband together with God.

Annie	Mary
Clarence Day Senr	Revd Dr Lloyd
Vinnie Day	Delia
Their sons: Clarence,	Nora
John, Whitney, Harlan	Dr Humphreys
Margaret	Dr Somers
Cora	Maggie

Lightnin'
Winchell Smith and Frank Bacon
Comedy 3 Acts
New York 1918

Name any vocation and old Lightnin' Bill Jones will have had a career in it; lawyer, engineer, soldier and now hotel keeper at Lake Tahoe on the California/Nevada border.

A young friend of the amiable braggart is John Marvin who is being swindled out of property by shyster lawyer Raymond Thomas and his confederate Hammond, and Lightnin' and John join forces when the hotel comes under threat too.

Thomas, using both legal and underhand methods, manages to involve Lightnin's wife in his schemes and gets her to sue him for divorce to gain control of the hotel. The old campaigner has a few tricks up his sleeve and he exposes the fraudulent Thomas after defending himself in court. His wife returns to him begging forgiveness and he even manipulates his daughter, Mildred, into marrying young Marvin.

Lightnin' Bill Jones	Everett Hammond
John Marvin	Sheriff Nevin Blodgett
Raymond Thomas	Oscar Nelson
Lemuel Townsend	Fred Peters
Rodney Harper	Walter Lennon

Zeb Crothers
Liveryman
Hotel clerk
Mildred Buckley
Mrs Jones
Mrs Margaret Davis
Mrs Harper
Freeda

Emily Jarvis
Mrs Moore
Mrs Jordan
Mrs Brainerd
Mrs Starr
Mrs Corshall
Mrs Brewer

Liliom
Ferenc Molnár
Legend 7 Scenes
New York 1921

Liliom, an amusement park barker in Budapest, marries Julie, although he cannot make enough money to keep her comfortably and sometimes beats her. He becomes desperate when his baby girl is born and attempts a bank robbery in which he is mortally wounded. Called to judgement in Heaven, Liliom defiantly defends his life on earth and is sentenced to sixteen years in Hell after which he is granted one day on earth to do 'something good' for his daughter Louise to prove that his soul has been purified.

Julie fails to recognize the 'tramp' Liliom who comes to her little house and relates to Louise that he used to know her father, who was a bully and used to beat her mother. Sweet Julie denies this vigorously and defends Liliom's memory. When Liliom offers his little girl a star he stole from Heaven she tells him to leave and he slaps her hand, but it does not hurt her. Liliom returns to his fate and Louise asks her mother how a slap cannot hurt; Julie explains 'someone may beat you, ... and beat you and not hurt you at all'.

Marie
Julie
Mrs Muskat
Liliom
Four servant girls
Policemen
Captain
Plainclothes man
Mother Hollunder
Ficsur 'The Sparrow'
Wolf Beifeld
Young Hollunder
Linzman

Two mounted policemen
Doctor
Carpenter
Two policemen of the
 beyond
Richly dressed man
Poorly dressed man
Old guard
Magistrate
Louise
Peasants
Townspeople

Linden Tree, The
J. B. Priestley
Drama 2 Acts
London 1947

The grown children of Professor Robert Linden and Isabel, his wife, return to the family home in Burmanley, a drab provincial university town, to celebrate their father's sixty-fifth birthday. The Professor's son Rex, who calls himself a city spiv, and his daughters Jean, a doctor, and Marion, living in France with her husband René de Vaury, have agreed to help Isabel persuade her husband to retire and leave Burmanley, which she hates for its grey post-war austerity.

Once they are assembled, the members of the family all fall into the behaviour that was habitual when they lived together. Jean, a dedicated, humourless left-winger, argues incessantly with Marion, whose life with the French Catholic gentry appals her, while Rex, who became a cynic during the war, tries to divert their attention into shallow amusements, his chosen refuge from life's difficulties. The Professor himself quickly assumes his former role as peacekeeper and confidant to the whole family, aided only by Dinah, at seventeen his youngest child, and by far the most sensitive.

Isabel, who has plotted with the Professor's old friend, Alfred Lockhart, the university secretary, to force her husband into retirement, is aghast when he refuses not only family advice, but also the opportunity to retire gracefully, and vows to resist all efforts to get him to abandon his passionate love of teaching history. To force his hand, Isabel decides to leave Burmanley and move into Rex's newly acquired country estate, but the old man digs in his heels and remains behind with Dinah and the housekeeper, Mrs Cotton.

Professor Robert Linden
Isabel Linden, his wife
Rex Linden, his son
Dr Jean Linden, his eldest daughter
Marion de Vaury, his daughter
Dinah Linden, his youngest daughter
Alfred Lockhart
Edith Westmore
Bernard Fawcett
Mrs Cotton

Lion in Winter, The
James Goldman
Comedy 2 Acts
New York 1966

Intrigue abounds at Henry II's castle at Chinon in France as the Plantagenets gather for Christmas 1183. Ageing but still-strong Henry has imprisoned his wife Eleanor (of Aquitaine) for treason, but she is out on parole for the festivities, and together and apart they plot and scheme for the succession; she favours strong son Richard, he favours weaker younger son John. Neither favours clever son Geoffrey whose allegiances and betrayals fly thick and fast. Also at Chinon are Henry's attractive and wise mistress, twenty-three-year-old French princess Alais (whom Henry wants Richard to wed), and seventeen-year-old King Philip of France, on his way to becoming a great monarch.

As the individual characters and relationships are explored in depth, the skirmishes increase to boiling point until Henry, fed up with his squabbling and treacherous sons, threatens to annul his marriage, wed Alais and beget a fresh dynasty. The three sons, helped by Eleanor, half-heartedly plot to kill him, but at the vital moment no one can strike the blow.

The great love of Henry and Eleanor has been buried beneath the weight of their individual embodiment of land and power, and submerged under bitter recriminations of emotional and political betrayal. Occasionally their love - or their memory of it - breaks through and affects each deeply until once again it gets buried beneath the tide of immediate political necessity. Eleanor goes back to prison in England and the family will meet again at Easter.

Henry II
Alais
John
Geoffrey
Richard 'Lionheart'
Eleanor
Philip

Little Eyolf
Henrik Ibsen
Drama 3 Acts
Berlin 1895

Wealthy man of letters, Alfred Allmers has been on a six-week hiking holiday, his first break in ten years from possessive wife Rita, and he returns home a changed man. Gone is his obsession with his Great Work, his book *The Responsibility of Man*, and he is now determined to remedy his neglect of crippled son Eyolf. Also there to greet him is his attractive half-sister Asta, a teacher who helps the couple with Eyolf. They are disconcerted by the arrival of local pest controller the Rat Wife, a weird old crone who, with dog Mopsemand, mesmerizes rats and leads them to be drowned. Rita becomes jealous of Eyolf's place in Allmers' affections, but soon after, the boy is drowned.

Guilt and recriminations fly thick and fast, and Allmers later finds some solace with Asta, reminiscing about their close and happy childhood when she would wear boy's clothes and he called her Eyolf. Asta is being pursued by solid engineer Borghejm, but although she likes him she cannot bring herself to marry him because of her affection for Allmers. Later she tells Allmers that she has found letters from her late mother which reveal that they are not brother and sister.

Now Eyolf is dead, Asta decides to leave, but Rita and Allmers beg her to stay and 'be their Eyolf'. She shrinks away and decides to leave with Borghejm. Rita and Allmers are left alone together with their 'gnawing consciences' (for neither of them truly loved little Eyolf), and they make plans to try to fill the void left by little Eyolf and big Eyolf.

Alfred Allmers
Rita
Eyolf
Asta Allmers
Borghejm
The Rat Wife

Little Foxes
Lillian Hellman
Drama 3 Acts
New York 1939

At the turn of the century, the Hubbards, a Southern business family, are determined to make a fortune by any means, fair or foul. Brothers Ben and Oscar and sister Regina are just concluding a big deal to build a cotton mill and discuss how to divide up the spoils. Regina's husband, Horace Giddens, a sick man, has a share in the business, but is not keen to get involved with the Hubbards whose attitudes he despises. The avaricious Regina is using his capital to her advantage and wants her daughter to marry Oscar's son, Leo, who works in Horace's bank. The boy has discovered that Horace's deposit box contains 88,000 dollars in negotiable bonds and Ben convinces him to 'borrow' it to conclude the deal.

When Horace discovers the theft, Regina sees it as a way of blackmailing more money out of her brothers and she precipitates her husband's death by withholding his medicine. She looks forward to a fortune, but has now lost the only love she ever had, that of her daughter.

Addie	*Regina Giddens*
Cal	*William Marshall*
Birdie Hubbard	*Benjamin Hubbard*
Oscar Hubbard	*Alexander Giddens*
Leo Hubbard	*Horace Giddens*

Little Hut, The
André Roussin and Nancy Mitford
Comedy 3 Acts
New York 1953

A married couple, Philip and Susan, have drifted ashore on a desert island, along with their closest friend, Henry, following the wreck of their cruise ship. Susan and Henry have for six years past been having a carefully concealed affair, but in the claustrophobic proximity of the island, Henry has been the odd man out for the three weeks since the wreck.

Unable to tolerate his enforced abstinence, Henry reveals the affair to Philip and they agree to share Susan by spending alternate weeks with her. The arrangement works brilliantly for Susan and Philip, but their easy contentment plunges Henry deep into jealousy. He approaches Philip again to suggest that they both live apart from Susan until rescuers arrive.

Their discussion is cut short by the arrival of an athletic, armed stranger who traps the two men in a net and then obliges Susan, who is not conspicuously unwilling, to make love to him. Her complicity further depresses Henry, who complains bitterly to Philip.

The stranger turns out to be the cook from their own cruise ship, and not the native Prince Susan imagined him to be. She traps him, in turn, and he is put to work as their servant. His very presence rankles Henry, whose carping only ceases when a ship arrives to rescue them all.

A chastened Henry makes Susan promise that, once rescued, they will feign a parting but resume their affair in utmost secrecy.

Henry	A stranger
Susan	The monkey
Philip, Susan's husband	

Little Mary Sunshine
Rick Besoyan
Musical 2 Acts
New York 1960

Mary Sunshine, proprietress of the Colorado Inn high in the Rocky Mountains at the turn of the century, faces eviction because the US government has ruled that her hotel is on federal land. As she is considering how to handle this crisis, her beau, Capt. 'Big Jim' Warrington of the Forest Rangers, arrives at the inn with a troop of his men. It is Big Jim's job to apprehend Yellow Feather, a renegade Indian and enemy of Mary's, who was raised by Yellow Feather's noble father Chief Brown Bear. She begs Big Jim not to let the old man discover that Yellow Feather is still alive, in order to spare the Chief from shame.

The Chief takes a strong liking to Big Jim's second-in-command, Cpl Billy Jester, dresses him in Yellow Feather's own clothing, and adopts him as his son. Unfortunately, though, Big Jim himself, along with Mary, who wishes to help capture the renegade, have both also disguised themselves as Yellow Feather. The three bogus Yellow Feathers meet the real one in the forest and almost confuse him into being captured, but the Indian sees through their plot just in time to capture Mary and tie her to a tree while he goes in search of his other would-be captors.

At the last gasp, Big Jim saves Mary and leads the capture of Yellow Feather. Mary's eviction is avoided when word arrives that the government have ceded the disputed land to Chief Brown Bear, who immediately grants Mary the right of occupation.

Chief Brown Bear,	Young ladies of
Mary's adoptive father	Eastchester Finishing
Cpl Billy Jester	School: Cora, Henrietta,
Capt. 'Big Jim'	Millicent, Mabel, Maud,
Warrington, Mary's	Gwendolyn and Blanche
beau	Nancy Twinkle, Mary's
Forest Rangers: Pete,	maid
Tex, Tom, Hank, Chuck,	Fleet Foot
Buster and Slim	Yellow Feather, Chief
Little Mary Sunshine	Brown Bear's son
Mme Ernestine Liebedich	Gen. Oscar Fairfax

Little Shop of Horrors
Howard Ashman and Alan Menken
Musical 2 Acts
New York 1982

Seymour has been in love for some time, rather hopelessly, with Audrey, his fellow clerk in Mushnik's Skid Row Florists, while she has been having a forlorn affair with Orin, a sadistic, motorcycle-crazy dentist. Business is so bad on Skid Row that Mr Mushnik, owner of the shop and Seymour's guardian, decides to close down. As Mushnik, Audrey and Seymour set about shutting up shop for the last time, a customer arrives, attracted by the look of a large plant, which Seymour calls Audrey Two, in honour of his great love. The plant is a sort of giant Venus Flytrap which Seymour purchased from a mysterious Chinese, and has been gently tending for several weeks. The customer purchases a hundred dollars' worth of roses but, more important, his admiration of the Audrey Two gives Mr Mushnik an idea. He contacts the Skid Row *Daily News* with the story of the strange plant, and within days Seymour is swamped with interviews and promotional offers, as well as a request from *Life* magazine to appear on its cover.

Meanwhile, though, Seymour has discovered that Audrey Two can only thrive on human blood and flesh. He feeds her from cuts he inflicts on himself, until he is on the verge of collapse. Then he decides to kill the odious Orin to provide the starving plant with a proper meal. Audrey Two thrives, Audrey herself sees Seymour in a new light and becomes his lover, but the plant, now several feet tall, is insatiable.

In his desire to keep Seymour's success on his own side, Mr Mushnik adopts the young man, but discovers that his ward has been involved in Orin's death. Seymour is obliged to get rid of Mushnik, so Audrey Two gets her second proper meal. Unfortunately, though, Audrey herself becomes the next victim of the plant's voracious hunger, and then Seymour is eaten trying to avenge her death by attacking Audrey Two with a machete.

As the play ends, the plant, now monstrous in size, moves on the audience, intent on world domination.

Chiffon	Derelict
Crystal	Orin, Audrey's lover
Ronette	Bernstein
Mushnik, florist owner	Snip
Audrey, his clerk	Luce
Seymour, a second clerk	Audrey Two

Living Room, The
Graham Greene
Drama 2 Acts
London 1953

Rose Pemberton, a recently orphaned young woman, arrives at the Holland Park home of her ageing aunts Teresa and Helen Browne, and of her uncle Father James Browne, a priest confined for many years to a wheelchair. She is in the company of Michael Dennis, a middle-aged family friend and the executor of her late mother's estate, with whom she has been having an affair. The three old people, all devout Catholics, are so much in the grip of fear of death that they have permanently locked every room in the house in which someone has, in the past, died. So few rooms are left open that a third floor bedroom is now the sitting room.

When the affair between Rose and Michael is revealed, both Rose's aunts are scandalized, not just because he is a Protestant, but because he is married. Father Browne, all too aware of the lack of compassion in the Church, tries to reason with the two young people, undermined all the while by Helen's attempts to play on Rose's guilt. Helen even goes so far as to provoke an attack of angina in Teresa, who suffers chronic heart trouble, hoping to force Rose to stay on and care for the old woman, rather than eloping with Michael.

Matters come to a head when Michael's wife discovers the affair, descends on the Browne home and makes an hysterical attempt at suicide by trying to swallow a bottle of pills, with Rose as her audience. Rose prevents her, but despairing of ever being more than Michael's lover, takes the pills herself and dies.

Teresa, brought to her senses by Rose's death, defies the tradition of years and insists on taking up residence in the room where her niece has died.

Mary	*Miss Helen Browne*
Michael Dennis	*Father James Browne*
Rose Pemberton	*Mrs Dennis*
Miss Teresa Browne	

Living Together (The Norman Conquests, Part I)
Alan Ayckbourn
Comedy 2 Acts
Scarborough 1973
See: *Round and Round the Garden; Table Manners*
One of *The Norman Conquests* trilogy in which the events during a single weekend, with the same set of characters, are viewed in a different setting in each play. *Living Together* is set in a sitting-room.

Annie lives alone with her invalid mother, for whom she acts as a nurse, in a rambling Victorian house. Her brother Reg, sister-in-law Sarah, and brother-in-law Norman all descend on Annie for a weekend which is meant to give her a respite from the daily nursing grind. All the visitors antagonize one another, and Annie's local boyfriend Tom, so much that the weekend becomes a perpetual conflict.

Annie has asked her family to stay so that she and Norman, with whom she is having an affair, can escape to the seaside for a while, but she loses her courage and decides to stay at home instead. A disgruntled Norman gets drunk and reveals all about the affair which leads Sarah, a busybody, to inform Norman's wife Ruth of his conduct; she also attacks Annie for her morals, mostly because she fancies Norman herself.

Unfortunately for both of the ladies, Ruth is unruffled by Norman's ways and ends up bedded down with him when she arrives in response to Sarah's call. As the weekend draws to a close the couples prepare to leave, and Sarah hopes Norman will ask her away next time.

Norman	*Annie*
Sarah	*Reg*
Tom	*Ruth*

Lloyd George Knew My Father
William Douglas Home
Drama 2 Acts
Boston, Lancs 1972
A dotty but very determined aristocrat, Lady Sheila Boothroyd, is outraged by a government plan to build a by-pass through the land surrounding her family's ancestral home. Even the intervention of her son, Hubert Boothroyd MP, with his colleagues in the government, fails to halt the plan, so Lady Boothroyd announces to the family that she will commit suicide the moment work on the by-pass commences.

With the help of her granddaughter Sally's boyfriend, reporter Simon Green, Lady Boothroyd publicizes her intentions by giving a number of press and television interviews, in the hope of embarrassing the government. When this too fails, she retires to bed on the evening before construction is due to start, after saying a brusque but heartfelt goodbye to her relatives.

In the morning, her door is found to be locked, and the family assume fearfully that she has indeed done away with herself. Her equally dotty husband, Gen. Sir William Boothroyd, has Robertson, the family butler and the General's former batman, play a halting version of the last post. But just as this odd tribute finishes, Lady Boothroyd appears for breakfast, saying she has been unable to carry out her intentions because she cannot bear the idea of separation from the General.

Gen. Sir William Boothroyd
Lady Sheila Boothroyd, the General's wife
Maud Boothroyd, their daughter-in-law
Sally Boothroyd, their granddaughter
Simon Green, Sally's boyfriend
Revd Trevor Simmonds
Robertson
Hubert Boothroyd MP

Lock Up Your Daughters
Bernard Miles
Music by Laurie Johnson
Lyrics by Lionel Bart
Musical 2 Acts
London 1959
Based on Henry Fielding's *Rape Upon Rape* (1730), the musical follows the fortunes of two sets of lovers, Capt. Constant and Capt. Hilaret, and Ramble and Cloris, Hilaret's maid.

Ramble, who believes that Cloris is dead, has come to London from the West Indies to drink and wench himself into forgetting her loss. On leaving a pub where he has been carousing he encounters Hilaret, who has been separated from Cloris by a public brawl, and attempts to ravish her in the mistaken belief that she is a streetwalker. He is arrested and taken before Squeezum, a corrupt justice, who tries to use Hilaret's accusation to wring a bribe out of Ramble. Hilaret, who was in fact on her way to elope with Constant, refuses to make a charge, Squeezum decides to seduce her by way of compensating himself.

Cloris, meanwhile, has been rescued from the brawl by Constant, but he too has been arrested for rape by Squeezum's agents who, anxious to extort money for their master, claim the rescue was a bawdy assault.

When Ramble is brought to the cell in which Constant is being held, the two greet each other effusively, having been friends years before. Ramble is rescued from his plight by Squeezum's lascivious and domineering wife, who arranges his release in return for his sexual attentions. Meanwhile, Hilaret has kept an assignation with the lecherous Squeezum, at which she arranges to be seen by a hidden friend, and witness. On the point of losing her virginity Hilaret cries out that she is being raped, and her witness steps forward.

But Hilaret's plan misfires when the justice pretends that he is the victim of a plot to discredit him, and Hilaret is committed for trial. She is saved at the last minute when Squeezum's wife produces his letter inviting Hilaret to their tryst. A happy resolution is reached when Squeezum is arrested, Hilaret and Constant are reunited, and Ramble discovers Cloris, the lover he thought was dead.

Songs include: 'A Proper Man'; 'Red Wine and a Wench'; 'When Does the Ravishing Begin?'

Staff, a constable	*Capt. Hilaret,*
A gentleman	*Constant's fiancé*
Watchman	*Cloris, Hilaret's maid*
Squeezum, a corrupt	*Dabble*
justice	*Faithful*
Sotmore	*Worthy*
Ramble	*Capt. Constant*
Brazencourt, an	*A servant*
innkeeper	
A wench	
Politic	

Long and the Short and the Tall, The
Willis Hall
Drama 2 Acts
Nottingham 1958

A seven-man British army patrol is lost in the Malayan jungle and unable to contact their base by radio. They come upon a crude jungle hut and take refuge in it for the night, while frantically trying to get through on their home frequency. During the night, a Japanese soldier, out alone having a covert cigarette, wanders into the hut and they take him prisoner. They realize they are very near the Japanese lines, send out a patrol and discover that there is a Japanese advance going on around them.

At first, they intend to take the prisoner back to base for interrogation, but the need for utter quiet persuades the brutal leader of the patrol, Sgt Mitcham, supported by his Corporal, Johnstone, to decide to murder their captive. L/Cpl MacLeish starts by opposing the plan, but gives in when the prisoner is found to have British issue cigarettes and a British cigarette case, suggesting that the Japanese had stolen them from British colleagues

elsewhere. This leaves Pte Bamforth, a rebellious, aggressive Cockney, as the only voice of opposition to the prisoner's death.

Just as Mitcham and Johnstone close in on Bamforth to disarm him, Pte Whitaker accidentally shoots the prisoner, whom he has been guarding, and the noise from his gun alerts the surrounding Japanese forces.

Sgt Mitcham
Cpl Johnstone
L/Cpl MacLeish
Pte Whitaker
Pte Evans
Pte Bamforth
Pte Smith
A Japanese soldier

Long Day's Journey into Night
Eugene O'Neill
Tragedy 4 Acts
New York 1956

In Connecticut in 1912, James Tyrone, a rich semi-retired actor, rules his family with a combination of extreme miserliness and grandiose self-obsession. These qualities have so undermined his wife Mary's sense of worth that she is gripped by a deepening neurosis along with alcoholism, both of which James simply ignores.

Jamie, their eldest son, is also sliding into a drink problem, and he becomes ever more resentful of his father's insensitivity. His younger brother Edmund, who has just come back after years at sea, is clearly dying of consumption, but their father is too proud to accept Edmund's condition and too mean to send him to a proper sanatorium, thus provoking Jamie to even further bouts of drunkenness.

James regards each new demonstration of Edmund's worsening condition with blithe disbelief, until Mary finally declines into total madness.

James Tyrone
Mary Cavan Tyrone
James (Jamie) Tyrone Jr
Edmund Tyrone
Cathleen

Long March to Jerusalem, A
Don Taylor
Drama 2 Acts
Watford 1977

The ill-fated Children's Crusade to Jerusalem (1212-13) forms the subject of this play designed for performance by school drama groups.

An ageing monk who had joined the Children's Crusade as a youth recounts the harrowing detail of his adventures on the long march from Paris to eventual captivity in Cairo. The early enthusiasm of the child crusaders is gradually worn away, during their march from Paris to Marseilles, by the political in-fighting of two rival groups who both wish to wrest control of the venture from Stephen, the devout boy whose visions inspired them all to action.

When Stephen's prayers that the sea should part to allow them passage go unanswered, two unscrupulous traders lure the youthful horde onto a fleet of ships with the promise of free passage to Jerusalem. Instead, the children who survive the crossing to Algiers are sold into slavery, and disperse with their new masters. Some of their number escape and march on to Cairo where they are forced into the service of Al-Kamil, son of the Governor of Cairo. It is one of these few who is eventually allowed to return to Europe, with news of the fate of the Crusade, and becomes the monk who narrates its history.

Children:	Adults:
Jackyboy	*The monk*
Boneyard	*A birdcatcher*
Beanpole	*King of France*
Princess	*The Archbishop*
Grizzle	*Lord Marshall*
Cleopatra	*Papal Legate*
Stephen	*An old man*
Sally Blackbird	*Guard Commander*
Troubadour	*The Mayor*
Clorinda	*William the Pig*
Cicero	*Hugh the Iron*
Big Warm Mavis	*A corporal*
One Leg	*Slave master*
Liz-from-London	*Al-Kamil*
Ranulf	*An old woman*
Eleanor	*Crusaders*
Clovis	*Soldiers*
Redhair	*Townspeople*
Guy	
A piper	
Geoffrey	
A drummer	
Jackdaw	
Pigface	
Ralph	
Ragbag	

Long Voyage Home, The
Eugene O'Neill
Drama 1 Act
New York 1921

Four tough merchant seamen, Olson, Driscoll, Cocky and Ivan arrive at a rough Docklands pub to celebrate the completion of a tour of duty. All but Olson, who wishes to stay sober, are soon so drunk that one of them, Ivan, slides into a stupor and has to be helped back to his lodgings by Driscoll and Cocky.

Olson stays in the pub to wait for Driscoll and Cocky to return, and the pub's landlord sends one of his barmaids, Freda, to engage Olson in conversation. Freda discovers that Olson has foregone drink in fear that, once he starts, he is likely to go too far, and thus disrupt his plan to quit the sea, return to his native Sweden, and put the wages he has saved for two years

into a small farm. Fat Joe, the landlord, has other plans. He has been offered a bribe by the Captain of a near derelict ship to provide a crewman for a gruelling trip around the Horn of Africa. Using Freda as cover, Fat Joe spikes Olson's ginger beer with a sleeping draught, robs him of his savings, and when he falls unconscious, turns him over to the Captain who had offered the bribe. Olson is dragged off to his fate just before Driscoll and Cocky, who might have saved him, come back to continue their binge.

Fat Joe, a publican
Nick
Mag, a barmaid
Olson, Driscoll, Cocky and Ivan
Kate and Freda, barmaids and tarts
Two roughs

Look Back in Anger
John Osborne
Drama 3 Acts
London 1956

In a dreary Midland town of the fifties, Jimmy Porter and his long suffering wife, Alison, share their tiny flat with Jimmy's mate and business partner, Cliff Lewis.

Bitter and resentful of the social system, Jimmy, a college graduate who runs a market stall and plays amateur trumpet, constantly taunts his upper-class wife and her family. Cliff acts as a buffer to the pair and when she becomes pregnant he helps keep Alison's secret, fearing Jimmy's response.

Helena, an actress friend of Alison's, arrives to stay; Jimmy detests her and insults both women when they want to go to church. While Jimmy goes to visit a sick friend, Helena brings Alison's father to take her away from this destructive situation. When he returns, Jimmy rails against Helena but his anger turns to passion after she hits him.

Several months later, Helena has replaced Alison as Jimmy continues his tirades against the class system; Cliff is about to leave. When Alison returns to visit, Jimmy scorns and ignores her as she tells Helena of her miscarriage. Jimmy is having self-doubt about his attitudes and when Alison describes how she lost her baby and how he would have relished seeing her suffer, the couple are reunited in mutual insecurity.

Jimmy Porter
Cliff Lewis
Alison Porter
Helena Charles
Colonel Redfern

Look Homeward, Angel
Ketti Frings based on the novel
by Thomas Wolfe
Comedy-drama 3 Acts
New York 1957

Eliza Gant runs the Dixieland Boarding House in Altamont, North Carolina, and amidst the intrigues and affairs of her disparate collection of boarders, her own family also live, with their dependence upon her financial acumen and resentment of her clinging authority. Her consumptive son Ben is the stable hero - protector of the family, and against the backdrop of his dying and eventual death is played the quest of her exploited younger son Eugene for independence, love and education.

Eliza's husband is a stonemason, both strong and self-pitying, saving a wonderful carving of an angel for his own headstone. Both Ben and Eugene are involved with older women, and after Ben's death Eliza and Gant vent their mutual pent-up fury against the boarders and boarding-house. Eugene, deserted by his love Laura, takes the opportunity then at last offered by Eliza and prepares to leave for the education and independence she has at last reconciled herself to giving him.

Mrs Gant	*Mrs Snowden*
Mrs Marie 'Fatty' Pert	*Mr Farrel*
Helen Gant Barton	*Miss Brown*
Hugh Barton	*Laura James*
Eliza Gant	*W.O. Gant*
Will Pentland	*Dr Maguire*
Eugene Gant	*Tarkinton*
Jake Clatt	*Mme Elizabeth*
Mrs Clatt	*Luke Gant*
Florry Mangle	

Loot
Joe Orton
Black Farce 2 Acts
London 1966

Hal and Dennis are lustful, thieving scamps. Dennis is a hearse driver for an undertaker. They have robbed the bank next door to the funeral parlour. Hal's mother - McLeavy's wife - has just died. Fay, the sexy young nurse who has seven deceased husbands behind her, is interested in marrying McLeavy. At the McLeavy house, where the embalmed Mrs McLeavy is lying in her coffin, Dennis has already had his way with Fay, is interested in marrying her and can offer her more financial 'security' than McLeavy. Truscott (of the Yard), a brutal, corrupt and devious police inspector, is on to the lads and calls at the house to search for loot but as he has no warrant he poses implausibly as an inspector for the Metropolitan Water Board.

The lads remove Hal's mother, all wrapped up, and lock her in a cupboard so that they can hide the money in the coffin which is shortly going to the cemetery. Later, when Truscott sees the 'mummy' he is told it is a bust on which Fay makes dresses. Fay gets cut in for a third of the loot but Truscott digs out the fact that Fay poisoned Mrs McLeavy. However, there is a car crash on the way to the cemetery and though the money is saved the casket containing the innards (removed during embalming) is destroyed so there is no evidence against Fay, who is released. Truscott finds the money and has to be cut in for his quarter. McLeavy threatens to expose

them so Truscott has him arrested and the others agree to give whatever evidence is necessary to have him put away. Fay agrees to marry Dennis.

McLeavy
Fay
Hal
Dennis
Inspector Truscott
Constable Meadows

Lord Arthur Savile's Crime
Constance Cox and Oscar Wilde
Comedy 3 Acts
London 1952

Lord Arthur Savile's quiet life in Grosvenor Square in 1890s' London is overturned when his prospective mother-in-law has his palm read by an unscrupulous chiromancer, Mr Podgers, who privately reveals to Lord Arthur that he will have a long, happy marriage, but will also kill someone. He decides, with the help of his butler Baines, to murder someone before marrying, so the crime will not sully his wife if it is found out.

With the help not just of Baines, who proves a hopeless murderer, but of the equally inept anarchist assassin, Herr Winkelkopf, Lord Arthur utterly bungles a series of murder attempts. He poisons himself trying to poison his aunt, blows up the front of his home with an exploding umbrella meant to kill his uncle, but eventually comes good when he murders Podgers, who turns out to be a blackmailer, instead. In a final blunder of epic proportions, though, Baines and Winkelkopf are jointly responsible for leaving an ignited bomb, meant for Arthur's uncle once more, in his lordship's carriage. Lord Arthur is then arrested when, on discovering the smouldering device, he throws it into the street where it explodes to devastating effect. The marriage is postponed.

Baines, the butler
Lord Arthur Savile
Sybil Merton, Lord Arthur's fiancée
The Dean of Paddington, Lord Arthur's uncle
Lady Windermere, Lord Arthur's aunt
Lady Clementina Beauchamp, Lord Arthur's great aunt
Lady Julia Merton, Sybil's mother
Mr Podgers, a palmist
Herr Winkelkopf, an anarchist

Love for Love
William Congreve
Comedy 5 Acts
London 1695

Riotous living and unsuccessful pursuit of lovely heiress Angelica have wasted Valentine's fortunes, and in this comedy of manners his angry father Sir Sampson is determined to force him to accept a lump sum to pay his debts in exchange for Valentine signing over his land inheritance to home-coming sailor brother Ben, the favoured son. Ben is supposed to wed country girl Miss Prue, a 'natural' wench lately spoiled by fickle beau Tattle, but earthily good-natured Ben wisely rejects her against his father's wishes.

To avoid signing over his property, Valentine feigns madness and also tries to use the ruse to net Angelica, who is not deceived. Meanwhile Prue's excessively superstitious father, Foresight, goes around spouting astrologies, seeing omens in everything and generally misunderstanding events, especially Valentine's friend Scandal's seduction of his young wife Mrs Foresight. Valentine's servant Jeremy tricks Tattle into marrying scheming Mrs Frail and vain old Sir Sampson imagines Angelica wants him as her husband. When Valentine declares that he will sign the paper because life without Angelica is hopeless, she relents and reveals her true feelings, impressed by his constancy towards her.

Sir Sampson Legend	*Buckram, a lawyer*
Valentine	*Angelica*
Scandal	*Mrs Foresight*
Tattle	*Miss Prue*
Ben	*Nurse to Miss Prue*
Foresight	*Mrs Frail, sister to Mrs*
Jeremy	* Foresight*
Trapland, a scrivener	*Jenny, maid to Angelica*

Love Match, The
Glenn Melvyn
Comedy 3 Acts
London 1953

Bill Brown, an irascible, brawling but fundamentally good-hearted Lancashire railwayman, fanatically supports his local football team, City, especially against their Derby rivals, United. His wife Sal and daughter Rose tolerate Bill's passion for City when they can, and grumble about it when he goes on too long.

With his commitment of twenty-five years to City's cause, Bill is left in a quandary when his son Percy wins a place to play for United. Bill's eventual shift of allegiance to United leaves him no less fanatical for his sport. So, when he is injured in a traffic mishap, and then bedridden for weeks with pneumonia during United's run to the Cup quarter-final, Sal, Rose and their neighbours Wally and Emma Binns, are run ragged trying to keep him at home to recuperate. They barely manage to keep him from attending the quarter-final, face his abuse when the radio breaks down just as the match starts, but end wildly celebrating a United victory in which Percy scores the decisive goal.

Sal Brown
Rose Brown
Arthur Ford
Percy Brown
Wally Binns
Emma Binns
Bill Brown
Alf Hall
A woman

Love of Four Colonels, The
Peter Ustinov
Fantasy 3 Acts
London 1951

This contemporary fairy tale is a reworking of the *Sleeping Beauty* theme. After the war an English, a French, an American and a Russian colonel are in dispute over a castle in the village Herzogenburg in the Harz mountains. They are stereotypes of their countries. Good and bad fairies transport the colonels to the castle where they are challenged to make the Sleeping Beauty fall in love with them using whatever transformations they feel necessary. The Frenchman becomes a restoration gallant, the Englishman an Elizabethan poet, the American a devil-defeating priest, and the Russian a weary Chekhovian uncle. Their attempts at courtship fail, due to the interference of the fairies, but they are given the chance of overhearing their own wives' secret thoughts about themselves. Given the choice of returning home or continuing to woo the Beauty, the English and Russian colonels choose their wives while the Frenchman and American stay, wondering if the others have made the right choice.

Col Desmond De S.	*The beauty*
* Rinder-Sparrow*	*Mrs Breitenspiegel*
Col Wesley Breitenspiegel	*Mme Frappot*
Col Aime Frappot	*Mrs Rinder-Sparrow*
Col Alexander Ikonenko	*Mme Ikonenko*
Mayor of Herzogenburg	
The wicked fairy	
The good fairy	

Love on the Dole
Ronald Gow and Walter Greenwood
Tragedy 3 Acts
Manchester 1934

Two young people from a northern industrial slum of the thirties, Hanky Park, fall in love on a hiking trip and plan to marry. The girl, Sarah Hardcastle, is a bright, courageous millworker, and her fiancé Larry Meath, a naive but intelligent socialist organizer, works in a foundry. Sarah is also coveted by the town's fat, corrupt but very influential bookmaker Sam Grundy, who destroys the couple's marriage plans by arranging to have Larry sacked from his job.

As Sarah's family sink deeper into the squalid poverty of the Depression, she is left their sole breadwinner. When Larry is killed in a demonstration against unemployment, Sarah decides, to general ridicule and her father's horror, to give in and become Grundy's mistress. In return, the bookmaker agrees a 'settlement' with her, and jobs for her unemployed father and brother.

Sarah Hardcastle	*Mrs Bull*
Larry Meath	*Mrs Dorbell*
Mr Hardcastle	*Mrs Jike*
Mrs Hardcastle	*Helen Hawkins*
Harry Hardcastle	*A policeman*

Charlie　　　　　*A newsboy*
Sam Grundy　　　*Men and women*
A young man

Love's Labour's Lost
William Shakespeare
Comedy 5 Acts
London 1595

Ferdinand, King of Navarre, decides to turn his court into a celibate congregation of intellectuals, and persuades three of his nobles, Berowne, Longaville and Dumaine, to join him in dedicating their next three years to ascetic study. For diversion they will have only the antics of the king's clown, Costard, and the wild conversation of Don Armado, an eccentric Spaniard.

The arrival of the Princess of France and her three beautiful ladies-in-waiting, Rosaline, Maria and Katherine, undermines the resolve not just of Ferdinand, who falls in love with the Princess, but of his lords as well, who quickly succumb to the charms of the Princess' companions.

When Costard is caught consorting with a country girl, he is placed under the guard of Don Armado, but the Spaniard, too, has fallen in love with Costard's chosen. Armado gives Costard a letter for the girl, which the clown mixes up with another letter Berowne has given him for delivery to Rosaline. So starts a series of muddled secrets being exposed, during which the courtiers and their King are all revealed as incapable of following the ascetic path.

The King and lords ruefully admit their weaknesses, and plunge into a round of revelling and courting. The women adopt disguises and trick their various suitors into pursuing the wrong targets. Finally, in the middle of a pageant, word arrives that the Princess' father has died. She and her ladies depart after extracting a promise from Ferdinand and his lords that they will forsake all pleasure for a year, after which the women will return.
Ferdinand, King of Navarre
Lords of Navarre: *Berowne, Longaville, Dumaine*
Lords of France: *Boyet and Marcade*
Don Adriano de Armado, a Spaniard
Sir Nathaniel, a curate
Holofernes, a schoolmaster
Dull, a constable
Costard, a clown
Moth, Armado's page
Forester
Ladies of France: *The Princess of France, Rosaline,*
　Maria and Katherine
Jacquenetta, a country wench
Lords, attendants, etc

Lover, The
Harold Pinter
Comedy Drama 1 Act
London 1963

Richard asks his wife, amiably, if her lover is coming today. Sarah says 'yes'. Richard says he will be back about six and goes out. When he comes back he asks how the afternoon went and wonders how she feels frolicking in their house while he is at his desk going through balance sheets and graphs. Sarah says she knew Richard would be with his mistress. He says he has not got one, just a convenient slut of a whore who comes in handy. He wants to know what the lover thinks of Sarah's husband and she says Richard is respected, which he finds rather moving. It is Richard she really loves and anyway the lover is happily married. Richard is not jealous so things are beautifully balanced.

Another afternoon: Sarah, sexily dressed, answers the door. It is John the milkman who soon goes away. The doorbell rings again and there is Max wearing a suede jacket and no tie. Max is Richard. He calls her Dolores, then Mary. They have quite a good time, though he does say she is too bony for his ideal taste. She insists she is plump. He says he likes them enormous. Max goes.

Richard, back in business suit, returns. Sarah, in sober dress, enquires about his whore and he says she is splendid, getting thinner by the day and he likes thin ladies. He is dissatisfied with the way she is neglecting her wifely duties and she must no longer entertain the lover in his home. If Richard catches him, his head will be kicked in. He has paid off his whore for being too bony. They quarrel, sort of. Sarah offers to change her clothes. After a few pauses he calls her a lovely whore.
Richard
Sarah
John

Lower Depths, The
Maxim Gorky
Drama 4 Acts
Moscow 1902

The residents of a Volga dosshouse at the turn of the century are a group of society's outcasts including a murderer, a thief, a prostitute, a decadent baron and a drunken actor. They live a hopeless existence coloured only by vodka, gambling and seduction.

Into this squalid scene comes an old pilgrim, Luka, who offers pity and hope of redemption, even if he preaches a gospel based on illusions. He comforts Anna, the dying wife of brutal and mean locksmith Kleshch telling her not to worry, 'Death quiets everything. It's kind to us humans.' To the drunken actor he tells of a free hospital for alcoholics, and he urges Pepel, a thief, to go to Siberia 'a land of gold'.

But the realities of life crowd in. Pepel kills the dosshouse owner and is dragged to off jail, and the drunken actor hangs himself. Satin, a card sharp, speaks eloquently for the old Luka, who has disappeared. 'He lied, but he lied out of sheer pity for you.'
Mikhail Ivanov Kostyliov, landlord of the dosshouse
Vassilissa Karpovna, his wife
Natasha, her sister

Abram Ivanich Medvediev, their uncle, a policeman
Vassily Pepel
Andrey Mitrich Kleshch, a locksmith
Anna, his wife
Nastya, a streetwalker
Kvashnia, a dumpling peddler
Bubnov, a cap-maker
Baron
Satin
Actor
Luka, a palmer
Alyoshka, a cobbler
Tartar, hook-man or porter
Krivoy Zob, hook-man or porter

Lulu
Peter Barnes
Tragedy 2 Acts
Nottingham 1970

A free adaptation of two Frank Wedekind texts, *Earth Spirit* and *Pandora's Box,* which were never played as one work during the author's lifetime.

In her teens Lulu was saved from a life of penury by Herr Schon, a newspaper proprietor, who made her his mistress at the same time as he took her from the gutter. Though she reserves her love entirely for her benefactor, he marries her off, first to a rich bourgeois, Dr Goll, and then to the painter Schwarz after Goll dies of heart failure brought on by the fury of catching the painter trying to seduce Lulu. Schon, a widower, cannot bring himself to marry Lulu because she is not of his own class and also shows a nearly male disregard for sexual fidelity. But he does nurture a bitter, ambivalent love for her in spite of himself.

When Schwarz discovers Lulu's love for Schon he commits suicide, and Lulu sets out to capture Schon once and for all. She snares him into marriage but her promiscuity drives him to despair, and when he finds her making love to his son Alwa, he tries to murder her. Lulu, however, turns the tables and shoots Schon, condemning herself to a life on the run from the law.

She goes first to Paris, with Alwa, where she falls in with a decadent set, one of whose members blackmails her and is quickly disposed of, requiring Lulu once again to flee. She ends up in London, with Alwa, her father and Countess Geschwitz, a lesbian who is madly in love with her. Her luck, though has run out, and she becomes a cheap streetwalker, the most dangerous occupation for a woman in 1890s' London. Her utter lack of discrimination leads her to pick up a man called Jack, who turns out to be the infamous 'Ripper'.

Ringmaster	*Schigolch, Lulu's father*
Lulu	*Escherich*
Schon	*Prince Escerny*
Schwarz	*Henriette*
Dr Goll, Lulu's first	*Countess Geschwitz*
* husband*	* Hugenburg*
Alwa, Schon's son	*Rodrigo Quast*

Ferdinand	*Puntschin*
Bianetta	*Bob*
Ludmilla	*Policeman*
Casti-Piani	*Hunidei*
Magelone	*Kungu-Poti*
Kadidja	*Dr Hilti*
Heilman	*Jack*

Luther
John Osborne
Drama 3 Acts
Nottingham 1961

This account of the life of the 'angry young man' of the Church, Martin Luther, constantly questioning God's word and confronting ungodly men, is historically accurate and uses many of his recorded words.

In early sixteenth-century Germany, Martin joins the Augustinian Order after having a vision. Although he has doubts about his revelation, he works hard despite being frequently troubled by chronic constipation.

He achieves considerable distinction as a scholar but begins to criticize aspects of Catholic dogma, and after producing a controversial thesis, which he refuses to withdraw, the Pope excommunicates him. He continues his critique of the Church, remaining steadfast to his interpretation of God's word and is blamed for inciting a peasant rebellion.

By 1530, his work is beginning to receive recognition by some church authorities, but he is still ravaged by self-doubt, despite the comfort provided by his wife, an ex-nun, and their small son.

Knight	*Leo*
Prior	*Eck*
Martin Luther	*Katherine*
Hans	*Hans, the younger*
Lucas	*Augustinians*
Weinand	*Dominicans*
Tetzel	*Herald*
Staupitz	*Emperor*
Cajetan	*Peasants*
Miltitz	

Luv
Murray Schisgal
Comedy 2 Acts
New York 1964

By a bridge in a park, old schoolfriends Harry Berlin and Milt Manville meet by accident. Ambitious Milt is amazed that his boyhood hero Harry, now a suicidal bum, has achieved nothing since school. Ragged Harry confesses he has been that way ever since a dog relieved itself on him when he was deciding on a career. Milt then tells Harry he wants to ditch his wife Ellen for girlfriend Linda, and suggests Harry and Ellen get together. Ellen arrives and instead of murdering her as planned, Milt is able to palm her off on Harry, both Ellen and Harry falling in love with love, as it were.

Several months later at the same spot they all meet again. Milt is disenchanted with Linda, who, he says, lies in bed all day and has grown a moustache, and Ellen is fed up with Harry - he also has done absolutely nothing, has not even made love to her. Milt and Ellen decide to get back together and attempt to drown poor Harry - instead Milt ends up in the drink. He emerges, desperate Harry jumps into the drink and Milt and Ellen run off, with dripping Harry yelling after him for the five bucks Milt borrowed months before. Their emotional posturing and affectation has now gone around full circle.

Harry Berlin
Milt Manville
Ellen Manville

Lysistrata
Aristophanes
Comedy 1 Act
Athens c. 415BC

It is usual to read this piece as Aristophanes' plea for an end to the continuing protracted war between Athens and Sparta.

The women of Athens, led by Lysistrata, convene a meeting of women from all over Greece at which all, Athenian and Spartan alike, vow to withold their sexual favours to their menfolk until a peace is concluded between the two states.

To underscore their commitment, the women occupy the Acropolis which they refuse to leave while the war continues. The occupation infuriates the Athenian males who attempt to light fires around the Acropolis, hoping to smoke out the women and also get access to the war funds hidden inside.

Undeterred, the women respond by dousing the men, and their fires, with pitcher after pitcher of water. Led by a magistrate, the men then try to arrest Lysistrata and her closest aides but instead they are thrashed by the determined women. A tenuous solidarity of purpose, bolstered by Lysistrata's resolution, holds the women to their course. When the Athenian men hear that in Sparta too the women have rebelled under the leadership of Lampito, Lysistrata's deputy, the men of both states finally relent and conclude the long awaited peace.

Athenian women: *Lysistrata, Calonice, Myrrhine*
Lampito, a Spartan woman
A magistrate
Cinesias, Myrrhine's husband
A Spartan ambassador
An Athenian negotiator
Chorus of women
Chorus of men
Stratyllis, leader of women's chorus
Ismenia, a Boetian woman
Policeman
Athenians
Spartan and Athenian women
Slaves

Macbeth
William Shakespeare
Tragedy 5 Acts
London 1606

While returning to King Duncan of Scotland after winning a great victory against the Norwegians and their ally, the treacherous thane of Cawdor, Generals Macbeth and Banquo come across the Weird Sisters, three prophesying witches, who predict Cawdor and the throne for Macbeth, and kingship for Banquo's descendences.

Neither is convinced until Duncan makes Macbeth thane of Cawdor as reward for his victory. Ambitious Macbeth decides to give fate a helping hand, and together with scheming Lady Macbeth secretly kills Duncan, whose son Malcolm then flees to England. Malcolm thus becomes a suspect in his father's murder, and Macbeth is made king. His conscience troubles him, yet he cannot now go back, and begins wading deeper and deeper in blood, first assassinating Banquo, whose son Fleance escapes, and then slaying the entire family of nobleman Macduff, who has fled to England to assist Malcolm. Further witches' prophesies seem to indicate Macbeth is safe, but as his recklessness increases, Lady Macbeth breaks, goes mad and kills herself. Confronted at last by Malcolm's army, Macbeth discovers that the prophecies, though true, were tricks; he is confronted by Macduff and slain.

Duncan, King of Scotland
Malcolm, Duncan's son
Donalbain, Duncan's son
Macbeth, a general of the King's army
Banquo, a general of the King's army
Noblemen of Scotland: *Macduff, Lenox, Rosse,*
  Menteth, Angus and Cathness
Fleance, son of Banquo
Siward, Earl of Northumberland
Young Siward, his son
Seyton, an officer attending on Macbeth
Son to Macduff
Lady Macbeth
Lady Macduff
Hecate
Three witches
An English doctor
A Scottish doctor
A soldier
A porter
An old man
Ghost of Banquo
Gentlewomen
Lords
Gentlemen
Officers
Soldiers
Murderers
Attendants
Messengers

Mack and Mabel
Michael Stewart and Jerry Herman
Musical 2 Acts
New York 1974

The great Hollywood comic director, Mack Sennett, reminisces about his career from the sound stage of the studios he once dominated. It is 1938, and the days of silent film are over, effectively ending Sennett's career.

In a series of flashbacks, Sennett relates the glory days of the Keystone Studios from 1911, when he discovered Mabel Normand, star of dozens of his early 'two reelers', through his invention of the Bathing Beauties and Keystone Cops, to Mabel's death from a heroin overdose in 1930.

Pride and a naturally hard, aggressive personality prevent Sennett from ever declaring openly the love he feels for Mabel. Although she is his mistress until 1920, Mabel eventually leaves him for the 'serious' director W. D. Taylor, who not only values her acting, but also treats her with kindness and consideration as well. However, when Taylor is murdered in Mabel's presence, the ensuing scandal wrecks her career. In an attempt to help her make a clean start, Sennett agrees to make her the star of a romantic drama, *Molly*, which he goes on to direct. The odium still attached to Mabel's name means, however, that no one will distribute the film.

Not content with this unhappy ending, Sennett plots a final scene in which he and Mabel marry, happily surrounded by a classic custard pie fight performed by the Keystone Cops.
Songs include: 'I Won't Send Roses'; 'Time Heals Everything'; 'Tap Your Troubles Away'

Eddie, the watchman	Mabel Normand
Mack Sennett	Mr Kleiman
Lottie Ames	Mr Fox
Ella	Iris, wardrobe mistress
Freddie	William Desmond Taylor
Charlie Muldson	Phyllis Foster
Wally	Serge
Frank Wyman	

Madwoman of Chaillot, The
Jean Giradoux
Adapted by Maurice Valency
Comedy 2 Acts
New York 1948

Sometime 'next year' two groups of people congregate on the terrace of the Chez Francis café in the stately Chaillot quarter of Paris; the unscrupulous capitalists, led by 'The President', and the poor and eccentric, including Countess Aurelia - the Madwoman of Chaillot. The eccentrics, headed by the Ragpicker, bring to the Countess' attention how everything in the world is now being 'pimped' by the faceless ones whose latest money-making venture is to destroy Paris in search of oil. The oil prospector himself, in league with the President, is blackmailing a young man to do his dirty work. When

the young man tries to drown himself, he is rescued and brought to the café where he and a waitress, Irma, fall in love. The Countess decides to save Paris, and after a mock trial of the capitalists, invites the greedy President and his gang down to the cellar beneath her house, enticing them with promises of oil. She has discovered, through her friend the King of the Sewers, a tunnel that goes on and on ... to death. Lured by their greed, the capitalists all troop to their doom and the Countess shuts the great stone door on them. Paris is saved, the birds can fly, shopkeepers smile again, and the young man and Irma are thrown together by the Countess who remembers her own thwarted love.

The waiter	The sewer man
The little man	Mme Constance, the
The prospector	madwoman of Passy
The baron	Mlle Gabrielle, the
Therese	madwoman of St Sulpice
The street singer	Mme Josephine, the
The flower girl	madwoman of La
The ragpicker	Concorde
Paulette	The Presidents (three)
The deaf-mute	The prospectors (three)
Irma	The press agents (three)
The shoelace peddler	The ladies (three)
The broker	The Adolphe Bertauts (three)
The street juggler	
Dr Jadin	
Countess Aurelia	
The doorman	
The policeman	
The young man	
The sergeant	

Magistrate, The
Arthur W. Pinero
Farce 3 Acts
London 1885

Agatha Posket's son Cis is extraordinarily precocious for his fourteen years. He flirts, drinks, gambles and is 'a regular young card'. He is actually nineteen but no one except his mother knows; she lied about her age when she married her second husband, good-hearted magistrate Mr Posket. One evening Cis secretly persuades Posket to accompany him for drinks at the Hotel des Princes, both imagining that Mrs Posket is visiting a sick friend. In fact she is with sister Charlotte at the same hotel in order to persuade Cis's godfather Capt. Lukan, just back from Bengal, not to reveal the truth about Cis's age. Nearby Cis and Posket are whooping it up, and when an after hours police raid nets all but Cis and Posket, next day the magistrate finds himself in his confusion sentencing his own wife to seven days for illegal drinking. His fellow magistrate Bullamy waives the sentence and afterwards Agatha confesses the truth. Then to Posket's shame the coat he left in the club is traced to him, but before he too must face the magistrate, he gives mischievous Cis permission to marry piano teacher Beatie, plus a thousand pounds to banish him to Canada.

Mr Posket, Mr Bullamy, magistrates of Mulberry
Street police court
Col Lukan from Bengal
Capt. Horace Vale, Shropshire Fusiliers
Cis Farringdon, Mrs Posket's son by her first
marriage
Achille Blond, proprietor of the Hotel des Princes
Isadore, a waiter
Mr Wormington, Chief Clerk at Mulburry Street
Inspector Messiter
Sgt Lugg
Constable Harris
Wyke, servant at Mr Posket's
Agatha Posket, late Farringdon, née Verrinder
Charlotte, her sister
Beatie Tomlinson, young lady, reduced to teaching
music
Popham

Brigands:
Carlo
Beppo
Pietro
Andrea
Zacch
Tonio
Angela, daughter of Gen. Malona
Crumpet, the General's attendant
Mayor of Santo
Lieut Rugini
Gianetta
Cpl Terroni
Dancers
Ladies-in-waiting
Citizens
Officers
Soldiers
Brigands
Fisherfolk

Maid of the Mountains, The
Frederick Lonsdale and Harry Graham
Musical 3 Acts
London 1917

A gang of Italian mountain brigands, led by the recklessly brave Baldasarre, are surrounded by the soldiers of the provincial governor, Gen. Malona, and look certain to face capture. To spare the only female member of the gang, Teresa, from prison, Baldasarre sends her away by a secret path. But she is captured and imprisoned, then offered her freedom in return for betraying her leader. She refuses the offer out of a loyalty born from her passionate love for Baldasarre.

Hearing of her capture, Baldasarre leads his men to intercept the new governor of the province, Count Orsino, who is on his way to take up Gen. Malona's post. He dons the Count's clothing, dresses his men as retainers, and, with Orsino's papers, presents himself to the General. The ruse works but Baldasarre puts everyone in danger when he falls in love with Malona's daughter, Angela, and refuses to leave with Teresa and the rest of the gang, as he had planned. Teresa, seeing Baldasarre is lost to her, reveals his true identity to the General out of spite, and they are all captured and sent to prison on Devil's Island.

There, the gang meet Lieut Rugini, who was given this very undesirable posting by the General for showing too much affection toward Angela. The Lieutenant decides to help the prisoners to escape, and to go with them himself. Baldasarre then realizes that he loves not Angela but Teresa, his maid of the mountains, when she selflessly offers to make amends for her earlier act of betrayal by aiding in the escape even if Baldasarre uses his freedom to return to her rival. They flee together to a new life.

Baldasarre, the Brigand Chief
Teresa, the Maid of the Mountains

Major Barbara
George Bernard Shaw
Drama 3 Acts
London 1905

In 1906 rich pragmatic munitions manufacturer Andrew Undershaft, who has been separated from his snobbish wife Lady Britomart for several years, visits his family and takes a great liking to one of his daughters, Barbara, who has become a Salvationist. He also gets on well with her fiancé, Professor Adolphus Cusins, who has joined the Salvation Army so that he can woo Barbara. She is a strong-willed and dedicated girl and knows well how to deal with the kind of ruffians who come to the Salvation Army shelter. Undershaft visits the shelter, and when a benefactor offers a large donation to help run the place, he matches it with a similar sum, much to Barbara's disgust as she does not approve of the way her father makes a fortune from armaments. She is, however, amazed when she later goes to her father's factory which has a model town attached and has every amenity for its worker inhabitants.

Professor Cusins is persuaded to join Undershaft's business, so that he can help the poor to help themselves, and Barbara, his future wife, will continue her good work by spreading the gospel among the well fed.

Lady Britomart
Undershaft
Stephen Undershaft
Barbara Undershaft
Sarah Undershaft
Andrew Undershaft
Morrison
Charles Lomax
Professor Adolphus
Cusins
Rummy Mitchens
Snobby Price
Jenny Hill
Peter Shirley
Bill Walker
Mrs Baines
Bilton

Majority of One, A
Leonard Spigelgass
Comedy 3 Acts
New York 1959

Young diplomat Jerry Black and his wife Alice are a liberal Jewish New York couple, and when he is posted to Japan they take along Alice's widowed mother Mrs Jacoby. On the boat, they meet Japanese business executive Koichi Asano, who will be discussing trade with Jerry. Mrs Jacoby is hostile to Mr Asano - her son was killed in the war - but after Asano reveals his two children also died in the conflict, they become good friends who obviously like and respect each other. This disturbs Jerry, who persuades his mother-in-law to cool it with Asano. In Japan, the talks do not go well and Mrs Jacoby visits Asano who is delighted to see her and treats her like an honoured guest - he also proposes to her. She asks for time to think, and when she tells this to Jerry and Alice their liberal anti-prejudice principles become highly strained. Mrs Jacoby refuses Asano, feeling he is too recently widowed to have a clear mind about such a commitment, but her commonsense suggestions help the trade talks to resume. She returns to Brooklyn and two months later is visited by Asano, and it is apparent their friendship will continue to deepen and ripen.

Mrs Rubin
Mrs Jacoby
Alice Black
Jerome Black
Lady passenger
Koicho Asano
Eddie
House boy
Tateshi (female)
Ayako Asano (female)
Noketi (female)
Servant girl
Chauffeur
Captain Norcross

Male Animal, The
James Thurber
Comedy 3 Acts
New York 1949

A group of old friends and acquaintances are reunited at the home of Tommy and Ellen Turner, in a middle American university town for a weekend celebration which they hope will culminate in the victory of their university's American football team over their arch rivals. The reunion offers Joe Ferguson, one of the town's former football greats, an excuse to return to the scene of his youthful glories, and to find out if his love for Ellen still burns as brightly as it once did.

But just as the celebrations get under way, Tommy, who lectures at the university, becomes embroiled with the reactionary university authorities over freedom of speech. Tommy's mood darkens as he watches Joe and Ellen light-heartedly dancing, while he himself tries to avoid either dismissal from his post or the loss of his integrity. His gloom and jealousy prompt Ellen to threaten to leave him for Joe. However, when Ellen realizes his bravery in facing down the authorities, she returns to him, leaving Joe in a mood of fondness for his own estranged wife.

Cleota, a housemaid
Ellen Turner
Tommy Turner, Ellen's husband
Patricia Stanley, Ellen's younger sister
Wally Myers
Dean Frederick Damon
Michael Barnes
Joe Ferguson
Mrs Blanche Damon
Ed Keller
Myrtle Keller
Nutsy Miller
Newspaper reporter

Mame
Jerome Lawrence and Robert E. Lee
Music by Jerry Herman
Musical 2 Acts
New York 1966
See: *Auntie Mame*
Songs include: 'Mame'; 'If He Walked into My Life'; 'The Man in the Moon'; 'Bosom Buddies'

Man and Superman
George Bernard Shaw
Comedy 4 Acts
London 1905

Staid and respected Roebuck Ramsden is sixty-ish; Jack Tanner is in his thirties, a rich socialist egoist whose advanced ideas Ramsden considers anarchist. Both have been appointed joint guardians of Ann Whitfield, whose father recently died, and who is being romantically pursued by a sensitive and poetic family friend, Octavius Robinson. Ann, though, is set on Jack, who is ignorant of her designs until his down-to-earth cockney chauffeur Straker points out the obvious. Frightened by Ann's predatory powers, Jack and Straker flee to Spain where they are captured by brigands, led by the flamboyant Mendoza.

Act Three is the dream 'Don Juan in Hell', often performed as a separate piece or as a reading. It features Tanner's ancestor Don Juan, his old flame Dona Ana, the Devil and Dona Ana's father the Statue, killed in a duel by Don Juan. The four engage in brilliant metaphysical speculations on life and death, heaven and hell and meaning; it ends with Don Juan's explanation of man's self-consciousness as the crowning glory of the 'Life Force' - thus, he intends to leave hell with its continuous round of empty pleasures and go to serve in the austere but more satisfying realm of heaven.

Upon awakening, Jack and Straker are rescued by

their friends, and although he goes on resisting the scheming Ann almost until the end, Jack knows that her vitality - the 'Life Force' - will conquer him, and finally he submits.

Roebuck Ramsden	*Mendoza*
Octavius Robinson	*Anarchist*
John Tanner	*Duval*
Henry Straker	*Rowdy Social Democrat*
Hector Malone	*Sulky Social Democrat*
Mr Malone	*Goatherd*
Ann Whitfield	*An officer*
Mrs Whitfield	*Don Juan (Tanner)*
Miss Ramsden	*Dona Ana de Ulla (Ann)*
Violet Robinson	*The Statue (Ramsden)*
Parlourmaid	*The Devil (Mendoza)*

Man Equals Man
Bertolt Brecht
Comedy 1 Act
Dusseldorf 1926

Galy Gay is a porter in the fictitious military enclave of Kilkoa in British India in 1925. He one day leaves home to fetch a flounder for lunch with his wife, is distracted by a woman who needs help carrying a load, and encounters a British machine-gun crew, one of whose number has gone missing while drunk. They persuade Galy to impersonate the missing man at roll-call, assuring him that he will be well paid and only slightly delayed. But after the roll is called and they still cannot find the missing man, it is decided that Galy must become his permanent replacement. The crew then lure him, with the promise of profit, into selling a ludicrous and obviously fake elephant, arrest him for fraud, and offer to let him escape execution if he will forego his own identity to become the missing man.

At first Galy refuses, but after a mock execution, decides he must fall in with the plan. The machine-gun crew are sent to help quell an uprising on the border with Tibet. Against all the odds, Galy distinguishes himself in the fighting and emerges a hero.

British soldiers:Uriah Shelly, Jesse Mahoney, Polly Baker and Jeriah Jip
Charles Fairchild, British sergeant
Galy Gay
Galy's wife
Mr Wang
Mah Sing
Leokadia Bagbick
Soldiers

Man for All Seasons, A
Robert Bolt
Drama 2 Acts
London 1960

This play is a reconstruction of the events leading to the execution of Sir Thomas More, Lord Chancellor of England, in 1535.

As the play opens, More, a Privy Councillor but not yet Lord Chancellor, is under pressure from his family and colleagues to approve Henry VIII's desire to divorce Catherine of Aragon. The King is about to arrive to discuss the matter. Although he is the King's devoted friend, More can only promise Henry that he will not oppose the divorce, and pleads loyalty to the Church and the Pope as his reasons. The King agrees to this compromise.

However, as opposition to the divorce grows amongst the common people, More's judicious silence comes to be seen as disapproval. So to trap More, the King sponsors the Act of Succession recognizing the children of his second wife, Anne Boleyn as his heirs, and requiring all his subjects to swear allegiance to them. More refuses to swear, but also refuses to take issue with the Act. To remove the embarrassment of More's stand, Henry instigates false charges against him. More is convicted by false evidence and put to death.

The common man
Thomas More, Lord Chancellor
Richard Rich
The Duke of Norfolk
Alice More, More's wife
Margaret More, their daughter
The Cardinal
Thomas Cromwell, Henry VIII's henchman
The Ambassador (M. Chapuys)
His attendant
William Roper
The King
A woman
The Archbishop

Man Most Likely To..., The
Joyce Rayburn
Comedy 3 Acts
London 1968

Successful businessman Victor Cadwallader finds his attempts to unwind at his Berkshire weekend cottage are continuously thwarted. First, wife Joan's irritatingly ever-doting ex-fiancé Martin turns up, and then son Giles' sexy girlfriend Shirley arrives, gets on rather too well with Victor and is mistaken by Joan for one of hubby's mistresses. When surly and rebellious Giles arrives, Shirley seems to prefer father to son, and that night the couple do not share the bedroom painstakingly arranged for them. Instead Giles sleeps downstairs, but when Victor mistakes his slumbering son for Shirley and makes a pass, the cat's out of the bag; vengeful Joan then implies that Giles isn't Victor's son but Martin's. Even so, Victor turns the situation to his own advantage by threatening to saddle Martin with Giles' school fees and other upbringing costs. Martin quickly leaves, Joan admits the paternity ploy was a bluff, and finally thwarts yet another liaison attempt by Victor and Shirley.

Victor Cadwallader	*Shirley Hughes*
Joan Cadwallader	*Giles Cadwallader*
Martin Morley	

Man of La Mancha
D. Wasserman, J. Darion and M. Leigh
Musical 1 Act
New York 1965

Don Miguel de Cervantes is brought to a dungeon full of thieves and murderers, charged with crimes against the Church because, as a tax collector, he had put a lien on a monastery which had refused to pay its due assessment.

He is arraigned before his fellow prisoners in a mock trial, and pleads his case by involving them all in a play using episodes from the manuscript of his great novel, *Don Quixote*. To show the liberating power of imagination, Cervantes, acting the part of Quixote, shows his hero imagining a windmill to be a giant enemy, an inn to be a castle and the innkeeper a knight errant, and a scullery maid to be his own true lady love.

Quixote's relatives and friends, desperate that his illusions may lead him to dissipate his small fortune, finally show him that his knightly quest is pure imagination. But on his deathbed he reverts to belief in his dream. As the play within a play closes, Cervantes is taken away to face his genuine trial by the Inquisition.

Don Quixote (Cervantes)
Sancho (The Manservant)
Captain of the Inquisition
Aldonza
The Innkeeper (Governor)
Dr Carrasco (Duke)
The Padre
Antonia
Housekeeper
Barber
Pedro, Anselmo, Jose, Juan, Paco and Tenorio,
  muleteers and convicts
Maria, innkeeper's wife
Fermina, servant girl
Guitarist
Horses
Guards
Inquisitors

Man Who Came to Dinner, The
Moss Hart and George S. Kaufman
Comedy 3 Acts
New York 1939

When internationally-famous thirties radio broadcaster and critic Sheridan Whiteside slips and injures his hip outside the Stanley residence in a small town in Ohio, the family have to put him up - and put up with him - over Christmas. Pompous, cunning and waspish, Whiteside completely takes over the house for his broadcasts, encourages the Stanley kids to defy their parents, attracts assorted wacky friends, and receives tons of fan mail and strange gifts, including an Egyptian mummy case. When his faithful secretary Maggie falls for local reporter and would-be playwright Bert Jefferson, Whiteside pulls out all the stops to block the romance, including using glamorous stage star Lorraine Sheldon to divert Bert. It does not work and when to everyone's relief Whiteside eventually leaves, he falls over again on the way out and has to be brought back in. The play's song 'What am I to do' sung by the Noel Coward-inspired character Beverly Carlton, was written by Cole Porter under the pseudonym 'Noël Porter'.

Mrs Ernest W. Stanley	*Three luncheon guests*
Miss Preen	*Mr Baker*
Richard Stanley	*Expressman*
June Stanley	*Lorraine Sheldon*
John	*Sandy*
Sarah	*Beverly Carlton*
Mrs Dexter	*Westcott*
Mrs McFutcheson	*Two radio technicians*
Mr Stanley	*Six young boys*
Maggie Cutler	*Banjo*
Dr Bradley	*Deputies*
Sheridan Whiteside	*A plainclothes man*
Harriet Stanley	
Bert Jefferson	
Professor Metz	

Man Who Stayed at Home, The
Lechmere Worrall and J. E. Harold Terry
Drama 3 Acts
London 1914

Christopher Brent, a gentleman of leisure and apparently very limited intelligence, continues his drone's life even though his friends of similar age are volunteering for service in the Great War. Brent is evidently content to continue the gentle daily round of life as a guest at the Wave Crest Hotel in East Anglia.

This nonchalance is upsetting to his girlfriend Molly Preston, who, although she tries to take Brent's part against those who believe him a coward, eventually comes to believe, with her jingoistic father, John, that he is shirking his duty. Brent's stupidity, though, is entirely affected. He is in fact a highly skilled government agent sent to the hotel to investigate its owner, Mrs Sanderson, her son Carl and two of her staff Fraulein Schroeder and Fritz, all of whom are suspected of being German spies. Assisting him is another agent, Miriam Leigh, and when Molly sees that the two are unusually close for people who have supposedly just met, her jealousy drives her further away from Brent.

Caught between his duty and his love for Molly, Brent still carries on his act, which is so effective that Mrs Sanderson and her group fail to take him seriously until it is, for them, too late. Only when he has unmasked the nest of spies can Brent reveal to Molly that he is, after all, a hero and not the bumbling coward he was thought to be.

John Preston JP
Miss Myrtle
Fraulein Schroeder, a spy
Percival Pennicuik
Daphne Kidlington

Molly Preston, Preston's daughter
Fritz, a spy
Miriam Leigh, a government agent
Christopher Brent, a government agent
Mrs Sanderson, a spy
Carl Sanderson, her son
Cpl Atkins

Marat/Sade
Peter Weiss
Verse Play 2 Acts
London 1964

This piece of 'theatre of cruelty' is a play within a play fully entitled *The Persecution and Assassination of Marat as Performed by the Inmates of the Asylum of Charenton under the Direction of the Marquis de Sade.*

Four years into the French Revolution, Marat sits in his bathtub, loudly defending the continuing executions and attacking the church. The straightjacketed priest Roux incites the people to further revolution much to the consternation of the asylum director. De Sade directs the play and debates with Marat, scorning patriotism and idealism, and masochistically encourages Charlotte Corday to beat him. Various historical characters such as Voltaire and Lavoissier become involved in the polemic and the action.

Marat addresses the National Assembly from his bathtub accusing the leaders of corruption and treason, and de Sade then brings in Charlotte to perform the stylized assassination of Marat. The patients become increasingly agitated and start to take over the asylum as de Sade watches the scene with delight.

M. Coulmier	*Abbot*
Mme Coulmier	*A mad animal*
Mlle Coulmier	*Schoolmaster*
Herald	*Mother*
Kokol	*Father*
Polpoch	*A newly-rich lady*
Cucurucu	*Voltaire*
Rossignol	*Lavoissier*
Jacques Roux	*Patients*
Charlotte Corday	*Nuns*
Jean Paul Marat	*Guards*
Simonne Everard	
Marquis de Sade	
Duperret	

Maria Marten or Murder in the Red Barn
Brian J. Burton
Melodrama/Musical 2 Acts
Worcester 1968

There are many anonymous versions of this real-life murder. Maria Marten, a poor Suffolk country girl with ideas beyond her station, is told by Nell Hatfield, a gypsy woman, that she will meet and marry a young gentleman of means, who will take her away from the boring farm life of the 1820s. Crazy Nell is in fact using Maria to gain revenge on William Corder, son of the

local squire, who had ravished and then abandoned Nell's sister. Maria's fate is sealed when Nell next tells Corder that Maria is in love with him.

Corder meets Maria on her way to the country fair, seduces her and, when she gives birth to his child, decides to abandon her. To prevent his upright father from discovering his paternity of the child, Corder murders the baby with poison, and goes on to shoot to death both Maria and Nell herself, who had obtained the poison for him. As she lies dying, Nell asks her gypsy friends to get word to her brother, Pharos, that Corder is her killer.

Maria was shot and buried next to the Corder family's Red Barn, and her body is discovered there by her father following a recurrent prophetic dream which has been troubling his wife, Maria's mother. When the police are notified of the murder, they send an officer, who turns out to be Pharos Lee, to apprehend Corder, who is tried and then hanged for his crimes.

William Corder, the squire's son
Thomas Marten
Tim Bobbin
Johnny Badger
Pharos Lee, a law officer
Maria Marten, Thomas' daughter
Mrs Marten, Thomas' wife
Anne Marten, Thomas' younger daughter
Meg Bobbin
Nell Hatfield, Pharos Lee's sister
Petro Andrews, Rosa Post, Carmen James, Nell's
  gypsy friends
Alice Rumble

Marriage à la Mode
John Dryden
Comedy 5 Acts
London 1673

Polydamas, Usurper of Sicily, discovers he has a grown-up child, and shortly afterwards Leonidas and Palmyra are brought to him. Their foster-father, old Hermogenes, swears princely Leonidas is Polydamas's son. The usurper rejoices and declares there shall be a double marriage - Palmyra with his favourite, Argaleon, and Leonidas with Amalthea, Argaleon's sister. But Leonidas and Palmyra are in love and sworn to one another, and when Leonidas rebels against Polydamas' wishes, the usurper decides to kill Palmyra. Hermogenes then reveals Palmyra is in fact Polydamas' daughter. She is reinstated and Leonidas forbidden to see her, but Amalthea, who still loves Leonidas, helps him meet Palmyra at a masqued ball. Shortly afterwards Leonidas discovers he is the rightful King of Sicily - there is a revolt, Polydamas is overthrown, and Leonidas becomes King with Palmyra as his Queen, and poor Amalthea resolves to enter a convent. In between these machinations, Captain of the Guards, Rhodophil, and courtier, Palamede, play the game of attempting to bed each other's wife or fiancée whilst attempting to stop the other from doing the same. The play's title comes from Palamede's francophile fiancée Melantha and her comically affected use of French words and phrases.

Polydamas
Leonidas
Argaleon
Hermogenes
Eubulus, his friend
 and companion
Rhodophil
Palamede

Palmyra
Amalthea
Doralice, wife of
 Rhodophil
Melantha
Philotis, woman to
 Melantha

Marriage of Figaro, The
Pierre Beaumarchais
Comedy 5 Acts
Paris 1784

Figaro, the wily cultivated valet to Count Almaviva, Governor of Andalucia, is on the point of marrying Suzanne, maid to the Count's wife. The Count has only recently given up his feudal right to possess, once before they marry, each of the women on his estates. Indeed, he is on the point of reinstituting the practice out of an overwhelming desire for Suzanne. A more telling obstacle for Figaro is the determination of the Count's housekeeper, Marceline, to force Figaro to honour a long-standing debt to her by agreeing to marry her instead.

With the help of the Countess, who is upset with the Count's philandering, Figaro tries to outmanoeuvre both the court which will try Marceline's claim, and his master. A series of ploys, based on disguises adopted by all the main characters, looks doomed to failure until it is fortuitously discovered that Figaro, orphaned as a babe-in-arms, is cousin to Marceline. His natural father then pays Figaro's debts, and he and Suzanne are free to marry. At the same time, the Count, caught intriguing for a night with Suzanne, is forced to forego his pleasure to placate the Countess.

Count Almaviva,
Governor of Andalucia
The Countess
Figaro, the Count's valet
Suzanne, the Countess's
 maid
Marceline
Antonio
Fanchette, Antonio's
 daughter
Chérubin
Bartholo, a doctor
Bazile, The Countess's
 music teacher
Don Guzman Brid'oison
Doublemain
Gripe-Soleil
Pedrillo
An usher
A shepherdess

An Alguazil
A magistrate
Servants and valets
Pages
Huntsmen and peasants

Marriage Proposal, The
Anton Chekhov
Comedy 1 Act
Moscow 1889

Ivan Lomov, a landowner with an exceedingly nervous disposition, arrives at the home of Stephen Chubukov to ask for the hand of Natasha, Chubukov's daughter. Left by themselves, Natasha and Lomov begin to quarrel about a tract of land both claim to own. Chubukov rejoins them, takes Natasha's side in the dispute, and so precipitates Lomov's angry departure.

Only following his departure does Natasha discover that Lomov had come to propose. She sends her father after him, but immediately the two men return, she starts another argument with Lomov, this time on the merits of their respective hunting dogs. Lomov becomes so upset that he collapses in a faint.

When he is revived and told that his proposal is accepted, Lomov barely has time to exchange a kiss with his new fiancée before they set to again. Chubukov, realizing that the couple thrive on conflict, orders champagne as the battle drags on.

Stephen Chubukov, a landowner
Natasha, Chubukov's daughter
Ivan Lomov

Mary, Mary
Jean Kerr
Comedy 3 Acts
London 1963

Bob McKellaway, a divorced New York publisher of modest means, is all set to marry rich, lovely and sweet Tiffany Richards, when accountant buddy Oscar warns of impending financial crisis. Ex-wife Mary is summoned to clarify unexplained cheques (hopefully tax-deductible) and upon arriving at Bob's, she is dated by movie-star neighbour Dirk who is hanging around trying to get his anecdotal memoirs published. That night a snowstorm forces Bob to cancel a trip and, after dining with Dirk, Mary has to stay at Bob's. They occupy separate rooms, but next day Tiffany believes the worst and is much too understanding. Mary is a straightforward joker with low self-esteem, and Bob hides his feelings, but underneath it all they still love each other. When Dirk returns and invites Mary to New Orleans, Bob locks her in a closet and Tiffany retreats gracefully, leaving the way clear for a reconciliation.

Bob McKellaway
Tiffany Richards
Oscar Nelson
Dirk Winston
Mary McKellaway

Master Builder, The
Henrik Ibsen
Tragedy 3 Acts
Copenhagen 1893

In late nineteenth-century Norway, middle-aged master architect Halvard Solness fears his talented young assistant Ragnar will leave his employ and usurp him, so he pretends affection to his clerk Kaia who is engaged to Ragner but infatuated with Solness. If Kaia stays, figures Solness, so will Ragnar. Then twenty-three-year-old Hilda Wangel appears; she met Solness ten years ago and saw him climb to the top of the last great tower he built and ever since has worshipped him - now, she is ready to be his 'princess'. Solness tells her his prosperity comes not from towers but from houses, which he began building when his wife Aline's house and all their possessions were destroyed by fire.

Later his twin sons died and guilt-ridden Solness feels his success has been achieved at the cost of his wife's fulfilment as a mother. Aline herself tells Hilda her sufferings are a punishment from God for loving her precious dolls (which were destroyed in the fire) more than her children. Solness has built a new house with a tower for himself and Aline, and Hilda, after persuading him to release Ragnar, wants him to climb the tower and crown it with a laurel wreath. He reveals he suffers from vertigo, but cannot resist Hilda's youth and her faith in him. He climbs, reaches the top, then falls to his death.

Kaia, clerk to Solness
Old Brovic
Ragnar, his son, assistant to Solness
Halvard Solness
Aline, his wife
Dr Herdel
Hilda Wangel

Matchmaker, The
Thornton Wilder
Comedy 4 Acts
Boston 1938

Horace Vandergelder, a rich merchant from Yonkers, just outside New York City, has decided in his sixties to remarry. His chosen bride is Irene Molly, a friend of his dead wife, who runs a millinery shop in New York City, this being one of the few occupations open to a respectable single woman in 1880s' America.

However, at the same time as he is bringing this affair to a head, with the help of Dolly Levi, another of his dead wife's friends, he is also desperate to prevent his lovely twenty-year-old daughter Ermengarde from marrying the man she loves, Ambrose Kemper, an artist the philistine Horace cannot help but loathe. In fact, though, Dolly herself is determined to marry the old man, and also to see Ermengarde and Ambrose happily wed, so she sets out to disrupt Horace's plan of sending his daughter out of town to forget about Ambrose.

Dolly's strategy is to encourage Horace in his pursuit of Irene, while waiting for those chances to subvert her rival which she is sure will crop up if only she is patient. Arriving at Irene's shop with Horace, who is on the point of proposing, Dolly finds that by coincidence the old man's two clerks, Cornelius Hackl and Barnaby Tucker, are already there trying to play the lovers with Irene and her assistant Minnie respectively.

She arranges, first, a dinner at which she hopes to expose Irene flirting with Cornelius, and, when this succeeds (to Horace's disgust) she then brings about a rendezvous of all the parties concerned at the home of Flora Van Huysen, where Ermengarde has been sent to isolate her from Ambrose. In due course, and after Horace's pig-headed tyranny has been flouted time and again, he and Dolly, Cornelius and Irene, Barnaby and Minnie and, of course, Ermengarde and Ambrose all happily pair off.

Horace Vandergelder
Cornelius Hackl, Barnaby Tucker, his clerks
Malachi Stack, his new clerk
Ambrose Kemper, an artist
Joe Scanlon
Rudolph
August
A cabman
Mrs Dolly Levi
Miss Flora Van Huysen
Miss Irene Molloy
Minnie Fay
Ermengarde, Kemper's betrothed
Gertrude
Miss Van Huysen's cook

Me and My Girl
Arthur L. Rose
Douglas Furber
Music by Noël Gay
Musical Comedy 2 Acts
London 1954

The lords and ladies gather at Hareford Hall to meet the new lord of the manor, who has been lost for years. Much to their horror he turns out to be a Cockney barrow-boy from Lambeth, one Bill Snibson, who in order to succeed to the title must convince his aunt, Maria Duchess of Dene, that he is a suitable person for such a task. Other members of the family hope he will not be up to it, as they will have to find work. Socialite beauty Jacqueline Carston has ideas of becoming the wife of the new heir, if she can prise him away from his Cockney girlfriend Sally Smith.

Despite efforts by his aunt to make him into an aristocrat, Bill is still a Lambeth lad at heart, and when he brings his old friends to the manor for a party, the Cockneys soon have the 'nobs' doing the 'Lambeth Walk' and talking in rhyming slang. Sally, conscious of her role in Bill's future, disappears for a while, and with the help of Lady Maria's old boyfriend, Sir John Tremayne, she returns as a fine lady, fit for any lord.

Gerald Bolingbroke, a good-looking young man

Lady Battersby
Lady Brighton
Lord Battersby
Jacqueline Carston, a dazzling young blonde
Charles, manservant
Mr Parchester, family solicitor
The Hon. Margaret Aikington
Lord Jasper Tring, a nonagenarian
Charles Boulting-Smythe
Maria, Duchess of Dene, a middle-aged martinet
Sir John Tremayne, a middle-aged baronet
Bill Snibson, Cockney Lord Hareford
Sally Smith, Bill's girl
Alf, Fred, Bert and Joe, servants
Telegraph boy
Mrs Brown, landlady
Bob Barking, Sally's friend
Police constable
Guests
Cockneys

Measure for Measure
William Shakespeare
Comedy 5 Acts
London 1604

Vienna's good-hearted Duke Vincentio decides to disguise himself as a friar and move about the city secretly in order to discover more about how his people think and feel. He appoints the cold-blooded and zealous adminstrator Angelo to rule temporarily in his place; Angelo's first act is to sentence to death a young Viennese named Claudio who has made his fiancée pregnant. Claudio's novitiate sister, Isabella, pleads with Angelo for her brother's life. Angelo is smitten with her and says she can only save Claudio if she gives herself to him. She refuses, and even Claudio cannot persuade his sister to dishonour herself in order to save his life. These goings-on eventually come to the attention of the Duke, who saves Claudio's life and Isabella's virtue through an ingenious if complex series of subterfuges. Everyone is duly rewarded or punished - justice being tempered with mercy - and the Duke weds Isabella.

Vincentio, the Duke	*Abhorson, an executioner*
Angelo, the Deputy	*Barnadine, a dissolute*
Escalus, an ancient Lord	* prisoner*
Claudio, a young	*Isabella, sister of Claudio*
* gentleman*	*Mariana, betrothed to*
Lucio, a fantastic	* Angelo*
Two other like gentlemen	*Juliet, betrothed to*
Varrius	* Claudio*
Provost	*Francisca, a nun*
Thomas, a friar	*Mistress Overdone,*
Peter, a friar	*Lords*
A justice	*Gentlemen*
Elbow, a simple constable	*Officers*
Froth, a foolish gentleman	*Guards*
Clown	*Other attendants*

Medea
Euripides
Tragedy 1 Act
Athens 431BC

In the course of his wanderings as Captain of the *Argo*, Jason met and took as his wife Medea, from Colchis in Asia Minor. After sharing desperate intrigues - the murders of Medea's brother and of King Pelius, sponsor of their voyage - the two found refuge in Corinth and raised two sons.

As the play opens, Jason has just left Medea to marry Glauce, daughter to King Creon of Corinth. Medea swears revenge on Jason, Creon and Glauce. Her threats come to Creon's attention, so to protect his daughter he banishes Medea and her sons. Medea pleads with Creon to spare her but continues to plot her revenge. Granted just one day's reprieve, Medea despairs of being able to prosecute her scheme when she meets Aegeus, King of Athens, who is so appalled by Jason's infidelity that he offers Medea refuge in his city.

Assured of an escape route, Medea lures Jason to a feigned reconciliation, agrees to leave Corinth and asks only that their sons be allowed to remain in Corinth. To this end she sends a golden coronet and a gown to Glauce, delivered by the two boys, as a supposed gesture of peace. The gifts, however, have been covered with a poison which kills both Glauce and Creon.

Jason realizes with Glauce's death that Medea has only feigned a reconciliation and fears for the life of his sons. He arrives too late to rescue them from Medea, who has murdered both to poison his life.

Nurse, to Medea and her sons
Tutor, to Medea's sons
Medea
Chorus
Creon, King of Corinth
Glauce, daughter of Creon
Jason, Medea's husband
Aegeus, King of Athens
Messenger
Medea's two sons

Melancholy Baby
S. K. Adams
Comedy 2 Acts
New York 1978

Rick and Kate, a young married couple living in New York City, have hit a rough patch in their marriage, largely brought on by Rick's refusal to hold a steady job, and Kate's consequent need to support them both by continuing to act in a soap opera she despises.

Kate throws Rick out of their flat just as her orphan sister, eleven-year-old Jane, is forced on her as a long-term house guest. In his annoyance at being evicted, Rick takes a job in California and insists that Kate must join him there if their marriage is to survive. At the same time he develops a close bond with Jane, an aspiring nightclub singer whose family, including Kate, are too self-absorbed to see how much emotional support such a young girl needs.

A final rupture between the couple is only narrowly avoided when Rick makes it clear that he will take Jane with him to California rather than leave her behind in the uncertain grasp of Kate's family, and Kate, impressed with his new good sense, agrees to go with them.

Rick
Kate, Rick's wife
Stephen, Kate's cousin
Debby, Kate's older sister
Jane, Kate's eleven-year-old sister
Dena, Kate's sister
Carlos, Dena's fiancé
Uncle David, Stephen's father

Member of the Wedding, A
Carson McCullers
Play 3 Acts
New York 1950

In a small Southern town in 1945, twelve-year-old Frankie Addams spends a lot of time sitting on the porch with the family negro cook, Bernice, and her playmate, John Henry, talking about her hopes for the future. She is a precocious girl and constantly changes her ideas and daydreams.

Her brother's forthcoming wedding is a source of confusion to her, and she decides that she will run away with the honeymoon couple. Kindly Bernice listens to her confused schemes with a mixture of disdain and pity and tries in her own simple way to set the girl straight. Although later a black acquaintance commits suicide through prejudice, little John Henry dies of illness, and the first atom bomb is dropped, these grave events make little difference to Frankie's egocentric pubescent attitudes. She makes new friends and plans new plans.

Bernice Sadie Brown	*Helen Fletcher*
Frankie Addams	*Doris*
John Henry West	*Sis Laura*
Jarvis, Frankie's brother	*T.T. Williams*
Janice, Jarvis's fiancée	*Honey Camden Brown*
Mr Addams	*Barney MacKean*
Mrs West	

Merchant of Venice, The
William Shakespeare
Comedy 5 Acts
London 1596

Bassanio, an impoverished Venetian noble, asks his friend Antonio, a wealthy trader, to lend him 3,000 ducats. The money is needed if Bassanio is to be able to marry Portia, a beautiful heiress whom he must woo in style. With his capital all committed, Antonio decides to borrow the sum from a Jewish usurer, Shylock, and agrees to forfeit a pound of his own flesh if he cannot make repayment on time.

Bassanio wins Portia's hand in a contest of wits devised by Portia's dead father, but his joy is cut short when news comes that Antonio's fortune has been lost with the destruction of his fleet at sea. Shylock claims his pound of flesh at the Venetian court, where Portia, disguised as a lawyer, argues successfully that the bond with Shylock is invalid since it constitutes a conspiracy against Antonio's life. The judge, the Duke of Venice, spares Shylock's life on condition that the usurer surrender half his estate to the state, half to Antonio. Antonio then surrenders his claim on condition that Shylock turn Christian and rescind the disinheritance of Jessica, Shylock's daughter, whom he had rejected for marrying a Christian.

Duke of Venice
Princes of Morocco and of Aragon, Portia's suitors
Antonio, Venetian merchant
Bassanio, Portia's preferred suitor
Solanio, Salerio, Gratiano, friends of Antonio and Bassanio
Lorenzo
Shylock, a Jewish usurer
Tubal
Launcelot Gobbo, Shylock's servant
Old Gobbo
Leonardo, Bassanio's servant
Balthasar and Stephano, Portia's servants
Portia, an heiress
Nerissa, Portia's confidante
Jessica, Shylock's daughter
Lords of Venice
Court officers
Gaolers
Servants
Attendants

Merry Wives of Windsor, The
William Shakespeare
Comedy 5 acts
London 1597

Sir John Falstaff, extravagant but without means, decides to seduce two married women, Mistress Ford and Mistress Page, who control their husbands' wealth. Two sycophants whom Falstaff has rejected betray him to the women's husbands. The women themselves turn on Falstaff when they discover that he has sent them identical love letters.

In a series of assignations designed by the women to humiliate him, Falstaff is dumped in a ditch, beaten by Ford while disguised as a woman, tormented by mock fairies in a wood and finally exposed to Ford and Page.

At the same time as Falstaff is pursuing his crude amours, Page's daughter Anne is the target of three suitors of roughly equal merit. Unlike Falstaff, whose tainted hopes come to nothing, Anne elopes from the forest scene of Falstaff's unmasking with her lover Fenton, and escapes the other two suitors, each of whom was championed by one of her parents.

Sir John Falstaff
Ford, a gentleman of Windsor
Page, a gentleman of Windsor
Mistress Ford, Ford's wife
Mistress Page, Page's wife
Anne Page, Pages's daughter
Fenton
Sir Hugh Evans
Doctor Caius
***Falstaff's men:** Bardolph, Pistol and Nym*
William Page
Shallow
Slender
Host of the Garter Inn
Robin
Simple
Rugby
Mistress Quickly
Servants

Middle-age Spread
Roger Hall
Play 10 Scenes
London 1979

Middle-aged, middle-class Colin and Elizabeth throw a dinner party, during which a series of flashbacks illustrate the background to the party's disastrous denouement.

Thoroughly nice Colin is promoted from assistant head to headmaster, but Elizabeth's apathy and domestic obsessions drive him into the arms of a teacher, Judy, who is separated from her solid but boring husband, Robert. Their affair is discovered by a neighbour, Reg, a leftie lecturer, who continually cheats on his wife Isobel; she is more interested in her arts and crafts.

The party begins well enough but when Colin and Elizabeth's daughter Judy is found to be pregnant by Reg and Isobel's son Stephen, Reg is so miffed at right-wing Robert that he reveals to all the affair between Colin and Judy. The party breaks up and the hosts go to do the dishes.

Elizabeth
Colin
Isobel
Reg
Judy
Robert

Midsummer Night's Dream, A
William Shakespeare
Comedy 5 Acts
London 1596

At Duke Theseus's palace in Athens, it is the day before the King's marriage to Hippolyta, Queen of the Amazons. Hermia and Lysander are in love, but her father Egeus wants her to wed Demetrius, loved by Hermia's friend Helena. When Theseus commands Hermia to obey her father, the lovers flee to a nearby forest, pursued by Demetrius and Helena. In the forest,

Fairy King Oberon is angry with his Queen Titania and orders Puck to sprinkle her eyes with juice from a magic flower which, when she wakes, will make her fall in love with the first creature she sees. Oberon also sees Demetrius and Helena blundering through the forest, and moved by her plight tells Puck to do the same to Demetrius that he may love Helena. Puck puts the juice on Titania's eyes while she sleeps, but mistakenly also uses it on the sleeping Lysander. When they wake he sees Helena and there is much confusion as everyone loves someone who does not love them.

Meanwhile a group of well-meaning, but artless, Athenian workmen are in the forest rehearsing a play *Pyramus and Thisbe* for the Duke's wedding entertainment, and naughty Puck conjures an ass's head onto lead player Bottom. His friends flee, and when Titania wakes, she falls in love with the ass, much to the merriment of Puck and Oberon, and Bottom is fêted and pampered by the fairies. Oberon orders Puck to undo the damage he has done with the lovers; he does so, and all is well between them - Lysander now loves Helena, and back at court Egeus gives them all his blessing.

Oberon decides he has had his sport with Titania and releases her from the spell. Bottom believes he had a fantastical dream and he and his naive colleagues play before the Duke and the court with great success and much merriment.

Theseus, Duke of Athens	*Hippolyta, Queen of the*
Egeus, father to Hermia	*Amazons*
Lysander	*Hermia*
Demetrius	*Helena*
Philostrate, master of the	*Oberon, King of the*
revels of Theseus	*Fairies*
Quince, the carpenter	*Titania, Queen of the*
Snug, the joiner	*Fairies*
Bottom, the weaver	***Fairies:**Puck (Robin*
Flute, the bellows-	*Goodfellow),*
mender	*Peaseblossom, Cobweb,*
Snout, the tinker	*Moth, Mustardseed*
Starveling, the tailor	*Other fairies, attendants*

Mikado, The
W.S. Gilbert and Arthur Sullivan
Comic Opera 2 Acts
London 1885

Subtitled *The Town of Titipu* this takes place in a mythical Japan. Nanki-Poo, a handsome young minstrel is in love with Yum-Yum, ward of the Lord High Executioner, Ko-Ko. Although only a cheap tailor by trade, he has become Lord High Executioner by a political manoeuvre from other officials. Now about to marry Yum-Yum, he is discussing marriage arrangements with Pooh-Bah, Lord Chief Justice. Yum-Yum and Nanki-Poo realize that their love is hopeless and he decides to hang himself, but Ko-Ko who has just had a letter from the Mikado complaining of a lack of executions, offers Nanki-Poo a deal. The young man can marry Yum-Yum for a month on condition he is executed for the Mikado's visit. He agrees, but when it transpires that the wife of an executed man must be buried alive, Ko-Ko who wishes to save Yum-Yum, sends the couple away and produces a document saying that the execution has taken place.

The Mikado visits Titipu and asks if anyone knows the whereabouts of his lost son - Nanki-Poo. The 'executed' prince must of course now come back to life with his new wife Yum-Yum and Ko-Ko by unarguable logic ensures a happy ending.

Songs include: 'If You Want to Know Who We Are'; 'Behold the Lord High Executioner'; 'Comes a Train of Little Ladies'; 'Three Little Maids from School are We'; 'The Sun Whose Rays'; 'The Flowers that Bloom in the Spring, Tra La'

The Mikado of Japan
Nanki-Poo, his son
Ko-Ko, Lord High Executioner
Pooh-Bah, Lord High Everything Else
Pish-Tush, a noble lord
Yum-Yum, Ward of Ko-Ko
Pitti-Sing, Yum-Yum's sisters
Peep-Bo,
Katisha
Schoolgirls
Nobles, guards, coolies

Militants, The
Norman Holland
Drama 3 Acts
Warrington 1969

Alderman Josiah Malin, mayor-elect of the Manchester suburb of Metringham, is caught up in support of Winston Churchill's anti-suffragette campaign to win Manchester for the Liberals in the spring of 1908. As Metringham's leading Liberal, Malin is also showing the ropes to the party's local candidate, Richard Ward, who is about to stand for Metringham.

Malin's pompous insensitivity has blinded him to the power of the suffragettes, but he begins to see his mistake when Ward resigns his candidacy in protest at the local Liberal's virulent anti-feminism. In rapid succession, Malin's daughter leaves home to work for the suffragettes in London, accompanied by Rachel Randall, wife of his Liberal colleague; Churchill loses the Manchester election through the efforts of the Women's Political and Social Union; and the mayor himself becomes the target of abuse from local feminists when he helps jail his wife's cousin, Sophie, for arson committed to protest for women's suffrage.

His humiliation is total when his wife of twenty-seven years, Lilian, leaves him after revealing that she has long been the secret leader of the Metringham branch of the women's movement. To avenge her cousin, Lilian organizes a women's assault on the Malin home, during which the mayor is ignominiously

dunked in a slimy horse trough he himself had donated to the town.

Alderman Joseph Malin
Reuben Randall, Liberal agent
Police Constable Thomas Dougan
Inspector Nathan Arkwright
Richard Ward, Liberal candidate
Nelly Brown, Malin's maid
Minnie Brown, Nelly's sister
Rachel Randall, Reuben's wife
Lilian Malin, Malin's wife
Vivian Malin, Malin's daughter
Sophie Ormesby, Lilian's cousin
Lady Honoria Cumberleigh
Eulalia Powle
'Captain' Ada Leyland
Suffragettes

Milk and Honey
Philip King
Comedy 3 Acts
Worthing 1959

Writer Basil Martin and wife Barbara live on the outskirts of Brighton; he is a bit of a bumbler, she is pleasant but houseproud. She is also mad that Basil has invited his hearty schoolchum George and his silly fiancée Delia to stay for a fortnight. Basil feels constantly in debt to George as he once saved him from drowning.

The domestic situation gets increasingly tense and inadvertently Barbara falls into the arms of their handsome young milkman. His attentions encourage her and she manages to relax, even ignoring an iron burn on the carpet. Meanwhile, Basil wants shapely local actress Faith Brantingham to star as a nun in his next play, and when George manages to save her from drowning (after pushing her off) she is brought back to the Martins. She quickly rushes off, however, revealing that she already has a part as a nun, in a new play; it seems that Basil's agent has done a good job.

When a trip to the Downs on the milkman's scooter fails to materialize for Barbara, Basil finds her sobbing in the kitchen. He imagines it is because he shouted at her for not appreciating his 'talent', but she responds affectionately to his sympathy and all seems well between them - until, that is, George runs into another old school chum and invites him and his wife, and his children, in for a drink...

Barbara Martin   *Delia Brown*
Basil Martin   *The milkman*
George Padstow   *Faith Brantingham*

Millionairess, The
George Bernard Shaw
Comedy 4 Acts
Vienna 1936

Flamboyant millionairess Epifania, her estranged husband Alastair, his mistress Patricia and Epifania's admirer Adrian all meet at the office of solicitor Julius

Sagamore. Epifania refuses to divorce Alastair and later throws over (literally) Adrian. Then she meets an Egyptian doctor who tends only to the poor and needy and she falls for him, but he will only marry her on his mother's condition she can earn her living unaided. She does so with great enterprise and ingenuity, and although in turn he does not strictly pass the test set by her father - turning 150 pounds into 50,000 pounds - she typically circumvents this, and attracted by her uniquely strong pulse, he agrees they should wed.

Julius Sagamore	Adrian Blenderbland
Epifania	The Doctor
Fitzfassenden	The man
Alastair	The woman
Fitzfassenden	The manager
Patricia Smith	

Miracle Worker
William Gibson
Drama 3 Acts
New York 1959

This dramatization is based on the true story of Helen Keller, struck deaf and blind by an infant illness towards the end of the last century in Tuscambia, Alabama. By the time she is a little girl, she is wild and uncontrollable and has the whole household in continual turmoil. No one can help, until at last a doctor sends them Annie Sullivan, a twenty-year-old formerly blind orphan. Annie's methods at first seem harsh to Helen's kindly mother Kate and even to her stern father Capt. Keller, and they doubt her suitability for the task. But when Annie begins to effectively discipline Helen, the family begin to relent. With infinite patience and courage, Annie teaches Helen to spell names of objects, although Helen cannot make the association between the word and the object. Finally, after Annie has had Helen alone for two whole weeks in the garden house, they return to the main house and the miracle occurs - Helen makes the fateful assocation and realizes everything has a name. The channel of communication between her and the outside world has at last been forged.

A doctor	James
Kate	Anagnos
Capt. Keller	Annie Sullivan
Helen	Viney
Martha	Seven blind girls
Percy	A servant
Aunt Ev	Offstage voices

Misalliance
George Bernard Shaw
Comedy 1 Act
London 1910

Lord Summerhays is well aware of his son Bentley's neurotic behaviour and can understand the exasperated attitude to him of Johnny Tarleton. Although Summerhays has proposed to her himself, it looks as if Johnny's sister, Hypatia, will probably marry his son

Bentley for his social status, although she really longs for a life of adventure and thrills. These both arrive together, when an aircraft crashes into the garden, the occupants being the handsome Joseph Percival and the beautiful Polish acrobat Lina Szczepanowska. Hypatia immediately falls in love with Percival.

Later, a gunman, who has come to kill Hypatia's father, John Tarleton, for seducing his mother, overhears her trying to seduce Percival and strongly reproaches her for such conduct with socialist speeches, before being disarmed by the lovely Lina.

Hypatia is now set on marrying Percival, of whom her father disapproves, while the nervous Bentley has found new strength in his pursuit of Lina who wants him to fly away with her.

John Tarleton, Jr	Joseph Percival
Bentley Summerhays	Lina Szczepanowska
Hypatia Tarleton	Julius Baker, gunman
Mrs Tarleton	
Lord Summerhays	
John Tarleton	

Misanthrope, The
Molière
Comedy 3 Acts
Paris 1666

To Alceste, frankness is everything. He despises society's flatterers and hypocrites, priding himself on his outspokenness. The trouble is, he takes it too far, often playing devil's advocate then switching sides when his opponents start to agree with him. When he criticizes Oronte's poetry, this determines Oronte to succeed in their rivalry for Célimène, whose loveliness masks the most hypocritical nature in Paris. Yet the contrary Alceste loves her, knowing her faults, and when Arsinoe, Célimène's rival for Alceste's affections, reveals letters from Célimène playing off one suitor against another, the disgusted Oronte quits the race.

After Alceste learns he has lost a lawsuit in which his cause was just, he decides not to appeal in order that he might make a martyr of himself, but it means he must flee Paris. Célimène is willing to marry him, but Alceste only wants her if she will join him. No, she says, she will marry him and live in Paris, but not in the countryside. He leaves, and his friends Philante and Eliante follow him to try to change his mind.

Arsinoe	Philante
Acaste	Alceste
Clitandre	Secretary of the Academy
Basque	Célimène
Oronte	Éliante
Dubois	

Miser, The
Molière
Comedy 2 Acts
Paris 1668

Harpagon is a rich old miser with two children, son

Cléante (in love with penniless neighbour Mariane), and daughter Elise (in love with Valère, posing as Harpagon's steward). Not knowing Cléante and Mariane's feelings, widower Harpagon himself decides to wed Mariane who must oblige him for her poor mother's sake. In order to thwart this, Cléante's servant La Flèche and his scheming girlfriend Frosine steal Harpagon's gold, intending to return it if he will break off the match. All this proves unnecessary; by an almost miraculous coincidence, it transpires Mariane and Valère are brother and sister, separated at childhood from their father, the Italian Count of Alberti, alias Harpagon's friend and neighbour Seigneur Anselm, who came to Paris to forget the tragic loss of his family. All are reunited - the Count and his family, the two pairs of lovers, and Harpagon and his darling gold.

Valère	Jacques, Harpagon's
Elise	servant
Cléante	First servant
Harpagon	Second servant
La Flèche	Mariane
Master Simon, a	Justice of the Peace
moneylender	Clerk to the Justice
Frosine	Seigneur Anselm

Misérables, Les
Alain Boublil, Claude-Michel Schönberg, Herbert Kretzmer and James Fenton
Musical 2 Acts
London 1980
Based on Victor Hugo's eponymous novel, the musical follows the life of the ex-convict Jean Valjean from his release after nineteen years on the chain gang until his quiet death seventeen years later, in the revolutionary year 1832.

On his release, Valjean finds that as an ex-convict he is unable to find honest employment. He resorts to stealing church silver, is caught in the act by the local bishop, pardoned by the old cleric and sent on his way. Astonished by the bishop's clemency, Valjean changes his name and by dint of hard work becomes a factory owner and Mayor of Montreuil-Sur-Mer in just eight years. But when he intercedes to help one of his ex-workers who is charged with prostitution, his nemesis, Inspector Javert, realizes his true identity and Valjean is forced once again to go on the run.

To keep a promise to the prostitute, made to her as she lay dying, Valjean retrieves her daughter, Cosette, from the abusive tavern keeper in whose care the child was left by her penniless mother.

By 1832, the child has grown into a beautiful young woman and falls in love with a young, aristocratic student revolutionary, Marius. During the uprising of that year, Marius is seriously wounded, and Valjean, who has been keeping a discreet eye on the young hothead rescues him from certain death, restores him to Cosette, explains to him the details of his sordid past, and resolves to leave the young couple to themselves.

Broken by the separation from his beloved Cosette, Valjean sinks into despondency and slides toward death. Marius discovers that it was Valjean who rescued him from death, and, spurred by both shame and gratitude, finds the dying old man just in time for a last reunion between him, Cosette and the noble ex-convict. Songs include: 'At the End of the Day'; 'Who Am I?'; 'Castle and Cloud'; 'In My Life'; 'On My Own'; 'A Little Fall of Rain'

Jean Valjean	Old couple
Police Inspector Javert	Travellers
Farmer	Drinkers
Labourer	Gavroche
Innkeeper	Old begger woman
Innkeeper's wife	Young prostitute
Bishop of Digne	Pimp
Constables	Eponine
Chain gang	**Thenardier's gang:**
Fantine	Montparnasse, Babet,
Foreman	Bryon, Clagueous
Workers	Enjolras
Factory girl	Marius
Old woman	Cosette
Crone	Combeferre
Pimp (Fauchelevent)	Feuilly
Bamatabois	Courfeyrac
Women workers	Joly
Whores	Grantaire
Young Cosette	Lesgles
Mme Thenardier	Jean Prouvaire
Young Eponine	
Drinker	
Young couple	
Drunk	
Diners	
Young man	
Young girls	

Miss Julie
August Strindberg
Tragedy 1 Act
Copenhagen 1888
Miss Julie is the daughter of a rural Swedish Count and his low-born but fiercely independent, intelligent, man-hating wife. Her mother's attitudes and the social differences between her mother and father have left Julie unable to form a 'normal' relationship with a man despite an intense desire to do so.

Left alone with the family servants to celebrate Midsummer's night, she taunts, and then is seduced by her father's valet, Jean. Jean is driven by an ambition to rise above his class and he and Julie plan an elopement. When they both realize, however, that their plans cannot succeed, Jean exploits Julie's dawning shame at their liaison to drive her to suicide.

Miss Julie
Jean, her father's valet
Kristine, her father's cook

Mister Roberts
Thomas Heggen and Joshua Logan
Drama 2 Acts
New York 1948

All is not happy aboard a drab US Navy cargo vessel tramping around the Pacific in World War Two. Cargo officer Lieut Roberts, desperate for active service, is continually thwarted by the despotic captain who blocks all his transfer applications. Then, after a year at sea without leave, the captain forbids the crew to go ashore at a South Seas liberty port. Roberts protests and the wily captain does a deal with him; no more letters requesting transfer (with their implied criticism of the ship's regime), and in return the captain will grant the crew leave. Roberts agrees, but later finds himself taking it out on the men, especially when seeing his chance of action slipping away after VE day. He gets so mad he dumps the captain's pet potted plant overboard, much to the captain's horror. Meanwhile, the crew discover Roberts' deal and send off another transfer letter, forging the captain's signature. Roberts gets the transfer and his place is taken by his sidekick Ensign Pulver. But when the news comes through that Roberts has been killed in action, Pulver uproots the two replacement palm trees and goes to confront the captain about his latest ban - on the crew's movie.

Chief Johnson	
Lieut (J.G.) Roberts	*Ensign Pulver*
Doc	*Dolan*
Dowdy	*Gerhart*
The Captain	*Payne*
Insignia	*Lieut Ann Girard*
Mannion	*Shore patrolman*
Lindstrom	*Military policeman*
Stefanowski	*Shore patrol officer*
Wiley	*Seaman*
Schlemmer	*Fireman*
Rober	*About twelve others*

Mixed Doubles
Fred Carmichael
Comedy 2 Acts
Dorset, USA 1972

Two distinct narratives interlock in this play, by focusing on the successive occupants of a set of rooms in the Casa Pericolo, a small Mexican tourist hotel.

First, Christopher and Shelley Sage, estranged and on the point of divorce, arrive at the hotel by coincidence, each with a new lover. Shelley has chosen, as has Christopher, someone temperamentally opposite to her estranged spouse. The accidental proximity in which they find themselves leads both of them to realize that they still belong together, and they are reunited when their respective lovers become vexed with their obvious need for one another and leave them to themselves.

The set of rooms they have occupied are given next to an elderly, but unmarried couple, Donald and Amy, who are hoodwinked by three other new guests into carrying a shipment of heroin into the US. The drug is disguised as the cremated remains of the bogus 'husband' of one of the three. The old couple, helped by their friend, Revd Glugg, discover and foil the plot, thus providing Amy, a writer of popular crime fiction, with her next subject, a retelling of their own improbable tale.

Luz
Wilma Burroughs, owner of the hotel
Shelley Sage
Howard Robertson, Shelley's lover
Julian, a handyman
Christopher Sage
Jackie, Christopher's lover
Donald Steed
Amy Dimston, Donald's lover
Revd Simon Glugg
Lilly Babber, a drug smuggler
George Ark, a drug smuggler

Mixed Doubles
George Melly, Alan Ayckbourn, John Bowen, Lyndon Brook, David Campton, Alun Owen, Harold Pinter, James Saunders, Fay Weldon
An Entertainment
London 1969

Eighteen sketches on the subject of marriage linked by monologues to unseen people.

The Vicar (Melly). An uplifting address at a wedding ceremony.

A Man's Best Friend (Saunders). A bride and groom in a railway carriage off on honeymoon. The groom is extremely agitated, tapping his feet and trying to tune a guitar he can't play. Clearly the night is not going to be all bliss.

The Bank Manager (Melly). He is talking to a client, himself, about his extravagant spending.

Score (Brook): Sheila and Harry are playing - miming - a game of tennis against unseen Jim and Jane, who are more beautiful and successful. On the surface, it's a friendly game, but underneath ...

The Lawyer (Melly). A lady wants a divorce. The lawyer only wants to help but is over-interested in the grotesque: 'Did he ever suggest you grace the marital chamber disguised as a nun, a schoolgirl, lady astronaut, or a circus equestrian ...?'

Norma (Owen). In a park shelter a man and woman are having a serious conversation about their affair, which he thinks is serious. Her husband, though, has found out about her adultery and she must end her little bit of fun.

The Nannie (Melly). In the park, a nanny is rocking a pram and reminiscing about an unsatisfactory holiday in Tangier.

Night (Pinter). A man and woman in their forties reminisce about their first meeting and the details of the ensuing fornication, apparently confusing each other with other women and men.

The Psychoanalyst (Melly). A heavily accented foreign psychiatrist is ostensibly listening to a (silent) woman on his couch but is mostly interested in his fee.

Permanence (Weldon). Peter and Helen are on a camping holiday in a tent. They are not getting on well, mostly because Helen's daughter Judy is not Peter's.

The Doctor (Melly). He deals with a man who has various aches and pains, a pregnant young girl, and a woman who cannot cope. When they have gone he gets stuck into the pills himself.

Countdown (Ayckbourn). A husband and wife hardly speak but we hear their thoughts. They are hostile.

The Union Official (Melly). An abrasive workers' representative is working over the management. He receives telephone calls from his bossy wife which make him more accommodating.

Silver Wedding (Bowen). Academic Julian is (perhaps deliberately) late home for the evening of his silver wedding anniversary. It is getting too late to go from Purley to a swank restaurant in London's West End. The couple discover that since the thrill of sex faded they don't like each other much. They stay at home.

The Director (Melly). A thoroughly 'professional', heartless TV director revels in the horrors of a hospital where old folk are dying.

Resting Place (Campton). An old man and an old woman think about a bit of grub, and what might have been, while contemplating death in a cemetery.

The Headmaster (Melly). Hopping mad that his school has been trounced at rugger by a day school, the headmaster proposes to thrash the whole school, starting with the captain of the first fifteen.

The Advertising Man (Melly). A ghastly late-sixties trendy exhorts his team to 'think square' because that's all that the admass can understand.

Linkman	Audrey
Jackie	Julian
Pete	The old man
Harry	The old woman
Sheila	
The woman	
The man	
The woman	
The man	
Helen	
Peter	
The husband	
The wife	

Month in the Country, A
Ivan Turgenev
Comedy 3 Acts
Moscow 1872

When the naive but attractive young Beliaev arrives at the estate of Yslaev to tutor young son Kolia, three women in the household all fall for him with disturbing results. Vera, ward of Yslaev's wife Natalia, confesses her love to Natalia who is herself smitten with Beliaev; the ensuing complications make Vera decide to wed rich old neighbouring landowner Bolshintsov, much to the delight of the cynical local doctor who will reap a team of carriage horses for his part in 'the deal'. Natalia herself confesses to her platonic lover, family friend and permanent guest Rakitin, and he decides he must leave. The sensuous maid Katia has also fallen for Beliaev and she postpones her decision to wed the servant Matvei. Beliaev himself soon quits his post, unable to cope with all these ramifications, and is followed by Lizaveta Bogdanova who leaves the employ of Yslaev's mother Anna to marry the scheming doctor.

Shaaf, Kolia's German tutor
Natalia
Anna Semyenovna, Natalia's mother-in-law
Lizaveta Bogdanova, her companion
Rakitin
Kolia
Beliaev
Matvei
Ignaty Illyich Shpichelsky, the doctor
Vera
Katia
Yslaev
Bolshintsov

Moon for the Misbegotten, A
Eugene O'Neill
Drama 4 Acts
USA 1952

Connecticut tenant farmer widower Phil Hogan is a little bull of an Irishman whose dominance has driven away his three sons, with sanctimonious Mike the last to leave. But Phil is dominated by strong daughter Josie, a big raw woman not without beauty. She pretends loose morals and loves their landlord, dissipated Jim Tyrone, an actor who inherited the land from his father. Jim loves Josie but wants to return to the bright lights of Broadway, and when Phil and Josie suspect him of going back on his word to sell them the farm at a reasonable price and instead sell it to their rich antagonistic neighbour Harder, they concoct a scheme. Josie will seduce Phil, and when the pair are discovered *in flagrante* by Hogan and witnesses, Jim will have to pay up. It does not work out that way; Jim has no intention of going back on his word, and all he wants to do is rest his weary head against Josie's welcoming bosom. This he does, and when Hogan turns up next morning without witnesses, she realizes Dad was playing a double game. But all he wanted was happiness for Josie, and when Jim leaves, grateful and revived with Josie's love, father and daughter are left alone together to tend their farm.

Josie Hogan
Phil Hogan
Mike Hogan
James Tyrone, Jr
T. Stedman Harder

Moon is Blue, The
Hugh F. Herbert
Comedy 3 Acts
New York 1951

Young architect Don picks up aspiring young actress Patty on the observation tower of the Empire State Building. She wants to be picked up and agrees to go back to his apartment for dinner provided he does not try to seduce her. She does not mind kissing, but that is all. Complications occur when upstairs neighbour Dave calls. He is rich, charming and a bit dissipated; he is also the father of Cynthia, Don's ex-girlfriend. They broke up the night before because Don did not want to go to bed with Cynthia. Patty likes Dave and Don gets the wrong idea, as does Patty's dad, Detective O'Neill, who arrives looking for her. He hits Don and knocks him out.

Later Patty returns to apologize - she has also been stung by Cynthia's taunt that she is a 'professional virgin' and wants to know what it means. Don tells her you only advertise something when you want to sell it. She leaves without giving him her telephone number, but next day they meet again 'coincidentally' on the observation tower. He proposes and she accepts.

Patty O'Neill
Donald Gresham
David Slater
Detective Michael O'Neill, Patty's father

Mornings at Seven
Paul Osborn
Drama 3 Acts
New York 1939

The relationships between all the members of a claustrophobically inward-looking American small town family have been moulded, for decades, by the youthful adultery of Amy Gibbs and her brother-in-law Thor Swanson. Amy, Thor and his wife Cora, Amy's sister, have lived their adult lives in the same house, immediately opposite the home of another sister, Ida Bolton, and her husband Carl and forty-year-old son Homer. Very close by, the eldest of the four sisters, Esty, lives with her husband David, a university professor who is entirely alienated from Esty's family.

When Homer brings home his fiancée of seven years, Myrtle Brown, to meet the family for the first time, and announces he will be taking over the house built for him by Carl years before, he sets off a series of emotional whirlwinds which first threaten, and then re-align, the emotional ties between every member of the family.

Amy, believed by her sisters to have been Thor's lover during the whole of their life together, moves in with Carl and Ida when she discovers their suspicions, and realizes she must abandon her forlorn love for Thor. David and Carl, who is in the grip of a spell of finding life empty, decide to live together when David, no longer able to tolerate Esty's absorption in her family, decides he must separate from her. And finally, Homer,

who almost loses his chance of a separate life with Myrtle, chooses instead to marry and claim the home Carl built for him. As the play ends, the beginnings of a new set of relationships emerge when Carl returns home, and David makes a tentative effort to bring Esty back into his life.

In the home on the left:
Theodore Swanson
Cora Swanson
Aaronetta Gibbs
In the home on the right:
Ida Bolton
Carl Bolton
Homer Bolton
Myrtle Brown, Homer's fiancée
Esther Crampton
David Crampton, Esther's husband

Mother Courage and Her Children
Bertolt Brecht
Tragedy 12 Scenes
Switzerland 1941

Written shortly before World War Two as a warning to the Danes against war profiteering - 'you need a long spoon to sup with the devil' - *Mother Courage* is set in the seventeenth-century during the Thirty Years' War which ravaged Germany.

Anna Fierling is serving with the Swedish army as a canteen woman, and with her wagon, drawn by her three children, she intends making a living from the war while keeping her kids out of it. One by one, however, they are taken from her; Eilif is recruited and later shot for killing one peasant too many; Swiss Cheese for defending the regimental cashbox too conscientiously; Kattrin when warning the town of Halle that the enemy are at the gates. The tenacious Mother Courage at first prospers, criss-crossing Europe with the hypocritical Chaplin and the womanizing Cook, but then her business declines. Finally, she is left hauling the wagon herself, still looking for business among the troops, the mud and the blood.

Mother Courage (Anna Fierling)	*A clerk*
	A young soldier
Kattrin, her dumb daughter	*An older soldier*
	A peasant
Eilif, her eldest son	*A peasant's wife*
Swiss Cheese, her younger son	*The young man*
	The old woman
The recruiter	*Another peasant*
The sergeant	*His wife*
The cook	*The young peasant*
The general	*The ensign*
The chaplin	*Soldiers*
The armourer	*A voice*
Yvette Pottier	
Man with patch	
Another sergeant	
The ancient colonel	

Mother, The
Bertolt Brecht
Drama 14 Scenes
Berlin 1931

Pelagea Vlasova, a worker's widow in Tzarist Russia, scrapes and sacrifices to feed her son Pavel, whose wages are increasingly cut by the Suchlinov works. When Pavel joins the revolutionary workers and begins to print leaflets at home, she is most disturbed, but to keep her son out of trouble she volunteers to distribute the leaflets herself.

Gradually she becomes more and more involved in the workers' cause and begins to understand the mechanics of repression. Her son is caught and imprisoned, and Vlasova's commitment increases. She learns to read, she helps striking workers, and when Pavel returns from Siberia, symbolically she carries on printing leaflets instead of cutting him his bread; they are now more united in their 'third cause' than they ever were as mother and son.

Later Pavel is arrested and shot and Vlasova becomes 'mother' to a whole militant class. Her dawning social awareness and understanding of Marxism culminate in cunning displays of dramatic dialectics aimed against her hypocritical neighbours and unaware women contributing to the war effort. Vlasova is rewarded when she carries the red flag through the streets during the October revolution.

Pelagea Vlasova	*Nikolai Vesovchikov*
Pavel Vlasova	*Sigorski*
Anton	*Prison warden*
Andrei	*Lushin*
Ivan	*Butcher*
Mascha	*Vasil Yefimovitch*
Policeman	*Butcher's wife*
Commissioner	*Workers*
Factory porter	*Neighbours*
Smilgin	*Strikebreakers*
Karpov	*Women*

Mourning Becomes Electra
Eugene O'Neill
3 Plays
New York 1932
See: *Homecoming; Hunted, The; Haunted, The*

Mousetrap, The
Agatha Christie
Mystery 2 Acts
London 1952

Giles and Mollie Ralston have inherited Monkswell Manor and converted it into a guest house. Their first guests arrive during a heavy snowstorm - the fussy Mrs Boyle, good-natured Maj. Metcalf, the neurotic young Christopher Wren, the rather masculine Miss Casewell, and unexpectedly because of the bad weather, the somewhat sinister Mr Paravicini.

Next morning they are snowbound and the local police phone to tell them to expect Detective Sergeant Trotter on a matter of some urgency. Trotter is young and efficient and arrives on skis. He reveals a connection between Monkswell Manor and a recent murder in London; several years ago three local children in need of care and protection were sent to a farming couple, the Stannings, who so mistreated them that one of the children died. Mr Stanning subsequently died in jail and it was Mrs Stanning who was the recent murder victim. Nobody takes this story too seriously until Mrs Boyle is strangled and it is revealed that she was the magistrate who sent the children to the Stannings. Suspicions mount, everyone distrusts everyone else and the *Three Blind Mice* motif indicates another likely murder ... until, that is, the culprit is discovered and apprehended.

Mollie Ralston	*Mr Paravicini*
Giles Ralston	*Detective Sergeant Trotter*
Christopher Wren	
Mrs Boyle	
Maj. Metcalf	
Miss Casewell	

Move Over Mrs Markham
Ray Cooney and John Chapman
Farce 2 Acts
London 1971

Joanna Markham and Linda Lodge, whose husbands are partners in a children's book company, meet in Joanna's elegant London flat. Linda persuades Joanna to lend her the flat that night for an assignation with her lover, Walter. At the same time Joanna's husband, Philip, has promised the flat to his partner, Henry, Linda's husband, for yet another assignation. The couples will also have to compete for space with the Markham's *au pair*, Sylvie, and her lover Alistair. When Philip finds a love note to Linda, from Walter, he wrongly accuses his wife of having a lover. In a fit of pique she tries to seduce Alistair.

When all the prospective partners start to arrive, and the ensuing chaos is at its height, Mrs Smythe, a staid, slightly dotty best-selling children's author, arrives unexpectedly to offer her books to the partners, in a deal that would make their fortunes. After many near misses with naked and semi-naked people nearly meeting the old lady, a deal is finally struck, and Philip is reconciled to Joanna, Henry to Linda, and Sylvie to Alistair.

Joanna Markham
Alistair Spenlow
Sylvie
Linda Lodge
Philip Markham
Henry Lodge
Walter Pangbourne
Olive Harriet Smythe
Miss Wilkinson

Mrs Warren's Profession
George Bernard Shaw
Drama 4 Acts
London 1902

Self-possessed Vivie Warren, twenty-two, was a maths genius at college and intends to make her fortune doing calculations for engineers, electricians and insurance companies. Her expensive upbringing and education was paid for by her mostly absent mother whom she hardly knows. While Vivie is staying with a family friend in the country, her mother arrives with the tough and slightly vicious Sir George Crofts, and platonic friend Praid, a romantic old artist. Viv introduces them to her charming, penniless local boyfriend Frank Gardner and when his father, the Revd Samuel, arrives it appears he knew Mrs Warren from the possibly murky old days.

Viv is slightly contemptuous of her blowsy mother, but when they are alone Mrs Warren tells her of her hard life and confesses she made her money from brothels, and Viv's contempt turns to admiration. However, Sir George is after Vivie, and her curt refusal leads him to tell her that he and her mother are still partners in the brothels which are still making a great deal of money. He also tells her that Frank, with whom she has been billing and cooing, is her half-brother, both sharing the Revd Gardner as their father. Poor Viv returns to London and refuses any more money from her mother. Frank arrives and when she tells him of her mother's profession it is clearly all over between them - he will not take Mrs Warren's money and he leaves Viv a goodbye note. Mrs Warren herself arrives attempting reconciliation, but Viv tells her goodbye; she must now go her own way and make her own money. As her mother leaves, Vivie sobs with relief.

Praed
Sir George Crofts
Revd Samuel Gardner
Frank Gardner
Vivie Warren
Mrs Kitty Warren

Much Ado About Nothing
William Shakespeare
Comedy 5 Acts
London 1598

Don Pedro, Prince of Aragon, arrives at the seat of Leonato, Governor of Messina, fresh from putting down a rebellion by his bastard brother, Don John. He has been reconciled with his brother and now travels with him and with Lord Benedick and Lord Claudio, a young Florentine whom Don John deeply resents. Benedick has long been in love with Leonato's niece, the spinster Beatrice, as Claudio is with Leonato's daughter, Hero. By trickery and disguise, Don John's comrade Borachio convinces Claudio that Hero has been unfaithful.

Borachio and Don John offer Don Pedro their bogus proof of Hero's duplicity, and Claudio denounces her at the altar where they have come to wed. The wise and cunning Friar Francis persuades Hero to hide away until he can prove her innocence, and then gives out that she is dead. Don John's plot is uncovered when Borachio boasts drunkenly of his part in it, and Leonato offers Claudio his 'niece' in place of Hero. The 'niece', of course, turns out to be Hero herself, whose reconciliation with her fiancé is followed by the welcome news that Don John has been arrested.

Don Pedro, Prince of Aragon
Don John, his bastard brother
Lord Claudio
Lord Benedick
Leonato, Governor of Messina
Antonio, Leonato's brother
Balthasar, Don Pedro's attendant
Borachio and Conrade, Don John's attendants
Friar Francis
Dogberry, a constable
Verges, a parish officer
A sexton
A boy
Hero, Leonato's daughter
Beatrice, Leonato's niece
Margaret and Ursula, Hero's attendants
Messengers
Watchman
Attendants

Murder at the Vicarage
Agatha Christie
Mystery 2 Acts
London 1949

Unpopular Col Protheroe is found shot dead in the vicarage at St Mary Mead and almost everyone is under suspicion - even Miss Marple, whom the Colonel was about to evict. But when local artist Lawrence Redding confesses, the case seems cut-and-dried. Further evidence seems to prove Redding innocent, but covering up for the Colonel's second wife, glamorous Mrs Anne Protheroe with whom he is having an affair. More evidence turns up - from Miss Marple herself - which then seems to clear Mrs Protheroe, but the real murderer has already made some telling mistakes - which are, of course, noticed and noted by Miss Marple. Other characters under suspicion include the Colonel's flighty teenage daughter Lettice, the vicar's wife Griselda who made a strange rendezvous with Redding, and Ronald Hawes, the nervy curate suspected of stealing church funds. When Miss Marple confronts the killer - or killers - with her evidence, there is yet more tragedy before justice triumphs.

The vicar, Revd Leonard   *Ronald Hawes*
  Clement   *Lettice Protheroe*
Griselda   *Miss Marple*
Dennis, the vicar's   *Mrs Price Ridley*
  nephew   *Anne Protheroe*
Mary, the maid   *Lawrence Redding*

Dr John Haydock
Inspector Slack
Police Constable Jennings

Murder has been Arranged, A
Emlyn Williams
Drama 3 Acts
London 1930

Under the terms of an eccentric will, Sir Charles Jasper will inherit two million pounds at the stroke of eleven pm on the day of his fortieth birthday. He decides to hold an equally eccentric party for himself on the day and chooses as the venue the stage of the St James's Theatre, once the scene of a murder Sir Charles has written a book about. The only possible beneficiary other than Sir Charles is Maurice Mullins, a distant cousin long since disappeared (or so Sir Charles thinks).

When Mullins arrives unexpectedly at the party, he seems the soul of charm, but has in fact come to murder Sir Charles and accede to the fortune. Sir Charles is duly poisoned, and Mullins' part in the crime, suspected by his young wife Beatrice, is confirmed when Sir Charles' ghost appears at the head of the dining-table in his place. The ghost so convinces Mullins it is real that he blurts out his confession, under the impression that the fortune is now lost to him anyway. The circumstances of Sir Charles' murder, and of Mullins' unmasking had, somewhat eerily, been predicted in Sir Charles' account of the earlier murder which had taken place in an almost identical way.

Miss Groze, Sir Charles Jasper's secretary
Cavendish
Mrs Wragg
Jimmy North
Beatrice Jasper, Sir Charles's wife
Mrs Arthur, Beatrice's mother
Sir Charles Jasper
Maurice Mullins, Sir Charles's cousin
A woman

Murder in the Cathedral
T. S. Eliot
Verse Play 2 Parts
Canterbury 1935

This play deals with the events that lead to the murder of Thomas à Becket. A chorus of poor women of Canterbury, sensing that something is about to disrupt their lives, shelter in the Cathedral. Becket, seven years in exile, is about to return. He has not properly made his peace with King Henry and although the clergy are optimistic, the Chorus has serious doubts.

Becket returns to face four temptations; compromise with the King, assume power as Chancellor, lead a nationalist struggle, or deliberately seek martydom. He gives himself up to the will of God, and in the Interlude preaches on birth and death, mourning and rejoicing.

Four days pass and the King's knights accuse Becket of treason with the Pope and the King of France, a charge which he denies and he refuses to exile himself from England.

The Chorus express their fears as Becket is murdered by the knights who justify their actions to the audience by reasoning that Becket was selfish in seeking martyrdom for himself rather than using his power as Archbishop to bring stability to the country. The priests and the Chorus praise the act of martyrdom as bringing new strength to the Church.

Chorus of the women of Canterbury
Archbishop Thomas à Becket
Three priests
Four tempters
Messenger
Attendants

Murder is Announced, A
Agatha Christie
Mystery 3 Acts
Brighton 1977

Letitia Blacklock and her companion Bunny live at Little Paddocks in the village of Chipping Cleghorn. Staying with them are Letitia's second cousins Patrick and Julia. On the morning of Friday 13th they see an astonishing insert in their local paper: 'A murder is announced and will take place on Friday 13th at Little Paddocks at 6.30. Friends please accept this the only intimation.' That evening several curious friends arrive and at 6.30 precisely the lights go out and three shots are fired. When the lights go on, the body of the mysterious Rudi Scherz is found shot dead. Villager and amateur sleuth Miss Marple decides to investigate; she subsequently uncovers a plot full of deception and double-identity revolving around a million pound inheritance. There is yet another murder before Miss Marple is able to satisfactorily unravel and explain the puzzles, exposing the guilty man - or woman.

Julia Simmons
Letitia Blacklock
Dora Bunner, 'Bunny'
Patrick Simmons
Mitzi
Miss Marple
Phillipa Haymes
Mrs Swettenham
Edmund Swettenham
Rudi Scherz
Inspector Craddock
Sergeant Mellors

Music Man, The
Meredith Willson
Musical 2 Acts
New York 1957

A fast-talking travelling salesman and conman, 'Professor' Harold Hill, arrives in River City, Iowa, posing as a music teacher and instrument salesman, and quickly obtains orders for both instruments and uniforms from most of the town's parents, all of them anxious that their sons should join the Boy's Band the 'Professor' undertakes to create.

His smooth chat and enthusiasm win the support of the whole town, except for the mayor, Mr Shinn, and the local librarian, Marian Paroo, who sets out to unearth Hill's credentials as part of her determination to expose him. His nearly magical capacity to motivate the boys of the town changes her mind, however, and even though she finds evidence to disprove Hill's claims of musical accomplishment, Marian is so taken by his charm that she suppresses the information so that the 'Professor' can carry on.

As the day arrives when the band will have to give its first performance another travelling salesman makes the truth about Hill known, and the townsfolk organize a party of searchers to hunt him down, but his escape is so well planned that he could easily evade them. Instead, having discovered Marian's complicity in concealing his musical ignorance, he realizes he is in love for the first time in his life, stays behind to meet her, and is captured by the town Constable.

Hill is on the point of being condemned for fraud when the band enters, uniformed and at the ready; he takes the part of conductor, and, to his amazed relief, the boys perform a terrible but satisfying version of the Minuet in G for the parents. Hill is saved and he and Marian can look forward to a happy, settled life together. Songs include: 'Seventy-six Trombones'; 'Goodnight, My Someone'; 'Lida Rose'; 'Till There Was You'

Charlie Cowell	Winthrop Paroo
Conductor	Eulalie Mackecknie Shinn
Harold Hill	Zaneeta Shinn
Mayor Shinn	Gracie Shinn
Ewart Dunlop	Alma Hix
Oliver Hix	Maud Dunlop
Jacey Squires	Ethel Toffelmier
Olin Britt	Mrs Squires
Marcellus Washburn	Constable Locke
Tommy Djilas	Townspeople and children
Marian Paroo	
Mrs Paroo	
Amaryllis	

Musical Chairs
Ronald Mackenzie
Play 3 Acts
London 1932

The Schindler family are prospecting for oil on their land in Poland and are desperate for a strike to save them from foreclosure. When Mrs Schindler's son Geoffrey (from her previous marriage) brings home American fiancée Irene, she has an affair with sensitive Joseph (Mr Schindler's son from his previous marriage), a cynic who plays piano beautifully but scorns the oil business. Oil is struck in the nick of time, but there is a great storm and a flood, and Mary (Mrs Schindler's daughter who is in love with Joseph) runs from the

house to drown herself, distraught over Joseph and Irene. Joseph saves her but is drowned; the family sell up and move out.

Wilhelm Schindler
Joseph Schindler
Irene Baumer
Mary Preston
Anna
Mrs Schindler
Geoffrey Preston
Samuel Plagett

My Fair Lady
Alan Jay Lerner and Frederick Loewe
Musical 2 Acts
New York 1956
See: *Pygmalion*
Songs include: 'On the Street Where You Live'; 'Wouldn't it be Luverly'; 'The Rain in Spain'; 'I Could Have Danced all Night'; 'Get Me to the Church On Time'

My Sister Eileen
Joseph Fields and Jerome Chodorov
Comedy 3 Acts
New York 1940
Sisters Ruth and Eileen Sherwood move from Columbus, Ohio to New York's Greenwich Village in search of fame and fortune. Ruth, the competent self-reliant one, is the leader and wants work as a writer; Eileen is stunningly beautiful and wants to be an actress. They are conned into living in a dank and noisy basement by landlord Appopolous, but help soon comes from many young men, usually attracted to Eileen. Frank from the local deli helps out with food; the 'wreck' from upstairs makes himself useful while his 'wife' Helen entertains her mother in the house above; reporter Chic Clark sends Ruth out on a story in order to get Eileen alone, and a misunderstanding with some Brazilian naval cadets brought home by Ruth after her assignment, leads to Eileen going to jail. In the midst of all this, their father Walter arrives and demands they return home. Lo and behold, when Eileen is released she is awarded a Brazilian medal and Ruth gets a newspaper job and a boyfriend, writer Robert Baker. The sisters can now tell Dad 'no thanks' - they have made it in New York. Just when everything seems hunky-dory, Appopolous cons them into renewing their lease, and the subway blasting beneath them turns into incessant drilling.

Mr Appopolous	Other street arabs
Ruth Sherwood	Capt. Fletcher
Eileen Sherwood	Helen Wadde
Jensen	Frank Lippencott
A street arab	Chic Clark
A pair of drunks	Cossack
Lonigan	Violet Shelton
The wreck	Mrs Wade

My Three Angels

Robert Baker   *The Consul*
Six future Admirals   *A workman*
Walter Sherwood   *Street vendors*
A prospective female   *Passers-by*
  tenant

My Three Angels
Bella and Samuel Spewack
Comedy 3 Acts
London 1955

Felix Dulay and his wife, Emilie, and daughter, Marie Louise, run a general store in French Guiana. It is owned by Felix's cousin, Gaston Lemare, who is about to arrive from France on a tour of inspection; he is avaricious and mean and is bringing with him his nephew, Paul, whom he has threatened to disinherit if he marries his love, Marie Louise. He is to announce to the Dulays his engagement to an heiress picked by Gaston. The Dulays are also apprehensive because they realize that Felix's habit of giving extended credit has led the business into a loss, and Gaston will sack him.

Fortunately for the Dulays, three members of the Guianese penal colony, whom they have treated well, are repairing their roof and these three 'angels' resolve to avert the impending trouble. In a climax of black humour, they kill firstly the odious Gaston, and then Paul, when he inherits Gaston's estate and looks set to jilt Marie Louise. The Dulay's future is left as assured as they could ever have hoped.

Felix Dulay
Emilie
Marie Louise Dulay
Mme Parole
Alfred
Jules
Joseph
Gaston Lemare
Paul Cassagon
Sub-Lieut Espoir

Mystery at Blackwater
Dan Sutherland
Drama 3 Acts
London 1954

Based on the novel *The Woman in White* by Wilkie Collins.

Walter Hartwright meets a young, very frightened woman, dressed entirely in white, on a Hampstead road in 1850s. Before disappearing, she reveals that her fear has something to do with Sir Percival Glyde who has, by coincidence, recently married the woman Hartwright loves, now Lady Laura Glyde, and whom this young woman exactly resembles.

Hartwright rushes to Laura's new home at Blackwater Park, Hampshire to see if she is in danger, and blunders into a plot, hatched by Glyde and his sinister friend Count Fosco, to defraud Laura of her considerable fortune. With the help of Laura's half-sister, Marian Halcombe, the fraud is prevented, leaving Glyde more desperate for the money than ever, and Hartwright, along with Marian, eager to discover the identity of the woman in white so that they can discover the cause of her fear of Sir Percival.

Operating together, they manage to corner Sir Percival into the claim that a young woman was the mad daughter of one of his local acquaintances, Mrs Cathrick, and that he has been paying her costs at an asylum out of pure altruism. Before they can go very far in attempting to disprove Sir Percival's story, both Hartwright and Marian are laid low by grief over Laura's sudden death.

Marian, however, quietly resumes her investigations, and manages to prove that it is not Laura who has died, but the young woman in white, whose place in the asylum Sir Percival has forced Laura to take. Confronted with Laura, whom Marian rescues, Sir Percival threatens to murder Marian, Laura and Hartwright - all witnesses. He trains a shotgun on Laura, but is himself fatally shot when Hartwright tries to wrestle the gun away.

Walter Hartwright
Anna Catherick, the woman in white
Doctor
Marian Halcombe, Laura's half-sister
Mrs Michelson
Alice
Laura Glyde
Count Fosco
Mme Fosco, Count Fosco's wife
Mrs Catherick

Nathan the Wise
Gotthold Lessing
Drama 5 Acts
Berlin 1793

A stoical Jewish merchant, Nathan, returns to Moslem-held Jerusalem to find that his adopted daughter, Recha, has been saved from a fire by a young German crusader, Conrade, himself just released from prison owing to his uncanny resemblance to the missing brother of Saladin, his captor.

Nathan finds the young hero to reward his bravery and discovers with evident surprise that Conrade's last name, von Stauffen, is the same as Recha's. Before he can do more than offer his gratitude, Nathan is called to court to provide a state loan for Saladin. A sum is agreed between the two and Saladin is moved when Nathan holds back only enough of his fortune to reward the young knight. Saladin remembers his former captive and orders him to court.

Meanwhile, Recha's bigoted Christian companion, Daya, has poisoned Conrade's faith in Nathan by claiming that the merchant had stolen his charge, in her infancy, from a Christian family. Conrade, who has fallen in love with Recha, repeats this story to the Christian Patriarch of Jerusalem, who sends a spy to Nathan's household for verification. By coincidence, the spy is the same man who had put Recha in Nathan's care, eighteen years before, after the death of her mother and disappearance of her father. Nathan discovers from the spy that Recha and Conrade are, in fact, brother and sister, and reveals their blood tie to Saladin, who has until this moment been favourably disposed to their plan to marry.

When Nathan goes on to reveal that the young couple's father had taken up a German name upon marrying their mother, a von Stauffen, but was by birth the Sultan's brother, the court is suffused with a sense of reconciliation between Jew, Christian and Moslem.

Saladin, the Sultan
Sittah, Saladin's sister
Nathan, a rich merchant
Recha, Nathan's adopted daughter
Daya, Recha's companion
Conrade, a Knight Templar
Hafi, a dervish
Athanasios, Patriarch of Jerusalem
Bonafides, a friar
An Emir
Mamelukes
Slaves

National Health, The
Peter Nichols
Comedy 2 Acts
London 1969

Two members of the staff in a London hospital, Dr Neil Boyd and Nurse Norton, a black West Indian, have fallen in love, each without the other knowing it. The halting progress they make toward declaring their love is narrated by Barnet, the cynical orderly who prepares deceased patients for the undertaker, in the style of a bad romantic novel.

The affair unfolds amidst the tragi-comic comings and goings of the patients on Dr Boyd's ward. He is prevented from declaring his love by the opposition of his father, Mr Boyd, the hospital's senior surgeon, who is determined his son shall marry Sister McPhee, a family friend for over thirty years.

Mr Boyd's opposition is overcome when his son falls seriously ill from kidney failure, and Nurse Norton offers to donate a kidney of her own to ensure that her lover survives. With the affair in the open, Sister McPhee is able to reveal to Mr Boyd that it is him, not his son, who has won her love. Since Mr Boyd is a widower of many years, they are free to marry, and Nurse Norton's bravery has even won the surgeon's approval for his son's choice.

Patients: Rees, Tyler, Ash, Foster, Ken, Flagg, Loach, Mackie
Nursing Staff: Matron, Sister McPhee, Staff Nurse Norton, Nurse Sweet, Nurse Lake, Oriental Nurse, Barnet, Michael and Prince
Doctors: Mr Boyd, Neil Boyd and Dr Bird
Indian student
Old woman

Chaplain
Theatre staff
Visitors

Native Son
Paul Green and Robert Wright
Tragedy I Act
New York 1941

A young Chicago black man, Bigger Thomas, is given a job as chauffeur to Henry G. Dalton, the slum landlord who owns Bigger's own tenement flat. Dalton's daughter Mary, a wilful young woman who feels profound guilt over her family's ruthless exploitation of blacks, fraternizes with Bigger during a night on the town, after which he takes her home, drunk. As he is nervously assisting Mary to her bed, Bigger is interrupted by her blind mother, Ellen. To keep Mary quiet and so avoid being discovered in her room, Bigger puts a pillow over her face and accidentally smothers her.

When his deed is discovered, Bigger flees into the ghetto and plans an escape to freedom with his girlfriend Clara, but is captured by the police in a gunfight during which Clara dies. He is wrongly found guilty of Mary's murder and sent for execution.

Bigger Thomas
Hannah Thomas, Bigger's mother
Vera Thomas, Bigger's sister
Buddy Thomas, Bigger's brother
Jack Henson
Gus Mitchell
'G. H.' Rankin
Ernie Jones
Henry G. Dalton, a slum landlord
Ellen Dalton, Dalton's wife
Mary Dalton, Dalton's daughter
Peggy MacAulife
Jeff Britten
Jan Erlone, Mary Dalton's boyfriend
Jed Norris
Clara Mears
Miss Emmet
David A. Buckley
Edward Max
Revd Hammond
Judge Alvin C. Hanley
Court stenographer
Reporters
Guards

Nerd, The
Larry Shue
Comedy 2 Acts
Milwaukee, USA 1982

Willum, a rather stolid, middle-class architect, is giving himself a birthday party. His guests, including his girlfriend and his most important client, are nonplussed when they are joined by Rick, who arrives dressed as a monster in the mistaken belief that he is coming to a

Halloween dress party. Willum feels obliged to ignore Rick's ridiculous mistake, and subsequent boorishness, because Rick had saved his life when they were both serving the the US forces in Vietnam. When Rick goes on to indicate that he is moving in with Willum, the latter's sense of indebtedness once more overcomes his grave doubts.

Rick's antics so disrupt Willum's formerly ordered life that he decides to drive out his erstwhile rescuer by making his life intolerable. But even with the help of Tansy, Willum's girlfriend, and Axel, his cynical but very loyal and lifelong friend, Rick remains unperturbed, so Willum must tell him to get out. Only after Rick leaves does the audience discover that 'Rick' was in fact an actor friend of Axel's, who conspired with him to upset Willum's life so much that he would lose his large but vulgar architectural commissions, and be obliged to apply himself to work with real merit.

Willum
Tansy
Axel
Waldgrave, Willum's client
Clelia, Waldgrave's wife
Thor, Waldgrave's son
Rick

Never Too Late
Sumner Arthur Long
Comedy 3 Acts
New York 1962

Middle-aged lumberyard boss Harry Lambert gets a shock when wife Edith becomes pregnant. Their married daughter Kate and husband Charlie (who works for Harry) live with them, and Edith usually does all the running around for everyone. Harry will not employ a maid (though he can afford it), so Kate takes over Mom's duties - and finds them tough.

Harry finds himself the butt of local jokes concerning his virility, and Charlie fares no better because Kate sees the only way out of her domestic slavery is to get pregnant herself.

Upset by Harry's attitude, Edith runs away for a night, and drunken Harry and Charlie upset their pompous, but useful, neighbour the Mayor. To everyone's joy Edith returns and Charlie placates the Mayor to earn himself a partnership in the business. He promises a home of their own to Kate, leaving Harry and Edith to bill and coo over their forthcoming offspring - and forthcoming maid (with uniform).

Grace Kimbrough
Harry Lambert
Edith Lambert
Dr James Kimbrough
Charlie
Kate
Mr Foley
Mayor Crane
Policeman

New Tenant, The
Eugene Ionesco
Play 1 Act
Paris 1957

A new tenant arrives at his London lodgings to find the caretaker, a tedious, babbling old woman, fussing about in his sitting-room.

He at first politely ignores her efforts to manipulate him into offering her a job but in the face of her persistence, he is finally obliged to put her out, and to endure her invective as she leaves.

Two furniture movers arrive as she is on her way and begin to unload the new tenant's possessions. His instructions to them are somewhat bizarre. His favourite chair is installed inside a chalk circle inscribed on the floor of the sitting-room, and he has himself completely walled in behind the rest of the furniture. The movers leave after first shutting off all the electric lights and the tenant is left in his darkened cocoon.

The gentleman
The caretaker
First furniture mover
Second furniture mover

Night and Day
Tom Stoppard
Drama 2 Acts
London 1978

In a former British African colony several reporters covering a rebellion congregate in a large house with a telex machine owned by Carson, a white mining executive.

Reporter Wagner and photographer Guthrie are with the *Sunday Globe*, while Jacob Milne is a freelance 'scab' whose anti-union idealism puts him at odds with Wagner. But it is Milne's exclusive interview with rebel leader Shimbu that has made the *Globe* front page, not Wagner's background piece. Carson's wife Ruth is unhappy at Wagner's presence; she coincidentally spent a casual night with him recently in London but is now attracted to Milne, and throughout the play the audience are privy to her thoughts. A plan for Shimbu to meet President Mageeba is arranged, and Milne and Guthrie leave for the rebel camp. Mageeba arrives and seems frank and open, but soon reveals psychopathic tendencies.

Guthrie returns with the news that Milne has been killed and the meeting thwarted; Mageeba leaves, followed by Carson and Guthrie. Ruth is left alone with Wagner.

Guthrie, a press photographer
Ruth
Alastair, son of Ruth and Carson
Wagner, an Australian reporter
Milne, a reporter
Carson, a mining engineer
Mageeba, the President
Francis, Carson's African servant

Night Must Fall
Emlyn Williams
Drama 3 Acts
London 1935

In a bungalow in a forest in Essex lives Mrs Bramson, a fussy hypochondriac. She pays her niece Olivia a small salary to act as her companion, and the household also includes her cook, Mrs Terence, and her maid Dora. When Dora gets pregnant, Mrs Bramson is determined to get the boyfriend to marry her, and at the same time a woman disappears from a nearby hotel.

The police begin investigations, and when Dora brings home boyfriend Dan, Olivia immediately suspects him of the crime. She observes Dan is always putting on an act, and soon he worms his way into the affections of Mrs Bramson, leaves his job as page boy at the hotel, and moves in. The woman's body is found, headless, and Olivia believes the head is in a hatbox Dan carries around with him, and although she is horrified of Dan, she is also fascinated by him. She knows he is after her aunt's money, and one night when everyone is out, Dan smothers Mrs Bramson. Olivia returns unexpectedly and Dan talks openly to her at last, intending to kill her also. But the police arrive and Olivia tries to cover up for Dan. He stops her from doing so, kisses her, and goes quietly.

Lord Chief Justice
Mrs Bramson
Olivia Grayne
Hubert Laurie
Nurse Libby
Mrs Terence
Dora Parkoe
Inspector Belsize
Dan

Night of the Iguana, The
Tennessee Williams
Drama 3 Acts
New York 1961

In 1940, sexy widow Maxine Faulk is running the Costa Verde, a small Mexican hotel on a jungle-covered hilltop overlooking the beach. Tour guide Shannon, a former priest, appears with a busload of female Baptist schoolteachers who have had enough of him - his speciality is showing off the local low-life and seducing the youngest girls in the party. He has got a fever and is having a breakdown. Maxine wants him to stay and help her run the hotel, but the arrival of attractively enigmatic painter Hannah and her grandfather Nonno, a famous poet aged ninety-seven, complicates matters. Hannah and Shannon are spiritually close and the jealous Maxine wants Hannah, who is broke, to leave.

The action is played against the powerful natural beauty of the region and the crude antics of a family of grotesque Germans crowing over Nazi broadcasts of their Battle of Britain 'victory'. Shannon vacillates between going back to the church, moving on with Hannah, or staying. He ends up staying because he has no strength to do otherwise. Nonno dies after writing his last great poem, and Hannah is left alone.

Maxine Faulk   *Judith Fellowes*
Pedro   *Hannah Jelkes*
Pancho   *Charlotte Goodall*
Revd Shannon   *Jonathan Coffin (Nonno)*
Hank   *Jake Latta*
Herr Fahrenkopf
Frau Fahrenkopf
Wolfgang
Hilda

Nine
A. Kopit, M. Yeston and M. Fratti
Musical 2 Acts
New York 1982

Guido Contini, a film director in the Fellini mould, has contracted with Liliane La Fleur to write and direct a film, but is unable to come up with a suitable plot. He is also, after recent box office failures, drifting towards a nervous breakdown, from which he is held back only by the support of his wife, Luisa. As his sanity disintegrates, he drifts into nostalgic reverie, eventually focusing on the formative sexual encounter of his life, which occurred at the age of nine.

He tries to lure the great actress Claudia Nardi into creating yet another version of the character that had launched her career in one of his earliest works, a character derived from Contini's precocious sexual encounters with a whore dressed as a nun. At the same time, he buys his mistress a nun's habit and encourages her to help him relive his childish passion.

La Fleur decides that the film should be a musical based on the life of Casanova, but Contini's rush into madness, which accelerates when his wife leaves him, throws the production into chaos. In the final scene, Contini has reverted to the personality he had at the age of nine.

Guido Contini, film director
Little Guido, Contini as a child
Luisa Contini, his wife
Carla Albanese, his mistress
Claudia Nardi, his protégée
Guido's mother
Liliane La Fleur, his producer
Lina Darling
Stephanie Necrophorus
Our Lady of the Spa
Mama Maddelena
Sarraghina, a prostitute
His Italian admirers: *Diana, Maria, Francesca, Annabella, Giulietta, Renata and Gondolier*
His German admirers: *Olga von Sturm, Heidi von Sturm, Ilsa von Hesse and Gretchen von Krupf*
Guido's three schoolmates
A nun

No Exit
Jean-Paul Sartre
Drama 1 Act
Paris 1944
See: *Huis Clos*

No Man's Land
Harold Pinter
Drama 2 Acts
London 1975

Spooner and Hirst, both in their sixties, meet in a pub and go back to Hirst's well-appointed home near Hampstead Heath. They drink heavily and at the end of their enigmatic and bleakly nostalgic conversation Hirst collapses. Then Fosters and the manservant Briggs enter; they belong to the household and attend to Hirst, who is, like Spooner, a poet and literary figure - but more successful. They are menacing and appear to resent Spooner's presence, their conversations consolidating the general air of doom and unspoken homosexuality - though at first Fosters claims Hirst is his father. Briggs locks Spooner in the room for the night and next day Hirst appears to remember Spooner from the past. They reminisce patchily about Oxford, their mutual acquaintances and lovers, and their war service. Hirst tells Spooner he had an affair with his wife. But did they really know each other? Spooner again offers his services and implies a way out of Hirst's no man's land where nothing changes.

Hirst

Spooner

Fosters, a man in his thirties

Briggs, a man in his forties

No Room at the Inn
Joan Temple
Drama 3 Acts
London 1945

Mary O'Rane, a delightful young schoolgirl, is placed in an appalling billet with four other evacuee children, Norma, Lily, Irene and Ronnie, when her mother dies and her father is away at sea fighting during the last war. Her teacher, Judith Drave, and her mother's friend, Kate Grant, try without success to get Mary an alternative home and push the authorities to take action against the unscrupulous landlady, Mrs Voray, who keeps her young charges in miserable circumstances.

Exposed to the coarsening influence of Mrs Voray, Mary's once lively, open personality becomes vulgar, cunning and cheap, although her fundamental goodness still shines through in the protection she affords to Ronnie, the particular target of Mrs Voray's abuse.

When in a drunken stupor, the sadistic Mrs Voray announces that Ronnie is to spend a night in the coal cellar for having damaged her new hat. Mary and Norma smother the woman with a pillow. The police are called in and it becomes clear that Mary will have to face the full force of the law.

Norma Smith
Judith Drave
Irene Saunders
Lily Robins
Ronnie Chilbury
Mary O'Rane
Kate Grant

Mr Burrels
Mrs Voray
Mrs Waters
Terence O'Rane
Mr Bowker
The Revd James Allworth

No Sex Please - We're British
Anthony Marriott and Alistair Foot
Farce 2 Acts
London 1971

Peter and Frances Hunter, newly married, have just set up home in the flat above the bank in the Thames Valley town where Peter has been made branch manager. Frances, in an attempt to bring extra cash into the household, has responded to a local advertisement offering to set people up in businesses they can run from home.

Peter points out that the bank would not be best pleased with such an arrangement, but too late, for the first shipment of goods arrives at the flat, along with Peter's overbearing and snobbish mother, Eleanor.

Frances' goods turn out to be pornographic postcards and she and Peter, panicking at the possibility that Eleanor will discover the material, involve Brian Runnicles in their attempt to dispose of it. Brian throws the shipment in the river, where it is discovered by the police, who determine to discover who owns it.

When Peter's superior, Mr Bromhead, and the bank's auditor, Mr Needham, both arrive at the flat, pandemonium ensues as Brian, Peter and Frances all try to prevent the two men from discovering yet another shipment of goods, this time a gross of sex manuals. Peter's position is made even more perilous when he and Frances realize that they have paid for the offending items, by mistake, with a cheque from one of the bank's clients. They have nearly finished loading the manuals into a van, for delivery to a public dump, when two young prostitutes arrive, sent by Frances' 'employers', the Scandinavian Import Company. Meanwhile, a third shipment, this time of risqué movies, is discovered in the back of a lorry, where Brian had thrown it, thinking thus to get rid of it.

Amidst utter chaos, the three naive conspirators frantically try to prevent Eleanor and Mr Bromhead, who return from a theatre engagement at just the wrong time, from meeting the two girls, and from discovering that they have been trying to seduce Mr Needham, who is staying the night in preparation for his audit.

It looks like their position is hopeless when Mr Bromhead discovers the two girls, but the day is saved when he turns out to be a 'Mr Smith', one of their regular clients. His utter embarrassment means he will not reveal the source of their discomfort, and when the two girls return the errant cheque, which their employer has been unable to cash, Peter, Frances and Brian are all in the clear.

Peter Hunter
Frances Hunter, Peter's wife
Eleanor Hunter, Peter's mother
Brian Runnicles, Peter's junior colleague
Leslie Bromhead, Peter's superior
Superintendent Paul
Mr Needham
Susan
Barbara
Delivery man

No Time for Sergeants
Ira Levin
Comedy 2 Acts
New York 1955

Will Stockdale, a well-meaning but astonishingly unintelligent and naive hillbilly, relates for the people of Callville, his hometown, the story of how he came to be decorated for services to the US Air Force, and we see the tale unfold in a series of flashbacks to his military career.

Will's father, Pa Stockdale, has been destroying letters from the US draft Board ordering his son to report for service, but the young man is eventually traced and taken for induction into the Air Force. The commanding officer of his barracks, Sgt King, takes advantage of Will's gullibility, makes the recruit Permanent Latrine Orderly, and plans to keep him unregistered so the job really will be permanent. When the Sergeant's superior, the Captain, discovers this ploy, he gives King one week to put the recruit through his registration tests, on pain of being reduced to the ranks should Will fail.

The Sergeant's frantic efforts to meet his target pay off, but only at the expense of getting himself into deep trouble and to his horror he is stripped of his stripes and sent, along with Will and his buddy Ben, to Air Force Gunnery School. There the sergeant soon ingratiates himself with the brass, wins back his stripes, and oversees Will's training into one of the worst gunners ever produced by the school. Will is heedless of the low level of his achievement, concerned only to help Ben achieve his aim of transferring to the infantry. Ben, however, is eventually forced to accept that he is in the Air Force for good.

Fate intervenes when Will's crew are sent on a flight to Colorado but end up instead, through incompetence, over the testing site for atomic bombs in Nevada. Their plane is blown out of the sky and Will, holding Ben, parachutes to safety in the desert. To disguise the crew's blunder, the brass decide to pretend they were on a secret mission, and to decorate the survivors, at the same time giving Will and Ben, no trace of whom is found, posthumous awards in front of a battery of newsmen.

Unfortunately for the brass, Will and Ben arrive back at base just as the ceremony ends, so efforts must be made to hide the existence of the two 'dead' heroes.

The brass arrange for Will and Ben, along with the hairless sergeant, to be transferred to the infantry.

Preacher	Three classification
Will Stockdale, a hillbilly	corporals
Pa Stockdale, Will's	A psychiatrist
father	Cigarette girl
Draft man	An infantryman
Bus driver	Air Force policeman
Iron Blauchard, a recruit	A colonel
Rosabelle	Lieut Bridges, pilot
Seven inductees	Lieut Gardella, co-pilot
Ben Whitledge, Will's	Lieut Kendall, engineer
buddy	Lieut Cover, navigator
A captain	Gen. Bush
A nurse	Gen. Pollard
A lieutenant	A senator
Sgt King	

No, No, Nanette
Frank Mandel, Otto Harbach and Irving Caesar
Music by Vincent Youmans
Musical Comedy 3 Acts
London 1925

Nanette, a flapper in the twenties is fed up with the restraints put on her by her guardian uncle Jimmy Smith and aunt Sue, so she runs off to Atlantic City. Smith, a rich Bible publisher, is himself a little unconventional, and has a weakness for sharing his wealth with three young ladies all of whose careers need financial encouragement. He is a kind of platonic sucker who gets no amorous return on his investments. He also comes to Atlantic City to meet his young friends and is pursued by his wife and Nanette's boyfriend Tom Trainor, who is not too happy about her free-wheeling ways. Billy Early, Fred's best friend, turns up as well to add to the confusion, and it takes his wife Lucille to sort him and Jimmy out and bring the young pair together, making sure that they are happily set up with a slice of uncle's fortune.

Songs include: 'My Boy and I'; 'I Want to be Happy'; 'Tea for Two'

Pauline, cook at the Smith's
Jimmy Smith
Sue Smith
Nanette, Sue's protégée
Billy Early, a lawyer
Lucille, his wife
Tom Trainor
Betty
Winnie
Flora

Noble Spaniard, The
W. Somerset Maugham adapted from the story by Grenet-Dancourt
Comedy 3 Acts
London 1909

In 1850 Marion and her sister, Lucy, are staying with

the Proudfoots at their villa in Boulogne. The Duke of Hermanos declares his love for her and asks her to marry him, and in desperation she invents a husband for herself to put him off. Hermanos is so determined that he sets out to find this husband and fight for her. Thinking that it is Proudfoot, he firstly approaches him, and declares his love for his wife, and poor Lady Proudfoot's fidelity is questioned further when roses intended for Marion are mistakenly given to her. Lucy's suitor, Capt. Chalford, sees Lucy with the flowers and suspects that she has another admirer. Hermanos takes Chalford for Marion's lover and proposes a duel, but she intervenes, assuring Hermanos that Proudfoot is not her husband nor Chalfont her lover. She hints that her husband has gone on a long journey, meaning he is dead, but Hermanos takes this literally, and when the Count de Moret returns from a long trip Hermanos demands his wife from him. Surprisingly the Count agrees, but he is insulted when Hermanos meets the real Countess and declines to elope with her.

Marion saves the day by coming back and throwing the roses out of the window, which Hermanos takes as a sign that she will marry him, and they all go off happily to dinner.

Mr Justice Proudfoot, an English judge
Lady Proudfoot
Marion Nairne, a young widow
Lucy, her younger sister
Capt. Chalford
Count de Moret, a French aristocrat
Countess de Moret, his English wife
The Duke of Hermanos
Mary Jane, a maid

Noises Off
Michael Frayn
Comedy 3 Acts
London 1982

Nothing On is a typically clichéd farce performed by a third-rate travelling theatre company, and at the dress rehearsal in Weston-super-Mare, a lot can and does go wrong. TV sitcom star Dolly Otley plays the 'char' and she is the biggest name in the cast. The others include her real-life younger lover Garry Lejeaune, lovely but dumb Brook Ashton, and drunken old trouper Seldon Mowbray who plays a burglar. Director Lloyd Dallas is having affairs with Brook - and his assistant Poppy.

Later the same act is seen from behind the stage during a performance in Goole, together with parallel backstage dramas among the cast including jealousy, drunkenness, missed cues and ad-libs, lost contact lenses, etc. Finally, the same act is presented as performed a couple of months later in Stockton-on-Tees. This time the script has been changed; real-life and farce have merged into a surreal variant on the original, a distorted caricature of a caricature.

Dolly Otley	*Garry Lejeaune*
Lloyd Dallas	*Brook Ashton*
Poppy Norton-Taylor	*Tim Allgood*
Frederick Fellowes	*Seldon Mowbray*
Belinda Blair	*Electrician*

Normal Heart, The
Larry Kramer
Drama 2 Acts
New York 1985

A promiscuous New York homosexual, Ned Weeks, is galvanized into the first responsible work of his life, as well as into his first proper love affair, by the appearance of AIDS amongst his friends in the gay community in 1981. Fuelled by his rage that the epidemic is being ignored by the community at large, and guided by the advice of Dr Emma Brookner, one of the first physicians to treat its victims, Ned forms a gay self-help group which quickly grows into a substantial organization.

In the course of seeking help for the cause from eminent gay men, Ned meets and falls in love with Felix Turner, fashion correspondent of the *New York Times*. But although he and Felix manage to establish stability in their personal lives, Ned's enraged and abrasive campaigning for victims of AIDS gradually alienates not just the leaders of the 'straight' community, but his fellow volunteers as well. An impasse is reached when Ned insists that the group must take Dr Brookner's advice and campaign in favour of temporary celibacy for all gay men, an anathema to a community only just discovering its sexual identity, and he is sacked from the organization he had founded.

At the same time, Felix is discovered to have the disease. Ned's only relief occurs when his beloved brother Ben, who has tortured him with his ambivalence about homosexuality, attends a death bed 'marriage' which joins Ned and Felix moments before Felix dies.

Craig Donner	*Ben Weeks*
Mickey Marcus	*Tommy Boatwright*
Ned Weeks	*Hiram Keebler*
David	*Grady*
Dr Emma Brookner	*Examining doctor*
Bruce Niles	*Two orderlies*
Felix Turner	

Norman Conquests, The
Alan Ayckbourn
3 Plays
Scarborough 1973

See: *Table Manners; Living Together; Round and Round the Garden*

Not Now Darling
Ray Cooney and John Chapman
Farce 2 Acts
Richmond 1967

Bodley, Bodley and Crouch is an exclusive Mayfair furriers run by philandering Gilbert Bodley, his formidable wife Maude, and their partner the bumbling Arnold Crouch. While Maude is away in Paris, Gilbert plans to seduce his new girlfriend Janie McMichael - but first he has to give her a mink coat. In order not to arouse the suspicions of her casino-owning husband Harry with the unexpected presence of a gratis full-length mink, Gilbert arranges for Janie to bring Harry to the salon where he will be offered the mink for 500 pounds, a fraction of its value. Gilbert then intends to pay the 4,500 pounds balance, Janie will get her coat - and Gilbert will get Janie. But of course things do not work out like that. In the subsequent farcical confusion, women strip, valuable furs come and go, people hide in small rooms, unexpected husbands, wives, lovers and mistresses appear and disappear, and innocent fall-guy Arnold ends up with a genuine marriage proposal.

Miss Whittington   *Maude Bodley*
Arnold Crouch   *Mr Lawson*
Miss Tipdale
Mrs Frencham
Gilbert Bodley
Cdr Frencham
Harry McMichael
Janie McMichael
Sue Lawson

Not Quite Jerusalem
Paul Kember
Drama 2 Acts
London 1980

At first, the four English volunteers at a kibbutz are sharply disillusioned. The work is hard and it seems more like a prison camp. Dave is a foul-mouthed typically English yob who does not even try to adapt; Pete is the same, but tries a bit. Mike is a Cambridge drop-out, articulate but confused, and Carrie has had mental problems and tells lies. Mike has an affair with Israeli Gila, but she cannot stabilize him, and when the English contingent have to contribute to Volunteers' Day theatricals representing their home culture, it is left to Dave and Pete. They sing some Flanagan and Allen, wave a flag, and bare their buttocks to the audience. They are told to leave the camp, but Mike explains to resident kibbutznik Ami the symbolism of their protest. The new Jerusalem was not built in England either, and the sort of cosmopolitan understanding promoted by the kibbutz is almost a different universe from where Dave and Pete - and Mike and Carrie - come from. Ami understands, and asks now-stable group leader Carrie what to do. She wants to give them a second chance, and to their delight, Dave and Pete are allowed to stay. Mike's problems, however, are more complex, cannot be solved at the Kibbutz and he leaves.

Dave
Mike
Carrie
Pete
Ami
Gila

Nothing but the Truth
James Montgomery
Comedy 3 Acts
London 1918

E. M. Ralston, Bob Bennett and Dick Donnelly are partners in a New York brokerage firm, and Ralston's daughter Gwen is involved in raising money for a children's seaside home. Her father is mean but cunning and has promised her he will double any sum she collects over 20,000 dollars. She has a week to go and only has 10,000 dollars, so she asks her sweetheart Bob to invest the money and try to double it. He cannot but accept, and later that day the partners and a customer, Van Dusen, discuss telling the truth. Bob says he believes he could tell the truth for any length of time, and Ralston bets he could not even for a day. Bob bets the 10,000 dollars he could, and the other three split the bet against him. The next twenty-four hours are chaos; in their attempts to get Bob to lie they pull out all the stops, and everything backfires on them. Friendships are broken, money won and lost, friends and relatives insulted, marriages almost destroyed...until Bob scrapes through and wins the bet, then tells a few white lies which put everything to rights.

Bob Bennett
E. M. Ralston
Revd Dr Doran
Clarence Van Dusen
Dick Donnelly
Gwen
Mrs Ralston
Ethel
Mabel
Sabel
Martha

Nude with Violin
Noël Coward
Comedy 3 Acts
London 1956

A modernist painter of huge reputation, Paul Sorodin, has died in his adopted Paris home in the mid-fifties. His prudish English wife, whom he had abandoned thirty years earlier, brings their children, Jane and Colin, and their daughter-in-law Pamela on a hypocritically pious trip to the funeral. All but Jane are really interested only in Sorodin's estate.

Under the guiding hand of Sorodin's devoted and devilishly cynical valet, Sebastien Lacreole, it is revealed to the family and to Sorodin's dealer Jacob Friedland, that Sorodin painted none of the pictures attributed to him. Instead his whole career had been a nose-thumbing hoax on the art business, and the paintings from his four 'periods' were done, respectively, by a Russian tart, an ex-chorus girl, a West Indian religious fanatic, and a boy of fourteen, Sebastien's son.

Sorodin's wish to expose the foolishness of modernist critics founders when Sebastien manages to buy off the real 'artists', and to suppress news of the hoax.

Sebastien Lacreole, Sorodin's valet
Marie-Celeste, Sorodin's maid
Clinton Preminger Jr, a journalist
Isobel Sorodin, Sorodin's wife
Jane and Colin, Sorodin's children
Pamela, Colin's wife
Jacob Friedland
Anya Pavlikov
Cherry-May Waterton
Fabrice
Obadiah Lewellyn
George
Lauderdale

Nunsense
Dan Goggin
Musical 2 Acts
New York 1985

An American order of nuns, the Little Sisters of Hoboken, in New Jersey, has been decimated by an outbreak of botulism, brought on by the carelessness of their own cook. Of the seventy-one sisters in the order, fifty-four have died of the infection, but the sisters have only buried forty-eight of the dead. Having spent a portion of the burial fund on a videotape machine, they are unable to afford services for the remaining four, whom they have secreted in the convent's freezer. They fear discovery by the public health inspectors, and decide to hold a musical revue, starring themselves in the hall of the convent school to raise another burial fund.

As the show gets underway, with Sister Amnesia, who has forgotten her past, as the star attraction, the Revd Mother discovers that the health inspectors have indeed, issued a summons against the Order, and have taken away Sister Ralph Marie, who is meant to do one of the main numbers in the review. The Revd Mother, along with several of the other nuns, leave to arrange release for Sister Ralph Marie. This gives the main understudy, Sister Robert Anne, a rough diamond with a Brooklyn slum background, an eagerly taken chance to get in and do her own, rather risqué, act.

The Revd Mother arrives back at the hall in time to witness part of Sister Robert Anne's ribaldry, and pulls her from the stage, sending Sister Amnesia on instead to ad lib a story for the audience. In the midst of her story, Sister Amnesia suddenly remembers that she is really Sister Mary Paul. When the Revd Mother realizes that Sister Mary Paul is the missing winner of a sweepstakes cash prize, the nuns start a wild celebration, realizing that they can finally bury their remaining dead and so avoid prosecution for health violations.

Sister Mary Regina, Mother Superior
Sister Mary Hubert
Sister Robert Anne
Sister Mary Amnesia
Sister Mary Leo

Nuts
Tom Topor
Drama 3 Acts
New York 1980

A young woman from a successful suburban family background, Claudia Draper, has been arraigned for manslaughter in New York City, where she now lives.

On the advice of her first lawyer, hired by her stepfather and quickly sacked by Claudia herself, she has been placed in Bellevue psychiatric hospital, where two doctors have summarily decided she is unfit to stand trial as she is a paranoid schizophrenic.

Realizing that she can be confined longer for being mad than for manslaughter, and rightly convinced that she is quite sane, Claudia hires her own counsel to challenge the diagnosis which, it turns out at a special hearing, has been very sloppily applied to her.

As one of her psychiatrists, Dr Rosenthal, and then her mother Rose and stepfather Arthur, give their evidence, it becomes clear that Claudia's withdrawal from her family and slide into prostitution - both offered as proof of her insanity - arose from her having been paid by her stepfather to tolerate his advances when she was a child. Although when giving her own evidence, Claudia adopts a cynical aggressive pose, the judge is persuaded that she is mentally competent, and sends her for trial where she is acquitted of the manslaughter charge.

Officer Harry Haggerty
Aaron Levinsky, Claudia's counsel
Franklin Macmillan, District Attorney
The Recorder
Rose Kirk, Claudia's mother
Arthur Kirk, Claudia's stepfather
Dr Herbert Rosenthal, a psychiatrist
Judge Murdoch
Claudia Faith Draper

Odd Couple, The
Neil Simon
Comedy 3 Acts
New York 1965

Oscar Madison, a sports writer, is an easygoing slob who lives alone in a large Manhattan apartment. The place is a mess, he is dangerously behind in his alimony, and he enjoys a weekly game of poker with his friends. During one game the guys realize that their friend Felix has not turned up. When he does, he is distraught - his wife has left him. Oscar invites Felix to stay and in no time at all Felix has everything spick and span, is cooking regular meals, and generally irritates Oscar.

When the two English women from the apartment above come down for dinner, it is the 'sensitive' Felix that they take to. Oscar has had enough, he throws Felix out, who lands on his feet and ends up with the girls.

However, as a result of Felix's economies, Oscar is able to pay off his alimony, and despite everything the guys still meet up for their weekly poker game.

Oscar Madison   Vinnie
Felix Ungar   Murray
Speed   Gwendoline Pigeon
Roy   Cecily Pigeon

Oedipus at Colonus
Sophocles
Tragedy 1 Act
Ahtens c. 406 BC
After their exile from Thebes, the blind Oedipus and his daughter, Antigone, have wandered together in destitution for many years. They have at last arrived at a grove sacred to the Eumenides near the gates of Athens where Apollo has prophesized that Oedipus will find refuge.

Oedipus sends a message to Theseus, King of Athens, asking for haven and pointing out that Apollo has promised to defeat the enemies of anyone who will take the old man in. To his surprise and delight his daughter Ismene, from whom he has long been separated, searches him out in Colonus. Her purpose is desperate - to warn Oedipus that Creon King of Thebes, means to abduct him. Creon has been told by the oracles that Oedipus's presence in Thebes will bring peace to the city and help to prevent civil war between the rival armies of Oedipus's sons, Eteocles and Polynices.

Creon appears and abducts Antigone and Ismene to force Oedipus to accompany him. Theseus arrives in time to prevent Creon from taking Oedipus as well and forces the return of the sisters to Athenian protection. Polynices also arrives and asks Oedipus to bless a campaign against Thebes. Outraged at his son's previous years of neglect, Oedipus instead curses Polynices' enterprise and predicts his death.

In line with Apollo's prophesy, a great storm gathers over the grove and Oedipus is summoned to the underworld by a ghostly voice. Before dying, he commends his daughters to Theseus's protection.
Oedipus, exiled former King of Thebes
Antigone, Oedipus' daughter
Ismene, Oedipus' daughter
Theseus, King of Athens
Creon, Oedipus' brother-in-law
Polynices, Oedipus' son
Chorus
Soldiers
Messenger
Attendants

Oedipus, The King
Sophocles
Tragedy 1 Act
Athens c. 425BC
In recognition of his services in ridding Thebes of control by the Sphinx, Oedipus has been made king, and married to Jocasta, wife of murdered former king, Laius. The defeat of the Sphinx has convinced Oedipus, and all of Thebes, that he is a man of destiny whose will is in harmony with the gods.

The play opens with Thebes in the grip of plague, and awaiting news from Creon, Jocasta's brother, who has been sent to Apollo's oracle in Delphi to discover why the gods have sent the plague. The oracle demands that the Thebans should discover and punish Laius' murderer. Oedipus pronounces a curse on the murderer, and swears before all Thebes to avenge Laius. Summoning Teiresias, he imperiously demands to be told whatever this blind prophet knows of the murder. Teiresias accuses the King himself of the foul deed, and Oedipus denounces the prophet and banishes Creon on the grounds that the two are in league to overthrow him.

Jocasta intervenes to save her brother, and tries to convince Oedipus of his own innocence since the oracle specified that Laius would be killed by his own son. But she also reveals that Laius was killed at the junction of three roads, and Oedipus, aghast, remembers that he killed a man at just such a place.

It gradually becomes clear that Oedipus is the dead king's son, and has, in fact, married his own mother. Jocasta, having deduced the truth of her position much sooner than Oedipus, commits suicide, and her bereft son/husband blinds himself and is replaced as king by Creon. He leaves Thebes, broken but still defiant.
Oedipus   Herdsman
Jocasta   Attendants
Creon   Chorus
Teiresias
Priest
Messenger

Of Mice and Men
John Steinbeck
Drama 3 Acts
New York 1937
George and Lennie are migrant workers travelling around together during the great American Depression. George is small and smart, Lennie is big and strong but feeble-minded. He loves to pet and stroke small animals but doesn't know his own strength and often kills them. Lennie dotes on George, particularly George's stories of the farm they will get together one day, 'living of the fat of the land'. They find work on a ranch in Northern California and everything seems ideal at first. They even find an old man, Candy, who has saved some money and would be willing to invest it with them in their dream farm.

But trouble comes in the shape of mean and nasty little Curley, the boss's son and his wife, a tart who is always making up to the men. Curley attacks Lennie who crushes his hand, and later, Curley's wife finds Lennie sulking in the barn where he is trying to hide a dead puppy. She lets Lennie stroke her hair, but then she panics; Lennie panics too and inadvertently breaks her neck. He flees, and men led by bloodthirsty Curley set out to lynch him. George finds Lennie first and gently calms him down, then talks to him about their dream farm. He is so convincing that Lennie imagines he can see the farm across the river and at that point George mercifully shoots him.

George	Curley's wife
Lennie	Slim
Candy	Carlson
The Boss	Whit
Curley	Crooks

Of Thee I Sing
George S. Kaufman and Morrie Ryskind
Music and Lyrics by George and Ira Gershwin
Musical 2 Acts
New York 1931

A group of cynical political writers meet in New York City to plan the election strategy for John P. Wintergreen, their chosen candidate to the US presidency. Lacking any real policy, they decide to galvanize the voters by holding a beauty contest to choose a wife for Wintergreen, hoping to make this pastiche of 'love' the main campaign theme. The winner of the contest, a southern belle called Diana Deveraux, has her hopes disappointed when Wintergreen suddenly falls in love with a minor aide, Mary Turner, and tours every state making public, vote-catching proposals of marriage.

The lovers duly wed and Wintergreen easily wins the election. Diana, though, launches a suit against the new President for breach of promise, and public opinion swings in favour of the jilted woman. Wintergreen's position becomes even more shaky when the French Ambassador, citing Deveraux's French antecedents as his reason, threatens to break off all relations with the US unless the President divorces Mary in favour of Diana. Mary seems to have outflanked her rival when she announces that she is pregnant, and thus starts a groundswell of public sympathy back in her own, and Wintergreen's side. The French, though, are not mollified until Wintergreen proposes that Deveraux should marry in his place the ineffectual Vice-President, Alexander Throttlebottom.

Louis Lippman	The French ambassador
Francis X. Gilhootey	Senate clerk
Maid	Guide
Matthew Arnold Fulton	Photographers
Senator Robert E. Lyons	Policemen
Senator Carver Jones	Supreme Court justices
Alexander Throttlebottom	Secretaries
John P. Wintergreen	Sightseers
Sam Jenkins	Newsmen
Diana Deveraux	Senators
Mary Turner	Flunkeys
Miss Benson	Guests
Vladimir Vidovitch	
Yussef Yussevitch	
Chief Justice	
The scrubwoman	

Off the Deep End
Dennis Driscoll
Comedy 3 Acts
Morecombe 1955

Mossop Vale is a northern town approaching its centenary in the fifties. The Dewsnap family are preparing; Fred plays in the band and Lily is a reluctant member of the Ladies Help Committee. Maurice Aubert has come to take part in the celebrations, and return to France with two representatives from Mossop Vale, Fred and Lily. At first Lily is sceptical about anything foreign, but comes around to the idea. Their daughter Maureen's fiancé, Edgar has been offered a job in Nottingham and does not consult Maureen about it which upsets her. He also turns his nose up at the idea of going to the centenary dance, so Maurice takes Maureen instead. On the way back they fall into the open air pool.

On the day of the main centenary parade Maurice is declaring his love to Maureen when Fred is brought home, apparently concussed by a mistimed throw of his conductor's mace. He quickly recovers, infuriated by officious Edgar. Suddenly, Mrs Ackworth rushes in with the story of the fall in the pool which someone has given to the local papers. To avoid the humiliation Edgar leaves for the job in Nottingham. Maureen refuses to accompany him and calls off their engagement. Instead she is invited to to go to France with Maurice and her parents, and she accepts.

Fred Dewsnap, open air swimming pool attendant
Lily Dewsnap, his wife
Maureen Dewsnap, their daughter
Elsie Hogarth, Lily's friend
Albert Hogarth
Edgar Jenkins, Maureen's fiancé
Mrs Ackworth, Chairman of the Ladies' Help
Committee
M. Maurice Aubert, Mayor of Touvrai

Oh, What a Lovely War!
Charles Chilton
Drama 1 Act
London 1963

This bitter satire on the Great War of 1914-18 is cast in the form of an old-style pierrot show. It uses, as well, back-projected action slides from the combat, and panels of contemporary news headlines, to carry the narrative on its frantic way.

The various pierrots play numerous short parts in a series of vignettes, all of which highlight some aspect of the stupidity of war. These vignettes depend for their impact on the stark contrast between the cruel determination of the Allied and German commanders (especially Gen. Sir Douglas Haig) and the devastation suffered by the the ordinary troops and citizens of both sides.

Fifteen to twenty pierrots

Oklahoma!
Richard Rodgers and Oscar Hammerstein
Musical 2 Acts
New York 1943

Curly arrives at the Oklahoma farmstead of Aunt Eller and his true love, Laurey, after a quarrel in the hope of making up with her and making a date to take her to the community social. His friend Will Parker also arrives at the farm, jubilant that the 50 dollars he has won in a Kansas City card game will allow him to pay the dowry demanded by his fiancée Ado Annie Carne's mean father. Curly asks Aunt Eller if anyone else is courting Laurey, and finds to his great annoyance that a churlish cowboy called Jud Fry has, in fact, already arranged to take Laurey to the social.

To cover his hurt, Curly invites another girl to the social, but then spends every penny he has to outbid Jud, in an auction, for the box lunch Laurey has prepared. Meanwhile, Ado Annie's father has forced his daughter to give up Will Parker in favour of her other beau, Ali Hakim, a Persian peddler, having discovered that Hakim has invited Annie to spend a night together in the local hotel. At the social, though, Annie cannot resist Will's advances, and ends by agreeing to marry him instead. Curly is not so lucky; though he wins Laurey's box lunch, she still dances with Jud Fry, who upsets her with his advances. Curly steps in and a fight ensues between the two rivals which ends in Jud's death . Luckily, the local judge witnesses the fight, convenes a frontier-style trial, and acquits Curly. He and Laurey ride happily off in a surrey with a fringe on top.

Songs include: 'Oklahoma!'; 'The Surrey with the Fringe on Top'; 'I Can't Say No'; 'Oh, What a Beautiful Mornin''; 'Many a New Day'; 'People Will Say We're in Love'; 'Lonely Room'

Aunt Eller	Ali Hakim
Curly	Gertie Cummings
Laurey	Ellen
Ike Skidmore	Andrew Carnes
Fred	Cord Elam
Slim	Mike
Will Parker	Joe
Jud Fry	Cowboy
Ado Annie Carnes	Sam

Old Country, The
Alan Bennett
Drama 2 Acts
London 1977

A shabby-genteel English couple, Hilary and his wife Bron, wait anxiously in their run-down 'cottage' for the arrival of their old friends Duff and Veronica, whom they have not seen in many years. Although the scene is apparently English - a profusion of books, Elgar on the gramophone - the location of the 'cottage' is vague.

While they await their guests, Hilary and Bron receive an unexpected and unwelcome visit from Eric, an obviously working-class Englishman, and his sour,

obviously foreign wife, Olga. Hilary offends Olga, who leaves to wait in her car. Annoyed with Hilary's rudeness, Bron remarks that they are all traitors, but before Hilary can do more than agree, they are interrupted by the arrival of Duff and Veronica.

A series of oblique references in the following conversation make it clear that the 'cottage' is somewhere in Russia, that Hilary is a retired Russian spy, and that Duff and Veronica have been sent jointly by the British and Soviet governments to persuade Hilary to return to Britain. When Hilary demurs, Olga returns to make it plain that she speaks for the Russians and that Hilary has no choice. With only minutes for packing, Hilary and Bron are whisked away.

Hilary
Bron
Eric
Olga
Duff
Veronica

Old Times
Harold Pinter
Drama 2 Acts
London 1971

Deeley and Kate, a married couple, are being visited in their London flat by Kate's friend Anna. The two women have not seen one another in many years and the strained atmosphere of their reunion is made worse by Deeley's suppressed jealousy of their former intimacy, along with his lust for Anna. The sexual tension is increased when Anna tells a story about watching Kate suffer through a clumsy seduction during the time they lived together, and then by a discussion between Deeley and Anna about the best way to help Kate to dry herself after her having bathed.

Following her bath, Kate gives her very different story of the same seduction, and Deeley, perhaps in pure fantasy, recalls meeting Anna years before and trying to catch a glimpse up her skirt. The strain becomes too much for Deeley, who begins to weep as silence descends on the two women.

Deeley
Kate
Anna

Oliver!
Lionel Bart
Musical 2 Acts
London 1960

This free adaptation of the Charles Dickens classic story follows in song and dance the adventures of young Oliver Twist starting in the workhouse, where he asks for more, through his experiences with Fagin as a member of a gang of pickpockets to his abduction by the evil Bill Sikes and his eventual happy restoration to his wealthy grandfather.

Songs include: 'Food, Glorious Food'; 'Oliver';

'Consider Yourself'; 'You've Got to Pick a Pocket or Two'; 'I'd Do Anything'; 'As Long as He Needs Me'; 'Who Will Buy?

Oliver Twist   *Bill Sikes*
Mr Bumble   *Bet*
Mrs Corney   *Mr Brownlow*
Old Sally   *Dr Grimwig*
Mr Sowerberry   *Mrs Bedwin*
Mrs Sowerberry   *Workhouse boys*
Charlotte   *Fagin's Gang*
Noah Claypole   *Londoners*
Fagin
The Artful Dodger
Nancy

On Approval
Frederick Lonsdale
Comedy 3 Acts
London 1927

Rich and nice young Helen Hayle is very fond of the conceited and penniless young Duke of Bristol. The Duke's older friend Richard Halton has loved bad-tempered widow Mrs Maria Wislack for twenty years but is too shy to propose. Eventually Maria suggests to Richard a trial marriage (without sex) of three weeks at her house in Scotland; if she discovers he is really as pleasant as he seems, she will marry him.

The Duke and Helen insist on coming along, Helen in the hope that the Duke will find marriage contagious. The results are contrary to expectations; Richard is appalled by Maria's ingrained bad-temper and declares he couldn't marry her, and when the Duke proposes to Helen, she refuses - she has seen through him. Richard and Helen hit upon the drastic solution of running off and leaving the Duke and Maria snowbound in the house. A few weeks of each other's enforced company should be enough to cure them of their selfish ways, making them fit to marry.

The Duke of Bristol
Richard Halton
Mrs Wislack
Helen Hayle

On Golden Pond
Ernest Thompson
Drama 2 Acts
New York 1978

A cantankerous old man, Norman Thayer, arrives for the summer at his retreat in rural Maine, accompanied by his wife Ethel. Norman is obsessed with death and has alienated all of the people in his life who might have made his old age happy by his unbending rudeness. The depth of his loneliness becomes apparent when his only daughter, Chelsea, arrives with her divorced boyfriend, Bill Ray and son Billy, all of whom Norman treats with undisguised contempt. Gradually, though, Norman warms to the young Billy and they form a bond based on Billy's eagerness to learn the old man's favourite

sport, game fishing.

The friendship between Norman and Billy leads to a partial thaw in relations between Norman and his daughter, and when Chelsea marries Billy's father, Norman is even guardedly happy. Indeed, as the summer draws to a close, Norman even allows himself to express some hope to Ethel that he will survive until the next year, if only to return with Billy to enjoy the fishing on Golden Pond.

Norman Thayer Jr
Ethel Thayer
Charlie Martin
Chelsea Thayer Wayne
Billy Ray
Bill Ray

On Monday Next
Philip King
Comedy 3 Acts
London 1949

A provincial repertory company from the Theatre Royal, Drossmouth, begins rehearsals of an appalling play written by a relative of one of the company's main patrons. The rehearsal is run by the inept, histrionic producer and his equally inept deputy, Jerry. The actors have all failed to learn their lines, the producer hates the play enough to cut and alter the text at will, and the bumbling theatre carpenter, George, constantly disrupts each attempt of Jerry's to organize proceedings.

The cast members blunder from personal misfortune through rivalry to scene stealing and petty confrontation as their hysteria over opening night gradually builds. Finally the producer throws a sandbag at the author, whom he can no longer tolerate, and the action ends in total chaos with the author being carted away by the ambulance brigade.

The producer   *Jackson Harley*
George   *Mary Manners*
Maud Barron   *Sandra Layton*
Jerry Winterton   *Norwood Beverly*
The Author   *A doctor*
Daphne Wray   *Two ambulancemen*
Avis Clare

On the Razzle
Tom Stoppard
Comedy 2 Acts
London 1981

High-class grocer Zangler leaves his small-town shop in the hands of assistants Weinberl and Christopher while he goes to Vienna to wine and dine his intended, fashion-house owner Mme Knorr. He also arranges to protect his ward Marie from the attentions of her impoverished lover Sonders. When he promises promotion to his two assistants, they decide on one last fling; they must get themselves 'a past' before being chained to the grocery business.

They go to Vienna, then in the grip of an infatuation for all things Scottish (after Verdi's *Macbeth*) where they pursue wine, women, food and song, dodging their employer all the way, and after a wonderful hell-raising day of plot and sub-plot, breathlessly return to the shop just before their boss.

They are promoted, Sonders is left a fortune and thus acquires Marie and a ragamuffin is employed in Christopher's place in the shop.

Weinberl	Citizens
Christopher	Waiters
Sonders	Customers,
Marie	German man
Zangler	German woman
Gertrud	Scotsman
Belgian foreigner	Scotswoman
Melchior	Constable
Hupfer	Lisette
Philippine	Miss Blumenblatt
Mme Knorr	Ragamuffin
Mrs Fischer	
Coachman	
Piper	

On the Spot
Edgar Wallace
Drama 3 Acts
London 1930

Two rival gangs, Tony Perrelli's and Mike Feeny's, are fighting for control of the bootleg liquor trade in thirties Chicago. Men from Perrelli's gang have murdered Feeny's partner, Shaun O'Donnell, and Feeny demands as the price of peace that the killers should be sacrificed to his vengeance. With cold duplicity, Perrelli agrees to Feeny's demands while at the same time behaving to the two doomed men as if they are his closest aides.

The youngest of the two, a disgraced Harvard undergraduate named Jimmy McGarth, falls in love with Perrelli's Chinese-American wife, Minn Lee, who warns him of the danger he faces. But McGarth goes happily to his death, sickened by his life of crime.

Minn Lee herself, aware that Perrelli is about to consign her to running one of his brothels, mortally stabs herself. Just as Perrelli is reading her suicide note, his nemesis, Detective John Kelly, arrives to question him about McGarth's murder. Seeing an opportunity finally to get his man, Kelly burns the suicide note and arrests Perrelli for the murder of Minn Lee.

A priest
An acolyte
Patrolman Ryan
An intern
A nurse
Shaun O'Donnell
Chief Detective Commissioner
John Kelly

Tony Perrelli
Kiriki, Perrelli's servant
Minn Lee
Con O'Hara, Perrelli's hired gun
Angelo Verona, Perrelli's lieutenant
Jimmy McGarth, Perrelli's hired gun
Maria Pouliski, O'Hara's mistress
Mike Feeny
Gangsters

On Your Toes
Richard Rodgers, George Abbott, Lorenz Hart
Musical 2 Acts
New York 1936

Phil Dolan III is removed from his family's vaudeville dance act as a youngster, by his mother, who wants him to have the benefit of a conventional education. He eventually becomes a teacher of music, but his love of dance is never far from his mind, so when one of his students shows him the outline of a ballet in which he sees great potential, Phil changes direction and arranges a production of the show with the help of Vera Barnova, a famous ballerina. He also finds his natural talent for the dance can flourish, and decides to understudy the male lead. It is fortunate for the production that he does so, since he must fill in for the star at short notice. But despite his success, he decides that the stage is not, after all, his destiny, and returns to a quiet life with his small town sweetheart, Frankie Frayne.

Songs include: 'Slaughter on 10th Avenue'; 'There's a Small Hotel'

Phil Dolan II	Snoopy
Lil Dolan	Policeman
Phil Dolan III	Nurse
Lola	Two thugs
New Year	Hoofer
Sergei Alexandrovitch	Striptease girl
Control man	Big boss
Announcer	
Footmen	
Peggy Porterfield	
Junior	
Frankie Frayne	
Sidney Cohen	
Vera Barnova	
Anushka	
Constantine Monossine	
Mischka	
Vassilli	
Dimitri	
Leon	
Call boy	
Princess Zenobia	
Beggar	
Old prince	
Young prince	
A singer	
A waiter	

Once a Catholic
Mary O'Malley
Comedy 2 Acts
London 1977

The lives of three fifth-form Catholic schoolgirls in 1956 and 1957 at the North London Convent of Our Lady of Fatima provide a battleground between the conflicting impulses of their burgeoning sexuality and the strictures of their faith. Busty blonde Mary McGinty cannnot wait to leave school to work in a shop, hangs out with 'teddy boy' Derek, but kissing is as far as she will go. Derek gets more satisfaction from naive Mary Mooney, plain and scruffy, whose mortal sin - helping Derek out - pushes her towards a future as a nun, despite music master Emmanuelli's encouragement of her fine voice.

Sensible and attractive Mary Gallagher plays the System, as does her spotty boyfriend Cuthbert, a Catholic sixth-former whose curious ambition is to be a non-celibate priest. They sleep together, she wears the forbidden tampons, and she gets away with it. Yet no matter what the girls' attitude towards their religion, and however much they see through the rantings of Mother Peter, Mother Basil and Father Mullarky, it is evident they have all been permanently affected, one way or another, by their faith.

Mother Thomas Aquinas	Mr Emmanuelli
Mother Peter	Derek
Mother Basil	Cuthbert
Mary Mooney	Mary O'Grady
Mary McGinty	Mary Hennessy
Mary Gallagher	Mary Murphy
Father Mullarky	Mary Flanagan

Once in a Lifetime
Moss Hart and George S. Kaufman
Comedy 3 Acts
New York 1930

Jerry, his fiancée May and their great friend George are a New York vaudeville act that is failing. When Jerry, the smart hustler of the trio, hears about the new 'talkies' he sells their act and persuades his partners to head west; they decide they can open up a school of voice culture.

On the train they meet May's old colleague Helen Hobart who is now a top Hollywood columnist and who wants in on the idea. Helen sets up a meeting with movie mogul Glogauer, and dumb George is made to pose as a silent intellectual 'Dr Lewis'. They get the job, but then lose it, and when George gives Glogauer a piece of his mind, the great man is so impressed he puts George in charge of production. May has already left for New York with Jerry in pursuit, but George cables them to return. George's dumbness, it seems, is just the thing for the movies and although everything he does seems stupid (like using the wrong movie script), it always turns out advantageously. May and Jerry make up and decide to marry, and 'Dr Lewis' blunders from one triumph to the next.

George Lewis	Miss Leighton
May Daniele	Lawrence Vail
Jerry Hyland	Weisskopf
The Porter	Meterstein
Helen Hobart	1st page
Susan Walker	2nd page
Cigarette girl	Scenario writers (three)
Coat check girl	Rudolph Kammerling
Phyllis Fontaine	1st electrician
Miss Fontaine's maid	2nd electrician
Miss Fontaine's	A voice pupil
chauffeur	Mr Flick
Florabel Leigh	Miss Chasen
Miss Leigh's maid	1st cameraman
Miss Leigh's chauffeur	The Bishop
Bellboy	The 6th bridesmaid
Mrs Walker	Script girl
Ernest	
George's secretary	
Herman Glogauer	

Ondine
Jean Giradoux
Fantasy-Drama 3 Acts
Paris 1939

Ondine, a lovely water-sprite changeling with magical powers, has been brought up by old fisherman Auguste and wife Eugenie. When knight-errant Hans arrives at their hut on his way back to his betrothed, Princess Bertha, Ondine falls in love with him and makes him fall for her. The other ondines (or undines) warn Ondine not to wed Hans and relinquish her watery ways. In order to procure Hans, she makes the bargain that the ondines can kill him if ever he is unfaithful. When the couple arrive at court, Bertha tries to win back Hans but cannot, and when she is revealed as Auguste and Eugene's real daughter she leaves court in shame, and Hans in pity allows her to live in his castle.

Later Ondine disappears and Hans and Bertha decide to wed; then on their wedding day Ondine reappears, caught in the water by a fisherman. She is put on trial and sentenced to death but rescued by the King of the Ondines.

Meanwhile Hans is having premonitions of doom and, half-crazy, approaches Ondine, his will to live sapped. He is dying of his love and with a final kiss he dies. Ondine is made to lose her memory of him by the Ondine King, and she is led back into the water.

Ondine	Bertram
Hans	The Poet
King of the Ondines	First Judge
Bertha	Second Judge
Auguste	Greta
Eugenie	Kitchen Maid
The King	First fisherman (Ulrich)
Queen Yseult	Second fisherman
Chamberlain	Seal-trainer

Superintendent of the   Matho
   Royal Theatres   Ondines
Swineherd   Knights
Violanta   Ladies
Salammbo

One Flew over the Cuckoo's Nest
Dale Wasserman
Drama 3 Acts
New York 1963

Everything is running smoothly at the State Mental Institution. The patients are tranquillized and docile under the iron-willed regime of the handsome but formidable Nurse Ratched. The arrival of McMurphy throws a spanner in the works. A strong, high-spirited extrovert, he has been committed after fighting at the prison work farm and deemed 'psychopathic'. A gambler and womanizer, he breathes life into the ward and his influence helps the patients one by one to assert themselves.

Ratched hates the challenge to her authority and finally, when McMurphy throws a party with alcohol and girlfriends smuggled in, she walks in on it and confronts McMurphy, taunting him. He tears open her dress and tries to strangle her, giving her the excuse she needed to have him lobotomized. After the operation, his friend Red Indian Chief Bromden finds his true strength, suffocates the lobotomized McMurphy and is helped by the others to escape.

Chief Bromden   Sefelt
Aide Warren   Col Matterson
Aide Williams   Randle P. McMurphy
Nurse Ratched   Dr Spivey
Nurse Flynn   Aide Turkle
Dale Harding   Candy Starr
Ellis   Nurse Nakamura
Billy Bibbit   Technician
Scanlon   Sandra
Cheswick   Aide
Martini
Ruckly
Fredericks

One for the Pot
Ray Cooney
Comedy 3 Acts
Richmond 1959

Jonathon Hardcastle draws up an agreement to give Billy Hickory Wood 10,000 pounds, because his father, Sam, helped make Hardcastle's mill a success. Unfortunately Billy will only get this sum if no other relatives turn up to claim it. On the night of Hardcastle's daughter Cynthia's birthday party, Billy's identical brothers Rupert and Michael arrive one by one to sign the agreement to collect the money. Jugg, the butler, conspires with Charlie, Billy's friend, for a price, to keep Hardcastle unaware of the existence of the brothers.

Chaos ensues as everyone confuses the brothers for Billy, including Winnie, his wife. Rupert and Cynthia fall in love - much to the disgust of Clifton Weaver who attempts to buy off Rupert's attentions, because he too is after Cynthia, that is, after her money. Michael attempts to get the 10,000 pounds for himself and they all come within a hair's breadth of signing the document during the course of the evening. Eventually, after several characters have been drugged, made drunk, and hidden in the cocktail cabinet the truth comes out. Hardcastle decides to fire Jugg, and has just enough time to be thankful that there are only three brothers - when Pierre arrives.

Billy Hickory Wood, a North Country lad
Rupert Hickory Wood, a well-spoken lad
Michael Hickory Wood, an Irish rogue
Pierre Hickory Wood, a Frenchman
Charlie Barnet, a middle-aged cockney
Jugg, the butler
Jonathon Hardcastle
Cynthia Hardcastle
Amy Hardcastle
Arnold Piper, Hardcastle's solicitor
Winnie
Clifton Weaver, an art critic
Jennifer Bowater-Smith, Cynthia's guest
Stanley Bowater-Smith, her husband

One for the Road
Willy Russell
Comedy 2 Acts
Nottingham 1979

Living in a dormer bungalow on a lower-middle-class Northern housing estate is driving Dennis crazy. Wife Pauline happily embraces the pretentiousness of the Tuppaware/John Denver crowd, but Dennis is almost thirty and can't let go his longings for freedom and open road. At a dinner party (when Dennis' parents get lost in the maze of bungalows and never arrive), their friends and neighbours Jane and Roger gang up with Pauline against 'childish' Dennis. Between talk of the local vandal - who artistically desecrates garden gnomes and vegetable plots - Roger suggests Dennis should relieve his frustrations by 'having a fling' with one of the local wives, like most of the other blokes on the estate. But Dennis's frustrations do eventually strike a chord with his friends and both, it transpires, want to join him for one last fling on the open road. But when their bohemian yearnings are diluted into a compromise plan to buy a shared mobile holiday home, disgusted Dennis reveals himself as the local vandal. The others, despite proof, refuse to believe him, and defeated Dennis is left stranded in suburbia with the consolation prize of a possible liaison with Jane.

Pauline Cain
Dennis Cain
Roger Fuller
Jane Fuller

One Mo' Time
Vernel Bagneris
Musical 2 Acts
New York 1979

Bertha's musical review arrives for a show at the Lyric Theatre in the black quarter of an American city. As always, Bertha, playing the star, is late for her own first number. One of the juniors in the company, Thelma, has ambitions and tries to persuade Bertha's lover, Papa Du, who is also the company manager, to let her take a star turn by doing Bertha's material. Wary as he is of Bertha's wrathful jealousy, he still grants Thelma's request, in the hope that she will be grateful enough to sleep with him.

Meanwhile, another member of the company, Agie, has disappeared with the money Bertha had provided to bail out the troupe's erotic dancer, Edna. Short by two members, the company is threatened with non-payment by the theatre manager. To keep to the letter of their contract, Papa Du himself does Agie's turn, and Ma Reed, a hefty older woman, is pressed into ludicrous service as a stripper. The manager is still not satisfied, and only agrees to pay when Bertha threatens him with a beating. Having dealt with the manager, Bertha turns her jealous attention on Thelma, but they eventually agree to share Papa Du's affection.

Bertha
Ma Reed
Thelma
Papa Du
Theatre owner

One Way Pendulum
N. F. Simpson
Comedy 2 Acts
Brighton 1959

Subtitled *A Farce in a New Dimension*, this surrealistic tale of the strange Groomkirby family centres around Kirby Groomkirby and his fixations. From babyhood he has always worn black and lately, to justify this, he has committed a large number of murders so that he may always be in mourning. His ultimate master-plan is to teach his collection of speak-your-weight machines to sing *The Hallelujah Chorus*, ship them to the North Pole, entice enough people along to hear them perform and then persuade these people to jump up and down in unison in order to create a shift in the earth's axis. This will cause a new ice age, many deaths, much mourning. All this is revealed in the trial sequence in Act 2, held in the Groomkirby living room. Other characters in the house include Aunt Mildred, whose fixaton is travelling, the enormous Myra Gantry who is employed by Mrs Groomkirby to eat the family leftovers, sweethearts Stan Honeyblock and Sylvia Groomkirby, and the eccentrically self-important Mr Groomkirby.

Kirby Groomkirby	*Sylvia Groomkirby*
Robert Barnes	*Aunt Mildred*
Mabel Groomkirby	*Myra Gantry*

Arthur Groomkirby	*Usher*
Stan Honeyblock	*Clerk of the court*
Judge	*Prosecuting counsel*
Policeman	*Defending counsel*

Oresteia Trilogy
Aeschylus
3 Plays
Athens 485BC

See: *Agamemnon; Choephori, The; Eumenides*

Orphée (Orpheus)
Jean Cocteau
Tragedy 1 Act
Paris 1926

Eurydice is jealous of the attention her husband, Orphée, gives to his horse, which inspires poetry he is entering for a competition in Thrace. She enlists the aid of Heurtebise, but due to a mistake by an old friend, Algaonice, she dies by poison intended for the horse.

Orphée is devastated by her death and Heurtebise arranges for him to visit her in death by going through a mirror. The couple emerge from death and resolve to start afresh, but they soon begin to argue and she disappears back through the mirror.

Algaonice has discovered secret meanings in Orphée's poetry and organizes the Bacchantes to kill him. He is decapitated and his severed head calls to Eurydice who comes through the mirror and takes his invisible body back with her. Heurtebise later follows and the trio arrive in heaven where they celebrate their salvation by Orphée reciting a prayer to poetry.

Orphée, a poet
Eurydice, his wife
The horse
Heurtebise, a glazier
Death
Azraël and Raphaël, Death's assistants
Commissioner of police
The scrivener

Orpheus Descending
Tennessee Williams
Tragedy 3 Acts
New York 1957

Val Xavier, blues guitarist, drifter and disillusioned ladies' man, finds himself stranded and penniless in a small town in the Southern USA. He is taken on as a clerk by Lady Torrance whose husband Jabe, owner of the town's general store, is dying of cancer.

Despite the attentions of the town's richest and loosest woman, Carol Cutrere, and the obvious interest of several other local women, Val maintains a laconic, wistful solitude until he and Lady fall in love. For Lady, this love is a release from the bitterness of her betrayal, years earlier, by her lover David Cutrere; and from the long, loveless marriage with Jabe.

As the result of a misunderstanding, the local sheriff

comes to suspect Val of trying to seduce his wife and orders the younger man to leave the town or face mob justice. At the same time Lady discovers, with joy, that she is pregnant by Val, and with fury, that Jabe had been one of the murderers of her own father. Lady begs Val to stay on, defying the sheriff, until she can have her revenge by opening a replica of her dead father's wine business and ignoring Jabe's slide into death. But just as she is revealing her pregnancy to Val, Jabe finds them together, shoots Lady, and rushes into the street, hurling accusation for the murder at Val, who is taken away to his death by a mob.

Dolly Hamma	Vee Talbot
Beulah Binnings	Lady Torrance
Pee Wee Binnings	Jabe Torrance
Dog Hamma	Sherrif Talbot
Carol Cutrere	Mr Dubinsky
Eva Temple	Woman
Sister Temple	
Uncle Pleasant	
Val Xavier	

Othello
William Shakespeare
Tragedy 5 Acts
London 1604

Iago, outwardly an honest soldier, is malevolently jealous when he is passed over for promotion by his master the great Othello, the Moor of Venice, in favour of Cassio. When Othello is posted to Cyprus, Iago and his wife Emilia follow and he wreaks terrible revenge, cunningly sowing seeds of jealousy into Othello's heart and leading him to believe his wife, Desdemona, is being unfaithful to him with Cassio. Iago's wickedly clever use of a magic handkerchief, given to Othello by his mother, finally breaks Othello's reason and the Moor kills the innocent Desdemona. Iago's treachery is unmasked by his wife Emilia, and Othello kills himself. The evil Iago is taken away to be tortured and Cassio rules over Cyprus.

Duke of Venice	Desdemona, wife to Iago
Brabanti, a Venetian	Emilia
senator	Bianca, a courtesan
Two other senators	Officers
Gratiano, brother to	Gentlemen
Brabantio	Messengers
Lodovico, kinsman to	Musicians
Brabantio	Sailors
Othello, the Moor	Attendants
Cassio, his lieutenant	
Iago	
Roderigo, a Venetian	
gentleman	
Montano, Othello's	
predecessor	
Clown	
Herald	

Otherwise Engaged
Simon Gray
Drama 2 Acts
Brighton 1959

Publisher Simon Hench lives in Islington with his sexy wife Beth and all their creature comforts in a deliberately childless marriage. He's sophisticated and cool and maintains a graceful distance from the problems and demands of his family, friends and associates. One day he sits down to play a new recording of *Parsifal* but interruptions mount in intensity from his boozy writer friend Jeff, hard and horrible young writer Davina Saunders, teacher brother Stephen, and pathetic middle-aged Wood whose young 'fiancée' Simon has recently 'had it off with'. He can handle these, but not the next ones; Beth admits adultery, which he knew about, and her pregnancy - father unknown - which he didn't. Then his lodger Dave, frenzied by Simon's supercilious attitude, states he won't be leaving but instead moving in two radical undesirables. Finally he hears something terrible on the telephone answering machine and the bubble of his selfishness is shattered. Jeff returns, having been arrested for drunk driving, and together they sit down and get to listen to *Parsifal*.

Simon Hench
Dave
Stephen Hench
Jeff Golding
Davina Saunders
Wood
Beth

Our Betters
W. Somerset Maugham
Comedy 3 Acts
London 1923

Young American heiress Bessie Saunders looks set to follow her sister Pearl, now Lady George Grayston, into the ranks of the often impoverished British aristocracy; the Americans get a title, and the British get the money. But despite the attentions of the attractive Lord Bleane, Bessie is undecided.

The arrival of her friend and ex-fiancé Fleming Harvey with his straightforward American ways only confirms her indecision. All around her she sees decadence, empty frivolity and adultery; Pearl is openly having an affair with the gross Arthur Fenwick to supplement her 'modest' income and enable her to be one of London's top society hostesses; the middle-aged Duchess de Surennes, originally from Chicago, has abandoned all pride and dotes on the heartless young gigolo Tony Paxton and the good-natured Principessa della Cercola is disillusion personified. When Pearl and Tony are caught *in flagrante* and Pearl wriggles out of considerable trouble with a series of unscrupulous and clever stratagems, the disgusted Bessie decides to return to the fresh air of America.

Lady George Grayston

Duchesse de Surennes
Principessa della Cercola
Elizabeth Saunders
Arthur Fenwick
Thornton Clay
Fleming Harvey
Anthony Paxton
Lord Bleane
Pole
Ernest

Our Boys
H. G. Bryon
Comedy 3 Acts
London 1875
This Victorian comedy details the triumph of true love over social pedigree and paternal pressure.

Sir Geoffry Champneys, a wealthy landowner, and Perkyn Middlewick, a retired dairy manufacturer, have come together to greet their returning sons, who have apparently become firm friends on their European travels. Whilst Middlewick is a friendly, demonstrative man, Champneys is typically superior and uncomfortable with those he feels are below his class. On the arrival of the boys, it is obvious that they have somewhat reversed the roles of their fathers. Charles Middlewick is well educated and eloquent, while Talbot Champneys is lazy and foppish.

Present at this homecoming are cousins Mary Melrose and heiress Violet who is Sir Geoffry's prospective bride for Talbot. Typically however, Charles and Violet fall in love, as do Talbot and the penniless Mary, to the chagrin of the fathers, who banish the boys into poverty.

Champneys and Middlewick cannot endure the loss of their dearly-loved sons for long and have a change of heart, and both couples and families are finally re-united.

Sir Geoffry Champneys, a county magistrate
Talbot Champneys, his son
Perkyn Middlewick, a retired butterman
Charles Middlewick, his son
Kempster, Sir Geoffry's manservant
Poddles, Middlewick's butler
Violet Melrose, an heiress
Mary Melrose, her poor cousin
Clarissa Champneys, Sir Geoffry's sister
Belinda, a lodging-house slave

Our Town
Thornton Wilder
Play 3 Acts
New York 1938
This American classic depicts the everyday life of two families in the town of Grovers Corner, New Hampshire 1901-13. In a representational form a narrator addresses the audience, describing, commenting on and participating in the three acts covering the 'daily life',

'love and marriage' and 'death and the meaning of life' of the Gibbs and the Webb families.

Flashbacks sketch in the everyday existence and work of the families, characters come and go, as the action focuses on the romance that develops between Emily Webb and George Gibbs from their schooldays through to their marriage.

Nine years on sees the end of their happy marriage when Emily dies in childbirth but she is resurrected to join the mourners at her own funeral and happily recall her twelfth birthday. She desperately wants to share her happiness with her mother, who cannot see her, so she returns to her grave full of admiration for life but saddened by how little people appreciate it.

Stage Manager	*Woman in the auditorium*
Dr Gibbs	*Man in the auditorium*
Joe Crowell	*Lady in a box*
Howie Newsome	*Simon Stimson*
Mrs Gibbs	*Mrs Soames*
Mrs Webb	*Constable Warren*
George Gibbs	*Si Crowell*
Rebecca Gibbs	*Three baseball players*
Wally Webb	*Sam Craig*
Emily Webb	*Joe Stoddard*
Professor Willard	
Mr Webb	
Woman on the balcony	

Outside Edge
Richard Harris
Comedy 2 Acts
London 1979
Boyish Roger's cricket team is playing British Rail Maintenance Division, Reading East, in the South-Western League and cricket and domestic problems run in tandem inside the ramshackle pavilion.

Roger's efficient wife Miriam is proud to a fault of her teas and refreshments; jovial 'sport' Dennis flirts with all the wives; worried Bob uses the match as an excuse to visit his ex-wife, and his present wife Ginnie turns up unexpectedly; arrogant young solicitor Alex brings his latest lovely but brainless girlfriend Sharon; little Kevin is smothered by loving wife big Maggie and then hurts his little finger so he can't bowl. During the course of the match Roger's bossiness upsets Miriam, who is further shocked when she discovers an unfortunate peccadillo he had in Dorking; tearful Sharon is locked in the loo; Ginnie gets happy again when Bob tells her his ex-wife is remarrying; and when Dennis is bowled for a duck, he is so obnoxious on the telephone to wife, Shirley, that she turns up and sets fire to his car. As a final blow, just as Roger's team is drawing even, the rain begins to fall...

Miriam	*Kevin*
Roger	*Ginnie*
Bob	*Alex*
Dennis	*Sharon*
Maggie	

Outsider, The
Dorothy Brandon
Drama 3 Acts
London 1923

The top surgeons at St Martha's hospital in the twenties are indignant at the claims of one of their number that the work of Anton Ragatzy should be recognized by the medical profession. Ragatzy's invention, a rack that can straighten crooked bones, has supposedly cured cases the surgeons pronounced incurable. Jasper Sturdee, the most eminent physician, adamantly refuses any possible meeting, as a quack doctor had crippled his baby daughter, Lalage, many years before.

The others, however, decide to meet Ragatzy. He does little to allay their suspicions. Arrogant and Svengali-like, he admits to making a profit, yet his invention definitely has merit. The surgeons reject him, and full of revenge he decides to cure the proud Sturdee's daughter.

Lalage Sturdee, though loyal to her father, is desperate to walk properly, as she loves Basil, a gauche young man who cannot see her nature beyond her crooked leg, and so accepts the persuasive Ragatzy's offer.

Over the next year, Ragatzy forgets his motives and falls in love with her, yet come the day of her release, he seems to have failed, to the fury of the assembled surgeons. However, Ragatzy's confession of his love for her moves Lalage to walk again as the play closes.

Anton Ragatzy
Jasper Sturdee MS
Sir Montague Tollemache FRCS
Sir Nathan Israel FRCS
Vincent Helmore
Frederick Ladd
Basil Owen
Mme Klost
Pritchard
Lalage Sturdee

Overcoat, The
Nikolai Gogol
Drama 1 Act
Yale 1973

In Tzarist Russia, Akaky Akakievich is a poor, but intensely dedicated copy clerk, who is constantly ridiculed by his colleagues for his tattered old overcoat, pitifully unsuited for the rigours of the St Petersburg winters. Akaky approaches the local tailor, Petrovich, only to be told it will cost him 200 roubles for a new coat, way beyond his means. He does, however, have some savings, and persuades his landlady to reduce his rent. Through flattery he also cajoles Petrovich to lower the price to 170 roubles. Six weeks later his new overcoat is finished and the envy of St Petersburg.

Akaky strays into a bad part of town and his overcoat is stolen. He begs the head of the civil service for help, but is cruelly rejected. The freezing conditions soon kill Akaky but his ghost returns to force the civil service boss to locate all stolen overcoats, to the delight of the citizens of St Petersburg.

Nikolai Gogol
Akaky Akakievich
Three men
Two women

Owl and the Pussycat, The
Bill Manhoff
Comedy 3 Acts
New York 1964

It is past midnight when F. Sherman, book-store clerk and would-be writer, opens his door to a very angry young woman. Doris Waverley storms in, hurling many and various insults at her unwilling host. She states that since it was his officious report to the landlord that got her evicted for taking paying gentlemen callers, she is now going to live in his apartment. They patently have nothing in common. She insists that though she is a prostitute, she is not promiscuous, and that she is an actress and model, between jobs. She is hurt and angry when Sherman questions her respectability. Sherman himself is no stranger to self-delusion. He is an arrogant pseudo-intellectual, whose delusions are amply reflected in his unsuccessful attempts as an author. Sherman is attracted to Doris and begins to admire her hidden intelligence. Theirs is a chaotic and turbulent relationship, yet by the end of the play they have both gained a valuable trust in each other, and a more realistic view of themselves.

F. Sherman
Doris Waverley

Pack of Lies
Hugh Whitemore
Drama 2 Acts
Brighton 1983

This play is based on the true story of Peter and Helen Kroger, an American couple living in a London suburb, who were convicted in 1961 of spying for the Russians.

The quietly respectable Jackson family, Bob, Barbara and their daughter Julie, live opposite the Krogers and consider them to be their closest friends. Julie in particular worships her 'Auntie' Helen. One day an MI5 official arrives and, after much coercion, persuades the Jacksons to let their house be used as a surveillance post, though who is to be watched he will not say.

Their previous quiet, happy existence is overtaken by a new world of deceit and intrigue through which Bob and Barbara slowly learn the truth about their good friends, the Krogers. On their arrest for espionage Julie's heart is broken, and Barbara reaches breaking point in the knowledge that the Krogers have betrayed her and she, in turn, has betrayed them.

Bob Jackson	*Peter Kroger*
Barbara Jackson	*Stewart*
Julie Jackson	*Thelma*
Helen Kroger	*Sally*

Paint Your Wagon
Alan Jay Lerner
Music by Frederick Loewe
Musical 2 Acts
New York 1951

Prospector Ben Rumson and his friends strike it rich in the Californian hill landscape of 1853 and Rumson Town booms with a population of seven hundred men. Jennifer, Ben's daughter, the only female, falls in love with Julio, the Mexican outsider, but is forced to leave for her own safety. When a Mormon, Jacob Woodling, arrives with two wives, one wife is auctioned off in fairness to everyone. Ben marries Elizabeth as the Fandango saloon girls arrive. Julio's hopes for his and Jennifer's future together seem doomed as we learn that the gold is drying up. As this news spreads, the population diminishes and Julio heads North to find a mythical lake of gold before Jennifer returns. Money-grabbing Ben accepts a bid for Elizabeth just as she elopes with Croker. News of a big strike in the South leaves the town unpopulated but Ben ever hopeful as Julio and Jennifer are reunited.

Songs include: 'Paint Your Wagon'; 'Wand'rin' Star'; 'I Talk to the Trees'

Walt	*Jacob Woodling*
Jennifer Rumson	*Sarah Woodling*
Salem Trumbull	*Elizabeth Woodling*
Jasper	*Dutchie*
Ben Rumson	*Carmellita*
Steve Bullnack	*Yvonne Sorel*
Pete Billings	*Suzanne Duval*
Cherry	*Raymond Janney*
Jake Whippany	*Rocky*
Mike Mooney	*Ed*
Lee Zen	*Jack*
Dr Newcomb	*Bill*
Edgar Croker	*Sam*
Sandy Twist	*Johansen*
Reuben Sloane	*Miners*
Julio Valveras	*Fandangoes*

Pajama Game, The
George Abbott and Richard Bissell
Music and lyrics by Richard Adler and Jerry Ross
Musical Comedy 2 Acts
New York 1954

Hasler, the wily boss of the Sleep-Tite Pajama Factory, is not keen to give a seven-and-a-half cent rise to the workers and he hires a time-and-motion man, Hines, and a new factory supervisor, Sid Sorokin, to speed up production. Sid begins negotiations with the union representative, Babe, but he is soon more interested in her romantically than professionally, and she feels exactly the same about him. The lovers' principles clash, however, and when Babe organizes a go-slow and tries to disrupt production, Sid dismisses her. Sid, still in love with Babe, takes the company bookkeeper, Gladys, out for an evening to Hernando's Hideaway and gets her to 'lend' him the keys to the office safe where he discovers that all is not what it should be with the firm's accounts. He confronts Hasler who decides that the workers should, of course, get their rise, and Sid gets his girl.

Songs include: 'I'm Not at All in Love'; 'Hey There'; 'Steam Heat'; 'Hernando's Hideaway'; 'There Once was a Man'

Hines	*Babe Williams*
Prez	*Mae*
Joe	*Brenda*
Hasler	*Poopsie*
Sid Sorokin	*Salesman*
Gladys	*Pop*
Mabel	*Dancers*
First helper	*Chorus*
Second helper	

Pajama Tops
Mauby Green and Ed Feilbert
Farce 3 Acts
New York 1954

Georges Chauvinet is preparing to leave his villa for a liaison with Babette Latouche on the pretext that her husband is his business partner. However, his wife has innocently invited the Latouches to dinner, signing with Georges' name.

Babette arrives with all her luggage, expecting a proposal from Georges, only to find he is married. In disgust she pretends (on Georges' behalf) that Leonard Joli-Joli, a friend of Georges, is in fact Jacques Latouche. The real Jacques, a swindler on the run, has also intercepted the invitation and arrives unexpectedly, taking a job as the butler. In the midst of this chaos, the maid Claudine phones Inspector Legrand to tell him that Latouche is on the premises (meaning Leonard).

After numerous plot twists, the truth is revealed, the couples are united and Georges escapes the discovery of his original intentions.

Claudine
Inspector Legrand
Yvonne Chauvinet
Georges Chauvinet
Leonard Joli-Joli
Babette Latouche
Jacques

Pal Joey
Lorenz Hart and Richard Rodgers
Musical 2 Acts
New York 1940

Joey Evans, a seedy nightclub dancer, begins a seduction of an innocent young girl, Linda English, by promising to write a book about her. He soon finds it expedient, though, to switch his attentions to Vera Simpson, an older but much more affluent woman, who gets him an expensive flat and then opens a nightclub in his name.

Even Vera, though, soon tires of Joey's rapacious selfishness, so when Linda informs her of a plan to tell Vera's husband about the affair with Joey, it seems the older woman is about to be blackmailed. As it happens, though, Linda has herself seen through Joey's facade and the two woman each reinforce the other's growing disenchantment with him. Joey, who has overheard their discussion, realizes he can no longer use either of them, and disappears into the night.

Songs include: 'I Could Write a Book'; 'Bewitched'; 'Take Him'; 'That Terrific Rainbow'; 'The Flower Garden of My Heart'; 'Do It the Hard Way'

Joey Evans	Ernest
Mike Spears	Max
Gladys	The Tenor
Agnes	Melba Snyder
The Kid	Waiter
Linda English	Ludlow Lowell
Valerie	Briefcase
Albert Doane	Commissioner O'Brien
Vera Simpson	Assistant hotel manager
Terry	Dancers
Victor	

Pandora's Box
Frank Wedekind
Tragedy 3 Acts
Vienna 1905

Originally dubbed 'pornographic', this tragedy is the second part of Wedekind's earlier work *Earth Spirit*.

The promiscuous Lulu, who has served a year in prison for killing her lover, Schon, is helped to escape by her lesbian admirer, Countess Geschwitz. Waiting for her is another lover, Rodrigo Quast, who wants to train her as an acrobat, but he is now repelled by her 'bag of gnawed bones' appearance. Also waiting is Alwa, Schon's son, whom she seduces.

Now moved to Paris, Lulu is threatened by the Marquis Casti-Piani who wants her for a prostitute in Cairo and she is also under pressure from her incestuous pimp father, Schigolch, who longs to sleep with her again; she agrees if he will 'dispose' of Rodrigo.

Later, in London, Lulu, Alwa and Schigolch are living in a squalid attic and desperate for money. Lulu goes on the streets as Geschwitz turns up. One of her clients kills Alwa and Schigolch leaves. Another client attacks Lulu and when Geschwitz tries to save her she is stabbed, before the murderer Jack 'the Ripper' drags Lulu away to deal with her.

Lulu
Alwa Schon, a writer
Rodrigo Quast, an acrobat
Schigolch
Alfred Hugenberg, an inmate of a reformatory
Countess Geschwitz
Marquis Casti-Piani
Banker Puntschu
Heilmann, a journalist
Magelone
Kadikja di Santa Croce, her daughter
Bianetta Gazil
Ludmilla Steinherz
Bob, a groom
A police inspector
Mr Hunidei
Kungu, Imperial Prince of Uahubee
Dr Hilti, a university lecturer
Jack (The Ripper)

Passage to India, A
Santha Rama Rau, from the novel
by E.M. Forster
Drama 3 Acts
London 1960

Fielding, an enlightened college principal in Imperial India during the twenties, has been warned by his superiors against fraternizing with the natives. Nevertheless he throws a tea party to bring together his new Muslim friend, Dr Aziz, with Hindi philosopher, Professor Godbole, and two newly arrived English ladies, wise old Mrs Moore, mother of local magistrate Ronnie Heaslop, and Ronnie's fiancée, Adela Quested.

Miss Quested is anxious to know all about the real India and the real Indians and finds Ronnie's colonialistic attitude offensive. Worse, she doesn't love him. So when Aziz invites them all on an expedition to the local Marabar Caves, she goes along with eagerness. But the caves are weird and sinister; Mrs Moore is upset by their strange echo and at the final cave only Adela goes in. She is overcome and her innermost anxieties make her imagine Aziz has followed her in and assaulted her.

Back at the club the Brits are out for Aziz's blood and a trial is mounted. Despite the locals' anti-British fury, Adela looks set to win, but at the last moment she comes to her senses and courageously withdraws the allegation. Everyone is furious with her, and only Fielding offers her protection. He persuades Aziz to drop costs against Miss Quested, but Aziz sees this as Fielding taking sides against him, and their friendship is broken.

Dr Aziz, Assistant Civil Surgeon
Mr Fielding, Principal, Government College of
  Chandrapore
Ranjit, Fielding's servant
Mrs Moore
Miss Adela Quested
Professor Godbole
Ronnie Heaslop
An Indian guide
Three Indian servants
Mrs Turton, wife of the collector
Mrs McBryde, wife of the Superintendent of Police
Mrs Leslie and Mrs Burton, wives of civil servants
Mrs Collins
A Lieutenant of the Indian Army

A club servant
Mr Fletcher
Maj. Callendar, Chief Surgeon of the Government
 Hospital
Mr McBryde, Superintendant of Police for
Chandrapore
Mr Hamidullah, a lawyer
Mr Amritrao
Mr Das, assistant magistrate for Chandrapore
An Indian guard
Nine Indian onlookers

Passing of the Third Floor Back, The
Jerome K. Jerome
Drama 3 Acts
London 1908
A charismatic, dignified and very refined old gentleman arrives at a Bloomsbury lodging house occupied by impoverished, and consequently embittered, members of the middle class.

His gentle manner and rather down-at-heel appearance attracts the immediate scorn of his new fellow lodgers, who set out to upset him into leaving by merciless teasing. Not only does the old man bear their taunts, but also manages by the moral force of his courtly kindness so to disarm each of his tormentors that they come very quickly to seek his approval by every means at their disposal. Each one, in turn, is so inspired by the old man, that they all eventually reform their lives and begin to live in a spirit of true compassion for their fellows, and confident commitment to the best in themselves. His work finished, the old man departs as quietly as he had arrived, and without ever revealing his true identity.
Joey Wright, a retired bookmaker
Christopher Penny, a young painter
Maj. Tompkins
Mrs Tompkins, his wife
Vivian, his daughter
Jape Samuels, a city trader
Harry Larkcom, his minion
Miss Kite, a spinster
Mrs Percival de Hooley, a poor society lady
Stasia, a servant
Mrs Sharpe, the landlady
The stranger, an old gentleman

Passion of Dracula, The
Bob Hall and David Richmond, from the novel
 by Bram Stoker
Drama 3 Acts
New York 1977
Count Dracula moves next door to a sanatorium for lunatics run by Dr Seward and strange things begin to happen in the area; women are killed at night by what seems to be a wild beast ripping out their throats; dogs howl, bats appear and sanatorium patient Renfield is found eating flies to prolong his life.

Seward is worried about his daughter Wilhemenia who is very weak and growing weaker by the day. He summons two doctors, Helga van Zandt and Van Helsing, but they are as baffled as he. One evening journalist Jonathan Harker is passing when his car breaks down and he goes inside. He meets Wilhemenia and soon they fall in love. That same evening Count Dracula pays a call and his presence makes both Renfield and Wilhemenia very agitated. Soon after he leaves, Wilhemenia faints, Helga's bloodstained body is found outside, and Seward realizes Dracula is a vampire. They kill Helga in the prescribed fashion by sticking a wooden stake through her heart, and cover the house with garlic and crucifixes, now realizing that Dracula is draining just a little of Wilhemenia's blood every night.

Dracula wants Wilhemenia to become his wife and live with him for all eternity, but she must go with him of her own free will. One night Dracula arrives at the Sewards, and Wilhemenia is weakened but tries to resist him. There is a fight as Harker tries to put a stake through Dracula, but he fails. Finally, as Wilhemenia pretends she will at last go with Dracula, she half embraces him, then plunges the stake through his heart. Other successful stage versions of *Dracula* include the 1927 dramatization by Hamilton Deane and John L. Balderton, and the 1971 adaptation by Ted Tiller.
Dr Cedric Seward   *Mr Renfield*
Jameson   *Wilhemenia Murray*
Professor Van Helsing   *Jonathan Harker*
Dr Helga Van Zandt   *Count Dracula*
Lord Godolming

Passion Play
Peter Nichols
Drama 2 Acts
London 1981
The marriage of James and Eleanor, a middle-aged professional London couple, apparently devoted to one another, starts to come apart when James is seduced by their mutual friend Kate, the former mistress of James' recently deceased best friend, and no older than the couple's own children.

As James starts the inevitable lying to Eleanor, they are both joined onstage by their *alter egos*, Jim and Nell, whose commentary reveals the violent passions beneath the surface of the couple's efforts to be 'civilized' about the affair. James persuades Eleanor that he has given Kate up, but Agnes, his best friend's ex-wife, still bitter at Kate's part in her own marriage break-up, reveals that the affair is still going on.

In a disingenuous attempt to help the couple patch things up, Kate insists on a visit to the couple's home, where she reveals a strong sexual desire not just for James, but for Eleanor as well. Unable to stand the pressure any longer, Eleanor attempts suicide by swallowing a bottle of pills, and although James watches over her recovery with tender solicitude, Jim's commentary, full of bitterness, shows the awful underside of his exemplary behaviour.

As Jim, watched over by Nell, reads a highly erotic letter from Kate to James, during what is supposed to be a Christmas party, it becomes clear that James and Eleanor are more drastically divided than ever. Kate, or perhaps her *alter ego* - it is left ambiguous - arrives at the party and makes love to Jim while the celebrations swirl around them.

Agnes, age fifty
Eleanor, age forty-five
James, Eleanor's husband, age fifty
Jim, James' alter ego
Kate, James' mistress, age twenty-five
Nell, Eleanor's alter ego

Past Imperfect
Hugh and Margaret Williams
Comedy 2 Acts
London 1964

The Earl of Flint, a fabulously rich and powerful businessman, falls in love with his temporary secretary, Miss Jones, as he watches her handle the preparations for a television interview he has to do. Flint is a radical Tory at odds with the trades unions, who he believes to be communist-led. After some initial reluctance, Miss Jones first becomes Flint's lover, and then his wife. The strain of newly-wed sex life with his much younger bride causes Flint to have a heart attack, and at the same time the audience discovers that Miss Jones is in fact a semi-professional communist agent, sent to provoke exactly such a breakdown of his health.

Miss Jones, however, has fallen in love with Flint, and refuses to continue her subterfuge, deciding instead to leave Flint rather than cause him more harm. Realizing that something is amiss, Flint tapes a conversation between Miss Jones and her 'control', in which she reveals her duplicity, but also her love. His love for her is unchanged, and he confronts her with the tape on which she admits her love for him, forgives her and decides to take her on holiday to the West Indies.

McVitie	*The Earl of Flint*
A cameraman	*A photographer*
Two electricians	*Sir William Hood*
Steven Pearson	*Ferdinand Jurescu*
Miss Jones	

Patience
W.S. Gilbert and Arthur Sullivan
Comic Opera 2 Acts
London 1881

Subtitled *Bunthorne's Bride* this tells the story of Reginald Bunthorne, an aesthete and poet, worshipped by twenty maidens who dote on his every word, while he only has eyes for a simple village milk maid, Patience. The maidens are in turn admired by the men of the 35th Dragoon Guards, who have just returned to town and cannot understand the girls' aesthetic interests.

Patience, who has no time for poetry, has however fallen in love with another poet, Archibald Grosvenor, but because she wishes to be truly unselfish she agrees to marry Bunthorne. The maidens now transfer their adulation to Grosvenor, but he has no wish for such attention and the girls straggle away and eventually marry some of the soldiers.

Patience undergoes several changes of heart and ends up married to Grosvenor. Only Bunthorne is wifeless, but he prefers it like that.

Songs include: 'Twenty Love-Sick Maidens We'; 'When I First Put This Uniform On'; 'Prithee, Pretty Maiden - Prithee Tell Me True'; 'If Saphir I Choose to Marry'

Officers of the Dragoon Guards: Col. Calverley,
Maj. Murgatroyd and Lieut the Duke of Dunstable
Reginald Bunthorne, poet
Archibald Grosvenor
Mr Bunthorne's solicitor
Maidens: Lady Angela, Lady Saphir, Lady Ella,
Lady Jane and Patience
Dairy maid
Maidens
Officers

Peer Gynt
Henrik Ibsen
Fantasy Comedy 5 Acts
Oslo 1876

Peer Gynt is a lovable rollicking rogue who when slighted by his true love Solveig, in revenge carries off the betrothed Ingrid from her wedding feast and seduces her. Solveig follows them to the mountains and warns Peer that the villagers are pursuing him and have already stripped his mother of all her possessions except for her bed. Peer steals to his dying mother's bedside and comforts her with his incredible stories, then he flees from Norway. He has a multitude of adventures and grows rich through slave-trading and other nefarious activities. In Africa he becomes entranced with Anitra, a dancing Arab girl who soon swindles him out of all his wealth. His tall tales land him in an asylum - where he becomes king - and back in Norway his life is endangered among the mountains by the wicked little Trolls. He returns home a disillusioned old man, wishing only to live an honest life, and he is reunited with the now-blind Solveig who has waited for him all her life. Her prayers have been his redemption. Music for this saga was written by Grieg in 1874.

Aase, a farmer's widow	*Solveig*
Peer Gynt, her son	*Helga, her sister*
Two old women with	*Ingrid's father, farmer at*
sacks of corn	*Heggstad*
Aslak, a smith	*Bridegroom*
Master Cook	*Bridegroom's father*
Solveig's mother,	*Bridegroom's mother*
immigrant	*Ingrid*
Solveig's father,	*Three Seater girls*
immigrant	*The Greenclad One*

Old Man of the
  Mountains
Oldest Troll courtier
Ugly Child
The Boyg
Kari, a cottar's wife
Travellers: Mr Cotton,
  M. Ballon, Herr Von
  Eberkopf, Herr
  Trumpeterstraale

Overseer
Thief
Receiver
Anitra, daughter of a
Bedouin chieftain

Peg O' My Heart
J. Hartley Manners
Comedy 3 Acts
Los Angeles 1912

Later produced as the musical *Peg* in 1967, this sentimental story is set in Scarborough in 1912.

The poor widow Mrs Chichester has taken in her niece from America, the beautiful but shabby eighteen-year-old Peg O'Connell. Mrs Chichester despises Peg's dear dead father and when Peg learns of this, and hears her girl cousin having an affair with a married man, she decides to take herself, and her little dog, back to the USA. But Jerry, a neighbour who is in love with Peg, persuades her to stay and against her aunt's wishes takes her dancing. When they return, her cousin is about to run off with the married bounder, who has also made advances to Peg. Peg convinces her of the errors of her ways but not before she is unfairly scolded by her snobbish aunt. It later transpires that Peg is really an heiress and the scheming Mrs Chichester tries to marry her off to her son. Peg refuses and prepares again to return to the USA, but a sudden thunderstorm convinces her that her real place is in the comfort of the arms of Jerry, in fact the rich Sir Gerald Adair.

Mrs Chichester
Footman
Ethel
Alarie
Christian Brent

Peg
Montgomery Hawkes
Maid
Jerry

Perchance to Dream
Ivor Novello
Musical Play 2 Acts
London 1945

This romantically-charged story follows the life and loves of the residents of the stately home of Huntersmoon.

In 1818 Sir Graham Rodney, a lovable rogue given to seduction and gambling, owns the house which is coveted by Lady Charlotte Fayre and her family. Rodney's lover, Lady Lydia, is seriously worried when Rodney takes up highway robbery as a profession and when he wagers that he can seduce Lady Charlotte's daughter, Melinda, whose cousin William schemes against Rodney to get the house. Rodney's career comes to an end when he is shot during a robbery and dies in Melinda's arms.

The house passes to the Fayres and in 1843 William's son Valentine is a successful musician and has fallen in love with and married Lady Lydia's daughter, Veronica, a singer; they both desperately love the magic of the house. However their wedded bliss is disturbed a few years later when Veronica's best friend, Melanie, turns up from Paris; a vivacious beauty, she falls passionately for Valentine. He tries hard to resist her but eventually can hide his feelings no longer and the lovers decide to run away together to London after Valentine and Veronica have performed at Windsor for the Royal family. However, Veronica's announcement that she is pregnant devastates Melanie and she drowns herself on the night of the Command Performance.

A century later Valentine's granddaughter Melody feels the magic of the house as she and her husband, reflect on the the tragic stories of Melinda and Melanie. Songs include: 'Love is My Reason'; 'We'll Gather Lilacs'

1818:
Friends of Sir Graham: *Mazelli, Edgar Peel, Sir*
  Aymas Wendell, Lord Failsham, Ernestine Flavelle,
  Susan Pell, Lydia Lyddington
Aiken, the butler
Sir Graham Rodney
Lady Charlotte Fayre, his aunt
Melinda, her daughter
William Fayre, her nephew
Bow Street official
1843:
Lady Charlotte Fayre
Miss Alice Connors, chorus mistress
Miss Rose, accompanist
Veronica, Lydia's daughter
Valentine Fayre, William's son
Mrs Bridport
Vicar
Melanie, Sir Graham's niece
Melanie's friends: *Amelia, Vivien, Lucy, Lavinia,*
  Lataitia, Sophia, Elizabeth, Caroline
Thomas, a footman
Modern Times:
Bill
Melody
Bray, her husband
Iris, Bill's wife
Flunkeys, Bow Street runners, dancers, Chorus

Pericles
William Shakespeare
Drama 5 Acts
London 1619

Pericles, Prince of Tyre, is forced to flee the wrath of Antiochus, the Greek emperor, who is aware that the Prince has discovered him in an incestuous affair.

Shipwrecked on the coast of Pentapolis, Pericles survives to win the hand of Thaisa, daughter of the King of Pentapolis. After his wedding he learns that Antiochus is dead and sets sail for the return to Tyre. Yet again he is caught in a storm, which brings on Thaisa's labour with their daughter, Marina. Thaisa herself seems to die in delivery. She is buried at sea, washed ashore and revived by a doctor, but believing Pericles has perished she enters the service of the Goddess Diana.

Pericles entrusts Marina's upbringing to Cleon, governor of Tarsus, and his wife Dionyza, but as Marina matures her beauty arouses jealousy and she leaves Tarsus, only to be captured by pirates and put into a brothel in Mitylene. Pericles arrives in Mitylene mourning her supposed death, but his pain turns to joy when he finds her alive.

Antiochus, King of	Marshal
Antioch	Antiochus' daughter
Pericles, Prince of Tyre	Dionyza, wife to Clean
Simonides, King of	Lychordia
Pentapolis	A Pander
Cleon	Boult
Thaisa, daughter of	A Bawd
Simonides	Lords
Marina, daughter to	Knights
Pericles and Thaisa	Gentleman
Helicanus	Sailors
Escanes	Pirates
Lysimachus	Fishermen
Cerimon	Messengers
Thaliard	The Goddess Diana
Philemon	Gower, as Chorus
Leonine	

Period of Adjustment
Tennessee Williams
Comedy 3 acts
New York 1960
Newly-weds Isabel and George Haverstick turn up on the doorstep of his Air Force war hero buddy Ralph Bates on a snowy Christmas Eve. It's one of 'those' evenings - Ralph's wife Dorothea has just left him, and Isabel and George's marriage has not yet 'got off the ground'. Ralph's problem is that Dorothea is his boss's daughter and Ralph just quit his job, so Dorothea quits him, taking their baby son. George's problem is that he has the shakes from his service days and cannot approach Isabel tenderly enough. Both women have a problem; they need to break away from their domineering fathers. When Dorothea's bulldozing parents come to take away her things, Dorothea has a change of heart and returns to Ralph. The two couples talk things out and a warm understanding grows between them - at the end of the play each couple is united or reunited in an atmosphere of tenderness and love.

Ralph Bates	Mr McGillicuddy
Isabel Haverstick	Police Officer
George Haverstick	Dorothea Bates
Susie	
Mrs McGillicuddy	

Personal Appearance
Lawrence Riley
Drama 3 Acts
New York 1934
Carole Arden, a famous cinema actress, along with her publicist Gene Tuttle, maid and chauffeuse, are all stranded near a rural Pennsylvania guest house after their car breaks down.

The guesthouse is run by Mrs Struthers, a proud New Englander, her daughter Joyce and Joyce's fiancé Bud Norton, a hardworking, very handsome young man. At first Carole is furious at the delay, but she soon decides that Bud is too tempting to miss, and decides to stay the night in order, or so she says, to see the young man's newly invented mechanism for improving the sound quality of moving pictures. Bud is unaware that Carole has set her sights on him, but Tuttle and Joyce, who both see the truth, decide that Carole's plan to take Bud to Hollywood for an introduction to Carole's husband, a major film producer, is only a cover for her real intentions.

The night before the intended departure, Carole stays up late into the night keeping Bud company while he works on his technical drawings. Joyce retires, convinced she has lost him to Carole, and faces the next morning with mounting anxiety.

Unknown to Joyce, however, her ageing Aunt Kate had seen through Carole's seduction plan, and sat with Carole and Bud long enough to drive Joyce's rival off to bed. Tuttle, in a masterly stroke of subterfuge, has led Carole to believe that a baby jacket Joyce has been crocheting proves the younger woman has a prior claim on Bud's loyalty. Carole cancels the Hollywood trip, Joyce discovers Bud's fidelity, and Tuttle promises to promote Bud's invention in Hollywood.

Gladys Kelcey
Aunt Kate Barnaby, Joyce's aunt
Joyce Struthers
Chester 'Bud' Norton, Joyce's fiancé
Mrs Struthers, Joyce's mother
Clyde Pelton
Gene Tuttle
Johnson
Carol Arden
Jessie

Peter Pan
J.M. Barrie
Comedy 5 Acts
London 1904
The Darling children - Michael, John and Wendy (the eldest) - are put to bed in the night nursery by their mother, gorgeous Mrs Darling, and their nurse, dog Nana. During the night they're woken by Peter Pan, the boy who never grew up, who has been hanging around to hear Mrs D's bedtime stories which he recounts back in Never Land to the Lost Boys, all of whom had once fallen out of their prams and not been reclaimed in time.

Wendy and Peter become friends, despite Peter's jealous fairy Tinkerbell, and Peter shows the children how to fly. He takes them to Never Land so that the Lost Boys may have Wendy as a mother; they build her a house, and all sorts of exciting adventures occur. The boys are pursued by a dreadful pirate gang led by Capt. Hook, who is in turn pursued by the bloodthirsty crocodile who, having eaten Hook's arm, now wants the rest. There are also Red Indians, and much fighting, all of which culminate in Peter beating Hook in a swordfight.

Eventually the Darling children return to London and their distraught parents, bringing back with them the Lost Boys who are happily reunited with their families. Peter himself stays on in Never Land, remains forever young and is sometimes visited by Wendy, and is looked after by the fairies. For some reason he is weightless, and only the fairies can touch him.

Nana
Michael Darling
Mrs Darling
John Darling
Wendy Darling
Mr Darling
Peter Pan
Tinkerbell
Liza
Slightly
Tootles
First twin, second twin
Nibs
Capt. James Hook
Cecco
Alf Mason
Canary Rob
Chas Turkey
Whibbles
Mullins
Bill Jukes
Flint
Cookson
Gentleman Starkey
Smee
Skylights
Noodler
Tiger Lily
Panther
Indian braves
Mermaids

Petrified Forest, The
Robert Emmet Sherwood
Drama 3 Acts
New York 1935

Three generations of the Maple family live and work at the Black Mesa Bar-B-Q gas station and lunch room in the Arizona desert - Gramp, an old pioneer who's happy to stay put, his son Jason, who wants to move the business to LA, and Jason's daughter Gabby. She reads poetry and dreams of going to France to join her mother, Jason's ex-wife, a Frenchwoman who couldn't stand Arizona and now has a new family.

When failed writer and ex-gigolo Alan Squier comes along, he and Gabby fall for each other, much to the annoyance of hired-hand Boze. Squier knows he's no good for Gabby and soon leaves, hitching a lift with the wealthy Chisholms, but soon they're all brought back by the notorious Duke Mantee and gang, on the run from a bank massacre in Oklahoma and heading for Mexico. Squier describes Mantee as 'the last great apostle of rugged individualism' and when Gabby is out of earshot he asks Duke a favour; he wants the gangster to kill him, after making out his life insurance policy to Gabby. Duke agrees, the Chisholms witness the signing of the document, and soon the police arrive. The gang escape and the Duke makes good his promise; Squier is killed, dies a hero's death and according to his wishes will be buried appropriately in the nearby petrified forest.

Gramp Maple
Boze Hertzlinger
A telegraph lineman
Another lineman
Jason Maple
Gabby Maple
Paula
Alan Squier
Herb
Mr Chisholm
Mrs Chisholm
Joseph
Jackie
Duke Mantee
Ruby
Pyles
Legion commander
Another legionnaire
Sheriff
Deputies

Phèdre
Jean Racine
Tragedy 5 Acts
Paris 1677

The goddess of love, Aphrodite, has developed an overwhelming hatred for Phèdre, wife of Theseus, King of Athens. The goddess causes Phèdre to fall into a passion for Hippolytus, her own stepson. A rumour spreads that Theseus has died while away from Athens, and Phèdre's nurse and confidante Oenone, persuades her mistress that her love for Hippolytus would no longer be adulterous. Unable to resist her passion, Phèdre confesses it to Hippolytus, but he, deeply in love with Aricia, an Athenian princess, is shocked and revolted by what she says.

Theseus returns unexpectedly and Phèdre is thrown into panic that he may discover her approach to Hippolytus. To pre-empt this discovery she inverts the truth, and tells Theseus that Hippolytus has tried to seduce her. In mixed rage and sorrow, Theseus curses Hippolytus and calls on the God Neptune to punish him. Remorse overtakes Phèdre and she begs Theseus to be merciful, but her jealousy is aroused when Theseus reveals that his son loves Princess Aricia.

Theseus, King of Athens
Phèdre, Theseus' wife
Hippolytus, Theseus' son by Antiope
Aricia, an Athenian princess
Oenone, Phedre's nurse
Theramenes, Hippolytus' tutor
Ismene, Aricia's friend
Panope, lady-in-waiting
Guards

Philadelphia Story, The
Philip Barry
Comedy 3 Acts
New York 1939

This comedy was later adapted as the successful musical High Society.

In 1939, in a beautiful mansion near Philadelphia, Tracy Lord, an attractive and wealthy divorcee, is preparing to remarry. She is an aloof perfectionist and her fiancé is a successful prig, quite unlike her former husband, C. K. Dexter Haven, whom she divorced for alleged cruelty and drinking. Her father is involved in a scandal and to divert society interest, the wedding is to receive considerable press coverage. Tracy becomes infatuated with the reporter on the story and begins to have second thoughts about the wedding, and when Dexter Haven turns up, still professing his love for her, she has further doubts. To relieve her problems, she gets drunk and goes swimming in the nude with the reporter, who decently refrains from taking advantage, but she is now aware of her fiancé's smugness and decides to call off the wedding at the last moment. At last tolerant and understanding, she and her father are finally reconciled as she walks down the aisle with Dexter Haven.

Tracy Lord	*George Kitteredge*
Dinah Lord	*C. K. Dexter Haven*
Margaret Lord	*Seth Lord*
Alexander Lord	*Elsie*
Thomas	*Mae*
William Tracy	*May*
Elizabeth Imbrie	*Edward*
Macaulay Connor	

Philanderer, The
George Bernard Shaw
Comedy 3 Acts
London 1893

The conflict between the new Ibsenite free-thinking philosophies of the 1890s, and conventional romance and marriage, is highlighted in this tale of Ibsenite Leonard Charteris, his self-possessed new love, widow Mrs Grace Tranfield, and his old love, fiery Julia Craven. Charteris is also in conflict with both girls' fathers, Craven and Cuthbertson, who still subscribe to the old notion of 'manly men and womenly women', but nevertheless belong to the Ibsen Club for its many conveniences.

It is at the club that family physician Dr Paramore reveals to Craven that he does not now suffer from 'Paramore's disease', the existence of which has just been disproved (enabling Shaw to take a swipe at vivisection). The general congratulations at the 'recovery' of Craven's health help Charteris to convince love-sick Paramore to propose to Julia, who accepts, thus getting her off his back. Grace, however, realizes that under the new Ibsenite regime she cannot have Charteris' love and his respect at the same time - so she plumps for the latter.

Leonard Charteris	*Sylvia Craven*
Mrs Grace Tranfield	*Dr Percy Paramore*
Julia Craven	*The club page*
Col Daniel Craven VC	
Joseph Cuthbertson	

Philanthropist, The
Christopher Hampton
Comedy 6 Scenes
London 1970

Philip is a bachelor don about to marry Celia, and a shadow is cast over his forthcoming dinner party when a few days previously would-be playwright John accidentally blows his brains out while arguing with Philip and his friend Don. Philip is a bumbling but amusing philologist, and his dinner-party guests are Don (who tells Philip he should actually marry Elizabeth), Celia, successful novelist Braham, Elizabeth and Araminta. Braham is cynical and unlikeable, Celia is hard, and the dinner-party brings out the worst in everybody - except Liz, who doesn't talk. Celia offers to stay and help Philip clear up, but he refuses and she leaves. Araminta, a nymphomaniac, forces herself on Philip and stays the night but he disappoints her. Next morning Celia discovers Araminta and tells Philip the wedding is off - anyway, she says, she spent the night with Braham but that's got nothing to do with it. Don arrives and Philip is again disappointed when he reveals he's taken up with Liz. But Philip is easily forgiving and fairly fatalistic, and invites them both to lunch...

Philip
Donald
John
Celia
Braham
Elizabeth
Araminta

Philistines, The
Maxim Gorky
Play 3 Acts
Moscow 1902
See: *Smug Citizens, The*

Philoctetes
Sophocles
Drama 1 Act
Athens 409 BC

Philoctetes, a great soldier who possesses a magic bow given him by the god Hercules, languishes on the island of Lemnos where he was abandoned by Odysseus. Odysseus had done so because Philoctetes' screaming agony from a footwound was hurting morale in the Greek force Odysseus was leading against Troy.

The gods have decreed, however, that the Greeks will not win the war unless they are led into battle by Philoctetes and his bow, so Odysseus is dispatched to bring him back to the war. Knowing that Philoctetes can only feel hatred for the Greeks, after being cast aside, Odysseus persuades Achilles' son, Neoptolemus to retrieve the bow by trickery. The trickery succeeds, but Neoptolemus is disgusted by his own treachery toward the wounded man, returns his weapon, and decides to take his part against Odysseus. Hercules intervenes and persuades the two new allies to forget their personal feelings and re-join the Greek Forces.

Odysseus, Greek naval leader
Neoptolemus
Philoctetes
Sailor
Hercules, demi-god and hero
Crew of sailors
Mate

Physicists, The
Friedreich Dürrenmatt
Comedy 2 Acts
Zurich 1962

At a sanatorium in the early sixties, the murders of nurses by two insane physicists appear to puzzle the director, the hunchbacked Dr Mathilde von Zahnd. She feels the diagnosis of their conditions has been wrong although she assures the police that Johan Mobius, another physicist, is quite harmless. The two murderers claim to be 'Sir Isaac Newton' and 'Albert Einstein' and it comes to light following a murder by Mobius, that they are in fact rival intelligence agents of the East and West, posing as madmen to gain access to Mobius and the secret device he has invented. The murders resulted from the nurses discovering their real identities.

Mobius, a scientist of conscience, tells the agents that he has destroyed the formulae, but Zahnd, herself a raving meglomaniac, has recorded all their conversations and copied the secret documents; she now has the potential to control the world. Mobius has now become 'poor King Solomon'.

Dr Mathilde von Zahnd, alienist
Marta Boll, head nurse
Monika Stettler, nurse
Uwe Sievers, chief male attendant
McArthur, male attendant
Murillo, male attendant
Herbert Georg Beutler (Newton), patient
Ernst Heinrich Ernesti (Einstein), patient
Johann Mobiu, patient
Oskar Rose, missionary
Lina Rose, his wife
Adolf-Friedrich, Wilfried-Kaspar, Jorg-Lukas, their sons
Richard Voss, Inspector of Police
Police doctors
Guhl, policeman
Blocher, policeman

Piaf
Pam Gems
Drama 2 Acts
Stratford-upon-Avon 1978

Potted dramatic biography of chanteuse Edith Piaf traces her remarkable rise from prostitute and amateur street singer to discovery by clubowner Louis Leplée and subsequent international stardom. Accompanied by her street friend Toine, Piaf artlessly and earthily develops as an enchanting entertainer while maintaining a pathetic dependence on increasingly younger men and later, on drugs. Her many troubles include her involvement in Leplee's murder, problems with German soldiers, and several major car accidents. At the end of her life she finds her great love in young Theo, and he is by her side when she dies. Her unaffected and indomitable spirit, her enduring friendships with Toine and Josephine (Baker) and finally her unique voice and dedication as a performer, emphasize a moving evocation of France's greatest singer.

Piaf	*Pierre*
Toine	*Sailor*
Josephine	*Marcel*
Manager	*Two American sailors*
Louis Leplée	*Barman*
Émil	*Madelaine*
Legionnaire	*Lucien*
Jacques	*Jean*
Louis	*Nurse*
Eddie	*Doctor*
Police Inspector	*Pianist*
Paul	*Angelo*
Two German soldiers	*Physiotherapist*
Georges	*Dope pusher*
Butcher	*Theo*

Picnic
William Inge
Play 3 Acts
New York 1953

In the yard of a drab house in a small Kansas town, Hal Carter, a handsome young drifter, is cleaning up for the kindly owner watched by several local women. As he strips off his T-shirt, he arouses a disdainful schoolteacher and shocks a neighbour Flo, but fascinates her daughters, precocious Millie, and beautiful shy Madge. Hal turns out to be an old friend of Madge's well-off suitor and Flo cordially invites him to a picnic.

On the outing, the women all have ideas about Hal; the schoolteacher makes a drunken advance which he repels and he dances with tomboy Millie, but it is obviously Madge to whom he is drawn and they are soon embracing passionately. After a night of love with her middle-aged suitor, the teacher begs him to marry her, to which he agrees. Madge and Hal have also spent the night together and are feeling guilty as he prepares to leave. Flo is very upset when Madge announces she will give up her rich suitor and follow him, but a neighbour points out that it is better if she finds out the ways of love for herself.

Helen Potts
Hal Carter
Millie Owen
Bomber, paperboy
Madge Owen, a beauty

Flo Owen
Rosemary Sydney, schoolteacher
Alan Seymour, Madge's boyfriend
Irma Kronkite, Christine Schoenwalder, teachers
Howard Bevans, friend of Miss Sydney

Picture of Dorian Gray, The

Constance Cox from the novel by Oscar Wilde
Drama 2 Acts
London 1947

Lord Henry Wotton, a decadent cynic, becomes fascinated by the beauty of Dorian Gray as depicted in a painting being done by their mutual friend, Basil Hallward, and decides he must meet the subject. When he does, he sets out to convert the younger man to decadent hedonism, and succeeds. Gray plunges into a sordid life of opium and clandestine sex, dragging with him a number of his close friends. As he grows older, Gray seems not to age at all, but the portrait by Hallward miraculously does so in his place.

Knowing that he has made a kind of infernal bargain for his soul, and that the portrait will become ever more grotesque as his debauches continue, Gray hides the painting. To win sympathy, Gray shows the now wretched portrait to Hallward, but instead of kindness the painter shows him only revulsion, and promises to expose the degrading life behind Gray's beauty. In desperation, Gray murders Hallward, blackmails a former friend into disposing of the corpse, and then, driven nearly mad with self-loathing, carves at the portrait with a knife. The destruction of his image releases the spell which has kept Gray's youthfulness, and he instantly turns into a hideous old man.

Lord Henry Wotton	*James Vane*
Dorian Gray	*Mrs Vane*
Basil Hallward	*Mr Isaacs*
Lady Gwendolin Wotton	*Women*
Lady Narborough	*Victor*
Adrian Singleton	*Helen Hallward*
Alan Campbell	*Parker*
Sibyl Vane	*Barman*

Pillars of Society

Henrik Ibsen
Drama 4 Acts
Copenhagen 1877

Shipbuilder Karsten Bernick is the moral and financial pillar of his community, a small coastal town in Norway, but his reputation and prosperity are built on a lie. Fifteen years earlier his wife's younger brother Johan had deliberately taken the blame for financial and moral incidents for which Karsten was responsible. Johan had fled to America with his half-sister Lona.

The pair now return and Karsten is terrified that they will reveal the truth, jeopardizing a crooked deal involving a new railway for the town. When Johan decides to return to the USA on the unseaworthy vessel *Indian Girl*, Karsten does nothing to stop him, but then discovers Johan has left with Dina Dorf, Karsten's ward. He is relieved when he finds the pair have in fact embarked on his own ship, the seaworthy *Palm Tree*, but relief turns to horror when he discovers his unhappy thirteen-year-old son Olaf has stowed away on the *Indian Girl*.

His wife finds the boy and stops the ship in time, and the shattered Karsten can no longer maintain his deceptions. When the local residents pay tribute to him, he shocks them with the truth about the railway and about himself, asking them to make up their own minds about what they wish to do with him. The truth brings his family closer together and Karsten finally realizes the worth of the women in his community.

Karsten Bernick
Mrs Bernick
Olaf
Martha Bernick, Karsten's sister
Johan Tonnesen, Mrs Bernick's younger brother
Lona Hessel, Mrs Bernick's elder half-sister
Hilmar Tonnesen, Mrs Bernick's cousin
Dina Dorf, young girl living with the Bernicks
Horlund, schoolmaster
Rummel, merchant
Vigeland and Sandstad, tradesmen
Krap, Bernick's confidential clerk
Aune, foreman of Bernick's shipbuilding yard
Mrs Rummel
Hilda Rummel, her daughter
Mrs Holt
Netta Holt, her daughter
Mrs Lyne
Townsfolk
Sailors
Passengers

Pink String and Sealing Wax

Roland Pertwee
Drama 3 Acts
London 1943

Edward Strachan, a typically austere, authoritarian father of the 1880s, watches in some anxiety as his two eldest children, Albert and Emily, grow further and further away from him. By dint of his own hard work, Edward has managed to become owner of a successful chemist's shop and also Public Analyst in Brighton, the family's home. He fondly hopes that Albert, who is studying for his examinations, will shortly join him in partnership, but his son has his heart set on becoming an inventor, a role for which the boy shows real aptitude.

Edward, however, regards both Albert's aspirations, along with Emily's passion for singing, to be thoroughly frivolous. Even when Emily manages to impress a visiting diva, who puts the girl in touch with a great singing master, Edward's only reaction is to refuse her the money for lessons with the master, and to insist that she go to work in a local drapers' shop where he has some influence. Meanwhile, Albert has secretly taken up with Pearl Bond, the wife of a publican, and carries on an affair with her under Edward's nose.

To allow Emily the chance of her chosen career, all of the Strachan children pool their savings to buy her a ticket to London, and an interview with the singing master. She is forced to give the money instead to Albert, so that he can consult a solicitor, when he reveals that Pearl has stolen strychnine from Edward's laboratory and used it to kill her husband. Because Albert is a minor, the solicitor reveals the boy's predicament to Edward who suddenly realizes that his children's real lives are being lived in almost complete isolation from his own.

He successfully confronts Pearl with the truth of her guilt, reverses his low opinion of Emily's skills as a singer, and resolves to curb his own ambition in favour of genuine intimacy with his family.

Eva Strachan
Mrs Strachan, her mother
Albert Strachan, the eldest Strachan child
Edward Strachan, the paterfamilias
Jessie Strachan, his daughter
Emily Strachan, his eldest daughter
Dr O'Shea
Ernest O'Shea, his son, Emily's suitor
Pearl Bond, Albert's married lover

Pirates of Penzance, The
W. S. Gilbert and Arthur Sullivan
Comic Opera 2 Acts
New York 1879

Subtitled *The Slave of Duty* this refers to Frederic, whose father, when he was a child, had instructed a servant, Ruth, that the sea-loving boy was to be apprenticed as a pilot, but she, being slightly deaf, misheard and set Frederic to work with a band of pirates and now at twenty-one he is a fully fledged brigand.

Frederic, an honourable lad, has decided to renounce his scholarship and become an honest citizen, and despite opposition from the Pirate King, he goes off to do so. He soon discovers women, he has never seen one before, and falls in love with Mabel, the daughter of a Major-General. When the pirates attack the home and daughters of the Major-General, Frederic joins with the police in the fight, but he soon has to change position for he learns that his pirate apprenticeship is not yet finished, and he is duty-bound.

The pirates win the battle, but their honour as Englishmen and their love of Queen Victoria, convinces them to renounce their evil profession and marry the Major-General's daughters.

Songs include: 'Poor Wandering One'; 'I am the Very Model of a Modern Major-General'; 'Oh, Dry the Glistening Tear'; 'With Cat-like Tread'.

Maj-Gen. Stanley
The Pirate King
Samuel, his lieutenant
Frederic, the pirate apprentice
Sergeant of Police
Mabel, Edith, Kate and Isabel, Maj-Gen. Stanley's daughters
Ruth, pirate maid of all work
Pirates
Police

Play it Again, Sam
Woody Allen
Comedy 3 Acts
New York 1969

Movie journalist Allan Felix's marriage has just broken up. He is insecure at the best of times and now is a total mass of hang-ups and daydreams. Throughout the play, dream situations of his (mainly erotic) hopes and fears keep occurring, punctuated by imaginary appearances from his hero, Humphrey Bogart, giving him macho advice to correct his painfully shy behaviour with women.

Allan's pals Dick and Linda Christie make lots of efforts to get him dates, but neurotic Allan just cannot 'be himself' and something always goes wrong. Eventually busy businessman Dick's inadvertent neglect of Linda throws Allan and her together. She knows the 'real' Allan and likes him a lot - they have a tremendous night together but neither wants the affair to continue, thus giving Allan the chance to use the immortal closing lines from Bogey's 'Casablanca'. Encouraged by his success with Linda, the new natural Allan immediately proves a hit with his new upstairs neighbour, film buff Barbara ...

Allan Felix	*Sharon Lake*
Nancy	*Gina*
Bogey	*Vanessa*
Dick Christie	*Go-go girl*
Linda Christie	*Intellectual girl*
Sharon	*Barbara*

Play's the Thing, The
Ferenc Molnár
Comedy 3 Acts
New York 1926

Sandor Turai, a dramatist, his collaborator Mansky, and their young composer Albert Adam, to whom Turai is guardian, arrive at an elegant hotel on the Italian Riviera to pay a surprise visit to Ilona Szabo, a glamorous diva who is also Albert's fiancée.

They overhear a steamy assignation between Ilona and her former lover, Almady, a famous actor. The intimacy between the two throws Albert into a suicidal depression, which Turai sets about dispelling. For the entire night, Turai writes away at fever pace in his room, elaborating a play which incorporates the overheard dialogue that has so downcast young Albert.

Taking Ilona and Almady into his confidence, he

has them play again the scene they had lived together the night before, under the watchful eye of both Albert and Mansky. The two, hearing the dialogue again, conclude that they overheard not a night of love but a rehearsal for the play they are now watching. Albert's suspicions naturally vanish, and he ruefully gives in once more to Ilona's charms.

Sandor Turai, a dramatist
Mansky, Turai's collaborator
Albert Adam, Turai's composer
Ilona Szabo, a diva
Almady, an actor
Johann Dwornitschek, a servant
Mell
Lackeys

Playboy of the Western World, The
J.M. Synge
Comedy 3 Acts
Dublin 1907

In a country pub near a village on the wild coast of Mayo in western Ireland live publican Michael James and his fiery daughter Pegeen. She is being courted by fat and cowardly Shawn Keogh whom she despises, and when young Christy Mahon appears with a tale of killing his bullying father with a single mighty blow of his spade, she is fascinated. So are all the other girls, and Christy becomes the local hero, even winning the village mule race. His credibility is destroyed when his father appears, nursing a fractured skull and telling tales of his miserable puny son. Christy is so upset at losing Pegeen's love that he attacks his dad again. The peasantry, thinking Christy has really killed his father this time - and with them as witnesses - try to string him up. But old Mahon recovers and father and son leave together with considerably more mutual respect, and Pegeen wailing the loss of her playboy.

Christopher Mahon
Old Mahon, his father, a squatter
Michael James Flaherty
Margaret Flaherty (Pegeen Mike)
Widow Quin
Shawn Keogh, her cousin
Philly Cullen and Jimmy Farrell, small farmers
Sara Tansey, Susan Brody and Honor Blake
A bellman
Peasants

Plaza Suite
Neil Simon
Comedy 3 Acts
New York 1968

Each of the three acts is a separate story but all take place in Suite 719 in New York's Plaza Hotel.

Visitor from Mamaroneck. A middle-aged couple, Karen and Sam Nash, are 'celebrating' their twenty-fourth wedding anniversary in the same suite they spent their honeymoon. It was Karen's idea and it all goes wrong; she got the date wrong, the room is wrong, and then worst of all, Sam (pathetically striving to hold off middle-age) confesses to an affair with his secretary.

Visitor from Hollywood. The visitor is successful movie producer Jesse Kiplinger. He has invited up small-town old flame Muriel Tate for a drink - she is married with three kids, he is three times divorced. She is lovely and unspoilt and has followed his career to the tiniest detail. They get drunk, he advances, she protests and makes to leave, but in the end they both get what they want - they go to bed together.

Visitor from Forest Hills. Mimsey Hubley has locked herself in the bathroom two minutes before her wedding. Her frantic parents Roy and Norma do, say and try everything possible to get her out. Actually, she is having second thoughts because she does not want to end up like them. Finally groom Borden Eisley comes along, says two little words through the door and Mimsey comes out looking radiant.

Visitor from
Mamaroneck:
Karen Nash
Sam Nash
Bellhop
Waiter
Jean McCormack
Visitor from
Hollywood:
Waiter
Jesse Kiplinger
Muriel Tate

Visitor from Forest Hills:
Norma Hubley
Roy Hubley
Borden Eisley
Mimsey Hubley

Plenty
David Hare
Drama 12 Scenes
London 1978

During World War Two, seventeen-year-old Susan Traherne was flown into France by Special Operations where she acted as a courier with the Resistance. The intensity of the experience marks her for life. It was, like Britain's, her finest hour and never again is she able to find fulfilment or satisfaction. Shortly after the war she meets and marries career diplomat Raymond Brock, but her deliberate semi-madness wears him down over the years and eventually she leaves him. She stays firm friends with Alice, a well-meaning girl with bohemian pretensions, and then after a radio interview she is traced by an old wartime comrade, Codename Lazar, and they spend a night together. In their own way both are tragic figures -he has opted for suburbia, she to be alone.

Susan Traherne
Alice Park
Raymond Brock
Codename Lazar
A Frenchman
Leonard Darwin
Mick

Louise
M. Wong
Mme Wong
Dorcas Frey
John Begley
Sir Andrew Charleson
Another Frenchman

Pocket Watch, The
Alvin Aronson
Comedy 2 Acts
New York 1966

Rachel Goldman, a suburban New York grandmother, is suffering a mild but vexing confusion of memory following a stroke. She develops a fixation on finding a gold pocket watch which her dead brother had given her husband, Chaim, decades before, at the time of their marriage. Although Chaim, her daughters Sophie and Freda, and her grandson Harold all tell her that her husband had been forced to pawn the watch thirty years earlier, during the Depression, she resolutely sticks to the search.

Her mental confusion increases as Freda announces her engagement, Harold searches for work, and Chaim is injured and forced into early retirement, but she refuses to abandon her quest for the watch. Harold, realizing that his grandmother will never rest until the watch is found, buys a replacement which he pretends to be the original, miraculously retrieved from the pawnbroker. It then emerges that Rachel's determination was born of her intense desire to pass the watch on to Harold. She dies happy, in the belief that her quest has been successful.

Rachel Goldman
Chaim Goldman, her husband
Sophie Schwartz, Freda Goldman, their daughters
Harold Schwartz, their grandson
Sam Schwartz, Sophie's husband
Irving Friedman, Freda's fiancé

Pope's Wedding, The
Edward Bond
Drama 16 Scenes
London 1962

Written in broad East Anglian dialect, Bond's first staged play shows the timeless lives of a gang of young farm workers, their jokes, their clichés, their poverty, their love of cricket, and focuses in on the romance between Scopey and village girl Pat. She falls for Scopey after seeing him 'beautiful in his whites', daringly winning the prestigious local match. But Pat has an inherited responsibility to look after Alen, an old hermit living in a corrugated iron hut outside the village. It was her mother's dying wish that she take care of Alen, although the reasons for this obligation are obscure. Pat's relationship towards the timid and tetchy old man upsets Scopey, who begins to take her duties upon himself as the old man's house is near his work. Gradually Scopey becomes obsessed with the old man, both fascinated and repelled by him. He spends so much time there he loses his job, and when Pat decides to visit Alen, she finds Scopey there ... and Alen murdered.

Scopey
Bill
Ron
Len
Lorry
Joe
Bye
Alen
Pat
June
Bowley
Wicket keeper
Umpire

Porgy and Bess
Dorothy and Du Bose Heywood
Drama 4 Acts
New York 1927 and 1935

An argument over a dice game played in the courtyard of Catfish Row, a Negro tenement in Charleston, South Carolina, leads to the murder of stevedore Robbins by the bullying Crown. He flees, leaving behind his ostracised girlfriend Bess, who takes up with crippled beggar Porgy. Despite being tempted by gambler/dope pusher Sporting Life, Bess settles down with Porgy and integrates with the community - but during a picnic outing to Kittiwah Island, Crown, in hiding, reveals himself to Bess, telling her she must soon leave with him. She returns to Porgy and falls delirious, revealing she met Crown. She recovers, then during a terrible storm Crown returns for her but apparently perishes trying to save fisherman Jake and his wife Clara. But in fact Crown has survived, and when he comes back for Bess, Porgy kills him. The police find the body nearby and when they ask Porgy to identify him, Sporting Life tricks him into fleeing. Sporting Life then persuades Bess that Porgy will be imprisoned and reluctantly she leaves with him for New York. Porgy returns, and determined to find Bess, sets off for New York in his goat-drawn cart.

In the folk-opera *Porgy and Bess*, the music is by George Gershwin, lyrics by Du Bose Heywood and Ira Gershwin. Songs include: 'I Got Plenty O' Nuttin''; 'It Ain't Necessarily So'; 'I Loves You Porgy'; 'Bess, You Is My Woman Now'; 'Summertime'

Maria, keeper of the cookshop
Jake, captain of the fishing fleet
Lili
Mingo
Annie
Sporting Life
Serena, Robbin's wife
Robbins, a young stevedore
Jim
Clara, Jake's wife
Peter, the honey-man
Porgy, a crippled beggar
Crown, a stevedore
Crown's Bess
A detective
Two policeman
Undertaker
Scipio
Simon Frazier, a lawyer
Nelson, a fisherman
Alan Archdale
The crab man
The coroner
Residents of Catfish Row
Fishermen
Children
Stevedores

Portrait of a Murder
Robert Bloomfield
Drama 2 Acts
London 1963

Paula Barlow, a famous popular novelist, returns to her Kent country home after months of convalescence from disfiguring injuries she received in a gas explosion, unaware that her husband Eliot had caused the disaster in an attempt to kill her, so that he would be free to marry his mistress, and Paula's friend, Denise Murray.

Instead of the irascible, over-bearing and selfish woman she was before the explosion, Paula's friends are shocked to find her cowed into passivity and victim of total amnesia. As she begins to question those around her - her agent, James Gutherie, her neighbour, Tod Logan, her secretary Agnes Webster, and the ever-present Denise - Paula begins to understand what an unpleasant women she was, and how loyal Eliot has been in bringing her back to health. But she also becomes uneasy about the day of the explosion, and begins to wonder if it really was accidental.

Under pressure from Denise, who is desperate to rid herself of Paula, Eliot casts around to find another way of killing his wife. When Gutherie, her agent, sends Paula a portable television, Denise suggests it be placed in the bathroom and tipped into her rival's bath to cause certain electrocution. Denise and Eliot are interrupted by Paula while they are discussing the murder, and a fight ensues in which Paula is knocked unconscious.

It is at this point that a second Paula, the real one, arrives to point out with all the bitterness at her command, that the Paula lying unconscious on the floor is in fact a secretary whom she had hired, on the day of the explosion, to replace Agnes, and that Denise and Eliot's plans are known to her and to the police, who are on their way to arrest the conspirators. The real Paula then repairs to the bathroom, trips over the television's cable on the way into her bath, and dies.

Tod Logan
Agnes Webster, Paula's secretary
Eliot Barlow, Paula's husband
Paula Burlow, a writer
Denise Murray, Eliot's mistress
James Gutherie, Paula's agent

Potash and Perlmutter
Montague Glass
Comedy 3 Acts
New York 1921

The good-natured quarrelling of business partners Potash and Perlmutter was first featured in *The Saturday Evening Post* and later had great stage success.

A new bookkeeper in their firm of clothing manufacturers is Russian refugee Boris Andrieff, a sensitive would-be opera composer who falls in love with young Irma Potash. Another of Boris' admirers is top dress designer Ruth Snyder; when Boris is threatened with extradition to Russia for a political murder, Miss Snyder stays to help, also increasing the fortunes of the firm. Boris is released on 20,000 dollar bail furnished by the firm, but Potash believes their legal representative Senator Murphy's assertion that there is a flaw in the papers which exempts the firm paying the bailbond if Boris skips. When it looks like Boris will be sent back to his death, Potash sends him to Canada, but soon the flaw in the bond is corrected. The consternation of Potash and Perlmutter when threatened with bankruptcy is terrific, but somewhat mitigated when Ruth Snyder realizes she loves the dynamic Perlmutter and agrees to marry him. Just before the bond is forfeited, Boris returns - he has heard of the firm's plight and intends to give himself up. At the same time a cable comes from Russia declaring he is innocent, and all is saved.

Mawruss Perlmutter *Ruth Snyder*
Abe Potash *Mrs Potash*
Mark Pasinsky *Miss Cohen*
Henry D. Feldman *Irma Potash*
Boris Andrieff *Expressman*
Mozart Rabiner *US Deputy Marshalls*
Henry Steurman *Miss Levin*
Senator Murphy *Miss O'Brien*
Miss Potchley
Miss Nelson
Book agent

Potting Shed, The
Graham Greene
Drama 3 Acts
London 1958

The famous atheist and sceptic H.C. Callifer lays dying and his family are summoned. Granddaughter Anne sees her Uncle James has been excluded so she wires him. He arrives, listless and alienated from the rest of the family, and his mother forbids him to see his dying father. He finds he is afraid to approach the old potting shed in the garden, but neither his mother nor his father's associate Dr Baston will enlighten him. He finally discovers the truth through his psychiatrist Dr Kreuzer, the late gardener's wife, Mrs Potter, and in the end his mother. James had hung himself in the potting shed aged eight, confused by his father's and uncle's contradictory philosophies, and was revived by his uncle, Father William Callifer, the 'black sheep' of this atheist family. The miracle had destroyed his father's 'faith'. He confronts his uncle, now a whisky priest, and the meeting gives Father William back his faith, traded with God for his nephew's life thirty years before.

Dr Frederick Baston *James Callifer*
Anne Callifer, John's *Corner, a journalist*
* daughter* *Dr Kreuzer, a psychiatrist*
Sara Callifer, James' *Mrs Potter*
* former wife* *Miss Connolly, William's*
Mrs Callifer, James' * housekeeper*
* and John's mother* *Father William Callifer,*
John Callifer * uncle to John and James*

Present Laughter
Noël Coward
Comedy 3 Acts
London 1947

Gary Essendine is the archetypal self-obsessed actor, hugely talented, a bit fey, charming, libidinous and emotionally immature. In his agitation over a pending tour of Africa, he has wound his life to a pitch of turbulence which is starting to swamp his closest friends and associates. His estranged but still loving wife, Liz, his secretary Monica, and his business associates, Roland and Henry, are all drawn into the swamp of histrionic anxiety which he creates around himself.

As he fusses about his departure, he indulges in brief love affairs to soothe his vain worries at having turned forty. Two of the women concerned, Henry's wife Joanna and Daphne, a young girl, show discomforting tenacity in pursuing him.

The ensuing emotional chaos, which is made worse by the pestering of a mad young man obsessed with Gary, leads the actor to flee back to his wife on the very eve of his departure for Africa.

Daphne Stillington, Gary's admirer
Miss Erikson, Gary's maid
Fred, Gary's valet
Monica Reed, Gary's secretary
Gary Essendine, a great actor
Liz Essendine, Gary's wife
Roland Maule, Henry Lyppiat and Morris Dixon,
Gary's Business associates
Joanna Lyppiat, Henry's wife
Lady Saltburn

Price, The
Arthur Miller
Drama 3 Acts
London 1968

Victor Franz is a cop in his early fifties waiting with his wife Esther in a condemned Manhattan brownstone for a valuation on their old family furniture. Ancient dealer Gregory Soloman arrives and quotes a price - too little for Esther, but Victor isn't pushy and is willing to accept it. He intends to split it with his brother Walter whom he hasn't seen for eighteen years. Both brothers were bright students, but under-achiever Victor sacrificed his schooling to look after their impoverished dad, a wealthy businessman who fell apart after the Wall Street crash and the subsequent death of his wife. Walter opted out of the responsibility, completed his education, and became a successful surgeon. But when Walter arrives and tries to appease his guilt by offering Victor friendship, money (in the form of a tax dodge involving the furniture) and a new job, disturbing new undercurrents are revealed about the family's past and about the brothers' individual relationships with their father. Victor may have sacrificed a promising career for his father, but he still has a happy marriage and a fine son. Walter is divorced, has suffered a breakdown, and

cannot make peace with his brother. He leaves in a fury, and the eccentric Soloman gets the furniture.

Victor Franz
Esther Franz
Gregory Soloman
Walter Franz

Pride and Prejudice
Helen Jerome, from the novel by Jane Austen
Drama 3 Acts
London 1936

A mid-nineteenth century married couple, the Bennetts, are much concerned to find husbands for their daughters Lizzie, Jane and Lydia. Mrs Bennett, for whom the marriage of her daughters has become an obsession, is therefore nearly ecstatic when a rich young man, Richard Bingley, takes an estate near their Hertfordshire home. She quickly decides to hold a ball, and is rewarded when Bingley pays court to Jane, the prettiest and most sweet-tempered of her girls. At the same time she is upset when Bingley's friend, the glacially aristocratic Mr Darcy, insults a dashing young officer, Mr Wickham, who shows an interest in Lizzie.

Unfortunately, though, the whole family sink into despondency when Bingley fails to follow up his interest, and Jane lapses into a heartsickness that actually reduces her to an invalid. Lizzie discovers that Mr Darcy and his sister have engineered Bingley's removal from the scene, and when she appreciates the extent of their involvement, her hatred of Darcy knows no bounds. As it happens, Lizzie has greatly attracted Darcy, who surprises her by offering marriage in spite of her relatively humble background. Lizzie haughtily refuses, upbraids Darcy for his hand in Jane's estrangement from Bingley, and pours scorn on his belief that Wickham is thoroughly immoral.

Shortly, though, Lizzie must herself revise her opinion of Wickham when word reaches the family that he and Lydia have run off together. To make amends to Lizzie, Darcy secretly arranges for Bingley to be restored to Jane, and then lends Mr Bennett funds sufficient to endow Lydia with a dowry that allows her to marry the wayward Wickham. When Lizzie discovers Darcy's selfless help to the family, she revises her opinion of him and agrees to marry him after all.

Mr Bennett	*Miss Bingley*
Mrs Bennett, his wife	*Lady Catherine de*
Lady Lucas	*Bourgh, Darcy's aunt*
Charlotte Lucas	*Col. the Hon. Guy*
The daughters:	*Fitswilliam*
Elizabeth (Lizzie) Bennett	*Mrs Gardiner*
Jane Bennett	*Hill*
Lydia Bennett	*A nurse (Mrs Lake)*
Mr Darcy, Lizzie's suitor	*Maggie*
Mr Bingley, Jane's suitor	
Mr Collins	
Mr Wickham, Lydia's	
suitor	

Prime of Miss Jean Brodie, The
Jay Presson Allen
Drama 3 Acts
New York 1969

Nun Sister Helena has been in retreat twenty-seven years and her book *The Transfiguration of the Common Place* has become an international bestseller. Interviewed (with Papal dispensation) by an American journalist, she reveals her chief influence: Jean Brodie. A teacher at the Marcia Blaine girls' academy in Edinburgh during the thirties, spinster Brodie lost her fiancé in World War One, and thereafter filled the heads of her impressionable girls with her high-flown notions of Goodness, Truth and Beauty. The hypnotic Brodie and her small coterie of 'special' girls - her crème de la crème - incurred the disapproval of staid head teacher Miss Mackay, but despite Brodie's eccentric amours with two male teachers, her position seemed safe. Then, fired by her admiration of the Fascist dictators, Brodie goes too far and her dullard pupil Mary McGregor, anxious for Brodie's admiration, fled to Spain with Brodie's connivance to join her brother. She is killed by a bomb. Brodie is sacked when her part in this is betrayed to Mackay by 'sensible' Sandy, smarting under imagined slights from Brodie. Sister Helena is in fact Sandy and years later has realized her book is just one more attempt to get Brodie's attention.

Sister Helena	*Gordon Lowther*
Mr Perry	*Teddy Lloyd*
Jean Brodie	*McCready*
Sandy	*Miss Campbell*
Jenny	*Citizens*
Monica	*Girl Guides*
Mary McGregor	*Schoolgirls*
Miss Mackay	

Prisoner of Second Avenue, The
Neil Simon
Comedy 3 Acts
New York 1971

Mel and Edna Edison live on the fourteenth floor of a cramped apartment house on New York's East Side. Mel is heading for a breakdown. He's bugged by the malfunctioning air conditioner, the party noises from the air hostesses next door, the garbage stink, and the city itself. Then they're burgled and when Mel goes on to the terrace and screams out his frustration his upstairs neighbour drenches him. He loses his job, becomes paranoid and plots a snowy revenge on his neighbour - but it's only mid-September.

Edna works as a secretary to help pay for their two girls to go through college and for a while she does well. Mel's family rally round and offer money for medical help, but when Edna suggests 25,000 dollars as a down-payment on a summer camp for the now-sedated Mel to run, they back off. After a while Mel recovers and a few weeks later brother Harry returns with the 25,000 dollars. Mel is touched but refuses, and life goes on; the building is out of water just when Edna needs a bath, just when she's lost her job. Mel gets drenched again, but then it begins to snow...

Mel Edison	*Pearl*
Edna Edison	*Jessie*
Harry Edison	*Pauline*

Private Ear, The
Peter Shaffer
Play 1 Act
London 1962

Bob, a shy sensitive office clerk, lives alone in a small bedsitter in North London and spends his time listening to classical music. He has managed to make his first date with a young lady, whom he met at a concert, and she is coming to his flat for dinner, but he has also invited a workmate, Ted, who has volunteered to do the cooking and help give him confidence.

Ted is worldly-wise and offers Bob advice about how to handle women before Doreen arrives. She is not, in fact, a classical music fan as Bob imagined and she is soon attracted to the extrovert charms of Ted and although Bob tries hard to charm her, he realizes that he is not the man for her; but he has learned a lot from the experience of disappointment.

Bob
Ted
Doreen

Private Lives
Noël Coward
Comedy 3 Acts
London 1930

Elyot Chase and Amanda Prynne, divorced from one another five years previously, arrive coincidentally at the same French hotel. They are honeymooning with their respective new spouses, Sybil Chase and Victor Prynne. Encountering one another by chance, both are at once horrified and fascinated.

Elyot begs Sibyl to leave for Paris with him, while Amanda does the same with Victor, and both new couples quarrel. When Sibyl goes to dine alone and Victor leaves for the bar, Elyot and Amanda meet again, realize they are still in love, and rush off to Paris together instead.

They enjoy a few passionate days together, but soon fall into the bickering which had originally driven them apart. After a spectacular row, they retire to bed only to be awoken early by Victor and Sibyl, who, while tracing them, have been giving one another sympathy.

Victor turns on Elyot, and Sibyl on Amanda. Their mutual sympathy dissolves in a row of their own, during which Elyot and Amanda once more run off together.

Sibyl Chase	*Amanda Prynne*
Elyot Chase	*Louise, a French servant*
Victor Prynne	

Private Secretary, The
Charles Hawtrey
Comedy 3 Acts
Cambridge 1883

Young gentleman Douglas Cattermole is attempting to 'sow his wild oats' to please his rich uncle Mr Cattermole who doesn't want his money going to a sissy. Among Doug's creditors is comical Sydney Gibson, a vulgar young tailor with pretentions to be a gentleman. When Doug's friend Harry arrives with his uncle Mr Marsland's new private secretary, the finicky ninny Revd Spalding, the two young blades decide it would be a wizard prank for Doug to substitute for Spalding for a few days at Mr Marsland's country home.

Shortly after they leave Doug's London flat, Mr Cattermole unexpectedly arrives and encounters the precious Spalding whom he takes to be his nephew - and is most disappointed. Down in the country all sorts of mix-ups and jolly japes occur. Doug falls for Edith, Marsland's daughter, and Harry falls for Eva, her pretty companion. Their tutor Miss Ashford is a spiritualist and when the real Spalding arrives he is mistaken for a medium. Gibson also arrives and demands to be taken for a gentleman or he will give the game away, but his inferior manners alienate the élite. Eventually all loose ends are wound up, everyone is happy, and the two pairs of lovers end up with marriage and money.

Douglas Cattermole
Mrs Stead, his landlady
Sydney Gibson, a tailor
Harry Marsland
Revd Robert Spalding
Mr Cattermole
Knox, a writ server
Miss Ashford
Mr Marsland
Edith Marsland
Eva Webster
John, the manservant

Privates on Parade
Peter Nichols
Comedy 2 Acts
London 1977

Pte Steven Flowers joins SADUSEA (Song and Dance Unit South East Asia) in 1948 and becomes an army entertainer, mixing with, among others, the outrageously camp Acting Capt. Terri Dennis, the criminally conniving Sgt Maj. Reg Drummond, good-natured foul-mouthed Cpl Len Bonny and his admirer L/Cpl Charles Bishop, and the only girl in the unit, anglophile Anglo-Indian beauty Sylvia Morgan. Some witty songs and lively performances punctuate the action in which paranoid Reg contrives his own (mock) murder in order to continue with his rackets (including working with the Communists). When blimpish Maj. Giles Flack sends the unit up country where, during a show that includes some inept conjuring, there is a shoot-out. Len

is killed and Flt Sgt Kevin Cartwright crippled. Steven is sexually initiated by Sylvia - they fall in love, she gets pregnant and they marry. Finally the battered remnants of the unit are gratefully shipped back to Blighty.

Maj. Giles Flack
Acting Capt. Terri Dennis
Sgt Maj. Reg Drummond
Sylvia Morgan
Flt Sgt Kevin Cartwright
Cpl Len Bonny
L/Cpl Charles Bishop
Leading Aircraftman Eric Young-Love
Pte Steven Flowers
Lee
Cheng

Promises, Promises
Neil Simon
Music by Burt Bacharach
Lyrics by Hal David
Musical 2 Acts
New York 1968

Chuck Baxter, a diffident, romantic junior executive in the giant Consolidated Life Insurance Company in New York City, becomes popular with his immediate superiors not for his talent or ambition, but because he is a single man with a mid-town flat which they can borrow for meetings with their mistresses. Although he feels diminished by this arrangement, he lets it continue in the hope that his colleagues will gratefully recommend him for promotion. And since his own love for Fran Kubelik, another Consolidated employee, is not even noticed by her, let alone reciprocated, his evenings out of the flat are an inconvenience he feels he can bear.

In due course, Chuck is promoted by the head of personnel, Mr Sheldrake, but only on condition that he returns the favour by allowing Sheldrake the privileges once enjoyed by Chuck's former superiors. So again, scruples are put aside and Chuck spends one night each week out of the flat to leave it free for his new boss. The arrangement is working smoothly when Chuck discovers, to his horror, that Sheldrake's mistress is, in fact, Fran Kubelik. Coming, as it does, on Christmas Eve, this discovery so dejects Chuck that he picks up a prostitute and heads home for a night of love. When he arrives, he finds Fran unconscious from an overdose of pills she had taken because of Sheldrake's refusal to divorce his wife.

Getting rid of the girl, Chuck nurses Fran back to health, with the aid of his neighbour Dr Dreyfuss, until she can return home. His hopes that Fran may now be his are dashed when, returning to work after the holiday, Sheldrake announces that he has left his wife to marry Fran, and asks for the use of Chuck's flat until they can arrange a new home. Dispirited beyond endurance, Chuck refuses, quits his job and goes home to pack up and move. But as he is doing so Fran appears, she too has had enough of Sheldrake.

Songs include: 'Promises, Promises'; 'I'll Never Fall in Love Again'

Chuck Baxter
J. D. Sheldrake
Fran Kubelik
Bartender Eddie
Mr Dobitch
Sylvia Gilhooley
Mr Kirkeby
Mr Eichelberger
Vivien Della Hoya
Dr Dreyfuss
Jesse Vanderhoff
Dentist's nurse
Company nurse
Company doctor
Peggy Olson
Lum Ding hostess
Waiter

Madison Square Garden attendant
Dining Room hostess
Miss Polansky
Miss Wong
Bartender Eugene
Marge Macdougall
Clancy's Lounge patrons
Clancy's employees
Helen Sheldrake
Karl Kubelik
New Young Executive
Interns and their dates
Orchestra voices

Provoked Wife, The
John Vanbrugh
Comedy 5 Acts
London 1697

Lady Brute has remained faithful to her foul-tempered, cowardly husband, Sir John, despite his constant drunkness, brawling and neglect. She has attracted the attention of Mr Constant, who has fallen in love with her and is in the process of courting her as the play opens. Constant's friend Heartfree has also fallen in love (although he professes total indifference to women) with Lady Brute's niece, Belinda. Somewhat in jest, the two women invite their suitors to meet them in Spring Garden, by way of an assignation.

Lady Brute is so affected by Constant's ardour that she is on the point of giving in to his advances when Lady Fancyfull, who is in love with Constant, interrupts them. To escape her attentions the two couples repair to Lady Brute's home to play cards, secure in the knowledge that Sir John is out on a drunken revel. Unfortunately, he has been brought before the magistrates for brawling and sent home after a dressing down. His normal belligerence dulled by the encounter with the magistrates, Sir John refuses to duel with Constant, and accepts the explanation that the men were in his home to propose the marriage of Heartfree and Belinda.

Constant
Heartfree
Sir John Brute
Treble
Rasor
Justice of the Peace
Lord Rake and Col. Bully
Constable and Watch
Lady Brute
Belinda, Lady Brute's niece

Lady Fancyfull
Mademoiselle
Cornet and Pipe, Lady Brute's servants

Public Eye, The
Peter Shaffer
Play 1 Act
London 1962

Charles Sidley, a tax consultant, has married vivacious young Belinda and has turned her from a nightclub waitress into a smart society wife. But he feels she is becoming tired of him and hires a private detective, Julian, to follow her, fearing she is having an affair.

Being constantly followed by a strange silent man proves fascinating for Belinda and the follower and the followed begin a strange silent relationship directing each other by eye and gesture.

When Julian reports his findings to Charles, he takes on the role of psychoanalyst and makes the jealous husband reveal the motives for his behaviour, and with the connivance of Belinda sets out to re-educate her husband in the art of love by making Charles follow Belinda everywhere, in total silence, for a month, while Julian takes over the running of the tax consultancy.

Julian Christoforou
Charles Sidley
Belinda Sidley

Purple Dust
Sean O'Casey
Comedy 3 Acts
Liverpool 1945

Two English financiers, Stoke and Poges, have acquired an old Irish Tudor mansion and have romantic plans to refurbish it and install themselves like country squires.

They bring their mistresses to the house and indulge in pastoral pursuits, like country dancing, much to the amusement of the shrewd local workmen who are repairing the dilapidated building.

Gradually their aspirations begin to fade in the face of rural discomforts and the increasing inefficiency of their Irish workforce, who are by stages reducing their dreamhouse to a pile of 'purple dust'. A garden roller demolishes a wall, antique furniture is destroyed, a horse is shot in the hall and the foreman rides off with Stoke's mistress.

The two Englishmen have totally failed to understand the Irish mentality which finally defeats them and they are forced to escape back to England as floodwaters engulf the house and their mistresses run off with their money to their Irish lovers.

Cyril Poges
Basil Stoke
Souhaun
Avril
Barney
Cloyne
O'Killigain
Three workmen
Revd George Canon
Chreehewel
Postmaster

Yellow-bearded man
The figure
The bull

Pygmalion
George Bernard Shaw
Comedy 5 Acts
London 1912

Outside Covent Garden Opera House one rainy night, Professor Higgins impresses a group of bystanders with his skill at phonetics. He can place anyone by their accent with remarkable accuracy and his skills frighten the coarse-speaking Eliza Doolittle, a guttersnipe Cockney flower-girl. Next day Higgins and his friend Col Pickering are astounded when she appears offering money for elocution lessons in order to get a job in a flower shop. Pickering bets Higgins won't be able to pass her off as a lady and Higgins accepts the bet. Although Eliza is shrill and excitable she is a quick learner and passes the test - she is accepted as a lady at the Ambassador's Garden Party and attracts the attention of the Eynsford Hill family. Eliza's opportunistic dustman father Doolittle soon appears and attempts to blackmail Higgins, but to his chagrin ends up a rich member of the middle-classes after being recommended to an American Reform Society. Despite their continual bickering, Eliza and Higgins find they are reluctantly attached to each other, but she escapes his domination and goes off to marry Freddy Eynsford Hill.

My Fair Lady follows the same basic story-line with the addition of songs (music by Frederick Loewe, lyrics by Alan Jay Lerner). They include:'On the Street Where You Live'; 'Wouldn't it be Luverly';' The Rain in Spain';'Just You Wait'; 'I Could've Danced All Night'.

Freddy Eynsford Hill
Mrs Eynsford Hill
Clara Eynsford Hill
Professor Henry Higgins
Col Pickering
Eliza Doolittle
Mrs Pearce
Bystanders
Alfred Doolittle
Mrs Higgins, Henry's mother

Quaker Girl, The
Lionel Monckton
Lyrics by Adrian Ross and Percy Greenbank
Musical 3 Acts
London 1910

An exiled French princess, Mathilde, waits for her fiancé, Captain Charteris, in a small English village which is also the home of a Quaker community. She has befriended a lovely Quaker girl, Prudence Pym, and asks her to attend the wedding, which will take place as soon as the Captain arrives. When he does so, he brings with him the Princess's former governess, Mme Blum, who is now a famous Parisian couturier.

After the wedding, Mathilde invites Prudence to accompany the wedding party to Paris, where Mme Blum wishes to re-create the 'Quaker style' as a fashion. Bored with small town life, Prudence agrees and is an instant hit in Paris's most fashionable circles. Unfortunately, though, the Princess's presence in Paris becomes known to M. Larose, the city's Chief of Police, who tries to lure her into the open. Prudence's worry for her friend is balanced by her love for Capt. Charteris's best man, Tony Chute, who frantically tries to rid himself of his lover, Diane, so that he should be free to court Prudence.

Diane, however, is not easily put off and she gives Prudence a bundle of letters, which, she claims, contain Tony's declarations of love made to her before Tony had met Prudence. It turns out, though, that Diane has mistakenly turned over not Tony's letters, but those from another of her lovers, M. Duhamel, a Minister of State. When Prudence offers the letters to the Minister with no thought of using them as blackmail, he is so impressed by her honesty that he quashes the order for the Princess's exile, and Prudence and Tony agree to marry.

Jarge
Mrs Lukyu
William
Nathaniel Pym, a Quaker
Rachel, his sister
Phoebe, Mathilde's maid
Capt. Charteris, Mathilde's fiance
Princess Mathilde
Mme Blum, Mathilde's former governess
Jeremiah
Prudence Pym, Nathaniel's niece
Toinette
M. Larose, Chief of Paris Police
Diane
Prince Carlo
M. Duhamel
Tony Chute

Quality Street
J. M. Barrie
Comedy 4 Acts
London 1902

Misses Susan and Phoebe Throssel live in Quality Street, a charming thoroughfare where everyone knows everyone else's business. Phoebe is in love with Valentine Brown, but he enlists in the army and goes off to the Napoleonic wars for ten years. The sisters are too proud to tell him his investment advice has caused them to lose all of their money. They start a little school, but by the time Valentine returns, Phoebe especially seems to have aged considerably. Sometimes, though, in secret, she dresses brightly, lets down her ringlets and becomes young again; when Valentine discovers her like this and does not immediately recognize her, she passes herself off as her own niece, Miss Livvy. He is charmed, so she flirts outrageously, determined eventually to humiliate him by refusing any proposal. However, when he declares Livvy's behaviour has made him realize how much he loves Phoebe, fresh complications occur. Miss Livvy must be got rid of - the neighbours are talking! Valentine, who knew the truth all along, does this charmingly, and finally proposes to Phoebe who modestly accepts.

Valentine Brown
Ensign Blades
Lieut Spice
A Recruiting Sergeant
Master Arthur Wellesley Thomson
Isabella
Miss Susan Throssel
Miss Phoebe Throssel
Miss Willoughby
Miss Henrietta Turnball
Miss Charlotte Parratt
Patty

Quare Fellow, The

Brendan Behan
Comedy-drama 3 Acts
London 1956

Tension mounts during the twenty-four hours before an execution in an Irish prison; two men have been sentenced to death - the wife-murderer is reprieved, but the man who killed his brother in cold blood and callously disposed of the body is to be hanged. He is 'the quare fellow' and although he never appears in the play, his unseen presence is the motive force of the play. The old lags drink meths and bet on the possibility of a reprieve; the young prisoners strain to see the women in the windows of the female prison; a man down in solitary sings plaintively. The hangman arrives from his English pub and describes to the warders some of the technical details of hanging a man such as sizing him up for weight and thickness of neck. The warders too are various - religious, compassionate, stern, sinister, backbiting and from the Governor downwards, the whole affair, from the beautifully-cooked last breakfast to the freshly-dug grave, sickens the whole prison community.

Prisoners:
Dunlavin
Neighbour
Prisoner A, hard case
Prisoner B, the man of thirty
Lifer
The Other Fellow
Mickser
English voice
Scholara, young prisoner
Shaybo, young prisoner
Prisoner C, the boy from the island
Prisoner D, the embezzler
Prisoner E, the bookie

Warders:
Chief Warder
Rega
Crimmin
Donelly, warder 1
The New One, warder 2
The Prison Governor
Holy Healey
The Hangman
Jenkinson

Quartermaine's Terms

Simon Gray
Comedy 2 Acts
London 1981

In the staff-room of a school of English for foreigners in Cambridge, the teachers come and go discussing their personal and professional problems, their social lives and their students. St John Quartermain drifts through it all in a good-natured daze, dozing off and skipping lessons and semi-oblivious to almost everything; Anita's consistently unfaithful husband Nigel, her abortions and finally her long-awaited pregnancy; new man Meadle's enthusiasm, accident proneness and exploitation by the management; Melanie's sick and tyrannical mother, her mother's death, and Melanie's subsequent religious conservation; Mark's marriage break-up and make-up and failure as a novelist; Windscape's over-achiever teenage daughter who goes mad and dies. Everyone likes Quartermaine and his innocent charm usually sees him through, but when the school's co-owner Thomas dies, partner Eddie Loomis hands over the job as Principal to Windscape, the 'cleverest' of the teachers and, just before Christmas, Quartermaine is dismissed.

St John Quartermaine
Anita Manchip
Mark Sackling
Eddie Loomis
Derek Meadle
Henry Windscape
Melanie Garth

Quiet Wedding

Esther McCracken
Comedy 3 Acts
London 1938

The tremendous fuss involved in what was supposed to be a quiet country wedding has unnerved bride-to-be Janet Royd. French dressmaker Mme Mirelle's continuous demands for fittings and the coy remarks about her honeymoon from Aunt Florence are among the many pressures that make her want to call the whole thing off. At the suggestion of worldly-wise family friend Mary, groom Dallas Chaytor takes Janet away to talk in private on the eve of the wedding. They end up at their flat - and stay the night. This convinces Janet she really loves Dallas, but their excursion causes commotions back home where father Arthur and Mary just about manage to hide Janet's absence from mother Mildred. Their car even breaks down on the return journey from their flat, but they get back in the nick of time - for a perfect wedding.

Miranda Bute, a schoolgirl, cousin of the bride
Florence Bute, Miranda's mother
Mme Mirelle
Bella
Mildred Royd
A maid

Mary Jarrow
Janet Royd
Arthur Royd
Dallas Chaytor
Denys Royd, the bride's brother, the best man
John Royd, another brother
Flower Lisle, John's fiancée
Marcia Brent, the bride's sister
Jim Brent, Marcia's husband

Quiet Weekend
Esther McCracken
Comedy 3 Acts
Newcastle 1941

When Arthur and Mildred Royd arrive for a quiet weekend at their country cottage, quiet it isn't. Seventeen-year-old niece Miranda Bute arrives unexpectedly; she is crazy about the Royd's son Denys and hates his new girlfriend, socialite Rowena Marriott, who is determined to drag Denys off to Hollywood. Then their neighbour Adrian, a magistrate who silently loves family friend and villager Mary Jarrow, is reluctantly forced by Arthur to go salmon poaching to honour a bet. The poaching takes place on the Saturday evening with the help of Royd's local handyman, poacher Sam Pecker - they catch a salmon but Adrian falls in and Sam is caught. Next day Arthur bails Sam out, and on Monday he will be up before the bench (and Adrian) who will fine him heavily, afterwards paying the fine. Adrian's humiliation is mitigated when he proposes to Mary and she accepts. The Royd's daughter Marcia nags her golf bore of a husband Jim until her family tell her to stop for the sake of their marriage. Denys and Rowena split up, much to Miranda's delight, and on Sunday evening he drives her back to London and, perhaps, romance. Finally, Sam Pecker drops in the salmon, which he'd hidden up a tree, and leaves Adrian and Arthur arguing over its weight.

Sam Pecker	*Marcia Brent*
Mary Jarrow	*Adrian Barasford*
Miranda Bute	*Jim Brent*
Sally Spender	*Ella Spender*
Mildred Royd	*Denys Royd*
Arthur Royd	*Rowena Marriott*
Bella Hitchins	

R U R
Karel Capek, adapted by Nigel Playfair
Play 3 Acts
Prague 1921

Rossum, a mad scientist, discovers the secret of creating living organisms and after his death his son manufactures robot workers in various grades and exports them all over the world.

Helena Glory, daughter of the president of Rossum's Universal Robots, visits the factory to try to stop the exploitation of the robot creatures, but she is reassured by, and later marries, the plant manager, Harry Domain.

Ten years later, problems are starting to occur, rebellion and bloodshed break out; humans beings, who are failing to reproduce, are being slaughtered by the robots who are taking on the characteristics of their former masters. Dr Gall, the factory physiologist, has been installing the qualities of resentment, irritability and pain into the robots, encouraged by Helena.

All human life is exterminated, except for Alquist, an old engineer, and the robot leader, Radius, orders him to dissect a robot body to find the secret of their life force but the old man cannot bring himself to kill something that now has beauty, feelings and the beginnings of love.

Harry Domain, General Manager of R U R
Fabry, Chief Engineer
Dr Gall, Head of Physiological Dept
Dr Helman, Psychologist-in-Chief
Jacob Berman, Managing Director
Alquist, Clerk of the Works
Helena Glory, daughter of Professor Glory
Emma, her maid
Marius, a robot
Sulla, a robotess
Radius, a robot
Primus, a robot
Helena, a robotess

Rain
John Colton and Clement Randolph based on a story by W. Somerset Maugham
Drama 3 Acts
London 1925

A party of Europeans are stranded at Joe Horn's hotel-store on the South Seas island of Pago-Pago during torrential rains, and a trial of moral strength ensues between the fanatical missionary Revd Davidson and prostitute Sadie Thompson. After being humiliated at the hands of Sadie's friends, Davidson persuades the island's governor to deport Sadie back to San Francisco where she will face prison. Davidson almost achieves total victory; Sadie repents of her past life and is prepared to return to face punishment. Then, on the night before departure, Davidson is unable to contain himself and falls for Sadie's charms. Next morning he is found dead, his throat cut. Sadie leaves for Sydney but despite her lesson in moral hypocrisy finds it in her heart to forgive Davidson.

Mrs Horn (Ameena)	*Natives*
Cpl Hodgeson	*A girl*
Pte Griggs	*A boy*
Sgt O'Hara	*An old man*
Joe Horn	*An old woman*
Mrs Davidson	*Policeman*
Dr Macphail	
Mrs Macphail	
Sadie Thompson	
Quartermaster Bates	
Revd Alfred Davidson	

Rainmaker, The

Richard N. Nash
Comedy 3 Acts
New York 1954

Lizzie Curry lives with her two brothers and their father in a Western state of the USA where there is a serious drought. However, the drought isn't the family's only problem - plain Lizzie looks like getting left on the shelf. The Currys invite Sheriff's assistant File to dinner, hoping to bring him and Lizzie a little closer, but when File gets wind of the plan he declines their offer.

Then Bill Starbuck arrives. He claims he can bring rain - at a price. He becomes friends with Lizzie and makes her feel special but when no rain arrives, Starbuck is revealed as a conman and must leave town to avoid arrest. He begs Lizzie to come with him, but when File, impressed by the 'new' Lizzie, asks her to stay, she stays. Then the rain comes; Starbuck is vindicated, for not only has the rain arrived, but his kindness and inspiration have saved Lizzie from spinsterhood.

A musical version of this play, *110 in the Shade*, opened in New York in 1963.

H.C. Curry
Noah Curry, his elder son
Jim Curry, his younger son
Lizzie Curry, his daughter
File
Sheriff Thomas
Bill Starbuck

Raisin in the Sun

Lorraine Hansberry
Drama 3 Acts
New York 1959

The Youngers are a poor black family living in Chicago. On the death of her husband, Mama receives a considerable sum of insurance money. She buys a house in an all-white area and this creates problems; a local white man asks them not to move in, but the family refuse to be intimidated. Mama's eldest son Walter is bitter about buying the house as he wanted to open a liquor store. However, his wife Ruth is delighted to move out of their old cockroach-infested hovel - she's pregnant, and breaking down under the pressures surrounding her. Sister Beneatha doesn't mind where they live; her main concern is her schooling and future medical studies. Mama finally gives in to Walter and lets him have the remainder of the money - including Beneatha's share - for the liquor store. Walter has two partners in the prospective business; one of them cheats him and runs off with the money. Scorned by his family, the humiliated Walter decides they should still move into their new house, and in doing so redeems his pride.

Walter Lee Younger	*Joseph Asagi*
Ruth Younger	*Karl Lindner*
Travis Younger	*Bobo*
Beneatha Younger	*Moving men*
Lena Younger, Mama	

Rape of the Belt, The

Benn W. Levy
Comedy 3 Acts
London 1957

As one of the labours imposed on him by the gods for helping humanity, Heracles, bastard son of Zeus, is sent to win from the supposedly fierce Amazons an especially beautiful belt which is their Queen's badge of office.

The Amazons are ruled jointly by two sisters, Antiope and Hippolyte, who nurture the myth that their exclusively female citizenry are fierce fighters, when in fact the queendom is virtually undefended, and given over to the most gentle pursuits. Heracles and his companion, the hero Theseus, fall in love with Antiope and Hippolyte, and bungle every attempt to win the belt by threat of war. Eventually the queens decide to make certain war is averted, and save face for Heracles, by relinquishing the belt. Theseus persuades Hippolyte to sail with him for Greece, but Antiope and Heracles regretfully part.

Hera, Queen of the gods	*Heracles, Zeus' bastard*
Zeus, King of the gods	*son*
Hippobomene	*Diasta*
Theseus, Heracles'	*Anthea*
companion	*Hippolyte, joint Amazon*
Antiope, joint Amazon	*queen*
queen	*Thalestris*

Rashomon

F. and M. Kanin
Drama 2 Acts
New York 1959

A Buddhist priest in eleventh-century Kyoto stands lost in disillusionment at the city's Rashomon gate, a dumping ground for corpses and a robber's hideout. He is approached by a woodcutter from his local area who tries to cheer him up and persuade him to stay in Kyoto.

Both priest and woodcutter, it turns out, have been witnesses at a recent murder trial which uncovered three different versions, each one self-seeking, of the events leading to the death of a local samurai. The 'murderer', a bandit called Tajomaru, boasts that he killed the samurai in combat for possession of the samurai's wife. The wife claims that the bandit raped her and murdered her husband. The ghost of the dead man says his wife led the bandit on by her coquetry.

Under the questioning of a cynical wigmaker who robs corpses of their hair, it emerges that the woodcutter was witness to the murder and robbed the dead man of his samurai sword. The truth is never established, but the priest comes to realize that his disillusionment is naive, and he must take men as they are.

Priest	*Wife*
Woodcutter	*Mother*
Wigmaker	*Medium*
Deputy, court official	
Bandit	
Husband, a ghost	

Rattle of a Simple Man
Charles Dyer
Drama 3 Acts
London 1962

Timid middle-aged football fan Percy is down from Manchester with the lads, and after the match he is picked up by lovely young prostitute Cyrenne. The lads bet he won't spend the night with her, but uncharacteristically he accepts the bet and goes to her basement flat. He is shy and gullible and believes all her lies about her exclusive education, her rich family and her exciting life. He would rather talk than 'do anything' and gradually they open up to one another - she learns about Percy's loneliness, his longing for love, his dull job, his hobby as a scoutmaster; eventually he discovers she's from an ordinary background, abused by her stepfather, struggling for some pride and independence. The secrets of their hearts somehow balance out, and at the end of the play it looks as if Percy might have the courage to...or will he?

Cyrenne
Percy
Ricard

Real Inspector Hound, The
Tom Stoppard
Comedy 1 Act
London 1967

Theatre critics Moon and Birdfoot are watching a clichéd murder-mystery while discussing their own preoccupations; Moon is moaning about being his paper's second-string critic - below Higgs but above MacCafferty - while Birdfoot is busy figuring out ways of trading good reviews for actresses' favours. As the plot (and the fog) thickens, both Birdfoot and Moon are drawn into the action of the play itself, where at the denouement all the loose ends of both the plot and the critics' predicaments are tied together into one neat solution - the true identity of the Real Inspector Hound.

Moon	*Felicity*
Birdfoot	*Cynthia*
Mrs Drudge	*Magnus*
Simon	*Inspector Hound*

Real Thing, The
Tom Stoppard
Comedy 2 Acts
London 1982

In the opening scene Max discovers Charlotte has been unfaithful, but in fact this is a scene from Henry's play; meanwhile, Max's real-life wife actress Annie really is having an affair with Henry, who is married to Charlotte. Henry is a successful writer, a romantic with refreshingly lowbrow musical tastes fixated on the fifties and sixties pop of his youth, and agonizing over his upcoming appearance on the radio show *Desert Island Discs*.

Both marriages break up and Henry and Annie marry. Two years later she meets AWOL squaddie Brodie and he goes with her to an anti-war demonstration; to impress her he burns the wreath on the Cenotaph and is jailed. She then becomes obsessed with presenting a protest play by Brodie which she gets the reluctant Henry to rewrite for TV. Henry then discovers she is having an affair with young actor Billy, who played Giovanni to her Annabella in *'Tis Pity She's a Whore* but somehow Henry and Annie stick it out together - it's 'the real thing'.

Max
Charlotte
Henry
Annie
Billy
Debbie
Brodie

Rebecca
Daphne du Maurier
Drama 3 Acts
Manchester 1940

The new Mrs de Winter feels out of her depth when she arrives at Manderley, the sumptuous country home of her rich and handsome husband Maxim. Their whirlwind romance, less than a year after the death of his first wife Rebecca, happened in the South of France where Mrs de Winter was working as companion to an American woman. Now she's back in England and mistress of a huge house and its estate constantly reminded of Rebecca, whose consummate beauty and good taste still dominate the house. Maxim seems particularly prickly when Rebecca is mentioned, and sinister housekeeper Mrs Danvers is obsessed with Rebecca's memory, maintaining an obsessive devotion to her late mistress's things. Her vehement hatred for the new Mrs de Winter, and for Maxim, almost destroys their marriage, and when Rebecca's body is found in a boat with holes drilled in the hull, things look black for Maxim. He confesses to his wife that Rebecca was evil and unfaithful and taunted him until he shot her. Rebecca's cousin and lover Jack Favell tries to blackmail Maxim, but it is found that Rebecca had an incurable disease. A verdict of suicide is brought in, and Maxim realizes that knowing she was doomed, Rebecca had set up her own murder.

Frith	*Mrs Coleman Fortesque*
Mrs Danvers	*Col Julyan*
Beatrice Lacy	*William Tabb*
Giles Lacy	
Frank Crawley	
Robert	
First maid	
Second maid	
Maxim de Winter	
Mrs de Winter	
Jack Favell	
Second Footman	
Mr Coleman Fortesque	

Recruiting Officer, The
George Farquhar
Comedy 5 Acts
London 1706

The charming Capt. Plume and the foppish Capt. Brazen are recruiting for the Army in Shrewsbury. Plume's Sgt Kite is a resourceful character who lies, cheats and dresses as a fortune-teller in order to enlist gullible men as soldiers. Plume is altogether more honourable and impresses would-be recruits with his own sterling qualities. Brazen is not so successful, neither at recruiting nor love. He is led on by the wayward Melinda, but she is merely using him against Plume's friend Mr Worthy, whom she will later wed.

Plume is smitten with Justice Balance's daughter Silvia, but when Balance's son dies and she is sole heir, her father forbids her to marry Plume, so she disguises herself as a man, gets recruited by Plume by contriving a situation concerning her 'rape' of country wench Rose, thereby making her father unwittingly hand her over to Plume. All is eventually revealed and Balance relents. Plume decides he will give up recruiting and settle down with Silvia 'to breed recruits', and generously he lets Brazen have all his latest recruits.

Mr Balance, Mr Scale, and Mr Brazen, Justices	A steward
	Servant
Mr Worthy, a gentleman of Shropshire	Melinda, a lady of fortune
Capt. Plume	Silvia
Capt. Brazen	Lucy, Melinda's maid
Kite	Rose
Bullock, a country clown	Poacher's wife
Costar Pearman	Collier's wife
Thomas Appletree	Drummer
Pluck, a butcher	Mob
Thomas, a smith	Servants
Bridewell	Attendants, etc
A poacher	
A collier	

Red Peppers
Noël Coward
Play 1 Act
London 1935
See: *Tonight at 8.30*

Rehearsal, The
Jean Anouilh
Comedy 3 Acts
Paris 1950

The Count de Febroques, approaching forty, sophisticated to the point of decadence and the lion of a 'set' dedicated to amusement, falls in love with his children's governess, Lucile, an unaffected and beautiful girl of only twenty.

The Count has transported his 'set' to the Chateau de Febroques in order to rehearse them as players in the French Classic comedy, *The Double Inconstancy*, (Pierre Coulet de Maravaux, 1723).

He assigns parts to each of his intimates - his wife, the countess, his lover, Hortensia, Villebosse, and Lucile's godfather, M. de Damiens so that they effectively play themselves, and so provide a screen for his declaration of love to Lucile.

Lucile resists the Count until she is convinced his regard is genuine. Once convinced, she refuses all offers of help from him but becomes his lover, tout court. His wife, worried that this particular affair of the Count's lacks style and is too earnest, plots to drive Lucile from the Chateau. After several failures, she succeeds finally by having the Count's friend, the drunken cynic Hero, offer Lucile money to leave on (fraudulent) orders from the Count. Hero then, to avenge himself on the Count for the latter's affair, seduces Lucile in turn.

Lucile, heartbroken, leaves the Chateau insisting she will see none of the 'set' again. In remorse for having betrayed the Count, Hero provokes the Countess's lover, Villebosse, who is a pistol champion, into a duel. The Count frantically leaves in search of Lucile, without knowing where she has gone.

The Count's Valet
M. de Damiens
The Countess
The Count
Hortensia
Hero
Villebosse
Lucile

Relative Values
Noël Coward
Comedy 3 Acts
London 1951

Nigel, Earl of Marshwood, is about to return to his family home with his fiancée, a Hollywood star named Miranda Frayle. His mother Felicity, Dowager Countess of Marshwood, who is bemused by her son's inappropriate choice of spouse, discovers that her own maid, Moxie, is in fact Miranda's sister. Bemusement turns to horror as the social humiliation in store for Moxie becomes clear, so the Countess and her unflappable butler Crestwell decide to pass Moxie off as an heiress and companion to Felicity.

Their plan comes unstuck when Moxie takes offence at Miranda's lies about her own supposed background and blurts out the truth. Into the ensuing chaos comes Don Lucas, Miranda's former lover who was also a Hollywood star. Felicity sees that Miranda still loves Don and cleverly contrives a reunion for them, and thus an escape from the proposed marriage for her son.

Crestwell, the butler
Alice, a maid
Mrs Dora Moxton (Moxie)
Felicity, Countess of Marshwood
Lady Cynthia Hayling

The Hon. Peter Ingleton
Admiral Sir John Hayling
Nigel, Earl of Marshwood
Miranda Frayle, Nigel's fiancée
Don Lucas

Jimmy Broadbent
Sheila Broadbent
Jane
Mabel Crosswaite
David Hoylake-Johnston
David Bulloch

Relatively Speaking
Alan Ayckbourn
Comedy 2 Acts
London 1967

As Ginny prepares to leave the London flat she shares with lover Greg on a Sunday morning in the sixties to visit her parents in the country, Greg discovers another man's slippers under her bed. Piqued by jealousy, he first taunts Ginny, then proposes marriage. After Ginny leaves, Greg decides to travel on the same train and surprise her by arriving unannounced at her parents'.

He arrives before she does, to a very puzzled reception, for in fact, Ginny's destination is the home of her older married lover, owner of the vagrant slippers, with whom she has decided to break. When she duly arrives, her shock at finding Greg is quickly replaced by a determination to continue the charade and so avoid exposure as her 'father's' lover in front of both Greg and her lover's wife.

All but Greg eventually realize their true positions, and part with an irony which highlights Greg's naivety.
Greg
Ginny
Philip
Sheila

Reluctant Debutante, The
William Douglas Home
Comedy 3 Acts
London 1955

Debutante Jane is disappointing her ambitious mother Sheila by appearing not particularly interested in all the eligible young men she is meeting during the current 'season'. Jane's own coming-out party is approaching and her usually obliging dad, Jimmy Broadment, is lamenting the immense amount of money it is costing him to secure Jane a suitable mate. By mistake, Sheila invites notorious rake David Hoylake-Johnston to dinner to partner Jane, and of course they fall for one another. Meanwhile, the originally-intended David, oversexed and dreary 'good' David Bulloch also pursues Jane, much to her annoyance. Sheila encourages this mismatch and discourages David Hoylake-Johnston, but when Jimmy talks to 'bad' David he discovers that he is really good David, while 'good' David is actually bad David. Bad David was responsible for Celia Barrington's infamous Swiss sojourn and compounded his villainy by laying the blame on good David. Luckily, good David has just inherited much money and an Italian title, so Jimmy is able to plot his daughter's future happiness with good David, knowing his wife's snobbery will soon help her accept the inevitable.

Reluctant Doctor, The
Molière
Comedy 3 Acts
Paris 1666

Scagnarelle is a lecherous, boozy woodcutter who used to work for a doctor and has learned some of the tricks of the trade. He likes to beat his wife Martine. When neighbour Robert tries to remonstrate, Martine and Scagnarelle turn on him and beat him. Martine has only pretended she likes a good beating; in truth, she is looking for revenge.

Valère, steward to local squire Géronte, turns up with his crony, Lucas, whose wife is the Gérontes' wet nurse, Jacqueline. They tell Martine that they are looking for a doctor to cure their master's daughter Lucinde of an affliction that has suddenly struck her dumb. Martine knows just the specialist but says he poses as a woodcutter, through eccentricity, but if beaten hard enough Scagnarelle will admit to his medical brilliance. They find him and, sure enough, after a good thrashing and the promise that he can name his own price, Scagnarelle is happy to 'remember' his skill.

At Géronte's, Scagnarelle takes a fancy to fondling Jacqueline's breasts and wants to sample her milk. When Lucas objects, Scagnarelle suggests that jealousy is bad form. Dazzling Géronte with fake Latin he manages to extract plenty of money. Then Léandre, who loves Lucinde, turns up and secretly offers the rascal more money, explaining that Lucinde is only faking loss of speech to avoid having to marry suitor Horace who is rich and approved by Géronte. Now Scagnarelle understands: up to this point he could not grasp why a husband should object to his wife being dumb, a quality he would much appreciate in Martine. Disguised as Scagnarelle's apothecary, Léandre helps effect a 'cure' and Scagnarelle obliquely recommends a purgative dose of Flight and Matrimonium Pills. The lovers slip away and Géronte discovers that Scagnarelle has deceived him so must hang. But the lovers return and Léandre asks for Lucinde's hand, saying he is now the heir to his just-deceased uncle's estates. Géronte is happy; Scagnarelle is spared the rope; Martine points out that it is she who helped elevate him to doctor status; Scagnarelle forgives her for her part in getting him beaten and points out that from now on she must show the proper respect for a man of his importance.
Géronte, father of Lucinde
Lucinde
Léandre, lover of Lucinde
Scagnarelle
Martine, wife of Scagnarelle

Robert, neighbour
Valère, steward to Géronte
Lucas, husband of Jacqueline
Jacqueline, wet nurse
Thibaut, a peasant
Perrin, his son

Reluctant Heroes
Colin Morris
Farce 3 Acts
London 1950

Reluctant conscripts Gregory, a Lancashire lad, Morgan the Cockney, and Tone the public school dandy, are bundled together in a draughty barrack room as they learn the facts of the National Service from A-Z under typically 'eloquent' Sgt Bell. Led by young Sandhurst officer Capt. Percy, Bell and his three men participate in war games (England versus Scotland) involving the WRAC corps, including Tone's ex-flame Gloria, now an officer. Billeted in an outbuilding of a farmhouse, the unit (an imaginary tank) is attacked by the serious Scots Sgt McKenzie and his men, and by a combination of bravado and blundering, Bell's 'tank' wins the day. Gregory is promoted, but immediately loses his stripes when he accidently blows up the farmhouse.

Morgan	Pat Thompson
Tone	Penny Raymond
Sgt Bell	Capt. Percy
Sgt McKenzie	Gloria Dennis
Gregory	Scots soldier
Medical Orderly	

Resistable Rise of Arturo Ui, The
Bertolt Brecht
Drama 15 Scenes
Stuttgart 1958

Arturo Ui is a small-time hoodlum whose callous manipulation of the Chicago greengrocery protection racket eventually raises him to city boss, on the lookout for yet more territories to dominate. The story is a parable of the rise of Hitler and his henchmen, with the white-haired ward boss Dogsborough representing President Hindenburg, the burning of the warehouse alluding to the Reichstag fire in 1933, and the massacre of Ui's lieutenant Roma combining the St Valentine's Day Massacre with Hitler's infamous Night of the Long Knives slaughter of Ernst Röhm and his brownshirts. The play is in verse, parodying the pretensions of the gangsters, but it is not a complete historical parellel. Ui's fanaticism, lies and violence, media manipulation and image promotion, give the play a wider scope for contemporary political analogy.

The announcer	Young Dogsborough
Flake, Caruthers,	Ernesto Roma, his
Butcher, Mulberry, Clark	lieutenant
and Sheet, businessmen	Guiseppe Givoli, florist,
Old Dogsborough	gangster

Arturo Ui, gang leader	Defendent Fish
Ted Ragg , reporter on	The Defence Counsel
The Star	The Judge
Dockdaisy	The Doctor
Bowl, Sheet's chief	The Prosecutor
accountant	A woman
Goodwill and Gaffles,	Young Inna, Roma's
City council members	familiar
O'Casey, investigator	A little man
An actor	Ignatius Dullfeet
Hook, wholesale	Betty Dullfeet, his wife
vegetable dealer	Dogsborough's butler

Resounding Tinkle, A
N.F. Simpson
Comedy 2 Acts
London 1957

In their suburban living-room, Bro and Middie (Mr and Mrs) Paradock drink their bright purple liquid and launch into a stream of non sequiturs and surreal comic abstractions, ably assisted by First Comedian (Hamster) and Second Comedian (Bug). Their intriguing speculations are interrupted by The Author and a Technician; Bro swaps the elephant in his garden with neighbour Mrs Nora Mortice for a more convenient tiny snake, and the Paradock's son Don returns home as a daughter. Finally a group of critics dissect the play and reach the conclusion that it's a parody of a skit on satire that's being burlesqued.

Bro Paradock	A technician
Middie Paradock	Don Paradock
First Comedian	Mustard Short
Hamster	Denzil Pepper
Second Comedian Bug	Miss Salt
The Author	Mrs Vinegar
Mrs Nora Mortice	Chairman
First cleaner	Man in bowler hat
Second cleaner	Producer

Rhinoceros
Eugene Ionesco
Play 3 Acts
Paris 1960

In a small modern French town the people sit in the cafés and ritually drink and chat. Berenger, slothful and weary, meets his fussy friend Jean, who chides him for his drinking and sloppy habits. Their encounter is interrupted by a rhinoceros thundering past, which causes mild interest in the locals, and Berenger continues justifying his drinking because he is paranoid and frustrated in his love of an office girl, Daisy. Another rhino blunders through and the next day Berenger and his colleague are discussing the events in their office when more reports come in and they hear that one of their number has turned into a pachyderm. Rhinoceroses are proliferating and transformations continue, and Berenger finds that Jean has wilfully become a vicious rhino himself.

Berenger thinks the whole affair is a gigantic nightmare, until his beloved Daisy suffers 'rhinoceritis' and he begins to find the creatures quite attractive. When he realizes that he is the last man in a world populated by rhinoceroses, his uniqueness gives him the resolve to remain so.

Jean	*Daisy*
Berenger	*Mr Papillon*
The waitress	*Duchard*
The grocer	*Botard*
The grocer's wife	*Mrs Boeuf*
The old gentleman	*A fireman*
The logician	*Little old man*
The housewife	*Little old man's wife*
The café proprietor	

Richard II
William Shakespeare
Drama 5 Acts
London 1595

Henry Bolingbroke, Richard's cousin, accuses the Duke of Norfolk of the murder of the king's uncle, the Duke of Gloucester, a crime which the king himself had arranged. Richard first orders that the issue be decided by a trial of combat between Bolingbroke and Norfolk, then instead banishes the duke for life, and Bolingbroke for six years. When, shortly thereafter, Bolingbroke's father, the Duke of Lancaster, dies, Richard seizes his estates to pay for a campaign against the Irish.

While the King is in Ireland, Bolingbroke and the Duke of Northumberland march on the Duke of York, Richard's regent, and execute two of the Royal favourites, Sir John Bushy and Sir Henry Green.

The people support Bolingbroke, and when Richard lands in Wales on his return from Ireland, he is taken prisoner. They return to London, where Richard yields the crown to Bolingbroke, who thereby becomes Henry IV. Richard's supporter the Duke of Aumerle, is caught in a plot against the new King, who has Richard poisoned to pre-empt further treachery.

Richard II, King of England	*Sir John Bagot*
	Lord Ross
John of Gaunt, Duke of Lancaster	*Lord Willoughby*
	Lord Berkeley
Henry Bolingbroke, Gaunt's son, later Henry IV	*Earl of Salisbury*
	Bishop of Carlisle
	Sir Stephen Scroop
Thomas Mowbray, Duke of Norfolk	*Lord Fitzwater*
	Duke of Surrey
Edmund of Langley, Duke of York, Richard's uncle	*Abbot of Westminster*
	Sir Pierce of Exton
	Lord Marshal
Duke of Aumerle, Duke of York's son	*A Welsh Captain*
	Two gardeners
Harry Percy, Earl of Northumberland	*A groom*
	Keeper of Pomfret prison
Sir John Bushy	*Queen Isabel*
Sir Henry Green	*The Duchess of York*
The Duchess of Gloucester	*Ladies*
	Guards
A Lord	*Soldiers*
Heralds	*Servants*

Richard III
William Shakespeare
Drama 5 Acts
London 1592

Richard, Duke of Gloucester, is willing to do anything to become king of England in place of his dying brother, Edward IV. He removes the rightful heir, his elder brother, the Duke of Clarence. The news of Clarence's murder causes Edward to die of grief, and Richard woos Lady Anne, widow of Edward, Prince of Wales, whose death, along with that of his father King Henry VI, Richard has had a hand in.

With Edward IV dead, Richard, helped by the Duke of Buckingham, imprisons and then murders Edward's heirs, the Prince of Wales and the Duke of York, and assumes the throne. As Richard sets about engineering yet more deaths, Buckingham deserts his cause, and swings his support to Henry, Earl of Richmond, who lands an army from France to attack Richard's forces. Richard's capture and execution of Buckingham precedes a final battle with Richmond at Bosworth Field, where the usurper is himself killed, leaving the field open to Richmond, who becomes Henry VII.

King Edward IV	*Lord Stanley*
Edward, Prince of Wales	*Lord Lovel*
	Sir Thomas Vaughan
Richard, Duke of York	*Elizabeth the Queen*
George, Duke of Clarence	*Margaret*
	Duchess of York
Richard, Duke of Gloucester	*Lady Anne*
	Sir Richard Ratcliff
Clarence's son	*Sir William Catesby*
Henry, Earl of Richmond	*Sir James Tyrrel*
	Sir James Blount
Cardinal Bourchier	*Sir Walter Herbert*
Thomas Rotherham	*Sir Robert Brackenbury*
John Morton	*Sir William Brandon*
Duke of Buckingham	*Christopher Ursick*
Duke of Norfolk	*Lord Mayor of London*
Earl of Surrey	*Sheriff of Wiltshire*
Anthony Woodville	*Hastings*
Marquess of Dorset	*Tressel*
Lord Grey	*Berkeley*
Earl of Oxford	*Ghosts, lords, gentlemen, attendants, etc..*
Lord Hastings	

Right Honourable Gentleman, The
Michael Dyne
Drama 2 Acts
London 1964

This play is a mainly factual account of the ruination of the political career of Sir Charles Dilke (1843-1911), who might have been Gladstone's successor had he not become entangled in an unpleasant divorce battle which involved his former mistress, Virginia Crawford.

Dilke's intelligence and smooth political competence have led him to the brink of being Gladstone's natural successor as leader of the Liberal party, when he is accused of adultery with Virginia in a divorce action with her husband, Donald Crawford. Although Dilke is innocent of the specific charge, he has in the past had affairs with both Virginia and with her mother, Mrs Rossiter, and Virginia's allegations are meant to avenge what she sees as Dilke's double treachery.

Dilke is absolved of blame but his career is ruined by the scandal surrounding the trial. As the truth behind Virginia's intrigue unfolds, it emerges that Dilke's sexual predations, far from being unusually sordid, are utterly typical of the clandestine sexuality of the Victorian middle and upper classes.

Mr Bodley
Sir Charles Dilke
A footman
Mrs Ashton Dilke (Maye)
Mrs Emilia Pattison (later Lady Dilke)
Mr Joseph Chamberlain, Dilke's colleague
Foreign Office messenger
Mrs Virginia Crawford (Nia), Dilke's accuser
Mr Donald Crawford
Sir Henry James
Mrs Sarsh Gray
Mrs Rossiter (Lila), Virginia's mother
Mrs Garland (Helen), Virginia's sister
Mrs Pelham
Capt. Harry Forster

Ring Round the Moon
Jean Anouilh
Charade with Music 3 Acts
London 1950

Heiress Diana Messerschmann is making her lovesick fiancé Frederic suffer, so his heartless but kind identical twin brother Hugo (who Diana really loves) has hired beautiful young ballet dancer Isabelle to turn Frederic's head at the ball and wake him from his destructive infatuation. Everything goes wrong. Isabelle's mother arrives and recognizes long-lost friend Capulet, companion to Mme Desmortes, aunt to Hugo and Frederic, and soon everyone knows about Hugo's scheme including Diana, her melancholy millionaire father Messerschmann, his mistress Lady India and her secret lover Patrice, Messerschmann's secretary. But it is Isabelle's innocence and guilessness that saves the day. She refuses payment from Hugo, whom she first believes she loves, and then refuses money from Messerschmann who is so astounded by her incorruptability he sells everything and becomes poor and hopefully happy (though he later learns this move has made him even richer). Hugo falls in love with the new 'poor' Diana, and finally Mme Desmortes brings Isabelle and Frederic together.

Joshua, a crumbling	*Capulet*
butler	*Messerschmann*
Hugo	*Romainville, lepidopterist*
Frederic	*Isabelle*
Diana Messerschmann	*Her mother*
Lady India	*A general*
Patrice	*Footmen*
Madame Desmortes	*Double for Hugo/Frederic*

Ringer, The
Edgar Wallace
Mystery 4 Acts
London 1926

It is panic stations at Scotland Yard when word is out that the notorious Ringer, alias Arthur Henry Milton, is back in London. Wanted for murdering several questionable types - white slavers, crooked moneylenders, etc - the Ringer is a master of disguise (he 'rings the changes'). On the case are nasty Detective Inspector Bliss and nice Detective Inspector Wembury overseen by Col Walford, Assistant Commissioner of Police, and divisional surgeon Dr Lomand, a Scotsman with recent experience of American crime-fighting techniques. They pull in small-time crook Sam Hackitt for information, but he stays mum, and they arrange around-the-clock protection for bent barrister Maurice Meister, a dandified fence and dope addict in whose hands the Ringer's sister recently killed herself. Despite their efforts, Meister is killed while all are present; thus, the Ringer must be one of the policemen. They question the Ringer's wife Cora, and despite his disguise she recognizes her husband whom she has not seen for three years. When the Ringer is finally unmasked, she helps him escape in a clever and daring manoeuvre.

Central Detective	*Station Sergeant Carter*
Inspector Bliss	*Benny*
Divisional Detective	*Mrs Hackitt*
Inspector Wembury,	*Police Constable Field*
DSO	*Detective Constable*
Col Walford, CB	*Graves*
Samuel Hackitt	*Detective Constable*
Maurice Meister	*Brown*
Dr Lomand	*Detective Constable*
Cora Ann Milton	*Atkins*
Mary Lenley	*Five policemen*
John Lenley	*Detective*

Rivals, The
Richard Brinsley Sheridan
Comedy 5 Acts
London 1775

Beautiful and headstrong heiress Lydia Languish wants to wed for love, not money, and plans to elope with penniless Ensign (2nd Lieut) Beverley. If she does, her formidable aunt, Mrs Malaprop, whose pretensions lead her to the now-famous hilarious mispronunciations, will disinherit her. Beverley is actually an alias for Capt. Jack Absolute. He loves Lydia and knows his suit will proceed better as a mere Ensign. But when Jack's father, Sir Anthony Absolute, suggests to Mrs Malaprop that Jack and Lydia should wed, Lydia discovers the truth and rejects Jack. Meanwhile, Jack's friend Falkland, a worrier, has alienated his fiancée, Lydia's lovely cousin Julia, by his cruel and continual testing of her affections. Rivals for Lydia's hand include Jack's friend Bob Acres who challenges Ensign Beverley to a duel. When he find out it is Jack, the dual is off, but next in line for Lydia is old Sir Lucius O'Trigger - he is enough to bring Lydia to her senses and return to Jack, her true love. Falkland and Julia are also reunited, with much merriment throughout.

Sir Anthony Absolute	*Mrs Malaprop*
Capt. Jack Absolute	*Lydia Languish*
(Ensign Beverley)	*Julia*
Falkland	*Lucy*
Acres	*Maid*
Sir Lucius O'Trigger	*Boy*
Fag	*Servants*
David	
Coachman (Thomas)	

Roar Like a Dove
Lesley Storm
Comedy 3 Acts
London 1957

The family estate in Scotland of Robert, Lord Dungavel, is a successful cattle and timber farm, but his lordship is worried. Family tradition decrees only a son can inherit, and so far his lovely American-born wife Emma has given birth to six girls in quick succession and cannot face the prospect of going on and on like a breeding machine. Dedicated farmer Robert knows the estate must go to someone with long-term farming interests, but when distant cousin Bernard is sent for, he proves useless.

Robert's obsession with the succession goads Emma into sending for her parents, Tom and Muriel, to help patch up her marriage, but after arriving they take different sides. Tom connives with Robert, advising him to seduce the unwilling Emma one last time. He does and she gets pregnant, but upon discovering the plot she decamps with her mum and the girls to the States. There, she indulges herself in becoming a glittering socialite, wearing her family jewels, appearing in newspapers and showing off her daughters. She returns when her pregnancy begins to show and slowly the entire family are happily reunited. Next Christmas Eve they all wait in trepidation for the actual birth, and just after midnight ... it's a boy.

Jane, Dungavel's	*Lord Dungavel (Robert)*
daughter	*Sheila and Shaw, servants*
Nurse	*Muriel Chadwick*
Mackintosh, manservant	*Tom Chadwick*
Lady Dungavel (Emma)	*Bernard Taggert-Stuart*
Cousin Edward	

Robert and Elizabeth
Fred G. Morrit and Ronald Millar
Music by Ron Grainer
Musical 2 Acts
London 1964
See: *Barretts of Wimpole Street, The*
Songs include: 'Wimpole Street Song'; 'Moon in My Pocket';' In a Simple Way'

Rock Garden, The
Sam Shepard
Drama 1 Act
New York 1964

A girl and boy share a glass of milk while a man sits reading a magazine. The boy is next seen in a bedroom, sitting on a chair beside a woman who is in bed suffering from a cold. The woman, apparently the boy's mother, reminisces about her father, an eccentric who looked very much like the boy, and complains about the draughts in the house.

A man arrives. He and the boy sit in the lounge, the man talking about the rock garden he has just built and trying to interest the boy in helping him. The boy is so bored he dozes off. When he does speak, he is interested only in talk about sex, and the man, in turn, dozes off.

A girl
The boy
The woman
The man

Rocky Horror Show, The
Richard O'Brien
Musical 11 Scenes
London 1973

Using themes and devices drawn from horror films, science fiction, and fantasy plus a generous dose of rock-and-roll, this loose story follows Janet and Brad as they encounter the various sexually ambivalent characters who inhabit a mysterious castle at which they seek refuge one dark and stormy night. These include the inevitable sinister butler, Riff Raff, his incestuous sister Magenta, fifties rocker-monster Eddie, and an all-purpose villain, Frank-n-Furter.
Songs include: 'Sweet Transvestite'; ' Damn It, Janet'; 'Science Fiction'

Narrator	*Columbia*
Brad Majors	*Eddie*
Janet Weiss	*Rocky Horror*
Riff-Raff	*Frank-n-Furter*
Magenta	*Dr Everett Scott*

Rollo
M. Achard and Felicity Douglas
Drama 3 Acts
London 1959

Leon Rollo and his wife Edith arrive at the luxurious Paris flat of Leon's lifelong friend, and sometime enemy, Noël Carradine. Leon's ambivalence towards

Noël stems from incidents in their shared youth, and especially from Carradine's having 'stolen' Leon's lover and wrested away control of his former business. The lover, Veronique, is now Noël's wife, the business is thriving and Leon has come to borrow 500,000 francs to launch a new venture in which he himself does not believe. When Noël shrewdly sees the virtues of the scheme and buys out Leon's interest, he is rewarded with his friend's envious hostility.

The hostility turns to raging hatred when Leon finds out that his beloved adopted daughter, Alexa, has been having an affair with Noël. Leon resolves to humiliate and blackmail Noël, but Edith and Alexa, with the help of a timely intervention from Veronique, eventually restore peace. Veronique takes Noël away on an extended holiday, Alexa decides to accept the marriage proposal of a suitor of her own age, and Edith persuades Leon to abandon his hateful envy once and for all.

Leon Rollo
Edith Rollo
Albert
Veronique Carradine
Noël Carradine
Alexa Rollo

Romance
Edward Sheldon
Drama 3 Acts
New York 1913

When young Harry tells grandfather Bishop Armstrong that he's crazy about an actress and intends marriage, the Bishop advises caution. Harry is stung and retorts that the old man has forgotten what it's like to be young. The Bishop in his turn tells Harry a long story that takes place in flashback.

Forty years earlier at a fashionable party held by worldly banker Cornelius Van Tuyl, young local rector Thomas Armstrong, who is engaged to Van Tuyl's niece Susan, meets prima donna Mme Margherita Cavallini (Rita), currently the toast of New York and all Europe, and secret mistress of Van Tuyl.

Thomas and Rita are opposites and fall in love, but he is hopelessly out of his depth in the relationship and becomes more and more fanatical as he discovers supposed evidence of her perfidy. She is more realistic and in the melodramatic finale of their relationship she makes him leave so that her soul may still be her own.

His grandfather's story makes Harry perversely decide to marry immediately, and at the same time the Bishop learns that Rita died recently in Italy. She never remarried and subsequently did much charitable work. He falls asleep listening to one of her records and holding her handkerchief.

Bishop Armstrong	*Susan Van Tuyl*
Harry	*Miss Armstrong*
Suzette	*Mrs Rutherford*
Thomas Armstrong	*Mrs Frothingham*
Cornelius Van Tuyl	*Mrs Gray*

Miss Snyder	*Eugene*
Mr Fred Livingstone	*Adolph*
Mr Harry Putnam	*Servant at Mr Van Tuyl's*
Signora Vannucci	*Butler at the rectory*
Baptiste	*Mme Margherita*
Louis	*Cavallini*
François	

Romanoff and Juliet
Peter Ustinov
Comedy 3 Acts
London 1956

Igor Romanoff, the son of Vadim Romanoff, Russian Ambassador to Europe's smallest country, has fallen in love with Juliet Moulsworth, daughter of the American Ambassador, Hooper Moulsworth. However, Juliet is engaged to marry Freddie Vanderstuyt, who has just arrived to visit from the US, and Igor's dour intended, Marfa Zlotochienko, has turned up from Moscow so confusion ensues.

The general, head of the local government, already under pressure to sign a pact with the Americans, fears that the Russian-American love affair will drive his country out of its neutrality by causing an incident. With his unctuous diplomacy, however, the General steers the lovers together, and is further reassured when Marfa and Freddie seem set to form an even more unlikely alliance.

First soldier
Second soldier
The General, head of government
Hooper Moulsworth, American ambassador
Vadim Romanoff, Russian ambassador
Igor Romanoff, Romanoff's son
Juliet Moulsworth, Moulsworth's daughter
The spy
Beulah Moulsworth
Evdokia Romanoff, Romanoff's wife
Jr Capt. Marfa Zlotochienko
Freddie Vanderstuyt
The Archbishop

Romeo and Juliet
William Shakespeare
Tragedy 5 Acts
London 1595

The two greatest families in Verona, the Montagues and the Capulets, are involved in a bitter feud. Romeo, the son of Lord Montague, goes in disguise to a feast hosted by the Capulets, where he falls in love with the beautiful Juliet Capulet. Waiting under her window after the feast, in the hope of seeing her, Romeo overhears Juliet confess her love for him. He decides to ask her to marry him secretly the next day.

Romeo's presence at the feast, discovered after he leaves, leads to a fight in which Romeo kills Tybalt Capulet, for which crime he is banished. Lord Capulet, unaware of Juliet's marriage, offers her to Count Paris.

With the help of Friar Laurence, who married her, Juliet plans to avoid marriage to the Count by swallowing a potion which will let her mimic death for forty-two hours. The friar will then contact Romeo, who will rescue her from the burial vault.

Instead, Romeo mistakes the Friar's message to mean that Juliet is truly dead, and commits suicide beside her sleeping form by swallowing poison. He dies, after killing Count Paris outside the vault, and when Juliet awakens to find his body beside her, she joins him in suicide.

Escalus, Prince of Verona	Friar John
Paris, The Prince's kinsman	Balthesar
	Sampson
	Gregory
Montague	Peter
Capulet	Abraham
Lady Montague	An apothecary
Lady Capulet	Three musicians
Romeo, Montague's son	Nurse to Juliet
	An officer
Juliet, Capulet's daughter	Pages
	Citizens
Mercutio, Romeo's friend	Various Montague and Capulet Relations
Tybalt, nephew of Lady Capulet	Maskers
	Guards
An old man	Watchmen
Friar Laurence	Chorus

La Ronde
Arthur Schnitzler
Drama 1 Act
Vienna 1921

A cycle of ten seductions begins with a young Viennese prostitute and a soldier she has attracted while out 'walking', and ends with the same prostitute making love to a count. In the series, which she both begins and ends, are played out most of the common self-deceptions by which turn-of-the-century lovers explained away their infidelities and indescretions.

Every social level is represented in the cycle. As well as the prostitute, a soldier, and a count, a housemaid, a gentleman, a young bourgeoise. A young wife, a poet, and an actress join the list of seducers and seduced, deceivers and deceived.

Soldier
Young gentleman
Husband
Poet
Count
Prostitute
Housemaid
Young woman
Sweet Young Thing
Actress

Rookery Nook
Ben Travers
Farce 3 Acts
London 1926

The formidable Mrs Gertrude Twine has arranged with her sister, Clara, and brother-in-law Clive Popkiss, recently married, to bring their ailing mother for a holiday near her Somerset home. They are to be joined by Clive's cousin Gerald, but although Gerald has arrived, Clara and Clive have been delayed, and when Clive eventually arrives it is with the news that Clara and her mother have temporarily stayed behind.

Clive moves into Rookery Nook, which Mrs Twine has rented for their holiday, and is on the point of retiring when a pajama-clad young woman arrives on the doorstep, having been thrown out of her own nearby home by her stepfather.

By taking the young woman, Rhoda, into the house overnight, Clive unleashes the fury of the priggish Mrs Twine, and sets in train a frantic series of evasions by which he and Gerald try, with diminishing success, to forestall the old lady's discovery of Clive's innocent but compromising gesture. Together, they involve Mrs Twine's hen-pecked husband, Harold, her neighbour Admiral Juddy, and a local girl, Poppy Dickey, in their ham-fisted efforts to avoid Mrs Twine's wrath.

Although their efforts fail, and the truth becomes clear, Clive's kindness is vindicated when the genuine innocence of his helpfulness to Rhoda becomes clear even to Mrs Twine.

Mrs Twine
Gertrude Twine
Mrs Leverett
Harold Twine, Gertrude's husband
Clive Popkiss
Gerald Popkiss, Clive's cousin
Rhoda Marley
Putz, Rhoda's stepfather
Admiral Juddy
Poppy Dickey
Clara Popkiss, Clive's wife
Mrs Possett

Room Service
John Murray and Allen Boretz
Comedy 3 Acts
New York 1937

Producer Gordon Miller has the entire cast of his forthcoming play *Godspeed* staying (and eating and rehearsing) at New York's White Way Hotel where the manager is his brother-in-law Joseph Gribble. Their unpaid bill is enormous, and when hotel supervising director Gregory Wagner turns up, he wants them all out and threatens to charge the bill to Gribble.

The gang contrive to stay put, but further complications occur when the play's young author Leo Davis shows up and has to be accommodated. A merry-go-round commences of Wagner trying to starve out the cast, and Miller's ingenious schemes to stay put. Eventually Wagner's animosity frightens off a bona-fide backer, but not before Miller has the soon-to-be-stopped cheque and gets five days credit. He puts on the show at the hotel's own disused theatre and holds off Wagner by faking Leo's death. When Wagner finally realizes he's been tricked and is about to close the production, hotel owner Senator Blake appears full of enthusiasm for *Godspeed* and all is saved.

Sasha Smirnoff	*Hilda Manney*
Gordon Miller	*Gregory Wagner*
Joseph Gribble	*Simon Jenkins*
Harry Binton	*Timothy Hogarth*
Faker Englung	*Dr Glass*
Christine Marlowe	*Bank Messenger*
Leo Davis	*Senator Blake*

Room, The
Harold Pinter
Drama 1 Act
London 1960

An elderly married couple, Bert and Rose Hudd, sit in their dingy bed-sitting room, Bert having his tea and Rose prattling to him about the cold weather. Bert says nothing at all, and eventually leaves to drive his van on some unspecified errand.

Shortly before Bert's departure, their ageing landlord, Mr Kidd, arrives and gets into disjointed conversation with Rose about the state of the other rooms in the house. Kidd is very agitated about something, but excuses himself without making clear what he wants. Immediately he is gone, Rose opens the door to the room, for no particular reason, and finds Mr and Mrs Sands standing in the hallway. She invites them in to warm themselves by the fire, and discovers that they are trying to find lodging in the house, but have been unable to locate the landlord.

After the Sands, in turn, depart, Mr Kidd reappears and tells Rose that a visitor had been waiting all weekend to speak to her alone, hoping that her husband would go out. Rose rather reluctantly agrees to meet the stranger, a blind black man called Riley who addresses her as Sal, and asks her to return home. Bert arrives back during their conversation and beats Riley insensible. Rose clutches at her own eyes and screams out that she has now gone blind as well.

Bert Hudd	*Mr Kidd, the Hudd's*
Rose, his wife	*landlord*
Mr Sands	*Riley, a black man*
Mrs Sands	

Roots
Arnold Wesker
Drama 3 Acts
Coventry 1959

The second part of The Wesker Trilogy takes place among the Bryant family in Norfolk in the mid-fifties.

Beatie Bryant comes up from London to stay first with her sister Jenny and husband Jimmy Beales and then with her parents. Beatie's kindly mother, neglected by her mean farm-labourer husband, is glad to see her daughter but Beatie is full of telling her family how small-minded they are, forever quoting her boyfriend Ronnie Kahn, a free-thinking Jewish socialist.

Beatie has arranged for Ronnie to come up and meet her family, and their preparations are elaborate. When, on the day he is expected, Beatie gets a letter from Ronnie breaking off their relationship, she blames her mother and her upbringing for not making her able to respond to Ronnie's encouragement. Her mother fiercely upbraids her, and then to her delight Beatie responds and finally finds her own voice, realizing Ronnie's lessons have actually taken root.

Beatie Bryant
Jenny Beales, her sister
Jimmy Beal, her brother-in-law
Mrs Bryant, her mother
Mr Bryant
Frankie Bryant
Pearl Bryant
Stan Mann, a neighbour of the Beales
Mr Healey, a manager at the farm

Rope
Patrick Hamilton
Drama 3 Acts
London 1929

Rich ex-undergraduate decadents Wyndham Brandon and his crony Charles Granillo have killed young Ronald Kentley for kicks, in a spurious Nietzschean notion of 'living dangerously'. They have stuffed his body in a trunk, and as extra spice have invited for dinner Ronald's father Sir Johnstone Kentley, his aunt Mrs Debenham, naive student Kenneth Raglan, pretentious young Leila Arden, and ex-student friend Rupert Cadell, a lame foppish poet. The guests arrive and dine off the trunk, then Brandon takes Sir Johnstone into another room to give him some rare books. Quite casually the talk turns to murder - everyone makes jokes about the trunk, and then the telephone rings to tell Sir Johnstone that the normally reliable Ronald, who went to the Coliseum cinema, is missing. Granillo gets drunker and drunker as the tension increases, and when Cadell sees Ronald's Coliseum ticket sticking out of Granillo's pocket his suspicions crystallize.

Everyone leaves, but Cadell returns and confronts the pair, forcing them to open the trunk. Brandon, the instigator, then pleads his 'philosophy' with Cadell. But Cadell is disgusted and unimpressed, and has no compunction in turning in the two murderers.

Wyndham Brandon	*Sir Johnstone Kentley*
Charles Granillo	*Mrs Debenham*
Sabot	*Rupert Cadell*
Kenneth Raglan	
Leila Arden	

Rose

Andrew Davies
Comedy 2 Acts
London 1980

Rose is unhappily married to dreary Geoffrey Fidgett, has two children, and likes her job teaching at an infant school. She describes her rather ordinary life in wry asides to the audience and we are presented with a portrait of a modern and eccentrically likeable young woman. Her attempts to bring about a more creative kind of learning into the school system are not appreciated by rigid head teacher Mrs Smale, whose relationship with emotionally suppressed teacher Mrs Malpass is slightly dubious. On one occasion Rose prompts her despairing mother to movingly evoke memories of the old-fashioned romance and shy sex between her and Rose's late father; on another occasion Rose visits her buddy Sheila, but the laughs are mitigated by the pathetic state of Sheila's alcoholic boyfriend, burnt-out folk-singer Jake. When Rose has a brief affair with attractive primary school advisor Jim Beam, self-pitying Geoffrey finds out and he threatens her with every possible kind of scandal in order to keep her. So she goes back to school and teaches the children.

Rose Fidgett	*Sally*
Mother	*Jake*
Mrs Smale	*Geoffrey Fidgett*
Mrs Malpass	*Father*
Jim Beam	

Rose Marie

Otto Harbach and Oscar Hammerstein
Musical 2 Acts
New York 1924

Rose Marie La Flamme, a beautiful young French Canadian girl, is passionately in love with Jim Kenyon, a wild young man known all over the Canadian northwest. Her brother, Emile, however, wants her to marry the respectable but dour Edward Hawley.

When Jim is framed for the murder of Black Eagle, a violent Indian chief, Rose Marie is given the choice of marrying Hawley, who will see to it that Jim escapes, or seeing her man go to jail or even the gallows. She chooses marriage to Hawley - and with it Jim's freedom. Just as Hawley and Rose Marie are on their way to the altar, however, the real killer, Black Eagle's former girl, Wanda, confesses and the wedding is called off. Rose Marie and Emile set off to search for Jim, find him and the lovers are reunited. Songs include: 'Vive la Canadienne'; 'Rose Marie'; 'Indian Call'; 'Why Shouldn't We?'; 'Only a Kiss'; 'One Man Woman'

Sgt Malone	*Hard-boiled Herman*
Lady Jane	*Jim Kenyon, a mountain*
Black Eagle	*man*
Edward Hawley	*Rose Marie La Flamme,*
Emile La Flamme,	*Emile's sister*
trapper	*Ethel Brander*
Wanda	

Rose Tattoo, The

Tennessee Williams
Drama 3 Acts
Chicago 1950

Serafina Delle Rosa is extraordinarily religious and romantic, even by the extreme standards of her little Sicilian community in New Orleans. She is around thirty, a dressmaker, sexy and plump, but when her handsome truck-driver husband Rosario is killed while transporting goods for the mob, she miscarries.

Three years later she is still in pieces; Rosario's ashes are in an urn which she talks to, and she has locked up her fifteen-year-old daughter Rosa to prevent her meeting her sailor boyfriend Jack. The priest and neighbours are worried for her sanity, and when two local gossips insinuate Rosario was having an affair with another woman (Estelle), Serafina appears to be on the verge of a breakdown. She is saved by the arrival of truck-driver Alvaro, a good-natured younger man who reminds her of Rosario and courts her avidly, even to the extent of copying Rosario's distinctive rose-tattoo. When Alvaro reveals he knows Estelle, Serafina insists he find out the truth. Estelle tells Alvaro that she too has the rose tattoo, and the distraught Serafina abandons herself to Alvaro. That night Rosa sees Alvaro after he has been with Serafina and she confronts her mother, calling her a hypocrite. Rosa's relationship with Jack has been decent and honest, and finally Serafina gives them her blessing. Then she feels the tattoo appear on her own breast and knows by this she has conceived - and goes to tell her new love, Alvaro.

Salvatore	*Teresa*
Vivi	*Father De Leo*
Bruno	*A doctor*
Assunta	*Miss Yorke*
Rosa Delle Rose	*Flora*
Serafina Delle Rose	*Bessie*
Estelle Hohengarten	*Jack Hunter*
The Strega	*The Salesman*
Guiseppina	*Alvaro Mangiacavello*
Peppina	*A man*
Violetta	*Another man*
Mariella	

Rose Without a Thorn, The

Clifford Bax
Drama 3 Acts
London 1932

King Henry VIII, in the process of having his marriage to Anne of Cleves annulled, has met and fallen in love with Katheryn Howard, niece of the Duke of Norfolk. The King's young friend, Thomas Culpepper, is likewise in thrall to Katheryn and, sensing the King's intentions, hurriedly proposes to her to pre-empt Henry. Katheryn, though, is so taken with the King's attentions that she refuses Culpepper and agrees to become Henry's queen.

Their marriage restores to the King the zest for life which had long since waned, and he reforms his habits so radically that he becomes, almost literally, a new man. Nemesis awaits both Henry and Katheryn, though, in the form of one of the Queen's childhood maids, the rigidly devout Mary Lassells whose religious convictions lead her to reveal that, as a girl, Katheryn had taken two lovers. When Mary's brother John, who is equally devout, reveals these dalliances to the King, an investigation is ordered and Katheryn's two affairs are confirmed. These, the King is of a mind to forgive, but interrogation of Katheryn's personal maid, Tilney, reveals that the Queen has shared a night of love with young Culpepper since her marriage.

Katherine Tilney, Culpepper and the Queen's two former lovers are all put to death and Henry is left to mourn the loss of the only woman he ever loved - his rose without a thorn.

Henry VIII
Thomas Cranmer, Archbishop of Canterbury
Sir Thomas Audley, Lord Chancellor
The Earl of Hertford
Thomas Culpepper, Henry's young friend
Francis Derham
John Lassells
Katheryn Howard, Queen of England
Katherine Tilney
Margery Morton
Anne of Cleves, former Queen of England
Mary Lassells

Rosencrantz and Guildenstern are Dead
Tom Stoppard
Comedy 3 Acts
Edinburgh 1966

The two attendant lords in *Hamlet* are cast as leads in this erudite, punning comedy, a play within a play, which touches upon both classical and modern dramatic themes. Rosencrantz and Guildenstern's universe is a kind of limbo where they exist between their pre-ordained appearances in *Hamlet*, appearances over which they have no control and the reasons for which they are largely unaware. They are trapped until events have played themselves out, and they while away the time by tossing coins (which always come up heads) engaging in frustrating banter with the motley and slightly sinister players, and by pondering together upon their existence, their purpose, and most of all upon death. Still confused they move on to their fate in the final scene of *Hamlet*.

Rosencrantz   *Polonius*
Guildenstern   *Horatio*
The player   *Fortinbras*
Alfred   *First Ambassador*
Tragedians   *Courtiers*
Hamlet   *Attendants*
Ophelia
Claudius
Gertrude

Rosmersholm
Henrik Ibsen
Drama 4 Acts
Oslo 1886

Former clergyman John Rosmer comes from a long and distinguished line of ancestors and lives in the family mansion Rosmerholm together with his dead wife's companion Rebecca West. With her support and encouragement he intends to join the progressive radical movement and begin his life's work 'ennobling souls', but his brother-in-law, Kroll, tries unsuccessfully at first to enlist him for the establishment cause. When imputations suggest Rosmer's barren wife Beata was not so much insane as driven to suicide by John and Rebecca, his guilt stultifies further radical activity. Rebecca, to free him, confesses her stratagems; not only has she pushed John into the radical posture, but she also, albeit subconsciously, encouraged Beata's suicide. Her goals have been fulfilled, but she cannot enjoy them. Rosmer has at least ennobled 'her' soul, but her happiness is destroyed. Furthermore, Kroll has revealed to her intimations of her illegitimacy. When she asks the disillusioned Rosmer what she must do for him to believe in her again, he says follow his wife. They declare their mutual love and go to the bridge over the millrace and drown together.

John Rosmer
Rebecca West
Kroll
Ulrik Brendel
Peter Mortensgaard
Mrs Helseth, Rosmer's housekeeper

Ross
Terence Rattigan
Drama 2 Acts
London 1960

This dramatic portrait of the scholar-soldier Lawrence of Arabia begins and ends in an RAF depot near London in 1922 where Lawrence has enlisted under the alias of Aircraftsman Ross - a refuge from himself and his legendary reputation. He is recognized by another RAF man who attempts to blackmail him, threatening Fleet Street exposure, but Lawrence won't pay, and at the end of the play the subsequent publicity forces him to leave the service. In between, the story of his army exploits, the triumphs and humiliations, are told in a series of short scenes highlighting his complex character; his support of Prince Feisal in the cause of pan-Arabism, his gruelling desert march to capture Akaba from the Turks, his stirring up of the Arab peoples against the Turks, his capture and physical and psychological humiliation by a clever Turkish general, his deep friendship with his Arab bodyguards, Hamed and Rashid, and their subsequent deaths, and finally his sensational capture of Damascus.

Flt Lieut Stoker   *Aircraftsman Parsons*
Flt Sgt Thompson   *Aircraftsman Dickinson*

Round and Round the Garden (The Norman Conquests)

Aircraftsman Ross
Franks, the lecturer
Gen. Allenby
Ronald Storrs
Colonel Barrington
Auda Aba Tayi
The Turkish Military
Governor, Deraa District
Hamed

Rashid
Turkish captain
Turkish sergeant
Turkish corporal
ADC
A photographer
An Australian soldier
Flt Lieut Higgins
Group Capt. Wood

Round and Round the Garden (The Norman Conquests)
Alan Ayckbourn
Comedy 2 Acts
Scarborough 1973
See: *Living Together; Table Manners*
One of *The Norman Conquests* trilogy in which events during a single weekend, with the same set of characters, are viewed in a different setting in each play. *Round and Round the Garden* is set in a garden

Norman arrives early for an assignation with his sister-in-law Annie, who is nurse to her invalid mother. The two have planned a dirty weekend, with Annie's mother left in the care of Reg and Sarah, Annie's brother and sister-in-law. But Norman's untimely arrival saps her courage and she cancels the trip.

As Norman alternately sulks and tries to seduce Annie, Reg and Sarah try to goad Tom, Annie's ineffectual boyfriend, into making a proposal of marriage. Sarah's true motive for doing so is her wish to supplant Annie as Norman's lover. However, her hope fades when Norman gets drunk and ignores her only to collapse weeping on Reg's shoulder. In revenge, Sarah telephones her sister-in-law, Norman's wife Ruth, and reveals his aborted plan with Annie. Ruth arrives and playfully declares a passion for Tom, which he takes seriously.

As the guests prepare to leave on Monday morning, Norman crashes the family cars in an attempt to delay everyone's departure so that he can continue his lechery. The women, tiring of him, turn their backs on him.
Norman
Tom, Annie's boyfriend
Sarah, Reg's wife
Annie, Ruth and Reg's sister
Reg, Ruth and Annie's brother, Sarah's husband
Ruth, Reg and Annie's sister, Norman's wife

Royal Hunt of the Sun, The
Peter Shaffer
Tragedy 2 Acts
London 1964
Francisco Pizarro, the Spanish conquistador, sets out in 1529 to conquer Peru for Spain and to win for himself the vast supplies of gold he knows the Inca kingdom to possess. His tiny band of less than two hundred men march, after an horrendous journey through the jungle, down the huge road into the centre of the Inca kingdom.

The Inca King, Atahuallpa, is impressed by Pizarro's boldness and convinced he is the white god spoken of in Inca legends, he lets the Spaniards surround and capture him.

Pizarro agrees to free Atahuallpa if the Incas fill a huge room with gold, but when they do so he reneges on his promise because the King swears vengeance on all but Pizarro. Goaded by fear of the Incas on one side and of his own restless troops on the other, Pizarro can see no way out of his dilemma until Atahuallpa offers to die and be reborn overnight to prove his own divinity. Pizarro half believes the King's claim to divinity, but sinks into sullen remorse and disillusionment when Atahuallpa fails to be resurrected by the morning sun which the Incas believed to be their King's brother.
Francisco Pizarro, conqueror of Peru
Hernando De Soto, Pizarro's deputy
Miguel Estete, the royal overseer
De Candia, master of artillery
Diego De Trujillo, master of horse
Martin Ruiz, Pizarro's page
Atahuallpa, Inca king
Villac Umu, Inca high priest
Challcuchima, Inca general
Young Martin Ruiz
Salinas
Rodas
Vasca
Domingo
Juan Chavez
Fray Vincente Valverde
Fray Marcos De Nizza
A chieftain
A headman
Felipillo
Manco
Inti Coussi
Oello

Ruffian on the Stair, The
Joe Orton
Comedy 5 Scenes
London 1967
This one-act surrealistic black comedy finds vicious, jealous Mike living in a tatty flat with ex-whore Joyce. Wilson arrives, purportedly looking for a room, but begins acting strangely, annoying Joyce and checking to make sure that Mike's revolver is loaded. When Mike returns he gets on fine with Wilson until he realizes Wilson is the brother (and homosexual lover) of a man he recently killed in a hit-and-run accident. Wilson leaves after ascertaining Mike would kill anyone interfering with Joyce, and next day he returns and stages his own murder, getting Mike to shoot him after pretending intimacy with Joyce.
Mike
Joyce
Wilson

Rules of the Game, The
Luigi Pirandello
Comedy 3 Acts
Rome 1918

When four drunks, including the Marquis Aldo Miglioritti, burst in mistakenly on lovely Silia Gala, she tells her lover Guido Venanzi to hide in the bedroom so she will not be compromised. The intrusion gives her the perfect excuse to make trouble for her husband Leone, from whom she is separated. Pretending near-rape, she calls the neighbours and takes the Marquis's card without accepting his apology, intending to tell Leone he must duel with the Marquis for her honour. After some protest, Guido goes along with this and arranges the terms of the duel most unfavourably to Leone. Leone himself is somewhat of a cool philosopher and insists that Guido act as his second. The rule is that Guido cannot refuse, and on the morning of the duel Leone says he will not fight and again, according to the rules, his second must stand in for him. Guido and Silia are then caught in the trap they have loaded for Leone. The Marquis is a superb marksman and swordsman and Guido is killed. In the aftermath of the tragedy, though, Leone begins to doubt his own philosophy.

Guido Venanzi   *Filippo*
Silia Gala   *Dr Spiga*
Clara   *Barelli*
Leone Gala
Marquis Aldo Miglioritti
Three drunks
Four neighbours

Run for Your Wife
Ray Cooney
Farce 2 Acts
Guildford 1982

This farce follows the ructions which develop in the life of John Smith, a bigamous London cabbie, when he is injured attempting to prevent a robbery and so disrupts the careful schedule which has prevented either of his wives from discovering the existence of the other.

Smith, with the bumbling help of his neighbour Stanley Gardner, creates chaos in both his households as one lie leads inexorably to the next. He traps himself in ever more implausible explanations when the police, the newspapers, and his neighbours give vent to a very natural curiosity about his affairs.

When he finally breaks down and admits his bigamy, the police refuse to believe him and he is left, ironically, in the wreckage his own panic has created.

Mary Smith, John's wife
Barbara Smith, John's wife
John Smith, a cabbie
Detective Sergeant Troughton
Stanley Gardner
Newspaper reporter
Detective Sergeant Porterhouse
Bobby Franklyn

Sabrina Fair or A Woman of the World
Samuel Taylor
Comedy 3 Acts
London 1954

Chauffeur Fairchild's daughter Sabrina returns to her father's house on the Long Island estate of his employers, the wealthy Larrabee family. She has been in Paris for five years and has blossomed from a 'mouse' into a vivacious and stylish young woman. She confides in ruthless and attractive elder son Linus, the business head of the family, that she has always had a crush on handsome younger son David. Linus throws them together and the enchanted David proposes, but realizing she does not love him, Sabrina turns him down, much to the delight of her father and the Larrabees. She also tells Linus that she is undecided about a recent marriage proposal from Paul, a charming and wealthy young French businessman - she does not love him, but she would love the lifestyle. Next day Paul appears and Linus gives him a plastics concession he has been after for years. Sabrina finally realizes it is Linus she wants to marry. He wants her too and, as a bonus, chauffeur Fairchild reveals he is a millionaire from investing in Larrabee stocks over the years - and it is all hers.

Maud Larrabee
Julia Ward McKinlock
Linus Larrabee, Jr
Linus Larrabee
Margaret
David Larrabee
Gretchen
Sabrina Fairchild
Fairchild
A young woman
A young man
Another young woman
Another young man
Paul D'Argenson

Sailor, Beware
Philip King and Falkland Cary
Comedy 3 Acts
London 1955

Emma Hornett is a domestic tyrant, domineering, houseproud, and self-righteous to a fault, and continuously bullies her ferret-fancier husband Henry and his live-in spinster sister, Edie. She is not happy with her precious daughter Shirley's choice of husband, orphan sailor Albert Tufnell, and makes sure everyone knows. When Albert and best man, Scots sailor Carnoustie Bligh, appear on the wedding eve, they go out to the pub and return with a drunken Henry. Emma throws a furious scene, and a little later Albert learns from Edie that his prospective mother-in-law has put down a deposit on a house a few doors away as a wedding present. Upset that Shirley did not tell him, Albert spends a sleepless night and next morning does not turn up at church. The distraught family return home and Albert appears to explain his actions to Shirley and the local Reverend. The fact is, he says, he could not bear to live so near his mother-in-law. Emma then repents after hearing henpecked Henry stick up for her, and the wedding goes ahead after all - but Albert insists they will not be moving in next door.

Edie Hornett
Emma Hornett
Mrs Lack
Henry Hornett
Albert Tufnell AB
Carnoustie Bligh AB
Daphne Pink
Shirley Hornett
The Revd Oliver Purefoy

Saint Joan
George Bernard Shaw
Chronicle Play 6 Scenes
London 1924

The play is an imaginative reconstruction of the main events in the life of Saint Joan of Arc (d. 1431) who was burnt at the stake, in Shaw's opinion, for nothing more than 'unwomanly and insufferable presumption' in a brutal male world she confronted as an equal.

A series of episodes follow Joan's career from her first arrival at the castle of her local squire claiming to have been sent by God to deliver France from the English, to her execution at Rouen. She dies abandoned by the King whose fortunes she rescued from defeat at the hands of the English, by the French Catholic church she thought she was defending, and even by Dunois, the royal bastard who knew her greatness better, perhaps, than anyone else.

In an epilogue, the ghosts of her main betrayers repent of their treachery to her, and celebrate her inauguration as a saint.

Robert de Baudricourt, Joan's feudal lord
Joan
Bertrand de Poulengey, Joan's first supporter
Archbishop of Rheims
La Trémouille, Constable of France
Gilles de Rais
Captain La Hire
The Dauphin (later Charles VII)
Dunois, Bastard of Orleans
Richard de Beauchamp, Earl of Warwick
Chaplain de Stogumber
Peter de Cauchon, Bishop of Beauvais
The Inquisitor
Brother Martin Ladvenu
Steward
Court Page
Duchesse de la Trémouille
Dunois' page
Warwick's page
D'Estivet
De Courcelles
Executioner
English soldier
Gentleman

Saint's Day
John Whiting
Drama 3 Acts
London 1951

On the day of his birthday Paul Southman, an ageing poet, is awaiting the arrival of Robert Procathren who is to take him to London for an honorary meal. Southman has been in self-imposed exile for many years with his granddaughter Stella and her husband Charles, due to adverse reaction to his controversial piece *The Abolition of Printing*. His bitterness extends to the local villagers, resulting in a state of feud. Their servant returns from the village with the news that three soldiers on the run have ransacked the village.

Stella hopes that Robert Procathren can restore her grandfather's respectability so that she and her future child can escape the misery of their solitary existence.

Procathren's arrival, however, has little effect on Southman who is rapidly approaching senility. Procathren discovers Southman's dead dog and the poet, convinced the villagers have poisoned it, demands that Procathren aid him in his revenge on the village, handing him a pistol. The pistol misfires, killing Stella.

Unable to accept the responsibility of Stella's death Procathren flees and orders the soldiers to kill Southman and Charles. The soldiers, happy to take orders once again, carry out the task with no remorse.

Stella Heberden, Paul's granddaughter
Charles Heberden, her husband
Paul Southman, an aged poet
John Winter, his manservant
Robert Procathren, an admirer of Paul
Giles Aldus, a recluse
Soldiers: Christian Melrose, Walter Killen, Henry Chater
Villagers: Hanah Trewin, Margaret Bant, Edith Tinson, Flora Baldon, Judith Warden, Thomas Cowper
A child

Salad Days
Dorothy Reynolds and Julian Slade
Musical 2 Acts
London 1954

Timothy and Jane, on graduating from university, find they have time on their hands. Timothy's parents tell him to get a job from one of his five uncles, but not to talk to Ba Ba, the black sheep uncle.

Jane's parents have planned a party for her at which they hope she will choose a suitable marriage partner. Having little time for plans, Jane and Timothy decide to get married, and accept a piano from a tramp in the park which seems to magically make people dance.

The piano is a great success with people in the park, and the newly-weds secretly earn a living with it, but the Minister of Pleasure and Pastime (Timothy's uncle

Augustine) is furious and sets the police force to tracking down the piano and its wilful owners.

Despite help from Tim's uncle Zed, and a passing spaceman in a flying saucer, Timothy and Jane (and the piano) are finally discovered by their parents and the police, but are soon forgiven when it transpires that the tramp is Timothy's long lost uncle Ba Ba. Although there is an offer to play the magic piano at the Royal Garden Party the happy couple pass the instrument to a couple of worthy friends. They may be going to visit another planet...

Songs include: 'Oh, Look at Me, I'm Dancing'; 'We're Looking for a Piano'; 'It's Easy to Sing'; 'We Said We Wouldn't Look Back'

The Tramp	American
Jane	Shopgirl
Timothy	Theatre-goers
Dons	Lady
Timothy's mother	Tom Smith
Timothy's father	Waitress
Aunt Prue	Slaves
Lady Raeburn	Arms dancers
Heloise	Augustine Williams
Assistant	Asphynxia
Manicurist	Pressmen
Police Constable Boot	Ladies
Rowena	Ambrose
The bishop	Marguerite
Troppo	Anthea
An artist	Electrode, the spaceman
A sunbather	Uncle Zed
A tennis player	Lady
Fosdyke	Butterfly catcher
Sir Clamsby Williams	Manager
Inspector	Pianist
Nigel	Fiona

Same Time, Next Year
Bernard Slade
Comedy 2 Acts
New York 1975
This play details the progression of an adulterous love affair and, through the protagonists, a reflection of twenty-five years of American life.

George and Doris begin their affair in a California Inn in 1951 and subsequently agree to meet once every year. Both, however, are happily married, have children, and are loyal but for their once-yearly fling.

We watch their characters progress over the years. When we first see him, George is a tense, nervous accountant becoming increasingly wealthy. He then drops out, has analysis, attends group therapy, becomes a hippie, only to finally rejoin the rat-race.

Doris begins as a clumsy *ingénue*, becomes a dissatisfied housewife, goes back to college, dabbles as a late flower-child, then a career woman, before finally settling down as a happy mother.

Throughout, the pairs' changes are in opposition, never in sync. After attempting to end the relationship, they both realize they cannot give it up.
George
Doris

Saved
Edward Bond
Comedy 13 Scenes
London 1965
Set in South London among the 'new poor' (where the poverty is spiritual and moral, not material), this traces the assimilation of good-natured Len into the family of Pam, a local 'slag' whose parents Harry and Mary have not spoken to each other for years. Pam ditches Len, who stays as a lodger, and takes up with his mate Fred. She becomes pregnant and has a baby but Fred does not want to know. One day she is pushing her unloved and unwanted offspring in the park when she bumps into Fred and his hooligan friends. Angrily she leaves the baby with him; the boys first begin shoving the pram around, then spitting in it, and finally they stone the baby to death.

Fred is arrested and sent to prison. On his release Pam wants him back but he is not interested. She also wants Len to leave but he will not go. There is a mild Oedipal scene between Mary and Len, which causes Mary and Harry to speak to each other, and later Harry tells Len he wants him to stay. He stays, and although there is barely any communication between any of them, they are at least together.

Len	Mike
Fred	Barry
Harry	Pam
Pete	Mary
Colin	Liz

Say Who You Are
Keith Waterhouse and Willis Hall
Comedy 3 Acts
Guildford 1965
Valerie Pitman, a young single London woman with a generous libido but no wish to settle, is carrying on an affair with Stuart Wheeler, a married man, in the home of her friend Sarah Lord, and under the pretence that she is married to Sarah's husband David. She thus hopes to prevent Stuart from wanting to become more than her occasional lover. Sarah has kept the arrangement secret from David, and takes him to a series of foreign films on the nights Valerie meets Stuart in their home, to his rather boorish annoyance.

Sarah treats Valerie's affair as if it is, vicariously, her own, as a kind of mild revenge on David, who has himself been caught out having a fling with a much younger woman.

On one of their outings, David becomes so upset that he insists they return home, earlier than expected, and he and Sarah only fail to confront the lovers because they, too, have quarrelled and Stuart has left for the local pub. David no sooner arrives in the flat than he leaves again, furious that Sarah, who has confessed, would let Valerie use the flat for her trysts. He too goes to the local pub, and falls into conversation with Stuart, both of them regaling one another with their different versions of Stuart's affair, without either of them being aware of the identity of the other.

Meanwhile Sarah, her anger reverting to jealousy, has mutilated David's suits, and leaves the flat herself just as he is trying to reach her from the pub phone. So starts a tightly-timed series of near misses as each of the men and women look frantically for one another.

David and Sarah resolve their differences after he has revealed, to her initial outrage, that he has never made love to his mistress. And Stuart, having discovered that Valerie is single, is unable to get her to agree to marriage but manages to convince her to see him three times each week.

David Lord
Sarah Lord, David's wife
Valerie Pitman, Sarah's friend
Stuart Wheeler, Valerie's lover

Scapino
Frank Dunlop
Comedy 2 Acts
New York 1965

Set in contemporary Naples this roistering comedy in the tradition of the Italian *commedia dell'arte* follows the escapades of the outrageously slippery servant, Scapino, as he outwits his own master, Geronte, and his master's associate and friend, Argante, in a series of plots on behalf of the two men's sons.

Geronte's son Leandro has fallen in love with a gypsy girl, Zorbinetta, and Argante's son, Ottavio, with an apparently penniless, abandoned young lady, Giacinta. Both affairs meet the disapproval of the older men, Ottavio's the more so because he and Argante have just agreed a marriage between Ottavio and Geronte's daughter, who has been brought up in Marseille, far from their native Naples. Scapino extracts from the two fathers the 700,000 lire the young men need to win their respective lovers in marriage, and at the same time gets Geronte to submit unwittingly to an ignominious thrashing, just for the pleasure of revenging a slight earlier humiliation at his master's hands.

A general reconciliation follows when it transpires that Giacinta is the daughter Geronte had intended for Ottavio, and that she had become separated from him by a storm at sea, which had prevented her scheduled arrival. Then Giacinta, who has become deeply attached to Zorbinetta, persuades Geronte that the girl will make Leandro a fine wife, despite her poverty.

Ottavio
Sylvestro, Ottavio's guardian
Scapino, Geronte's servant
Giacinta, Ottavio's betrothed
Argante, Ottavio's father
Geronte
Leandro, Geronte's son
Carlo
Zorbinetta, Leandro's lover
Nurse
Headwaiter
Two harrassed waiters
One waitress

Scarecrow, The
Percy Mackaye
Drama 4 Acts
New York 1914

In a small town in Massachusetts in the late seventeenth century, Goody Rickby (Blacksmith Bess) connives with Dickon (Lucifer) to exact her revenge on Justice Merton, who many years before left her with a son, who subsequently died. Together they build a scarecrow and give it life, calling it Lord Ravensbone. Merton's daughter Rachel is betrothed to Richard Talbot, but on meeting Ravensbone the two fall in love according to Goody Rickby's plan.

Ravensbone is tragically unaware of his true origins, and slowly rejects the machinations of the wily Dickon and assumes his own character. Rachel however, possesses a magical mirror which reflects the true form or nature of the beholder, and Ravensbone is inadvertently revealed in it as a scarecrow. Dejected, he asks for one last meeting and through his love for Rachel is revealed in the mirror again, as a man.

Justice Gilead Merton
Goody Rickby
Lord Ravensbone
Dickon
Rachel Merton
Mistress Cecilia Merton
Richard Talbot
Sir Charles Reddington
Mistress Reddington
Amelia Reddington
Capt. Bugby
Minister Dodge
Mistress Dodge
Revd Master Rand
Revd Master Todd
Micah

School for Scandal, The
Richard Brinsley Sheridan
Comedy 5 Acts
London 1777

This comedy of manners has the general theme of the absurd behaviour of scandalmongers. Lady Sneerwell opens the play by complaining of how she has been wounded by slander while she is plotting with Joseph Surface to discredit his brother Charles in order to stop him marrying Maria, an heiress and ward of Sir Peter Teazle. Joseph is an arch hypocrite and is paying court to Lady Teazle, an ex-country maid and now leading scandalmonger, in order to get to Maria himself. Maria, however, loves Charles, a wastrel but an honest one.

In disguise, Sir Oliver Surface, the boys' rich uncle makes a secret trial of his nephews, and, deciding on Charles' basic honesty he helps him financially while Joseph is exposed by a penitent Lady Teazle who is finally reconciled with her husband.

Sir Peter Teazle, an elderly aristocrat
Sir Oliver Surface, an elderly aristocrat
Joseph Surface, a young gentleman
Charles Surface, a young gentleman
Maria, Sir Peter Teazle's ward
Lady Sneerwell, Mrs Candour, Sir Benjamin
  Backbite, scandalmongers
Lady Teazle, wife of Sir Peter
Crabtree
Snake
Moses, a moneylender
Rowley, friend of Sir Peter
Careless, friend of Charles Surface
Trip, Charles' servant
Two maids

School for Wives, The
Molière
Comedy 3 Acts
Paris 1662

A middle-aged Parisian cynic, M. Arnolphe, who obsessively impugns the sexual fidelity of all women, has secretly been having a bride prepared for himself, in the shape of the girl, now a young woman, of whom he is the official guardian. To ensure, as he hopes, her perpetual innocence, Arnolphe has had the girl, Agnes, raised very strictly by nuns.

Unfortunately for Arnolphe, the nuns are only too successful, and Agnes innocently falls in love with the son of one of Arnolphe's oldest friends. Arnolphe discovers the affair and, while pretending to further the young man's interests, undermines him instead, secure in the knowledge that his rival is not aware that they have designs on the same woman.

Only after Arnolphe's jealousy leads him nearly to murder the younger man, Horace, is his rage tamed by the timely arrival and wise counsel of his old friend, Horace's father Oronte.

The lovers are left free to marry, and Arnolphe to rue his stupidity and wonder at his escape from disaster.

Arnolphe
Chrysalde, Arnolphe's friend
Alain, Arnolphe's servant
Georgette, Arnolphe's servant
Agnes
Horace
Enrique
Oronte, Horace's father

Seagull, The
Anton Chekhov
Drama 4 Acts
St Petersburg 1896

Young would-be author Konstantin Trevlev stages an experimental play starring his girlfriend Nina in an open-air theatre on his uncle Sorin's country estate; it is generally derided, especially by his selfish but lovable mother Arkadina and her lover, the successful writer Trigorin. Even Nina does not like the play, and when her affections begin to switch towards Trigorin, the desperate Trevlev casually kills a seagull and lays it at her feet. She shows it to Trigorin who has an idea to work it into a story about a girl casually destroyed by a man, and then he does just that; he takes Nina as his new mistress, but after the death of their baby and the failure of her career as an actress, leaves her and returns to Arkadina. Everyone's love is thwarted, and when the half-crazy Nina returns to still-faithful Trevlev to say goodbye, she tells him she still loves Trigorin. Trevlev goes out and shoots himself.

Simon Medvedenke
Peter Sorin
Konstantin Trevlev
Yakov
Elya Shamrayev
Doctor Dorn
Boris Trigorin
Masha
Nina Zarechnaya
Polena Andreyevna
Irena Arkadina
Cook
Maid

Seagulls over Sorrento
Hugh Hastings
Comedy 3 Acts
London 1949

In a disused fortress on a rocky little island near Scapa Flow, an experimental naval station has been set up shortly after World War Two. Four disparate ratings - Haggis, Badger, Sprog and Lofty - are engaged in a constant battle with the snide and authoritarian Petty Officer Herbert. Bonds of friendship and sympathy grow between the men, and when a fifth member arrives - highly-educated Able Seaman Hudson ('Radar') - he is able to coax silent Scot Haggis out of his dour shell. Quick-tempered cockney Badger's mistrust of middle-class Radar is never resolved because Radar is accidentally killed by his own torpedo explosives. Sub-Lieut Granger then needs a volunteer for the new torpedo tests and courageous Lofty fiddles the draw and gets picked, but before the dangerous mission manages to slug Herbert. A telegraphist, 'Sparks', arrives to help with the tests and proves to be Badger's mortal enemy Cleland - the man who ran off with his wife. But when flashy Cleland sides with the men against Herbert, all is forgiven. Lofty returns safe from his mission, and instead of punishment for their defiance, all the men (except Herbert) get a fourteen-day leave from sympathetic Lieut-Com. Redmond and a new posting.

Able Seaman McIntosh ('Haggis')
Able Seaman Sims ('Sprog')
Able Seaman Turner ('Lofty')
Able Seaman Badger
Petty Officer Herbert
Lieut-Com. Redmond DSO DSC RN
Sub-Lieut Granger RN
Able Seaman Hudson ('Radar')
A telegraphist ('Sparks') Cleland

Second Mrs Tanqueray, The
Arthur Wing Pinero
Drama 4 Acts
London 1893

Aubrey Tanqueray's first marriage was a disaster; his late wife was frigid and his daughter Ellean, now eighteen, is in a convent. He decides to remarry, but his intended, the beautiful Paula, has a 'past', and rather than be socially ostracised the couple move to his Surrey country home. But they are bored and bicker, and events reach a head when Ellean leaves the convent and comes home. Her purity and innocence contrast with Paula's cynicism and wordliness, and when Ellean falls in love with Capt. Hugh Ardale, Paula has to reveal to Aubrey that she and Hugh once had an affair. Righteous Ellean (who has despised Paula) learns the truth, but her recent experiences of worldly affairs have given her more understanding and compassion. She goes to Paula intending to apologize, but it is too late. Her stepmother has already killed herself.

Aubrey Tanqueray
Paula
Ellean
Cayley Drummle
Mrs Cortelyon
Capt. Hugh Ardale
Gordon Jayne MD
Frank Misqueth QC MP
Sir George Orreyed, Bart.
Lady Orreyed
Morse

Secret Life of Walter Mitty, The
James Thurber
Musical 2 Acts
New York 1963

On reaching his fortieth birthday Walter Mitty reflects on his dull and ordinary life. Tied down by responsibility to his family, a routine job and a certain lack of drive; Mitty daydreams elaborate fantasies in which he is always the conquering hero. His secret world is so attractive that he often confuses dream and reality as he slips into the world of his imagination.

An attractive aspiring singer, Willa de Wisp, encourages him to leave his nagging but devoted wife Agnes and really live 'the secret life'. Unfortunately for Mitty, that life is ultimately unreachable, and the would-be hero discovers his commitment is to the real world and his wife.

Walter Mitty	*Ruthie*
Cdr MacMilolan	*Fred Dorman*
Firing squad	*Hazel*
Peasant woman	*Crêpe Suzette*
Agnes Mitty	*Tortoni*
Peninnah Mitty	*Apple Turnover*
Space command	*Townspeople*
lieutenant	*Male dancers*
Surgical patient	*Blind date*
(MacMillan)	*Customers*
Head nurse	*Psychiatric patients*
Dr Renshaw	*Sylvia*
Dr Bendow	
Professor Remington	
Dr Pritchard-Mitford	
First nurse	
Second nurse	
Willa	
Irving	

Secretary Bird, The
William Douglas Home
Comedy 2 Acts
Swanage 1967

Hugh Walford, an urbane writer in late middle-age, is shocked when his much younger wife Liz announces her intention to divorce him in favour of her lover, John Brownlow.

Although he has been secretly aware of Liz's affair for some time, her decision to leave him catches Hugh off guard. He recovers his composure as best he can and decides to invite not just Brownlow but his own beautiful secretary, Molly Forsyth, to spend the weekend at their country home. He explains to Liz that he intends to make love with Molly, arranging to be caught *in flagrante* by their housekeeper, Mrs Gray, in order honourably to provide his wife with grounds for divorce.

Over the course of the weekend, he tries, with some success, to undermine Brownlow's assurance by obliquely showing him Liz's less attractive qualities, while at the same time arousing her jealousy of Molly. By Monday morning, however, he seems to have lost his gamble, and Liz prepares to depart. At the last minute, though, she realizes her mistake, changes her mind and watches as Brownlow leaves with Molly, all to Hugh's tremendous relief.

Hugh Walford
Liz Walford, his wife
Mrs Gray, their housekeeper
Molly Forsyth, Hugh's secretary
John Brownlow, Liz's lover

Seduced
Sam Shepard
Drama 2 Acts
New York 1978

In a hotel suite on the Mexican border, the infinitely rich Henry Hackamore waits in failing health, with only his manservant Raul as company, for a private plane to take him to Las Vegas.

While Raul follows Henry's obsessive instructions about cleanliness, order and secrecy, the old man receives Luna, a beautiful lover from his youth, who seems to be as young as ever. They are joined by another of Henry's lovers, Miami, and Henry obliges the two women to write a contract in the air, with their fingers, by which they agree to do whatever he wants.

Because his memory is disintegrating along with his health, Henry obliges each of the women to act out a scene from their shared past. Part way through the story, Henry forgets who the women are, calls Raul to remove them and sends him for a transfusion of plasma. He then puts on a flying kit from World War One, only to have Raul, suddenly transformed from servant to master, refuse to let him leave Mexico and then make him sign over his fortune.

As witnesses to the contract, Raul brings back the two women, with two doctors, and a gangster, who leaves with the contract. Henry straddles a chair, believing it to be an airplane he can fly to safety, as Raul shoots him again and again with a pistol.

Henry Hackamore
Raul, his servant
Luna, his lover
Miami, his lover

See How They Run
Philip King
Farce 3 Acts
London 1945

Ex-actress Penelope Toop lives in a country vicarage with her husband, the Revd Lionel Toop. When he is unexpectedly called to assist the local Glee singers, along comes L/Cpl Clive Winton, one of Penny's former thespian friends. They decide to go out and visit a nearby village production of *Private Lives* for old times' sake, but as that particular village is out of bounds for Clive, he dresses as a vicar, impersonating Lionel's stand-in, Revd Arthur Humphrey.

Upon their return they lark around practising their own old roles in *Private Lives* and when snoopy local old maid Miss Skillon gets in the way, she is accidentally floored.

The scene is now set for total confusion aided and abetted by saucy maid Ida. Penny's uncle, the Bishop of Lax, arrives plus an escaped Nazi airman, plus the real Revd Humphrey. Vicars chase each other all over the house, Miss Skillon gets wildly drunk, clothes and uniforms are lost and found, and, of course, all is eventually explained to everyone's satisfaction - except the nasty Nazi and the unfortunate Miss Skillon.

Ida
Miss Skillon
The Revd Lionel Toop
Penelope Toop
L/Cpl Clive Winton
The Intruder
The Bishop of Lax
The Revd Arthur Humphrey
Sgt Towers

See Naples and Die
Elmer Rice
Comedy 3 Acts
London 1928

Charles Carroll, a guest in a small pension on the Bay of Naples in the twenties, prepares to leave the hotel with the new lover he has acquired at the expense of a Rumanian general who has been living opposite with the woman, Kunnie Wandl. He imagines himself jilted by a rich American, Nanette Dodge, who has interrupted their love affair to run off, as he sees it, and marry Prince Kosoff, a Russian *émigré*.

When Nanette, the Prince and his sinister valet, Stepan, arrive by coincidence at the pension, Charles discovers from Nanette that she has been blackmailed into the marriage to save her sister's reputation.

In a fury, Charles attacks the Prince, who then resolves to abduct Nanette to remove her from her lover's influence. Charles rescues her from the Prince, and they are released from fear of the Russian when he is shot by assassins sent to murder Kunnie's Rumanian general, who also dies in the attack. Kunnie is so happy to be free of the general that she quickly recovers from Charles' return to Nanette.

Mrs Evans, Basil Rowlinson, pension guests
Mr De'Medici, pension owner
Hugo von Klaus
Charles Carroll, Princess Kosoff's lover
Luisa, pension maid
Kunegunde Wandl
Mrs De'Medici
Princess Nanette Dodge Kosoff
A coachman
Two chess players (assassins)
Postman
Prince Ivan Ivanovich Kosoff
Stepan, Prince Kosoff's servant
Marie Elizabeth Dodge Norton, Princess Kosoff's sister
Gen Jan Skulany

Separate Rooms
J. Carole and A. Dinehart
Comedy 3 Acts
New York 1942

Jim Stackhouse, a cynical, misogynistic New York newspaper columnist, tries to destroy a love affair between his brother Don and Pamela Barry, a rising young actress, by arranging that Gary Bryce, a wealthy financier, should back a play written by Don and starring Pamela. Jim is convinced that his brother's play is so bad that it will utterly fail, and that its failure will persuade Pamela that her stage ambitions will be better served by taking up with Bryce who can at least offer her the luxuries of life she so craves.

Jim's plan comes unstuck when the play is such a hit that Pamela and Don marry, and Pamela sets out on a social whirl which leaves Don isolated and unhappy. To protect his brother's interests, Jim threatens to expose Pamela's wild past in his column unless she becomes the ideal wife. At first Pamela bridles under his regimen, but gradually she comes to see Don's merits and settles into her new and unfamiliar role.

Pamela in turn has her revenge on Jim by blackmailing him into proposing to his Girl Friday, Linda Roberts, who has long been in love with him.

Gary Bryce, a financier
Taggart
Don Stackhouse, a playwright
Scoop Davis
Pamela Barry, an actress
Jim Stackhouse, Don's brother
Linda Roberts, Jim's Girl Friday
Leona Sharpe

Separate Tables
Terence Rattigan
Drama 2 Acts
London 1954

The 'regulars' and the 'casuals' sit at the tables in the dining-room of the Beauregard Hotel in Bournemouth; each has a story, each of the regulars are coming to terms in their own way with age, despair or loneliness.
Table by the Window. Hard-drinking journalist and disgraced former politician John Malcolm has entombed himself in the hotel and is having a comfortable affair with manageress Miss Cooper. Sparks fly when his ex-wife, model Mrs Shankland, 'discovers' him. Their relationship had been stormy and violent but he still loves her and they leave together, realizing they have more hope with each other than apart.
Table Number Seven. Busybody Mrs Railton-Bell discovers fellow-resident Maj. Pollock has been convicted of annoying a woman in a local cinema and that his military credentials are phoney. She righteously rallies the other residents against him including her nervy daughter Sibyl who likes the Major. When Sibyl confronts Pollock he breaks down and explains his action, telling her they have much in common; both are scared of life, of sex, of people. He decides to leave, but during his last dinner the other residents including Sibyl defy Mrs Railton-Bell and their unspoken compassion persuades him to stay.

Mabel
Lady Matheson

Doreen
Mr Fowler
Mrs Shankland
Miss Cooper
Mr Malcolm

Mrs Railton-Bell
Miss Meacham

Charles Stratton
Jean Tanner
Maj. Pollock
Miss Railton-Bell

Serjeant Musgrave's Dance
John Arden
Drama 3 Acts
London 1959

Towards the end of the last century, four soldiers serving in the colonies are sickened by violent reprisals against innocent civilians for the death of their comrade Billy Hicks. They desert, and under the leadership of Sjt Musgrave return to Billy's home town, a northern mining community in the grip of a coal strike and cut off by winter snow. The soldiers intend to show Billy's skeleton and convince people that the colonial war and its attendant repression is wrong. But after lack of sympathy towards them by the striking miners and the accidental death of one of their number, Sparky, who tried to run away with Billy's old girlfriend Annie, the soldiers attempt to kill five times five townsfolk with their Gatling gun as a lesson and a warning. They fight among themselves, another is killed, and at the last moment the dragoons arrive just in time to prevent a massacre. The two remaining soldiers, Musgrave and the pacifist Attercliffe, are arrested. Innkeeper Mrs Hitchcock visits them in jail and sums up the play's anti-violence message... 'you can't cure the pox with further whoring.'

Pte Sparky
Pte Hurst
Pte Attercliffe
Budgeon, a bargee
Sjt Musgrave
The parson
Mrs Hitchcock
Annie

The constable
The major
A slow collier
A pugnacious collier
Walsh, an earnest collier
A trooper of the dragoons
An officer of the dragoons

Servant of Two Masters, The
Carlo Goldoni
Comedy 2 Acts
Venice 1740

This slapstick from the *commedia dell'arte* tradition centres on the extravagantly contradictory character of Truffaldino, the servant of the title, and on his finally unsuccessful attempts to serve two masters while keeping each one unaware of the other's existence.

He is engaged first by Beatrice Rasponi, a gentlewoman who arrives in Venice disguised as her own brother. Beatrice has come to collect the dowry which her dead brother had been promised by Sr Pantalone, a rich merchant, whose daughter Clarice was meant to become the dead man's bride. Out of greed and a sense of bravado, Truffaldino then agrees to serve as well another new arrival to Venice, Florindo

Aretusi, who turns out to be Beatrice's fiancé, and who is a fugitive from Turin where he faces a murder charge over the death of Beatrice's brother.

Truffaldino's need to conceal one master from the other keeps each one ignorant of the other's presence in Venice until very nearly the end of the play, when, in a welter of revelations, the true identities of Beatrice and Florindo are revealed, and Beatrice is forgiven her attempted fraud.

Dr Lombardi, a lawyer
Brighella, an innkeeper
Silvio, Lombardi's son
Pantalone, a rich merchant
Smeraldina
Clarice, Pantalone's daughter
Truffaldino, a servant
Beatrice Rasponi
Florindo Aretusi, Beatrice's fiancé
Two porters
Two waiters
Servants
Musicians

Seven Year Itch, The
George Axelrod
Comedy 3 Acts
New York 1952

Richard Sherman is thirty-eight, vice-president of a book publishing company, a compulsive fantasist, and lives in a Manhattan apartment. He has been married for seven years to Helen, who is away for the summer with son Ricky. One evening he is out on the balcony, listening to the sports, fantasizing about women, and trying not to smoke when suddenly a heavy iron pot containing a tomato plant falls from the balcony above and almost kills him, giving him the chance to meet the apartment's occupant, a vivacious young woman.

For the next few days there is an on-off-on flirtation between them, interrupted by Richard's business meetings with zany psychiatrist Dr Brubaker whose book he is publishing, and also by his own fantasies about Helen and her friend Tom Mackenzie. He spends a night with the girl and next morning is consumed with guilt and worry. But the girl is cool; they say goodbye and it is all over. He realizes how much he loves Helen, and when Tom Mackenzie arrives to collect a skirt for her that Richard forgot to send, he insults the hapless Tom and decides to take her the skirt himself.

Richard Sherman   *Richard's voice*
Ricky   *The girl's voice*
Helen Sherman
Miss Morris
Elaine
Pat
Marie
The girl
Dr Brubaker
Tom Mackenzie

1776
Peter Stone and Sherman Edwards
Musical 1 Act
New York 1969

The play follows the manoeuverings of the two main blocs in the Second Continental Congress which is debating the proposal that the thirteen American colonies should, in this year 1776, declare their independence from Great Britain.

Instead of the dignified unanimity on the question which is taught to American schoolchildren, we see the intense in-fighting between the pro- and anti-factions, much of it based on divergent self-interest. The great champion of independence, John Adams of Massachusetts, so annoys the other delegates with his relentless carping on the issue that he endangers the whole movement; although he has the support of eminent colonists like Dr Benjamin Franklin.

To pacify the 'anti' faction, and to stall for time, Franklin proposes that a declaration should be written, clearly putting the case for independence, opening the issue for full, detailed debate. The job of drafting the declaration is given to Thomas Jefferson, who includes in it a call for the abolition of slavery, and is supported by the fiery Adams. This proposal threatens the entire enterprise, since it is vigorously opposed by the southern colonies with their slave economy. At Franklin's urging, the clauses on slavery are deleted, and the Declaration of Independence unanimously agreed by the Congress, while, in New York, Gen. Washington prepares to meet the British forces of Gen. Howe who have been sent to crush the revolutionary army.

Songs include: 'Sit Down John'; 'The Lees of Old Virginia'; 'Yours, Yours, Yours'

Delegates to the Second Continental Congress:
President John Hancock, Dr Josiah Bartlett, John
Adams, Stephen Hopkins, Roger Sherman, Lewis
Morris, Robert Livingston, Revd Jonathan
Witherspoon, Dr Benjamin Franklin, John
Dickinson, James Wilson, Caesar Rodney,
Col Thomas McKean, George Read, Samuel Chase,
Richard Henry Lee, Thomas Jefferson, Joseph
Hewes, Edward Rutledge, Dr Lyman Hall
Congressional Secretary Charles Thomson
Congressional Custodian Andrew McNair
A Leather Apron
Courier
Abigail Adams
Martha Jefferson

Seventh Heaven
Austin Strong
Drama 3 Acts
New York 1922

Orphaned sisters Nana and Diane are two of the shady inhabitants of the low-life Paris cul-de-sac known as 'the hole in the sock'. Bullying Nana forces Diane to trade stolen trinkets to satisfy her absinthe habit, but when their puritan uncle Georges appears and offers them a home and money, Diane tells him the truth about their criminal life and he rejects them. The furious Nana savagely attacks Diane, but she is rescued by dashing sewer-worker Chico. Later that day when the police come to arrest Diane for theft, Chico claims she is his wife and takes her off to his attic flat. They fall in love and for a few days are blissfully happy, and Chico manages to imbue Diane with some of his own courage; he considers himself 'someone special' and is a self-proclaimed athiest.

Then World War One breaks out and Chico is conscripted. Diane endures great hardship but with the courage she has learned from Chico she finally stands up to Nana. Then the war ends; there is no word from Chico and she loses her sustaining faith in 'the Bon Dieu'. But when Chico reappears, severely wounded and blinded, the miracle of his return has convinced him of the existence of 'the Bon Dieu', and Diane, too, has her faith restored.

Boul	*Blonde*
The rat	*Père Chevillon*
Arlette	*Sergeant of Police*
Maximilian Gobin	*Uncle Georges*
Nana	*Aunt Valentine*
Recan	*Chico*
Diane	*Lamplighter*
Brissac	

Severed Head, A
Iris Murdoch and J.B. Priestley
Drama 3 Acts
Bristol 1963

Wine merchant Martin Lynch-Gibbon is married to the voluptuous Antonia but having an affair with young university lecturer Georgie Hands. She is unhappy with the furtiveness of the affair, especially when Martin's hole-and-corner attitude persists even after Antonia tells Martin she wants a divorce. Antonia is crazy about her psychoanalyst, Martin's friend Palmer Anderson, but the pair of them seem somehow to need Martin's approval for their match. They become most upset when Palmer's half-sister, anthropologist Honor Klein, discovers Martin's affair with Georgie and reveals it. This, they feel, is not playing the game with sufficient 'openness'. With the arrival of Alexander, Martin's attractive sculptor brother, events speed up to an almost farce-like pace; almost everybody has an affair with almost everybody else, not excluding a touch of incest, and by the end of the play Antonia is with Alexander, Palmer in New York with Georgie, and Martin, surprisingly, with Honor.

Martin Lynch-Gibbon	*Rosemary, Martin's sister*
Georgie Hands	*Alexander*
Palmer Anderson	*Honor Klein*
Antonia	

Shadow of a Gunman, The
Sean O'Casey
Drama 2 Acts
Dublin 1925

Donal Davoren, an ineffectual young poet, and Seumus Shields, a pedlar in cheap goods, share a tenement basement in Dublin in 1920 during 'the troubles'. The local residents, including landlord Mr Mulligan and attractive and self-confident young Minnie Powell, believe that Davoren is an IRA gunman on the run and they treat him like a hero. Timid neighbour Mr Gallagher, assisted by hefty Mrs Henderson even presents Davoren with a letter petitioning the IRA to do something about his foul-mouthed neighbours. One morning, Shields' fellow-pedlar Mr Maguire rushes in and leaves his case of samples and then rushes out. Later that day they learn he was an IRA man and has been shot. When the British army raids the house that night, Davoren and Shields discover Maguire's case is full of bombs. Both are paralysed with fear, but plucky Minnie, who is sweet on Davoren, takes the case to hide in her room. She is caught and when the army lorry she is in is ambushed by the IRA, Minnie tries to escape, shouting 'Up the republic!' But she is shot dead ... a real hero.

Donal Davoren	*Mr Mulligan*
Seumus Shields	*Mr Maguire*
Tommy Owens	*Mrs Henderson*
Adolphus Grigson	*Mr Gallagher*
Mrs Grigson	*An auxiliary*
Minnie Powell	

Shadow Play
Noël Coward
Play 1 Act
London 1935

See: *Tonight at 8.30*

Shawl, The
David Mamet
Drama 4 Acts
Chicago 1985

A seedy, apparently bogus clairvoyant, John, sits interviewing Miss A., a prospective client, observed by his assistant Charles. By what appear to be clever, oblique suggestions, John elicits from the girl enough information to locate her area of concern - the disposition of her dead mother's estate. When the girl leaves, John discusses his technique with Charles, who is impatient to begin fleecing her, and they agree to try to coax money out of her at their next session.

Miss A. returns, and once again John manages to provide enough intimate details about the girl's life seemingly to impress her greatly. But when he moves on to the subject of payment, the girl laughs in his face and points out that the picture of her 'mother' on which his pronouncements are based is one she cut randomly out of a magazine. To the girl's astonishment, though, John then pours out a mass of detail about her mother which culminates in the revelation that Miss A. had five years past burnt a red shawl belonging to her mother, in a fury of resentment.

Charles
Miss A
John

She Stoops to Conquer
Oliver Goldsmith
Comedy 5 Acts
London 1773

Mr Hardcastle and his old friend Sir Charles Marlowe have high hopes of a match between young Marlowe and Hardcastle's daughter Kate. Young Marlowe sets off to meet Kate together with his friend Hastings, but they lose their way and stray into a tavern where Hardcastle's boorish stepson Tony Lumpkin sends them to the nearest inn, actually the Hardcastle residence.

All hell breaks loose as Marlowe and Hastings treat Hardcastle as an innkeeper, while he in turn is outraged and baffled at their behaviour. Marlowe is painfully shy with women of his own class but has no such inhibitions with serving wenches and, mistakenly believing Kate to be a maid, proceeds to court her avidly. At the same time, Hastings pursues Kate's cousin Constance whom Tony's doting mother Mrs Hardcastle intends for her reluctant son. All misunderstandings are cleared up by the arrival of Sir Charles, much to his son's embarrassment, and when devious Lumpkin tells his outraged mother he does not intend to marry Constance, the way is open for the two pairs of lovers to wed.

Mr Hardcastle
Tony Lumpkin
Hastings
Marlowe
Sir Charles Marlowe
Diggory
Roger
Four servants
Jeremy, Marlowe's servant
Landlord of the inn
Four fellows
Mrs Hardcastle
Miss Kate Hardcastle
Miss Constance Neville
Pimple, Miss Hardcastle's maid

Shop at Sly Corner, The
Edward Percy
Drama 3 Acts
London 1945

Descius Heiss is a middle-aged European *émigré* who runs an antique/curio shop. He lives with his sister Mathilde Heiss and his beloved daughter Margaret. After a visit by burglar Corder Morris, Heiss' slimy young assistant Archie discovers his employer is not only a receiver of stolen property, a fence, but has a

foreign criminal record including a charge of murder. He blackmails Heiss but goes too far in demanding marriage with Margaret, who is already engaged to ship's doctor Robert Graham. Heiss attempts to kill Archie with a blow-pipe and poison darts, left by Graham after a recent voyage, but fails; instead he throttles him and together with Morris dumps the body. As the police investigations continue, Robert discovers the truth, but Heiss is relieved that he still intends to wed Margaret. When, unexpectedly, the police inspector returns, Heiss believes he has been discovered and pierces himself with the other poison dart. Just before he dies he realizes the policeman had returned merely to buy a suit of armour. Margaret returns and sees her dead father, but at least will never know his secrets.

Descius Heiss	*Mrs Catt*
Archie Fellowes	*Robert Graham*
Margaret Heiss	*Corder Morris*
Joan Deal	*Steve Hubbard*
Mathilde Heiss	*John Elliot*

Show Boat
Oscar Hammerstein
Music by Jerome Kern
Musical Play 2 Acts
New York 1927

This story starts in the 1880s on one of the many American riverboats that featured travelling shows. It follows the lives and loves of the troupe that work aboard the *Cotton Blossom* under the command of Cap'n Andy and his wife Parthy. In Natchez they come up against racial prejudice when the sheriff discovers that the leading lady, Julie, is a half-caste and he does not allow 'mixed shows' in his town. The Captain's daughter, Magnolia, steps in to save the show along with her love, handsome gambler Gaylord Ravenal, who also has problems with the sheriff. The lovers marry and go to live in Chicago, where they are happy for a few years until Gaylord's gambling losses makes him desert his wife and their daughter Kim. But two old showboat troupers, Ellie and Frank, who have become successful, turn up and save the day by getting Magnolia a job as a singer at the Trocadero to replace the now boozy old Julie (who sacrifices her position).

Years later, both Magnolia and Kim are radio stars, and when Cap'n Andy organizes a reunion of the old team on board the *Cotton Blossom* and invites them, it is of course the ideal opportunity for them to be reunited with the now reformed Gaylord. Frank and Ellie stop off to greet their old colleagues on route to Hollywood. Songs include: 'Ol' Man River'; 'Can't Help Lovin' That Man'; 'Why Do I Love You'; 'Bill'; 'Only Make Believe'

Windy	*Cap'n Andy*
Steve	*Ellie*
Pete	*Frank*
Queenie	*Rubber Face*
Parthy Ann Hawks	*Julie*

Gaylord Ravenal
Vallon
Magnolia
Joe
Faro dealer
Gambler
Backwoodsman
Jeb
Three barkers
Old sport
Landlady

Ethel
Jake
Announcer at Trocadero
Lottie
Kim
Drunks
Children
Men

Show-off, The
George Kelly
Comedy 3 Acts
New York 1924

It is a true love-match between Amy Fisher and Aubrey Piper, but her parents cannot stand him. He is a 'character': an impulsive liar, a braggart, a dreamer and laughs too heartily at his own often bad jokes. Notwithstanding his lowly clerical position, the couple marry, but when demolition threatens their cheap rooms they must find other accommodation. Then Aubrey borrows a car, injures a policeman, and is fined 1,000 dollars, which is paid by his brother-in-law Frank Hyland, married to Amy's sister Clara. Frank likes Aubrey and Clara is beginning to come around, but when Mr Fisher dies, Aubrey and Amy move in, much to Mrs Fisher's disgust. When younger brother Joe, an engineer, tries to market his invention (with which Aubrey has inadvertently helped), Aubrey brazenly tackles the lawyers about the contract and succeeds in getting Joe's advances doubled with better royalties. Joe offers money to Aubrey, who grandly tells him to give it to Mrs Fisher, who, silently fuming, is forced to keep her peace, while Amy gazes admiringly at wonderful Aubrey.

Clara
Mrs Fisher
Amy
Frank Hyland
Mr Fisher
Joe
Aubrey Piper
Mr Gill
Mr Rogers

Shrivings
Peter Shaffer
Drama 3 Acts
London 1970

Shaffer has said of this play that it is his attempt to deal with the politically-inspired violence of the late-sixties.

Shrivings is the home of Gideon Petrie, a world-famous pacifist philosopher and ascetic. Gideon sees Shrivings as a sanctuary which extends a welcome to all. His central beliefs are challenged by the arrival of his former pupil and friend, Mark Askelon, a poet celebrated for his work and notorious for his intemperance and violence. Mark inveigles Gideon and the Shrivings' other guests, including his own son David, into a game designed to goad Gideon into violence. He finally succeeds after exposing Gideon's character and beliefs to ruthless abuse during a weekend of drunken persecution. Gideon ends up shorn of belief and Mark plunged into self-loathing.

Gideon, President - World League of Peace
Lois Neal, Gideon's secretary
Mark Askelon, poet and former pupil of Gideon's
David Askelon, Mark's son and Gideon's lover

Shut Your Eyes and Think of England
John Chapman and Anthony Marriott
Farce 2 Acts
London 1977

When accountant Arthur Pullen catches his City investment firm's chairman Sir Justin Holbrook with call-girl Stella, farcical repercussions proliferate. Holbrook soon collapses and stays gaga throughout, and when senior civil servant Sir Frederick Goudhurst turns up to warn of the impending arrival of Sheik Marami, Pullen is forced to impersonate Holbrook for the good of his country. Unless the Sheik does a deal with Holbrook Investments, he will pull his millions out of the City, so will all the other Arabs, and Britain will collapse. The Sheik arrives and so does Lady Holbrook, followed by Mrs Pullen, and the Sheik mistakenly believes Holbrook (Pullen) is gay, resulting in much limp-wristing. The Sheik also fancies Mrs Pullen and much to her delight she is thrown in with the deal, and Pullen is left with the lovely Lady Holbrook.

Sir Justin Holbrook
Stella Richards
Arthur Pullen
Lady Holbrook
The Rt Hon. Sir Frederick Goudhurst
His Highness Sheik Marami
Mrs Joyce Pullen
Mr Rubenstein
Dr Vornish

Siegfried
Jean Giradoux
Drama 4 Acts
Paris 1928

In this drama of ideas, Giraudoux explores the fascinated antagonism which, he believes, rules relations between France and Germany.

A French poet, Jacques Forestier, has received a head wound, which has left him amnesiac, while serving against the Germans in the Great War. He is mistaken for a German, Siegfried, nursed back to health in a German hospital, and sets out after his convalesence on a political career which sees him rise to be the German Secretary of State in just seven years. Along the way he has come to personify everything German for the common people.

One of his political opponents, Baron Von Zelten, discovers Siegried's true identity and enlists the help of Forestier's former fiancée, Genevieve, to break down his amnesia. She slowly manages to spur Siegfried's memory of being Forestier, and he resigns all his German posts to return to France, reluctantly abandoning his adopted home to the political chaos which he alone had the charismatic authority to control.

Genevieve	*Muck*
Eva	*A Schupo*
Frau Patchkoffer	*Kratz*
Frau Hoepfl	*Meyr*
Siegfried (Forestier)	*Herr Schmitt*
Baron Von Zelton	*Herr Patchkoffer*
Robineau	*Herr Keller*
Gen. de Fontgeloy	*Segt of the Schupos*
Gen.Von Waldorf	*Schuman*
Gen. Leduiger	*A servant*
Pietri	

Silver Tassie, The
Sean O'Casey
Tragi-Comedy 4 Acts
London 1928

Two close friends, Harry Heegan and Barney Bagnal, along with their Avondale neighbour Teddy Foran, return home for a few days' leave from duty on the Western Front in the Great War. Harry leads the local football team to their third local Cup win in as many years, and then races with Barney to pack for the ship back to France.

The Front is full of the horrors and waste of war, and Harry receives a crippling wound. He is saved from death only by Barney's heroism in carrying him back to their lines while under fire. When Harry's girlfriend Jessie, a feckless, self-indulgent girl, realizes Harry's condition, she switches her affection to Barney, and Harry's hopes for the future are thus destroyed, and he sinks into rancour. As a last desperate show of strength, Harry mangles the Cup, the Silver Tassie, which his now-vanished prowess had won for the local team.

Sylvester Heegan	*Two casualties*
Mrs Heegan, his wife	*Surgeon Forby Maxwell*
Simon Norton	*The ward sister*
Susie Monican, a nurse	
Mrs Foran	
Teddy Foran	
Harry Heegan	
Jessie Taite	
Barney Bagnal, Harry's friend	
The croucher	
Four soldiers	
The corporal	
The visitor	
The staff wallah	
Two stretcher-bearers	

Simon and Laura
Alan Melville
Comedy 3 Acts
London 1954

Simon Foster and his wife Laura, both of them actors, are on the point of permanently breaking up when they are offered the lead roles in a pseudo-documentary television series in which they are to play a blissfully happy married couple. They take the jobs out of sheer financial need and despite their continued off-screen bickering, turn the series into a hit.

On the night of the series' two hundredth broadcast, though, while the cast and crew begin preparations for a celebration, Laura, furious that Simon has been seen with their scriptwriter, Janet Honeyman, on a dirty weekend, departs from the script to hurl abuse at him. Fortunately, her outburst is cut short by a power failure, but she leaves Simon anyway when he provokes a fight with their producer, David Prentice, claiming that Prentice and Laura have been having an affair.

The following day, when Laura is not back for rehearsals, it seems to the rest of the cast and crew that they must somehow reconcile the two stars or face the end of their own jobs. Wilson, their real-life butler, and the butler in the series, arranges with the help of Timothy, who plays their orphaned nephew, secretly to record each of the two stars in conversation about the other. Both fall into the trap and separately reveal that, despite their constant rows they are still very much in love. To the chagrin, but benefit, of both, the tapes are then played to the whole crew, harmony is restored, and the series goes happily on.

Simon Foster, an actor
Laura Foster, his wife, an actress
Wilson, their butler
Jessie
Mr Wolfstein, their agent
David Prentice, their producer
Janet Honeyman, their scriptwriter
Timothy, their co-star
Barney
Joe
Bert
Miss Mills
Mabel
Archie

Simple Spymen
John Chapman
Comedy 3 Acts
London 1958

A group of incompetent War Office counter-espionage specialists, led by their hare-brained Col Gray-Balding, mistakenly send a pair of down-at-heel street singers, George Chuffer and Percy Pringle, on an assignment working undercover in Dover.

The 'spies' are meant to intercept a M. Grobchick whose latest invention, an Atomic Pile restorer, the

War Office is very keen to acquire. Percy and George face keen competition from a gang of foreign spies led by Max, a brutal killer and skilled espionage specialist. Led by George, whose bravado is equalled only by his bungling, the two men so thoroughly disorientate their opponents that they eventually win the day, and recover the Atomic Pile restorer for HM Government.

Unfortunately for all concerned, the restorer has nothing to do with atomic weapons, but is instead a patented mixture for restoring carpet pile.

Cpl Flight
Lieut Fosgrove
Col Gray-Balding
Mr Forester Stand
George Chuffer, a street singer
Percy Pringle, a street singer
Mrs Byng
Smogs
Max, a foreign spy
Crab, a trained killer
Mr Grobchick, an inventor

Sisterly Feelings
Alan Ayckbourn
Comedy 2 Acts
Scarborough 1980

On a damp day in February after the funeral of his wife Amy, Dr Ralph Matthews drags his unwilling family and mourners to the remote corner of Pendon where he proposed to her. Ralph's son Melvyn is smitten with seemingly-daft Brenda, but her brother, handsome athletic Simon, is fancied by both Ralph's daughters, unmarried Dorcas, and Abigail, married to Patrick. When Patrick leaves early for a business meeting, there is not enough room for all the mourners in one car, so one of the sisters must walk back with Simon. They toss a coin, and the alternative possibilities of either Dorcas or Abigail going with Simon are intriguingly explored in two separate scenes. Complications arise when Dorcas' poet boyfriend Stafford still pursues her, and her deliberate choice at a picnic between Simon and Stafford determines the parallel set of possibilities in the next two scenes; a farcical camping sojourn for Abigail, or an involvement in a long-distance race for Dorcas. Eventually the status quo is resumed, with the play ending in the wedding of Melvyn and Brenda.

Dr Ralph Matthews
Len Coker
Rita Coker
Abigail Smythe
Patrick Smythe
Dorcas Matthews
Melvyn Matthews
Brenda Grimshaw
Simon Grimshaw
Stafford Wilkins
Murphy
Maj. Lidgett

Six Characters in Search of an Author
Luigi Pirandello
Tragedy 3 Acts,
Rome 1921

As the producer and his cast are rehearsing the second act of Pirandello's hit play *Rules of the Game* they are interrupted when six strange personages enter the theatre and tell the producer they are looking for an author. They proceed to explain and act out for the increasingly indulgent producer and the astonished actors their own personal drama.

In this drama, the father, who has been separated from his former family for many years, is reunited with his stepdaughter, at a brothel. Realizing the desperate situation the family are in, he takes them back, but later the silent little girl is drowned while the silent little boy looks on, and then shoots his older stepbrother. During this exposition, the grotesque brothel-keeper Mme Pace is 'called into being' and the mother remains eternally suffering and downtrodden. The producer is so impressed he decides to work on this story at once, and have his own cast play the part of each character. Naturally, the characters complain that the actors are far less realistic than themselves, and at the end of the day the producer and the actors go home, but the characters remain, frozen forever in their roles.

The father
The mother
The stepdaughter
The son
The boy
The little girl
Mme Pace
The producer
The leading lady
The commissionaire
The leading man
The second female lead

The ingénue
The juvenile lead
Other actors and
actresses
The stage manager
The prompter
The property man
The foreman of the stage
crew
The producer's secretary
Stagehands

Skin Game, The
John Galsworthy
Drama 3 Acts
London 1920

Squire Hillcrist is most conscious of his position as a civilized member of the gentry and consequently contemptuous of his neighbour, the blustering self-made industrialist Hornblower. When, against their verbal agreement, Hornblower evicts the tenants from cottages bought from Hillcrist, the two men meet and snooty Mrs Hillcrist enrages Hornblower by snubbing his daughter-in-law Chloe. Hornblower then threatens to buy the land overlooking the Hillcrist house and build clay kilns with chimneys.

From here on it is 'the skin game', fighting with the gloves off. Hornblower buys the land at an inflated price at an auction, but meanwhile Hillcrist's agent, Dawker, digs up some dirt on Chloe; she used to be a 'professional co-respondent'. Hillcrist is reluctant to use blackmail but his wife insists. Upon hearing the information Hornblower caves in and agrees to sell the land to Hillcrist at a loss, and reinstate the tenants, providing the secret is kept. But Chloe's husband Charles smells a rat and bullies Dawker into revealing the secret, resulting in the pregnant Chloe attempting suicide and the break-up of their marriage. Hillcrist has won, but is deeply ashamed. When it came to the crunch, he abandoned his life-long principles.

Hillcrist, a country gentleman
Amy, his wife
Jill, his daughter
Dawker, his agent
Hornblower, a man newly-rich
Charles, his elder son
Chloe, wife to Charles
Rolf, Charles' younger son
Fellows, Hillcrist's butler
Anna, Chloe's maid
The Jackmans, man and wife
An auctioneer
A solicitor
Two strangers

Skin of our Teeth, The
Thornton Wilder
Comedy 3 Acts
New York 1942

The Antrobus family, along with their maid, are meant to be Everyman figures in a play which uses anachronism as the basis of its humour. George and Maggie, the mother, live in a town in New Jersey, USA and go through all the trials attributed variously to Adam and Eve, Noah, and so on, up to suffering as victims of the Napoleonic wars. Mr Antrobus doggedly pursues the improvement of the race by inventing the wheel, the alphabet and higher mathematics, all the while enduring his son Henry's growing animosity. Maggie, for her part, is left to fend for the family when Henry's projects keep him away from home. During the Ice Age, for example, she and her brood are reduced to burning the household furniture to stay warm. Again when Antrobus is made President of the Order of Mammals, Maggie and the family must follow him on his political rounds.

The play ends in modern times with the maid sitting, as she has immemorially, waiting for Antrobus to get home from work.

Announcer
Sabina, Antrobus' maid
Mrs Antrobus
Gladys, Antrobus'
  daughter
Henry, Antrobus' son
Mr Antrobus
Fortune teller
Mr Fitzpatrick
Dinosaur
Mammoth
Telegraph boy
Doctor
Professor
Judge Homer
Miss E. Muse
Miss T. Muse
Miss M. Muse
Two ushers
Two drum majorettes

Two chair pushers
Five convention
  delegates
Broadcast official
Defeated candidate
Mr Tremayne
Hester
Ivy
Fred Bailey

Skirmishes
Catherine Hayes
Drama 1 Act
Liverpool 1981

Rita returns home to be with her mother, who is on the point of dying from a stroke. She and her sister Jean, who has been nursing Mother for some months, argue bitterly over their responsibilities toward the dying woman, Jean resentful that the hard slog of caring and nursing has fallen on her, Rita incensed that Mother's large house has been left to her sister.

The old woman spends most of her time unconscious, waking slightly only when the bickering between her two daughters is at its worst. They rehearse all the squabbles of their past, within the framework of Jean's barrenness and Rita's good fortune in having two children and a loving husband, and reach a peak of mutual vindictiveness just as Mother breathes her last.

Jean
Rita
Mother

Slab Boys, The
John Byrne
Comedy 2 Acts
Edinburgh 1978

The Slab Boys - Phil McCann, Spanky Farrell, Hector McKenzie and Alan Downie, a new employee - are all none too hard at work mixing the colours for their designer colleagues at a carpet manufacturers' on a winter Friday afternoon in the fifties. They are all, as well, looking forward to the staff dance that same night.

McCann and Farrell, the wise-cracking, utterly irreverent senior boys, decide to spruce up Hector's outmoded style of dress, so that he can make a date for the dance with Lucille Bentley, a buxom sketch artist in the design department. Hector resists the plan, so the much larger McCann drags him off to the toilets, makes him submit to a haircut during which Hector's ear is badly lacerated, and leaves him waiting, naked but for his underwear while his clothes are re-styled by the sewing machine operators. Crudely bandaged and freezing, the hapless Hector makes his way stealthily back to the slab room, where Lucille sees him through the window and thinks he is a monster - so foul has McCann left his appearance.

With Downie's unwilling help, McCann and Farrell hide Hector in a closet while the restyling of his clothes is completed, but Hector keeps popping out each time Lucille enters the slab room, and only barely escapes detection several times.

As the working day draws to a close, McCann is

sacked for consistent malingering, and it appears that Hector will be joining him in the dole queue. Ironically, though, Hector is promoted to the design room and given a large pay rise, thus easing his pain when it becomes clear that Downie has managed to get Lucille to accompany him to the dance instead. Farrell becomes the senior slab boy, and McCann is left the odd man out with nothing to sustain him but his great self-belief and the hope that he will be accepted into art school.

The Slab Boys: Phil McCann, George 'Spanky'
  Farrell, Hector McKenzie
Jack Hogg, a designer
Lucille Bentley, a sketch artist
Alan Downie, a new slab boy
Willie Curry, the manager of design
Sadie, the tea lady

Sleuth
Anthony Shaffer
Drama 2 Acts
London 1970

Andrew Wyke is a successful middle-aged writer of detective fiction and lives, appropriately, in a Norman manor house in Wiltshire surrounded by his impressive collection of games and toys. He is a cynic and games player, and when his wife Marguerite's lover Milo Tindle visits him in order to clarify their relationships (Milo and Marguerite wish to marry), Wyke plays a game. Knowing Milo is broke and Marguerite is extravagant, Wyke persuades Tindle to burgle her jewels; thus, explains Wyke, Tindle gets the jewels which he can sell, and Wyke gets rid of Marguerite and cops the insurance. Wyke even persuades Tindle to dress as a clown for the event, but then turns the tables and humiliates Tindle, scaring him into a faint. Stung by this humiliation, Tindle returns several days later disguised as a police detective and plays a series of even cleverer games on Wyke. The sexual conflict and jealousy, the racism (Tindle is half-Italian) and the intellectual one-upmanship crystallize at the moment when Wyke shoots and kills Tindle, believing him to be bluffing, then, as he hears the police approaching, realizes he was not.

Andrew Wyke
Milo Tindle
Inspector Doppler
Detective Sergeant Tarrant
Police Constable Higgs

Small Hotel
Rex Frost
Comedy 3 Acts
London 1954

Alan Pryor and his wife Sheila manage The Jolly Fiddler, a small country hotel in the Midlands, for a hotel group. They have just hired a new waitress to assist their ageing but highly professional waiter Albert, of whom they and their customers are very fond. But their area supervisor arrives and insists Albert must retire and be replaced by the bustling, heartlessly efficient Caroline Mallett.

The young assistant gives offence to the hotel's only permanent resident, Mrs Samson-Box, who threatens the hotel with legal action when she catches the girl sipping wine while under age. Miss Mallett so annoys the Pryors that Alan threatens resignation if the supervisor will not relent over Albert's fate.

The old waiter remains calm and cunning throughout and manages to pit the formidable Mrs Samson-Box against both the supervisor and Miss Mallett, at the same time winning the old woman's forgiveness for his hapless young assistant. Albert's position is saved when Mrs Samson-Box outfaces the supervisor and blackmails him into recalling Miss Mallett and reinstating the old man.

Hotel customers: Spencer Crouch, Gladys Spiller,
  Mr Barrington
Alan Pryor, hotel manager
Albert, the waiter
Sheila Pryor, Alan's wife
Mr Finch, Alan's supervisor
Mrs Samson-Box, hotel resident
Effie Rigler, a waitress
Mrs Gammon, hotel cook
Caroline Mallett, a waitress

Smug Citizens, The or Philistines, The
Maxim Gorky
Play 3 acts
Moscow 1902

In a small provincial Russian town at the turn of the century, the middle-class Besemenov family is ruled over with an iron rod by father Vasilevich. A boring and tedious man himself, he nevertheless constantly decries the attitudes of his family, his meek wife, their failed student son, and spinster schoolteacher daughter. Their life is quite unlike the boarders and visitors they have, who are cheerful and optimistic and find the Besemenov's totally negative. Among these are a lively and beautiful young widow of a prison officer (who prefers convicts), a choir singer, and Vasilevich's foster son Nil who has become the fiancé of a poor, but vivacious seamstress rather than marry the schoolteacher daughter, who in desperation tries to commit suicide. Besemenov's intellectual son Pyotr, who is petrified by his father, is in love with the young widow, and she possibly has sufficient spirit to get him to stand up to the tyrant and marry her. The smug Besemenov cannot understand how ungrateful his family can be when he has done so much for them.

Vasily Vasilevich Besemenov, a prosperous house-
  painter
Akulina Ivanovna, his wife
Pyotr, their son, an expelled student
Tatyana, their daughter, a schoolmistress
Nil, their foster son, a train driver

Perchikin, *a relative*
Poyla, *a seamstress*
Yelena Krivtsova, *a prison officer's widow*
Teterev, *a choir singer*
Shishkin, *a lodger*
Tsvetaeva, *a friend of Tatyana*
Stepanida, *cook*
An old woman
A doctor
A young boy

Snow Job, The
George Eastman
and Jack Perry
Comedy 3 Acts
New York 1973

Norman Hammond, a New York advertising copywriter, takes his wife Sally to their New Hampshire cottage retreat for an intimate weekend away from their children prior to his departure for a three-month business trip. Sally has invited their neighbours, Madge and Stanley Miller, to drop by the cottage en route to their own weekend away, further upstate.

To Norman's annoyance, a blizzard traps the Millers overnight, and annoyance turns to fury when, the next morning, Stanley's car breaks down and must be hauled away for repairs. While Sally and Norman are in town, Stanley invites Ernie and Lois Jackson, to whose home he and Madge were bound before the storm, to join them at the Millers. They arrive, along with their house guests Gunther Durgin, a ski bum, and Wendy Forsythe, a beautiful young student, and set about drinking and preparing a meal.

When Norman and Sally return, it is all she can do to prevent her unhappy spouse from throwing everyone out of the house. She persuades Norman that they must offer to put the whole crew up for the night on the grounds that Lois, who has fallen ill, cannot possibly travel. Norman endures yet another night deprived of Sally's favours, for she is too inhibited to make love while they have so many guests.

When, by the next afternoon, their guests are still with them, Norman gets so drunk that he is unable to contemplate driving back to New York. He resolves to stay over Sunday night, but Sally, now thoroughly piqued with his behaviour, leaves for the city with their departing guests.

Just as Norman is tottering off to bed, Wendy returns, having made an excuse to the other guests, and tries to seduce him. He only just manages to refuse her blandishments, but faces terrible embarrassment the next morning when Sally unexpectedly returns to find Wendy preparing breakfast. After some lengthy recriminations, Sally believes Norman's claims of innocence, sends Wendy packing, and announces that she has arranged that they will stay at the cottage, alone, for a full week.
Norman Hammond

Sally Hammond, *Norman's wife*
Bert Sprinker
Madge Miller, Stanley Miller, *the Hammonds'*
  neighbours
Willis Fry
Harold Bartlett
Murph
Vic
The Hammonds' unexpected guests:
Ernie Jackson
Lois Jackson
Gunther Durgin
Wendy Forsythe
Chester Ollander

Solid Gold Cadillac, The
Howard Teichmann
and George S. Kaufman
Comedy 2 Acts
Connecticut 1954

When 'Big Ed' McKeever, hard-working president of General Products Corporation of America, is offered a post in Washington, he sells his shares and quits the company.

The four remaining directors then see a chance to feather their own nests. Unfortunately for them, small stockholder old Mrs Partridge turns up at their first stockholders' meeting and asks awkward questions, especially about the outrageous rise in directors' salaries. They fob her off with a newly-created job, 'stockholder relations', and she sets to work with zeal.

When 'Big Ed' does not wangle them any government work, they send Mrs Partridge to lobby him; the two become friends and she tells Ed that General Products is going down the drain. He returns to the company but the greedy foursome chuck him out - until, that is, he discovers that Mrs Partridge's homely overtures to the shareholders have resulted in them giving her proxy voting for almost the entire company. She is now boss, sacks the greedies and reinstates McKeever. Then, at the next stockholders' meeting, another little old lady begins asking questions ...
T. John Blessington
Alfred Metcalfe
Warren Gillie
Clifford Snell
Mrs Laura Partridge
Miss Amelia Shotgraven
Mark Jenkins
Miss L'Arriere
Edward L. McKeever
Miss Logan
The A.P.
The U.P.
I.N.S.
A little old lady
News broadcasters (three)
The voice

Sound of Music, The

Howard Lindsay, Russell Crouse, Richard
Rodgers and Oscar Hammerstein
Musical 2 Acts
New York 1959

Maria Rainer, a postulant at Nonnberg Abbey in Austria in 1938, is sent by her abbess to act as governess to the seven children of Capt. Georg Von Trapp, a widower deeply grieved at the loss of his wife. The abbess intends that Maria, a very high-spirited girl, should discover by spending time away from the abbey whether or not she is suited to a religious vocation.

Maria's gaiety and love of music soon brings cheer back to the Captain's estate as she uses singing to impart the lessons she feels the children need. Without being quite aware of it, the Captain falls in love with Maria, although he is engaged to Elsa Schraeder, a rich Viennese. When Maria realizes that she has fallen in love with the Captain, she rushes back to the Abbey in confusion, but is sent back to the Von Trapps by the abbess, who realizes that domesticity is the girl's true *métier*.

As the Nazis invade Austria, it becomes clear to Elsa that the Captain will never accommodate the new regime, and she breaks with him out of fear for her position in the Third Reich. The Captain, at last forthcoming with his feelings for Maria, proposes to her. Their honeymoon is cut short by the invasion and on returning home, the Captain finds a virtual press gang of German officers waiting to commission him into the navy.

He, Maria and the children use an appearance at Salzburg Festival of music, where they sing as The Von Trapp Family Singers, to provide cover for their escape over the mountains into Switzerland, and a new life free from the Nazi tyranny.

Songs include: 'The Sound of Music'; 'Climb Every Mountain'; 'My Favourite Things': 'Do Re Mi'

Sister Berthe
Maria Rainer
Sister Sophia
Sister Margaretta
The Mother Abbess
Capt. Georg Von Trapp
Franz, his butler
His children: *Liel, Friedrich,*
Louisa, Kurt, Marta,
Grett and Brigitta
Rolf Gruber
Elsa Schrader, his fiancée
Ursula
Max Detweiler
Baron Elberfeld
Herr Zeller
Baroness Elberfeld
Admiral von Scheiber
Neighbours, nuns, novices, postulants, contestants
in the Salzburg Festival

South Pacific

Joshua Logan and Oscar Hammerstein
Music by Richard Rodgers
Musical Play 2 Acts
New York 1947

On a Pacific island during World War Two ageing Emile de Becque, a widower with two Eurasian children, is attracted to nurse Nellie Forbush. He has reservations when asked by pilot Lieut Joseph Cable to go on a dangerous mission to a nearby Japanese-held island. Cable is romantically involved with an islander Liat, daughter of Bloody Mary, but his natural prejudices emerge which he cannot overcome, despite pleas for racial reconciliation. Becque and Cable go off on the mission and are reported missing. Cable is killed, but Becque manages to return to find Nellie has been caring for his orphaned children and is waiting for him.

Songs include: 'Some Enchanted Evening'; 'Cockeyed Optimist'; 'There is Nothing Like a Dame'; 'I'm Gonna Wash that Man Right Outa My Hair'; 'Younger than Springtime'

Ngana	*Staff Sgt Thomas*
Jerome	*Hassinger*
Henry	*Pte Victor Jerome*
Ensign Nellie Forbush	*Pte Sven Larson*
Emile de Becque	*Lieut Genevieve Marshall*
Bloody Mary	***Ensigns:*** *Lisa Manelli,*
Abner	*Connie Walewska, Janet*
Stewpot	*McGregor, Bessie*
Luther Billis	*Noonan, Pamela*
Professor	*Whitmore, Rita Adams,*
Lieut Joseph Cable	*Sue Yaeger, Betty Pitt,*
USMC	*Cora MacRae, Dinah*
Capt. George Brackett	*Murphy*
USN	*Liat*
Cdr William Harbison	*Marcel*
Yeoman Herbert Quale	*Lieut Buzz Adams*
Sgt Kenneth Johnson	*Islanders*
Seabee Richard West	*Sailors, marines*
Seabee Morton Wise	*Officers*
Seabee Tom O'Brien	
Radio Op., Bob	
McCaffrey	
Cpl Hamilton Steeves	

Spider's Web

Agatha Christie
Drama 3 Acts
London 1954

Diplomatic family the Hailsham-Browns have a cheap lease on Copplestone Court, a large house in Kent. When Henry Hailsham-Brown's imaginative wife Clarissa finds the body of Oliver Costello, dope-dealer husband of Henry's neurotic first wife, she thinks the culprit is her beloved stepdaughter Pippa, who did not want to go back to her mother and Costello. Clarissa cannot call the police because Henry is due back with a VIP, so she persuades three local friends, Sir Roland

Delahaye, Hugo Birch and her admirer Jeremy Warrender, to hide the body in a secret cubby-hole. But someone has called the police, and resident gardener Miss Peake inadvertently shows them the body. Clarissa tells Inspector Lord the truth but he does not believe her, so she lies and confesses self defence, but then the body mysteriously disappears. Who is the real murderer and why? The key to the mystery is an antique desk, and something valuable hidden inside it. Miss Peake, it transpires, is really Mrs Brown, the owner of the house, and she has been using the Hailsham-Brown family as bait to catch the murderer of her antiques partner. Clarissa concludes her real life adventure by helping unmask the real murderer before he has time to smother little Pippa, and by the time hubby Henry returns with his VIP, all is calm again.

Sir Roland Delahaye
Hugo Birch
Jeremy Warrender
Clarissa Hailsham-Brown
Pippa Hailsham-Brown
Mildred Peake
Elgin, the butler
Henry Hailsham-Brown
Inspector Lord
Constable Jones

Spring and Port Wine
Bill Naughton
Comedy 2 Acts
London 1965

The respectable working-class Crompton household is dominated by father Rafe, a benevolent dictator whose family often find it difficult to live up to his high standards. His four children feel humiliated at having to hand over their pay-packets every week; wife Daisy has to resort to fiddling the housekeeping accounts; elder son Harold cannot smoke at home and when younger daughter Hilda refuses to eat a kipper for tea, Rafe insists it be served up for her until she does eat it. This provokes general mutiny among the family and elder sister Florence's boyfriend, Arthur, tells Rafe some home truths before leaving with Florence, who is usually on her dad's side. Even younger son Wilfred decides to leave home after being frightened and humiliated by his father. Rafe relents after seeing the dangers of his rigid attitudes and reveals to Daisy for the first time that it was his own deprived childhood and his mother's sufferings that determined him to make a stable and respectable situation for his own family. For all their conflicts, there is no lack of love in the Crompton family, and when Rafe realizes his mistakes and becomes more tolerant, they are reunited.

Daisy Crompton	*Hilda Crompton*
Florence Crompton	*Rafe Crompton*
Betsy Jane	*Arthur*
Wilfred Crompton	
Harold Crompton	

Stage Struck
Simon Gray
Drama 2 Acts
London 1979

Robert Simon was a first-rate stage manager, but after failing as an actor and writer he now runs a large country house for himself and his successful West End actress wife Anne. Their cottage-tenant, Herman, tells Robert he is having problems with strange girlfriend Griselda, but Robert thinks no more of this when that evening Anne informs him she wants a divorce; her exclusive shrink Widdecombe has put her up to it, citing especially Robert's frequent peccadillos. Next day Robert invites Widdecombe over, and after some terrifying theatricals, fools the analyst into 'killing' him. Anne returns with Herman and the frightened Widdecombe leaves; we realize he is not a shrink but a private detective, and the whole thing was a put-up job by Anne and her lover Herman to get rid of Robert. But Robert has been playing possum and revives; he calls the police and TV news telling them a murder has occurred and with split-second timing arranges for Anne and Herman to kill him moments before the police and TV cameras arrive. This time, however, he really is dead.

Robert
Herman
Anne
Widdecombe

Stags and Hens
Willy Russell
Comedy 2 Acts
Liverpool 1978

On the night before the marriage of working-class Liverpudlians Dave and Linda, his friends and her friends coincidentally arrange to spend their respective stag- and hen- nights at the same seedy dance hall. The action takes place almost entirely in the Ladies' and Gents' toilets, and throughout the play Dave is comatose, his head stuck down a lavatory pan. His friends drink, dance and pull the 'tarts', while Linda's drink, dance, get pulled and get both sentimental and sceptical about marriage. Things go really wrong when Linda's ex-lover Peter turns up. He is now a musician in a successful rock group and when Linda dances with him, the stags and hens are horrified. Dave's tough mate Eddy warns off Peter, but Linda herself is different from the other girls, perhaps not quite so prepared for Liverpool domesticity. The others try to hold her back but she makes a run for it and escapes in Peter's van.

Linda	*Billy*
Maureen	*Kav*
Bernadette	*Eddy*
Carol	*Peter*
Frances	*Roadie*
Dave	
Robbie	

Staircase
Charles Dyer
Drama 2 Acts
London 1966

A lonely, middle-aged homosexual couple, Charles Dyer and Harry C. Leeds, sit in the barber shop they run, and bicker with one another. Charlie, a former actor, is nervously awaiting the arrival of a summons, and takes his nervousness out on Harry by poking merciless fun at him for wearing swathes of bandages on his head to disguise his baldness.

As they argue, it emerges that Charlie has been arrested for grossly importuning while dressed in 'drag' at a seedy club. He worries not just on his own account, but because his daughter, Cassy, whom he has not seen in twenty years and who is unaware of his homosexuality, is expected to arrive that very day for a visit. Charlie sinks further and further into a frenzy of worry, which he relieves by redoubling his taunts at Harry. The strain of trying to calm Charlie eventually affects Harry, who has a fainting fit in their storeroom. When Charlie finds Harry lying on the storeroom floor, he believes his partner has committed suicide, and begins to weep in lonely frustration. But Harry revives and they start their eternal squabbling over again.

Charles Dyer
Harry C. Leeds

State of Siege
Albert Camus
Play 3 Parts
Paris 1948

The Plague, a fat uniformed brutal man, easily takes control of Cadiz, in modern Spain, from its despicable government. His secretary, Death, sets up a vicious structure of power with mass executions, death patrols, crooked elections and propaganda. In change of terror and death, is the nihilistic drunk Nada.

Only one person, a courageous young medical student, Diego, resists this tyranny. He sacrifices his life and happiness with Victoria, his sweetheart, to force the regime of the Plague into retreat. Life and freedom return to the city but the menace of enslavement is always present and must be resisted, constantly.

The Plague	*A fisherman*
The Secretary	*An astrologer*
Nada	*An actor*
Victoria	*A merchant*
The judge	*A priest*
The judge's wife	*A boatman*
The judge's daughter	*Beggars*
Diego	*Guards*
The governor	*Town criers*
The alcalde	
Women of Cadiz	
Men of Cadiz	
An officer	
A herald	

State of the Union
Howard Lindsay and Robert Crouse
Comedy 3 Acts
New York 1945

This post-World War Two political comedy shows Grant Matthews, an airplane manufacturer with a national reputation for integrity, being eased (or shoved) into the post of Republican presidential candidate by smoothly unscrupulous political boss James Conover. Aided by Matthews' mistress, millionaire publisher Kay Thorndyke, and with the help of sympathetic newsman, Spike Macmanus, Conover almost gets Matthews to compromise his principles. Unfortunately for Conover, Matthews must present a united matrimonial front to the nation and thus must be seen with wife Mary although lately their relationship has been somewhat frosty. Of course, Matthews and Mary really still love each other and with her incorruptible support he finally rebels against Conover, culminating in a scene where Mary gets drunk and mouths off against the Republican big-wigs at their party. Grant assures her, 'We've got something great to work for !'

James Conover	*Sam Parrish*
Spike Macmanus	*Swenson*
Kay Thorndyke	*Judge Jefferson Davis*
Grant Matthews	*Alexander*
Norah	*Mrs Alexander*
Mary Matthews	*Jenny*
Stevens	*Mrs Draper*
Bellboy	*Senator Lauterback*
Waiter	

Steaming
Nell Dunn
Drama 2 Acts
London 1981

Six women, including Violet, its custodian, have become very fond of the time they regularly spend in council-run Turkish baths in London's East End. For Josie, a good-time girl, the baths are her only respite from constant man troubles; for Nancy and Jane, they are a haven where their lapsed friendship can be brought back to life; and for Mrs Meadow and Dawn, her backward daughter, they provide the only warm refuge in a life of dire poverty.

The council decides, on a flimsy pretext, that the baths are unsafe and must be shut down prior to being converted into a library. The woman band together, petition the council, and are at last given a hearing where they can make the case against closure. They agree that Josie should present their case, and she grows in stature and confidence under what is, for her, a rare commitment to seeing through her responsibility. Even Dawn, spurred into action by the crisis, delivers a personal plea to the council members, but to no effect. The order for closure is reaffirmed. Instead of meekly complying with the order, the women barricade themselves into the building, determined to resist expulsion at any cost.

Violet, custodian of the baths

Patrons of the baths:

Josie
Mrs Meadow
Dawn
Nancy
Jane
Bill, caretaker of the baths

Stevie
Hugh Whitemore
Drama 2 Acts
London 1977

Set in the sitting-room of a small semi-detached house in Palmers Green, North London, this takes the form of an autobiography of the poet Stevie Smith, told by herself in anecdote, reminiscence and poetry, helped along by her 'Lion Aunt' with whom she lived, and, offstage, The Man, representing several characters in her life, and also commenting on certain events. Her childhood, her schooldays, her work, her brief romances, her suicide attempt, her successes: all are told with a unique mixture of humour and pathos, interspersed with revealing comments about the nature of her poetry and her tragi-comic attitude towards life. The action takes place in the fifties and sixties and contains some of her most famous poems.

Stevie
Lion Aunt
The man

Still Life
Noël Coward
Play 1 Act
London 1935
See: *Tonight at 8.30*

Strange Interlude
Eugene O'Neill
Play 9 Acts
New York 1928

After World War One, Nina Leeds bitterly resents her father, Professor Henry Leeds, for not allowing her to marry her sportsman, and war-hero fiancé Gordon Shaw. She becomes a nurse in a hospital for crippled soldiers and covers her sorrow by excessive promiscuity with the patients, but later marries ineffectual Sam Evans hoping for a stable marriage and children. However, her joy of becoming pregnant is shortlived for her mother-in-law tells her of insanity in the family and insists she has an abortion. Dr Edmund Darrell becomes her lover and she has his child, Gordon, which she convinces Evans is his. Although happy as a mother, Nina still longs for her old lover, who is in Europe, but when he returns she will not break up her happy home for him.

As the young Gordon grows up, he comes to resent the attention his mother gets from Darrell, while she is growing to hate Evans, now a successful businessman. Evans dies and Gordon leaves to get married. Nina refuses to marry Darrell and settles for an old friend of her father, Charles Marsden who has admired her from afar for years.

Charles Marsden
Professor Henry Leeds
Nina Leeds, his daughter
Edmund Darrell
Sam Evans
Mrs Amos Evans, Sam's mother
Gordon Evans
Madeline Arnold

Street Scene
Elmer Rice
Play 3 Acts
New York 1929

In a New York tenement of the 1920 families of many ethnic and national groups, Germans, Italians, Swedes, Jewish and Irish, chat and argue on a hot summer night. They are mainly gossiping about the extramarital affair of Irish Anna Maurrant, but they are equally disapproving of her daughter Rose's romance with Jewish boy Sam Kaplan, a law student. Rose is also courted by a rich businessman, but all she really wants is to get away from the city slums and start a new life.

Returning unexpectedly, Frank Maurrant discovers his wife with her lover and shoots them both. Although he escapes briefly, he is soon arrested and as he bids farewell he pleads with Rose to look after her young brother. Sam offers to give up college to marry Rose, but she declines and leaves him heartbroken as she heads for a new life with her brother.

The cynical neighbours suspect that she will be looked after by her rich admirer. A couple enquire about the now empty apartment.

Abraham Kaplan	*Rose Maurrant*
Greta Fiorentino	*Harry Easter*
Emma Jones	*Mae Jones*
Olga Olsen	*Dick McGann*
Willie Maurrant	*Vincent Jones*
Anna Maurrant	*Dr John Wilson*
Daniel Buchanan	*Officer Harry Murphy*
Frank Maurrant	*A milkman*
George Jones	*A letter-carrier*
Steve Sankey	*An ice-man*
Agnes Cushing	*Two college girls*
Carl Olsen	*A music student*
Shirley Kaplan	*Marshal James Henry*
Filippa Fiorentino	*Fred Cullen*
Alice Simpson	*An old-clothes man*
Laura Hildebrand	
Mary Hildebrand	
Charlie Hildebrand	
Samuel Kaplan (Sam)	

Streetcar Named Desire, A
Tennessee Williams
Tragedy 11 Scenes
New York 1947

Blanche DuBois, genteel and highly strung, is at the end of a sordid downhill path and comes to live with her sister Stella and husband Stanley Kowalski in New Orleans. The sisters are from a refined plantation family and have had an educated upbringing; Blanche vainly holds on to their old values and attitudes, while Stella has adapted to a new way of life. Blanche is openly critical of Stella's marriage, considering Stanley coarse and brutish, and is contemptuous of his virile attractions. When she finds a last chance for happiness with Stanley's friend Mitch, Stanley uncovers the details of Blanche's past life and uses this knowledge to destroy her. Our sympathies are divided, and although we understand Stanley's blunt expediency, there is a heroism in Blanche's uncompromising sensitivity that excites admiration and compassion.

Blanche DuBois, a faded Southern belle
Stella Kowalski, Blanche's sister
Stanley Kowalski, Stella's husband
Harold (Mitch) Mitchell, Stanley's friend
Eunice Hubbel, landlady
Steve Hubbel, husband
Pablo Gonzales, Stanley's friend
Negro woman
Doctor
Nurse
A young collector
A Mexican woman
A tamale vendor

Strictly Dishonourable
Preston Sturges
Comedy 3 Acts
New York 1929

A conventional young couple, Henry Greene and Isabelle Parry, who are engaged to be married, arrive at a New York City speakeasy for a Saturday night drink. The pair are not yet married, and Henry's somewhat pious temperament takes offence at the rather sleazy atmosphere. Isabelle, though, decides she loves the place and, to Henry's growing annoyance, settles down for a few drinks and a chat with the owner, Tomasso, and one of his regulars, Judge Dempsey.

When Henry is called by a policeman to move his car, which is parked blocking a fire hydrant, Isabelle falls into conversation with a new arrival, a handsome opera singer called Count di Ruvo who is a friend of Tomasso's and of the judge. On his return, Henry is furiously jealous and demands that Isabelle leave with him immediately. She refuses, and Henry storms off without her. Her interest in di Ruvo has become noticeably intense, and even when a policeman arrives, sent by Henry with the claim that she is being held against her will, she still refuses to leave and retires instead to the Count's apartment.

There she is faced with the di Ruvo seduction technique, but just as he is on the point of having his way with her, di Ruvo realizes he has fallen in love and leaves her alone to spend a chaste night with his friend Dempsey. The next day, Henry returns full of apologies, but the Count wins Isabelle's hand instead, and Henry is left to rue his loss.

Giovanni
Mario
Tomasso Antiovi, speakeasy owner
Judge Dempsey, his regular patron
Henry Greene
Isabelle Parry, Henry's fiancée
Count di Ruvo
Patrolman Mulligan

Strife
John Galsworthy
Drama 3 Acts
London 1909

In a little Welsh village at the turn of the century, there is a long-running strike at the Trenartha Tin Plate Works. Fiercely capitalist chairman and firm's founder John Anthony will not give in, despite substantial losses in revenue and share value, as well as the emotional pressures from incredible hardship suffered by the workforce - especially by their women and children. Led by impassioned firebrand Roberts, the men have even gone against their union; their cause seems just, and like Anthony, Roberts will not compromise, neither with the firm nor the union.

The firm's directors come up from London in a final desperate attempt to stop the strike, but both Anthony and Roberts remain implacable. But when Roberts' wife Annie dies of cold and malnutrition, the weary men take advantage of his brief absence to effect a compromise deal through union negotiator Harness; the board of directors accept it but in doing so have to force Anthony to resign. In the final scene the two strongest men, both broken, acknowledge their respect towards each other.

John Anthony, Chairman of the Trenarth Tin Plate
  Works
Directors: *Edgar Anthony, Frederick H. Wilder*
  and William Scantlebury
Oliver Wanklin
Henry Tench, secretary
Francis Underwood CE, manager
Simon Harness, trade union official
Workmans' committee: *David Roberts,*
  James Green, John Bulgin
  and Henry Thomas
Workmen: *George Rous,*
  Henry Rous, Lewis,
  Jago and Evans
A blacksmith
Davis

Strippers

Peter Terson
Comedy 2 Acts
Newcastle 1984

A Newcastle lathe operator, Bernard Robson, has been made redundant during the industrial closures of the early 1980s. His wife Wendy takes a second job herself, waiting on tables in a local café, to alleviate the family's financial strain, but her extra responsibilities leave her so little time at home that she is obliged to leave Bernard in charge of their baby and most of the domestic work. Even with the help of Bernard's Aunt Ada, the housework suffers and Bernard comes to feel at once superfluous and resentful.

While working in the café, Wendy meets Buffy, Michelle and Cilla, three strippers who work the local working men's clubs and they introduce her to their manager, Harry, with the suggestion that she consider switching to their own much more lucrative employment. She does so, reluctantly at first but with gradually increasing confidence as she hones her act in preparation for her first engagement. Her only worry is that Bernard will discover what she is doing and forbid it to continue, so she arranges to perform only in parts of the city her husband does not frequent. As luck would have it though, Bernard makes an unprecedented visit to the club in which she is making her debút, causes a scene and drags her away, his pride in tatters. No amount of explaining that she is mindful only of the family's future, can persuade Bernard to accept her new work, but she perseveres anyway, and Bernard at least comes to tolerate her decision, and to find some satisfaction himself in mastering domestic routine.

Cilla, a stripper
Wendy Robson, Bernard's wife
Aunt Ada, Bernard's aunt
Bernard Robson
Dougie, Bernard's friend
Harry, the strippers' agent
Paulie, Harry's secretary
Michelle, Buffy, strippers
Barmaid

Subject was Roses, The

Frank D. Gilroy
Comedy-Drama 2 Acts
New York 1964

When infantryman Timmy Cleary returns from Europe to his parents' apartment in the West Bronx after World War Two, their fragile family relationship is brought into sharp focus. Doted on by his sensitive mother Nettie, only child Tim had always blamed his father, hard gregarious businessman John, for the family problems and his own constant sickliness. In the army, Timmy was not sickly at all and earned decorations and commendations. His parents do all they can to make him feel at home, but he is not comfortable; he drinks, gets sick again, and despite establishing a better rapport with his father, decides to leave home after a few days. His parents are not suited to each other and there is nothing he can do about it.

John Cleary
Nettie Cleary
Timmy Cleary

Suddenly Last Summer

Tennessee Williams
Drama 2 Acts
New York 1958

Wealthy Mrs Veneble promises the local mental asylum enough money for their much-needed neuro-surgery wing, to be dedicated to her dead son Sebastian, on condition that top surgeon Dr Cukrowicz lobotomizes her niece Cathy who has been languishing in a convent hospital after a severe breakdown.

Last summer when the exotic Sebastian went for his usual three-month holiday, instead of taking his mother he took Cathy, then died in Europe in mysterious circumstances. Cathy has a memory block and Cukrowicz begins to work towards freeing her mind, but Mrs Veneble - whose relationship with her sensitive poet son was unnaturally close - puts on the pressure for Cathy's brain surgery. Cukrowicz resists until he is able to help Cathy remember what happened, and then arranges for the two women to confront one another. Cathy reveals that 'chaste' Sebastian had been using first his mother, then her, as 'bait' to attract boys for himself; suddenly, last summer, Sebastian got sick, and the frenzied hungry boys chased him in the blinding midday heat until his weak heart gave way: they then cannibalized him. The Doctor believes her story and Mrs Veneble is led away.

Mrs Veneble
Dr Cukrowicz
Miss Foxhill
Mrs Holly
George Holly
Catharine Holly
Sister Felicity

Suicide in B Flat

Sam Shepard
Drama 1 Act
New Haven 1976

Two rather hysterical detectives are investigating the apparent suicide of a gigantic avant-garde jazz composer, Niles, whose face has been blown off by a gunshot. The detectives, Pablo and Louis, try to reconstruct the crime, Louis convinced that Niles has really just disappeared, and Pablo that he was murdered.

They are joined by Petrone, one of Niles' musicians, and then by Laureen, another player, both of whom try to explain the dead man's odd musical theories. As the four of them ramble on inconsequentially, Niles and his girlfriend Paulettea join them, unseen, and begin to kill off Niles' musical heroes, with Niles taking the imaginary role of each hero and Paulettea acting the part of the killer. When Paulettea shoots an arrow at Niles, it lodges in Louis' back, and, likewise, when she fires a pistol, the shot hits Pablo.

When the two detectives are suddenly able to see Niles, until then invisible to them, they quickly handcuff him, one of them on each side of his massive frame. He claims to be dead, and the detectives drag him away.

Pianist
Pablo, a detective
Louis, a detective
Petrone, a jazz player
Laureen, another jazz player
Niles, a jazz composer
Paulettea, Niles' girlfriend

Summer in the Country
Anton Chekhov
Comedy 1 Act
Moscow 1889

Chekhov adapted his own story *One of Many* for the dialogue in this short farce.

Tolkachov enters his friend Murashkin's St Petersburg flat laden like a donkey with everything from a glass lamp and child's bicycle to parcels of clothes and a bottle of beer. He threatens suicide and demands to borrow Murashkin's pistol for the purpose. His friend refuses but asks to know why he is upset. Tolkachov explains that his family's summers in the country, which leave him to commute by train, are the purest hell for him. He is obliged to fetch endless 'necessities' not just for his wife and children, but for all the summer neighbours as well. Moreover, his wife, refreshed from sleeping late, excites her imagination singing late into the night and then demands his attentions at four a.m. Murashkin calms him, but then asks him to take a few things out to the country, since he is going that way. He screams for blood and chases Murashkin with murderous intent.

Murashkin
Tolkachov

Summer of the Seventeenth Doll
Ray Lawler
Drama 3 Acts
Melbourne 1955

For seven winter months the cane-cutters of Queensland, mighty men with mighty muscles, are isolated from the rest of humanity. When the summer heat comes, they return to Melbourne and tough cane-gang leader Roo and his sidekick Barney, the great ladies' man, have for the last sixteen years spent those five riotous months with Olive and Nancy. Now Nancy's off and married, and Olive has recruited dull widower Pearl to replace her. When Roo and Barney return for their seventeenth summer, Roo with his customary kewpie doll for Olive, none of the exciting stories Olive told Pearl about this five-month annual honeymoon - 'better than any dull

marriage' - are fulfilled. Old age has crept in; Roo has been displaced as gang boss by young Johnnie Dowd, and Barney is now no great lover. The two men mercilessly expose each others' weaknesses, and their young neighbour Bubba - Kathie - who for years has vicariously enjoyed the foursome's lifestyle goes off with Dowd. Roo and Barney can no longer return to the cane-cutting or to Olive; the good times have gone. Distraught, the two men leave together.

Bubba Ryan (Kathie)
Pearl Cunningham
Olive Leech
Emma Leech, Olive's mother
Barney Ibbot
Roo Webber
Johnnie Dowd

Sunrise at Campobello
Doré Schary
Drama 3 Acts
New York 1958

Franklin Delano Roosevelt and his family are spending summer 1921 at their lake-and-forest lodge in Campobello, New Brunswick, Canada. F.D.R. was the vice-Presidential candidate for the recently defeated Democratic party, and one evening after swimming and picnicking with his children, he gets a bad back twinge. It is polio and Roosevelt is soon crippled. Friction develops between his mother Sara and his friend Louis Howe; one wants him to rest and be comfortable, the other to take an active part in politics. Despite his disability, F.D.R. does his best to keep up a good relationship with his children, all the while making tremendous efforts to regain mobility. His devoted wife Eleanor goes out and makes speeches and becomes more and more effective, and eventually F.D.R.'s warmth and courage enable him to make a political comeback.

Anna Roosevelt	*Daly*
Eleanor Roosevelt	*Policeman*
Franklin D. Roosevelt, Jr	*Senator*
James Roosevelt	*A speaker*
Elliot Roosevelt	
Edward	
Franklin Delano	
Roosevelt, F.D.R.	
John Roosevelt	
Marie	
Louis McHenry Howe	
Mrs Sara Delano	
Roosevelt	
Miss Marguerite	
Dr Bennet	
Franklin Calder	
Stretcher bearers	
Mr Brimmer	
Mr Lassiter	
Governor Alfred E. Smith	

Sunshine Boys, The
Neil Simon
Comedy 2 Acts
New York 1972

Willie Clark and Al Lewis are two cantankerous old comedians whose vaudeville double-act is a legend. They have not worked together for eleven years and now Willie is holed up in an old Broadway hotel, visited every Wednesday by his nephew, heir and agent Ben, who brings him various goodies including *Variety* so he can scan the show-biz obits. He does not get much work and when Ben receives an offer from CBS-TV for a one-sketch Lewis-Clark reunion, he railroads the reluctant Willie into seeing Al, now living in New Jersey with his daughter and family. Willie and Al do not get on; Willie hates the way Al prods him and spits at him during their 'doctor' sketch, but in the middle of the CBS rehearsals things really get out of hand. They fight so much that Willie has a heart attack and CBS eventually end up showing an old film clip of the pair. Later at the hotel, Ben tells the recuperating Willie that he has arranged for him to move to the Actors' Home in New Brunswick, where he can be well looked after; then Al arrives to see Willie, revealing that his daughter is having another baby, so he will be moving out - to the Actors' Home in New Brunswick.

Willie Clark *Eddie*
Ben Silverman *Nurse*
Al Lewis   *Registered nurse*
Patient

Sus
Barrie Keefe
Drama 2 Acts
London 1979

In a sparse interview room in a London police station, detectives Karn and Wilby are interrogating Delroy, a black suspect who has been picked up under the notorious 'sus' (suspicion) laws. What they know (and he does not) is that his wife has been found dead in a pool of blood. The interview begins with deceptively friendly macho sexual fantasies bandied about, and throughout the whole interrogation the results of the current (1979) general election come through in dribs and drabs, promising a Tory landslide much to Karn's delight, who believes the coming Thatcher government will herald a new dawn for the beleaguered police. The proceedings become more and more menacing and after the detectives tell Delroy of his wife's death, he realizes he is under suspicion of murder. Taking advantage of his supposed guilt, Karn and Wilby give full verbal rein to their racist and sadistic impulses until the post-mortem reveals that Delroy's wife was not murdered. She died of an ectopic pregnancy.

Karn
Wilby
Delroy

Sweeney Todd - The Demon Barber of Fleet Street
Hugh Wheeler, based on the story by George Dibdin Pitt,
Music and Lyrics by Stephen Sondheim
Musical Thriller 2 Acts
New York 1979

This ghastly tale begins as Todd (Barker) returns to nineteenth century London with a young sailor, Anthony. He quickly sets up his barber shop above Mrs Lovatt's pie-shop and pledges revenge upon Judge Turpin and the Beadle, who fifteen years previously had Todd exiled and molested his beautiful wife, Lucy, who later poisoned herself. Their daughter, Johanna, now a ward of the judge, falls in love with Anthony and they plan to elope. Meanwhile, the blackmailing Pirelli is silenced by Sweeney's deadly razor, whereupon Todd and Lovatt devise a scheme combining body disposal and quality meat pies!

As sales boom, the beggar woman suspects foul play. Anthony rescues Johanna from an asylum and conceals her at Todd's place, where she witnesses the murders of the beggar woman and judge. Tension mounts as Lovatt discloses the true identity of the beggar woman - Lucy. One death follows another leaving only the young hopefuls to survive this carnage. Songs include: 'Johanna'; 'Not While I'm Around'; 'A Little Priest'

Anthony Hope *The Beadle*
Sweeney Todd (Barker) *Johanna*
Beggar woman *Tobias Ragg*
Mrs Lovatt   *Pirelli*
Judge Turpin *Jonas Fogg*

Sweet Bird of Youth
Tennessee Williams
Drama 3 Acts
New York 1959

Chance Wayne returns to St Cloud as gigolo to faded film star Princess Kosmonopolis; he was once 'the most beautiful boy in town', but was driven away by corrupt local politician Boss Finlay to prevent him marrying Finlay's daughter, Heavenly. Chance's hopes of movie stardom have diminished over the years, and after each failure he returned to the arms of Heavenly. Unknown to him, during his last visit he infected Heavenly who has had to be 'spayed like a dawg', and now Finlay, his son Tom and his men, are seeking revenge. When Chance discovers what has happened to Heavenly he declines to leave town with the Princess and awaits retribution with dignity. He is aware that Finlay was recently involved in castrating an innocent black man - and he knows this will be his fate also.

Chance Wayne *Hatcher*
Princess Kosmonopolis *Boss Finlay*
Fly   *Tom Junior*
Maid   *Aunt Nonnie*
George Scudder *Heavenly Finlay*

Charles	Edna
Stuff	Scotty
Miss Lucy	Bud
The Heckler	Men in bar
Violet	Page

Sweet Charity
Neil Simon
Lyrics by Dorothy Fields
Music by Cy Coleman
Musical 2 Acts
New York 1966

Charity Hope Valentine is the type of tart who has a heart of gold. Although she is a hostess at the Fan-Dango Ballroom, and part of its rough world, she chases her dream of marriage with total determination in spite of numerous disappointments.

As the play opens, she is waiting in New York's Central Park for her lover Charlie. When he arrives, Charlie pushes her into a pond and steals her money, then runs off. Back at the Ballroom, she pretends Charlie merely borrowed the money, to general disbelief. After completing her shift, she finds herself outside the glamorous Pompeii Club, and receives a sudden invitation to join Vittorio Vidal, a movie star whose girlfriend has just left him, for a drink and dinner. She spends the night with Vidal discussing his emotional problems, but secretly leaves in the morning, when his girlfriend comes back to him, with nothing but a signed photograph of the great man and a walking stick he used in one of his films.

Luck seems to turn her way when she is caught in a lift with a desperately shy young man, Oscar, whose terrified reaction to being trapped she manages to soothe. At first, she pretends to work in a bank, but when she realizes she is in love with Oscar, her scruples force her to admit her true occupation. Oscar, who had already accidentally learned the truth, assures her that he wants to marry her anyway but after a farewell party from the Ballroom staff, when she and Oscar are on the way to the ceremony, he breaks with her out of jealousy for her previous lovers. She is left to go hopefully on. Songs include: 'Big Spender'; 'Baby, Dream Your Dream'

Charity Hope Valentine	Herman
Dark Glasses (Charlie)	Doorman
Bystander	Ursula
Married couple	Vittorio Vidal
Woman with hat	Waiter
Ice cream vendor	Manfred
Football player	Receptionist
Ballplayers	Old maid
Career girl	Oscar
Spanish young man	Daddy Johann Sebastian
Two cops	Brubeck
Helene	Brother Harold
Nickie	Brother Eddie
Carmen	Policeman

Rosie	Good Fairy
Barney	Singers and Dancers
Mike	

Table Manners (The Norman Conquests)
Alan Ayckbourn
Comedy 2 Acts
Scarborough 1973
See: *Living Room; Round and Round the Garden*
One of *The Norman Conquests* trilogy in which events during a single weekend, with the same set of characters, are viewed in a different setting in each play. *Table Manners* is set in a dining-room.

A married couple, Reg and Sarah, arrive at Reg's mother's house to care for Reg's invalid mother in order to leave Annie, Reg's sister, a weekend free from caring for the old woman. Shortly after they arrive, they are joined by Norman, Reg and Annie's brother-in-law, and by Annie's ineffectual admirer, Tom. Reg and Sarah are surprised to see Norman, and even more surprised when they find out he has come to take Annie away for a dirty weekend, unknown to his wife, Reg and Annie's sister, Ruth. When Annie gets cold feet for the plan, Norman gets drunk and causes a scene, melodramatically proclaiming himself misunderstood.

Sarah, revolted by Annie and Norman's plan, rings Ruth, who arrives the next day quite unperturbed. The family decide, under Sarah's desperate prodding, to have a cosy Sunday lunch. They quickly break apart in acrimony and, when on Monday they are all about to part, Norman and Annie promise one another to pursue their original plan another time.

Norman	Annie
Tom	Reg
Sarah	Ruth

Taking Steps
Alan Ayckbourn
Comedy 2 Acts
Scarborough 1979
Hard-drinking bucket tycoon Roland has been renting The Pines, a large Victorian manor house and former brothel said to be haunted by ghostly prostitute Scarlet Lucy. He intends to buy the house, unaware that his wife, ex-dancer Elizabeth, is on the point of leaving him. His bumbling solicitor Tristram and the house's owner, builder Leslie, are ready for Roland's signature when he discovers Elizabeth's goodbye note. He postpones the deal and persuades Tristram to stay the night in the master bedroom - he is too upset to stay there himself.

From this point, events speed up to a farce-like velocity; Elizabeth returns and inadvertently beds with Tristram, who believes she is Scarlet Lucy; Elizabeth's brother Mark brings back his wayward fiancée Lizzie, who is accidentally locked up all night in an attic cupboard by drunken Roland; Leslie is assaulted, his motor-bike wrecked; there are various suicide complications; Lizzie ends up in bed with Tristram and leaves Mark yet again - to be followed by Tristram. Elizabeth just cannot make up her mind whether to stay or go.

All this takes place in an ingenious setting where all the rooms, passages and stairs are on the same level.

Elizabeth
Mark
Tristram
Roland
Leslie
Lizzie

Tales from Hollywood
Christopher Hampton
Drama 2 Acts
London 1983
This seamless blend of fact and fiction is narrated by Odon von Horvath, who in reality died in 1938, and follows his imaginary career in Hollywood, as a script writer, from 1938-50.

Horvath moves mainly in the world of *émigré* writers and artists - Brecht, Thomas Mann, his brother Heinrich, Lion Feuchtwanger and their families - who found ready work in Hollywood as World War Two approached. None of them, however, was really understood by the studio bosses who hired them, and there result hilarious confrontations of the high-brow and low-brow.

As these fine creative minds become ground down, as with Heinrich Mann, or learn ruthless methods of survival, like Brecht, Horvath senses that he can love Hollywood precisely for its grand tackiness. Even this cynical element in his love of the place, though, cannot prevent his disillusionment when the communism scares of the immediate post-war years start. He is saved from seeing the worst of these when he dies an absurd death by crashing headlong into the end of a swimming pool.

Odon von Horvath, the	*Helen Schwartz*
narrator	*Bertolt Brecht*
Young man	*Helene Weige, Brecht's*
Johnny Weissmuller	*wife*
Thomas Mann	*Hal*
Chico Marx	*Angel*
Harpo Marx	*Jacob Lomakhin*
Greta Garbo	*Robert E. Stripling*
Charles Money	*Art Nicely*
Heinrich Mann, Thomas	
Mann's brother	
Nelly Mann, Heinrich's	
wife	
Salka Viertl	
Walter	
Lion Feuchtwanger	
Marta Feuchtwanger	
Tony Spuhler	
Katja Mann, Thomas	
Mann's wife	

Tamburlaine the Great
Christopher Marlowe
Drama 2 Parts, Each 5 Acts
London 1587
Based on the true story of fourteenth-century conqueror Timur the Lame, Marlowe's Tamburlaine has arisen from humble beginnings as a Scythian shepherd. First he grabs the Persian throne from weakling King Mycetes and his scheming brother Cosroe, gaining alliance from powerful Persian Lord Theridamas. Then Turkey, Egypt, Arabia, northern Africa and Greece all fall to his superb military prowess. Tamburlaine calls himself 'the Scourge of God' though his enemies, Moslem and Christian alike, consider him an atheist; in fact, he believes himself to have God-like powers and qualities. He humiliates his captured enemies (caging Turkish emperor Bajazeth, making other great kings pull his chariot), drowns whole cities, massacres every inhabitant, roars and blusters everywhere. His sentimental love for Zenocrate, daughter of the Soldan of Egypt, does not stop him from slaughtering everyone in her home town of Damascus - except her father. He is rewarded with three sons, but when one proves cowardly, Tamburlaine stabs him. After capturing Babylon, Tamburlaine sneers at the prophet Mahomet and orders the sacred scriptures burned, but a few moments later is struck down by a fatal sickness. This is as well, because his enemies, led by Callapine, son of Bajazeth, look like finally overcoming him. Marlowe's 'mighty line' resounds relentlessly throughout this sensationalised portrait of martial man incarnate.

Part One:
Mycetes, King of Persia
Cosroe, his brother
Persian lords and captains: Ceneus, Ortygius,
Meander, Menaphon, Theridamas
Tamburlaine, a Scythian shepherd
Techelles
Usumcasane
Bajazeth, Emperor of Turkey
King of Arabia
King of Fez
King of Morocco
King of Algiers
Soldan of Egypt
Governor of Damascus
Agydas, Magnetes, Median Lords
Capolin, an Egyptian captain
A spy
Messengers
Philemus, messenger
Zenocrate, daughter of the Soldan of Egypt
Anippe, her maid
Zabina, wife of Bajazeth
Ebea, her maid
Virgins of Damascus
Bassoes
Lords

Citizens
Moors
Soldiers
Attendants
Part Two:
Tamburlaine, King of Persia
Calyphas, Amyras, Celebinus, his sons
Theridamas, King of Algiers
Techelles, King of Fez
Usumcasane, King of Morocco
Orcanes, King of Natolia (Asia Minor)
King of Jerusalem
King of Tyre
King of Amasia
King of Trebizond
Gazellus, viceroy of Byron
Uribassa, a captain
Sigismund, king of Hungary
Frederick, lord of Buda and Bohemia
Baldwin
Callapine, son of Bajazath
Almeda, his keeper
Perdicas, servant to Calyphas
Governor of Babylon
Capt. of Balsera
His son
Another captain
Maximus, a captain
Perdicas
Zenocrate, wife of Tamburlaine
Olympia, wife of the Capt. of Balsera
Turkish concubines
Lords
Citizens
Physicians
Messengers
Attendants

Taming of the Shrew, The
William Shakespeare
Comedy 5 Acts
Published 1594

Christopher Sly, a drunken tinker, is duped by a group of noblemen into believing that he is an aristocrat. They bring before him a band of players who present a comedy. This is the story of the two daughters of a Paduan merchant Baptista; the elder one Katherina is a shrew whom no one will marry, while her sister Bianca is pursued and wooed by many, but cannot marry until her elder sister is wedded off. Along comes a fortune hunter Petruchio, who pursues the unwilling Katherina avidly, and despite many rebuttals and a series of impersonations involving Bianca's suitors, eventually marries her and carries her off to his home in Verona. Here he sets about taming her, his principal weapon being laughter, and the cynic finds himself blessed with a loving wife who ends up lecturing to Bianca, now married to Lucentio, on the duties of good wifehood.

Christopher Sly, a tinker
Baptista Minola, a wealthy Paduan
Vincento, a merchant of Padua
Lucentio, son of Vincento
Petruchio, a gentleman of Verona
Katherina
Bianca, her sister
Grumio, Curtis, servants to Petruchio
Gremio, Hortensio, gentlemen of Padua
Tranio, Biondello, servants to Lucentio
A lord
A pedant
A widow
A hostess
A page
A tailor
A haberdasher
Servants

Tartuffe or The Imposter
Molière
Comedy 5 Acts
Paris 1669

Tartuffe, a rogue posing as a pious puritan, has wormed his way into the admiration and affections of gullible merchant Orgon. Deaf to the warnings of his horrified family, Orgon promises his daughter Mariane in marriage to Tartuffe, despite her already being betrothed to her true love Valère.

When Orgon's son Damis hears Tartuffe making overtures to his beautiful stepmother Elmire, he tells Orgon who chooses to believe Tartuffe's innocence and to spite his family makes out his estate to the imposter. Finally, Elmire convinces her husband to hide under a table while she sees Tartuffe alone. Smitten with Elmire, he makes a play for her and the enraged and enlightened Orgon throws him out.

Tartuffe retaliates by claiming Orgon's house and fortune as his own, and then betrays Orgon to the King using some traitorous documents left in Orgon's safekeeping which he has entrusted to Tartuffe. The King, however, (perhaps with help from Tartuffe's turncoat servant Laurent) sees through the imposter, discovers his past criminal record, and restores Orgon's fortunes to him.

Mme Pernelle, Orgon's mother
Orgon
Elmire, Orgon's wife
Damis, Orgon's son
Mariane, Orgon's daughter
Valère
Cléante, Valere's father and Orgon's brother-in-law
Tartuffe
Dorine, Mariane's maid
Monsieur Loyal, a bailiff
Flipote, Mme Parnelle's maidservant
Laurent, Tartuffe's manservant
An officer

Taste of Honey, A
Shelagh Delaney
Drama 2 Acts
London 1958

Helen and teenage daughter Jo move into a dingy Manchester flat; Helen is an indifferent mother and the pair have an amusing but semi-hostile relationship. When Helen's boyfriend Peter - a used-car salesman - appears and spontaneously proposes, she goes off with him. Jo feels upset and neglected and finds comfort with Jimmy, her black serviceman boyfriend who she lets stay with her over Christmas, although she knows he will not be coming back. Some months later, pregnant and working, she befriends Geoff, a homosexual art student with tender feelings towards her; he moves in and enjoys preparing for the baby but misguidedly sends for Helen who appears, then leaves again when an irate Peter turns up. Jo and Geoff continue their happy preparations but Helen reappears after a final row with Peter. Jo is asleep and Helen makes Geoff leave. Jo wakes and begins labour, but when she mentions to Helen that the baby's father was black, her mother becomes distraught and rushes out to the pub, leaving Jo alone and thinking of Geoff and his gentleness.
Helen
Josephine, her daughter
Peter, her friend, later husband
The boy (Jimmy)
Geoffrey

Tea and Sympathy
Robert Anderson
Drama 3 Acts
London 1957

In a New England boys' boarding school, the only intimacy encouraged between the pupils and the masters' wives is 'tea and sympathy'. Laura, though, has more than sympathy for young Tom; he reminds her of her first husband, a sensitive boy who died in the war proving his courage and manhood. Tom, too, is persecuted for his 'differentness' and branded homosexual. In fact he is quite normal and is secretly crazy about Laura, whose marriage to her second husband, macho-teacher Bill, is distinctly rocky. Rejected by his father, friends and teachers, Tom tries to prove his manhood with the local whore but is impotent and tries to kill himself. For this he must quit the school but on his last day Laura declares she is leaving Bill, whose intense persecution of Tom has made her see what Bill himself is covering up. She goes to Tom and finds him doubting his own manhood. She offers herself to him ... and he responds.

Laura Reynolds	*Steve*
Lilly Sears	*Bill Reynolds*
Tom Lee	*Phil*
David Harris	*Herbert Lee*
Ralph	*Paul*
Al	

Tea Party, The
Harold Pinter
Comedy 1 Act
London 1970

Disson, head of a firm that manufactures sanitary hardware, hires sexy secretary Wendy who left her last job because of her boss's unwanted attentions. Widower Disson has two sons, John and Tom, and he remarries - his new wife is the lovely Diana. Her brother Willy makes the wedding speeches and Disson is so impressed he takes Willy into partnership with him, explaining his philosophy of clear intentions and precise execution. Soon Disson begins having trouble with his eyesight, although his optician friend Disley says his sight is normal - better than normal, in fact. Disson gets worse and likes having bandages, or Wendy's scarves, tied tight over his eyes. There is a tea-party in his office attended by his family and friends and blindfolded Disson imagines Willy touching the swelling bodies of his wife and secretary. Or does he? He then collapses.
Disson
Wendy
Diana
Willy
Disley
Lois
Father
Mother
Tom
John

Teahouse of the August Moon, The
John Patrick
Comedy 3 Acts
New York 1953

Wise and wily Sakini is interpreter to Col Purdy of the US Army of Occupation in Okinawa after World War Two. Purdy sends the goofily good-natured Capt. Fisby of the Psychological Warfare Unit off to Tobiki village to indoctrinate the natives with democracy, to build a schoolhouse and organize various committees, and along goes Sakini to interpret. Okinawa is an island in the China Seas between Japan and Taiwan and over the centuries has been constantly invaded; thus, the locals are experts at handling meddlesome foreigners. With the help of luscious geisha Lotus Blossom, they soon get Fisby to 'go native', build a lovely teahouse, and start producing the local brandy on a big scale. When Purdy's suspicions are aroused he sends along Capt. McLean, but he too is ensnared, finding Tobiki ideal for his chemical-free crop experiments.

Eventually Purdy himself arrives and orders everything destroyed - but then hears that Tobiki has been heralded in Washington as a supreme example of American get-up-and-go. Luckily the natives did not destroy the brandy stills and teahouse screens - they only hid them, and the play ends with Purdy musing on the wonders of the Orient, and Sakini - who acts as a chorus throughout - reiterating his philosophy.

Sakini	*Mr Sumata's father*
Sgt Gregovich	*Mr Hokaida*
Col Wainwright Purdy	*Mr Seiko*
II	*Mr Oshura*
Capt. Fisby	*Mr Omura*
Old woman	*Mr Keora*
Old woman's daughter	*Villagers (6)*
The daughter's	*Miss Higa Jiga*
children (4)	*Ladies' League For*
Angela	*Democratic Action (4)*
Ancient man	*Lotus Blossom*
Mr Sumata	*Capt. McLean*

Tempest, The
William Shakespeare
Comedy 5 Acts
London 1611

A strange tempest wrecks a ship on an enchanted island in the Mediterranean, ruled by the magician Prospero, the rightful Duke of Milan. Usurped and cast adrift fifteen years previously by his wicked brother Antonio and the ambitious Alonso, King of Naples, Prospero lives with his beautiful daughter Miranda, their monster servant Caliban (a dead witch's son) and the sprite Ariel, imprisoned by the witch and freed by Prospero.

Aboard the vessel are all Prospero's enemies including Alonso, his son Ferdinand, his brother Sebastian, the usurper Antonio, and the honest Gonzalo. With the help of Ariel, who must pay off his debt to Prospero, the magician separates the crew and passengers and firstly reveals himself to Ferdinand who falls in love with Miranda. She returns his love and Prospero approves of the romance. Alonso's party search in vain for Ferdinand, and Antonio and Sebastian engage in further plots, but Ariel hears all and reports back to his master. Then Caliban meets Stephano the butler and Trinculo the jester; they get him drunk and he determines to rebel against Prospero whom he hates. Prospero finally orchestrates the situation so that everyone meets up and justice is done and seen to be done. Alonso gives his blessing to the marriage, the traitors are forgiven, Prospero will return as rightful Duke of Milan, and Caliban regrets his drunkenness. Faithful Ariel gets his freedom, and in the epilogue of his penultimate play, Shakespeare closes with an expositional plea for mercy.

Alonso, King of Naples
Sebastian, his brother
Prospero, rightful Duke of Milan
Antonio, his brother, the usurping Duke of Milan
Ferdinand, son to the King of Naples
Gonzalo, an honest old Counsellor of Naples
Adrian, Francisco, lords
Caliban, a savage and deformed slave
Trinculo, a jester
Stephano, a drunken butler
Miranda, daughter of Prospero
Ariel, an airy spirit
Iris
Ceres
Juno
Nymps
Reapers
Spirits
Master of the ship
Boatswain
Mariners

Ten Little Indians or And Then There Were None
Agatha Christie
Mystery 3 Acts
London 1944

Nine disparate guests are invited on various pretexts to the house on Indian Island off the Devon coast. They are met by manservant and cook, Mr and Mrs Rogers, but their hosts, Mr and Mrs Owen, are delayed. It transpired that no-one, not even the newly-hired Rogers, have ever met their hosts, and when, according to instructions, Rogers puts on a certain gramophone record, the puzzle falls into place. According to the voice on the record, each of the guests and the Rogers have committed a murder or murders and seemingly got away with it. Their mad host is revealed as an 'avenging angel', and one by one the guests and the Rogers are murdered, each in the manner specified by the old nursery rhyme *Ten Little Indians*.

They quickly realize one of their number must be the mysterious Owen, but despite all precautions the plan succeeds perfectly until only Vera and Lombard - the two who are actually innocent - are left. She shoots him, thinking him to be Owen, but then the real Owen appears - a 'murdered' guest who played dead. Luckily, Lombard is only wounded and manages to kill 'Owen' before he is able to complete the final stanza of the deadly rhyme.

Rogers
Narracot
Mrs Rogers
Vera Claythorne
Philip Lombard
Anthony Marston
William Blore
Gen. Mackenzie
Emily Brent
Sir Lawrence Wargrave
Dr Armstrong

Ten Minute Alibi
Anthony Armstrong
Drama 3 Acts
London 1933

Philip Sevilla, a handsome half-Latin cad, has bewitched naive Betty Findon into taking a mock 'honeymoon' with him in Paris - his wife (he says) is insane and divorce impossible. Actually he intends Betty for something unspeakable in South America after having his fling. When Bet's upright admirer Colin Derwent tries to persuade Sevilla to relent, a drugged cigarette sends him into a dream where ironically he works out the perfect method for killing the vile Sevilla. Upon awakening he puts the plan in action - it all depends on manipulating the clock to provide a perfect alibi involving respected barrister Sir Miles Standing. With a couple of minor snags the murder goes according to plan, and although cops Pember and Brace suspect Derwent, his alibi is watertight; anyway they've discovered Sevilla's evil habits and convince themselves Derwent is innocent. Then, at the last minute, an extra clock chime gives the game away. Betty saves Derwent from discovery but afterwards is not sure whether or not she wishes to continue their association.

Hunter
Philip Sevilla
Betty Findon
Colin Derwent
Sir Miles Standing
Inspector Pember
Sergeant Brace

Ten Times Table
Alan Ayckbourn
Comedy 2 Acts
Scarborough 1977
The gloomy old Swan Hotel ballroom is being used as a committee room for the Pendon Civic Society meeting, and Chairman Ray proposes a fund-raising pageant based on the obscure local martyrdom of 'the Pendon Twelve'. The attitude of Ray's snobby wife Helen enrages Marxist schoolteacher Eric who determines to turn the event into a piece of political propaganda. The committee splits into two factions - purportedly friendly - one side responsible for the workers, the other for the military. Worker chief Eric's organization is superior, so Ray's group, representing the forces of law and order, recruit Tim - neo-fascist ex-Army brother of Helen's friend Sophie; Tim's miffed because Sophie is developing a soft spot for Eric. Armed with a real revolver (rumoured to be kept under his pillow), Tim plans his side of the pageant like a military campaign. On the day of the event there is much bludgeoning, shooting and general disarray, followed by Sophie's disillusion with Eric, and optimistic Ray contemplating a future pageant of Romans versus Ancient Britons.

Ray   *Philippa*
Donald   *Max Kirkov*
Helen
Sophie
Eric
Audrey
Lawrence
Tim

Tenth Man, The
Paddy Chayefsky
Drama 3 Acts
New York 1959
On a bitterly cold morning in a poor Orthodox synagogue somewhere in New York, some men - mostly old - are trying to make up the requisite quorum of ten for morning prayers. Before they can do so, one of their number, Foreman, comes in with his lunatic granddaughter. He has kidnapped her to save her from the asylum, convinced she is possessed by a *dybbuk*, a soul in torment; indeed, in a harsh voice the *dybbuk* reveals some sexual secrets of those present. The quorum is then completed when the Sexton drags in Arthur from the street. He is a cynical young Jewish lawyer who has been on a three-day drinking binge and is desperate to see his analyst. After morning prayers, Arthur and the sometime-lucid girl Evelyn start talking and are attracted to one another. Her condition, however, visibly worsens, and the others decide on an exorcism which is duly performed. To everyone's astonishment, it is Arthur, not Evelyn, who falls down screaming. When he revives, his cynicism and lovelessness are gone and he pledges to love and care for the still-crazy Evelyn.

The Cabalist
The Sexton
Schlissel
Zitorsky
Alper
Foreman
The girl (Evelyn Foreman)
Arthur Landau
The Rabbi
Kessler boys (two)
The policeman

Thark
Ben Travers
Farce 3 Acts
London 1927
Sir Hector Benbow, a peer with a roving eye, picks up shop-assistant Cherry Buck and invites her to dinner at his Mayfair flat, but her arrival coincides with that of Mrs Frush and her son Lionel who have just bought the country house, Thark, from Sir Hector, who has sold it on behalf of his niece Kitty.

When Sir Hector's wife Lady Benbow also arrives, he coerces Ronny Gamble, Kitty's fiancé, into taking Cherry off his hands for the evening and also involves his long-suffering servants in his chicanery. Mrs Frush has complaints about Thark, she thinks it is haunted, so the whole party goes down to the country to investigate. A tangled web of romantic affairs and mistaken identities ensues against a background of haunting, thunder and lightning. Sir Hector bluffs his way through all this, with a shotgun at the ready, while a sinister butler and a prying newspaper reporter add to the general confusion which sorts itself out in the end with Kitty in the arms of Ronny and Cherry finding romance with Lionel.

Hook, the Benbows' butler
Warner, the maid
Cherry Buck
Lionel Frush
Mrs Frush
Sir Hector Benbow
Ronald Gamble (Ronny)
Lady Benbow
Kitty Stratton
Jones, Mrs Frush's butler
Whittle, a reporter

That Championship Season
Jason Miller
Drama 2 Acts
New York 1972

In the midst of the American moral collapse of the early seventies, four middle-aged men meet at the home of their high school basketball coach to plot the re-election of one of their number, George Sikowski, as mayor of their city. The coach, who had moulded them into a championship basketball team twenty years earlier, still holds his place as their mentor. But now, the focus of his attention is domination of the corrupt local politics, not the basketball court.

One of the old team, Phil Romano, now a rich political patron, has lost faith in George's performance as mayor, and threatens not to support the current election campaign. This would ruin both George and James Daley, another member of the old team who is George's campaign manager.

As the coach scuttles between the members of the team, patching up a deal in the worst traditions of American backroom politics, it is revealed that even their championship victory was won by cheating.

Tom Daley
George Sikowski
James Daley
Phil Romano
Coach

There Was an Old Woman....
David Wood
Musical 2 Acts
Leicester 1979

This family entertainment weaves the stories of *Jack and Jill* and *Old Mother Hubbard* into a story meant mainly for children.

Old Mother Shipton lives with Jack, Jill and a large number of children whose parents have been enslaved by an evil Giant. Their home is the Giant's huge shoe, which he lost when taking away the parents. A magician called The Great Boon arrives at their home looking for a circus in which he is meant to perform. When the Giant returns, Boon reduces him to human size with a magic spell, but in doing so reduces the shoe-home to normal size as well.

Jack and Jill are off fetching a pail of water while this is going on, and when they meet the shrunken Giant by the well, they trade him Cocky, their family rooster, for a pail of apples which turn out to be rotten. The giant becomes angry when they pursue him, seeking the return of Cocky, and knocks them both down the hill. They return home with nothing to show for their efforts, but Boon again comes to the rescue by creating a magic apple tree loaded with fruit. Boon's next trick, though, misfires when, in a spell which returns the giant's shoe to its original size, he inadvertently returns the Giant to his original stature as well.

The children save the day by singing a lullaby which sends the Giant off to sleep, giving Boon time to reduce him once again. Boon's new spell turns the Giant into a midget, and the magician decides to make him part of a circus act. In his final spell, Boon brings back all the missing parents, and everyone goes off to live happily in the former giant's castle.

Cocky
Mother Shipton
Jill, her daughter
Jack, her son
The Great Boon
Giant
A crowd of children

There's a Girl in My Soup
Terence Frisby
Comedy 3 Acts
London 1966

Famous food writer and broadcaster Robert Danvers is in his early forties, vain and pompous and a compulsive womanizer. But then he goes to the wrong party and meets nineteen-year-old Marion whose bright fresh charm floors him. She has just walked out on her boyfriend, Jimmy, an oaf who wanted to move in another girl so both his girlfriends 'could live under the same roof'.

Naturally, Marion is impressed with Robert's lifestyle, especially when he takes her wine-tasting in France. But upon their return she hears from an apologetic Jimmy and decides to go back. Robert is pragmatic about this, having learned much from his short but intense fling with Marion. But when the objectionable Jimmy arrives to take Marion, she dithers. Robert's editor Andrew suggests to Jimmy that he and Robert share Marion. Jimmy is disgusted and leaves with Marion, who, it seems, may well be back. Then the phone rings and Robert is off and running with his new conquest - Andrew's *au pair*.

Robert Danvers
Clare Dorlaton-Finch
Andrew Hunter
Porter
Paola
Marion
Jimmy

Thérèse Raquin
Emile Zola
Drama 4 Acts
Paris 1873
In the Paris of 1860, Mme Raquin adores her son Camille and is devastated when he is killed in a boating accident. Devoted to the man who tried to save her son's life, painter Laurent, she suggests that he should marry Camille's widow Thérèse unaware that the pair are lovers and have plotted her son's murder.

The wedding night, however, turns out to be disastrous as the couple find that their crime has destroyed their ardour; Mme Raquin overhears them discussing the killing and has a paralysing stroke. Although immobile, she watches the criminals constantly and during a friend's visit, she starts to write a message to them but does not finish. Later, Thérèse and Laurent begin to accuse each other of the crime to the point of trying to murder each other, but Mme Raquin recovers and tells them she did not finish the message because she wants to watch them suffer slowly for their crime. They find their own answer to their anguish after Mme Raquin refuses to hand them over to the police.

Thérèse
Laurent
Mme Raquin
Camille
Grivet
Michaud

They're Playing Our Song
Neil Simon
Music by Marvin Hamlisch
Lyrics by Carole Bayer Sager
Musical 2 Acts
Los Angeles 1979
Sonia Walsk, a neurotic song lyricist, arrives at the New York apartment of Vernon Gersch, an equally neurotic and very successful popular composer, for a meeting which is meant to inaugurate a period of creative collaboration between them. As is her habit, Sonia arrives late and anxiety-ridden, then rushes off after having time only to set a date for their next meeting.

Vernon finds himself smitten with Sonia's odd personality, but their every attempt to meet is dogged by interruptions from Leon, Sonia's ex-boyfriend, who is suicidal as a result of losing her. Even when Vernon takes her away for a weekend on Long Island, Sonia is in constant touch with Leon. Their mutual attraction is strong enough, however, that Sonia leaves her apartment to Leon and moves with Vernon. They dive into a period of intense work which culminates in a recording session for which Sonia arrives hours late, to find Vernon furious.

The session goes so badly that they break up, and both end up working separately in Los Angeles, where Vernon breaks his leg and ends up, by coincidence, in a ward where Leon is also hospitalized. Leon's fond description of Sonia's earlier years inspires Vernon to catch up with her some months later in New York, and they decide to live together again under a new regimen of mutual respect.

Vernon Gersch
Sonia Walsk
Voices of Vernon
Voices of Sonia
Voice of Phil the Engineer.

This Happy Breed
Noël Coward
Drama 3 Acts
London 1939
Patriotic saga of the ups and downs of a working-class family in London from 1919 to 1939. After demob, Frank and Ethel Gibbons move into their own house in Clapham together with Frank's dismal spinster sister Sylvia, Ethel's mum Mrs Flint, and their children Reg, Queenie and Vi. Next door is Frank's old army chum Bob Mitchell, whose sailor son Billy takes a shine to the flashy Queenie. Frank and Bob become drinking buddies, Reg marries his sweetheart Phyllis but both are later killed in a car crash. Queenie, discontent with her humble lot, runs off with a married man, is abandoned in France, and is brought home by Billy whom she weds. She is then touchingly reconciled with her family, especially her mother. Vi weds ex-Marxist Sam Leadbitter, and Sylvia brightens up to become a smug Christian Scientist. With the kids all gone, Frank and Ethel move to a smaller and more convenient flat, and as compensation are left looking after grandson little Frankie while Queenie joins Billy in India.

Mrs Ethel Flint
Ethel
Sylvia
Frank Gibbons
Bob Mitchell
Reg
Queenie
Vi
Sam Leadbitter
Phyllis Blake
Edie
Billy

Three Men on a Horse
John Cecil Holm and George Abbot
Comedy 3 Acts
New York 1935
Erwin Trowbridge is a modest young writer of greetings-card verses living with his loving wife Audrey in Ozone Heights, New Jersey. Unfortunately, meddlesome brother-in-law Clarence is a pain; he built their house and he despises poetic Erwin. As a hobby, Erwin plays the horses - but only on paper. He never actually bets, but always wins, and one day after a set-to with Clarence,

he drowns his sorrows and meets a crowd of gamblers who pick up on his talent. Led by Patsy and his moll Mabel, the gang encourage Erwin to abscond from work while he makes their fortune. The action assumes a farce-like velocity as Erwin is chased by his wife, his brother-in-law, the betting fraternity and his boss Mr Carver. Finally, Erwin breaks his successful run when he has a bet himself, and returns home to Audrey, kicks out Clarence, and gets a raise and the respect he deserves from his boss.

Audrey Trowbridge
The tailor
Erwin Trowbridge
Clarence Dobbins
Delivery boy
Harry
Charlie
Frankie
Patsy
Mabel
Moses
Gloria
Al
Hotel maid
Mr Carver

Three Sisters, The
Anton Chekhov
Drama 4 Acts
Moscow 1901

The three Prozorov sisters, Olga, Masha (Maria) and Irina live with their brother Andrey in their large house in a provincial capital of Tzarist Russia at the end of the last century. The frustrations and hopes of their lives are set against the effects of the financial irresponsibility of gambler Andrey and the increasing tiresomeness of his stupid fiancée - and later wife - Natasha.

The presence of the Imperial Army seems to provide at least limited opportunities to relieve the stifling oppressions of their lives; Masha, bored by modest schoolteacher husband Kuligin, finds solace in the company of Lieut Col Vershinin, an older married man with a neurotic wife, whose domestic misfortunes and fanciful imaginings at first arouse her pity, then her love. Though Irina has abandoned her young dreams of love, she agrees to marry kind Lieut Baron Tusenbach who can give her a new life.

But the army moves on, Vershinin leaves, and the Baron is killed in a duel with Irina's other military admirer, the jealous and immature subaltern Solyony. For schoolmistress Olga there is promotion to headmistress and an end to her dreams of Moscow, but in the end the sisters still stand together, consoling one another with their optimism and determination to live, to work, and to understand.

Andrey Sergyevich Prozorov
Natasha (Natalie Ivanovna)
Olga
Masha (Maria)
Irina
Fyodor Ilyich Kuligin, secondary schoolteacher, Masha's husband
Lieut Col Alexander Ignatyevich Vershinin, battery commander
Lieut Com Baron Nikolai (Nicholas) Lvovich Tusenbach
Vasily Vasilyevich Solyony, subaltern
Ivan Romanivich Chebutykin, army doctor
Second Lieut Alexy Petrovich Fedotik
Second Lieut Vladimir Karlovich Rode
Ferapont, an old District Council porter
Anfisa, an old nurse
Two army officers
Two musicians
A soldier
A maid

Threepenny Opera, The
Bertold Brecht
Music by Kurt Weill
Musical 3 Acts
Berlin 1928

Based on John Gay's *Beggars' Opera*, this interpretation opens with the hit standard 'Mack the Knife'.

Among the criminal fraternity in London's Soho, Mr Peacham, 'friend of the poor' and organizer of the city's beggars is horrified to learn his lovely daughter, Polly, has wed sinister villain Macheath (Mackie). He plots with the police to catch Mackie, who leaves his gang under Polly's command and flees. He stops at a brothel and is betrayed by a whore, his ex-girlfriend Jenny, is imprisoned but escapes with help of another girlfriend Lucy Brown, then unwisely spends the night with Suki Tawdrey in her flat in Oxford Street and is again betrayed. His gang have now gone into legitimate banking and everyone is reluctant to bail him out. However, just before Mackie's hanging, Brecht tacks on his happy ending - it is the Queen's coronation and Mackie is pardoned.

Narrator
Dolly
Mr Peacham
Filch
Mrs Peacham
Matt
Macheath
Polly Peacham
Bob
Walt
Jake
Revd Kimball
Tiger Brown
Betty
Coaxer
Nelly
Smith
Lucy Brown
Three constables
Four beggars

Ticket of Leave Man, The
Tom Taylor
Drama 4 Acts
London 1863

Robert Brierly, an honest but thoroughly naive young Lancastrian, arrives in London with nothing but a small inheritance and a thirst for high living. He falls in with James Dalton, an utter rogue, and is arrested for passing a counterfeit twenty pound note provided by this very false friend.

After serving just one year of his sentence, he is given a 'ticket of leave' from prison for his exemplary conduct. Returning to London, he goes to the lodgings of May Edwards, a poor but upright street singer with whom he is in love. His evidently good character spurs May's benefactor, the banker and bill broker Mr Gibson, to offer him a modest position. With his past now behind him, Robert and May plan to marry and are on their way to the registry office when Melter Moss, a corrupt associate of Dalton, reveals Robert's past to Mr Gibson, who feels obliged to dismiss him.

With his employment gone, Robert and May sink ever deeper into poverty, and Robert's every attempt to find new work is sabotaged, without him being aware, by Dalton and Moss. The two criminals are determined to bring him to his knees, break his resolve to live an upright life, and then bring him into their conspiracy to rob Mr Gibson of the large sum of cash in his office safe. Robert pretends to join their enterprise, intending to turn them over to the police at the crucial moment. His intentions are discovered by Dalton's bitter enemy, Detective Hawkshaw, who helps the plan to a successful conclusion.

Moss and Dalton are captured, Robert is given a new position by a grateful Mr Gibson and at last he is free to marry May.

Robert Brierly, a Lancashire lad
James Dalton (alias Downy, alias The Tiger), a criminal
Detective Hawkshaw
Melter Moss, a criminal
Green Jones
Mr Gibson
Sam Willoughby
Maltby
Burton
May Edwards
Emily St Evremond
Mrs Willoughby

Tiger at the Gates or Trojan War Will not Take Place, The
Jean Giradoux
Drama 2 Acts
Paris 1948

Hector, Troy's greatest soldier, returns home from an eastern war victorious but converted to keeping future peace by a new found revulsion to slaughter. In Troy he finds that the Greek navy under Odysseus are about to descend on the city to force his own brother, Paris, to return the beautiful Helen to her Greek husband King Menelaus, from whom Paris abducted her.

The Trojan populace clamours for war, urged on by the vainglorious poet Demokos. Hector endures the taunts of the Greek hero Ajax, overides the blood lust of his countrymen, and negotiates a face-saving return of Helen with Odysseus. But just as peace looks set to prevail, Demokos pretends to have been attacked by Ajax, the negotiations unravel, and war is declared.

Andromache, Hector's wife	Troilus
Cassandra, Priam's wife	Abneos
Laundress	Busiris
Hector, Trojan general	Olipdes
Paris, Hector's brother	Iris
Priam, King of Troy	Peace
Demokos, a poet	Senator
Hecuba, Priam's wife	Servants
Helen	Messengers
Ajax	Sailor
Odysseus	Two old men
Mathematician	A top man
Polyxene	Guard
	Crowd

Time and the Conways
J. B. Priestley
Drama 3 Acts
London 1937

Well-off middle-class family the Conways celebrate daughter Kay's twenty-first birthday in the autumn of 1919. They are a fun family and the future is full of promise; Kay wants to be a novelist, lovely Hazel to marry a rich and handsome man, serious Madge to work for socialism, while demobbed officer Robin returns home and immediately starts courting pretty family friend Joan Helford. Only son Alan is unambitious, and youngest daughter Carol, the most charming of them all, has not yet made up her mind. Widow Mrs Conway delights in her brood and is a little upset when, during charades, family friend and solicitor Gerald Thornton brings along Ernest Beevers, a hard young businessman fascinated by the scornful Hazel.

Nearly twenty years later disillusionment has set in; Hazel is married to the bully Beevers, Madge is a soured schoolmistress spinster, Robin a sponging drunk whose marriage is on the rocks, Kay a cheap magazine journalist, and Alan still a clerk. Carol is dead and Mrs Conway in financial difficulties. Kay and Alan reminisce, and Alan explains the theory of time as a continuum and this comforts her. Act Three is a continuation of Act One, the irony of foreknowledge of the future made more poignant as the seeds of the family's downfall can be seen to be sown.

Hazel
Carol

Alan
Madge
Kay
Robin
Mrs Conway
Joan Helford
Gerald Thornton
Ernest Beevers

Time and Time Again
Alan Ayckbourn
Comedy 2 Acts
London 1972

When Anna's mother dies, she and her husband Graham inherit not only their house, but also its lodger - Anna's brother, slightly eccentric ex-school teacher Leonard, a poetic ditherer who works in the council parks department and holds conversations with the garden gnome. The action takes place entirely in the family garden and conservatory.

When Graham's sports-mad employee Peter brings over fiancée Joan, lecherous bullying Graham makes a bee-line for her. To his horror, Joan becomes entangled with Leonard, and their furtive affair arouses Peter's suspicions. But it is Graham he suspects. Only after Peter has half-strangled Graham does Leonard tell him the truth and the disgusted Joan walks out on them both. Fortunately for Leonard, friendship - and various mutual sporting activities - negates Peter's wrath, even though he has lost his job, his girlfriend, and several times been accidently injured at the hands of his Jonah-like friend.
Graham
Anna
Leonard
Joan
Peter

Time of Your Life, The
William Saroyan
Comedy 5 Acts
New York 1939

Nick's Pacific Street Saloon, Restaurant and Entertainment Palace in San Francisco is a good-time bar with a host of genial regulars, each with a story. They reflect Nick's own expansive and generous personality; Joe is an eccentric young loafer with plenty of money, exploring the possibilities of living a life which does not hurt anyone; Tom is his friend, admirer, stooge and errand-boy who falls in love with Kitty, a street-walker still clinging to her girlish dreams. Joe sets it up so they can marry and escape the streets, but their relationship is threatened by vice-squad sadist Blick. Set against a background of Wesley's atmospheric blues-and-boogie piano, unfunny comic Harry's excellent hoofing and the philosophic Arab's harmonica, everything works out fine. Blick gets killed, shot perhaps or perhaps not by the likeably boastful old Indian fighter Kit Carson. Side-plots include the romance of Dudley and Elsie, and the dilemma of waterfront cop Krupp and his friend the striking McCarthy.

Joe	*Willie*
Tom	*Blick*
Kitty Duval	*Ma, Nick's mother*
Nick	*A street walker*
Arab	*Her sidekick*
Kit Carson	*A cop*
McCarthy	*Another cop*
Krupp	*A sailor*
Harry	*A society gentleman*
Wesley	*A society lady*
Dudley	*A drunkard*
Elsie	*The newsboy*
Lorene	*Ann, Nick's daughter*
Mary L.	

Timon of Athens
William Shakespeare
Tragedy 5 Acts
London 1608

Timon is a generous Athenian aristocrat, entertaining with lavish feasts and always ready to help the needy. But when his own wealth is exhausted and he asks help from his friends, one after another they turn him down. So he invites them to yet another feast; they arrive, thinking he has recovered his wealth, but instead he belabours them with withering sarcasm, overturns the tables and attacks them. He then casts off the trappings of civilization and becomes a hermit, embracing a kind of nirvana. While digging for roots to eat, he finds gold, and gives it away to stragglers, to his steward, and even to robbers, whom he reforms. Others hear of his gold and even believe his retreat has been a mere testing of his friends. Then the rebel general Alcibiades, fighting against the corrupt Athenians, is about to storm the city, and the Senators ask Timon for help. He refuses - he is now beyond Mankind, and returning to the world of the spirit he dies. Athens surrenders to Alciabades, who promises peace.

Timon, a noble Athenian
Lords and flatterers of Timon: *Lucius, Lucullus and*
  Sempronius
Ventidius, one of Timon's false friends
Apemantus, a churlish philosopher
Alcibiades, an Athenian general
Flavius, steward to Timon
Timon's servants: *Flaminius, Lucilius, Servilius*
Servants to Timon's creditors: *Caphis, Philotus,*
  Titus and Hortensius
Cupid and maskers
Three strangers
Poet
Painter
Jeweller
Merchant
Mercer
An old Athenian

A page
A fool
Phrynia, Timandra, mistresses to Alcibiades
Lords
Senators
Officers
Servants
Creditors
Soldiers
Banditti
Attendants

'Tis Pity She's a Whore
John Ford
Tragedy 5 Acts
London 1633

The incestuous love of Giovanni and his sister Annabella is known only to his confessor Friar Bonaventura, and to her tutoress Putana. The Friar, with all his threats of hellish torments, cannot sway Giovanni from his fatalistic convictions, so he encourages Annabella to mitigate her sin by marrying one of her many suitors. They include the cream of Parma society, and in the tussles for her hand ex-soldier Grimaldi tries to kill nobleman Sorenzo, but mistakenly slays likeable young oaf Bergetto, heir and nephew to the rich Donado. Soranzo's cunning Spanish servant Vasques is in the midst of the intrigues and saves his master from a death plot by Hippolita, whom Soranzo had wronged. Soranzo marries Annabella but is enraged upon discovering she is pregnant; Vasques gleans from Putana that Giovanni is responsible, and master and servant set a trap. They lure Giovanni to Soranzo's birthday feast and send him to see his sister, intending to slay him *in flagrante*. But Giovanni knows he and Annabella are doomed and he kills her. He reappears at the feast with her heart on the point of his sword. Their father Floria dies of a broken heart as Giovanni makes his confessions then kills Soranzo. Vasques and his bandits kill Giovanni and the spoils of the dead are claimed by the corrupt Cardinal.

Bonaventura, a friar
A Cardinal, nuncio to the Pope
Soranzo, a nobleman
Florio, a citizen of Parma
Donado, another citizen
Grimaldi, a Roman gentleman
Giovanni, son to Florio
Bergetto, nephew to Donado
Richardetto, a supposed physician
Vasques, servant to Soranzo
Poggio, servant to Bergetto
Banditti
Officers
Servants
Annabella, daughter to Florio
Hippolita, wife to Richardetto
Philotis, Richardetto's niece
Putana, tutoress to Annabella

Titus Andronicus
William Shakespeare
Tragedy 5 Acts
London 1594

Brothers Bassianus and Saturninus are rivals for the Roman throne. Rome's greatest general, Titus Andronicus, favours Saturninus and the issue is thus decided in his favour.

The appointment is a tragic mistake. Saturninus is a murderous tyrant and plots with his concubine Tamora, Queen of the Goths, even against Titus. With the new emperor's complicity, Bassianus is murdered, Titus' daughter Lavinia is raped and has her tongue cut out by Tamora's sons, while her brothers are falsely denounced and executed and Titus himself is tricked into sacrificing his sword hand.

When Titus' only remaining son, Lucius, rides north to raise an army of Goths to overthrow Saturninus, Titus unleashes his private revenge. He kills one of Tamora's sons as a sacrifice at the tomb of his own son, Mutius, whom he himself had been tricked into murdering, and cooks her remaining sons in a pie which he serves to Tamora and Saturninus. Turning on Lavinia, he inflicts a mortal wound to spare her further shame, then stabs Tamora before falling to Saturninus. Lucius, who has just returned to Rome, runs Saturninus through and is then declared Governor of the city.

Saturninus, declared Emperor
Bassianus, his brother
Titus Andronicus, a Roman general
Marcus Andronicus, his brother
Titus' sons: *Lucius, Quintus, Martius and Mutius*
Young Lucius, Lucius' son
Titus' relatives: *Sempronius, Caius and Valentine*
Aemelius, a Roman noble
Tamora's sons: *Alarbus, Demetrius and Chiron*
Aaron, Tamora's lover
Tamora, queen of the Goths
Lavinia, Titus' daughter
Capt. Tribune
Messenger
Clown
Romans
Goths
Nurse
Senators
Officers
Soldiers
Attendants

To Damascus, Part I
August Strindberg
Drama 1 Act
Stockholm 1900

This first part of the *To Damascus* trilogy focuses on the anguished wandering and searching of a Stranger who is desperately trying to rid himself of the belief that he has been too evil ever to merit redemption.

The Stranger, having abandoned his own wife and children, meets, falls in love with and is joined in his quest by a Lady who, by coincidence, is the wife of a man whom the Stranger had betrayed many years before. Everywhere they travel, the Stranger is shunned by the people they meet, all of whom are deeply disturbed by the aura of hopeless damnation he carries around with him.

They return penniless and in disgrace, to the humble mountain home of the Lady, but her Mother and Grandfather, kind as they are, cannot accept the Stranger either, so he sets out alone on another round of wandering. Losing his way, the Stranger contracts a fever and is taken in by the Abbess of St Saviour, a charity hospital, where he only recovers his senses after a three-month convalescence.

After his recovery, he sets out again to find the Lady, but although they eventually meet again, poverty forces them once more to wandering. They eventually return to the street corner where they had first met, and the Lady suggests that the Stranger go to the local post office and retrieve a letter which has been waiting for him since that meeting. He does so, and makes the ironic discovery that the letter contains royalties from his books - sufficient to have spared them the privations they have suffered.

Before they set off once more for the mountains, the Lady persuades the Stranger to join her in lighting a candle, in the local church, to her patroness St Elizabeth.

The Stranger
The Lady
The Beggar
The Doctor, the Lady's Husband
His sister
An old man
A mother, the Lady's Mother
An abbess
A confessor
Three mourners
Landlord
Ceasar
Waiter
A smith
Miller's wife
Funeral attendants

To Damascus, Part II
August Strindberg
Drama 4 Acts
Stockholm 1916

In this, the second part of the *To Damascus* trilogy, the Stranger is being discussed by a Dominican confessor from St Saviour's Abbey with the mother of the Lady, who is now about to give birth to the Stranger's child. A letter arrives for the Stranger, containing a picture of his six-year-old son by his first marriage, but the Lady hides it in fear that their expected child will be denied the Stranger's love if he sees the picture. The Lady's

former husband arrives on the scene, broken by the loss of her love and become a beggar. He reveals to the Stranger that the Lady has been giving his own former garments to the Stranger. The Stranger considers this to be a sure sign of the Lady's contempt.

Rather than await the birth of his child, the Stranger goes to a laboratory where he makes gold by an alchemical process. He is then fêted by a committee of supposed intellectuals, who turn out to be nothing but drunks, beggars and whores.

Returning home, he bids a bitter farewell to the Lady's mother and returns to his drinking with the committee, vowing never again to see the Lady. He meets the Lady's former husband again, and discovers that her early life was scandalously debauched. Broken by this news, he breaks his vow and returns home again, to find that the Lady has given birth to a beautiful daughter.

Plagued by the belief that he can only bring misery to the child, the Stranger once again prepares to depart. The Dominican confessor appears and persuades the Stranger to go once again to the Abbey of St Saviour, for solace.

The Stranger
The Lady, his wife
The Mother to the Lady
The Father to the Lady
The Confessor
*The Doctor, the Lady's former
  husband*
Ceasar
Maid
Professor
Ragged person
Another ragged person
Two women
Waitress
Policeman

To Damascus, Part III
August Strindberg
Drama 4 Acts
Stockholm 1916

In this final part of the *To Damascus* trilogy, the Stranger has decided to seek redemption in a mountain monastery and to leave forever behind him the overpowering sorrow of his life.

As he prepares to cross the river which stands between him and the mountain, he is met by his firstborn, his daughter Sylvia, now a young woman. They speak dispiritedly of the past and she leaves him sitting alone. He is then joined by his Confessor, who gives him the last glass of wine he will have as the Stranger, by way of a rite of passage to a new identity. A series of figures from his past - the Lady, his children, his former maid - appear to him and seem to tempt him back into his former life.

While he is talking to the Lady, she is transformed

into his mother, and he must face his own powerful urge to take succour from her, and forego his spiritual quest. Again he resists, but his will weakens and he moves down the mountain for a last period of domestic happiness with the Lady/Mother.

Finally, his restlessness reasserts itself, he feels himself again the Stranger and, after a sad reconciliation with his first wife, climbs the mountain one last time to face his death, and rebirth.

The Stranger
The Lady, his wife
The Confessor
The Magistrate
The Prior
The Tempter
The Daughter, the Stranger's firstborn
Hostess
Two voices
Worshippers of Venus
Maria, the Stranger's former maid
Pilgrim
Father
Woman
Eve
Prior
Pater Isidor, the Doctor of Part I
Pater Clemens
Pater Melcher

To Dorothy, a Son
Roger MacDougall
Farcical Comedy 2 Acts
London 1950

Penniless composer Toni Rigi is trying to fend off his creditors and write documentary theme music, while his wife Dorothy is bedbound and about to give birth.

Who should turn up but Toni's American ex-wife, glamorous Myrtle, with news that their Brazilian divorce is invalid and that if Toni has a son within a year, he will inherit a million dollars from an eccentric uncle. Fortunately the terms of this rich misogynist's will do not specify any particular female to bear and give birth to the precocious manling.

Unfortunately the time for producing the heir is almost up, but despite the invalidity of her marriage, Dorothy produces twins -a boy and a girl- who qualify under the conditions of the will. Then Toni discovers that he and Myrtle were never properly married anyway, and after finding out she has a husband and family back in the USA, agrees to split the million.

Toni Rigi
Dorothy Rigi
Taxi driver
Second taxi driver
Myrtle
Landlord
Dr Cameron
Nurse

Tobacco Road
Erskine Caldwell
Drama 3 Acts
New York 1933

In a squalid shack in Georgia live the poor Lester family, dirty reprobate Jeeter, his feeble wife Ada, and his old crone of a mother. From their fifteen children only three remain on the farm, Ellie May, a harelipped eighteen-year-old tomboy, Dude an impudent sixteen-year-old, and fourteen-year-old married daughter Pearl.

As the family lounge around on the porch, Pearl's husband Lov arrives complaining of her lack of marital qualities, and begins to flirt with sister Ellie May who fancies him. Another visitor is a forty-year-old preacher woman, Bessie Rice, who is looking to marry Dude.

Pearl runs away and Jeeter schemes with Lov to get her back but is not averse to letting him have Ellie May, for a price. When Ada tries to resist this move, she is run over and killed in the struggle, and Jeeter decides to bury her out at the back as he sits and watches the continuing deterioration of his land.

Dude Lester
Ada Lester
Jeeter Lester
Ellie May
Grandma Lester
Lov Bensey
Henry Peabody
Sister Bessie Rice
Pearl
Captain Tim
George Payne

Tom Jones
Joan Macalpine based on the novel
by Henry Fielding
Comedy 3 Acts
Leatherhead 1965

Tom Jones, a handsome orphan and the adopted son of the upright Squire Allworthy, brings disgrace on his benefactor by making a local Somerset wench pregnant. Allworthy forgives him, but when Tom is caught once again *in flagrante*, and appears incapable of curbing his amorous nature, the Squire sends him packing. Although he is as aware as anyone else of his lack of self-control, Tom's main regret in leaving is that he must be parted from Sophia Western, daughter of Squire Western, with whom he has long been secretly in love. Their separation is even harder to bear when Tom discovers that Allworthy and Western have decided she should marry Blifil, Allworthy's sanctimonious and hypocritical nephew.

Tom and Sophia say their goodbyes and he sets off to join the army, but on his first stopover he falls in with a lusty woman, Mrs Waters, whom he is on the point of seducing when Sophia, having fled home to find him, coincidentally arrives at the same inn. Discovering Tom's lechery is unabated, she sets off with Mrs

Fitzpatrick, who is also, coincidentally both a guest at the inn and one of Sophia's childhood friends. They travel to London, pursued by Tom.

But though he searches for weeks Tom finds no trace of Sophia, and falls instead into the role of Mrs Fitzpatrick's lover. Here too, he comes unstuck when Capt. Fitzpatrick discovers the affair, challenges Tom to a duel and is killed. Although he acted in self-defence, Tom is expertly framed by Blifil, who secretly hates him and has been in London waiting to do him down, and trying, with Western and Allworthy, to find Sophia for himself.

Tom is mounting the scaffold, having been condemned for murder, when Allworthy, Western, Sophia and Mrs Waters arrive with a reprieve. Mrs. Waters, it transpires, has witnessed Blifil's treachery, revealed it to the two Squires and, with their help, convinced the authorities of Tom's innocence. She then reveals that under her maiden name, Jenny Jones, she was maid to Allworthy's sister, Bridget, and that Tom is Bridget's natural son. So the young rascal is not only saved, but is Allworthy's heir, and free at last to marry Sophia.

Tom Jones
Squire Allworthy, Tom's guardian
Bridget Allworthy, Allworthy's sister
Thwackum
Blifil, Allworthy's nephew
Squire Western
Sophia Western, his daughter
George Seagrim
Doctor
Honour
Susan
Mrs Waters
Mrs Fitzpatrick
Lord Fellerman, Mrs Fitzpatrick's husband
Constable
First Bystander
Second Bystander
Woman with basket
Andrews
Allworthy's servant
Executioner
Priest

Tonight at 8.30
Noël Coward
Nine One-act Plays
London 1935-6
A series of one-act plays, the parts depict the decline of Western civilization, and are performed in different combinations to make up three shows.

We Were Dancing
Comedy 2 Scenes
After spending an evening trying to convince her husband to let her go to Australia with her lover, next morning, a young wife has second thoughts about the affair and decides against it.
Louise Chateris
Hubert Chateris
Karl Sandys
Clara Bethel
George Davies
Eva Blake
Maj. Blake
Ippaga
Country club members

The Astonished Heart
Play 6 Scenes
Through a series of flashbacks, in reverse order, the stormy passionate affair of a psychiatrist and his wife's friend is shown culminating in his death by suicide.
Christian Faber
Barbara Faber
Leonora Vail
Tim Verney
Susan Birch
Sir Reginald French
Ernest

Red Peppers
Sketch with music
George and Lily Pepper have a music-hall act which is decidedly not up to scratch. They row with the manager after a poor first house, and during the second the musical director makes their act look ridiculous.
George and Lily Pepper, a music-hall duo
Mr Edwards, House Manager
Bert Bently, Musical Director
Alf, call boy
Mabel Grace, an old actress

Hands Across the Sea
Comedy
Colonial couple, the Wadhursts, are mistakenly at the London party given by the scatterbrained Piggie Gilpin. Piggy has just returned from a world tour and takes them for people she met on her travels. They are subjected to meaningless conversations about people they do not know by a hostess who has forgotten who they are.
Peter Gilpin, a young navy man
Alistair Corbett, a young navy man
Mr Wadhurst, a pleasant middle aged man
Mrs Wadhurst, his wife
Mr Burnham,
'Bogey' Gosling, handsome young marine
Lady Maureen 'Piggie' Gilpin
Claire Wedderburn
Walters, parlour maid

Fumed Oak
Unpleasant Comedy 2 Acts
Henry Gow is a poor down-trodden male in a household

of dreadful women, a sloppy wife, a snivelling daughter, and a hideous nagging mother-in-law. After a few drinks at the pub he tells them all what he thinks, takes his savings, and leaves them to it for good.

Henry Gow
Doris, his wife
Elsie, their daughter
Mrs Rockett, mother-in-law

Shadow Play
Musical Fantasy
A woman, about to be divorced, takes an overdose of pills and relives the happiness the couple had in the early years. Her memories bring them back together.

Victoria Gayforth
Simon Gayforth
Martha Cunningham
George Cunningham
Lena
Sibyl Heston
Michael Doyle
A young man
Hodge

Family Album
Comedy
In 1860 when the Featherways family gather to hear the will of their deceased father, drink makes them reveal what they all thought about the old boy, a mean, pompous, and profligate bounder. Daughter Lavinia and butler Burrows liven up the proceedings even more by admitting that they have burnt the will that would have left the family fortune to father's mistress.

Jasper Featherways
Richard Featherways
Jane Featherways
Lavinia Featherways
Charles Winter
Harriet Winter
Edward Valance
Emily Valance
Burrows

Ways and Means
Comedy 3 Scenes
The Cartwrights have become unwelcome guests at Olive's Riviera house; they are broke. Their difficulties are solved when their host is robbed by a friendly chauffeur who goes halves with them, leaving them bound and gagged to allay suspicion.

Toby Cartwright
Stella Cartwright, his wife
Lord Chapworth
Olive Lloyd-Ransome
Princess Elena Krasiloff
Gaston, French valet
Stevens, chauffeur
Nanny

Still Life
Play 5 Scenes
Set in a railway station refreshment room with the comic activities of its personel, Alec and Laura, both married, meet and fall in love, have a few furtive moments of happiness and the agonies of guilt, and then finally part, their farewell being cruelly spoilt by a garrulous friend.

Alec Harvey
Laura Jesson
Albert Godby, ticket collector
Bill and Johnny, soldiers
Myrtle Bagot
Beryl Waters
Mildred
Stanley, a young man
Dolly Messiter

Tons of Money
Will Evans and Valentine
Farce 3 Acts
Southport 1922
Profligate inventor and toff Aubrey Allington is besieged by creditors. When he gets news of a fortune left to him by his brother who has died in Mexico, he realizes the legacy will be swallowed in his debts. Together with scheming wife Louise he concocts a plan; he will 'die' and return as his cousin George Maitland, named as second beneficiary in the will. George, so Aubrey believes, also perished abroad. So Aubrey blows himself up and returns as George, and the complications begin. George's wife Jean turns up, followed by another imposter called Henory, foisted on the proceedings by the wily servants. Not realizing Henory is a phoney, Aubrey 'perishes' again, this time by drowning, and reincarnates as a fey clergyman. When the real George Maitland turns up, lured by the will, he chases off Henory but is thwarted by Aubrey who confesses all in order to keep the inheritance. But all is to no avail because solicitor James Chesterman reveals that the Mexican government have annexed the fortune.

Sprules, a butler
Simpson, a parlourmaid
Miss Benita Mullett
Louise Allington
Aubrey Henry Maitland Allington
Giles, a gardener
James Chesterman
Jean Everard
Henory
George Maitland

Tooth of Crime, The
Sam Shepard
Drama 2 Acts
London 1972
Set in a near future dominated by violent anarchy, this play follows the harrowing overthrow of a contract

killer, Hoss, by a much younger killer, Crow, who is intent on ousting Hoss from the top of a hit parade of killers which has replaced the pop hit parade. Hoss and his stable of assistants, all of them caught up in their employer's drug-raddled paranoia, try to whip up a sense of their own inviolable strength to cover feelings of impending disaster.

When Crow eventually arrives, it is agreed that he and Hoss will meet in a bizarre form of single combat, to be judged by a referee, in which they slowly circle round one another mounting ritualized insults meant to undermine the confidence of their opponent. As he is on the point of losing, Hoss gives up the battle and kills himself, leaving Crow free to inherit his mantle as the ultimate killer.

Hoss, a contract killer
Becky Lou, his girlfriend
Star-man
Galactic Jack
Referee
Cheyenne
Doc
Crow, Hoss's sworn enemy

Torch Song Trilogy
Harvey Fierstein
Comedy 3 Plays
New York 1982

Three connected plays about homosexuality which revolve around the on-off-on romance of Arnold, a witty twenty-four-year-old who works in a nightclub as a drag queen, and Ed, a handsome boyish bisexual of thirty-four. In the first play, Lady Blues sings twenties' and thirties' torch songs between the scenes *á la* Helen Morgan or Ruth Etting, and there are also several long monologues from Arnold, including a pre-AIDS ramble on Arnold's experiences in the back room of the bar.

The International Stud: Arnold and Ed meet in 'The International Stud' bar, and soon become lovers, but after a few months Ed's attracted to Laurel, the kind of gal who always lands a bisexual. Ed has not come out of the closet in front of his folks and is happy because he can conduct his romance in the open.

Fugue in a Nursery: Ed and Laurel wed. Laurel invites Arnold and his new boyfriend Alan - presumably to study the opposition.

Widows and Children First: Several years have passed. Alan has been murdered by queer-bashers and Arnold has no lover but is about to adopt David, an ex-delinquent fifteen-year-old. Ed is through with Laurel and comes to stay for a few days. Arnold's Ma arrives. She is not impressed with Arnold's life-style, they fight, reach a kind of truce, and after she leaves it looks as if Arnold and Ed will get back together.

Arnold   *Alan*
Ed   *David*
Lady Blues   *Mrs Beckoff*
Laurel

Towards Zero
Agatha Christie
Drama 3 Acts
London 1956

Neville Strange, an urbane, sporty, rich young man arrives, with his second wife, Kay, at the Cornish home of his aunt, Lady Tressilian. His ostensible reason for visiting is that he hopes Kay will have a chance to meet and befriend his first wife, Audrey, who is taking her regular yearly holiday with Lady Tressilian, to whom Audrey is devoted. They are joined by Thomas Royde, Neville's cousin, and mix with Mary Aldin, Lady Tressilian's secretary, and Mathew Treves, a retired lawyer and lifelong family friend who lives nearby.

All of the guests but Neville find the atmosphere oppressive and threatening on account, they believe, of the embarrassing proximity of Kay and Audrey. And Neville's apparent preference for Audrey's company further clouds the atmosphere, and sends Kay into a despairing rage.

On the morning after the Strange's arrival it is discovered that Mary has been drugged and Lady Tressilian brutally murdered. The evidence points strongly to Neville's guilt, but he escapes prosecution by providing an evidently cast-iron alibi. The detective in charge of the investigation then switches his attention to Audrey, whose motive appears to be revenge on Neville, by 'framing' him, for deserting her. Audrey is led away and the family, guests and servants appear to accept her guilt.

However, in a typical Christie final scene, Mathew Treves brings the household together, traps the guilty party into an admission of guilt, and reveals that his suspicions were aroused when he discovered that Audrey had abandoned Neville, not vice versa. The motive, therefore, was revenge.

Thomas Royde, Lady Tressilian's nephew
Kay Strange
Mary Aldin, Lady Tressilian's secretary
Mathew Treves, a retired solicitor
Neville Strange, Kay's husband
Lady Tressilian
Audrey Strange, Neville's ex-wife
Ted Latimer
Superintendent Battle
Inspector Leach
Police Constable Benson

Toys in the Attic
Lillian Hellman
Drama 3 Acts
New York 1960

Middle-aged spinster sisters Carrie and Anna Berniers live in their old family house in New Orleans which they detest. They dream of going to Europe and worry why their beloved younger brother Julian has not been in touch since his marriage to the delicate and highly-strung Lily. They have been bailing Julian out financially for years - it gives them pleasure to do so - and when he does arrive they are amazed to see he has lots of money 150,000 dollars in cash; he has also bought them tickets to Europe, paid off the mortgage and bought them exotic gifts. They discover he had an inside tip from an old mistress about a land deal, and he has to leave briefly to pay off his old girlfriend. He plans afterwards to go to New York with Lily, and his friend will also be able to escape from her brutal lawyer husband. Lily is afraid she will lose Julian, and in collusion with Carrie tips off the lawyer. Julian is robbed and beaten, his friend slashed; he returns with no money and the status quo is resumed - seemingly to everyone's satisfaction.

Carrie Berniers
Anna Berniers, her sister
Gus
Albertine Prine, Lily's mother
Henry Simpson
Julian Berniers
Lily Berniers
Taxi driver
Three removal men

Trafford Tanzi
Claire Luckham and Chris Monks
Musical 2 Acts
Manchester 1980

This play uses a ten-round wrestling match, in which a girl named Trafford Tanzi fights a round each with her mother, one of her childhood friends, the local school psychiatrist, her father, her boyfriend and eventual husband Dean Rebel, her husband's mistress, her mother again, and so on, as a metaphor for the struggle women face if they wish to achieve independence.

In the final round, Tanzi meets her husband again, having already become European Ladies Champion Wrestler, with the loser being obliged to become a housewife while the winner follows his, or her, chosen career. Tanzi wins.

The referee
Tanzi's mum
Tanzi's dad
Platinum Sue
Dean Rebel
Trafford Tanzi

Travesties
Tom Stoppard
Comedy 2 Acts
London 1974

Lenin, James Joyce and Dada-ist Tristan Tzara were all in Zurich during World War One, and *Travesties* ties these characters together with the leading figure of Henry Carr, a minor British consulate official. Carr played Algy in Joyce's production of Wilde's *The Importance of Being Earnest* by the English Players in Zurich, and this elaborate story, set mostly in the Zurich library, moves in and out of the dialogue and action of the play combining pastiche, political history, artistic argument, time shifts and reminiscences. Papers from Joyce's *Ulysses* and Lenin's great work on Imperialism are mixed up, Carr and Joyce litigate over theatrical expenses, and Carr is unable to prevent Lenin from leaving for Russia with all the consequent historical ramifications. True to Wilde's story he does however marry the bolshevik librarian Cecily.

Henry Carr
Tristan Tzara
James Joyce
Lenin
Bennett, Carr's manservant
Gwendolen, Carr's younger sister
Cecily
Nadya, Lenin's wife

Trelawney of the 'Wells'
Arthur Wing Pinero
Drama 4 Acts
London 1898

Rose Trelawney, an actress of Clerkenwell, is about to leave the profession to marry Arthur Gower, but prior to the wedding she is to live with the Gower family in the West End to familiarize herself with her new life style. Friends from the theatre visit Rose and discuss performances and attitudes to their work. Imogen Parrott and Tom Wrench are prominent.

Rose is not happy in her new genteel surroundings, it is too quiet, and she joins in a song with a street barrel-organ, which is silenced by Arthur's father Sir William. She plays a piano, sings some opera and is secretly joined by her old friends who are on a trip to the West End. Some drinking is followed by a confrontation with Sir William who order the actors out. Rose decides to join them.

Six months later Rose is not the actress she was and Arthur has joined the acting profession himself. Things are changing in the theatre, and Rose's friends are fearful for their jobs.

Tom and Imogen are to produce a play themselves, but need more finance. Sir William, in search of his son, has an encounter with another actress, Avonia Bunn, who manages to soften his attitudes to the point of getting more money for the show from him. He is astonished to find Arthur is the leading man.

James Telfer
Augustus Colpoys
Ferdinand Gadd
Tom Wrench
Mrs Telfer
Avonia Bunn
Rose Trelawney
Imogen Parrott
O'Dwyer
Sir William Gower
Arthur Gower
Clara de Foenix
Miss Trafalgar Gower
Capt. Foenix
Mrs Mossop
Mr Ablett
Charles
Sarah

Trial by Jury
W.S. Gilbert and Arthur Sullivan
Comic Opera 1 Act
London 1875

This Dramatic Cantata takes place in a court of justice, where the jury are instructed on their duties as they prepare to hear a breach of promise case brought by Angelina against Edwin. The jury is biased against Edwin, but he pleads with them to hear his case, and tells of his youthful inexperience. The judge enters to a chorus of praise from all, and tells of his own rise to fame and love life.

After the jury is sworn in, the plaintiff enters accompanied by a chorus of bridesmaids, with whom the jury fall in love. She tells her sad story and the jury is deeply moved. The defendant then gives his side and suggests that he is such a bad lot that the girl could not have loved him and a solution could be that he marries her today and then another tomorrow.

The judge has the answer, he will marry pretty Angelina himself.

Songs include: 'All hail, great Judge'; 'When I, Good Friends, Was Called to the Bar'; 'Oh, Gentlemen, Listen, I Pray'; 'I love him - I love him - with Fervour Unceasing'

The learned judge
Angelina, the plaintiff
Edwin, the defendant
Counsel for the plaintiff
Usher
Foreman of the jury
Associate
First bridesmaid
Chorus of bridesmaids
Jury
Barristers

Trilby
Paul M. Potter
Melodrama 4 Acts
London 1895

Talbot 'Taffy' Wynne, Sandy McAlister and William Bagot, three British gentlemen painters who live an a rooming house in Paris' Latin Quarter in the gay 1890s, are all in love with Trilby O'Ferrall, an impoverished but proud and very beautiful artist's model. When Taffy and McAlister realize that Trilby has eyes only for Bagot, whom she calls Little Billee, they happily defer to her choice, and the young couple decide to wed.

On the night before the wedding, though, Bagot's parents arrive unexpectedly and are appalled at Little Billee's choice, preferring that he should marry a proper English girl. They are thus overjoyed when Svengali, an evil stage magician and hypnotist, puts Trilby in a trance and spirits her out of Paris.

For five years, Trilby is kept in a trance by the magician who turns her by his power from a tone-deaf croaker into a true diva, but only at the expense of her general health. By coincidence, the three British friends return to Paris and stumble upon one of Trilby's performances, still believing that she deserted Little Billee for the sake of fame and fortune. When they discover that her departure and absence were the result of Svengali's strange power over her, they are appalled, but relief comes quickly with Svengali's death from the stress of his years of controlling Trilby's every mood and mannerism.

The lovers plan to carry through with their former marriage plans, but when they are left alone to contemplate the happy prospect, they are interrupted by the delivery of a painting from a stranger who says it is a gift for Trilby. She uncovers the picture and, finding it to be a portrait of the dead magician, falls into a trance, mumbles his names and dies.

Svengali, an evil stage magician
Gentlemen painters:
  Talbot 'Taffy' Wynne
  Sandy 'The Laird' McAlister
  William 'Little Billee' Bagot
Gecko, Svengali's lackey
Zouzou
Dodor
Anthony Oliver
Lorimer
Revd Thomas Bagot
Col Kaur
Trilby O'Ferrall
Mrs Bagot
Mme Vinard
Angele Honorine
Mimi
Musette

Troilus and Cressida
William Shakespeare
Tragedy 5 Acts
London 1601

The Greek siege of Troy, meant to win the return of Helen of Troy to her Greek husband, has been going on for seven years. The Trojan prince, Troilus, is in love with Cressida, the daughter of a Trojan priest who has defected to the Greeks.

Just as the war reaches the crucial point where the Greek hero Achilles is about to fight Hector of Troy in single combat, the Greeks agree to exchange a Trojan prisoner for Cressida, so that she may rejoin her father. When she reaches the Greek camp, Cressida soon forgets her love for Troilus, and gives his last token of love to the Greek Diomedes.

Troilus, hiding nearby, is heartbroken when he sees the exchange, and determines to challenge Diomedes in battle the next day. He is defeated, as is Hector, and Troy mourns its dead.

Priam, King of Troy
Priam's sons: *Hector, Troilus, Paris, Deiphobus and Helenus*

Margarelon, Priam's bastard son
Trojan commanders: *Aeneas, Antenor*
Calchas, Cressida's father
Pandarus, Cressida's uncle
Agamemnon, Greek general
Menelaus, Agamemnon's brother
Greek commanders: *Achilles, Ajax, Ulysses, Nestor,*
  Diomedes, Patroclus
Thersites, a Greek
Alexander, Cressida's servant
Helen, Menelaus' wife
Andromache, Hector's wife
Cressida, Calchas' daughter
Cassandra, Priam's daughter
Soldiers
Attendants
Servants

Trojan Women, The
Euripides
Tragedy 1 Act
415BC

Troy lies smashed and burning, its men put to the sword, its women and children allotted as slaves to the victorious Greeks under the command of Menelaus and Agamemnon.

The play unfolds the sorrows, suffered already and still to come, of the Trojan survivors, chief amongst whom is their Queen, Hecuba. She has already been made a slave of Odysseus who she hates most amongst the Greeks, and we see her learn of the murder of one of her daughters, Polyxena; the degredation of another, Cassandra, who is made a concubine to Agamemnon; and the murder of her grandson, Astyanax.

Half mad, Cassandra rejoices in her fate since it has angered the Goddess Athene, who in revenge will wreck the Greek fleet in a sea storm. Andromache, her sister-in-law and Astyanax' mother, is made a slave and sets sail with her master, forcibly leaving Astyanax to be buried by Hecuba.

Hecuba encounters the victorious Menelaus and Helen, his beautiful wife, whose desertion to Hecuba's son, Paris, was the cause of the war. Hecuba pleads with Menelaus to execute Helen and he, more out of injured vanity then jealousy, agrees to do so.

As Hecuba gently prepares Astyanax's infant body for burial, the Greeks put Troy to the torch and, surrounded by the wailing Trojan women, load their fleet for the homeward journey.
Poseidon, god of the sea
Athena, a goddess
Hecuba, Queen of Troy
Chorus, captured Trojan women
Talthybins, a Greek herald
Cassandra, Hecuba's daughter
Andromache, Hecuba's daughter-in-law
Menelaus, a Greek king
Helen, Menelaus' wife

True West
Sam Shepard
Drama 2 Acts
London 1981

Under pressure of deadlines Austin, a screen writer transplanted from the 'true west' of the title to suburban Southern California, moves into his mother's house while she is on holiday. He has unexpectedly been joined there by his older brother Lee, a petty criminal and drifter in the classic American 'greaser' mould.

As Austin tries to finish a draft script he is writing for Saul Kimmer, a Hollywood producer, Lee wheedles out of Austin the impressive details of his deal with Saul. When Saul comes for a meeting with Austin, Lee upstages his brother's work with a storyline based on his own experience. He goes on to cajole and bully Saul into backing the story as a film project.

In order to present the story professionally, Lee is obliged to get Austin's help with writing a script. They write, quarrel and are alternatively depressed or elated by the collaboration. Just as their rivalry reaches its sourest point, their mother returns home early from holiday. Her presence increases the tension between the two men and Austin attacks Lee, nearly strangling him. Their mother pleads with Austin to release Lee, but when he does so, Lee blocks his exit and the two men square off to continue their fight.
Austin
Lee
Saul Kimmer
Mom

Trumpets and Raspberries
Dario Fo
Comedy 2 Acts
Rome 1981

Urban guerrillas kidnap Italy's leading capitalist, Gianni Agnelli, owner of Fiat and proponent of 'strong' right-wing government. In trying to make their escape the guerrillas crash their car and are killed. Agnelli survives, the victim of disfiguring burns. The attempted escape is seen by a left-wing Fiat worker, Antonio Berardi, who is at the time keeping a tryst with his lover Lucia.

When Antonio flees after taking Agnelli to hospital, the injured man is wrongly identified as his humble worker, treated as the chief suspect in his own kidnapping, and given plastic surgery which leaves him looking like Berardi's double. While Antonio goes underground, his wife Rosa joins with Lucia in a series of hapless attempts to prove sometimes that the double is, and sometimes that he is not, the real Antonio.

Only after the real Antonio is captured and tortured by the police is the mistake in identity accepted by the authorities, who are left to rue their blunder.
Four orderlies
Doctor
Rosa Berardi, Antonio Berardi's wife
Antonio Berardi, Fiat worker

Lucia, Antonio's mistress
Agnelli, a leading capitalist
Inspector
Examining magistrate
Group leader
Two secret agents
Man with dishwasher

Turista, La
Sam Shepard
Drama 2 Acts
New York 1967

An American couple, Salem and Kent, languish in a Mexican hotel room, both of them victims of acute dysentry, known as La Turista. A Mexican boy arrives unbidden at the room offering to shine their shoes, but instead involves himself in finding a local witch doctor to cure their malady. The cure involves chants and dancing by the witch doctor and his apprentice son, followed by the sacrifice of two chickens whose blood is sprayed over Kent's recumbent body. The cure fails.

In the play's second act the couple are found in an American hotel room, still in the grip of their disease. This time they are treated, with the same lack of results, by an American doctor dressed incongruously in the style of a Civil War military medic. Kent, in a delirium of sickness and anxiety, escapes and is not seen again.

Salem	*Son*
Kent	*Doc*
Boy	*Sonny*
Doctor	

Turn of the Screw, The
Ken Whitmore, adapted from a story by Henry James
Drama 2 Acts
Oldham 1982

Miles, ten, and Flora, eight, are orphans living in a large country house at Bly, Essex, in 1875. Their only relative is their uncle Mr Crimond; he has no time for them and appoints the young Miss Grey as their governess. The children are sweet and clever - too sweet and clever - and shortly after her arrival Miss Grey sees two ghosts. She describes them to housekeeper Mrs Grose who tells her they must be Quint, the valet, and Miss Jessel, the former governess, both of whom are dead. There was an affair between them resulting in pregnancy, exceptionally scandalous because of their difference in rank. Miss Grey soon realizes it is not her the ghosts are after - it is the children. Quint and Jessel were kind and loving to them, and they are still attached to the two tormented souls. Miss Grey manages to get Flora and Mrs Grose away from the house, but one fateful night all her efforts cannot prevent Miles from tragedy.

Flora	*Mr Crimond*
Miss Grey	*Peter Quint*
Miles	*Miss Jessell*
Mrs Grose	

Twelfth Night or What You Will
William Shakespeare
Comedy 5 Acts
London 1601

Viola and Sebastian are almost identical twins. In a storm at sea they are separated and washed ashore at different places on the coast of Illyria. Viola disguises herself as a boy, calls herself Cesario, and goes to work for the Count Orsino as a page - soon she has fallen in love with him. Orsino is in love with the beautiful countess Olivia and sends Cesario to plead his suit, but on meeting Cesario, Olivia falls in love with 'him'. During this time, Sebastian is exploring the island with his friend Antonio, who has to be careful in Illyria as he is wanted by Duke Orsino. One day Antonio sees Viola and mistakes her for Sebastian and is then arrested by Orsino's officers. When Olivia meets Sebastian for the first time, she thinks he is Cesario and proposes; he promises to accept. Eventually Viola and Sebastian meet, Antonio is pardoned and all of the mistakes explained. The Duke and Viola marry.

Meanwhile, Olivia's uncle Sir Toby Belch, his companion Sir Andrew Aguecheek and Maria the maid play a trick on Malvolio, Olivia's haughty steward. Cunningly they send him a love letter pretending it is from Olivia. The letter recommends he dress in a strange fashion to win her love. He does, and is treated as a fool and a madman.

Orsino, Duke of Illyria
Sebastian, Violas's brother
Viola
Antonio, a sea captain
Valentine, Curio, gentlemen attending the Duke
Sir Toby Belch, Olivia's uncle
Sir Andrew Aguecheek
Malvolio, Olivia's steward
A sea captain, Viola's friend
Olivia, a rich countess
Maria, Olivia's woman
Lords
Priests
Sailors
Officers
Musicians
Attendants

Twelve Angry Men
Reginald Rose
Play 3 Acts
New York 1956

The twelve men of an American jury gather to make their verdict after hearing the case against a nineteen-year-old boy accused of killing his father. The prosecution has presented a mass of circumstancial evidence that makes a guilty decision look certain.

But one juror, Number 8, has nagging doubts about the way the case has been presented and, despite objections from his colleagues, requests that they go over the whole evidence again. His skilled re-examination reveals that the facts can be interpreted in quite a different way and that the boy could well be innocent. There is certainly no justification for a quick and easy guilty decision.

Only one juror, Number 3, remains unconvinced. Himself a violent man who tyrannizes his family, he wants a vengeful guilty decision and the others have a hard time to make him realize his own deep-seated prejudices before they can announce their verdict.
Guard
Foreman of the jury
Eleven jurors
Voice of judge

Twin Rivals, The
George Farquhar
Comedy 5 Acts
London 1702

When ne'er-do-well Ben Wouldbe's kind and wealthy father dies, he seizes the opportunity to defraud his absent elder twin brother Hermes of his rightful inheritance. With the connivance of midwife and procuress Mrs Mandrake, steward Clearaccount, and attorney Subtleman, Ben contrives a false will. Unfortunately for him, one of the witnesses is Hermes' faithful Irish servant Teague, the pair having just returned from Germany. Ben immediately begins squandering the estate and manages to get Hermes thrown into prison, to be rescued by his fiancée Constance and his friend Trueman.

An elaborate sub-plot concerns the machinations of Trueman's lascivious uncle Richmore towards his abandoned love Clelia, whom he attempts to pass on to his nephew. At the same time Richmore attempts to discredit Trueman's true love Aurelia in order to have her for himself. Trueman rescues Aurelia from his uncle's clutches, and his youthful virtue inspires Richmore to repent his slimy ways. Meanwhile Hermes finally retains his birthright and inheritance, and brother Ben leaves in high dudgeon, deciding poverty is preferable to obligation towards his hated twin.
Elder Wouldbe (Hermes)
Young Wouldbe (Benjamin)
Richmore
Trueman
Subtleman
Balderdash
Alderman
Clearaccount, a steward
Fairbank, a goldsmith
Teague
Constance
Aurelia
Mandrake
Steward's wife
Constable
Watch

Two for the Seesaw
William Gibson
Comedy-Drama 3 Acts
New York 1958

Nebraska lawyer Jerry Ryan is desperate in New York City. He is divorcing his rich wife Tess back home, he is lonely and hates the city. Then he meets attractive and vulnerable Gittel Mosca at a party, and the play follows their affair from beginning to end, in their respective rooms a few miles apart (both of which are on stage). Gittel is a kind of cause for Jerry - she undervalues herself, she suffers from stomach ulcers which cause internal haemorrhages, and she lets men walk all over her. He nurses her and helps her regain her self-respect and she in turn demolishes his self-pity. Trouble is, he still loves Tess, and she wants him back. Gittel knows that Jerry will stay as long as she needs him, and she does not want that. So they say goodbye, with love, each coming out of the relationship with more than they went in with.
Jerry Ryan
Gittel Mosca

Two Gentlemen of Verona, The
William Shakespeare
Comedy 5 Acts
London 1594

Valentine and Proteus, two young friends, leave home in Verona for Milan, Valentine to learn sophistication, and Proteus because his father is sending him away from Julia, his lover. Valentine falls in love with Silvia, daughter of the Duke of Milan. When Proteus joins them, they reveal that they must elope because the Duke prefers another suitor, Thurio, to Valentine. Proteus is smitten by Silvia's beauty, and betrays the couple's intention to the Duke, who banishes Valentine. An outcast, Valentine becomes an elegant outlaw leader. Meanwhile, Julia, disguised as a boy, has been following Proteus, and must tolerate her lover's attempts to win Silvia's regard. As his page, Julia even carries Proteus' entreaties to Silvia, to be met with scornful refusal.

The Duke is captured by outlaws in pursuit of his daughter, while Proteus rescues her. When Valentine, who has been following the action from cover, steps out and contemptuously renounces Silvia, Julia, still in the guise of a page, faints dead away. The Duke is brought on by the outlaws, whom he pardons after being freed. In a gentle denouement, Valentine and Silvia, Proteus and Julia, are all reconciled to one another.
Duke of Milan, Silvia's father
Valentine, Proteus, two young Veronese
Antonio, Proteus' father
Thurio, Valentine's rival
Sir Eglamour
Speed, Valentine's servant
Launce, Proteus' servant
Panthino, Antonio's servant
Julia's host

Julia, Proteus' lover
Silvia, The Duke's daughter
Lucetta, Julia's servant
Host
Outlaws
Servants, musicians

Two Mrs Carrolls, The
Martin Vale
Drama 3 Acts
London 1935

Everything looks rosy for highly-strung painter Geoffrey Carroll and his lovely new wife Sally at their elegant villa in the Alpes Maritime in France. Then he meets beautiful neighbour Cecily Harden and instead of painting Sally's portrait, he paints Cecily's. Geoffrey begins an affair with Cecily and at the same time Sally's health begins to deteriorate, but despite the suspicions of Sally's old boyfriend Pennington, useless local Dr Tuttle insists Sally is merely run down. Then Geoffrey is called away on a pretext and his ex-wife Harriet turns up, warning ailing Sally she is being poisoned; she explains that exactly the same thing happened to her, and reveals she has in her possession a confession from Geoffrey of attempted murder. After their divorce she threatened to use the confession unless Geoffrey remained faithful to Sally. Sally refuses to believe Harriet, but the seeds of doubt are sown. When Geoffrey returns he realizes Sally knows the truth and prepares to kill her, intending to lay the blame on a local burglar. He fails, and when discovered and confronted with prison, he kills himself.

Clemence
Pennington
Sally Carroll
Geoffrey Carroll
Mrs Latham
Cecily Harden
Dr Tuttle
Harriet Carroll

Two Noble Kinsmen, The
William Shakespeare and John Fletcher
Tragedy 5 Acts,
London 1613

The marriage of Theseus, Duke of Athens, to Hippolyta, Queen of the Amazons, is interrupted by three widowed queens who beg the duke to avenge their husbands, slain unjustly by Creon, King of Thebes. Theseus agrees and in the war which follows, Theseus captures Creon's nephews Palamon and Arcite.

From their prison cells both of them see and fall in love with Hippolyta's sister, Emilia. Arcite is released from prison but banished from Athens, so he disguises himself and becomes Emilia's servant. At the same time, Palamon escapes from prison with the help of his gaoler's daughter, who is madly in love with him.

The two cousins meet in a duel to decide who will have Emilia, but they are interrupted by an enraged Theseus who, because Emilia cannot decide between them, orders that they must fight again in a month's time. The winner will have Emilia, the loser will die.

Arcite wins the second fight, but is then mortally wounded in a fall from his horse. Palamon is saved from execution when the dying Arcite requests that Emilia should become his cousin's wife instead.

Theseus, Duke of Athens
Pirithous, Theseus' friend
Palamon, Arcite, two cousins
Artesius
Valerius
Gaoler
A doctor
Hyman, god of marriage
Hippolyta, Queen of the Amazons
Emilia, Hippolyta's sister
The gaoler's daughter
Three queens
Herald
Boy
Gentleman
Six knights
Wooer of gaoler's daughter
Two friends of gaoler
Gaoler's brother
Six countrymen
Schoolmaster
Nell
Four country wenches
Emilia's servant
Nymphs
Attendants
Countrymen
Garland-bearer
Hunters
Maids
Executioner
Soldiers

Ubu Roi
Alfred Jarry
Play 5 Acts
Paris 1896
See: King Ubu

Uncle Tom's Cabin
George L. Aiken, based on the story by Harriet Beecher Stowe
Drama 3 Acts
New York 1933

This play takes place in the old South where George and his wife Eliza are slaves but on different plantations. When Eliza's owner, facing the loss of his land, is about to sell her son Harry, the pair flee to Canada pursued by the vicious slave trader Haley.

Uncle Tom, devoted to his master, stays behind and later befriends little Eva, a sick white child, who makes her father promise to free the slaves before she dies. Her father is unfortunately killed and Tom and young slave Emmeline fall into the hands of his evil murderer Simon Legree who beats them mercilessly.

Uncle Tom's original owner Shelby returns, hoping to restore the old slave to his family but he is too late to prevent the brave and good Uncle Tom being struck by Legree. Tom forgives his tormentor as he looks up to Heaven and sees little Eva on a white dove waiting to greet him.

Uncle Tom
Simon Legree
George Harris
St Clair
Marks
Phineas Fletcher
Shelby
Haley
Tom Loker
Gumption Cute
Mr Wilson
Harry
George Shelby Jr
Maj. Mann
George Fisk
Adolph
Caesar
Skeggs
Auctioneer

First bidder
Second bidder
Clerk
Sambo
Quimbo
Overseer
Eliza
Aunt Chloe
Marie
Eva
Aunt Ophelia
Topsy
Nurse
Emmeline
Aunt Hagar
Cassy
Ladies, Slaves, Planters,
Overseers, Singers

Uncle Vanya
Anton Chekhov
Drama 4 Acts
Moscow 1899

Dreary old Professor Serebryakov and his beautiful young wife Yelena have retired to the country estate he inherited from his deceased first wife, whose brother, Vanya, is the estate manager. Also living there are Vanya's mother Maria Vasilyevna and the Professor's grown-up daughter Sonya. For twenty-five years Vanya has revered the Professor's writings and scrimped to send him every spare kopek from the estate; now he is disillusioned and in despair, feeling he has wasted his life on a charlatan. To make matters worse he is jealous, enraptured by the indolent Yelena, whose beauty has also captured Astrov, the sensitive local doctor fascinated by ecology. The rather plain Sonya loves Astrov, but he cannot return her love, and matters come to a head when the Professor, who hates the countryside, suggests selling the estate and moving nearer St Petersburg. Vanya goes crazy and tries to shoot the Professor but misses; subsequent to an apology it is decided that the Professor and his wife should leave, and everything remain as before with Vanya continuing to send them the estate monies. Left to endure their lifelong desperation, Sonya comforts her Uncle Vanya with a moving evocation of God's mercy and the joys of the afterlife.

Serebryakov
Yelena
Sonya
Maria Vasilyevna
Vanya
Astrov
Telegin, an impoverished landowner
Marina, the old nurse
Workman
Watchman

Under Milk Wood
Dylan Thomas
Edinburgh 1956

This 'Play For Voices' commissioned by BBC Radio has subsequently proved equally successful on stage. Through night-time to dawn, then morning, daytime, afternoon, dusk, evening and back to night-time, the inhabitants and ghosts of a tiny Welsh village tell of themselves and each other in delightful prose-poetry and song; the characters are deep and rich and universal, and despite Thomas' death in 1953 preventing his final revision, the cycle of the work stands fairly complete. Particularly memorable characters are the blind seafarer and narrator Capt. Cat and his ghostly girlfriend Rosie Probert; houseproud Mrs Ogmore-Pritchard and her two dead husbands; local bard Revd Eli Jenkins; Dai Bread and his two wives; and local bawd Polly Garter.

Onlooker (Narrator)
Capt. Cat
Five drowned people
Rosie Probert
Myfanwy Price
Mog Edwards
Jack Black
Mr Waldo
Waldo's mother
Waldo's wife
Four neighbours
Little boy Waldo
Matti Richards
Matti's mother
Revd Eli Jenkins
Mrs Ogmore-Pritchard
Mr Ogmore
Mr Pritchard
Gossamer Beynon
Organ Morgan
Mrs Organ Morgan
Utah Watkins
Willy Nilly
Mrs Willy Nilly
PC Attila Rees
Sinbad
Lily Smalls
Mae Rose Cottage
Bessie Bighead

Ocky Milkman
Cherry Owen
Butcher Beynon
Mr Pugh
Mrs Pugh
Mary Ann Sailors
Dai Bread
Polly Garter
Nogood Boyo
Lord Cut-Glass
The Guide Book
Mrs Dai Bread One
Mrs Dai Bread Two
Mrs Cherry Owen
Mrs Beynon
Maggy Richards
Ricky Rees
Our Sal
Nasty Humphrey
Billy Swansea
One of Mr Waldo's
Jackie with the sniff
Four women
Evans the death
Fishermen
Gwenny
Child
Mother

Unexpected Guest, The
Agatha Christie
Mystery 2 Acts
London 1958

When Michael Starkwedder drives into a ditch in the fog and goes to the nearest house for help, he finds Laura Warwick standing over her dead husband, Richard, with a gun. Unwilling to immediately call the police, he helps her concoct a story blaming the murder on the vengeful father of a child the brutish Richard killed in a careless road accident some years back. But when the police make enquiries, they find the father is dead, and suspicions shift to the household. Starkwedder realizes Laura is innocent when he sees she cannot use a gun; in fact, she had been covering up for her lover, would-be politician Julian. But he did not do it either. Then Richard's retarded younger brother Jan, under the suggestive influence of housekeeper Miss Bennett, also confesses, and during a shoot-out with the police is accidentally killed. The police are satisfied Jan was the murderer, but in fact Miss Bennett had only blamed him in order to protect the gentle and lovable Laura. So who did it? The startling truth is revealed with typical Christie virtuosity in the last few minutes of the play.

Richard Warwick
Laura Warwick
Michael Starkwedder
Miss Bennett
Jan Warwick
Mrs Warwick
Henry Angell
Sergeant Cadwallader
Inspector Thomas
Julian Farrar

Unseen Hand, The
Sam Shepard
Drama 1 Act
New York 1971

Blue Morphan, an old cowboy who has seen better days, lives in a derelict '51 Chevrolet automobile abandoned just outside a California dormitory town. On his way to bed one night he is approached by a Space Age punk with a hand print burnt into his skull. The punk wants Blue to rescue him from control by space creatures he calls the High Commission of the Nogo, who control him through an unseen hand which squeezes his brain if he attempts free will.

The punk, called Willie, brings back the ghosts of Blue's long dead brothers Cisco and Sycamore, to help with the rescue. A passing cheerleader stops and gives the brothers instruction in guerrilla warfare, but before they can set out for Nogo, Willie frees himself from the hand's control. Cisco, Blue and the cheerleader drift away after Willie leaves, and Sycamore is left alone in Blue's former home.

Blue Morphan
Willie
Cisco Morphan
The Kid
Sycamore Morphan

Unsinkable Molly Brown, The
Meredith Willson and Richard Morris
Musical 2 Acts
New York 1960

Molly Tobin, daughter of the drunken but amiable Irishman Shamus Tobin, leaves her home in Hannibal, Missouri, bound for the Colorado goldfields with the determined belief that she can rise to be a proper lady. In the rough mining town of Leadville, where she works in the Saddle Rock Saloon, she meets the formidable but gentle and very lucky Leadville Johnny Brown. Initially, she refuses his advances because Johnny is poor, but he produces a wad of 300,000 dollars in cash, a home for her and her father, and the marital brass bed of her romantic dreams, all on the strength of a gold claim he finds by good fortune and sells without a qualm. Even when Johnny burns their hoard in the stove fire, unaware that Molly had hidden it there, he simply finds a huge claim, moves them to a mansion in Denver's finest street, and glories in providing whatever Molly wants.

Molly's attempts to gain acceptance by the Denver *nouveau riche* come unstuck, though, and she decides to seek polish by making a tour of Europe. Her natural charm and energy, supported by Johnny's fortune, win her the friendship of a very sophisticated Paris set led by the Prince and Princess Delong. She brings the set back to Denver and gives a huge party to impress her snooty neighbours, but it turns to social disgrace when Johnny's Leadville drinking friends get involved in a brawl with the other guests. Molly leaves for France in what she feels is disgrace, but Johnny, hungry for home, stays sadly behind.

After years of frantic but unhappy socializing in France, she is cajoled into an engagement by Prince Delong, who has long loved her. At the last minute she breaks off the engagement, sails for America, is shipwrecked in the Atlantic but saves her own life and that of everyone in her lifeboat by selfless heroism. Back in Denver, she is reconciled with Johnny and returns to Leadville to take up the life she realizes she should never have left.

Songs include: 'I Ain't Down Yet'; 'I'll Never Say No'
Molly Tobin
Michael, Aloysius, Patric, her brothers
Father Flynn
Shamus Tobin, Molly's father
Brawling miners
Charlie
Christmas Morgan
Burt
Banjo
Prostitutes
Leadville Johnny Brown
Gittan
A boy
Sheriff
Denver policemen
Mrs McGlone
Mgr Ryan
Roberts
Professor Gardella
Germaine
Princess Delong

Prince Delong
Countess Ethanotous
Jenab-Ashros
The Grand Duchess Marie Nicholaiovna
Count Feranti
Duchess of Burlingame
Duke of Burlingame
The Baron of Auld
Malcolm Broderick
Mrs Wadlington
Mr Wadlington
Young waiter
Maître D'
Page
Male passenger
Mother
Wounded sailor

Variations on a Theme
Terence Rattigan
Drama 2 Acts
London 1958
The 'theme' is that of the older woman and the younger man, in this case Rose Fish, a beautiful socialite who through her purposeful marriages now resides in a crumbling villa outside Cannes, where she drinks her fragile health away, gambles her money, and plans to marry hard-headed German industrialist millionaire Kurt. When she meets and falls for young ballet dancer Ron Vale, her companion Hettie warns her against him, thinking him a gigolo. But Ron, like Rose herself, is a native Brummie; underneath they have much in common and he needs her in a way no other man has done. Despite pressures not only from Hettie, but also Rose's daughter Fiona, Ron's ballet patron and 'friend' Sam, and the on-off relationship with Kurt, Rose finally decides not to convalesce in Switzerland during the winter. She will stay in Cannes with Ron, whom she loves 'more than life', knowing she will probably die.
Rose
Hettie
Ron
Kurt
Fiona
Mona
Adrian
Sam

Venus Observed
Christopher Fry
Comedy 3 Acts
London 1950
The middle-aged Duke of Altair decides to remarry, and on the day of All-Hallows Eve invites three old flames, Rosabel, Jessie and Hilda to view an eclipse of the sun from his observatory. Rather unromantically he leaves the choice of his new bride to his grown-up son Edgar, who is to play Paris by giving an apple to

whichever he thinks most suitable. He chooses Rosabel, but she gets mad at the Duke for having his head in the stars. The Duke then falls for Perpetua (youth itself), newly-arrived daughter of his agent Reedbeck, and that night they go to canoodle in the observatory. But Perpetua doesn't love the Duke - she only goes along with him because she's after getting her swindling dad off the hook, and she actually loves Edgar. Hot-blooded Rosabel sets fire to the observatory determined to bring the Duke down to earth, not knowing he's inside. The Duke and Perpetua escape, and Rosabel gives herself up for a six-month arson sentence. The Duke is so impressed with Rosabel's devotion he declares he'll wed her when she's free; Edgar goes off with Perpetua.
The Duke of Altair
Edgar, his son
Herbert Reedbeck, his agent
Dominic, Reedbeck's son
Rosabel Fleming
Jessie Dill
Hilda Snell-Taylor
Capt. Fox Reddleman, the Duke's butler
Bates, the Duke's footman
Perpetua, Reedbeck's daughter

Verdict
Agatha Christie
Drama 2 Acts
London 1958
Refugee Professor Karl Hendryk lives in his Bloomsbury flat together with his ailing wife Anya and her cousin Lisa. The Professor and Lisa are in love, but it is unspoken - they are both devoted to the once-beautiful Anya. When rich and lovely Helen Rollander wants private tuition from the Professor, he refuses. He knows that she is not serious and his time is valuable. But Helen is in love with the Professor and does not give up easily; she persuades her father Sir William to offer an expensive new treatment in the USA which could cure Anya. The professor accepts Helen as pupil, but one day when Helen is alone with Anya she gives her an overdose of heart medicine. Helen seemingly gets away with it, then confesses her crime and her love to Karl. He is horrified, but against Lisa's wishes does not call the police. After the inquest the police become suspicious and arrest Lisa. Karl tells them about Helen and they show him a paragraph in his newspaper; Helen is dead after having walked under a lorry. They disbelieve his story and Lisa is tried for murder. She is acquitted and intends to leave Karl, whom she has come to believe prizes principles above people. In the end, however, she relents - against her better judgement.

Lester Cole	Helen Rollander
Mrs Roper	Sir William Rollander
Lisa Koletzky	Detective Inspector
Professor Karl Hendryk	Ogden
Dr Stoner	Police Sergeant Pearce
Anya Hendryk	

View from the Bridge, A
Arthur Miller
Tragedy 2 Acts
New York 1960

Eddie Carbone is a longshoreman working the docks down from Brooklyn Bridge. He lives with his wife Beatrice and orphaned niece Catherine. They've brought up Catherine since she was a baby; she loves Eddie like a father, but his love for her is becoming too possessive as she grows into a woman. Two illegal immigrant brothers, relatives of Beatrice's from Sicily, come to live with them; the elder, Marco, has a family in the old country; the younger, Rodolpho is attractive and single and he and Catherine fall in love. Eddie gets jealous and faced with the possibility of losing Catherine accuses Rodolpho of being homosexual, only interested in Catherine in order to marry her and get a US passport. Eddie loses all sense of reason and denounces the brothers to the immigration authorities. There is a fight with Marco and Eddie dies. In this, a modern version of a Greek tragedy, the local lawyer, Alfieri, represents the Greek chorus.

Eddie	Tony
Beatrice	Louis
Catherine	Mike
Marco	Two immigration officers
Rodolpho	Neighbours
Mr Alfieri	

Visit to a Small Planet
Gore Vidal
Farce 3 Acts
New York 1957

It is the fifties, war scares and UFO sightings are becoming frequent, and Roger Spelding, TV pundit, is preparing to tell the American public on his evening show that it is all mass hysteria. He is, therefore, totally bewildered when an old army friend, Gen. Powers, arrives to inform him that there is a flying saucer hovering in the sky near his house. A pleasant looking alien emerges from the spacecraft but Roger's family soon learn that Kreton, as he is called, has come to pursue his hobby of watching the wars of Earth's history and he enjoys the vibrations of aggression that man possesses and constantly uses. Kreton demonstrates his telepathic and kinetic abilities to Roger's daughter Ellen, and makes her pacifist fiancé, Conrad, have a fight with one of the soldiers who have now surrounded the house. Powers is sure that Kreton is part of a hostile extra-terrestrial force that is about to invade Earth but the mischevious spaceman convinces him that the Russians are about to invade the USA and the scenario is set for a world war.

Ellen deduces from his conversation that Kreton is being sought by others of his kind and she makes contact with them using thought transmissions. Delton 4, Kreton's superior, turns up in another flying saucer and orders the war-loving alien to return home. He apologizes for Kreton's behaviour and explains that time will be reversed till before their arrival, but Kreton has plans to return one day.

Roger Spelding
Ellen Spelding
Reba Spelding
Kreton
Gen. Tom Powers
Conrad Mayberry
Aide
Delton 4
Two television technicians

Visit, The
Freidrich Dürrenmatt
Drama 3 Acts
New York 1958

Anticipation runs riot in the run-down Central European town of Gullen following news of a visit by its most illustrious daughter - renowned charitable multi-millionairess Claire Zachanassian. She arrives with a strange entourage of bodyguards and blind men, and after the official greetings she meets with her childhood sweetheart, shopkeeper Anton Schill. They reminisce over their young love affair and its tragic consequences; Claire got pregnant and Schill bribed two boys to say they had also been with her. She was forced to leave town and put her baby up for adoption where it soon died; Schill married the shopkeeper's daughter and inherited the shop.

Claire calls a public meeting and promises the town millions of marks, plus a substantial sum for each of the townsfolk. Her condition, she says, is 'justice' - she wants the life of Anton Schill. At first the townspeople consider the notion immoral and preposterous, but they are inevitably corrupted. When they start buying things on credit from Schill's shop, the penny drops and, deserted by friends and family, he abandons himself to his fate and is murdered by the townspeople.

Claire Zachanassian	Two women
Bobby	The Frai Burgomaster
Pedro	The two grandchildren
Max	Station master
Mike	Conductor
First blind man	Reporter
Second blind man	Photographer
Anton Schill	Radio reporter
Frau Schill	Cameraman
The son	Truck driver
The daughter	Athlete
Burgomaster	Delivery man
Pastor	First townsman
Teacher	Second townsman
Doctor	
Policeman	
Painter	
Four men	

Vivat! Vivat Regina!
Robert Bolt
Tragedy 2 Acts
Chichester 1970

Mary, Queen of Scots, has just succeeded to the Scottish throne. Her position is tenuous since much of her country, led by the puritanical John Knox, has converted from the Queen's Catholicism to the Protestant faith of the kirk.

In England, Elizabeth rules over a country equally divided on the same religious lines. Thus, though the English monarch wishes, at least, to prevent an alliance between Mary and the Continental Catholic powers against Tudor England, she must treat her potential rival with circumspection.

Mary's sensual character and habits so offend the Scots that they conspire with Elizabeth to unseat their glamorous monarch.

At the same time Elizabeth insists that she will not act against Mary, her half-sister, unless proof of the Scottish Queen's complicity with renegade English Catholics can be produced. Instead, she confines her to Sheffield Castle.

Mary's feckless nature cannot tolerate confinement and she half-knowingly falls into the trap of giving the English Catholics support against their Queen. Her execution inevitably follows.

Mary, Queen of Scots
Claud Nau, Mary's secretary
William Cecil,
 Elizabeth's confidant
Elizabeth I of England
Robert Dudley, Elizabeth's lover
John Knox, Scottish divine
David Rizzio, Mary's lover
Lord Bothwell, Mary's suitor
Sir Francis Walsingham,
 Elizabeth's henchman
Bagpiper
Lord Morton
Lord Bishop of Durham
A Cleric
De Quadra
Davison
Lord Darnley
Lord Mor
Ruthven
Lindsey
A doctor
Tala
Ormiston
A prisoner
Scots Archbishop
Philip of Spain
The Pope
Jailers
Brewer
The Courts of England and Scotland

Voice of the Turtle, The
John Van Druten
Comedy 3 Acts
New York 1947

Pretty young actress Sally Middleton is embarrassed when her apartment is used by her friend Olive for a brush-off scene with Olive's recent beau, serviceman Bill Page. Olive leaves for her new date, so glum Bill wines and dines Sally instead. They fall in love, but Sally is still smarting from a recent broken affair and according to Bill 'the voice of the turtle (dove) is heard in our land'. His open-heartedness eventually wins Sally around to opening up and admitting her feelings, and finally making a commitment.

Sally Middleton
Olive Lashbrooke
Bill Page

Volpone or The Fox
Ben Jonson
Comedy 5 Acts
London 1606

Volpone, a rich Venetian Magnifico, is greed incarnate. When his cunning servant Mosca - his 'parasite' - draws the morning curtains, it's not the sun but Volpone's hoard of gold that's revealed. To further enrich himself, the unwed and childless Volpone feigns sickness to the point of death, and with Mosca's connivance obtains a stream of valuable gifts from three avaricious Venetians who each hope to be his heir - Voltare, the advocate, Corbaccio, an old Gentleman, and Corvino the merchant. Corbaccio even disinherits his own son Bonario in favour of Volpone in order to convince him of his loyalty, and Corvino overcomes his marital possessiveness to offer his unwilling wife Celia to the lustful Volpone. However, Bonario rescues Celia in the nick of time, but Volpone and Mosca have the pair flung into prison on false charges. When they finally over-reach themselves with their greed and crowing over others' misfortunes, the Avocatori (magistrates) deal out appropriate punishment to all - Volpone himself is sent to jail, his fortune given to the infirm; Mosca is flogged and sent to the galleys.

Volpone, a magnifico
Mosca, his parasite
Voltore, an advocate
Corvino, a merchant
Corbaccio, an old gentleman
Avocatori, four magistrates
Notario, the register
Nano, a dwarf
Castrone, a eunuch
Servitore, a servant
(Sir) Politic Would-be, a knight
Peregrine, a gentleman-traveller
Baonario, a young gentleman, son of Corbaccio
Fine Mme Would-Be, the knight's wife
Celia, the merchant's wife

Commendatori, officers
Mercatori
Androgyno, an hermaphrodite
Grege
Crowd

Vortex, The
Noël Coward
Drama 3 Acts
London 1924

Socialite Florence Lancaster lives only for her own great beauty, which is fading. She is having an affair with young, athletic, Tom Veryan almost under the nose of her husband, the amiable David, and will not heed the warnings of her friend Helen Saville. When her grown-up son Nicky returns from France with his new fiancée Bunty Mainwaring, an old friend of Tom Veryan, they all go to their house in the country for a small party. Bunty realizes she and Nicky are not suited and they break off their fairly casual 'engagement'; more seriously Tom and Bunty are discovered kissing by Florence, who throws a scene and humiliates herself. At the end of the party, Nicky confronts his mother with her selfishness, her affairs, and his drug addiction. She breaks down, promising she will try to be a real mother.

Preston
Helen Saville
Pauncefort Quentin
Clara Hibbert
Florence Lancaster
Tom Veryan
Nicky Lancaster
David Lancaster
Bunty Mainwaring
Bruce Fairlight

Voyage Round My Father, A
John Mortimer
Drama 2 Acts
Greenwich 1970

A narrator, the only son of the main character of the play, conducts the audience through a series of vignettes which reveal the extraordinary personality of the older man.

Blinded in an accident pursuing his passion for gardening, the father, a barrister specializing in divorce, decides to ignore his disability- the family never allude to it - and carry on as normal. He is utterly without pretence, instils in his son a wry disregard for all accepted wisdom and engages with life in a manner at once aloof and oddly intimate. The latter trait is most poignant when he innocently and incessantly asks those around him to 'paint' for him in words what they are seeing, which he does most enthusiastically when strolling in his beloved garden.

When his father dies peacefully of old age, the narrator feels none of the sense of release, and broader horizons beckoning, which he believes the psychologists say he should, but only a deep loneliness.

Father	*Miss Baker*
Son/Narrator	*First ATS witness*
Mother	*Ringer Lean*
Elizabeth, the son's wife	*Thong*
Son, as boy	*Film director*
Headmaster	*Japhet*
Ham	*Judges (two)*
George	*Cameraman*
Boustead	*Doctor*
Sparks	*Second ATS*
Mr Morrow	*Reigate*
Matron Miss Cox	*Iris*
Doris	*Three children*
Social worker	*Ushers and technicians*
Mrs Reigate	

Voysey Inheritance, The
Harley Granville-Barker
Comedy 5 Acts
London 1905

Edward Voysey is a partner in the family business, a firm of prestigious solicitors in Lincoln's Inn. He is horrified to discover that his father, the senior partner, has been speculating with clients' monies and stocks, and that the firm is hundreds of thousands of pounds in debt. His father, by always paying the appropriate dividends, has so far avoided discovery. Edward, however, is not such a buccaneer and becomes worried and distraught. When his father unexpectedly dies, Edward calls a meeting with his large family and informs them of the situation, intending to come clean with the law. They do not see it from this point of view, and try to dissuade him. Eventually he decides to brazen it out and gradually clear up the mess; it is a difficult course of action but wins the respect and hand in marriage of his sweetheart, Alice Maitland.

Mr Voysey	*Ethel Voysey*
Mrs Voysey	*Denis Tregoning*
Trenchard Voysey KC	*Alice Maitland*
Honor Voysey	*Mr Booth*
Maj. Booth Voysey	*The Revd Evan Colpus*
Christopher	*Peacey*
Edward Voysey	*Phoebe*
Hugh Voysey	*Mary*
Mrs Hugh Voysey	

Wait until Dark
Frederick Knott
Drama 3 Acts
London 1966

Small-time confidence tricksters Mike and Croker have just come out of jail and are summoned to a flat in London's Notting Hill Gate by former accomplice Lisa, who informed on them. Instead of Lisa, they are met by the sinister Roat. He explains he wants them to find a doll stuffed with heroin left somewhere in the flat by photographer Sam Henderson who was conned into bringing it through Customs. When Mike and Croker discover Roat has murdered Lisa they want out, but Roat blackmails them - their fingerprints are now all over the flat. The three of them set up an elaborate scheme intended to get Sam out of the way on a fictitious assignment and then persuade his wife Susy to hand over the doll. But Susy is blind - she returns to the flat and despite their precautions she smells a rat. Together with little helper Gloria (who took the doll from the flat in the first place), she outwits the criminals. Mike and Croker are killed by Roat, but in a tense denouement, Susy gets the better of Roat just before the police and Sam arrive.

Mike
Croker
Roat
Susy Henderson
Sam Henderson
Gloria
Two policemen

Waiting for Godot
Samuel Beckett
Tragicomedy 2 Acts
London 1955

Vladimir and Estragon, two old men now almost tramps, wait by a country road for a message from Godot. They consider hanging themselves but have no rope and their dialogue, ordinary yet enigmatic, is capable of infinite degrees of interpretation. Along the road comes Pozzo, a bully inclined toward lyricism, with his willing slave Lucky, who is both furtive and pathetic. They stay awhile exchanging banter, and Lucky gives an interminable speech. As they depart a boy arrives to tell Vladimir and Estragon that Godot has been delayed and will arrive tomorrow.

Next day the proceedings are repeated with a few changes; Pozzo is now blind and cannot remember the events of the previous day, but Lucky is still willing to serve him. The boy comes with the same message from Godot. Vladimir and Estragon again consider hanging themselves but have no rope.

Vladimir
Estragon
Lucky
Pozzo
A boy

Waiting Room, The
John Bowen
Play 1 Act
London 1970

A woman in her thirties and a younger man are shown into an anonymous waiting room, where there is no indication of what they are waiting for or why they are there. They fall into desultory conversation, and both have the impression that they have met before. It gradually transpires that the woman, Harriet, has been married to, and left by, the same man who has 'picked up' and seduced the young man, Paul. Though they mutually dislike each other, a strange bond develops between them as they describe their relationship with the husband and each other. Finally a corpse is brought in which they are asked to identify, which they do, and as they depart the woman offers her hand.

Harriet
Paul
A man
A woman cleaner

Waltz of the Toreadors, The
Jean Anouilh
Comedy 3 Acts
London 1956

Philandering Gen. St Pé is saddled with malingering wife Emily who pretends to be crippled. Not brave enought to leave her, the General has kept the real love of his life, Mlle Ghislaine de Ste-Euverte, waiting seventeen years. Somehow Ghislaine obtains love letters from Emily to her doctor, and demands the General leave 'unfaithful' Emily. The General dithers so much that despairing Ghislaine throws herself from a window but lands in the arms of the General's attractive young secretary Gaston. They fall in love and to Ghislaine's delight immediately make love. This disappoints the General's two daughters Estella and Sidonia who both fancy Gaston, but then Father Ambrose reveals that Gaston is the General's illegitimate son from one of his many casual flings. The General reluctantly gives permission for Gaston and Ghislaine to marry and faced with the awful prospect of remaining with Emily, begins an affair with their maid.

Gen. St Pé
Emily
Gaston
Estella
Sidonia
Doctor
Mlle Ghislaine de Ste-Euverte
Eugenie
Mme Dupont-Fredaine
Father Ambrose
Pamela

Wandering Jew, The
E. Temple Thurston
Play 4 Phases
London 1920

Phase 1. A Jew, Matathias, spits in the face of Christ on His way to the Crucifixion and is told 'I will not wait for thee, but thou wilt wait for Me until I come to thee again'.

Phase 2. During the First Crusade in Antioch, the Jew, in a passionate love scene with the wife of a defeated knight repeats that he would spit again 'If He did cross my way'. But hearing a leper's bell and the cry 'Unclean', he realizes that this applies to himself, the first awakening of his mind to the purpose of his soul, and he releases the horrified lady.

Phase 3. In 1290 the Jew is now a prosperous merchant in Palermo. His son has died and persecution has begun. He prepares to flee with his wife, but she has just been converted to Christianity and goes to a convent. After nearly deciding to kill her he admits that she is making her way to Christ.

Phase 4. It is now 1560 and the Inquisition is in Seville, where the Jew is Matteos Battadios, a famous doctor. A family, after pretending to be Christian admit to being Jews when leprosy is diagnosed in their son. Matteos is tried before the Inquisition for a remark that 'It would go hard with Christ to know his own if He should come again'. He now claims to be a Jew who has watched the growth of Christianity for over a thousand years and achieves release by being burnt at the stake.

Phase 1:
Judith
Rachel
Matathias, the Jew

Phase 2:
Du Guesclin
Boemond Prince of Tarentum
Godfrey Duke of Normandy
Raymond of Toulouse
Joanne de Baudricourt
The unknown knight
Phirous, a man-at-arms
Yeoman
Ladies
Knights
Men-at-arms

Phase 3:
Mario, a servant
Andrea Michelotti, a merchant of Messina
Matteos Battadios, the Jew
Gianella Battadios, his wife
Pietro Morelli, a padre

Phase 4:
Matteos Battadios, the Jew
Juan de Texeda
Gonzaales Ferera
Alonzo Castro
Lazzaro Zapportas
Al Kazar, a servant
Maria Zapportas
Olalla Quintana, a harlot
Usher, Bellman's crier
Councillors of the Inquisition
Soldiers
Citizens of Seville
A messenger

Wasps, The
Aristophanes
Comedy 1 Act
Athens 422BC

Anticleon has imprisoned his father Procleon using slaves and netting to keep him at home. Old Procleon has gone crazy on judicial business and spends his entire life on jury duty, believing the flatteries of the demagogues who declare that the jurymen are Lords of Athens and Masters of the World. The chorus is Procleon's fellow-jurors, dressed like wasps with sharp stings, but despite their assaults they are unable to free Procleon. Both sides then decide to listen to reason, and Anticleon wins, arguing that this father is deluded - a tool and slave of the grasping demagogues. No longer a juryman, Procleon gets so downcast that Anticleon sets up a home court for his father's amusement, and first they try the dog for stealing cheese. Eventually the son teaches the father to take part in friendly parties and fashionable life; the old man learns his lesson too well, becomes noisy and naughty and brings a shower of lawsuits on his head ... he also demonstrates he is the champion dancer of his day.

Anticleon, an Athenian citizen
Procleon, his father
Xanthias, Sosias, slaves
Two dogs
A reveller
A baking woman
A citizen
Chorus
Boy's chorus
Midas
Phryx
Masyntias
Dardanis
Chaerophon
Witness
Puppies
Revellers
The three sons of Carcinus

Watch on the Rhine
Lillian Hellman
Drama 3 Acts
New York 1941

In 1940 Sara returns from Europe with her impoverished family and arrives back at the Farrelly country house near Washington DC where her eccentric mother Fanny and her brother David live. Already staying with them is Rumanian aristocrat Teck de Brancovis and his wife Marthe; they are broke and their marriage is on the rocks - Marthe and David are in love. Everyone is enchanted with Sara's children, Joshua, Babette and Bodo, but her enigmatic husband Kurt is investigated by Teck, a gambler who frequents the poker games at the German embassy. He discovers Kurt is a member of the anti-Nazi resistance with a price on his head, and when Kurt decides to return to Germany and try to free his closest comrade, Teck blackmails him, demanding 10,000 dollars to keep his silence. He has already discovered Kurt carried large sums of money contributed by anti-Fascists in order to help victims of the Nazis. But there is no guarantee Teck will not take the money and then betray Kurt, who has no alternative but to kill Teck. Kurt bids goodbye to his family and leaves for Germany, arranging to dispose of Teck's body en route.

Anise	*Sara Muller*
Joseph	*Joshua Muller*
Fanny Farrelly	*Bodo Muller*
David Farrelly	*Babette Muller*
Marthe de Brancovis	*Kurt Muller*
Teck de Brancovis	

Waters of the Moon
N. C. Hunter
Comedy 3 Acts
London 1951

The wealthy Lancaster family are marooned during a heavy snowstorm in late December at a small hotel on the edge of Dartmoor. Mrs Daly and her daughter Evelyn who run the hotel and their four resident guests are all affected in various ways, especially by vivacious Helen Lancaster whose determined attitude towards life contrasts with that of these impoverished gentry vegetating in this backwater. A friendship is struck up between Helen's daughter Tonetta and Mrs Daly's son John, an attractive and over-protected consumptive, and when Austrian musician Julius Winterhalter begins to dote unashamedly on Helen, it arouses the jealousy of Evelyn. The residents both resent and admire the Lancasters, who leave for London after an emotional New Year's Eve party, and Evelyn and Julius then come to their senses, realizing they still have each other.

John Daly
Evelyn Daly
Mrs Whyte
Col Selby
Mrs Daly
Mrs Ashworth
Julius Winterhalter
Helen Lancaster
Tonetta Landi, her daughter
Robert Lancaster

Way of the World, The
William Congreve
Comedy 5 Acts
London 1700

Mirabell and Fainall are opponents, firstly at cards, then over inheritances and estates. Both are masters of repartee, but while Mirabell is generous, Fainall is ruthless. Mirabell and gorgeous Mrs Millimant are in love, but he has alienated her aunt Lady Wishfort by paying court to her in order to conceal his forbidden suit to her niece. Witwoud and Petulant (names in this play identify their character types) also favour Mrs Millimant, but Lady Wishfort, who controls Millimant's fortune, is determined her niece should marry Witwoud's brother Sir Wilfull. However, when Fainall and his mistress Mrs Marwood attempt to blackmail Lady Wishfort by threatening to expose the reputation of her daughter Mrs Fainall (formerly Mirabell's mistress), Lady Wishfort turns to Mirabell for help. Prudently, he has already acted to protect Mrs Fainall's fortune against her husband, and his proof destroys Fainall's plot. The drunken Sir Wilfull confesses he would rather travel abroad than wed, and so Lady Wishfort relents and allows Mirabell and Millimant to marry. In this prime Restoration comedy there is much plotting, scheming, high and low humour and caricature, and all the society ladies, married or single, are addressed as 'Mrs'.

Fainall
Mirabell
Witwoud
Petulant
Sir Wilfull Witwoud
Waitwell, servant to Mirabell
Lady Wishfort
Mrs Millimant
Mrs Marwood
Mrs Fainall
Foible, woman to Lady Wishfort
Mincing, woman to Mrs Millimant

Way Upstream
Alan Ayckbourn
Comedy 2 Acts
Scarborough 1981

Two English married couples, Keith and June and Alistair and Emma, set out on a canal boating holiday with Keith rather pompously playing weekend skipper. As they proceed upriver, they are joined at regular intervals by Mrs Hatfield, the secretary in Keith and Alistair's business, who reports on a growing labour crisis in their factory.

The couples wrangle bitterly, especially Keith and June, until Keith is forced to leave the holiday to deal with the labour force. The remaining three soon run the boat aground, and are rescued from their predicament by Vince, an expert on the canal who assumes control of the boat, brings his friend Fleur aboard, and seduces a very willing June.

Alistair and Emma are scandalized and frightened by Vince's antics, and the men come to blows. To escape the growing unpleasantness, Alistair suggests, and Emma agrees, that they should leave everyone else behind and press on alone.

Keith	*Vince*
June	*Fleur*
Alistair	
Emma	
Mrs Hatfield	

Ways and Means
Noël Coward
Play 1 Act
London 1935
See: *Tonight at 8.30*

We Were Dancing
Noël Coward
Play 1 Act
New York 1935
See: *Tonight at 8.30*

Wedding, The
Anton Chekhov
Drama 1 Act
Moscow 1889
A minor civil servant and his wife are celebrating the marriage of their daughter Dasha to one Epaminondas Aplombov with a miscellaneous collection of characters, a telegraph clerk, a Greek confectioner, a midwife and among others, an insurance agent who has undertaken to bring a General to give dignity to the proceedings.

The best man sets the dances going while they await his arrival. The bridegroom complains that two lottery tickets are missing from the dowry.

After further confusion the guest of honour arrives. He turns out to be only a retired naval Commander, deaf and rather drunk, who after complaining that the bread and herrings are 'sour' monopolizes the party with non-stop naval chatter, which is only checked when he discovers that the twenty-five roubles which should have been his fee, has been diverted into the pocket of the insurance agent.

Yevdokim Zhigalov, a minor
civil servant, retired
Nastasya, his wife
Dasha, their daughter
Epaminondas Aplombov, her fiancé
Cdr Theodore Revunov-Karaulov, Imperial Russian
navy, retired
Andrew Nyunin, insurance agent
Mrs Ana Zmeyukin, a midwife
Ivan Yat, telegraph clerk
Kharlampy Dymba, Greek confectioner
Dmitry Mozgovoy, sailor
The best man
Other young men
Servants etc

Wesker Trilogy
Arnold Wesker
3 Plays
Coventry 1958/60
See: *Chicken Soup with Barley*
Roots
I'm Talking about Jerusalem

West Side Story
From the book by Arthur Laurents
Music by Leonard Bernstein
Lyrics by Stephen Sondheim
Musical 2 Acts
New York 1957
This is a contemporary reworking of the familiar Romeo and Juliet theme. In the slums of Manhattan, the old-established European immigrant kids have their gang, the 'Jets'. Their enemies on the streets are the police and the Puerto Rican 'Sharks'. Feuds are frequent and after an altercation at a dance the gangs arrange a 'rumble'.

Jet member Tony, however, is deeply in love with Maria, the sister of Bernardo, the Shark's chief, and promises her that he will stop the fight. He cannot, though, and becomes involved in the vicious fighting himself in which one of his gang is killed and he accidentally stabs Bernardo. Maria is devastated by her brother's death, but still loves Tony and they plan to escape the city, but revenge is in the air and Chino, a Shark, is looking to kill Tony.

Anita, Bernardo's girl, tries to intervene, but after being taunted by the Jets, lies to Tony that Chino has murdered Maria. Tony goes to find her, only to be shot by Chino and he dies in Maria's arms.

Songs include: 'Something's Coming'; 'Tonight'; 'I Feel Pretty'; 'Gee, Officer Krupke'; 'America'.

The Jets: Riff, the Jet's leader, Tony, Action, A-Rab,
Baby John, Snowboy, Big Deal, Diesel, Gee-Tar,
Mouth Piece
Jets' girls: Graziella, Velma, Minnie, Clarice,
Anybodys
The Sharks: Bernardo, the Sharks' Leader, Chino,
Pepe, Indio, Luis, Anxious, Nibbles, Juano
Sharks' girls: Anita, Rosalia, Tresita, Francisca,
Estella, Marguerita
Maria, Bernardo's sister
Doc
Schrank, Krupke, policemen
Glad Hand

What Every Woman Knows
J. M. Barrie
Comedy 4 Acts
London 1908
In a small town in Scotland, wealthy Alick Wylie and his two sons David and James despair that their adored Maggie will ever make a match. She is plain, but shrewd and loving, and the canny Wylies do a deal with local up-and-coming politician John Shand to sponsor him if he will wed Maggie in five years. The strong but humourless Shand agrees and so does Maggie, and six years later, when Shand becomes an MP, they marry. The key to Shand's success is in his speeches - the combination of his knowledge and eloquence combined with 'Shandisms', witty touches supplied by 'secretary' Maggie but which John is unaware of. When he falls for the beautiful Lady Sybil, Maggie throws them together

and John discovers Sybil is no inspiration at all. His latest speech is set to be flop, but Maggie re-types it, adds the 'Shandisms' and saves the day. At last John realizes what she has been doing and wakes up to her charm - and actually laughs.

John Shand
Alick Wylie
David Wylie, James Wylie, his sons
Maggie Wylie, his daughter
Mr Venebles
Comtesse de la Briere
Lady Sybil Tenterden
Grace, a maid
An elector
A manservant

What Makes Sammy Run?
Budd Schulberg
Music and lyrics by Ervin Drake
Musical Play
New York 1964

As the play opens, Sammy Glick is the copy-boy for the *New York Record*. He befriends Al Manheim, the Drama Editor, with his ready wit and easy smile, yet it soon becomes obvious that this is a very ambitious young man. He has soon impressed enough to get Al's job and from there on there is no turning back. The light of Hollywood beckons and Sammy makes the trip to Los Angeles. He fights his way to the top, using anyone along the way, particularly Kit Sargent, who he romanced because she was a scriptwriter. He steals the scripts of a naive young writer and soon becomes a film producer. At this point he recalls his trusting friend Al, who has fallen in love with Kit, to force them into working for him, and they fall for his trap.

Sammy is soon head of the studio, and married to the boss' daughter. But he has used up too much luck and too many friends; and when he finds his new bride with another man he has no one to turn to; Al and Kit have deserted him. Sammy is left alone in his mansion, which has become his prison, and tastes for the first time the real price of his success.
Songs include: 'My Hometown'; 'A Room Without Windows'

Al Manheim	*Guard*
Osborn	*Columnist*
Sammy Glick	*Kit Sargent*
O'Brien	*Grip*
Reporter	*H. L. Harrinton*
Henry	*Seymour Glick*
Julian Blumberg	*Gino*
Tracy Clark	*Philippe Grandel*
Rita Rio	*Photographer*
Slave Master	
Lucky Dugan	
Sheik Orsini	
Technical advisor	
Sidney Fineman	

What the Butler Saw
Joe Orton
Comedy 2 Acts
London 1969

Lecherous Dr Prentice runs a private clinic, and when interviewing Geraldine Barclay to become his secretary asks her to get undressed. She obliges, goes behind a curtain and then Mrs Prentice arrives. She complains that during her stay at the Station Hotel, page boy Nicholas Beckett tried to rape her and that her dress and wig were stolen. Dr Prentice leaves the room and Nicholas himself arrives, reveals to Mrs Prentice that he took some obscene photographs of her, and attempts blackmail. The Freudian farce gathers pace with lots of dressing and undressing, accusations of transvestism, infidelity and madness; during the fuss, Sergeant Match comes to arrest Geraldine and Nicholas who at that point are dressed as each other. State psychiatrist Dr Rance also appears, expounding his theories of why Geraldine is crazy and the link this has with her father. But as the play draws to a close and everyone is either in a straitjacket, has been shot, or is just exhausted, a coincidence is revealed; Geraldine and Nicholas are in fact twins, and their long-lost parents are Dr and Mrs Prentice. Rance's theories are accidentally validated and the Prentice family happily reunited.

Dr Prentice
Geraldine Barclay
Mrs Prentice
Nicholas Beckett
Dr Rance
Sergeant Match

When We Are Married
J. B. Priestley
Comedy 3 Acts
London 1938

Three middle-aged Yorkshire couples gather in the house of Alderman Joseph Helliwell to celebrate their twenty-fifth wedding anniversary. All were married on the same day in the same church, and they have invited the local press to take a 'twenty-five years of married life' picture. Helliwell and wife Maria are rounded and self-satisfied, Councillor Albert Parker is tall, thin and stingy, his wife Annie is a mouse; lastly, Mr Soppitt is neat and reasonable but wife Clara is a battleaxe. After gorging themselves at high tea, they bring in new local chapel organist Gerald Forbes, a despised Londoner, with the intention of sacking him. He has committed the sin of being seen with a girl (actually Helliwell's niece Nancy), but they change their tune when he reveals that due to the ignorance of a young cleric twenty-five years ago, none of them is actually married. All hell breaks loose - Gerald is reinstated and all three couples examine their relationships in a different light, with Soppitt establishing a more equal relationship with Clara, and Annie puncturing Parker's stinginess - to the extent that when redundant press photographer Ormonroyd reveals that all three couples are actually still married, Parker sets him up in business and thereafter determines to 'have some fun'.

Ruby Birtles
Gerald Forbes
Nancy Holmes
Alderman Joseph
Helliwell
Councillor Albert
Parker
Annie Parker

Maria Helliwell
Herbert Soppitt
Clara Soppitt
Mrs Northrop
Fred Dyson
Henry Ormonroyd
Lottie Grady
Revd Clement Mercer

The sea witch
The slacker
The woodmouse
The fairy queen
The black bear
Two elves
The slitherslime
The spirit of the lake
Two green dragons
Two red dragons
Rabbits, elves, fairies, frogs, hyenas, dragon-flies, green dragons, red dragons, rainbow children.

Where the Rainbow Ends
Clifford Mills and John Ramsay
Music by Roger Quilter
Musical Play 4 Acts
London 1932

Rosamund, Crispian and his pet lion, Cubs, reside in Maidenhead in the home of their late Uncle Matthew. They are now governed by their evil Aunt Matilda and Uncle Joseph since the disappearance of their parents, in a plane crash, six months ago. Uncle Matthew's house, soon to be converted into a hotel, holds many treasures from his extensive travels, the greatest of which is a book, *Where the Rainbow Ends*. Finding the book, Rosamund discovers the path to finding lost loved ones, and excitedly tells Crispian of her desire to find their mother and father. Only Matilda, Joseph and William, their servant boy, stand in their way.

By accident, Rosamund discovers the Persian rug in the library is a magic carpet, containing a genie with the power to grant four wishes. They summon two friends, Jim and Betty Blunders, and Saint George of England, as their companions.

We follow them on their quest for their lost parents at the end of the rainbow through the terrible Dragon's Wood; through encounters with countless enemies, Will-o'-the-Wisp, wild beasts and the Dragon King himself. With the aid of Saint George they reach where the rainbow ends and are re-united with their parents.

Mortals
Rosamund Carey, a child
Crispian Carey, her brother
Matilda Flint, their aunt
Joseph Flint, her brother
M. Betrand, a curio dealer
William, the 'boots'
Jim Blunders, Crispian's friend
Betty Blunders, his sister
John Carey, Rosamund and Crispian's father
Vera Carey, his wife
Cubs, a baby lion
Saint George
The Dragon King
Dunks, his chief minister
Genie of the carpet
Will-o'-the-Wisp

Where's Charley?
Music and lyrics by George Abbott and Frank Loesser
Musical 2 Acts
New York 1948

See: *Charley's Aunt*

Songs include: 'Make me a Miracle'; 'My Darling, my Darling'; 'Once in Love With Amy'

While the Sun Shines
Terence Rattigan
Comedy 3 Acts
London 1943

It is wartime; young millionaire the Earl of Harpenden who lives in chambers at the Albany, London, is on leave from the Navy and set to marry childhood sweetheart Lady Elisabeth Randall. On the day before the wedding, she becomes beset by doubts, planted firstly by amorous Free French Lieut Colbert who convinces her that the affection she feels for Harpenden is not 'white-hot' enough, and then by Harpenden's guest, US Air Force bombardier Lieut Mulvaney who, thinking she is Harpenden's old mistress Mabel Crum, gets her drunk and kisses her. By the time confused Elisabeth realizes it is Harpenden she really wants, he has proposed to Mabel Crum, who very wisely rejects him and brings the two sweethearts together again, all with no thanks to her meddlesome father, insolvent gambler the Duke of Ayr and Stirling.

Horton
The Earl of Harpenden
Lieut Mulvaney
Lady Elisabeth Randall
The Duke of Ayr and Stirling
Lieut Colbert
Mabel Crum

White Cargo
Leon Gordon
Drama 3 Acts
London 1927

Situated in a ramshackle trader's bungalow in colonial West Africa, this is the story of three men's struggle against the unremitting harshness of the climate and lack of companionship.

The doctor and Weston have both been in Africa for nearly twenty years, relying respectively on alcohol and bitterness to get them through the months between relief boats. Into this bleak atmosphere arrives Allen Langford, a naive young Englishman on his first trip. He immediately states his intentions; that he will remain civilised and not succumb to drink, women, or the cynicism on which Weston survives. Weston sneeringly prophesies that he will fall prey to all three, especially women. From that point on, their enmity thrives.

Langford does indeed deteriorate, falling for the charms of the beautiful Tondeleyo, a half-breed native, who passes among the male community in return for jewellery. Out of an obsession for keeping face with Weston, Langford marries Tondeleyo, who is ill-informed as to what this entails. When she realizes it is 'till death us do part', she poisons Langford in the form of the regular anti-malarial drug. Weston saves Langford just in time, putting him aboard the next boat, the *White Cargo* of the title, and waits for the next unfortunate replacement.

Allen Langford	*Skipper*
Fred Ashley	*Engineer*
Harry Weston	*Worthing*
Doctor	*Tondeleyo*
Missionary	*Jim Fish*

White Devil, The
John Webster
Tragedy 5 Acts
London 1612

Loosely based on real events in sixteenth century Italy, *The White Devil* chronicles the tragic passion of the Duke of Bracciano and the Venetian lady Vittoria Corobona. Aided in his adulterous desire by his pandering secretary Flamineo, who is Vittoria's brother, Bracciano is inspired by a dream of Vittoria's and kills both his own wife Isabella and Vittoria's cuckolded husband Camillo. Their love is doomed and revenge is exacted by Francisco de Medici, Duke of Florence and brother of Isabella, and by Camillo's cousin Cardinal Monticelso. Another avenger is Count Ludovico who was in love with Isabella. Slaughter, ghosts, torture and intrigue pave the way to the bloody finale.

Monticelso, a cardinal, later Pope Paul IV
Francisco de Medici, Duke of Florence
The Duke of Bracciano, Paulo Giodani Orsino, first husband of Isabella, later of Vittoria
Giovanni, his son by Isabella
Count Lodovico
Camillo, first husband of Vittoria
Antonelli, Gasparo, friends of Lodovico
Carlo, Pedro, Hortensio, of Bracciano's household
Flamineo, brother of Vittoria
Marcello, his younger brother
Arragon, a cardinal
Julio, a doctor
Isabella, first wife of Bracciano, sister to Francisco

Vittoria Corobona, first wife of Camillo, later of Bracciano
Cornelia, mother to Vittoria, Marcello and Flamineo
Zanche, a moor, servant to Vittoria
Ambassadors
Courtiers
Officers
Guards
Attendants
Conjuror
Chancellor
Register
Lawyers
Conclavist
Armourer
Physicians
Page
Matron of the House of Convertites
Ladies

White Horse Inn
Hans Müller, Erik Charell, Ralph Benatzky, Robert Stolz and Robert Gilbert
Lyrics by Harry Graham
Musical 2 Acts
London 1931

Leopold, the headwaiter at the White Horse Inn high in the Austrian Alps, is madly in love with Josepha Vogelhuber, its widowed owner. She, however, is equally passionate about Valentine Sutton, an English solicitor and regular guest at the Inn, who is about to descend on them for his annual leave.

John Ebenezer Grinkle and his daughter Ottoline are placed in rooms set aside for Sutton by a jealous Leopold, who will do anything to inconvenience his rival. When Sutton arrives he makes as if to evict the interlopers, but stays his hand when he is smitten by Ottoline's charms. Unfortunately for Sutton, it soom emerges that he represents Grinkle's chief commercial rival in the men's underwear business, the Shirtopants firm of Hammersmith, owned by the Smith family, whose eldest son, Sigismund, is also a guest at the inn.

Realizing that he will never get Grinkle's blessing to approach Ottoline, Sutton cleverly pretends to the old man that he will arrange a marriage between her and Sigismund, thus ending the ruinous rivalry between the two families. The plan suits Sigismund, who is himself in love with Gretel Hinzel, a lovely Austrian girl, and the two happy couples spend blissful days together walking in the mountains.

Meanwhile, Leopold, certain he will never win Josepha's hand, prepares to leave the Inn to work abroad. Josepha manages to persuade him to stay on to welcome the Emperor, who is arriving at the Inn to see in the new shooting season. Finding herself alone with the Emperor, Josepha asks his advice about her love life and is advised to accept Leopold. She agrees, to Leopold's delight, not only to marry him but also to make him her co-proprietor. And the other two love affairs also come to a happy conclusion when Grinkle accepts Sutton as his son-in-law, and Gretel's father does the same for Sigismund.

Kathi	The Mayor
Karl	The Mayor's secretary
A forester	The Emperor
Zenzi	Ketterl
A courier	Landlord of the Travellers
Franz	Rest
Leopold	Villagers
Josepha Vogelhuber	Chambermaids
The steamer captain	Tourists
Bridegroom	Waiters
Bride	Waitresses
John Ebenezer Grinkle	Guides
Ottoline	Sailors
Valentine Sutton	Travellers
Sigismund Smith	Dairymaids
Professor Hinzel	Farmhands
Gretel	

Who is Sylvia?
Terence Rattigan
Comedy 3 Acts
London 1950

Seven years into his marriage, Mark St Neots, diplomat, talented sculptor and heir to a viscountcy, meets a girl on a bus who reminds him of his first, lost, juvenile love. He invites her to the home of his friend, Capt. Oscar Philipson, who is away fighting on the Western Front in World War One. In the midst of trying to seduce the girl, his first fling since marrying, Mark is interrupted by Oscar's sudden return on leave, and is forced to involve Oscar in the pretence that he is Mark Wright, sculptor. So taken is Mark with his new identity that he persuades Oscar to leave the flat, takes over Williams, Oscar's valet, and embarks on a dual existence, despite Oscar's warning that the arrangement can only end in discovery, and disaster.

For the next thirty years, Mark and Oscar indulge themselves with a series of ever more tarty girls, and, although Mark is several times nearly discovered by members of his own circle, meets his own son at one of his wild parties, and nearly gives up his career to live permanently with a much younger woman, he reaches old age without apparently arousing his wife's suspicions.

Nearing the age of seventy, though, he and Oscar are one night surprised by the arrival of his wife, Caroline, while they are in the process of trying to seduce yet another pair of young ladies. Caroline apologizes for interrupting, but insists that Mark take her to the opening night of their son's first appearance as lead in a West End play. She then playfully deflates his swollen ego by revealing that she has always been aware of his philandering - has indeed conspired with his friends and colleagues to keep him out of scandals - and is

perfectly happy with the odd double life he has chosen to lead.

Mark St Neots/Wright
Williams, his valet
Daphne, his first affair
Sidney, her brother
Ethel
Oscar Philipson, Mark's best friend
Bubbles
Nora
Denis
Wilberforce
Doris
Chloe
Caroline, Mark's wife

Who's Afraid of Virginia Woolf?
Edward Albee
Drama 3 Acts
New York 1962

At two in the morning in a house on the campus of a small New England college, middle-aged Martha has invited over new biology lecturer Nick (whom she fancies) and wife Honey, after a party given by Martha's dad, the College head, to welcome the young couple. Her husband George, assistant professor of history, who has not been able to fill his father-in-law's shoes, is not at all pleased, and the night degenerates into a liquor-soaked four-sided battle. George and Martha are experts, treacherously humiliating the new couple and prizing out and revealing their secrets and their weaknesses, at the same time wounding themselves and each other. When Martha reveals - for the first time to strangers - they have a son, George hits the roof. The boy is actually a fantasy, a small comfort to them, and George takes the last trick by 'killing' the boy off. For better of for worse they now have to live without him.

Martha
George
Nick
Honey

Whole Truth, The
Philip Mackie
Drama 3 Acts
London 1955

It is early evening when Mr Lewis Paulton, a film producer, arrives home to his house in Hampstead. Deenie, the Dutch maid, is preparing the dinner-table for two guests. Paulton's wife, Brenda, joins her husband and reminds him of the guests that will be dining - Tony, an old friend, and Marion, a beautiful but ruthlessly ambitious actress. As Brenda changes for dinner, Paulton is visited by Carliss, who confides in him alone that he is a detective investigating the murder of Marion. It soon becomes apparent that Paulton was having an affair with the actress and had visited her at the apartment at the time of the murder. After brief questioning,

Carliss leaves Paulton to cancel the dinner party only after he removes a paper knife and broken cuff-link without being seen.

Shocked by the news, Paulton confesses the affair to Brenda and convinces her that he did not murder Marion. Much to their amazement, Marion arrives for dinner only to be confronted with hostility from her guests. Paulton escorts Marion to the door alone and soon returns to his wife. Their suspicions are aroused when they realize that Marion has not driven away. On investigation they find her stabbed.

Inspector Brett having found the incriminating evidence of the murder weapon - the paper knife - and cuff-link in the car, arrests Paulton for murder, only after Carliss' alibi appears to be more than perfect.

Paulton, concerned for his wife's safety, persuades the Inspector to telephone her to ensure she has arrived home safely from the police station. The phone is answered by Carliss who has returned to their home and killed Deenie - who had evidence that would incriminate him. He makes his only error by doing so and is finally caught by Brett.

Deenie
Lewis Paulton
Brenda Paulton
Carliss
A visitor
Briggs
Inspector Brett
Petty

Whose Life is it Anyway?
Brian Clark
Drama 2 Acts
London 1978

Ken Harrison is a young man paralysed from the neck downwards after a road accident. Because of this he has to be permanently in hospital and no longer feels properly and fully alive - he wants to die. The story tells of his struggle to achieve this, and how the medical profession react to his request. The play ends with a judge and two doctors in his hospital room, one doctor declaring him sane enough to make such a decision and the other declaring him mentally unstable. Finally he is allowed to stay and have all treatment and food stopped.

Ken Harrison
Sister Anderson
Kay Sadler, a probationer nurse
John, a West Indian ward orderly
Dr Clare Scott, junior registrar
Dr Michael Emerson, consultant physician
Mrs Gillian Boyle, a medical social worker
Philip Hill, Ken's solicitor
Dr Paul Travers, consultant psychiatrist
Peter Kershaw, Ken's barrister
Dr Barr, consultant psychiatrist
Andrew Eden, hospital's barrister
Mr Justice Millhouse

Wild Duck, The
Henrik Ibsen
Drama 5 Acts
Bergen 1885

When prosperous manufacturer Haakon Werle's almost-estranged son Gregers is guest of honour at his father's dinner party, he takes along boyhood friend Hjalmar Ekdal, son of Haakon's disgraced former partner Old Ekdal. Gregers is astonished to learn that his father has set up Hjalmar as a photographer and has been most generous to his family - wife Gina, formerly Haakon's housekeeper, and Hedvig, their fourteen-year-old daughter. Hedvig is slowly going blind and so is Haakon, and Gregers realizes Hedvig must be Haakon's natural daughter - his half-sister. An obnoxious 'new thinker' who believes marriages must be founded upon complete truth, Gregers tells the immature Hjalmar of his discovery, resulting in Hjalmar turning against Hedvig - who worships him. Among their family menagerie of pets is a wild duck, particularly beloved of Hedvig because it has no family and must live now in a strange place. Gregers suggests to Hedvig that she shoot her pet to prove to her father she is willing to sacrifice her greatest treasure for him. Instead, she shoots herself.

Haakon Werle
Gregers Werle
Old Ekdal
Hjalmar Ekdal
Gina Ekdal
Hedvig Ekdal
Mrs Bertha Sorby, Haakon Werle's housekeeper
Dr Reeling
Molvik, an ex-student of theology
Graaberg, Werle's book-keeper
Petterson, Werle's manservant
Jenson, a hired waiter
Other hired waiters
A flabby gentleman
A bald gentleman
A shortsighted gentleman
Six other gentlemen

Wild Oats
John O'Keefe
Comedy 5 Acts
London 1798

This play based on mistaken identities and misunderstandings has Sir George Thunder, formerly in the Navy, with his bo'sun John Dory, much given to naval lingo, searching for some deserters. They find themselves near the house of Sir George's niece, a wealthy Quaker, and he sends for his son Harry from Portsmouth. Harry under another name, Dick, has joined a (disbanded) company of actors whose principal player is apparently an orphan, Rover, much given to quotations. They part and for some time Rover is taken for Harry, and Rover's cousin falls in love with him. Rover, meanwhile, helps an unfortunate ex-parson and his sister whose goods and chattels are being seized by bailiffs at the behest of a rough farmer. Rover is taken to the house of the Quaker who befriends any deserving poor person. After numerous misunderstandings and adventures, Rover turns out to be the long lost son of Sir George Thunder, his mother being the sister of the unfortunate parson. He happily marries his cousin.

Sir George Thunder	Muz
Rover	Trap
Harry	Twitch
Banks	Waiter
John Dory	Landlord
Farmer Gammon	Sheriff's Officer
Lamp	Three ruffians
Ephraim Smooth	Lady Amaranth
Sim	Amelia
Zachariah	Jane

Wind and the Rain, The
Merton Hodge
Drama 3 Acts
London 1933

Londoner Charles Tritton arrives at Mrs McFie's boarding house in Edinburgh to study medicine. He meets and befriends fellow-lodgers and students Gilbert, John and Frenchman Paul. He also meets and falls in love with Anne Hargreaves, a sculptor from New Zealand living nearby. His mother, however, is set upon him marrying Jill Mannering, an orphan who has grown up with their family, but when she comes up to visit Charles it becomes obvious they are more like brother and sister. After five years Charles passes his exams, and Anne declares she must return to New Zealand now her support for Charles is unnecessary, and he can go back to London and to Jill. Suddenly Charles' mother falls sick and he rushes down to London where she dies; Jill goes abroad to recover, and he accepts a post back up at the Royal Infirmary, Edinburgh. When he arrives, Anne is still there. She had postponed her departure not knowing Charles was returning. He is delighted but contrite, realizing how much his successful studies owe to her love and support. He proposes, and she accepts.

Mrs McFie	Anne Hargreaves
Gilbert Raymond	Jill Mannering
John Williams	Roger Cole
Charles Tritten	Peter Morgan
Dr Paul Duhamel	

Winslow Boy, The
Terence Rattigan
Drama 2 Acts
London 1946

Fourteen-year-old Ronnie Winslow is expelled from Osborne Naval College accused of stealing a postal order. Ronnie swears he did not do it, and so his father Arthur begins a fight to prove his son's innocence. A

further Admiralty inquiry only confirms the 'guilty' verdict, but official high-handedness in the case arouses nation-wide controversy. When Arthur decides to employ top barrister Sir Robert Morton, the family is split; high legal fees prevent eldest son Dickie from continuing at Oxford, and only daughter Kate supports her father. She admires the supercilious Morton but considers him 'a cold fish' who has only taken on the case to further his already glittering career. Kate's support costs her dearly - her fiancé's father threatens to withdraw his son's allowance, essential for their marriage, if the case continues. Arthur is not prepared to jeopardize his daughter's happiness and leaves the decision to her - she decides to go ahead. Eventually Morton wins the case, Ronnie's name is cleared, 'right is done' and Kate discovers she has been wrong about Morton; he turned down the post of Lord Chief Justice in order to conclude the Winslow case.

Ronnie Winslow
Grace Winslow
Violet
Catherine Winslow (Kate)
Dickie Winslow
John Watherstone
Desmond Curry
Miss Barnes
Fred
Sir Robert Morton

Winter's Tale, The
William Shakespeare
Comedy 5 Acts
London 1611

Hermione, Queen of Sicily, is about to give birth to a child her wildly jealous husband, King Leontes, believes to have been fathered by their guest, Polixenes, King of Bohemia. Leontes' plot to poison Polixenes is revealed to the Bohemian, who flees. When Hermione delivers a girl, Leontes has the child abandoned in the wilds.

Hermione is tried for adultery, but declared innocent by the Delphic oracle. When Leontes refuses to believe the oracle, he is told in quick succession that his son Mamillius, and Hermione, have both died, concludes that his wife was innocent and vows lifelong mourning.

The abandoned daughter, Perdita, is raised by shepherds until, grown into a young woman, she attracts the love of Polixenes' son Florizel. Fearing what he believes would be incest, Polixenes threatens to execute Perdita unless Florizel leaves her. The lovers flee to Sicily, followed by Polixenes, where they learn from the penitent Leontes that they are not related by blood, and so are free to marry. Polixenes and Leontes are reconciled, and Leontes discovers to his delight that Hermione is still alive, still in love with him.

Leontes, King of Sicily
Mamillius, his son
Sicilian lords: Camillo, Antigonus, Cleomenes, Dion
Polixenes, King of Bohemia

Florizel, his son
Archidamus, Bohemian lord
Hermione, Queen of Sicily
Perdita, Leontes' and Hermione's daughter
Paulina
Emilia
Old shepherd
Clown
Autolycus
A mariner
A gaoler
Mopsa
Dorcas
Lords
Ladies
Shepherds, Shepherdesses
Servants
Time, chorus

Within the Law
Bayard Veiller
Drama 4 Acts
New York 1912

Shopgirl Mary Turner is wrongly jailed for theft for three years and made a special example of by vindictive proprietor Edward Gilder. She swears revenge, and after release becomes a kind of confidence trickster working entirely within the law, helped by former criminals Joe Garson and Agnes Lynch. Mary is wooed by Gilder's son Dick who is ignorant of her background and they secretly marry; Mary now has her revenge and prepares to desert Dick, but when he discovers the truth he is determined to keep her. Police Inspector Burke, egged on by Gilder Sr, contrives a plan to incriminate Mary - he has stool pigeon 'English' Eddie Griggs arrange a burglary in the Gilder home. Mary tells Garson not to do it, but Eddie convinces him it will be easy money. Burke then tips off Mary just before the job, knowing she will arrive at Gilder's to warn Garson, and thus enable the police to catch the whole gang red-handed. But when Mary arrives, Dick is there - they talk, and realize it is a trap. Garson kills Eddie and escapes, but Mary and Dick are arrested. Burke then finds an apologetic letter to Mary from Helen Morris, the real shopgirl thief, and offers to show it to Gilder if Mary tells him who killed Eddie. She refuses, but when Garson is brought in he confesses to save Mary, and she and Dick leave together now as a couple.

Sarah, Edward Gilder's private secretary
Smithson, floorwalker at 'The Emporium'
Richard Gilder
Edward Gilder
George Demarest, Edward Gilder's lawyer
Helen Morris
Detective Sergeant Cassidy
Mary Turner
Agnes Lynch
Joe Garson

Fannie, a maid
William Irwin, a lawyer
Eddie Griggs
Police Inspector Burke
Thomas, a butler
Chicago Red, Tom Dacey, two crooks
Williams, police stenographer
Thompson, police detective
Dan, police doorman

Witness for the Prosecution
Agatha Christie
Drama 3 Acts
London 1953

Leonard Vole, an evidently naive young man, is arraigned for the murder of an elderly, and rich spinster, Miss Emily French, whom Vole had met by saving her dropped parcels from being run over when she panicked crossing Oxford Street in London. Vole is implicated by Miss French's severe Scottish housekeeper, Janet Mackenzie, who claims to have heard Vole chatting with the old lady moments before her death. When it is revealed that Vole had been named Miss French's main beneficiary in a will written only days before her death, his position begins to look hopeless.

Despite further incriminating evidence which comes out at the trial, it seems that Vole, represented by the eminent barrister Sir Wilfrid Robarts, QC, will escape conviction. His hopes are apparently dashed, though, when his wife testifies against him. But just as the judge is about to send the jury out, new evidence is provided by a streetwalker who gives Sir Wilfrid a bunch of letters, written by Vole's wife to her lover, which clear Vole and prove his wife to be the murderer.

Once he is acquitted, Vole is joined in court by his young lover, to the sudden, clear horror of his wife, who reveals that the woman who gave Sir Wilfrid the letters was she herself in disguise. Her plan had been to save Vole, who was the real killer, by casting suspicion on herself. His treachery in love, though, is too much for her to bear, and she stabs Vole to death in front of a horrified Sir Wilfrid.

Greta
Carter
Mr Mayhew, a solicitor
Leonard Vole, the
  accused
Sir Wilfrid Robarts QC
Inspector Hearne
Plain clothes detective
Romaine, Vole's wife
Clerk of the court
Mr Justice Wainwright
Alderman
Mr Myers QC, the
  prosecutor
Court usher
Court stenographer

Warder
The judge's clerk
Six barristers
Three jurymen
A policeman
Dr Wyatt
Janet Mackenzie
Mr Clegg
The other woman

Wizard of Oz, The

Book by Frank L. Baum
Music by Harold Arlen
Lyrics by E. Y. Harburg
Fantasy Musical 2 Acts
New York 1875

Other stage versions of this classic story include *The Wiz* with music and lyrics by Charlie Smalls.

From her farm home in Kansas, Dorothy and her pet, Toto, are transported to the land of Oz during a cyclone, where she accidentally kills the Wicked Witch of the East, much to the delight of the Good Witches. Her wish to return home can only be granted by the Wizard, thus begins her journey along the Yellow Brick Road. On her travels she befriends the Scarecrow (who wishes for brains), the Tin Man (who wants a heart) and the Lion (who wants courage). They are waylaid by obstacles on their path conjured up by the Wicked Witch of the West. The Wizard, however, will only grant their wishes once they have killed the Wicked Witch, which Dorothy succeeds in doing after a short imprisonment. On returning to the Wizard, the foursome uncover his fraudulence whilst discovering that their wishes are granted. Dorothy's wish is made possible by her silver shoes and she returns home.

Songs include: 'We're Off to See the Wizard'; 'Ding Dong the Witch is Dead'; 'Over the Rainbow'

Dorothy
The Scarecrow
The Tin Man
The Cowardly Lion
Aunt Em
Uncle Henry
The Good Witch of the North
The Guardian of the Gates
The Wizard of Oz
The Queen of the Fieldmice
The Wicked Witch of the West
The witch's cat
Glinda, the Good Witch of the South

Wolfsbane

Georgina Reid
Drama 2 Acts
London 1982

Joan Meredith, an accomplished sculptor but inept homemaker, hires a forbidding, narrowly religious home-help and cook, Mrs Bond, who arrives with her teenage daughter, Sarah, both of whom are to live in.

The Meredith family try to enliven Sarah's closely regulated life, and Joan even has the girl model for a bust of Aphrodite, but when Mrs Bond discovers what Joan is doing, her rigid morality is offended, and a serious row ensues, with Gran Meredith defending the value of Joan's work. Soon after, Gran suffers what seems to be a stroke, but turns out to be poisoning. Mrs Bond is arrested for attempted murder, amidst a welter of veiled hints from Sarah that her mother has been guilty of similar conduct in the past. While the rest of the family are being interviewed by the police, Gran traps Sarah into an admission that it was she who administered the poison. Sarah mocks the old women, claiming that Mrs Bond will take the blame, out of her profound, if smothering, motherly love. But Mrs Bond, having lost her previous post by protecting Sarah in a similar incident, returns with the Merediths and the police, and turns the girl over to justice.

Joan Meredith
Luke Meredith, Joan's son
Howard Meredith, Joan's husband
Gran (Mrs Blackwell), Joan's mother
Sarah Bond
Mrs Bond

Woman in a Dressing Gown

Ted Willis
Play 2 Acts
Bromley 1963

The Prestons are an average family living in a council flat in the fifties. Mum Amy, though, is a daydreamer spending time listening to classical music on the radio and letting the flat get into a mess, but this is largely ignored by son Brian and husband Jim, who finds solace in the arms of Georgie, an intelligent and positive young lady; she wants him to leave Amy and start a new life in Australia. Jim's reluctance to leave Amy arises out of a genuine affection for her; he is a kind person who finds it difficult to think for himself.

When, eventually, Jim does reveal his intentions Amy is confused and unwilling to accept the situation imagining that her untidiness is the cause of friction. She tries unsuccessfully to tidy herself up and ends up drunk with her friend Hilda. A confrontation with Jim and Georgie follows in which Amy resorts to insults and self-recrimination, and although son Brian tries to take a detatched view of the proceedings, he does not hesitate to tell Georgie to leave. The status quo returns with Amy promising to make an effort.

Amy Preston
Brian Preston
Jim Preston
Georgie Barlow
Hilda
Willie
Christine

Woman of No Importance, A

Oscar Wilde
Drama 3 Acts
London 1893

Among the guests at Hunstanton Chase are opinionated young American Hester Worsley and eager Gerald Arbuthnot who delights hostess Lady Hunstanton with the news that he is to become secretary to charming but selfish bachelor Lord Illingworth (who is being pursued by vivacious Mrs Allonby). But when Gerald's normally reticent mother Mrs Arbuthnot appears, she discourages his ambition, though she cannot forbid it. Left alone with Lord Illingworth, she reveals that Gerald is his son, born of their old affair after Illingworth had gone back on his promise to marry her. His Lordship is naturally now even more anxious to employ Gerald, but commits the error of making a pass at Hester who cries out to Gerald for assistance. In order to stop Gerald striking Illingworth, Mrs Arbuthnot is forced to reveal the truth to her son. Gerald then demands his parents wed, but although his father is willing for Gerald's sake, his mother is persuaded otherwise by righteous Hester who demands Mrs Arbuthnot should not compromise herself. Gerald and Hester announce their engagement and Mrs Arbuthnot dismisses Illingworth, telling him he is neither wanted nor needed by herself or the sweethearts.

Lady Caroline Pontefract
Miss Hester Worsley
Sir John Pontefract
Lady Hunstanton
The Ven. Archdeacon Daubeny, DD
Gerald Arbuthnot
James, Footman
Mrs Allonby
Lady Stutfield
Mr Kelvil, MP
Lord Illingworth
Lord Alfred Rufford
Farquar, the butler
Francis, the footman
Mrs Arbuthnot
Alice, the maid

Woman of the Year
Peter Stone
Music and lyrics by John Kander and Fred Ebb
Musical Comedy 2 Acts
New York 1981

Tess Harding is an internationally known TV hostess and her work has earned her the award as 'Woman of the Year'. We follow a few days in her hectic life, where her activities include interviewing various people, mainly by phone, and in several languages, getting married to a cartoonist whose own life goes on in parallel, having a huge party instead of going to bed, and returning to her former husband in the country for a bit of peace and quiet. This does not work as the second wife objects. Returning to the studio she finds that her husband does not want to give up all the glamour and excitement, and they end up as 'Couple of the Year'.

Tess Harding, Woman of the Year
Gerald, Tess's secretary
Helga, her German housekeeper
Chip Salisbury, a network anchorman
Phil, Ellis, Abbot and Pinky, cartoonists and Sam's friends

Sam Craig, a cartoonist
Maury, bar keeper
Tony, doorman
Prescott, FBI agent
Alexi Petnikov, Russian ballet dancer
Larry, Tess' first husband
Jan, Larry's wife
Chairwoman
Committee women
TV technicians
Patrons of Maury's bar
Others

Women, The
Clare Boothe Luce
Drama 3 Acts
New York 1936

Mary Haines, one of a group of pampered thirties New York society women, has her world torn apart when her friends reveal to her that her husband Stephen is conducting an affair with Crystal Allen, a glamorous younger woman. On the advice of her mother, Mary decides to ignore Stephen's behaviour, but, again, the interference of her friends leads to a welter of damaging gossip and, much worse, to the appearance of the story in the gossip columns.

Feeling herself cornered, Mary insists on a divorce, to which Stephen reluctantly agrees, on the grounds of his adultery. While Mary is in Reno, Nevada, arranging the 'quickie' divorce that is a Nevada speciality, she meets the much-married Countess de Lage, who has just taken up with Buck Windsor, a cowboy whom the Countess intends to turn into a cinema star.

Back in New York, Mary and the Countess begin to see one another socially, and Mary finds out, from the innocent conversation of her daughter, Little Mary, that Crystal, now married to Stephen, is conducting an affair with Buck. With considerable cunning, Mary traps Crystal into admitting the affair during a night club party, and looks forward to forgetting her pride and winning her husband back.

***Mary Haines' group of friends:** Jane, Nancy, Peggy, Sylvia, Edith*	*Mrs Morehead, Mary's mother*
Mary Haines	*Another saleswoman*
Mrs Wagstaff	*A fitter*
Two hairdressers	*Corset model*
Pedicurist	*Princess Tamara*
Olga	*Crystal Allen*
Euphie	*Exercise instructress*
A Mud Mask	*Maggie*
Cook (Ingrid)	*Miss Trimmerback*
Miss Fordyce	*Miss Watts*
Little Mary, Mary's daughter	*A nurse*
Two salesgirls	*Lucy*
Head saleswoman	*Countess De Lage*
Model	*Miriam Aarons*
	Helene
	Two cuties

Two society women	A dowager
Sadie	A débutante
Cigarette girl	Girl in distress

Woods, The
David Mamet
Drama 1 Act
Chicago 1977

Two lovers, Ruth and Nick, have come to the summer cottage of Nick's family for a break from the pressures of city life just at the end of the summer season.

Left alone, though, they quickly fall into a feeling of mutual isolation, and no amount of talking seems able to restore to either of them the sense of intimacy their holiday was meant to deepen. Eventually they argue bitterly when Ruth rebuffs Nick's crude sexual advances, and she decides to leave for the city alone. Just as she is going, they are partially reconciled, Nick falls into her arms, and she tries to soothe him into sleep.

Ruth
Nick

Worm's Eye View
R. F. Delderfield
Comedy 3 Acts
London 1945

Five young airmen are billeted in the home of Mrs Bounty, an imperious, affected Northern landlady, in the middle of World War Two. With her equally affected son Sydney, Mrs Bounty makes the young men's lives as unpleasant and barren of pleasure as she can.

Her rigid control over the household begins to slip when her daughter Bella, a shy twenty-one-year-old, falls in love with Mark, the non-commissioned officer who is in command of the billet. Despite the efforts of Mrs Bounty and her son to break up the relationship, the young couple persevere in meeting one another. Bella's father, Mrs Bounty's second husband, is inspired by the young airmen and their jaunty air of freedom to escape his wife's domination, and he leaves home to find work in London.

Tension reaches a peak when Bella and Mark, returning from a secret night out, are caught by Mrs Bounty and Sydney. When Sydney calls Bella a slut, Mark knocks him to the ground, and is put on a charge by the vengeful pair. Unknown to the entire household, though, Mr Bounty, who has just returned from London with a new sense of self-respect, hears of the charge, intercedes with Mark's commanding officer, and arranges that Mark should be let off.

He, Bella and Mrs Bounty's harrassed maid, Thelma, all depart, the billet is closed and the airmen transferred elsewhere, and Sydney and Mrs Bounty are left to nurse their injured pride. Mr Bounty, now as self-assured as he once was docile, throws Sydney out of the house and demands that his wife start behaving like his wife and not his boss.

Pop, an older airman

| *Mark, Corporal of the billet* |
| *Mrs Bounty, landlady of the billet* |
| *Thelma, her maid* |
| *Mr Bounty, her husband* |
| *Sydney Spooner, Mrs Bounty's son* |
| *Taffy, Porter, two young recruits* |
| *Bella, the Bountys' daughter* |
| *Sqn Ldr Briarly* |

Write Me a Murder
Frederick Knott
Drama 3 Acts
London 1962

Upon the death of Lord Rodingham, eldest son Clive immediately sells the family estate and all its contents to local self-made businessman Charles Sturrock, then goes off to Texas with his new American wife, a millionairess. Younger brother David, a well-known short-story writer, is disappointed, but strikes up a friendship with Sturrock's wife Julia. She is a would-be writer and he helps her plot a murder story set in the study of Rodingham Manor for an *Evening News* competition...but when her husband becomes objectionable, they decide to carry out the plot in earnest. It proves unnecessary; Charles is killed in a car smash, David and Julia marry, and she begins a new story set on a houseboat.

A year later while Julia is up in London, Clive returns - he is broke and his marriage has failed. When he discovers David is interested in following through Sturrock's plans to exploit the estate, he threatens to blackmail him and expose the development plans to the local villagers. David then kills him according to the original story, but when Julia returns she reveals to David she has won first prize and was published in the *Evening News* - only it was not the houseboat story she entered - it was their murder collaboration. David looks out of the window and sees the police with the newspaper on the point of finding the incriminating evidence buried beneath a sundial.

Clive Rodingham
Dr Elizabeth Wooley
David Rodingham
Nurse
Charles Sturrock
Julia Sturrock
Mr Tibbit, the builder
Police Constable Hacket
Two men

You Can't Take It With You
Moss Hart and George S. Kaufman
Comedy 3 Acts
New York 1936

Grandpa Martin Vanderhof has a house in New York City near Columbia University and a long time ago he gave up the rat-race and became a happy man. His family are equally eccentric - daughter Penelope writes plays and paints, son-in-law Paul makes fireworks with family friend Mr De Pinna (who also poses for Penelope), pixie-like granddaughter Essie studies ballet with volatile Russian bear Boris Kolenkhov, and her husband Ed is a musician. Grandpa is also being heavily hustled by the Internal Revenue for not paying taxes, but gets out of it by proving he is dead - the family buried a permanent guest, their milkman, some years ago under Grandpa's name. Their activities go on, all at once, all the time, and youngest granddaughter Alice tells them to behave more conventionally when she invites over the staid parents of her fiancé, boss's son Tony. But Tony deliberately brings them over on the wrong night and when they get the full eccentric treatment they leave quite disgusted and shocked. Alice tells Tony their marriage would never work, and to cap it all the fireworks operation is busted by G-men. Next evening Tony returns attempting to change Alice's mind and is followed by his dad, Mr Kirby. When Grandpa and Mr Kirby manage to sit down and talk, they reach an understanding and Kirby relaxes and begins to enjoy himself. Alice and Tony are now free to marry.

Penelope Sycamore
Essie
Rheba
Paul Sycamore
Mr De Pinna
Ed
Donald
Martin Vanderhof
Alice
Henderson
Tony Kirby
Boris Kolenkhov
Gay Wellington
Mr Kirby
Mrs Kirby
Three men
Olga

You Know I Can't Hear You When The Water's Running
Robert Anderson
Drama 4 Acts
New York 1967

Four one-act plays are held together by their joint theme; namely, the sexual alienation which afflicts all of their main characters.

In the first, Jack Barnstaple, a successful playwright, argues with his rather philistine producer, Herb Miller, about the acceptability of a scene in Jack's latest play, which shows the 'hero' in an unflattering state of nakedness.

The second follows a middle-aged married couple, George and Harriet, on a visit to a bedding store where Harriet tries to persuade George, using the excuse of their differing taste in mattresses, that they should abandon their double bed for a pair of single ones.

Chuck Berringer's isolation from his own sexual identity, and inability to deal with his son's coming of age, dominates the third play. What would have been a difficult transition for Chuck anyway is made intolerably sad by his wife, Edith's, constant pressure on him to talk openly with their children about the role of sex in their lives.

Finally, Herbert and Muriel, a doddering old couple, both of whom have been married several times, sit in rocking chairs confusing their affairs and previous marriages so completely that each is nostalgic for the other while remembering passion actually shared with former partners.

Act One:
Jack Barnstaple
Herb Miller
Dorothy
Richard Pawling
Act Two:
Salesman
Harriet
George
Jill

Act Three:
Chuck
Edith
Clarice
Act Four:
Herbert
Muriel

You Never Can Tell
George Bernard Shaw
Comedy 4 Acts
London 1899

Valentine's first dentistry patient is pert Dolly Clandon, who together with her twin Philip invite him to lunch with their family. They have moved from Madeira to Torbay, Devon, together with elder sister Gloria and mother Mrs Lanfrey Clandon, authoress of the *Twentieth Century Treatises* (famous in Madeira) on just about everything - cooking, creeds, conduct, parents, children, etc. Their mother, however, has always kept them in absolute ignorance about their absent father, philosophically maintaining an individual's right to privacy. Valentine falls in love with Gloria, a thoroughly modern young woman brought up on her mother's treatises who goes against her feelings and ignores his sentimentality. When the children insist on knowing the identity of their father, their mother lets family friend Finch M'Comas explain. Their dad is coincidentally Valentine's grumpy landlord Mr Crampton, who has no manners but a heart of gold. With the help of the diplomatic hotel waiter and his barrister son, the Clandon/Crampton family are eventually reunited. Valentine and Gloria are set for nuptials and various conflicting philosophies and generations reconciled.

Fergus Crampton
Bohun, QC
Finch M'Comas
The waiter
Valentine
Philip Clandon

Parlourmaid
Mrs Clandon
Dolly Clandon
Gloria Clandon

You're a Good Man, Charlie Brown
Clark Gesner
Musical 2 Acts
New York 1967

This series of loosely connected vignettes is based on the comic strip *Charlie Brown* by Charles Schulz and features all its main characters - Linus, his sister Lucy, Charlie himself, his dog Snoopy, Charlie's flame Patty, and Schroeder, the boy genius.

Charlie pursues his amiable, self-deprecating way through confrontations with the wilful Lucy, the preparation of a book report on Peter Rabbit, a championship baseball game which he loses for the home team, and his hopeless love for Patty.

He at last wins Lucy's grudging admission 'You're a good man Charlie Brown'.

Linus
Charlie Brown
Patty
Schroeder
Snoopy
Lucy

Young Elizabeth, The
Jeannette Dowling and Francis Letton
Drama 2 Acts
London 1952

Fast-moving historical drama of Good Queen Bess's life from the death of her father Henry VIII to her accession on the death of half-sister Mary.

At first, Elizabeth is protected by the patronage of her father's widow, Katherine Parr, who weds Lord Thomas Seymour. Both love Elizabeth, but thing. go almost too far between her and Seymour. When Queen Katherine dies in childbirth, Thomas is soon seized on the pretext of corrupting Elizabeth and beheaded by his brother, protector of sickly young King Edward. When Edward dies and pro-Spanish fanatical Roman Catholic Mary takes the throne, things go from bad to worse for Elizabeth; her sister's jealousy leads her to imprison her in the Tower.

Luckily, Elizabeth is madly popular with the English people, and is surrounded by a crowd of aristocratic young men willing to die for her at the drop of a feathered hat. There are plenty of impetuous tossings of Tudor-red hair, fade-outs on forbidden embraces, and last-minute reprieves.

Elizabeth is expecting her mad and murderous sister to behead her, but instead poor old Mary dies after a series of phantom/miracle pregnancies, and Elizabeth goes on to preside over the most glorious reign in English history.

Two palace guards	*William Cecil*
A page	*Bishop Gardiner*
Lord Thomas Seymour	*Amy, a serving maid*
Lord Robert Tyrwhitt	*Katherine Ashley*
Katherine Parr	*Elizabeth Tudor*
Mary Tudor	*Thomas Parry*

Robert Dudley	*Two gentlemen*
Lady Tyrwhitt	*Lord William Howard*
Sir Francis Verney	
Sir Thomas Wyatt	
Sir Peter Carew	
Abel Cousins	

Young Wives' Tale
Ronald Jeans
Comedy 3 Acts
London 1949

Two young couples, Rodney and Sabina Pennant and Bruce and Mary Banning, are obliged by post-war austerity to share a London house, along with Valentine, the Pennants' baby son, Elizabeth, the Bannings' baby daughter and a lodger, twenty-year-old Eve.

Their chaotic attempts at domestic routine (a particular muddle for Sabina, a retired actress with none of the then normal womanly skills) have sunk to a new low with the departure of their shared nanny. The household stumbles from mishap to mishap, with meals ruined, clothing uncleaned and clutter everywhere, to the particular annoyance of Rodney, a scriptwriter who is obliged to work from home. As the tension built up by the disarray steadily increases, Victor Manifold, a professional man with an obviously romantic interest in Sabina, drops by the house more frequently to press his attentions on her. One of his visits follows by moments a row between Rodney and Sabina over her latest botched meal, which has finished with Rodney storming out of the house.

In her distress over the row, Sabina allows Victor to give her a lingering kiss. They are caught in the act by Bruce, who throws Victor out but then, in an effort to calm Sabina, finds himself embracing her instead. Returning at just the wrong moment, Rodney sees their clinch and again storms out. Even worse, their new nanny, Nurse Gallop, finds the two in each other's arms and, not having yet met Sabina's husband, naturally assumes that Bruce is he.

For fear of losing her, the household is obliged to carry on the pretence, and the resultant round of jealousy is only cut short when Nurse Blott discovers Rodney making up with Sabina, decides she is in a disreputable home, and quits her job on the spot. The two couples settle their differences, and Victor, arriving just as they do so, goes off to dinner with Eve when he realizes that Sabina is out of reach.

Rodney Pennant
Sabina Pennant, his wife
Nurse Blott
Eve Lester
German woman
Mary Banning
Bruce Banning, her husband
Victor Manifold
Nurse Gallop

Zigger Zagger
Peter Terson
Drama 1 Act
London 1967

Zigger Zagger, leader of a group of football hooligans who support the fictitious 'City' in London's East End, narrates the life of Harry Philton, a typical City supporter of the sixties, who becomes a fanatic and hooligan.

To earn money to supplement the income his mother brings in from prostitution, Harry, at age fifteen, is up every morning at five am to start his paper round. This leaves him far too tired to do well in his lessons at Millwall Secondary School, and he leaves with no qualifications. His only interest in life is as a member of the gang of City supporters led by Zigger Zagger, until he decides to try the army, which rejects him on health grounds.

His mother, anxious to have him out of the house while her clients visit, encourages him to spend time with his sister, Edna, and her husband Les, both of them DIY fanatics. Harry is quite fond of Les, who encourages him to enjoy his youth, but they eventually fall out over Harry's growing passion for City, and frequent brushes with the law. After one of his appearances, with Zigger Zagger, before the magistrates, Harry is sent to a youth club, where he meets and falls in love with Sandra who, at this stage, knows nothing of football. Under Harry's guidance, though, Sandra soon becomes even more fanatical than he is, and falls in love with Vincent, City's flashy centre-forward.

Harry, facing the growing realization that there must be more to life than football, allows Les to persuade him to start an apprenticeship, and hopes to emulate the domestic contentment Les and Edna have built. Unfortunately, though, Harry loses Sandra when Vincent meets her, and sweeps her into the high life. Harry is left bewildered and alone.

Zigger Zagger, a football hooligan
Harry Philton
Two policemen
School dentist
Headmaster
Caretaker
Teacher
Newsagent
Mrs Philton, Harry's mother
Uncle Albert
Edna, Harry's sister
Les, Edna's husband
Chairman of City
Youth Careers Officer
Uncle Brian
Four students
Recruiting Sergeant
Medical Officer
Four letter readers
Old soldier
Magistrate

Youth Club Leader
Sandra
Glenice
Stanley
Vincent
Two girls on bus
Bus conductor
Vicar
Three apprentices
Football crowd
Supporters
Police

Zip Goes a Million
Emile Littler, Eric Maschwitz and George Posford
Musical 2 Acts
Coventry 1951

A Lancashire window cleaner, Percy Piggott, arrives in Piggottsville, Texas, to take receipt of a fortune left to him as the only surviving relative of Old Man Piggott, the local oil baron.

Percy, a normally careful young man, discovers that he has been left not the one million dollars he anticipates, but eight million. But there are conditions. Percy must spend one million dollars in four months, must not 'go courting' and must tell no one of these conditions. He sets out to lose as much money as he can by backing a dreadful Broadway musical, buying stock in a nearly defunct fertilizer company and keeping his cash on deposit in a very shaky bank. His girlfriend Sally Whittle and her father Motty, who have come with him from Lancashire, are both appalled by Percy's apparent loss of good sense, but nothing they say can staunch the outward flow of his cash.

They move with him from Piggottsville to New York and then on to *The Pleasure Cruise*, a ruinously expensive yacht on which Percy tours the South Seas. There, news reaches them that Percy's apparently foolish investments have turned to gold: the Broadway show is a hit, the fertilizer company makes a freak recovery and the shaky bank survives a near crash. No one can understand when Percy is desolated by this apparent good news, and acts as if his fortune is lost. However, with only two weeks to go until his deadline, Percy is saved when his yacht runs aground, wiping out 500,000 dollars of his assets, he closes the Broadway show and manages to spend his last cash just before the four months are over. He inherits the balance of Old Man Piggott's estate, reveals the reason for his strange behaviour to Sally and Motty, and proposes marriage followed by a Blackpool honeymoon.

Sheriff MacOwen
Lilac Delany, an actress
Buddy Delany, her husband
Jed Harper
Motty Whittle, a Lancashire window cleaner
Sally Whittle, his daughter

Percy Piggott, Motty's friend and employee
George Connelly
Paula Van Nordon, a socialite
Hairdresser
Manicurist
Barber
Shoe shine boy
Eddie
James Van Norden, Paula's father
The musical director
Two policemen
Lefty
Touch
Elevator boy
Captain
Wireless operator
Kelly
Singers
Dancers

Zoo Story, The
Edward Albee
Drama 1 Act
New York 1960

Peter, a New York publishing executive, is sitting on a bench in Central Park, quietly reading a book, as he does every Sunday afternoon. He is approached by Jerry, a slightly shabby young man who clearly wants a bit of conversation. Jerry asks Peter a series of pointed and rather personal questions and discovers that Peter is a married man with two daughters, a fine apartment and a good job. He then relates the horrific details of his own life in a dingy West Side rooming house, and finishes with the story of his attempt to poison his landlady's dog because the animal had so often tried to bite him.

All the while he is telling his story, Jerry creates a measure of curiosity by promising to tell Peter, in due course, the story of his afternoon at the zoo where, he broadly hints, something extraordinary occurred. After finishing the tale of the dog, though, he infuriates Peter by trying to force him off his park bench. They argue over the bench, and Jerry offers Peter a knife, saying he will need it if they are to fight. Peter holds the knife in front of himself, in a defensive stance, but Jerry rushes at him anyway, purposely impales himself and dies.
Peter
Jerry

Index of Authors

Index of Authors

Index of Authors

Gazzo, Michael V.
Hatful of Rain, A
Gelbart, Larry
*Funny Thing Happened on the Way to
 the Forum, A*
Gelber, Jack
Connection, The
Gems, Pam
Camille
Piaf
Genet, Jean
Balcony, The
Blacks, The
Gershe, Leonard
Butterflies are Free
Gershwin, George and Ira
Of Thee I Sing
Gesner, Clark
You're a Good Man Charlie Brown
Gibson, William
Miracle Worker, The
Two for the Seesaw
Gilbert, Willie
*How to Succeed in Business Without
 Really Trying*
Gilbert, Robert
White Horse Inn
Gilbert, W.S.
Gondoliers, The
HMS Pinafore
Iolanthe
Mikado, The
Patience
Pirates of Penzance, The
Trial by Jury
Gilroy, Frank D.
Subject was Roses, The
Giradoux, Jean
Amphitryon
Intermezzo
Mad Woman of Chaillot, The
Ondine
Siegfried
*Tiger at the Gates, or, Trojan War
 Will not Take Place, The*
Glass, Montague
Potash and Perlmutter
Goetz, Ruth and Augustus
Heiress, The
Goggin, Dan
Nunsense
Gogol, Nikolai
Government Inspector, The
Overcoat, The
Goldman, James
Lion in Winter, The
Goldoni, Carlo
Servant of Two Masters, The
Goldsby, Angela and Robert
Let's Get a Divorce
Goldsmith, Oliver
She Stoops to Conquer
Goodritch, Frances
Diary of Anne Frank, The
Gordon, Leon

White Cargo
Gorky, Maxim
Enemies
Lower Depths, The
Smug Citizens, The or Philistines, The
Gow, Ronald
Love on the Dole
Graham, Harry
Maid of the Mountains, The
White Horse Inn
Grainer, Ron
Robert and Elizabeth
Granville-Barker, Harley
Voysey Inheritance, The
Gray, Simon
Butley
Idiot, The
Otherwise Engaged
Quartermaine's Terms
Stage Struck
Gredy, Jean Pierre
Forty Carats
Green, Adolph
Applause
Bells Are Ringing
Green, Mauby
Pajama Tops
Green, Paul
Native Son
Greenbank, Percy
Quaker Girl, The
Greene, Graham
Complaisant Lover, The
Living Room, The
Potting Shed, The
Greenwood, Walter
Love on the Dole
Griffiths, Trevor
Comedians
Gurney Jr, A.R.
Dining Room, The
Hackett, Albert
Diary of Anne Frank, The
Hall, Bob
Passion of Dracula, The
Hall, Carol
Best Little Whorehouse in Texas, The
Hall, Peter
Animal Farm
Hall, Roger
Middle-age Spread
Hall, Willis
Billy Liar
Long and the Short and the Tall, The
Say Who You Are
Hamilton, Patrick
Gaslight
Rope
Hamlisch, Marvin
Chorus Line, A
They're Playing Our Song
Hammerstein, Oscar
Annie Get Your Gun
Carmen Jones
Carousel

Desert Song, The
King and I, The
Oklahoma!
Rose Marie
Show Boat
Sound of Music, The
South Pacific
Hampton, Christopher
Liasons Dangereuses, Les
Philanthropist, The
Tales from Hollywood
Hanau, John
Johnny Belinda
Hansberry, Lorraine
Raisin in the Sun
Harbach, Otto
Desert Song, The
No, No, Nanette
Rose Marie
E. Y. Harburg
Wizard of Oz, The
Harding, John
Golden Pathway Annual, The
Harding, Mike
Fur Coat and No Knickers
Hare, David
Plenty
Harnick, Sheldon
Fiddler on the Roof
Fiorello!
Harold Terry, J.E.
Man Who Stayed at Home, The
Harris, Elmer
Johnny Belinda
Harris, Richard
Business of Murder, The
Outside Edge
Hart, Lorenz
Babes in Arms
Boys from Syracuse, The
On Your Toes
Pal Joey
Hart, Moss
Man Who Came to Dinner, The
Once in a Lifetime
You Can't Take It With You
Harwood, Ronald
Dresser, The
Hassal, Christopher
Dancing Years, The
King's Rhapsody
Hastings, B. Macdonald
If Winter Comes
Hastings, Hugh
Seagulls over Sorrento
Hawtrey, Charles
Private Secretary, The
Hayes, Catherine
Skirmishes
Hecht, Ben
Front Page, The
Heggen, Thomas
Mister Roberts
Heller, Joseph
Catch 22

Index of Authors

Index of Authors

Verneuil, Louis
Affairs of State
Vidal, Gore
Best Man, The
Visit to a Small Planet
Vosburgh, Dick
Day in Hollywood, a Night in the Ukraine, A
Wallace, Edgar
On the Spot
Ringer, The
Warren, Harry
42nd Street
Wasserman, Dale
Man of La Mancha
One Flew over the Cuckoo's Nest
Waterhouse, Keith
Billy Liar
Say Who You Are
Watkins, Maurine Dallas
Chicago
Watkyn, Arthur
Amber for Anna
For Better for Worse
Webster, John
Duchess of Malfi, The
White Devil, The
Webster, Paul
Calamity Jane
Wedekind, Frank
Pandora's Box
Weidman, Jerome
Fiorello!
Weill, Kurt
Threepenny Opera, The
Weinstock, Jack
How to Succeed in Business Without Really Trying
Weiss, Peter
Marat / Sade
Weldon, Fay
Action Replay
Mixed Doubles
Wesker, Arnold
Chicken Soup with Barley
Chips with Everything
Friends, The
I'm Talking about Jerusalem
Kitchen, The
Roots
Wesker Trilogy
Wheeler, Hugh
Irene
Sweeney Todd - The Demon Barber of Fleet Street
Whelan, Peter
Accrington Pals, The
Whitemore, Hugh
Stevie
Pack of Lies
Whiting, John
Devils, The
Saint's Day
Whitmore, Ken
Turn of the Screw, The

Wilber, Richard
Candide
Wilde, Oscar
Ideal Husband, An
Importance of Being Earnest, The
Lady Windermere's Fan
Lord Arthur Savile's Crime
Woman of No Importance, A
Wilder, Thornton
Matchmaker, The
Our Town
Skin of our Teeth, The
Willard, John
Cat and the Canary, The
Williams, Emlyn
Corn is Green, The
Murder has been Arranged, A
Night Must Fall
Williams, Hugh and Margaret
Past Imperfect
Williams, Nigel
Class Enemy
Williams, Tennessee
Camino Real
Cat on a Hot Tin Roof
Glass Menagerie, The
Night of the Iguana, The
Orpheus Descending
Period of Adjustment
Rose Tattoo, The
Streetcar Named Desire, A
Suddenly Last Summer
Sweet Bird of Youth
Willis, Ted
Doctor in the House
Woman in a Dressing Gown
Willson, Meredith
Music Man, The
Unsinkable Molly Brown, The
Wilson, August
Fences
Wilson, John
Hamp
Wilson, Sandy
Boyfriend, The
Wodehouse, P.G.
Anything Goes
Wood, David
Gingerbread Man, The
There was an Old Woman ...
Wood, Mrs Henry
East Lynne
Woods, Phil
Canterbury Tales, The
Worrall, Lechmere
Man Who Stayed at Home, The
Wouk, Herman
Caine Mutiny Court Martial, The
Wright, Robert
Kismet
Native Son
Wycherly, William
Country Wife, The
Yeston, M.
Nine

Yordan, Philip
Anna Lucasta
Youmans, Vincent
No, No, Nanette
Zindel, Paul
Effect of Gamma Rays on Man-in-the-Moon Marigolds, The
Zola, Emile
Thérèse Raquin